THE UNITED FRONT

SOVIET AND EAST EUROPEAN STUDIES

Editorial Board

The National Association for Soviet and East European Studies exists for the purpose of promoting study and research on the social sciences as they relate to the Soviet Union and the countries of Eastern Europe. The Monograph Series is intended to promote the publication of works presenting substantial and original research in the economics, politics, sociology and modern history of the USSR and Eastern Europe.

SOVIET AND EAST EUROPEAN STUDIES

THE
UNITED FRONT

THE TUC AND THE
RUSSIANS 1923–1928

DANIEL F. CALHOUN

Professor of History
The College of Wooster, Ohio

CAMBRIDGE UNIVERSITY PRESS

CAMBRIDGE

LONDON · NEW YORK · MELBOURNE

Published by the Syndics of the Cambridge University Press
The Pitt Building, Trumpington Street, Cambridge CB2 1RP
Bentley House, 200 Euston Road, London NW1 2DB
32 East 57th Street, New York, NY 10022, USA
296 Beaconsfield Parade, Middle Park, Melbourne 3206, Australia

First published 1976

Printed in Great Britain
by W & J Mackay Limited, Chatham

Library of Congress Cataloguing in Publication Data
Calhoun, Daniel Fairchild, 1929–
United Front.

(Soviet and East European studies)

Bibliography: p.

1. Trade-unions and communism – Great Britain – History.
2. Trades Union Congress. 3. Communist international – History.
4. Trade-unions – Great Britain – Political activity – History. I.
Title. II. Series.

HX544.C34   331.88'33'0941   75–23846

ISBN 0 521 21056 9

To
E. H. CARR *and* H. J. COPELAND

Unity Song*

Long the slaves endured their fetters
Cowed by fear, afraid to rise.
Till they saw the mystic letters
Glow before their up-turned eyes

Chorus

Then unite, ye sons of labour
Yours the world, to take and mould.
Into plough-shares beat the sabre
Strive for Peace, and not for gold.

Forward! With your eyes on Zion;
Hark! The Tramping of your feet,
Like the roaring of the lion
Shakes the earth with thunderous beat.

(*Chorus*)

Hark! The dawn now fast appearing,
Breaks the sun through blood-red sky;
Greetings Brothers! – Home we're nearing –
Let your banners upwards fly!

(*Chorus*)

* *Lansbury's Labour Weekly* February 19, 1927.
  Words © W. Gillion

Contents

Contents

Preface

This study derives from the most elemental of human weaknesses – curiosity. I was reading Isaac Deutscher's admirable biography of Trotsky, and it became apparent that something called the Anglo–Russian Committee played a conspicuous role in the great man's life during the middle years of the 1920s, just before he was expelled from the Party. Since my teaching responsibilities have involved both Russia and England – and I have often found their interrelationship absorbing – my interest was piqued. The standard secondary sources, however, in both British and Russian history, had almost nothing to say on the subject, so I decided to check into it myself, and perhaps write a short article. The subject expanded, as any good topic will, into a more general investigation of the whole fascinating flirtation between the Soviets and the Trades Union Congress in the mid-20s, and of the impact that aborted relationship had on the Comintern's doctrine of the 'united front.' The result is this book.

Scholars often have to work by themselves, but they never work in isolation, and I am happy to be able to acknowledge here all the help I have received in bringing this project to fruition. I am especially grateful to the trustees and administration of the College of Wooster, who supported me in the style to which I had become accustomed during 18 months of research leave. They also helped finance some of the incidental expenses any researcher encounters. Without their generosity, this book could never have been. I also appreciate the tolerance, consideration and support of my much esteemed colleagues in the College of Wooster history department, who proved, to my dismay, how effortlessly they could carry on without me while I was away. They restore one's faith in the tenure system.

All scholars love to read books, and historians in addition are addicted to reading old newspapers and dead people's mail. I am most appreciative, therefore, of those instititutions – and those who labour in them – which preserve such treasures. The following have been particularly useful to me: The British Museum; the British Museum Newspaper Library; the Marx Memorial Library; the London Library of Economics and

Political Science; the Trades Union Congress Library; the Library of the School of Slavonic and East European Studies, University of London; the Senate House Library, University of London; the Houghton Library, Harvard University; the Cleveland Public Library; and the Library of the College of Wooster. Material from the Trotsky Archive is quoted by permission of the Houghton Library, Harvard University. I am especially grateful to the following individuals connected with various of these institutions: Miss M. Nesbitt, Mr W. Kellaway, Mr E. Brown, Mr R. Jones, Mr J. Williamson. I have also exploited, profitably, the resources of the Trades Union Congress Archives, the Labour Research Department, the Public Record Office, Somerset House, the National Register of Archives, and the British Museum Manuscript Department. The Institute of Historical Research of the University of London has provided me a useful reference library, a comfortable chair, an enormous desk, light, heat, and enough isolation to get some writing done. It has been a real refuge.

Many individuals, apart from libraries, have been kind enough to assist me in this effort. The late Professor Charles L. Mowat was an inspiration to me when I was doing graduate work, and a kind patron of this project in its initial stages. Baron Citrine of Wembley was good enough to clear up a number of special problems for me. Mr Andrew Rothstein and Mr R. Page Arnot were helpful on the affairs of the Communist Party of Great Britain in the 1920s. Mr George Woodcock cleared my way into the wilderness of the TUC Archives. Mr B. Averlianov of the International Committee of the All-Union Central Trade Union Council responded to enquiries of mine, as did Mr O. H. Parsons, Mr Leslie H. Thomas, Mr W. D. Pugh, Mr J. Conway, Mr W. R. Drumm, and others. I owe a special debt of gratitude to Professor E. H. Carr of Cambridge University, who took time out from his own splendid work to read this effort in its entirety, and offer helpful comments and suggestions throughout. My meetings and conversations with him were as inspiring as they were entertaining. My students over the years at the College of Wooster have sustained and deepened my interest in Russian history by the intelligence and insistence with which they have demanded I make it all make sense to them. Finally, my deepest appreciation must be reserved for a caring and sympathetic wife and family, a collection of cheer-leaders anybody would be happy to perform for. They labelled this elephantine monster 'Spunky,' and celebrated its birth with an enthusiasm and panache that made the whole two years' labour instantly worth it all. They, and especially my wife, are singular blessings. Needless to say, all the individuals listed above are responsible for all deficiencies that may be apparent in this book: I take sole credit for its virtues. Or is it supposed to be the other way around?

I will, in any event, conclude with a cheerful confession to two failings. I have sacrificed consistency to comprehensibility in matters of transliteration from the Russian. Trotsky, therefore, is Trotsky, not Trotskii; and Zinoviev is preferred to Zinov'ev. I do not think anybody who speaks Russian will have any trouble identifying the individuals named, nor I hope, will he have to strain to make out the original Russian titles of sources cited in that language. Non-Russian speakers will not care. Second, I have, solely for the sake of 'elegant variation,' used the terms 'Russian' and 'Soviet' and the terms 'English' and 'British,' interchangeably. I can only beg all Welshmen, Ukrainians, etc. to forgive my callous assault on their sensibilities. It did seem to make the writing flow more smoothly, and I doubt it will cause genuine confusion. The Soviet press did, in the 1920s, commonly refer to Great Britain as 'Angliia' (England) and the British press most generally designated the USSR 'Russia'. I am afraid I picked up the bad habits of my sources.

DANIEL F. CALHOUN

Wooster, Ohio: March 1, 1975

1
Background (1921–1924)

By 1921, the revolutionary firestorm that had seemed about to consume all Europe four years earlier had died back to a few smouldering embers – in Soviet Russia only. Even there, in the 'proletarian fatherland,' the introduction of the New Economic Policy (NEP) in 1921 could be interpreted as a retreat to capitalism, marking the end of any real effort to achieve the totality of the Marxist dream. The great international workingman's revolution was not, then, to be international at all, it appeared, and might not even be especially revolutionary.

And yet, internationalism was at the very core of Marxist doctrine, its most unchallenged tenet. The enemy – capitalism – was no national monopoly. In his search for labour to exploit and markets to plunder, the capitalist had penetrated every continent, every country. The manifestation of capitalist internationalism was imperialism, and it was Lenin's great theoretical contribution to Marxism to show how imperialism was inevitable to capitalism, and a source of short-term strength to it, but equally, the guarantee of its ultimate overthrow. It was in the backward nations, the colonial and semi-colonial countries most ruthlessly ravaged for bourgeois gain, that the weakest link in the capitalist chain would be found, and broken, Lenin wrote. And when it broke, the whole interconnected system would break with it. The revolution had to begin somewhere specific, of course, in some country or other, probably a backward one, but it could not stop there. The capitalists would not let it. They could not, for the system was composed of interdependent parts, and for it to survive anywhere it had to flourish everywhere. So a capitalist counter-revolution would quickly confront any proletarian revolution with a decisive challenge. If the revolution could not overpower capitalism's bastions of economic and military strength, in the west, it would fail that challenge and be crushed. To survive, then, it had to spread. The proletarian had to be as internationalist as his bourgeois enemy.

Somewhat crudely stated, that had been the dogma, and it remained so into 1921. But it was increasingly difficult to square what the theories indicated should happen with what the facts demonstrated had not. The bourgeoisie had exhibited no great delight in the persistence of Soviet power but had abandoned the direct assault on it. Soviet leaders were convinced the respite was only temporary. They credited it, publicly, to the efforts of sympathetic western workers' organizations which had campaigned against the intervention. Less openly, however, many nurtured suspicions that bourgeois restraint might also be attributable to the distasteful concessions to capitalism Soviet Russia had to make in adopting NEP. The enemy might tolerate a Russia which was revolutionary in name only, in which Nepmen flourished and kulaks waxed fat and cynicism grew and revolutionary fervour evaporated. The bourgeoisie might feel it did not have to murder the revolution; it was in the process of committing suicide. Lev Trotsky surely felt the force of that argument, and probably Lev Kamenev and Grigorii Zinoviev did, too.

The Cause, in any event, was clearly in jeopardy. The west would either crush it in combat or let it crush itself in compromise. The only escape from the tragic dilemma was to spread the revolution, to take the offensive, to arouse the workers to action in the European centres of capitalist power. The proletarians of all nations had to unite on behalf of their beleaguered brothers in the first workers' republic. The question was how to unite them. Bravely sounding the tocsin in 1917 and 1918 had produced disappointing results. Revolutionary phrase-making and flag-waving from the east had not been enough. The bourgeoisie had been too clever to let itself be overthrown by such elementary tactics. Something more subtle, more compelling, and more permanent had to be found – a new tactic, good for the temporary ebb of revolutionary enthusiasm as well as for the long-term surge of dialectical necessity. It was in 1921 that the Communist International, since 1919 the self-appointed general staff of the world-wide revolutionary army, came up with its recommendation – the tactics of the united front.

II

The united front was a device, an expedient, a contrivance. The intensity with which Communists themselves stressed such descriptions testified to their concern that misguided comrades might distort the united front into something it was not supposed to be, an end in itself. It was a tactic of the moment, for temporary use only in set, specific, historical circumstances. When the circumstances changed, the tactic would have to be reconsidered, and altered to suit the new realities.

At the moment, however, western Europe was in a state of suspended political animation. The bourgeoisie had managed to stabilize its position, partially and provisionally, and thus earned itself a brief respite from revolutionary nightmares. Bolshevik-controlled organizations had nowhere succeeded in winning a majority, even of urban factory workers, and in most countries Communists constituted a tiny, feeble, divided and discouraged minority of the population at large. In such conditions, even though the long-term revolutionary pressures would continue to mount, capitalism might remain entrenched and apparently secure not for months, but for a matter of years. The recovery could not be permanent, of course. The inexorable laws of Marxist science proved beyond question that revolutionary opportunities would open up in the future as they had in the past. When they did, therefore, Communist parties had to be prepared to take advantage of them. They had to build bridges, now, bridges across which the masses, the 'broad proletarian masses' as the orators invariably put it, could be led, at the right time, to their historic destiny. The united front tactic was designed to build those bridges, during the current respite, for use in the future.[1]

It consisted, most simply, in winning over the workers by making common cause with them and their leaders on basic and not especially revolutionary issues – often bread-and-butter issues of wages, hours and working conditions, occasionally broader issues such as the struggle against Fascism or the agitation against war. On such issues, the Communist stand coincided with that of the social-democratic politicians and trade union bureaucrats to whom most western workers, unfortunately, still pledged their allegiance. So Communists could offer the reformist organizations an alliance. However much we may differ from one another in theoretical fundamentals, they could propose, we are as one on these practical, immediate issues. Let us therefore sit down together and discuss how we might work together to achieve the results we both say we want.

Common action to achieve common objectives, that was the kernel of it. It involved no compromise of principle, no dilution of dogma, no

---

[1] The outline of united front tactics which follows derives mostly from documents in Karl Radek, *Piat' Let Kominterna*, Two Parts (Moscow: Izdatel'stvo 'Krasnaia Nov',' 1924), Part II, pp. 140–53, 274–8, 417–19, 461–74. The most helpful summary in Russian is Iu. L. Molchanov, *Komintern: u Istokov Politiki Edinogo Proletarskogo Fronta* (Moscow: Izdatel'stvo 'Mysl',' 1969). In English, see Cyril L. R. James, *World Revolution, 1917–1936: The Rise and Fall of the Communist International* (London: M. Secker and Warburg, 1937), pp. 168–74. I have also profited from ideas and materials in Jane Degras, ed., *The Communist International 1919–1943: Documents* (London–New York: Oxford University Press, 1956–65), II, 1–3, 22–23, and *passim*, and Isaac Deutscher, *The Prophet Unarmed: Trotsky 1921–1929* (London–New York: Oxford University Press, 1959), pp. 56–65.

organic union with quitters, defeatists or traitors. Indeed, the whole purpose of it was to expose the temporary allies, to their own followers, as the cowards and renegades they were, and thus to storm the reformist citadel from within. Communists knew the social democrats were reluctant to take the fight for any of their professed goals very far, not so far as to provoke the bourgeoisie into retaliatory action. When it came to a crisis, when, in spite of their reluctance, the battle was joined, reformists would – inevitably and conspicuously – abandon the battlefield and flee to the enemy. Communists knew all this, and said so quite openly, even as they offered such potential renegades the united front.

Of course, the social democrats could refuse even to talk with men who execrated and pilloried them so mercilessly. But to do so would seem to prove they were more concerned for their dignity than for their professed principles. Rejecting the united front, then, would give the Communists valuable propaganda ammunition. So would accepting it. Communists would then insist the battle had to be fought totally, unconditionally, no matter what the cost and however extreme the methods. Inevitably, the workers would note the Communists' energy and devotion and single-minded ruthlessness and contrast it with the passivity and empty rhetoric of their own leaders. At the decisive moment, when the Communists appealed to the workers directly over the heads of the reformist functionaries, they would respond. They would come over. The bridge would have been prepared for them.

If countering the united front challenge involved risks for the social democrats, however, posing it successfully put the Communists in jeopardy as well. Pose it too aggressively and too militantly and the reformists could rightfully dub the proletarian vanguard a band of sectarians and dogmatists, not worth associating with. Pose it too moderately and with too much deference to delicate reformist sensibilities and it would probably be accepted, but the acceptance could trap the Communists in a maze of opportunism which would obscure their own principles and muffle any compelling call to the proletariat when the crisis came. The menace of sectarianism on the left, then, and the catastrophe of opportunism on the right, delineated the very straight and very narrow path of Communist orthodoxy in the employment of united front tactics.

To avoid either trap, Communist organizations had to remain united, disciplined, and absolutely true to their principles. They had to devote especially diligent study to the experience of their sure-footed Russian comrades, who had so triumphantly avoided all ideological pitfalls.[1] They had to be acutely sensitive to timing, to know precisely when to pass from passivity to action, from preparing the revolution to waging it. All negotiations with the reformists had to be conducted in the open, without camouflage or secrecy, so that the responsibility for the break-down of the talks, or for the subsequent betrayal of agreements reached, could be clearly placed. Prior to that *dénouement*, and in preparation for it, Communists should maintain their separate identity, continue to propagandize their own ultimate objectives, and most essentially of all, insist on their absolute right and duty to criticize – indeed, to revile – those whom they had made their temporary allies.

The whole matter of collaborating with the ideologically corrupted became a major preoccupation of the Communist International, the Comintern, in 1921.[2] The issue was too immediate to be avoided. The relationship of the Chinese Communist Party to the Kuomintang, for example, hung on its resolution. So did the future of the comrades in Germany. Recent revolutionary efforts there had smacked more of farce than drama, but the Party had scored promising gains at the polls in both Saxony and Thuringia, posing the problem of how to react to Social Democratic offers of parliamentary coalitions in the state legislatures.

That the decision was made for the united front we know. How and by whom it was made is not so clear. Angelica Balabanova, at one time very close to the Comintern inner circle, reported later all significant Comintern decisions were made in fact by a secret committee of the Russian Communist Party.[3] If such a committee did exist, its membership surely included Zinoviev, the Comintern chairman, and the two Soviet

[1] This educational process was dubbed 'Bolshevization' and came strongly into vogue in 1924, in circumstances we shall be concerned with later. See below, p. 63.

[2] My information on the adoption of united front tactics by the Comintern in the years 1921–3 derives from Radek, *Piat' Let Kominterna*, Part II, *passim*; Deutscher, *Trotsky*, pp. 56–65; Jane Degras, 'United Front Tactics in the Comintern, 1921–8,' in David Footman, ed., *International Communism* (London: Chatto and Windus, 1960), pp. 9–22; Franz Borkenau, *The Communist International* (London: Faber and Faber, 1938), pp. 164, 226–37; Michael T. Florinsky, *World Revolution and the USSR* (London: Macmillan, 1933), pp. 87–106; Degras, *Communist International: Documents*, II, 26–51; Lewis Lorwin, *Labor and Internationalism* (London: George Allen and Unwin, 1929), pp. 235–40; and U.S. Congress, House, Committee on Un-American Activities, *The Communist Conspiracy: Strategy and Tactics of World Communism*, Part 1. *Communism Outside the United States*, Section C. *The World Congresses of the Communist International*, House Report 2242 (Washington, D.C.: U.S. Government Printing Office, 1956), pp. 106–52.

[3] Angelica Balabanova (Balabanoff), *My Life as a Rebel* (London: Hamish Hamilton, 1938), p. 246.

members of the Comintern's Executive Committee (the ECCI), Nikolai Bukharin and Karl Radek. For matters of high policy, Trotsky would be brought in, and of course, if he were well enough, Lenin. At the risk of unduly stressing a negative, one must emphasize that Stalin was not in the inner circle at all. He had little use for the International anyway. He was convinced it was incapable of organizing a successful revolution anywhere, and dreaded the possibility it might interfere in the internal affairs of the Russian party and government. He shunned Comintern meetings, consistently declined invitations to address Comintern Congresses, and after securing his grip on the movement in the late 1920s, allowed only one more Congress to take place at all.[1]

So any decision on whether to implement the united front would have been made by Zinoviev, Bukharin, Radek, Trotsky and Lenin. The first two, antagonists on so many other issues, were allies on this one: both opposed the new line. They were overridden by Lenin, Trotsky and Radek, all three of whom spoke for the new line at the 3rd Comintern Congress in June and July, 1921. Although no precise commitment to the united front was adopted at the Congress, the slogan that emerged, 'To the Masses!' clearly implied a change of course. The theses on tactics as much as acknowledged that workers, far from being in a militant mood, were docilely following their reformist leaders, and that a frontal attack by Communists on those leaders would net the Party precisely nothing. To get 'to the masses' in such circumstances, without making distasteful overtures to the leaders, was clearly impossible. The united front was not specifically mentioned, much less precisely delineated, but it followed inevitably from the conclusions of the Congress.

The details were worked out by December, 1921, when the ECCI issued specific directions for achieving the united front, and the whole new line was ratified by the 4th Comintern Congress in November, 1922 after Trotsky made a strenuous appeal on its behalf. Opposition to the new line was conspicuously vocal. The French, Italian, and Spanish parties were particularly bitter about being obliged to cooperate with social-democratic elements they had long damned as the worst enemies of the working classes. The Congress labelled their position 'sectarian,' even though Radek threw them a sop in his assurance the leadership intended no merger with the social democrats, but rather 'to stifle them in our embrace.'[2] The final resolutions adopted proclaimed united front

---

[1] The material on Stalin is from Isaac Deutscher, *Stalin: A Political Biography*, Rev. Ed. (Harmondsworth: Penguin Books, 1966), pp. 388–93.

[2] Cited by Degras, 'United Front Tactics' in Footman, *International Communism*, p. 11.

tactics indispensible, and the delegates even approved active Communist participation in coalition 'workers' governments,' an ambiguous phrase left diplomatically undefined. A decisive test of the new line seemed to be emerging in Germany.[1] A bitter party wrangle had developed there centered around the question of how far the German Communist Party, the KPD, should go in co-operative efforts with the Social Democratic party, the SPD. The KPD right, including the Party leader, Heinrich Brandler, interpreted the somewhat equivocal wording of the 4th Comintern Congress's united front resolutions as authorizing parliamentary coalitions with the SPD, even to the point of participation in SPD-controlled state governments. The left wing, led by Ruth Fischer and Arkadi Maslow, denounced the whole idea of parliamentary methods as basically alien to Communist principles, and condemned the SPD in particular as a front organization for the bourgeoisie. The row was conducted with uncomradely vigour, and Moscow had to step in in April, 1923 to call a halt to the argument. Four leftists were added to the KPD Central Committee, in return for which the left wing toned down its overt protests against the united front.

Unity was essential if the party were to rise to the revolutionary possibilities that seemed to be opening up so rapidly in Germany. The French occupation of the Ruhr had produced an accelerating economic and political crisis culminating, in August, in a massive strike effort, the fall of the federal government, and the emergence of a new government, under Stresemann, in which the SPD agreed to participate. Communist Party membership grew dramatically over the summer, and to sanguine enthusiasts, the 'German October' was at last in sight.

As early as July, 1923 the KPD called for a Comintern decision on revolution. Radek, the International's representative in Germany, felt the situation was not yet ripe, and counselled caution. So did Stalin, from the sidelines and with no great energy, and then shrugged off the problem for others to resolve. Zinoviev and Bukharin, vague about details, were nevertheless strongly for action. So too, with somewhat less enthusiasm but somewhat more willingness to work out the practical

---

[1] For the immediate impact of the German revolution of 1923 on Comintern policy, I have relied on the following: Ruth Fischer, *Stalin and German Communism* (London: Oxford University Press, 1948), pp. 291–383; Radek, *Piat' Let Kominterna*, Part II, pp. 409–502; Deutscher, *Trotsky*, pp. 141–6; Deutscher, *Stalin*, pp. 390–3; Borkenau, *Communist International*, pp. 235–53; Degras, *Communist International: Documents*, II, 18–22, 62–5, 68–72, 90; Victor Serge, *Memoirs of a Revolutionary, 1901–1941*, trans. and ed. by Peter Sedgwick (London: Oxford University Press, 1963), pp. 169–75.

details, was Trotsky. So that is the way the decision went, in late August, 1923, and the following month Brandler showed up in Moscow, doubtful about the whole affair – he never claimed to be a revolutionary commander and was nervous in the role – but willing to yield to the superior wisdom of such crafty veterans as Trotsky.

The plans were duly elaborated, and Radek and Georgii Piatakov, the former Kiev sugar millionaire, were delegated Comintern agents-in-charge. Brandler was to return to Saxony and accept the SPD invitation to join the state government there. He would then take advantage of his official status to, first, arm the workers, and then, proclaim the revolution. It was assumed the rank-and-file of the SPD and the trade unions, and perhaps many of their leaders as well, would answer the call. Thus, for the first – and last – time, the Comintern did precisely what it had been established to do: decide scientifically when, where, and how a revolution should be launched, and dispatch the experts to make sure the plan was carried through smoothly.

But it was a clumsy plan, drawn up at too great a distance by men who knew little of local conditions. The specific instructions that went with it were contradictory, confused and impracticable. The result was a fiasco from beginning to end. Very shortly after Brandler joined the Saxon 'Government of Proletarian Defence,' the German army marched in – armed with weapons supplied from the Soviet Union! – and deposed it. There was practically no resistance. The Social Democrats and the trade unions rejected Communist proposals for a retaliatory general strike and proclamation of armed insurrection, and it was soon clear the masses of workers were unprepared to back any such extreme reactions. At the last minute Brandler asked permission to cancel the call for revolution, and Zinoviev, back in Moscow, quickly agreed. But the news of the change of plans did not get to Hamburg on time, where the workers, with more spirit than good sense, rose, fought, and were crushed. In the aftermath German Communism lost its legal status for a matter of months and its soul forever. And as for the Comintern, nobody but rabid right-wing western politicians – and its own functionaries – could ever take it very seriously again. 'The Comintern was a corpse,' Ruth Fischer wrote.[1]

The attempt to assess the blame for the disaster produced minor masterpieces of comradely vituperation, or 'self-criticism,' as the official thesaurus prefers. Stalin and Zinoviev, well-launched on their campaign to destroy Trotsky's political influence, blamed him on the ground that

---

[1] Fischer, *Stalin and German Communism*, p. 365.

it was his plan that had failed, his supporter, Radek, who was on the spot, and his protégé, Brandler, who had capitulated at the eleventh hour. Trotsky responded that since his plan had been cancelled, with Zinoviev's consent, it had never been given a proper trial, and attributed the failure to Stalin, who had opposed the revolution from the beginning, and Zinoviev, who had betrayed it in the crucial final hours. The German leftists, Fischer and Maslow, blamed Brandler and his 'opportunism', a transparent euphemism for his adherence to the united front tactics which were the official Comintern line. They also attacked Trotsky, who was assumed to be Brandler's protector. The revolutionary plan could have succeeded, they claimed (thus, in effect, complimenting the work of the author of the plan, Trotsky) had not Brandler cancelled it. With the backing of Zinoviev and Bukharin, they got Brandler ousted from the KPD leadership in 1924.

All this was nightmarishly distorted, and the political line-ups that emerged in early 1924 defy all the standard generalizations in elementary textbooks of Soviet history. The 'leftist' Trotsky, the advocate of permanent revolution, with his 'rightist' associate Brandler, were condemned by the 'rightist' Bukharin and the 'leftist' Zinoviev for not being revolutionary enough, in spite of the fact it had been Zinoviev who cancelled Trotsky's revolutionary plan. Only two men had assessed events accurately, Stalin and Radek, both of whom had urged caution: now each blamed the other for the failure of the revolution neither had wanted. One can make no sense out of all this, except to note all major participants found themselves innocent of all blame for the debacle.

Clearly, however, the rout required reconsideration of those united front tactics which had been so central to the whole effort. Two of the three authors of the united front doctrine, Trotsky and Radek, had been disgraced following the German debacle, and the third, Lenin, died in January, 1924. The united front could not be publicly repudiated, however. That would imply a propensity to err in both Lenin and the Comintern leadership generally. But dexterous reinterpretation of authoritative texts can accomplish the same results as repeal, and that was the direction the Comintern seemed to be moving in early 1924. An Executive Committee statement noted that alliances with social democrats and parliamentary coalitions with anybody were, of course, foreign to the essential spirit of the united front. The united front must be pursued not so much from above, through overtures to reformist leaders, as from below, by agitation among the working masses. Brandler was blamed for the German failure. He was pronounced guilty of opportunism and of failure to realise that the united front was 'only a method of revolutionary agitation and mobilisation.'[1] The aim had always been to destroy the social-democratic factions, not support them. Social democracy was merely 'fascism wearing a socialist mask.'[2] Left-wing leaders, with their strong and subtle appeal to the masses, were more dangerous than rightists, and the object should be their 'political annihilation.'[3] It would seem that if the united front concept were not already dead, such language would quickly kill it. But such was not to be the case. Ideology showed its usual remarkable power to recuperate from reality. By the end of the year 1924 Communist leaders were developing a new project to be achieved through united front tactics, the penetration of the international trade union movement.

Efforts to rally trade unions to more than merely national organizational banners date back to at least the end of the nineteenth century. Some degree of success in what was called 'vertical organization' had been achieved prior to the First World War through the so-called International Trade Secretariats, the Miners' International, the Transport Workers' International, and so on – organizations of trade unionists in specific industries. Attempts to go beyond that and achieve a 'horizontal organization,' incorporating complete national trade union federations, produced, in 1901, the International Secretariat of Trade Unions, a very loosely constructed affair which did little more than hold annual conferences for the exchange of advice, information and anecdotes. The organization was of no great importance, and collapsed ignominiously under the strain of Sarajevo.

Even while the war was on, however, plans were developed for establishing a newer and stronger international when the fighting stopped.[4] The details were worked out by a conference meeting at Amsterdam in July and August of 1919. It was, in part, an unedifying and indeed degrading display. The representatives from the Entente

---

[1] Degras, *Communist International: Documents*, II, 72.
[2] *Ibid.*, p. 77.   [3] *Ibid.*, p. 78.
[4] A scholarly history of the IFTU does not yet exist. Somewhat surprisingly, one of the most competent surveys of the earliest history of the IFTU is by the leader of its rival organization, the RILU. See Alexander Lozovsky, *The World's Trade Union Movement* (London: National Minority Movement, 1925), pp. 9–24, 54–72. I have also used Georges Lefranc, *Les Expériences syndicales internationals, des origines à nos jours* (Paris: Aubier, 1952), pp. 7–35; G. D. H. Cole, *A History of Socialist Thought*, Vol. IV, *Communism and Social Democracy, 1914–1931*, Two Parts (London: Macmillan, 1958), Part I, Chapter IX, pp. 287–342; and Walther Schevenals, *Quarante-cinq années: Fédération syndicale internationale, 1901–1945* ([Brussels]: Editions de l'Institut E. Vandervelde, 1964), pp. 1–87.

powers refused to have anything to do with their German proletarian brothers until the Germans apologized for and explained away – on the grounds they had been misled and misinformed – their previous support of the 'injustices' committed against Belgium from 1914 to 1918. Only after that fatuous ritual (which, in any event, the German unions subsequently repudiated) could the Congress get down to business and elaborate a constitution for an International Federation of Trade Unions (IFTU).

Basic policies of the IFTU were to be decided by majority vote of triennial General Congresses, but enforcement of agreed decisions by individual national centres was to be purely voluntary. Between Congresses, the IFTU's Executive Committee and General Council were entrusted with management of the organization's affairs. The Executive Committee consisted of the IFTU's president, vice-presidents and secretaries, seven officials altogether as of 1924. It was responsible for routine IFTU business, and was supposed to meet six times a year. Questions of higher priority, including admissions to the organization and exclusions from it, were entrusted to the General Council, meeting twice a year and consisting of the Executive Committee plus twelve additional members chosen to represent regional groupings of affiliated members. In addition, after 1924, the revived International Trade Secretariats were entitled to designate three General Council members, so that its total membership, then, was 22.

The young Russian trade union movement seemed, at first, very interested in joining an international organization of IFTU's type.[1] A resolution of the Menshevik-dominated 3rd All-Russian Trade Union Conference in June, 1917, calling for just such a venture, had been reaffirmed by the Bolshevik-controlled 1st All-Russian Trade Union Congress in January, 1918. But a subordinate role in an association dominated by the sort of legalists and compromisers who assembled at Amsterdam was not what the Russian revolutionary militants had in mind at all, and when they were invited to participate in the IFTU's

---

[1] Information on the first Russian reactions to IFTU, and the formation of the rival RILU organization, is derived from the following sources: Lozovsky, *World's Trade Union Movement*, pp. 126–44; S. Sorbonsky, comp. and A. Lozovsky, ed., *Desiat' Let Profinterna v Rezoliutsiiakh, Dokumentakh i Tsifrakh* (Moscow: Izdatel'stvo VTsSPS, 1930), pp. 17–77; Lefranc, *Les Expériences syndicales internationales*, pp. 52–64; Borkenau, *Communist International*, pp. 196–8; International Labour Office, *The Trade Union Movement in Soviet Russia*, Studies and Reports, Series A (Industrial Relations), No. 26 (Geneva: International Labour Office, 1927), pp. 216–30; and J. T. Murphy, *New Horizons* (London: John Lane, 1941), pp. 157–61, 172–6.

inaugural congress, their response was to hurl abuse at the imperialist agents and lackeys of bourgeois capitalism there represented. As early as October of 1919, just two months after the founding of the IFTU, the All-Russian Central Council of Trade Unions appealed to the workers of the world 'to break with the international union of conciliators' at Amsterdam and 'cooperate in a really revolutionary attempt to liberate the workers from the capitalist yoke and to establish the dictatorship of the proletariat...'[1]

It seemed, at first, that the rival organization to the IFTU was going to be the Third International itself and not any separate trade union federation. In early 1920, the Russian unions resolved to 'affiliate' with the Comintern and to encourage others to follow their example. But just a few months later, Lenin apparently decided on different tactics. While condemning the 'yellow' Amsterdam International ('yellow,' in trade union jargon, implying that the IFTU and its member unions were paid agents of international capitalism), and encouraging creation of a more agreeable alternative to it, the Comintern would not itself become a centre of trade unionism. Its function was to be the proletariat's vanguard, not its caretaker. A new organization would be founded, subject of course to Comintern's general oversight and maintaining the closest ties with it, but structurally separate.

The man designated to implement the new policy and see to the new institution was a singular choice. He was Aleksandr Lozovsky, born Solomon Abramovich Dridzo, the son of a teacher, an active Menshevik as late as 1919,[2] an exhaustingly prolific orator and pamphleteer, and a major rival of the genial chairman of the All-Russian Central Council of Trade Unions, Mikhail Tomsky, for command of the Soviet trade union movement. Lozovsky always seemed out-of-place among the rough-hewn trade union militants whom he hoped to lead. He had never been a manual worker himself, and his only previous trade union experience had been the two years he spent as secretary-general of the Hatters' Union in France from 1909 to 1911. He was too much the intellectual to play his part convincingly. He looked more like a 'slightly fastidious schoolmaster,'[3] as one colleague put it, than a labourer. And

---

[1] Otchet VTsSPS, Moscow, 1920, p. 58, cited in International Labour Office, *Trade Union Movement in Soviet Russia*, p. 217.

[2] Lozovsky's political perambulations are difficult to follow. He was apparently a Menshevik from 1903 to 1909, a Bolshevik for a few years after 1909, but a member of the Trotskyite *mezhraiontsy* group as of 1917. He became a Bolshevik in August of that year, resigned (or was expelled) from the Bolshevik organization in 1918, and was readmitted to it in 1919.   [3] Serge, *Memoirs*, p. 146.

sounded more like one. He enjoyed showing off his knowledge of languages, of German, French and English. He relished his pose as cosmopolitan sophisticate, in marked contrast to the native, blunt, sometimes raw openness of a Tomsky. Ideologically, he was, after 1919, the total convert, more Bolshevik than the Bolsheviks, far more 'hard-line' than was Tomsky, even though Tomsky had been an undeviating Leninist for almost two decades. Few took Lozovsky altogether seriously, however, and almost everybody who knew them both preferred dealing with Tomsky.[1] The choice of Lozovsky as Communism's leader-designate in international trade unionism was very much of a surprise, therefore, and perhaps in retrospect, a tactical error.

Chosen he was, however, and authorized to begin preparations, in the late spring of 1920, for a new international trade union organization. On June 15, 1920, after a month of negotiations on the details, an interim propaganda body called the International Council of Trade and Industrial Unions, the forbear of the later Red International, was declared in existence, and a Provisional Committee named to run it consisting of Lozovsky, Tomsky, and the British Communist leader, J. T. Murphy. The very first manifesto issued by the new organization, on August 1, rejected any compromise with Amsterdam and demanded the IFTU be smashed.[2] The workers of the world were to be required to make their choice one way or the other, Moscow or Amsterdam, and Moscow was confident of the result.

The intention, however, was not to split European trade unionism. The 2nd Comintern Congress specifically condemned any mass withdrawals from IFTU affiliates. Lenin's pamphlet, *Left-Wing Communism: An Infantile Disorder*, was similarly explicit. The aim was not to break up, or desert, IFTU-associated trade union movements, but to stay with them, penetrate them further, take them over, and finally transfer them from the Amsterdam affiliation to a Moscow one. The revolutionary tide was still flowing, it was assumed, and would continue to swell. The trade unions were moving rapidly to the left, far to the left of the IFTU's leadership. Moscow had only to be patient, then, and to be patient only briefly. Under the pressure of just a few ferocious manifestos, Amsterdam would fall apart, and its affiliates would come meekly over to the new international. There, accepting the leadership of the

---

[1] See, for example, Murphy, *New Horizons*, p. 161; Borkenau, *Communist International*, pp. 196–8.

[2] Aleksandr Lozovsky, ed., *Profintern v Rezoliutsiakh*, compiled, and with a commentary by S. V. Girinis (Moscow: Izd. Profinterna, 1928), pp. 12–15.

Russian trade unions, they would come under the effective control of the Comintern.

So the fledgling International was launched, even if only provisionally, and it promptly opened an acrimonious assault on the IFTU. Representatives were sent to western Europe to establish national bureaus of the new organization, to force the Moscow-versus-Amsterdam decision, and finally, to detach the unions from Amsterdam and affiliate them to Moscow. The formal founding Congress of the new organization was announced for the following year. To IFTU suggestions that perhaps it could collaborate with the Russians, Lozovsky replied that 'the hand held out to us will...be ignored.'[1] Amsterdam's attitude toward its antagonist had, at first, been quite casual, as if it did not take the challenge very seriously. It had termed the Moscow organization just a lot of 'bluff and bluster,'[2] and indicated the Russian unions could calm down and join IFTU whenever they liked. But as the attacks from the east continued and intensified, and Moscow began to receive some membership applications – from Finland, Bulgaria, Latvia, Yugoslavia – the Amsterdam line hardened. In May, 1921, it adopted a resolution bitterly condemning the Russians for organizing dissension within its member centres, and specifically forbidding any of its direct affiliates, or affiliates of International Trade Secretariats associated with it, to become members of the Moscow organization as well. Some of the IFTU's national centres, notably the French, took an even stronger retaliatory line. They ordered Communists excluded from trade union organizations altogether, hoping to isolate the Red hard-liners, and thus render them comparatively ineffective. Both sides, then, had now put the issue in the same fundamental and uncompromising terms: it was indeed to be Moscow or Amsterdam.

The inaugural Congress of the Russian-sponsored International was held at Moscow in July, 1921. The formal name of the association was to be the Red International of Labour Unions, RILU, or in the somewhat startling Russian abbreviation, Profintern. 350 delegates from 38 countries participated in the founding meeting. A basic organizational structure was approved institutionalizing Russia's pre-eminent position in the International in the arrangements for finance and in provision for extra Soviet membership in the RILU's executive organs. Hostility toward Amsterdam was reaffirmed in the most militant terms – unity

---

[1] International Labour Office, *Trade Union Movement in Soviet Russia*, p. 219, citing the journal *International Communist* for November, 1920.

[2] Lorwin, *Labor and Internationalism*, p. 232.

with it was certainly out of the question[1] – but the Congress confirmed, after some debate, that the older unions in the west should be won over, conquered by the usual cell-building tactics, rather than repudiated, split or abandoned. Comrades were strictly enjoined, once again, to stay in IFTU affiliates, not desert them.[2] Moscow's inevitable triumph might take some time. The buoyant confidence of a year earlier, when the effort to build the new organization had begun, had subsided markedly. A new and cautious realism was reflected in the debates of the RILU's 1st Congress, if not so clearly in all its resolutions.

In terms of raw membership statistics, the new organization probably made fairly good progress in the years after 1921, especially when its performance is contrasted with IFTU's dreary reports of annual shrinkages.[3] Boasting a membership of 23 million at the time of its founding, IFTU had shrunk to just 15 million – almost all of them European – by early 1924. Comparable RILU statistics are hard to come by. Lozovsky was making wholly fanciful claims of 17 million 'adherents' in 1921, and had come down to a more realistic 13 million 'members' in 1927. It would be reasonable to assume, however, that Profintern began with roughly 8 million direct affiliations plus an indeterminate number of sympathizers in IFTU unions. By 1924 membership may have reached 9 million (plus sympathizers) and by 1927, 12 million. Only one-third the size of the IFTU at its founding, then, RILU was over half as large by 1924 and had come close to drawing even with the older organization as of 1927. The figures must be evaluated cautiously, however. Much of the increase over the last three years, for example, represented the growth of just one component of the organization, the unions of Soviet Russia, which swelled from $6\frac{1}{2}$ million to over 9 million members between 1924 and 1926, and which always made up at least two-thirds, often more, of the Profintern membership. Such an imbalance was clearly no source of strength to the new organization, and in this respect, Amsterdam

---

[1] *Profintern v Rezoliutsiakh*, pp. 16–20.

[2] *Ibid.*, pp. 68–70.

[3] Much of the decline in IFTU membership was due to affiliates dropping out of the organization altogether, as did the AF of L. Precise figures for IFTU and RILU memberships are hard to come by. Those quoted in Communist International, *Jahrbuch für Wirtschaft, Politik und Arbeiterbewegung, 1925–1926* (Hamburg: Hoym, 1926) are remarkably different from the estimates in International Federation of Trade Unions, *Fifth Year Book, 1925* (Amsterdam, 1925). For other guesses, see Ludwig Heyde, ed., *Internationales Handwörterbuch des Gewerkschaftswesens* (Berlin: Werk und Wirtschafts-Verlagsaktiengesellschaft, 1931–2) and Lorwin, *Labor and Internationalism*. In 1924, Profintern was claiming 13 million supporters: IFTU would only concede it something over 7 million.

statistics looked a good deal healthier; neither of the two largest national components of IFTU, Great Britain or Germany, contributed as much as 35 per cent of the federation's total membership.

Theoretically, no 'double membership' was possible. A trade union federation had to adhere either to Amsterdam or to Moscow, one or the other, not both. On the other hand, it was Profintern policy to capture IFTU affiliates, not split them, which brought up the problem of whether to claim as an RILU member the sympathetic individual enrolled in an IFTU affiliate. Even more complicated was the question of whole unions that wanted to affiliate to RILU, but would be expelled from their national federation if they were to do so. The Comintern Executive Committee resolved the question in March of 1922 by establishing a category of what was called 'only ideological' allegiance to Profintern for sympathizers who would be ousted from their organizations for overt RILU membership.[1]

The agonizing position of the good Party member writhing under reformist leadership in a compromising trade union was fully recognized, but the comrade was counselled to persevere. Splitting the union, or abandoning it to the reformists, would only strengthen the enemy, and 'impatient comrades' would just have to learn to bear their burden cheerfully.[2] Of course, where splits were unavoidable, where they were forced on the Communists by reformist leaders, as in Czechoslovakia and France, a home was found in Profintern for the excluded Red loyalists. But even there, the appeal was always for re-union, in return for which any direct RILU-association would be dropped.

The Red International aimed at winning over, not only the individual unions and federations of unions, but the International Trade Secretariats as well. To supervise the infiltration of those organizations and lure them away from IFTU's influence, Profintern established a series of International Propaganda Committees, IPCs, one for each Secretariat. The IPCs were not competing with the Secretariats for membership, RILU emphasized. They were not alternatives to the Secretariats. They merely sought to persuade the Secretariats to open their membership rolls to RILU affiliates. Once the revolutionary unions had been admitted to the International's charmed circle, and the struggle against reformism could proceed from within, the corresponding IPC would presumably close down.[3]

---

[1] *Kommunisticheskii Internatsional v Dokumentakh*, p. 270.
[2] See, for example, *Desiat' Let Profinterna*, p. 107.
[3] For this material, and that which follows on the International Trade Secretariats

The effort met determined resistance from Amsterdam. Delegates to the federation's Rome Congress in April of 1922 agreed the IFTU should oppose any Trade Secretariat's admitting a union not affiliated to Amsterdam through its national centre. IFTU could not dictate to the trade Secretariats and compel them to agree to any such policy, of course, but it could exert a good deal of influence, and in November of 1923 a majority of trade Secretariat representatives did consent to a policy conforming to the Rome recommendations, and agreed, as well, that the Secretariats should confine their policy declarations to issues of immediate concern to their own trades. Broader statements on matters of more general interest should be left to IFTU, it was acknowledged.

Amsterdam's pressure was sufficient to checkmate IPC efforts in most Secretariats. Such victories as the revolutionaries won tended to be incomplete, temporary or inconsequential. They did effect admission of the Russian unions into the International Food and Drink Workers' Federation in the autumn of 1923, and towards the end of the year, the entrance of all RILU affiliates to the International of Educational Workers. But revolutionary waiters, wine-stewards and school-teachers, gratifying though they might be, would hardly constitute the core of the proletarian class army, and in the larger Secretariats, the efforts of Profintern and its IPCs were frustrated at every turning.

Their major attention was devoted to the Transport Workers' International, a powerful organization and one with pronounced left-wing leanings. Rebuffed at first, the transport workers' IPC finally seemed to be making progress in 1923. The International agreed to a conference with the Russian transport workers on the dangers of war and of fascism. The conference, at Berlin on May 23 and 24, resulted in an action committee to direct a campaign against the twin menaces and a call for a unity congress of all transport workers' organizations, IFTU and RILU, to meet in the autumn.

The Russians were ecstatic. Lozovsky modestly hailed his work as a triumph of united front tactics carefully applied, and the Comintern's Enlarged Executive solemnly agreed that the Berlin success marked the utter defeat of Amsterdam's policy of nipping off revolutionary buds in the trade unions.[1] All the Muscovite rapture, however, proved premature. Amsterdam pressure finally persuaded the General Council of the

and the IPCs, I am especially indebted to the scrupulous research in E. H. Carr, *A History of Soviet Russia, Socialism in One Country, 1924–26*, Vol. III, Two Parts (New York–London: Macmillan, 1964), Part I, pp. 530–4, 540, 545–9.

[1] *Kommunisticheskii Internatsional v Dokumentakh*, p. 377.

Transport Workers' International to disown the work of its representatives at Berlin. It resolutely supported a united front against war, reaction and fascism, the General Council affirmed, but before it could agree to admit Profintern unions to the International, RILU had to pledge itself to discontinue its attacks on IFTU affiliates, and the Russian trade unions had to promise to fight war, reaction and fascism at home as well as abroad. The Russians of course refused to submit to such verbal humiliation, and the whole effort collapsed.

A major casualty of the struggle was the Dutchman, Edo Fimmen, one of the secretaries of the Amsterdam Federation, a member of its Executive Committee, and a powerful voice in the Transport Workers' International as well. Fimmen was an energetic and eloquent spokesman for reconciliation between the European and Russian trade unions – too energetic and eloquent, apparently, for his colleagues on the IFTU Executive Committee to tolerate. His indiscreet public attacks on their policies – and, they felt, on their integrity – provoked reaction. J. H. Thomas, the IFTU President, berated Fimmen soundly at the Executive Committee's March, 1923 meeting. A month later, the German trade union centre formally demanded his dismissal, a demand the Executive rejected only because the IFTU constitution did not provide such conveniently drastic penalties for dissent. His colleagues' expressions of chill contempt, however, finally provoked Fimmen's resignation, amidst mutual recriminations and IFTU charges he was disloyal, had disclosed confidential information, and committed various other enormities.[1] The unity campaign had lost its strongest voice in Amsterdam's highest councils.

While the Profintern's lesser effort, directed at the International Trade Secretariats, was faltering, its greater effort, aimed at the IFTU as a whole, was collapsing altogether. The RILU's Central Council swung into action with the new united front tactics as early as February, 1922, just two months after they were officially proclaimed. The first specific proposals, however, were couched in such brutal language that the possibility of any positive response from Amsterdam was minimal. Profintern was always ready to join in a united effort against capitalist exploitation, the resolution pledged, but the IFTU bosses lacked both the will and the determination to participate in any such effort, and

---

[1] Trades Union Congress, General Council, Minutes, 31 Oct., 1923; International Committee, Minutes, 19 Feb., 1924, file 901, Doc. 1.C.2. Borkenau, *Communist International*, pp. 277–8, an otherwise useful summary of the affair, wrongly identifies Fimmen as president of the IFTU: he was in fact one of the secretaries.

would therefore reject the offer.[1] That was a self-fulfilling prophecy, of course, and Lozovsky must have known it would be.

In addition to the standard united front manoeuvres, however, the RILU also began to hint at the possibility of organic unity with IFTU – which was something else altogether – in its 1922 resolutions. The split in the international trade union movement was not of our making and was not to our liking, the RILU insisted. Our movement was a forced response to Amsterdam's policy of political expulsions. The deep split in international trade unionism that had resulted, the RILU observed, might be healed by the convocation of an international unity conference. If Amsterdam would agree to participate in such a conference, so would Moscow.[2] The IFTU's tangential response to the overture, at its Rome Congress in April, 1922, was to invite the Russian trade unions to drop their RILU affiliation and join IFTU, a suggestion Lozovsky damned as hypocritical.[3] The Amsterdam delegates rejected any deals with RILU as a whole. Profintern's outrageous slanders against IFTU affiliates and their leaders were embedded in the very constitution and rules of RILU, it was observed, and the divisive, cell-building activities of revolutionary militants allowed to penetrate established organizations were too well known to require comment. Only if the Russians would desert these renegade splinter groups was a united organization possible.

Undeterred, the RILU repeated the old proposals, if perhaps with somewhat less conviction, in the resolutions of its 2nd Congress in November of 1922. It once again suggested international trade union unity but this time did not bother to be specific on how to achieve it. It was sufficient to note that the workers wanted and needed unity, and Amsterdam rejected it, proving that Amsterdam represented the class enemy. The united front policy was reaffirmed, however, and absolute discipline in its administration demanded. The united front must be pursued with even greater devotion, the directives suggested, and went on to offer a new list of specific issues on which revolutionaries and reformists might come together – bread-and-butter economic issues, anti-fascism, anti-imperialism, the struggle for peace, even the campaign against the Ku Klux Klan.[4]

All these proposals were hurled at Amsterdam, one by one, through December and January of 1922–3. An IFTU-sponsored conference on

---

[1] *Profintern v Rezoliutsiakh*, pp. 37–43.
[2] *Ibid.*, pp. 71–3; *Desiat' Let Profinterna*, pp. 83–4.
[3] Lozovsky, *World's Trade Union Movement*, pp. 66–9.
[4] *Desiat' Let Profinterna*, pp. 104–9; *Profintern v Rezoliutsiakh*, pp. 44–7.

peace at the Hague in December provided an especially irresistible opportunity. Three unwanted Soviet delegates, headed by Lozovsky, attended, made fervent, uncompromising speeches demanding the united front, and then cast the only votes against the final resolutions adopted. When the conference was over, and talk was no longer possible, Profintern turned to manifestos and letters. The IFTU Executive finally decided to call an abrupt half to the irritating dialogue. A rude, brusque letter dated January 30, 1923 announced the IFTU did not believe Profintern proposals were meant seriously and it would therefore refuse to waste its time replying to any further Profintern correspondence. Mutual confidence, which alone could provide the basis for common action, was, unhappily, lacking.[1]

Amsterdam was as good as its word. It never again communicated directly with the rival international. Lozovsky's repeated challenges for a united front met only a frigid silence. The result was that the major responsibility for pursuing united front tactics shifted – as of the spring of 1923 – from Profintern to its major affiliate, the Russian trade union organization – in effect, then, from Lozovsky to Tomsky. Amsterdam had rebuffed only RILU, not the Russians. It had indicated it was always ready to talk to the Soviet labour leaders. That provided an opening, and Tomsky seemed delighted to step through it. The whole shift in emphasis might be advantageous to him personally, in maintaining his political lead over Lozovsky. And it might serve to maintain his power base, the Soviet trade unions, as against the encroachments of the Red International.[2]

The Russian trade union movement had not found it easy to maintain a meaningful and autonomous role for itself in a society in which exploitation or oppression of the proletariat was theoretically quite impossible.[3] The traditional trade union function, after all, had been to

[1] International Federation of Trade Unions, *Report on Activities during the Years 1924, 1925, and 1926: Submitted to the Fourth Ordinary Congress, Paris, August, 1927* (Amsterdam, 1927), p. 43.

[2] See, for example, *Profintern v Rezoliutsiakh*, p. 75 and Degras, *Communist International: Documents*, ii, 33–5.

[3] Material on the Soviet trade union movement is derived primarily from *Profsoiuzy SSSR; Dokumenty i Materialy*, 4 vols., Vol. ii, *Profsoiuzy v Period Postroeniia Sotsializma v SSSR, Oktiabria 1917g–1937g* (Moscow–Leningrad: Izdatel'stvo VTs-SPS–Profizdat, 1963), *passim*; Isaac Deutscher, *Soviet Trade Unions: Their Place in Soviet Labour Policy* (London: Royal Institute of International Affairs, 1950); E. H. Carr, *A History of Soviet Russia, The Bolshevik Revolution 1917–1923*, Vol. ii (London: Macmillan, 1952), pp. 198–227, 317–31; N. Rytikov, 'Sovetskie Profsoiuzy' *Bol'shaia Sovetskaia Entsiklopediia*, ed. S. I. Vavilov et al. (Moscow: Institut 'Sovetskaia Entsiklopediia,' 1947), pp. 1743–60; and I. Yuzepovich,

champion the workers' cause. In the new Soviet Russia, under a proletarian dictatorship and led by the proletarian vanguard, that cause was presumably more than adequately championed by the state itself, and by the Party in command of the state apparatus. Thus Zinoviev had openly urged suicide on the 1st All-Russian Trade Union Congress in January, 1918, suggesting to the delegates that they turn their unions into integral subsidiary organs of state power, subject to the soviets. The precarious compromise finally arranged maintained the unions' separate identity and their right to make binding decisions in matters of detail, but pledged in return their full support to the government in essentials, rejected any claim to political independence, and conceded that their ultimate role, after the revolution was complete, would indeed be as just part of the state apparatus.

The 10th Party Congress, in 1921, reaffirmed that decision. The Russian labour organizations were neither to be absorbed by the state nor to be totally detached from it. In a society which was not yet 'classless,' they were to be autonomous – but subordinate – 'schools of Communism.' They would function as a 'transmission belt,' to convey the Party's messages to the masses, and by their enforcement of the strictest labour discipline, they would ensure the success of the Party programme.

If the 10th Congress exorcised the spectre of 'statification' of the unions, however, it threatened them with the prospect of all the more vigorous supervision by the Party. Ideologically, the unions would submit absolutely to the Party, the Congress decreed, and the Party would even exercise 'direct control' over the selection of trade union leaders.[1] When, two months later, at the 4th All-Russian Trade Union Congress, Tomsky appeared to be challenging that decision, he was not only reprimanded but temporarily removed from the trade union leadership and packed off to Central Asia for a half year of reflection and penitence in dusty Tashkent. His disgrace was short-lived, however. He was back in Moscow by the end of 1921, and completely re-established

---

'Professional'nye Soiuzy,' *Bol'shaia Sovetskaia Entsiklopediia*, 1st Edition, Gen. Ed. O. Iu. Shmidt, Vol. XLVII (Moscow: Aktsionernoe Obshchestvo 'Sovetskaia Entsiklopediia,' 1940), pp. 403–26. A more recent (1957) edition of the *Bol'shaia Sovetskaia Entsiklopediia* limits its article on the trade unions to two scant pages.

[1] See Ihstitut Marksa–Engel'sa–Lenina pri TsK, VKP(B), *Vsesoiuznaia Kommunisticheskaia Partiia (Bol'shevikov) v Rezoliutsiiakh i Resheniiakh S''ezdov, Konferentsii i Plenumov TsK*, ed. M. B. Mitin, A. N. Poskrebyshev, P. N. Pospelov, Sixth Edition, Two Parts ([Leningrad]: Politizdat pri TsK, VKP (B), 1941), Part 1, pp. 372–3.

in his old pre-eminence by the time of the next Trade Union Congress in
September of 1922. His ideological deviation seemed fully corrected. He
fulsomely acknowledged the Party's supremacy over the trade unions.
The dogma thus securely established would be expounded most succinctly by Stalin in an article written in 1926. The trade unions were
allowed to exist solely for the convenience of the Party, he argued. It was
unthinkable that 'a single important political or organizational decision'
should be made by the unions 'without guiding directives from the
Party.'[1] To such unpalatable doctrine, Tomsky, and the trade unions,
were obliged to submit.

Tomsky, surely, submitted only with reluctance, however. Not that he
did not believe in the Party's right to direct the unions ideologically.
Clearly he did. He never challenged, even by implication, the right of
that organization to delineate the limits of acceptable political debate,
and to set the direction of future overall policy. But the deference thus
due the Party did not justify petty tyranny over responsible elected trade
union officials by officious local Party bureaucrats anxious to flaunt
their prerogatives. The workers had a right to be defended against such
tawdry meddling. Tomsky always felt he had a special responsibility to
assume their defence, accounting for Trotsky's taunt in 1920 that Tomsky
was just an old-fashioned trade-unionist type. In the special Russian
sense of that phrase – not the western – he was, and in a way that his
rival Lozovsky, for example, definitely was not.[2]

Why, given his attitude, he was restored to power after the 1921
disgrace is not entirely clear. His personal popularity may have had
something to do with it, but a simpler explanation seems most likely.
The triumvirate, Kamenev, Zinoviev and Stalin, were preparing their
assault on Trotsky. Though modest, soft-spoken, and diffident about
getting deeply involved in debate, Tomsky could be absolutely relied
upon to follow the anti-Trotsky line every time. And Tomsky was a
member of the Party's Politburo, where Trotsky's future would be
decided. It would have been folly for the triumvirate to alienate, for
long, such valuable support, over an issue which, as NEP became

---

[1] Josef Stalin, *Sochineniia* (Moscow: Institut Marksa–Engel'sa–Lenina pri TsK, VKP
(B): Gosudarstvennoe Izdatel'stvo Politicheskoi Literatury, 1946–54), VIII, 33–8.

[2] Biographical material on Tomsky, and estimates of his personality, policies and
rivalries, is drawn from a number of sources, but see, especially Deutscher, *Trotsky*,
pp. 81–2 and Fischer, *Stalin and German Communism*, p. 370. A quasi-official
sketch of Tomsky's life, as of 1925, may be found in 'Mikhail Tomsky: A Biography,' *Communist Review*, VI, 5 (Sept., 1925), 208–10. An interesting contemporary British evaluation may be found in 'Who's Who in Soviet Russia,' prepared
for Foreign Office officials: N275/275/38, F.O. 371. 10485, 11 Jan., 1924.

established, seemed less important than it had back in 1920.

Over the years after 1923, western trade unionists speculated quite openly and indiscreetly on Tomsky's 'real' motives in negotiating with them so enthusiastically and apparently sincerely. They suggested – though none of them could ever document it – that his aim must surely have been to use the contemplated alliance with his European counterparts to put the Soviet trade unions in a stronger position as against the Party, indeed, to enable them to establish their independence of the Party. That is what they would have done in his position, and they assumed any good trade unionist – surely Tomsky *was* a good trade unionist – would behave as they would. It seems clear such suggestions were only half accurate. That Tomsky was concerned for the position of the Russian trade unions, in the sense already indicated, is indisputable. That he could have been so naive as to cherish the illusion that the backing of reformist labour leaders would really help him resist Party encroachments on the unions hardly seems probable. Western support would scarcely be an asset in those Party councils where the unions' position would be determined, and the reformists' noisy conjectures on his motives for courting their support doubtless were a source of considerable embarrassment to Tomsky.

There seems to be no reason to doubt, on the other hand, that Tomsky did hope to gain domestic political advantage from the negotiations. Skilfully conducted diplomacy producing results demonstrably advantageous to the Party and state would enhance his prestige within the governing elite and his power to influence that elite in directions he favoured. His successes, contrasted with Lozovsky's previous failures, would strengthen his control over the trade union movement. They would perpetuate that movement's independence of Profintern, a possibility he surely dreaded as much as Stalin did Comintern's technical right to exercise control over the Russian Communist Party.

The question is what would constitute a demonstrably advantageous result. Two possibilities suggest themselves. One would be the amalgamation of all RILU and IFTU affiliates into a single trade union international. Within such an organization, Communists could freely proceed with their cell-building campaign, work for the ouster of the reformist leaders, agitate among the masses, and ultimately transform the trade unions everywhere into a united fighting agent of world proletarian revolution. Another advantageous result – not so spectacular but perhaps more practicable – would be to propagandize the unity effort within Amsterdam so successfully that, even if it failed, IFTU would be torn apart by the strain of the debate. Revolutionaries could then gather in the remnants of it at their leisure. There seems no reason to doubt that these were Tomsky's 'real' objectives. They were the ones he openly acknowledged. And if he also still hoped, as well, to win additional dispensations for the Russian trade unions back home, a diplomatic victory abroad might put him in a position to do so.

To start with, however, such victories proved disagreeably elusive.[1] A letter of March 4, 1923 urging the IFTU to cooperate with the Russian unions in a campaign in support of the Ruhr strikers met with glacial silence. So did a May 12 suggestion for a common rebuke to British Foreign Secretary Lord Curzon for his harsh 'ultimatum' to the USSR.

These proposals were all preliminary, however, to the major effort, outlined in a letter from the presidium of the All-Russian Central Council of Trade Unions to the IFTU on June 10, 1923.[2] Deploring Amsterdam's past failures to make common cause with Communists in the workers' interest, and expressing grave doubts whether Amsterdam was really interested in unity anyway, the Russians nevertheless noted with satisfaction IFTU's statement of willingness to recognize, and respond to, overtures from the Soviet trade union centre, even while denying such favours to RILU. It therefore proposed convening a conference of all IFTU and RILU national affiliates to agree to a positive action programme against the dangers of war and fascist reaction. Such a conference should assemble, the Central Council suggested, that very month.

The IFTU waited until the following month, July 2, before replying. After noting, with some rancour, the Red International's pungent anti-Amsterdam propaganda, the IFTU enquired whether the proposal for a conference emanated from that organization or from just the Russians. The plain truth, of course, was that Profintern officials had been consulted on the proposal, and in any event, the Party set policy for both Profintern and the Russian trade unions. The Central Council response did not try to deny such elementary facts. It merely demanded a definite decision from Amsterdam, and a degree of elementary courtesy toward an organization (the RILU) of which it was a loyal part.

---

[1] The efforts to win them may be followed in the weekly issues of the Comintern's publication, *International Press Correspondence* (*Inprecorr*), in the organ of the British Bureau of the Red International, *The Worker*, and in *Profsoiuzy SSSR*, II, 421, 424–7, 429. For comment see Lorwin, *Labor and Internationalism*, pp. 245–6; Carr, *Socialism in One Country*, III, Part I, 550–2; and International Labour Office, *Trade Union Movement in Soviet Russia*, pp. 224–30.

[2] The text of the letter may be found in *The Worker* for 7 July, 1923.

The IFTU General Council considered the whole matter in its meeting of November 8, 1923. A resolution was passed authorizing the Executive Committee to participate in negotiations only with the Russian trade union centre, not, under any circumstances, with Profintern, and negotiations would have to be conducted 'on the sole basis of the rules and general policy'[1] of the IFTU – a stipulation not precisely defined but one nicely calculated to cool the ardour of the embarrassing eastern wooer.

Not until over a month later, December 11, 1923, did IFTU's Executive even bother to dispatch a copy of the resolution to the Russians. When they did, they coupled it with an expression of feigned surprise that good members of RILU like the Russians could possibly be so illogical as to want to enter into relations with the IFTU when Article 4 of the RILU constitution clearly declared war to the death on IFTU. But if, nevertheless, the Russians wanted to talk – just the Russians, not their revolutionary colleagues in the Red International – Amsterdam was willing.

The Russians answered on February 7, 1924. They confirmed their earlier proposals for a united front. They were ready to meet IFTU representatives at any time and any place to engage in serious discussions on how to resist the capitalist offensive jointly. They could not, however, accept those strictures in the November 8 resolution about the rules and general policy of IFTU – rules and policies in the elaboration of which they, after all, had taken no part. If Amsterdam was willing to talk without preliminary conditions, a discussion could begin immediately.

The IFTU Executive decided its one condition for negotiations had not been met by the Russians, and that it would therefore be futile to prolong the correspondence. It referred the whole matter to the forthcoming General Congress of the IFTU, scheduled to meet in Vienna in June. The Executive was bored with the exchange and wanted to see it lapse. Tomsky was bored, too. He later called the correspondence between the Central Council and Amsterdam during this period 'a kind of cheap rubbish novel in letter form.'[2] It was at this low point in negotiations for unity that help arrived from an unexpected source – the most ancient and tradition-bound trade union movement in the world – the British.

---

[1] *The Labour Year Book, 1925*, p. 425. One gets the impression the delay in transmitting the resolution, and the note that was transmitted with it, represented a not very subtle effort by the IFTU's Executive to sabotage the work of the resolution's proponents. See General Council Minutes, 12 Dec., 1923.

[2] *Inprecorr*, IV, 85 (16 Dec., 1924), 981.

III

That so stout a bourgeois bastion as Britain could produce a *deus ex machina* to save the Russian campaign for the united front and trade union unity doubtless seemed quite unthinkable prior to 1924. Relations between the two countries were icy, barely attaining the most elementary levels of ordinary civility. British political leaders could hardly forget that their Soviet counterparts were pledged to their liquidation by violent revolution. Repeated manifestos of the Communist International, endorsed by every influential functionary in the Soviet government, made that aim perfectly clear. Equally obviously, Soviet political leaders could hardly forget that their British counterparts had undertaken an active military effort against them from 1918 through 1920. The fervent professions since then, from almost every politically responsible English leader, of how utterly abhorrent he found Communism, hardly guaranteed the effort would never be renewed.

The 1921 agreements winding up the intervention, establishing trade relations, and extending to the Soviet government *de facto* diplomatic recognition, had produced no real thaw between the two states. London was especially exercised over alleged violations by the Third International's agents of the pledge Moscow made in 1921 not to interfere in Britain's domestic affairs or to distribute anti-British propaganda. Statements from the Foreign Commissariat denying the Soviet government could be charged with any responsibility for Comintern activities were greeted with incredulity, derision and contempt. When, in 1923, those activities seemed to be producing results, especially in Persia and Afghanistan where Britain was especially sensitive and where British and Russian ambitions had traditionally collided, Lord Curzon, the Foreign Secretary, resolved to take decisive action.

The resulting document, the so-called Curzon Ultimatum, produced the sharpest crisis in Anglo-Soviet relations since the intervention.[1]

---

[1] Standard English-language references on Anglo-Soviet relations in this period are William P. and Zelda K. Coates, *A History of Anglo-Soviet Relations*, Two Vols. (London: Lawrence and Wishart, 1943–58) and Louis Fischer, *The Soviets in World Affairs: A History of the Relations between the Soviet Union and the Rest of the World, 1917–1929*, Two Vols. (New York: J. Cope and H. Smith, 1930). The Curzon Ultimatum incident is recounted in Fischer, I, 435–49 and Coates, I, 102–29. X. J. Eudin and H. H. Fischer, *Soviet Russia and the West, 1920–1927*, reprint the official Soviet reply. For Comintern reaction, Degras, *Communist International Documents*, II, 35–7. For Soviet documents in the original language, USSR, Narodnyi Komissariat po Inostrannym Delam, *Anglo-Sovetskie Otnosheniia so Dnia Podpisaniia Torgovogo Soglasheniia do Razryva* (1921–1927 gg): *Noty i Dokumenty* (Moscow: Izdanie Litizdata Narodnogo Komissariata po Inostrannym Delam, 1927).

Recounting all London's grievances since 1921, the note threatened cancellation of the trade agreements unless, within ten days, the Soviets made a satisfactory reply and pledged an end to the alleged offences. The British seemed unwilling to accept anything less than ignominious surrender, and it was widely assumed that London had already resolved to break trade relations with the Russians, and probably to sever diplomatic ties as well. Moscow seemed to fear even more drastic action was contemplated. The Comintern alerted proletarians everywhere to the danger of war, and called on them to rally to the defence of the revolution.

The Soviet reply, on May 17, 1923, was conciliatory. Rejecting most of the charges, it nevertheless proposed to discuss London's grievances, offered concessions on some pending minor matters, and was couched in comparatively gentle language. To push the issue to a break after such a note would have been technically justifiable from London's point of view, but politically unwise. In any event, Bonar Law, the Prime Minister at the time the note was sent, did not remain in office long enough to see the matter through. He resigned on May 22. Lord Curzon, who had expected he would succeed him, was passed over (much to the relief of the Russians), and the new government leader, Stanley Baldwin, was not disposed to continue the wrangling. The cabinet officially declared the incident closed on June 13, 1923. The immediate crisis was past, but the atmosphere had hardly been cleared on either side, and relations between the two states remained tense for the rest of the year.

The hostility of the British government might have been more tolerable to the Soviets if they could point confidently to the devotion of the British masses. But they could not, at least not insofar as Communist Party strength was, for them, the most reliable measure of mass allegiance. The Communist Party of Great Britain (CPGB) could claim only four thousand members as of 1924, one of the feeblest stars in the Comintern constellation.[1] Its financial position was ludicrous. Of some

---

[1] The standard treatments of the history of the Communist Party of Great Britain are Henry Pelling, *The British Communist Party: A Historical Profile* (London: Adam and Charles Black, 1958), as corrected and amplified by L. J. MacFarlane, *The British Communist Party: Its Origin and Development until 1929* (London: MacGibbon and Kee, 1966). A review of Dr MacFarlane's book in the *Times Literary Supplement* produced an instructive correspondence in that journal, to which R. Palme Dutt contributed some fascinating sidelights. See the issues of 28 April, 5, 12, 19 May, 2, 9 June, 1966. Since neither Dr Pelling nor Dr MacFarlane are at home in Russian sources, Carr, *History of Soviet Russia*, provides useful supplementary material. Historians of the CPGB have been especially well supplied with memoirs by participants. The best are those by William G. Gallacher, *Revolt*

seventeen thousand pounds it spent in 1925, it could raise only a thousand from its own members: the Comintern had to make up the rest.[1] No attempt to explain such figures by dubbing them glorious examples of international proletarian solidarity[2] could hide the weakness they evidenced. And the CPGB seemed intellectually bankrupt, as well. Its sole theoretician of any consequence internationally was the detached, reserved, somewhat sickly Balliol graduate – always a bit of a mystery man even to his Party comrades – Rajani Palme Dutt, editor of the journal *Labour Monthly*, and he was no Britisher but an Indo-Swede!

Still, the Third International never despaired of its British section. The leaders might not be first-class dialecticians but they were able, energetic, honest, and rarely quarrelled among themselves in public. Ideologically, their very weakness could be construed as an organizational asset. No party was more docile, more deferential to suggestions from headquarters, than was the English. Aside from a 1923 effort to establish its financial independence of the Comintern – condemned as 'anti-international' and surely, in view of the circumstances, fiscally suicidal – it fell into no ideological error, not during the early years, anyway. Schisms that tore other Communist Parties to shreds in the 1920s left the British Party untouched. It dutifully if unenthusiastically condemned, in turn, Trotsky, Zinoviev, Bukharin, whomever it was asked to condemn, and never too soon, never too late.

Such deference to Moscow was less a product of timidity than of indifference. British Communists made fewer doctrinal mistakes because matters of doctrine really did not interest them very much. Their leaders – Harry Pollitt, William Gallacher, Arthur MacManus, Tom Bell, Jack Murphy, Albert Inkpin, William Paul – were not doctrinaires but first-class agitators, pamphleteers, propagandists. They might not be subtle interpreters of dogma, but they had wit, enthusiasm, fire and energy. Almost anywhere else they might have made a revolution, anywhere but in Britain.

on the Clyde (London: Lawrence and Wishart, 1936), *Rolling of the Thunder* (London: Lawrence and Wishart, 1947), and *The Last Memoirs of William Gallacher* (London: Lawrence and Wishart, 1966). See also Harry Pollitt, *Serving My Time: An Apprenticeship to Politics* (London: Lawrence and Wishart, 1940); Murphy, *New Horizons*; and Wal Hannington, *Never on our Knees* (London: Lawrence and Wishart, 1967).

[1] Great Britain, Parliament, *Communist Papers: Documents Selected from those Obtained on the Arrest of the Communist Leaders on the 14th and 21st October, 1925*, Cmd. 2682 (1926) (London: H.M.S.O., 1926), pp. 61–3.
[2] *Workers' Weekly*, 22 July 1926.

The British Party acquired more experience earlier in united front tactics than did any other Comintern section. As early as 1920 the CPGB agreed to follow Lenin's advice in *Left-Wing Communism* and apply for Labour party affiliation. Support Ramsay MacDonald, the Soviet leader had counselled, 'as the rope supports the hanging man.' Although they followed it, not all British comrades found the suggestion palatable, and when, towards the end of 1921, the Comintern insisted on continued and even more vigorous application of the united front line, the CPGB had to endure a number of painful resignations. The leadership, however, persisted. No real reconciliation with class traitors was involved. 'We must take them [Labour] by the hand as a preliminary to taking them by the throat,' a spokesman explained. In spite of statements such as that, Communists professed to find Labour's annual rejection of their application for affiliation surprising and infuriating. They continued, nevertheless, in a policy of uninvited collaboration, withdrawing the Communist candidate in any Parliamentary constituency in which Labour produced one, for example, so that the proletarian vote would not be split. Their restraint netted them no credits in Labour circles. The united front seemed no more productive of positive results in Britain, then, where it was pursued most energetically, than it did in France, for example, where it was barely pursued at all.[1]

For a time Party stalwarts seemed to do rather better agitating in the workshops and factories than they did knocking down the gates of the Labour party. The CPGB was especially zealous in getting through to the workingman. Its own leadership, after all, came overwhelmingly from the working class. It was not, as so many continental Parties were, a Party of the intelligentsia. A Harry Pollitt or a Tom Bell might receive scant attention in the overstuffed leather world of the Fabian intellectuals; outside the factory gate, on a soapbox, he was in his element, speaking to his own in his, and their, language. There the Communist Party might win, not masses of recruits perhaps – the British workingman was distressingly loyal to his traditional organizational allegiances – but understanding, support on specific issues, and a degree of sympathy which might one day produce the mass party dreamed of, once conditions were right, at a time of major industrial unrest, perhaps.

The most obvious way to get to the factory workers was, of course, to capture their trade unions, and that was Profintern's primary responsibility.[2] Jack Murphy had come back from Moscow in December of

[1] Murphy, *New Horizons*, p. 181.
[2] Material on the early Profintern effort in Britain is derived from the following

1920 to establish a British Bureau of RILU, and within a month, a skeleton organization was in existence. The figurehead president was Tom Mann, an elder statesman in the councils of revolution with more than three decades of agitation behind him. Within six months, by the time of RILU's 1st Congress, he and his associates were claiming control over 460 trade union branches. In early 1922 they were publishing their own periodical, *All Power*! By the end of that year they were estimating 180,000 adherents in South Wales and 150,000 in Fife, almost surely an exaggeration, and yet the South Wales Miners' Federation had voted in favour of RILU affiliation by a 2-to-1 majority. Superficially, it might have seemed Profintern's organization in Britain was making more progress than the CPGB itself.

In spite of appearances, however, the campaign had failed in its major objective, a failure the tough headquarters realists back in Moscow were bluntly acknowledging by the end of 1922. It had failed because most British trade unions were clearly not going to abandon the Amsterdam Federation, and the Trades Union Congress was not, therefore, to become an RILU affiliate. And yet, the unsuccessful campaign was no total write-off. Local organizations had been mobilized, recruits had been enlisted, and great enthusiasm had been discovered – even in circles wholly opposed to renouncing IFTU for RILU – for a much more militant, even revolutionary, trade unionism than was favoured by the TUC's current leadership. To abandon such splendid zealots just because they were not CPGB members, or because the trade unions to which they belonged would never join Profintern, would constitute gross mis-management of valuable resources. A new organizational base had to be created for them, a base from which they could plan the takeover of the existing trade union structure, beef the revolutionary minorities in the unions up into revolutionary majorities, and finally transform the unions into true organs of class war. And thus the name for the new coalition, a name in common use from the end of 1922 on even though no formal national organization was yet in existence, the Minority Movement.

Profintern approved the idea behind the Minority Movement and urged its speedy organization on a national basis. The orders to that effect went out to the British Bureau of RILU at the end of 1922, but

sources: Roderick Martin, *Communism and the British Trade Unions, 1924–1933* (Oxford: Clarendon Press, 1969), pp. 1–36; Murphy, *New Horizons*, pp. 167ff.; George Allen Hutt, *The Post-War History of the British Working Class* (London: Victor Gollancz, 1937), pp. 72ff.; Pollitt, *Serving My Time*, Chapter X, pp. 164–88; Pelling, *British Communist Party*, pp. 24–33; MacFarlane, *British Communist Party*, pp. 112–17; and Carr, *Socialism in One Country*, III, Part I, 117–24.

progress was practically non-existent and Moscow grew impatient. A major behind-the-scenes conference of British Communist Party and Profintern leaders was held in Moscow in June and July of 1923 at which Lozovsky rebuked all concerned for sluggishness and delay. The RILU British Bureau was reorganized, and Gallacher assigned responsibility for implementing plans for the Minority Movement. It was not designed to compete with TUC, to break away from it, or to move it over to RILU allegiance, the propaganda for the new organization was to emphasize. Its purpose was solely to convert TUC to revolution, to vigorous prosecution of the class war.

Not for almost a year were the organizational plans completed. It seems likely that a major cause of the delay was disagreement on the relationship of the Minority Movement and the Party. How could Communists maintain control of the organization while seeming to stand apart from it? Would the proletarian vanguard be fatally diluted by contact with hundreds of thousands of ideologically amorphous 'leftist' malcontents willing to join the Minority Movement? Such questions could not easily be answered. Gallacher took excessively long answering them.[1] Not until June of 1924 was the first convention of the National Minority Movement announced. The British Bureau of the RILU – too closely identified with the single issue of affiliation to Profintern – was to dissolve itself in favour of the new organization. And when the convention met, in August, Gallacher, who had delayed summoning it too long, found himself displaced, as General Secretary, by Harry Pollitt.

Profintern's failure was thus even clearer than that of the CPGB, to the point it had been required to commit organizational suicide to further the cause. None of Soviet Russia's most wholly committed friends in Britain seemed able to build and sustain a mass organization for themselves. And yet, if professions of non-Communists could ever be accepted at face value, revolutionary Russia was not without backing in Britain – far from it. The Communist leader, Harry Pollitt, surely exaggerated only somewhat when he spoke of the ecstatic excitement 'that comes over a worker when he realises for the first time that our class owns one-sixth of the world – the Soviet Union.'[2] Later academic scholarship would confirm that judgement, and only somewhat less extravagantly. A recent historian finds a 'Russia complex' in labour and trade unionist circles in

---

[1] The principal resolution on the topic may be found in Communist Party of Great Britain, *Speeches and Documents of the Sixth (Manchester) Conference of the Communist Party of Great Britain. May 17, 18 and 19, 1924* (London: Communist Party of Great Britain, [1924]), p. 34.

[2] Pollitt, *Serving My Time*, p. 46.

the early twenties, 'a tenderness towards Russia alternately fanned by Tory gibes and cooled by Russian rebuffs.'[1]

Manifestations of this attachment were less evident in the official Labour party than they were in the trade unions. Marxist and non-Marxist trade unionists alike had acclaimed the overthrow of tsardom and the advent of socialism in Russia, and when their own country seemed determined to overwhelm the revolution by force, they organized to defend it, even from their own country. The Hands Off Russia movement, first appearing in early 1919 and formally organized on a national level that autumn, won massive trade union support from the beginning.[2] The movement's demands, evacuation of British troops from Soviet territory, withdrawal of support from the White generals, an end to the blockade of Russian ports and the establishment of diplomatic relations with the Bolshevik government, became trade unionism's demands. The annual Trades Union Congress meeting in Glasgow that September affirmed its opposition to the intervention, commissioned a deputation to apprise the Prime Minister of its stand, and approved convocation of a special Congress in December to hear the deputation's report and take appropriate action. The deputation got little satisfaction from Lloyd George, and the special TUC convened to consider its statement expressed profound unhappiness at the whole situation. Rather than authorizing any immediate action, however, the Congress demanded only the right to send a delegation to Soviet Russia to make an 'independent and impartial enquiry' into conditions there. In case the

[1] Charles L. Mowat, *Britain Between the Wars, 1918–40* (London: Methuen, 1956), pp. 50–1.
[2] The Hands Off Russia campaign is dealt with most authoritatively in Coates, *Anglo-Soviet Relations*, I, 135–52. William P. Coates was national secretary of the movement. The most detailed secondary treatment is Stephen R. Graubard, *British Labour and the Russian Revolution, 1917–1924* (London: Oxford University Press, [1956]), pp. 64–114. Other more or less useful accounts include Robin Page Arnot, *The Impact of the Russian Revolution in Britain* (London: Lawrence and Wishart, 1967), pp. 149–50, 160–5; B. Vinogradov, *Mirovoi Proletariat i SSSR*, Book 5 of *Desiat' Let Kapitalisticheskogo Okruzheniia SSSR*, Gen. Eds. E. Pashukanio and M. Spektator (Moscow: Izdatel'stvo Kommunisticheskoi Akademii, 1928), pp. 82–90; Pollitt, *Serving My Time*, pp. 111–21; William P. Maddox, *Foreign Relations in British Labour Politics* (Cambridge, Mass.: Harvard University Press, 1934), pp. 192–5; and Hutt, *British Working Class*, pp. 34–40. For the Councils of Action, see, in addition to the above, Fenner Brockway, *Inside the Left: Thirty Years of Platform, Press, Prison and Parliament* (London: George Allen and Unwin, 1942), p. 133 and Wilfrid H. Crook, *The General Strike: A Study of Labor's Tragic Weapon in Theory and Practice* (Chapel Hill, N.C.: University of North Carolina Press, 1931), pp. 263–70. For a fine recent study, see Stephen White, 'Labour's Council of Action 1920,' *Journal of Contemporary History*, vol. 9, no. 4 (Oct., 1974), pp. 99–122.

government might misinterpret the cautious resolution as, in fact, an obituary for the whole anti-intervention effort, a number of rightist and moderate TUC leaders published a manifesto in January, 1920, warning sternly against any open war on Soviet Russia and noting labour would decide for itself, if such war were declared, whether or not to let it continue. *The Times* called the manifesto an open summons to extra-constitutional action and 'a great infringement of the most fundamental of democratic principles.'

The delegation to Russia – it finally emerged as a joint TUC–Labour party delegation – did not set out until May 1920. In the meantime, the national Hands Off Russia committee maintained momentum in the anti-intervention campaign. Its major weapon was George Lansbury, the handsome and fiercely independent Labour party maverick who came back from a brief Russian visit in March of 1920 to preach the New Jerusalem to packed halls with a rhetorical brilliance gloriously untarnished by factual accuracy. When Poland attacked Soviet Russia towards the end of April, 1920 – reportedly with British approval and backing – Lansbury and the committee urged workers to put pressure on the government to call off the Poles. The appeal got a positive response. On May 10, London dockers refused to load the *Jolly George* with munitions for Poland. Not only did the ship eventually have to leave with an empty hold, but the success of the venture prompted the Dockers' Union to order a general embargo on arms shipments to Russia's enemies. Previously labour had just threatened; now it had acted, and even more drastic action seemed impending. On May 22, the *Daily Herald* published a manifesto signed by moderate and left-wing trade union leaders appealing for a nation-wide 24-hour strike to punctuate the demand for peace with Soviet Russia. Nothing came of the suggestion, for the time being, but the broad support for it was an indication of the direction in which opinion was moving.

While the Russo-Polish War was still on, the TUC and Labour party delegates set out for Russia to see conditions for themselves.[1] With one or two exceptions, the delegates were not committed pro-Bolsheviks, although most of them were anxious to be impressed. Among the

---

[1] The report is Labour Party, *British Labour Delegation to Russia, 1920: Report* (London: Trades Union Congress and Labour Party, 1921.) The best short accounts of the trip are, from the Russian point of view, Vinogradov, *Mirovoi Proletariat i SSSR*, pp. 70–4 and Balabanova, *My Life*, pp. 283–7, and from the British, Margaret Bondfield, *A Life's Work* (London: Hutchinson, 1949), pp. 189–240. See also Bertrand Russell, *The Autobiography of Bertrand Russell*, II (London: George Allen and Unwin, 1968), 101–10, and *Inprecorr*, v, 9 (29 Jan., 1925), 101–3.

well-known trade unionists included were A. A. Purcell of the Furnishing Trades' Federation (whom Lozovsky would consult, while he was there, on the formation of the RILU), Margaret Bondfield, Ben Tillett and Ben Turner. The formidable and vocal Mrs Philip Snowden was the most forceful of the Labour party's representatives. Bertrand Russell accompanied the delegates, unofficially, as far as Petrograd. 'No one paid any attention to him,' Balabanova later recalled.

The delegates got a rousing reception – as rousing as a desperately crippled, economically broken Russia could provide. Mass demonstrations to greet them, parades in their honour, were almost daily occurrences. Intended to impress the visitors, the ceremonial was also designed to reassure the Russians themselves. They were not alone. Proletarians all over the world were their brothers, and would not allow their governments to trample the revolution to dust. The English delegates did not announce any such policy: they did not have to. Their very presence in Russia was enough. The government had only to dramatize that presence.

Aside from a noisy and dramatic outburst by Menshevik stalwarts at a meeting of the Moscow Printers' Union the delegates attended, the tour went smoothly enough and the official account of it represented fine reporting. It covered a wide range of data cautiously, impartially and informatively. It showed sympathetic awareness of the difficulties which the Soviets had to surmount, difficulties not all of their making. It showed also how the commissars had compounded their agonies by occasional stupidities and sometimes by pure blind dogmatism. All in all, it was an enlightening document produced by enlightened people, and stands up well even five decades after its compilation. The Soviets, although not happy at being scolded by Mrs Snowden for their anti-religious campaign, were delighted to have respectable and influential people tell the British worker that his press had been deceiving him all along on what conditions were really like in revolutionary Russia, that Lenin had not nationalized women, that Bolshevik power was well-established, and that no alternative political arrangement was in sight.

The anti-intervention campaign reached a climax shortly after the delegation to Russia returned. A special Trades Union Congress meeting July 13, 1920 passed a peace resolution unanimously and warned the government not to proceed with any programme of military aid, overt or clandestine, to the Poles. The warning came none too soon, but perhaps it lacked force. In any event, the government seemed oblivious to it. As Soviet troops crossed the old frontiers and advanced on Warsaw, Lord Curzon demanded a pull-back and bluntly threatened war to save

Poland. The Labour party secretary, Arthur Henderson, appealed to workers to act. On Sunday, August 8, hundreds of mass meetings and demonstrations all over the country demanded peace with Russia and non-interference in the Russo–Polish war. The *Daily Herald*, appearing on Sunday for the first time, headlined 'Not a Man, Not a Gun, Not a Sou!'

The following day the Parliamentary Committee of the TUC met with the Labour party Executive and the Parliamentary Labour party. The government was engineering a war with Russia over the issue of Poland, they declared, an 'intolerable crime against humanity' that organized labour would resist by a general strike, if necessary. A Council of Action was named to deliver labour's ultimatum to the Prime Minister on August 10, and to direct the subsequent strike effort if it came to that. It spawned local Councils of Action, some 350 of them, all over the country. What amounted to a complete revolutionary apparatus was created in an incredibly short time.

Over a thousand delegates turned out for the meeting called by the Council of Action on August 13 to report on the unsatisfactory conversations with Lord Curzon and Lloyd George. J. H. Thomas, the president of the TUC and considered among the staunchest of right wingers, was in the chair. For the first, last and only time in his career, he sounded like a subversive. He proudly affirmed, 'with a full sense of responsibility,' that the decision to use the general strike weapon was revolutionary. Labour was ready, he said, to challenge not just the government of the day, but the constitution itself, an announcement the delegates greeted with cheers.

The challenge was never accepted. On Sunday, August 15, 1920, the Russian army lost the great battle for Warsaw, and could no longer seriously threaten the Polish state. Within a few weeks, the whole issue had resolved itself – as so many issues do – by becoming obsolete. Soviet leaders were convinced, however – or said they were – that the Councils of Action had saved their revolution from a combined Anglo-Polish assault. They also noted the whole experience had contributed hugely to promoting a revolutionary spirit in Britain itself. The situation in England in August, 1920, Lenin wrote, very much resembled the situation in Russia in the spring of 1917. The councils of action were nothing more nor less than soviets, even if they were not explicitly given that name. England had experienced, if briefly, the dual power, the first stage in the transition to a workers' dictatorship. The very fact that the 'malicious Mensheviks' who ran the TUC, even such out-and-out reactionaries as J. H. Thomas, had been whipped into leading such an effort, indicated how potent was the feeling of the masses. Lenin was confident the whole experience had advanced the Bolshevik cause in Britain enormously.[1]

Although the end of the intervention and the conclusion of the 1921 Anglo-Soviet trade agreement deprived trade unionists of the opportunity to intercede in Russia's behalf as forcefully and dramatically as they had in 1919–20, they did what they could, especially in the area of promoting international labour unity. In 1923 and 24, they alone among IFTU's affiliates seemed willing to listen to Russian proposals for a united front. It was, for example, the British delegates on IFTU's General Council who persuaded that body in November of 1923, and only 'after great difficulty,' to agree to negotiate the whole unity question with the Russian trade union centre.[2] These initiatives may have been timid, tentative, and in retrospect, unproductive; it is still a fact that of all Amsterdam's affiliates, only the British showed any disposition to react other than totally negatively to the idea of east–west trade union unity.

The degree of power the TUC could exert in behalf of any cause, however, seemed constantly diminishing during the first half of the twenties. British trade unionism seemed to be wasting away, especially after the psychological disaster of 'Black Friday,' April 15, 1921. On that day, on the initiative of J. H. Thomas, the railwaymen and transport workers withdrew from a pledge to back the wage demands of the miners, by concerted strike action if necessary. They thus broke up the so-called Triple Alliance on which workers in many industries had based their hopes for the maintenance of wage rates. A fragmented trade unionism seemed unable, thereafter, to resist the employers' pressure, pressure all the heavier in an era of contracting markets and intense foreign competition, for lower wages and longer hours. Between 1921 and 1924 TUC membership dropped by more than a third, from 8,346,000 at the beginning of 1921 to 5,428,000 at the beginning of 1924.[3] Those left in the movement seemed spiritless and inactive. In reckless, enthusiastic 1921, employers had been deprived of almost 86 million working days by strike action. In quiet 1924 the corresponding figure was 8,424,000 working days, less than 10 per cent.[4]

---

[1] V. I. Lenin, *Sobranie Sochinenii* (Moscow: 1926) XVII, 309.

[2] General Council Minutes, 12 December 1923; International Committee Minutes, 10 December 1923, file 901, doc. T 1 06. See above, p. 25.

[3] *Statistical Abstract for the United Kingdom*, For each of the fifteen years 1913 and 1920 to 1933, Seventy-eighth Number, Cmd. 4801 (London: H.M.S.O., 1935), p. 117. [4] *Ibid.*, p. 121.

Trade unionism made use of the lull to try to tone up its organizational muscles. The focus of that effort was the TUC's General Council, established in 1921 to replace the almost powerless old Parliamentary Committee. Its supporters had hoped the General Council would provide the movement that brisk, forceful, and most of all, centralized leadership it had previously so conspicuously lacked. Such a Council, directing the work of a bright, efficient staff headed by a competent and respected General Secretary, could unify trade unionism in a way patchy and ill-defined combinations such as the Triple Alliance clearly could not.

Such hopes had proved ill-founded. The failing was not in the staff. The General Secretary, Fred Bramley, though no master organizer, was nevertheless a bold and eloquent speaker and his drive, his vision and his personal magnetism attracted a staff of able and intelligent people whose only failing was a tendency to stumble all over one another in their efforts to get things done. The fault was not there. The fault was in the General Council. Its members were chosen more for seniority than for ability. It became a kind of haven for trade unionism's elderly has-beens. The rules and conventions of TUC elections were such that, once chosen, a General Council member could be almost sure of serving as long as he liked. Vigorously contested elections were rare; unseating an incumbent candidate even rarer. Many General Council members hardly ever spoke in meetings at all. Those meetings, ordinarily once a month, usually made decisions only in matters on which decisions could no longer be avoided, and adjourned. There might be much talking but rarely was much said. The General Council chairmen, who might have provided it with some creative, imaginative leadership, hardly ever did so, and since they were selected not because of their executive aptitudes but because it was their turn in a complex rotation system, their failure was hardly surprising. When basic policy issues did get raised in the Council and recommendations for their resolution adopted, it was most likely to be at the initiative of the General Secretary, but that initiative had to be exercised with discretion. Up against respected veterans of a hundred past industrial wars, a somewhat younger and less experienced Bramley clearly had to play his cards with care and some diffidence.

In retrospect, it is arguable that the General Council's ineffectiveness was more a product of its membership than of any constitutional limitations on its power. But that is not how trade union militants saw it at the time. They hoped to renovate and activate the Council by enlarging its competence and expanding its authority. It was in support of such an effort that the trade union left appeared as an organized and coherent force in the early twenties. And it was this same left, devoted to trade union unity at home, which would take up the cause of world trade union unity so enthusiastically somewhat later on.

Its leaders on the General Council were Purcell, Hicks, Swales and Tillett. A. A. Purcell was a French-polisher, 56 years old as of 1924, a strong, forceful person, blunt and often extreme in expressing his opinions, rather too obviously contemptuous of those who refused to accept them, totally lacking in tact, finesse or diplomacy. Few men could get close to him, but many men took their inspiration from him. He had called himself a guild socialist in his younger days, and expressed great enthusiasm for Bolshevik doctrines right after the revolution. He even attended the inaugural congress of the CPGB, but found it politically expedient, subsequently, to remain in the Labour party, on the left wing, of course. Ernest George Hicks, who rarely used his first name, was 45 years old, a bricklayer, a clever and witty speaker, and the first general secretary of the Amalgamated Union of Building Trade Workers. He had been a member of the old Social Democratic Federation and professed himself to be a devoted Marxist. His devotion was more a matter of sentiment than reflection, however; he had certainly made no extended study of doctrine, and perhaps that – or perhaps his strong empirical streak – accounts for the flexibility verging on unreliability that characterized his politics in the mid-twenties. Alonso Beaumont Swales, who understandably preferred to be known as simply A.B., was a great mountain of a man, full 20 stone. He looked and occasionally sounded something like a highly-placed churchman. He was, however, totally incapable of pomposity, show or pretence. He was 54 years old, general secretary of the Amalgamated Engineering Union, and the left's most impressive orator, whose speeches expressed with power and ringing sincerity what he himself felt so deeply. He did not speak often, but when he did he was worth hearing. Ben Tillett was one of labour's elder statesmen by this time. Sixty-four years old in 1924, he had first achieved notoriety 35 years earlier as the dynamic, energizing leader of the great dockers' strike of 1889. His rich experience in the movement, his continued untiring zest for it, and his evangelistic eloquence for it, especially after two or three drinks, won him a wide following, both in his own organization, the Transport and General Workers' Union, and in trade unionism generally.

The trade union right was not blessed, or cursed, with quite so many leaders. It tended to be less concerned with purely political issues and could therefore abdicate leadership claims there to such trustworthy

Labour party politicians as MacDonald and Philip Snowden. It devoted itself more to purely trade union questions. It prided itself in its attention to the bread-and-butter demands of its constituency, and preferred to satisfy those demands by negotiation rather than by preaching class war. Negotiations were cheaper, less disruptive of the normal routine, gentler on union treasuries and less offensive to public opinion. It was zealous of the authority of the individual unions, suspicious of General Council encroachments on their independence, and bored with the whole topic of international trade unionism.

Its most well-known spokesman – the Russians and the CPGB would try to make him into a kind of arch-villain of English trade unionism – was J. H. Thomas of the Railwaymen. With his precisely trimmed moustache, his rich Cockney accent, and his exuberant delight in horse-racing, good food and drink, people with titles, and sartorial splendour, Thomas was an apt subject for caricature and ridicule. It was easy to make him out a clown or buffoon; it was rather more difficult to persuade his devoted brethren in the NUR that he was a renegade or a scoundrel. His failings were, for his fellows, completely understandable. In his position they would have succumbed to the same temptations, and as blissfully as he had. And they appreciated his very real strengths, his devotion to his work, his tireless energy, and his jovial good humour. Most of all, they appreciated the immense finesse and skill he displayed on their behalf at the negotiating table, where his apparent artlessness never prevented him from striking an advantageous bargain.

It would be impossible to classify all the major trade union leaders as of 1924 as right, centre, and left. Too many of them were unidentifiable, and in any event, ideological lines were blurred by that characteristically English pragmatism, empiricism, and indifference to dogma so irritating to foreigners and to the CPGB. Within the General Council, in 'the club,' a certain sense of corporate solidarity inhibited or even precluded taking inflexible positions, forming irreversible alliances, and thus acquiring unyielding enemies. Only very rarely would a Council member criticize a colleague by name in public. So the political niches which not only historians, but even their own contemporaries, have devised for the trade union leaders in the twenties, will not fit all of them, and must be taken tentatively and sceptically even for such as Purcell, Swales and Thomas, who seem to fit them the best.

Admitting all that, it must still be affirmed that there nevertheless was a point-of-view identifiable as the left in British trade unionism in the twenties, and a point-of-view identifiable as the right, and that the left was marked by a greater interest in international trade unionism and a more benign attitude toward the Soviet experiment. Any clear and decisive shift to the left position, then, would constitute a major victory in the Russian effort to employ united front tactics in the campaign for the merger of RILU and IFTU into a single trade union international. British trade unionism had already demonstrated sympathetic understanding toward the Russian proposal. Given a movement to the left, it might be persuaded to take a truly active role in the struggle.

v

The Baldwin Government resigned November 13, 1923, ostensibly to get a popular mandate for its economic policies. The subsequent elections produced an unprecedented political result. Baldwin's Conservatives remained the largest single party in the Commons, but they were outnumbered by the combined Labour and Liberal oppositions. Since the Liberal leader, H. H. Asquith, made it clear as early as December 17 he would not maintain the Tories in office, it was soon evident that the new year and the new Parliament would produce a new government, the first Labour government, a government representing a minority of the voters and a minority of the Commons but prepared, provided the Liberals would acquiesce, to prove once and for all that socialists could indeed administer the country sanely, responsibly, and efficiently.

To the Russians, and to the British Communist Party, the election results were highly suspicious. While allowing Labour to take office, the bourgeoisie had somehow managed to ensure a Liberal veto on socialist experimentation. A result so satisfactory to the capitalists must be the result of a plot. Why else would Baldwin have gone to the country on an issue so unpopular as that of tariffs? It was surely to ensure a minority Labour government now rather than face the prospect of a majority Labour government in 1926, when elections would otherwise be due. The minority government could put through certain distasteful measures which the Tories favoured but for which they did not want to take responsibility. Labour could mend relations with the leftist government of France, for example. It could extend *de jure* recognition to Russia, opening up a lucrative new market for profitable exploitation by Tory merchants and bankers. Any Labour effort to do anything more revolutionary, however, would be frustrated by the Liberals. British workers would soon become disillusioned with political action, which apparently produced no tangible benefits for them even when they won elections, and would lose interest in politics altogether. The bourgeois hold on the state apparatus would be thus secured, and a Conservative (or Liberal) government would resume office after the next elections. 'It was a daring solution,' wrote one fervent Party member, 'requiring all the skill in political manoeuvring in which the British governing class has so long excelled.' And it worked.[1]

Such pathological suspicions in Moscow did not bode well for good relations with the MacDonald government. They were reinforced, moreover, by the hesitations of the new government in the matter of *de jure* recognition of the Soviet state. Both Labour and Liberal spokesmen had pledged such recognition during the election campaign, and since to extend it required no more than a simple proclamation, an announcement was generally expected sometime during the first day or two of the new administration. It did not come. Rumours began to circulate of strong opposition to recognition from certain 'highly placed circles.'[2] The Labour and trade union left took alarm. Duncan Carmichael, secretary of the London Trades Council, booked a hall, provisionally, for a mass meeting of protest, and warned MacDonald to move quickly or suffer the indignity of the labour movement demonstrating against its own government. On January 30, Downing Street officially denied that Russian policy was being reconsidered, and two days later, on February 1, *de jure* recognition was extended. The Russians were invited to send a negotiating team to London to discuss a financial settlement and trade relations.[3]

In fact, MacDonald had put off his recognition statement on purely technical grounds, mostly to tell Britain's partners in the Commonwealth what he was about to do. Carmichael's talk of demonstrations might, then, have speeded up the announcement of the new policy, but no more. Indeed, when the prime minister finally decided to go ahead with recognition, he did not even wait to consult with his cabinet colleagues before

[1] The quotation is from Hutt, *British Working Class*, p. 77. For a Russian statement of the same unlikely theory, see A. Lozovsky, *Angliiskii Proletariat na Rasputi: Sbornik Statei* (Moscow: Izdanie Profinterna, 1926), pp. 46–83.

[2] Coates, *Anglo-Soviet Relations*, I, 131.

[3] The flurry of speculation over recognition is summarized in *ibid.*, I, 131–3. The charge that MacDonald only went through with recognition because of the workers' pressure is stated quite explicitly in D. Petrowski, *Das Anglo-Russische Komitee und die Opposition in der KPSU* (Hamburg–Berlin: Verlag Carl Hoym Nachfolger, [1927], p. 6. Petrovsky (Bennet) was the chief resident Comintern agent in Britain. See also Hutt, *British Working Class*, p. 90, and Vinogradov, *Mirovoi Proletariat i SSSR*, pp. 106–7. For a contrary view, Richard Lyman, *The First Labour Government, 1924* (London: Chapman and Hall, 1957), pp. 185–6, and for strong support for his thesis, see the documents cited in note 1, p. 42 below.

implementing it, setting a precedent he was to follow for the rest of his government. He always managed relations with the Russians personally, kept his own counsels, almost never solicited the opinions of his ministers, and only rarely even bothered to keep them informed.[1]

The whole delay, however, had aroused Soviet suspicions – always easily aroused in the best of circumstances. Communist spokesmen could not quite make up their minds whether the workers had forced Mac-Donald into recognition or whether the bourgeoisie had, in hopes of profiting by Russian trade. Both theories were advanced simultaneously. The Soviet government credited the recognition not to the Labour party leadership, but to the pressure of the English proletarian masses, whose previous aid at the time of the intervention was now warmly recalled. The Soviets also suggested that Britain's precarious economic position and the need to find new markets had much to do with the policy adopted by His Majesty's Government. Recognition, then, was a forced response to external pressures not a conscious act of policy.[2]

Such statements represented a manifestation of international Communism's new harsh line on the Labour party. Earlier reactions to the MacDonald victory had been much more conciliatory. Even though Labourites had turned down the CPGB's application for affiliation by almost 8 to 1 in 1923, British Communists were willing to cooperate in the great common battle of workers *versus* capitalists, a Party organ had announced.[3] Labour might be ideologically myopic, but it was on the side of the angels in the decisive dialectical division of proletariat and bourgeoisie, and for as long as it remained there, Communists would support it.

Such tolerance of compromisers went rapidly out of fashion in the early days of 1924, largely as a result of the comrades' appraisals of mistakes made in the recent German revolution. If it had proven politically disastrous to make common cause with Social Democrats in Germany, it could hardly be wise to repeat the error in Britain. The Comintern's Executive Committee set forth the new line in its resolution of February 6, 1924. The Labour government was not a government of proletarian class struggle at all. It aimed not at destroying the capitalist state but strengthening it. Its leaders were ideologically bankrupt petty-bourgeois backsliders and would inevitably betray the workers who had elected them.

---

[1] The relevant documents are Cabinet Conclusions, 1924, CAB 23.47, Conclusions 7 (24) 19, 23 Jan., 1924, 8 (24) 10, 28 Jan., 1924 and 9 (24) 1, 4 Feb., 1924.

[2] The text of the Soviet Congress' response is in Narodnyi Komissariat Po Inostrannym Delam, *Anglo-Sovetskie Otnosheniia*, pp. 61–2.

[3] *Communist Review*, IV, 10 (Feb., 1924), pp. 423–4.

MacDonald's failure would enormously enhance the prospects for creating a mass Communist movement in Britain. The workers would have to surrender their democratic illusions. It would become clear to them the class war could not be won in Parliament. They would turn from the ballot box to revolutionary struggle, from the Labour party, then, to the CPGB. The tasks of the CPGB in such circumstances were clear: maintain its organizational identity and its ideological purity, support MacDonald only when he took some hesitant step forward, demand that he take more resolute steps, revile him when he refused, and finally, force him to reveal himself as the class traitor he was.[1] After some hesitations, the British comrades got accustomed to the new line, and by the time of their Party conference in May, 1924, were preaching it with zest and abandon. The resolutions adopted, condemning any united front with the likes of MacDonald, Snowden and Thomas, urged instead a campaign to liberate the workers from the influence of such renegades, the united front from below only.[2]

Pursuing their harsh line, British Communists participated fiercely and tirelessly in every major industrial dispute in which the workers involved would let them play a part. The new government was plagued by what seemed unusually virulent labour troubles in the first half of 1924. The locomotive engineers and firemen struck the railways in January, the dockers went out in February, municipal transport was hit in March, the shipyards in April, and a mass walkout of miners was only narrowly averted in May. The troubles persisted right into the summer months: the London Underground system was struck in June and the builders downed tools in July. It seemed like a good time for labour to flex its muscles. The government was reluctant to support management as against its own constituency and the employers knew it. A compromise settlement, even if costly, often seemed more advantageous to them than fighting a long industrial war without official backing. Union leaders could therefore expect to get good results via stubbornness and militancy. The Communist Party could hardly have devised a situation more to its advantage.[3]

[1] The ECCI resolution is reprinted in Degras, *Communist International: Documents*, II, 82–4. Excellent examples of subsequent Communist abuse of MacDonald are to be found in Lozovsky, *Angliiskii Proletariat na Rasputi*, pp. 46–83.

[2] *CPGB, Speeches and Documents: 6th CPGB Conference.* Bell's speech is on pp. 17–30. The relevant resolutions are on pp. 31–3.

[3] A good survey of the labour unrest in early 1924 and the government's predicament in dealing with it is in G. D. H. Cole and Raymond William Postgate, *The Common People*, 4th Ed. (London: Methuen, 1956), pp. 572–3. See also *The Annual Register*, 1924, Ed. by M. Epstein, New Series (London: Longmans, Green, 1925), pp. 21–3.

MacDonald smarted under all the labour troubles and was prone to attribute them to Communist malevolence. The cabinet appointed a special committee in April of 1924 to enquire into CPGB responsibility for the strikes. It reported two weeks later in a 'most secret' document what the comrades had hardly tried to conceal anyway, that they intended to overthrow existing institutions violently and unconstitutionally, that they received substantial financial aid from non-British sources, and that they had intervened in and promoted recent industrial unrest. What perhaps justified the strict security surrounding the report was its appendix, nine pages long, citing passages from Harry Pollitt's correspondence with a friend in Moscow, even letters from Gallacher to his own wife. But all the demonstrated contempt for the sanctity of the mails failed to prove any impressive conspiracy theory. The CPGB was small, getting smaller, and in considerable financial distress, the committee found. While it had tried to prolong and extend industrial disputes, there was no evidence it had actually been able to initiate them. Its influence in the labour world had been greatly exaggerated, and it had been credited with results proceeding in fact from quite different causes. To subject the Party's leaders to criminal charges would serve no useful purpose.

While the committee's recommendations were cautious, it did not suggest the information it had gathered should be wholly disregarded. Responsible trade union leaders could, for example, be appraised of the efforts of Communist agitators to penetrate and take control of their organizations. And Foreign Office negotiators could use the report in their talks with the Russians. It was 'common knowledge,' the committee reported, that the Comintern and the Soviet Government were identical in all but name, and Comintern subsidies to the CPGB could hardly be reconciled, therefore, with Soviet promises to abstain from anti-British propaganda. Moscow's efforts to foment labour troubles in Britain might not be notably successful, the report indicated, but the effort was being made, made through the agency of the British Communist Party, and Britain had the right to demand it be abandoned.[1]

The committee's recognition that Communist agitation was not a major cause of industrial unrest was realistic and wise. In fact, British workers seemed to be moving to the left *en masse* in 1924, on their own initiative, without much CPGB help. Management efforts to freeze wage

---

[1] Cabinet Conclusions, 1924, CAB 23.48, Conclusions 27 (24) 8, 15 April, 1924 and 32 (24) 5, 14 May, 1924. The Committee's 'interim report' (there was in fact no subsequent report) is in Cabinet Papers, 1924, CAB 24.166, C.P. 273 (24), 30 Apr., 1924.

levels, or even reduce them, had not let up. A minority Labour government was in no position to diminish the pressure by proclaiming the socialist commonwealth, even assuming it wanted to. Militant action seemed to be producing results: most strikes in 1924 were won. In such circumstances, a general shift of attitudes leftward was hardly surprising.

Its most dramatic manifestation was the election of A. J. Cook to the position of secretary of the Miners' Federation of Great Britain on April 10, 1924. A. J. Cook was the son of a soldier, brought up in the barracks. He had gone directly from primary school to the pits, where he worked for 21 years. Ideologically, after passing through a stage of fervent religion, he put all the accumulated evangelistic eloquence at the service of trade unionism and his own rather romantic vision of Communism. Beatrice Webb called him the 'Billy Sunday of the Labour Movement,... an inspired idiot, drunk with his own words, dominated by his own slogans.' Although by most standards an ugly man, with lanky yellow hair, large-lipped mouth and gangly gait, he was nevertheless 'not without personal attractiveness,' Mrs Webb observed. His 'glittering, china-blue eyes, set close together,' and his extravagance of gesture and expression made it impossible to ignore him, made him, indeed, strangely compelling.[1]

He got his chance when the Miners' Federation secretary, Frank Hodges, resigned to contest a seat in Parliament. The Communist Party pledged Cook its support as Hodges' replacement, even though he had resigned his own membership in the CPGB back in 1921. The Minority Movement, not yet organized on a national scale but already strong in the mining areas, also backed him. By a majority of just over a half of one per cent he won the endorsement of his district organization, the South Wales Mining Federation, and by a majority of less than a half of one per cent he carried the final election.[2] The ultra-militants had won their first great success. 'A raving, tearing Communist' – the expression was TUC General Secretary Fred Bramley's – had taken over one of the most powerful positions in British trade unionism. For some it appeared that the only man standing in the way of Cook's handing over the miners' union to Moscow was the MFGB president (since 1922), Herbert Smith, the man famous for his cloth cap and his blunt obstinacy. Neither

---

[1] Beatrice Webb, *Beatrice Webb's Diaries, 1924–32*, Ed. by Margaret Cole (London: Longmans Green, 1956), p. 116. For other descriptions of Cook, see Murphy, *New Horizons*, pp. 202–3 and George Hardy, *Those Stormy Years: Memories of the Fight for Freedom on Five Continents* (London: Lawrence and Wishart, 1956), p. 174. A modern full-scale biography of Cook would be useful.

[2] MacFarlane, *British Communist Party*, p. 131.

had improved with advancing age. 'He was a man of few words, mostly no,' one commentator has written.[1] Beatrice Webb despaired at what the future might hold for the miners. 'An honest mule and an inspired goose make bad leadership for any herd,' she confided to her diary.[2]

The trade union leadership lagged behind the rank-and-file in the turn leftward in early 1924, but it clearly moved in the same direction. Communists tended to attribute the shift to unprincipled opportunism. Men who had assumed responsible positions by pretending to be leaders were now careening frantically about trying to overtake those whom they had the temerity to ask to follow them. Put thus, it all seemed disreputable and hypocritical, but it surely would be no slander to suggest trade union leaders could not and should not have been coldly insensitive to the changing attitudes and opinions of those they led. Clearly there was some such interaction.

Most of the change in the official Trade Union Congress line, however, derived from a factor much easier to explain and reflecting credit or discredit on nobody. In February 1924 the General Council required resignations of all its members accepting official positions in the Mac-Donald government. The absolute independence of the trade union movement from government supervision or interference – an article of faith hallowed by over half a century's repetition – surely required that none of the movement's general staff risk divided loyalties or be encumbered by possibly conflicting responsibilities as political leaders. In compliance with the decision, five Council members resigned. All of them represented moderate to right-wing opinion. They included J. H. Thomas, far and away the right's most influential spokesman. Margaret Bondfield also resigned. She had been serving as the General Council's chairman, and would therefore have presided at the next Congress.

Deprived of most of its leadership as well as five of its votes, the right wing in the General Council was substantially weakened by the resignations. The new General Council chairman, replacing the moderate Miss Bondfield, was A. A. Purcell, the left's most vigorous and irrepressible pulpiteer. Purcell also succeeded J. H. Thomas as president of the International Federation of Trade Unions, a position which had been reserved, by custom, for whomever the General Council designated. Replacing Thomas on the TUC's key International Committee was George Hicks,

---

[1] As quoted by W. M. Citrine (Baron Citrine), *Men and Work: An Autobiography* (London: Hutchinson, 1964), p. 77.
[2] Julian Symons, *The General Strike* (London: The Cresset Press, 1957), p. 6. The only full-scale biography is Jack Lawson, *The Man in the Cap: The Life of Herbert Smith* (London: Methuen, 1941).

another forceful advocate for the left. The whole look of the TUC leader-ship was different, then, after the formation of the Labour government. Its spokesmen spoke a different sort of language. The resignations and replacements were not numerically startling, but in the General Council many members rarely spoke anyway; on matters of indifference to them many were willing to defer to the strongest voice, and a few assertive, emphatic personalities could thus seem to dominate proceedings.

The General Council's new left look was intensified by a certain dis-illusionment with the Labour government. The backbone of the Labour party, after all, was the solid support of millions of trade unionists, and their representatives on the General Council felt they should therefore enjoy a special intimacy with the MacDonald administration. They soon discovered otherwise. Purcell had been rebuffed, for example, when he had asked in Commons in late February whether British trades unionism would be represented at the pending treaty negotiations with the Rus-sians.[1] A month later, a more wide-ranging General Council request to inspect several draft bills under consideration by the Home Secretary and the Labour Ministry was also rejected, a setback all the more stinging because it was delivered by Tom Shaw, the Minister of Labour, himself a trade unionist.[2] In June the government intervened to stop the strike in the London Underground as abruptly and decisively as any Con-servative government might have. It was all a bit baffling and most lamentable.

It was in such an atmosphere that a Soviet negotiating team arrived in Britain to hammer out the new treaty governing trade and diplomatic relations between the two powers. The Red diplomats landed on April 10, the same day A. J. Cook won the secretaryship of the MFGB. That happy event just added to Russian confidence, which was already at a high level anyway. The British masses were turning to the Soviets for inspiration even if their government were not. Zinoviev's circular letter convening the 5th Comintern Congress, issued a few days after the negotiating team's arrival, breathed a brisk satisfaction typical of the time. The rapid progress being made among English workers was far more significant than the recent setback in Germany, he wrote. A mass Communist Party in Britain was imminent. Conditions were now right for it.[3] If the prediction proved accurate, British proletarians would

[1] Hansard, *Parliamentary Debates, House of Commons*, 5th Series, Vol. 170, c. 505 (hereafter cited as 170 H.C. Deb. 5s. at c. 505).

[2] Cabinet Papers, 1924, CAB 24.166, C.P. 204 (24), 24 Mar., 1924 and C.P. 210 (24), 25 Mar., 1924. Also Cabinet Conclusions, 1924, CAB 23.47, Conclusion 22 (24) 9, 26 Mar., 1924.   [3] Degras, *Communist International: Documents*, II, 89–91.

presumably stand by their class homeland, Soviet Russia, even as against the Labour party representatives of the land of their birth. No diplomat could ask for a more advantageous position at the bargaining table than that – to be able to call for, and get, the backing of his adversary's constituency.

Just as, from Moscow's viewpoint, the British were in a weak negotiating position, so the Soviets were in a strong one. Political rivalries at home were apparently under control. Trotsky had made no energetic bid to succeed Lenin. The 13th Party Congress would condemn him for sectarianism early the following month, thereby ratifying his political oblivion. The Kamenev–Zinoviev–Stalin triumvirate appeared firmly established.

It remained, then, only to exploit Soviet strengths and assumed British weaknesses to extract an advantageous treaty from the MacDonald government. That meant, primarily, enlisting the support of the leftward-moving trade unions. Contact with them would prove additionally useful anyway in the campaign for international trade union unity. The Russian negotiating team had been carefully selected to make such contacts both easy and natural. At least four of the eleven Russians were prominent trade unionists; one of them, Tomsky, was chairman of the All-Russian Central Council of Trade Unions. It would surely be gross discourtesy for British trade unionists to ignore his presence in the country. And from the Soviet point of view, it would be a betrayal of international proletarian solidarity if they did not back him in the pending negotiations. In case the British might forget that obligation, the Soviet Railwaymen's Union reminded them of it the beginning of May.[1] The TUC hardly needed reminding, however, not so long as Purcell and Hicks spoke for it. By early May the first contacts with Tomsky had been made, and the first formal confrontation of British and Russian trade unionists arranged.

[1] *Workers' Weekly*, 9 May, 1924.

2
Courtship (May 1924–February, 1925)

The prospects were never very good for the 1924 Anglo–Soviet negotiations. Both sides were anxious, it is true, to regularize their diplomatic relations, to replace their makeshift 1921 trade agreement with a fully-fledged commercial treaty, and to resolve the irritating issues of inter-governmental financial claims. But much else – too much else, it seemed – divided them. Moscow was determined to secure a sizeable loan to enable her to buy badly-needed British capital equipment. Such a demand, coming from brigands who had stolen private property and defaulted on legitimate debts, was deemed outrageous impudence by the high priests of financial orthodoxy in the City temples. London was determined to extract from the Soviets some binding pledge to dam the flood of scurrilous anti-British propaganda spewing out of Comintern headquarters. No Soviet leader would have dared suggest acceding to any such suggestion. To surrender the dream of world revolution to win some fragile national diplomatic advantage would have been the grossest betrayal of all they stood for.

The discords all became painfully apparent on the very first day of talks, April 14, 1924. MacDonald chilled the Russians with his speech of 'greeting,' emphasizing what most divided the two sides and stressing, in particular, British insistence that the agreement reached on 'propaganda' be something more than an empty formality.[1] The subsequent talks only confirmed those initial negative impressions. In spite of undertakings by both sides to set strict limits on press releases, it was soon common knowledge that progress – if any – was almost imperceptible. In such dreary circumstances some members of the TUC's General Council approached the General Secretary, Fred Bramley, suggesting he invite the trade unionists on the Russian negotiating team to have dinner with some of their British counterparts. Bramley agreed, the invitation was extended, and the Russians accepted it with a gusto that was surely more than merely gastronomical.[2]

Fifteen of the General Council's 32 members attended, including all

[1] *The Times*, 15 Apr., 1924.
[2] General Council Minutes, 28 May, 1924.

the most articulate left wingers except Hicks. The more conservative group within the Council was represented by Arthur Pugh of the Iron and Steel Trades Confederation and John Turner of the Shop Assistants. Purcell presided, and pronounced the official welcome.[1] The General Council stood ready to offer the Russian workers every possible help, he averred. A closer relationship between the two countries was essential. All the councillors were agreed on that, he said, and would do all they could to establish it. 'One and all look forward to the time when the working class will be master of its own destiny, and will be freed from the yoke of capitalism.'[2]

Tomsky responded in the same vein. Although superficial differences might temporarily separate British and Russian trade unionists, he declared, the basic 'motive forces' that united them would remain. Those forces were 'the imminent struggle between the working class and the capitalist class...all over the world' and 'the imminent and inevitable necessity that the working class shall organize to deliver itself from the yoke of capitalism.'[3] For the proletariat to triumph in the historic battle against capitalism, it had to be as organized as the capitalists.

He brought his listeners up-to-date on the diplomatic negotiations in which he was so closely involved. He denied the Soviets came only to secure a loan, although a loan would be advantageous – for both sides. The primary mission, however, was to secure peace. The obstacles in the way of agreement were many, and he explained them in some detail, indicating the Russian position on each. 'I know,' he confided, 'that if we could discuss the matters at issue with the British workers themselves, instead of with officials of the Ministry for Foreign Affairs, we could come to a satisfactory agreement in four or five hours. Unfortunately, however, the people with whom we have to deal are a very different type from yourselves.'[4] Smoothly, genially, as one unpretentious working-man to another, Tomsky made his points, made them with a minimum of polemics and without any dogmatic unctuousness. It was a polished performance. He suggested, neither too subtly nor too peremptorily, both the short-term Soviet goal, TUC pressure on the English negotia-

[1] The record of the meeting is in Mikhail P. Tomsky, *Getting Together: Speeches Delivered in Russia and England, 1924–1925* (London: Labour Research Department, [1925]). Purcell's speech of welcome is on pp. 14–15. Inexplicably, *Getting Together* dates the dinner for the Russian trade unionists as Mar., 14, 1924. The Russian delegation did not even arrive until April, and General Council records clearly establish the date as May 14.

[2] *Ibid.*, p. 14.

[3] Tomsky's speech is in *ibid.*, pp. 16–34. The quotations are from p. 17.

[4] *Ibid.*, p. 33.

tors, and the longer-range Communist objective, trade union solidarity against capitalism.

The enthusiastic response of his hosts testifies to the quality either of Tomsky's rhetoric or of the restaurant's wine list.[1] One assumes it was a little of each. Ben Tillett's remarks, for example, were lavish, flowery, and unhappily, largely autobiographical. E. L. Poulton of the Boot and Shoe Operatives was more to the point, indeed, quite explicit. Russians and British could hardly agree on everything, he said, but the General Council should undertake to help smooth over any disputes arising out of the negotiations. Predictably, Purcell was most emphatic of all. If the negotiations seemed to be breaking down, the Russians should inform the Council, which could then exert its influence to effect an understanding. 'The [General] Council will give you its full and unconditional support,' he promised. 'However much work you demand of us, whatever the call you make on our energies, whatever the support you need from us – all is yours for the asking!...We want you to maintain direct contact with us...so...we may be in continuous consultation. We are fully prepared to collaborate with you in this way.'[2] Fred Bramley, the last of the speakers, was almost as effusive as Purcell. He too emphasized that 'uninterrupted contact must be maintained between our British trade union centre and the trade union members of the Soviet Delegation.' The Labour government, he pointed out, were 'the servants of the trade union movement,' and could therefore not fail to be responsive to it. 'All that the Soviet Delegation wants, will be undertaken by the General Council of the Trades Union Congress,' he pledged.[3] Tomsky was clearly moved by the warmth of the feelings he had generated, so moved, indeed, he made a truly extraordinary reply, unprecedented in the annals of diplomacy. 'I can pledge my word,' he declared, 'that the Soviet Delegation will not undertake any important step at the conference without having first of all, come to an understanding with the General Council of the Trades Union Congress.'[4]

The minutes of the General Council and of its International Committee contain no reference to any subsequent meetings between TUC officials and Russian trade-unionist-diplomats. Such conversations as occurred must have been informal. Reporting to the Hull Congress that September, the General Council noted the May meeting had been 'very cordial and frank,' that it demonstrated the value of such direct confrontations, and that 'contact has been maintained' over the period of

[1] The responses are in *ibid.*, pp. 34–40.
[2] *Ibid.*, p. 35. [3] *Ibid.*, pp. 39–40. [4] *Ibid.*, pp. 40–2.

the Russian delegation's stay in Britain. 'It is in the interests of the Trade Unionists of both countries,' the Council felt, 'that it should be continued.'[1]

The Russian diplomats were doubtless delighted to recruit all the help they could, even though the influence the TUC could bring to bear on the independently-minded Mr MacDonald and Arthur Ponsonby, his chief negotiator, was not all that had been implied that heady evening of May 14. It was gratifying to have some support in reserve, nevertheless, and on the pivotal issue of whether the British government would agree to guarantee repayment of that loan the Soviets hoped to negotiate in the City, W. H. Hutchinson of the Engineers, John Hill of the Boilermakers, and Purcell himself all endorsed the Soviet position emphatically in late May and June.[2] Even the British Communist Party noted, with admiration, the General Council's efforts on behalf of better Anglo-Soviet understanding. The Party programme, published just two days after the Russian trade unionists and their British opposite numbers shared that dinner, urged MacDonald to appoint a trade unionist as Ambassador to Moscow, and suggested the General Council be authorized to designate the most appropriate individual.[3] Downing Street ignored the proposal.

The General Council's efforts in behalf of the Anglo-Soviet diplomatic negotiations produced only a modest yield at first, however. Its record in support of Tomsky's other suggestion, international trade union unity, was more immediately impressive. That cause was no Bolshevik monopoly, of course. The British labour movement had urged it for quite as long and with quite as much energy as had the Russian. Soviet arguments about class interests crossing national lines hardly needed repetition in Britain: they seemed self-evident. If, after all, the wages of a non-unionized textile worker in Kyoto were a fraction of those paid in Lancashire, Japanese capitalists were in a position to cut international price levels and force an eventual reduction in British wages. Precisely that sort of squeeze was being applied to British wages during the twenties. Or if steel workers struck in Sheffield, it was clearly to their advantage that American workers refuse to permit steel shipments from Pittsburgh to relieve the pressure. A single trade union international

---

[1] Trades Union Congress, *Report of Proceedings at the 56th Annual Trades Union Congress* (1924), Ed. by Fred Bramley (London: Cooperative Printing Society [1924]), p. 244.

[2] Lyman, *First Labour Government*, p. 188.

[3] *Workers' Weekly*, 16 May, 1924; Tom Bell, *The British Communist Party: A Short History* (London: Lawrence and Wishart, 1937), pp. 98–9.

could undertake such projects. It could sponsor and promote trade union movements in low-wage areas not previously organized or inadequately organized. It could coordinate international boycott actions in support of major strikes. It could accumulate financial reserves to sustain work stoppages otherwise wholly beyond the capacity of any single national centre. Unlike the Russians, then, who dreamed of a trade union international pursuing basically political goals by revolutionary class war methods, the British envisaged an organization employing traditional trade union techniques, on a larger scale, to achieve purely economic objectives.

The basis of any all-inclusive trade union international would have to be built in Europe, which meant, first of all, Russia would have to be brought in. The TUC was in a peculiarly advantageous position to achieve that end. It had unity at home. It was un-troubled by Communist-led breakaway unions such as plagued its counterpart organizations on the continent. While few British labour leaders were pro-Communist, then, almost none of them were anti-Russian. They had evidenced genuine enthusiasm for the Bolshevik revolution and the Soviet state in 1917 and honest good wishes for their success ever since. For them, Soviet Russia was a workers' republic, the first in history, and just as it was damned and reviled by all those who lived by exploitation, by industrialists, bankers, monopolists, and the lackeys who served them, so, clearly, must it be defended by the workers. Its example might have little or no relevance to Britain, whose traditions were so different. It might show a woeful insensitivity to the delicacies and gentilities of diplomacy and of debate. But it belonged to those who toiled, it preached the unity of all who toiled, and its participation in any all-inclusive trade union international would surely be wholehearted and resolute.

The attitude toward the Russians among British trade unionists, then, was much milder than the attitude of their opposite numbers on the continent. The TUC might therefore hope to be able to exert some influence in Moscow. It could presumably exert even more in Amsterdam. It was almost surely – after the mass withdrawals from German trade unions following the revolutionary follies of 1923 – the largest single affiliate of the International Federation of Trade Unions, and indisputably the richest. If Britain ever left IFTU, IFTU would be dead. So the TUC had a kind of ultimate weapon to wield in any negotiations with IFTU, a weapon so decisive it should not even need to be brandished ostentatiously. The application of gentle pressure should be enough to persuade the IFTU to accept any application by the Russian trade union centre for membership. But could the Russians be persuaded to apply at all? Hopefully, they could, if the IFTU would amend its constitution enough to allow Russia's fellow members of the rival Red International to troop into Amsterdam too, and on conditions short of unconditional surrender. The British aim, then, was to persuade the Russians to make such an application, on reasonable terms, and to persuade Amsterdam to accept it. Neither goal seemed inaccessibly remote.

The position outlined above was that of almost all TUC leaders who had taken any position at all as of 1924. The organization as a whole, however, had never bothered to prepare any formal statement on trade union unity. Its representatives at Amsterdam had pursued the campaign in whatever way they thought best, pretty much unrestrained by General Council directives. That situation was unchanged in June of 1924 when Purcell, Bramley and their fellow delegates from the TUC set off for the triennial IFTU Congress at Vienna. The General Council would later, almost casually, approve everything its representatives did for unity at Vienna.[1] But there was no advance plan behind it all; the achievement must be credited to the personal initiative of Purcell and Bramley.

The IFTU Executive Committee came to Vienna resolved to put an end to its correspondence with the Communists.[2] The exchange with Tomsky and the Russian trade unionists had proved time-consuming and unproductive, no more worthwhile, it was felt, than those earlier exchanges with Lozovsky and the RILU. The most recent Russian letter, that of February 7, 1924, was especially disappointing.[3] 'There is no object in the International Federation of Trade Unions taking any further steps so long as it has only replies of this kind to expect,' the Executive's report concluded.

The British delegation objected to that sentence, and moved to strike it, substituting an instruction to the Executive 'to continue consultations with the All-Russian Trade Union Council.' Urging the amendment from the podium, Purcell called attention to the negotiations in London between the Soviets and the Labour Government, negotiations which the Trades Union Congress had urged and in which it took a great interest. For the British movement to press its own government to talk with the

[1] General Council Minutes, 25 June, 1924.
[2] I have been unable to locate a stenographic transcript of the IFTU Vienna Congress. My main source for the Congress debates on the Russian question is Bramley's report to the 1924 Hull TUC Congress. See 1924 *TUC: Report of Proceedings*, pp. 246–7. All quotations cited from the Vienna resolutions may be found there. See also Schevenels, *Quarante-cinq années*, pp. 87–8.
[3] See above, p. 25.

Russians, while acquiescing in IFTU's breaking off just such talks, would be anomalous, he said. The IFTU's rules guaranteed the autonomy of individual national centres, guaranteed that no one affiliate could impose its politics on the others without their consent. Russian membership in Amsterdam need not be feared, therefore, and would clearly strengthen the organization. To a sceptical audience, he insisted Moscow might be sincere about unity, might be seeking something more than mere propaganda advantage. 'We believe,' he said, 'that the All-Russian Trade Union Congress, by force of circumstances, and after reasonable discussion, might be persuaded to accept the policy of the I.F.T.U.'

The British intervention was enough to forestall any immediate acceptance of the Executive's recommendation, but it is doubtful whether the TUC delegation could have managed to achieve much more than a delay had not the Russians themselves acted. The Central Council of Trade Unions in Moscow moved with commendable speed to intervene in support of the British position. A telegram went out to Purcell within a matter of hours of his speech noting 'with satisfaction' the British proposals 'in favour of bringing together the Amsterdam unions and the unions of Soviet Russia.' The Central Council 'declares its full readiness, under certain conditions, to meet the desires of the British unions,' the wire continued, 'which undoubtedly coincide with the desires of the better part of the workers of the world...'[1] The reference to 'certain conditions' was a bit ominous, but the telegram did make it seem the Russian position on unity might not be nearly as rigidly unyielding as the IFTU Executive had pictured it. Moscow might indeed be willing to join that very organization her leaders had pilloried so savagely for half a decade past. The Congress therefore declined to slam the door shut on her. The final compromise resolution adopted, after intensive unofficial consultations, regretted 'the continued absence of the Russian trade union organizations from the International Federation due to their refusal to accept its rules and constitution' and recommended to the new Executive 'to continue consultations in so far as this is possible without prejudicing the dignity of the IFTU, with the object of securing the inclusion of Russia in the International Trade Union Movement,

---

[1] The telegram was never made public by the British, but the delegates were made aware of its contents. For the English text, see All-Russian Central Council of Trade Unions, *Trade Unions in the USSR, 1922–1924: Short Report* (Moscow: ACCTU, 1924), p. 55. The Russian-language text is in M. P. Tomsky, *K Probleme Edinstva Mezhdunarodnogo Professional'nogo Dvizheniia* (Moscow: Izdatel'stvo VTsSPS, 1926), p. 34.

through the necessary acceptance of the IFTU rules and conditions.'
The resolution made no provision for Profintern affiliates other than the
Russian to apply for IFTU membership, and the demand that Russia
acquiesce unconditionally in 'rules and conditions' she had had no part
in formulating was surely unrealistic. The British effort had nevertheless
ensured the possibility of further talks and guaranteed the unity campaign would not be abruptly terminated by Amsterdam's unilateral fiat.
Fred Bramley, anyway, was optimistic. The compromise resolution was
not all that had been hoped for, he wrote, but if the Russians could
accept 'rules for international procedure which meet with the approval
of the vast majority of Trade Union representatives,' an agreement was
possible.[1]

First reactions from the Communist press were not so positive. The
IFTU was a decaying monument to the cowardice, timidity and stupidity
of the reformist trade union leaders, who showed signs of energy only
when they were attacking the Russians, Communism or the RILU. Most
resolutions approved at Vienna were worthless, mere phrase-making.
The resolution on maintaining peace, advocating use of the general
strike weapon to oppose any war declaration, was especially mischievous.
To decree a general strike was to decree a revolution. By postponing
decreeing revolution until the bourgeoisie decided on a war declaration,
the IFTU was in effect authorizing the bourgeois governments to set the
day for the workers to revolt against them. Such tactics typified the
idiocy of IFTU's leadership. True, the left wing had made indisputable
gains at Vienna, notably Purcell's election as IFTU president and the
compromise resolution on the Russian trade unions. But all three vice-
presidents of IFTU, Léon Jouhaux of France, Corneille Mertens of
Belgium and Theodor Leipart of Germany, stood clearly on the right
wing, and among the three secretaries, Jan Oudegeest of the Netherlands,
Johann Sassenbach of Germany and John W. Brown of Great Britain,
only Brown was associated with the left-wing group. Brown and Purcell
stood alone, then, on a predominantly rightist seven-man Executive.

And even what left wing there was seemed vague and confused on
many key issues, and too prone to believe a few new words and some
new formulas represented a real change in policies. The unity resolution
was a case in point. The real issue was not how to get the Russian unions
into IFTU, but how to fuse all affiliates of the two internationals, IFTU
and RILU, into a single, new, world organization. In that effort, insist-

[1] Fred Bramley, 'A Workers' Parliament of Europe,' *The Labour Magazine*, III, 3
(July, 1924), 100.

ence on respect for IFTU's 'dignity' and the strict maintenance of its 'rules and conditions' scarcely represented a positive contribution at all. The way to unity was not through Russian surrender to Amsterdam, but through a joint conference of both internationals on how to effect a merger. The TUC General Council had taken one positive step forward at Vienna by preventing any collapse of the dialogue between Amsterdam and Moscow. It should now take the next step and demand that world conference. The RILU would surely agree; it had always favoured such a meeting. In case anybody doubted it, Lozovsky spoke out once again. We sincerely want real unity, he wrote. We want to 'force our way' into the reformist unions in order to get in closer touch with the working masses. We want to see if it is possible, 'at the risk of enduring two or three days in the company of Messrs. Jouhaux and Co., to win more sympathy from the working class.' That policy involved no 'liquidation' of RILU, he wrote. Quite the contrary. In the projected new organization, RILU's programme would be fulfilled. It would be the Amsterdam social democrats whose policies would be liquidated. We are for unity, then, he concluded, 'because it offers a possibility of widening the sphere of action of Communism.'[1] Opponents of unity within Amsterdam would translate and reprint such indiscretions with relish.

Lozovsky, of course, who stood to lose his job as Profintern chairman if the unity campaign ever bore fruit, did not necessarily speak for the Communist Party, the Soviet government or the Russian trade unions, and as far as the British were concerned, nothing in the first Communist reactions to the Vienna resolutions absolutely and irrevocably ruled out an eventual Russian application for IFTU membership. They still felt, therefore, that they had made a positive contribution to trade union unity by the Vienna resolution. At the same time, however, their efforts back home in behalf of the Anglo-Soviet diplomatic negotiations seemed more and more ineffectual. The talks were adjourned in early June while the Soviet delegates met representatives of private British bondholders to try to put together some compromise financial settlement

---

[1] Lozovsky's article was published in *Pravda*, 15 June, 1924. Other typical Communist commentary on the Vienna Congress can be found in Lozovsky's *World's Trade Union Movement*, pp. 69–72; in August Enderle, 'The Congress of the Amsterdamers in Vienna,' *Inprecorr*, IV, 33 (12 June, 1924), 329–31; in Leon Trotsky, 'The Amsterdam International and War,' *ibid.*, IV, 35 (19 June, 1924), 349–50 and 36 (26 June, 1924), 361–2; and in the British RILU organ, *The Worker*, for 28 June 1924 (article by Harry Pollitt) and 5 July, 1924. For a more recent but not very different Soviet evaluation of Vienna, see P. V. Gurovich, *Vseobshchaia Stachka v Anglii 1926 g.* (Moscow: Izd. Akad. Nauk SSSR, 1959), p. 30.

agreeable to both. Prospects seemed bleak. Rakovsky's statements to the British press were pessimistic.[1] Back in Moscow, *Pravda* was trying to explain to its readers why the British working masses had not intervened more energetically to support the Russian diplomats. It was not that the English worker was not 'sympathetically inclined' to the Soviet stand, *Pravda* noted. He was, 'thanks chiefly to his class instincts.' Why, then, did the masses seem unable to exert much influence on their Labour government? Why could they not compel it to acquiesce in the Soviet position? In the first place, *Pravda* answered, the Communist Party of Great Britain was very weak, little more than a clique of propagandists, not a truly influential mass political organization. The British worker entrusted his allegiance not to the CPGB but to his trade union. He was stubborn about his union; he would neither defy nor abandon it. The leaders of the unions, however, who could thus speak for the workers, were 'much more to the right' than those they represented. It was the leaders who had failed to support the Soviet diplomats unambiguously and forcefully. The clearly indicated Soviet response was to find a way to 'a closer community' and 'more intimate contact' with the masses themselves. 'We must use every suitable expedient,' *Pravda* concluded, 'to obtain this end.'[2]

Such rebukes, and implied threats, had little impact at TUC headquarters. General Council members did not subscribe to *Pravda*. In any event, they did not need to be reminded the treaty was in danger, nor reproached into speaking out for it. Some of them apparently put strong new pressure on the government in mid-June, with special emphasis on how opening up the Russian market could help solve Britain's unemployment problem.[3] Their greatest effort, however, came on August 5–6, 1924. After a 20-hour negotiating session stretching into the early hours of August 5, the talks had deadlocked completely on the question of the compensation to be offered British owners of nationalised Russian properties. Philip Snowden, Chancellor of the Exchequer and a longtime sceptic on the value of any Russian connection, felt the treaty

---

[1] See, for example, the interview in *The Observer*, 1 June, 1924, reprinted in Jane Degras, ed., *Soviet Documents on Foreign Policy*, issued under the auspices of the Royal Institute of International Affairs, I (1917–24) (London–New York–Toronto: Oxford University Press, 1951), 452–3.

[2] *Pravda*, 21 June, 1924. The British Embassy in Moscow translated and transmitted large extracts from the article, with interesting comment: N 6043/5799/38, 22 July, 1924, F.O. 371.10498.

[3] There is no evidence in TUC records of any formal intervention in June. The approaches were presumably, therefore, personal and unofficial. See Fischer, *Soviets in World Affairs*, II, 482–3 and Carr, *Socialism in One Country*, II, Part I, 129.

might as well be scrapped.[1] MacDonald agreed. A public announcement was made that the negotiations had broken down.

The chief Soviet negotiator, Rakovsky, quickly summoned his reserves from among the left-wingers in Parliament and in the TUC. He and his entire delegation met with some 25 of them, MPs and trade unionists, on the evening of the 5th. He enlisted their good offices, Snowden noted sarcastically, with 'fairy-tales about the hundreds of millions of Russian orders which were waiting to be given to British industrialists just as soon as a Treaty was signed.'[2] Four of them, including Purcell, worked out a compromise formula on the disputed treaty point. Snowden thought it 'meaningless' and 'a mere face-saving device' but accepted it, reluctantly, to avoid a complete collapse of the talks. So did MacDonald and Ponsonby, after some stormy scenes. So, finally, did Rakovsky, although it was less than he had hoped for. By the time the *Daily Herald* appeared the morning of the 6th, with a strong call to the labour movement to urge resumption of the negotiations, the editorial was already obsolete. The two sides were back at the conference table. A second intervention by the same unofficial intermediaries that very day helped the diplomats surmount one last hurdle, and by the end of the day Ponsonby could tell the Commons the settlement was complete. It was formally signed August 8.[3]

Almost immediately Moscow began affirming that it was only the indignation of the English working class which had forced a reluctant MacDonald to sign a treaty he had hoped to avoid. 'The intervention of the trade union leaders,' Kamenev said a month later, had saved the agreement, which was signed only 'under the big stick of the workers.'[4] D. A. Petrovsky, the chief Comintern agent for Britain, seconded that interpretation. When the *Daily Herald* sounded the tocsin, the 'active elements of the English workers' movement answered immediately' and

---

[1] The early debate in the Cabinet may be followed in Cabinet Conclusions, 1924, CAB.23.48, Conclusions 44 (24) 6, 30 July, 1924 and 47 (24) 20, 5 Aug., 1924, and in Cabinet Papers, 1924, CAB.24.168, C.P. 415 (24), 29 July, 1924.

[2] Philip Snowden (Viscount Snowden of Ickornshaw), *An Autobiography*, II (1919–1934) (London: Ivor Nicholson and Watson, 1934), 682.

[3] For the last-minute crisis, the authoritative account is E. D. Morel's article in *Forward*, 23 Aug., 1924. See also Lyman, *First Labour Government*, pp. 193–5; Coates, *Anglo-Soviet Relations*, I, 166–8; Fischer, *Soviets in World Affairs*, II, 489–90; Snowden, *Autobiography*, II, 682–4; Carr, *Socialism in One Country*, III, Part I, 25–7; Arnold Toynbee, *Survey of International Affairs, 1924*, issued under the auspices of the British Institute of International Affairs (London: Oxford University Press, 1926), pp. 241–4.

[4] Cited in Carr, *Socialism in One Country*, III, Part I, 26.

MacDonald caved in to their pressure.[1] Later Soviet scholarship improved the legend almost beyond recognition. It was the British Communist Party, apparently, which called out the British proletariat in defence of the treaty. Inspired by the CPGB, 'the workers in many enterprises stopped work' on the morning of August 6, the revised standard version has disclosed, 'demanding an answer from the Labour party and trade union leaders on why the MacDonald government was breaking off negotiations with the USSR.' These mass protests aroused the frightened left wing of the Labour party which in turn brought pressure to bear on the MacDonald-dominated right wing. Thus emerged the final agreement, according to this remarkable example of 'scientific history.' It was not behind-the-scenes manoeuvring by leaders but demonstrations by the masses that made the difference. The role of a Purcell has almost been lost sight of altogether, and what remains of it attributed not to good will, nor to personal resolution, but to craven surrender before the insistent demands of the rank and file.[2]

The facts were well enough known at the time, however, and the Russians were generous enough in their praise, to persuade the TUC leaders to continue the campaign for the treaty so long as Parliament was still debating ratification. At the Hull Congress, in early September, John Bromley of the General Council moved a resolution welcoming the treaty as 'of paramount importance to world peace and world economic recovery' and authorizing a press campaign in support of it. His speech was full of admiration for the Russians for achieving so quickly the abolition of capitalism, 'our ultimate aim' as well. The resolution was passed, according to the minutes, 'with considerable fervour.'[3]

Eight days later the *Daily Herald* printed the first apparent result of that decision, a joint manifesto from the TUC General Council and the Executive Committee of the Labour party urging support for the Russian treaty and for a general *détente* with the Soviets. Actually,

[1] Petrowski, *Anglo-Russische Komitee*, pp. 6–7. For the same point of view, see Vinogradov, *Mirovoi Proletariat i SSSR*, pp. 106–7.

[2] F. D. Volkov, *Anglo-Sovetskie Otnosheniia, 1924–1928 gg.* (Moscow: Gosudarst-vennoe Izdatel'stvo Politicheskoi Literatury, 1958), pp. 65–78. The quotations are from pp. 69 and 78. Volkov refers with some awe to the involvement of 'the whole Communist press of England' in the campaign for the treaty. He presumably refers to the *Worker's Weekly* and *The Worker* (also a weekly). Neither of those publications appeared during the crisis. *The Worker* was published Aug. 2 and 9; the *Workers' Weekly* Aug. 1 and 8.

[3] *1924 TUC: Report of Proceedings*, pp. 434–7. Vinogradov (*Mirovoi Proletariat i SSSR*, p. 113) says the TUC leaders were forced to support the treaty in order to maintain their position with the masses. I can find no evidence, however, their position was threatened at all on this occasion.

the General Council had begun preparing that statement even before the passage of the enabling resolution at Hull, and ironically, it was the trade unions, not the Labour party, which took the initiative on the document. The unions seemed more strongly and militantly for the treaty than did the political party directly responsible for it.[1]

On September 24, the General Council agreed to publish a new resolution favouring the pact and to dispatch a delegation to the Prime Minister to state its case orally. 'The whole power of the Trade Union Movement,' the new General Council chairman, A. B. Swales, said a day later, was to be mobilized in behalf of the treaty.[2] Even after the fall of the government in October – in large part due to its Russian policy – the campaign continued. On the eve of the subsequent elections, a special General Council appeal to the affiliated societies urging support for the Labour party laid particular stress on the government's record in foreign policy. The proposed treaty would reduce unemployment and lower food costs, the appeal emphasized. It deserved support 'not because we approve the policy, methods, or principles of Soviet rule' but because it was in the clear economic interests of British workers.[3] Even when Labour lost the election anyway and Stanley Baldwin moved into Number 10, the General Council continued to recommend the treaty to the new government. Not until Baldwin made it crisply and bluntly clear that any such agreement was out of the question did the unions call off their efforts in support of the aborted pact.

Perhaps, at the time, it all seemed like an exercise in futility, a great deal of energy and anguish expended on a campaign producing nothing. It may have seemed that way in TUC headquarters at Eccleston Square, but it seemed rather different in Moscow. The Anglo-Soviet negotiations had collapsed, no treaty was in prospect at all, but it had not all been fruitless. Rakovsky told a teachers' conference in Moscow in January 1925 that the most important positive result of the negotiations was that they had provided the occasion for establishing close relations between the Soviet diplomats on the one hand and the British trade unionists and left Labourites on the other. Those contacts, becoming closer and more meaningful since, were 'a great asset in the Soviet political balance-sheet for 1924,' he concluded. To have the chance to know the English workers,

---

[1] General Council Minutes, 28 Aug., 1924; *Daily Herald*, 13 Sept., 1924.
[2] General Council Minutes, 24 Sept., 1924, 26 Nov., 1924; *Daily Herald*, 26 Sept., 1924.
[3] Trades Union Congress, *Report of Proceedings at the 57th Annual Trades Union Congress (1925)*, Ed. by Walter Citrine (London: Co-operative Printing Society, 1925), pp. 337–9.

he seemed to be saying, it was even worth enduring the likes of Ramsay MacDonald.[1]

II

The 5th Congress of the Communist International assembled in Moscow in June, 1924.[2] Eighteen crowded and critical months had intervened since the previous Congress. The German revolution had ingloriously and ostentatiously fizzled. Treacherous social democrats and reformists, moving out from their power base in the trade unions, had come triumphantly to power in both London and Paris. Amsterdam had begun gesturing suggestively, practically indecently, at the Russian trade unions. A chaotically untidy mass of circumstances had piled up, some of them promising, some ominous, all perplexing and challenging. Some dialectical order had to be imposed on the anarchy of events. The past demanded interpretation, and the future preparation. If the International were to move ahead, it had to know where it had already been, where it was now, in what direction and at what pace it was to proceed, and who was going to lead it. Lenin, who had manipulated history so surely and confidently and finally made it yield to his will, was dead. The Movement would have to fend for itself.

The centre of attention at the Congress was the question of the united front. The right-wing leadership of the German Communist Party, headed by Brandler, had cited united front doctrines to justify a parliamentary coalition with the social democrats. Out of that coalition had come the 1923 humiliation, a setback which demanded explanation.[3] To repeal the Comintern's past resolutions on the united front was out of the question. Practically every top leader in the organization had committed

[1] *The Times*, 30 Jan., 1925.
[2] The authoritative source for the Congress is Communist International, 5th Congress, *Piatyi Vsemirnyi Kongress Kommunisticheskogo Internatsionala, 17 iiunia–8 iiulia 1924 g. Stenograficheskii Otchet*, Two parts (Moscow–Leningrad: Gosudarstvennoe Izdatel'stvo, 1925). Further footnote references to the Congress will derive from this source. There is also a transcript in German, *Protokoll des 5 Kongresses der Kommunistischen Internationale*, 2 Vols. (Hamburg: C. Hoym, 1924). An abbreviated version is available in English: *Fifth Congress of the Communist International: Abridged Report of Meetings held at Moscow June 17th to July 8 1924.* ([London]: Published for the Communist International by the Communist Party of Great Britain, [1924]). Zinoviev's speech on the trade union question was published separately in English: G. Zinoviev, *Towards Trade Union Unity!* (London: Published for the Communist International by the Communist Party of Great Britain, [1925]). For a later Soviet summary of the Congress's achievements, see N. Popov, *Outline History of the Communist Party of the Soviet Union*, ed. by A. Fineberg and H. C. Scott, II (London: Martin Lawrence, [1935]), 211–14.
[3] See above, pp. 7–8.

himself to them publicly. Rather than change the canon, the leadership preferred to attack Brandler for misinterpreting it. That procedure offered two obvious advantages. It provided convenient scapegoats for the German failure, drawing attention away from the equally glaring errors made by more prominent Comintern functionaries. And it compromised Trotsky and Radek, Brandler's friends and patrons in the International.

Zinoviev led off the attack the opening day of the Congress.[1] Brandler's opportunism plus Radek's distortion of united front tactics had produced the disaster. A united front from above only, a front just with reformist overlords, was absolutely inadmissible. Primary emphasis must be placed on the united front from below, splitting the misguided rank and file in the leftist parties from their treacherous leaders. In special situations, where Communists were a tiny minority and social democracy was especially strong, the tactics of the united front from above *and* below, an appeal to the leaders and the led simultaneously, might be justifiable, but it must be employed with great caution and only after elaborate safeguards against it being applied opportunistically.

The antidote to opportunism in the Communist movement, Zinoviev suggested, was 'Bolshevization,' a term more often acclaimed than clarified. On a later occasion, Zinoviev defined Bolshevization as 'making use of the experience of the Bolshevik party in the three Russian revolutions' and applying the lessons thus learned 'to the concrete situation of each particular country.'[2] The essential message behind the verbal delicacies was clear: follow the Soviet example, learn from the Russians, take Muscovite directions. In the first instance, Bolshevization would involve quick and explicit condemnation of Trotsky's supporters in all Communist Parties where they still held influential positions. After that, it meant taking no decisive step without the explicit agreement of the CPSU. Only after such thorough training in Bolshevization could a Party confidently employ the whole approved range of united front weapons, safe from the perils of opportunism.

Zinoviev's radical redefinition of united front doctrine – Radek called it 'liquidation' of the doctrine – provoked its defenders into replying. The British defence was cautious and self-effacing. The CPGB conceded that the united front could be abused and could infect a Party with opportunism. Blanket restrictions on its use, however, might be ill-advised, and the International would do better to specify the limits of the

[1] His speech is in *Piatyi Kongress, Stenograficheskii Otchet*, I, 45–91.
[2] *Inprecorr*, v, (22 Jan. 1925), 63–4.

united front separately, for each national Party, to accord with special local conditions.[1] Radek was more forceful.[2] He scoffed at Zinoviev's cheerful estimates on the growing strength of Communist Parties in the west. The social democrats still controlled millions of workers, he said, and to follow the chairman in all but abandoning united front tactics was to surrender masses of proletarians to the reformists.

Predictably, the final resolutions closely followed Zinoviev's recommendations.[3] Although the validity of united front tactics was reaffirmed *pro forma*, the comrades were strenuously warned to avoid the associated dangers of opportunism and revisionism. The united front was solely 'a method of agitation and revolutionary mobilization of the masses,' a 'method of revolution' rather than of 'peaceful evolution,' and to be undertaken solely for the purpose of 'agitating for a proletarian dictatorship.' It was best pursued only from below. To pursue it from above alone, to unite with social-democratic renegades or form coalitions with them or surrender the right to revile and execrate them, was sternly forbidden.

The new line posed especially difficult problems for the British Party, which had embraced united front doctrines more enthusiastically than had any other section of the International. Every year the CPGB applied to the Labour party for affiliation, renewing the application regularly in spite of the humiliation of seeing it consistently rejected. At election time, it withdrew its own Parliamentary candidates to leave Labour a clear field. In the 1924 atmosphere, such spiritless submission to reformism inevitably attracted unpleasant attention. Zinoviev, wildly optimistic about revolutionary prospects in England, did not think the local comrades were taking full advantage of their opportunities.[4] MacDonald was the 'British Kerensky,' whose 'bourgeois and anti-worker' government would soon disintegrate. The CPGB could speed his fall by launching an immediate and vigorous offensive against him. In such conditions the British party, presently 'the most important section of the Com-

---

[1] *Piatyi Kongress, Stenograficheskii Otchet*, I, 265–8 (Murphy) and 349–57 (Mac-Manus).

[2] *Ibid.*, I, 158–72. The German left Communist leader, Ruth Fischer, defended Zinoviev on this occasion. See *ibid.*, I, 173–92.

[3] The resolution is reprinted in *Kommunisticheskii Internatsional v Dokumentakh*, pp. 407–9.

[4] For sections of Zinoviev's opening speech referring specifically to England see *Piatyi Kongress, Stenograficheskii Otchet*, I, 65–7, 80–1. The famous reference to the other possible doors to a mass party than the Stewart–MacManus door (quoted below) came in a subsequent speech in connection with the discussion on trade union policy (*ibid.*, p. 879).

munist International,' should press its advantages ruthlessly, devoting special attention to the significant leftward movement evident in the trade unions, and transform itself into a true mass organization.

To the chagrin of his British comrades, Zinoviev implied that the transformation he had in mind might involve a whole new orientation, abandoning the existing revolutionary machinery and building anew from within the trade union organizations on the Labour party left. The rapid growth of the Minority Movement, and the clear swing to the left evidenced by Cook's victory and the TUC's behaviour at Vienna, opened up possibilities not previously even contemplated. Zinoviev was not explicit, but nobody could miss the drift of his argument. The key sentences would be much quoted thereafter. 'We do not know,' he said, 'exactly whence the Communist mass party of England will come, whether only through the Stewart–MacManus door [the current CPGB leaders], or through some other door. And it is entirely possible, comrades, that the Communist mass party may appear through still another door – we cannot lose sight of that.' The existing CPGB, he implied, might have to be written off as a failure. Trotsky, very much subdued while attending the Congress, would seize on those words three months later and rebuke their author. The key to revolution was a party, not trade unions, he said. 'Without a party, apart from a party, over the head of a party, or with a substitute for a party, the proletarian revolution cannot conquer,' he wrote. 'It is true that the English trade unions may become a mighty lever of the proletarian revolution.... They can, however, fill such a role, not apart from a Communist party, and certainly not *against* the party, but only on the condition that Communist influence becomes the decisive influence in the trade unions. We have paid far too dearly for this conclusion – with regard to the role and importance of a party in a proletarian revolution – to renounce it so lightly or even to minimize its significance.'[1]

The reprimand, however merited, was not voiced publicly at the Congress. The British delegates there, without being abusive, were still stubborn.[2] The MacDonald government was as bad as everybody said it was, they confessed, but it was not weak, and it might even gain further support at the next elections. Even if it did fall, the fall would bring

---

[1] Leon Trotsky, *The Lessons of October*, Trans. by John G. Wright (New York: Pioneer Publishers, 1937), pp. 98–100.
[2] The relevant speeches in *Piatyi Kongress, Stenograficheskii Otchet*, are those of Murphy (I, 265–8) and MacManus (I, 349–57). Brown's speech, mysteriously omitted from the Russian transcript, may be found in the English 'summary,' *Fifth Congress: Abridged Report*, pp. 74–5.

down only the government, not the party. The Labour party would stand, still the sole political organization commanding the support of the entire British working class. To remain outside of it, to surrender its five million members to their reformist leaders, was to condemn the CPGB to sectarian ineffectiveness. The aim must be not to destroy the Labour party, but to capture it and transform it into a mass Communist Party. To capture it required first getting admitted to it. Setting Communist Parliamentary candidates in opposition to Labour's candidates would hardly further that objective. Instead, the CPGB should concentrate on the trade unions, the core of Labour party strength. Through the mechanism of the Minority Movement the old trade union leadership could be challenged and replaced. The Labour party left wing could thus be strengthened and the MacDonald rightists neutralized. Finally, when the Communist Party application for affiliation had been granted, and objective conditions were right, the Labour party could be made over into the overwhelming and irresistible revolutionary instrument Zinoviev had urged.

The resolution adopted[1] gently chided the British comrades for 'right-wing deviations' on the question of the united front and an overly solicitous attitude toward the Labour party leadership. The CPGB was too important a part of the International to afford such ideological luxuries, the Comintern declared, and would 'need much greater attention in the future from the international leadership' to prevent further abuses.

The Comintern's concern for a more restricted application of united front tactics apparently extended only to pacts with reformist political parties. Trade union policy would remain the same.[2] There could be no deserting reformist-dominated trade unions, meekly yielding them to the social democrats, or attempting to split them, Lozovsky said. The unions must be held together, unified, and finally captured for Communism. The campaign had already brought results in the emergence of a left wing within the IFTU leadership. The leftists were no revolutionaries, he confessed, and their timidity, inconsistency, and hesitancy must be relentlessly exposed and condemned. But they were moving in a progressive direction and they reflected an even more fundamental movement among the masses. To give up the struggle for the unions in such favourable circumstances was not only unnecessary, it was absurd.[3]

[1] *Inprecorr*, IV, 62 (29 Aug. 1924), 651–3.
[2] Lozovsky told the delegates so a month before they arrived: *Communist International*, New Series, No. 4 (1924), pp. 41–54.
[3] *Piatyi Kongress, Stenograficheskii Otchet*, I, 801–29.

The German delegates led off the debate on Lozovsky's theses by vigorously attacking them.[1] German experience demonstrated that trade union left wingers were even more dangerous than rightists. To put any faith in any of them was to wallow in illusion, they warned. Zinoviev himself finally had to rise in Lozovsky's defence.[2] However difficult it was to imagine a trade union serving any revolutionary purpose, it still could, he said. Russian experience proved it. The unions were, after all, the proletariat's only true mass organizations, the sole 'historically inevitable' expressions of proletarian unity. Within them, the proletarian vanguard could find its class brothers, and mobilize them to struggle for their own liberation. Any other course was anti-Leninist.

The achievement of national trade union unity was just a beginning. International unity came next. It could be attained in part, Lozovsky suggested, by bilateral committees uniting, for example, French and Italian miners, or German and Czech transport workers. On a still larger scale, he proposed establishing committees linking workers in all industries, a Russo-Polish committee, perhaps, or an Anglo-Russian one. Such committees could help neutralize the propaganda in the bourgeois press and, in 'the tensest moments of struggle, play a tremendous part in uniting and mobilizing the workers.'[3]

However off-handedly and casually it was mentioned, the reference to an 'Anglo-Russian committee' – the first such in published Soviet sources – could hardly have been accidental. Indeed, it was repeated in the final theses adopted. Nobody at the Congress was unaware of the recent contacts between British and Russian trade unionists, and indeed, many delegates deplored them. The Germans were especially suspicious, suggesting quite openly that the talks might have been inspired by officials of the Soviet Foreign Commissariat, seeking to gain a point or two in the London treaty negotiations.[4] Zinoviev met such slanders head on. The trade union leftists in Britain were not revolutionaries, he admitted, but their appearance and growing strength were still of historic importance and neither the Russian trade unions nor the Comintern could just

---

[1] See *ibid.*, pp. 830–43 (Heckert), pp. 844–52 (Schumacher) and pp. 853–8 (Seelig).

[2] *Ibid.*, pp. 869-84. The final theses adopted of course reflected the Lozovsky–Zinoviev point of view: *Kommunisticheskii Internatsional v Dokumentakh*, pp. 438–44.

[3] *Piatyi Kongress, Stenograficheskii Otchet*, I, 824–5.

[4] Bukharin discussed these suspicions quite openly in the 6th ECCI meeting in February 1926. See Communist International, Enlarged Executive, *Shestoi Rasshirennyi Plenum Ispolkoma Kominterna (17 Febralia–15 Marta 1926g)*. *Stenograficheskii Otchet* (Moscow–Leningrad: Gosudarstvennoe Izdatel'stvo, 1927), pp. 201–13.

ignore them. Their overtures demanded some sort of response. That response would, of course, have repercussions on the diplomatic negotiations in London, but diplomatic considerations had not, should not, and would not dictate the response. 'The response should be that decided by the whole International.'[1]

The 'overture' to which Zinoviev referred was, of course, the resolution the British had pushed through the Vienna IFTU Congress inviting the Russian trade unions to join Amsterdam. Lozovsky had evaded that issue in introducing the trade union discussion, but the debates got out of control subsequently and an exploration of the problem was unavoidable.[2] Delegates were soon blurting out indiscretions at a horrendous rate, including the revelation that the Russian trade unions were for saying yes to Amsterdam, apparently unconditionally. That was making a fetish of unity, said an American delegate, and he was against it. An Italian comrade went still further. He was against any new trade union international even if it included all Profintern's affiliates. Any such unity would be spurious and artificial, he said. The new German leaders, predictably, were most vociferous on the subject. Amsterdam would never agree to a revolutionary trade union international, they said, and any other kind was not worth the effort. The proper response to IFTU's unity gestures was to show them up for what they were, a mere game, not intended seriously. The Amsterdam leftists had to be exposed to the masses as hypocrites and frauds. Any ignominious surrender of the Red International was out of the question. The extreme leftists were especially vocal on that last possibility. 'I declare,' one of them thundered, 'that whoever thinks of liquidating the R.I.L.U. ultimately liquidates the Communist International.'[3]

Zinoviev had to reassure the delegates.[4] In the course of a lengthy exposition he twice promised them that no 'marriage' with Amsterdam was contemplated. The Russian unions would never apply for IFTU membership by themselves, abandoning the other Profintern affiliates, he pledged. That would be sheer capitulation and was out of the question. But it would be no moral defeat for the Russian unions to make unity proposals to Amsterdam on behalf of Profintern as a whole, even if those proposals were rejected. Profintern was expendable, given

---

[1] *Piatyi Kongress, Stenograficheskii Otchet*, I, 869–84. The quotations are from p. 880.
[2] The debate is in *ibid.*, pp. 830–99.
[3] Schumacher, in *ibid.*, p. 894.
[4] The relevant portions of his speech are in *ibid.*, pp. 877–81. The quotations cited are from p. 879.

the right terms. The workers would understand. They realized, he said, that the class struggle required strategic manoeuvring just like any other war.

Lozovsky – with less feeling, perhaps – seconded Zinoviev's remarks.[1] The IFTU had made a definite political proposal, he said, requiring a definite political answer. It had proposed the Russian trade unions join IFTU on the basis of IFTU's programme and statutes. The Russian trade unions wanted to accept the proposal, he noted, even though acceptance would mean dissolution of RILU. He could not agree, nor did he think anybody else at the Congress would agree either. 'I believe we are all against this solution, because the Russian trade unions are an integral part of the international revolutionary trade union movement. They cannot have tactics of their own, differing from those of the Communist International and the Red Trade Union International.' On the other hand, to reject IFTU's proposals, to seem to reject unity outright, would be to just play into the hands of the reformist enemy. The middle course was the wisest, Lozovsky urged, to endorse the campaign for unity but seek it on Moscow's terms, not Amsterdam's – unity via a world congress including all affiliates of both IFTU and RILU.

The Congress finally shrugged off the controversial issue of the response to IFTU onto its Executive Committee, instructing it 'to examine the question thoroughly and to draw up the required instructions.'[2] The resolution adopted on trade union policy was splendidly vague on unity, urging it, but cautiously side-stepping the issue of how to achieve it.[3] Pride in the emergence of an IFTU left wing was balanced by conspicuous reluctance to find any virtue in it. Its inconsistencies, vagueness and half-heartedness were solemnly noted and its insistence on some middle way between reformism and Communism specifically condemned. The proper revolutionary response to it was to test it, to make it show its good intentions in practice by whole-hearted participation in joint demonstrations against the programme and tactics of the Amsterdam old guard.

The Executive Committee's supplementary resolution, approved just a few days later, added very little to the Congress's equivocal response.[4] The German demand that the unity campaign be carefully prepared from below, by a massive propaganda barrage, before it was consummated in negotiations at the summit, was conceded. On the other hand, the basic

---

[1] *Ibid.*, pp. 899–911. The quotation is from p. 909.   [2] *Ibid.*, p. 980.
[3] *Kommunisticheskii Internatsional v Dokumentakh*, pp. 438–44.
[4] *Piatyi Kongress, Stenograficheskii Otchet*, ii, 10–11.

proposition favouring merger of RILU and IFTU was confirmed. The fusion should be effected by a joint congress with proportional representation. Each side must retain full freedom within the projected new organization to agitate for and propagandize its viewpoint, but strictest discipline must be observed in all actions directed against the bourgeoisie. Until unity on such a basis was achieved, Comintern should continue to support and strengthen Profintern. In no circumstances should the Russian unions be permitted to negotiate for unity independently.

The 3rd Congress of the Red International of Labour Unions assembled immediately following the adjournment of the Comintern Congress.[1] Many of the same delegates yawned through reports by the same leaders rehashing the same grave issues and parroting the same considered judgements on them. In return for a degree of tedium, the revolutionary movement thus achieved a considerable saving in travel expenses. The decisions on united front tactics rubber-stamped the strictures of the Comintern Congress. The manoeuvre was a sound one but it had been misunderstood and abused. It should be pursued primarily from below and never from above only. Backstage negotiations with reformist leaders, or secret agreements with them, were forbidden. Any dealings with them must be openly conducted and the working masses kept fully informed of the results. Communists should never blunt their sharp criticisms of reformists, nor ease their struggle against imperialists, merely to achieve understandings with them. So long as that was understood, united front arrangements were permissible, and through them, Communism could 'involve wide masses of the unorganized in the struggle against capital.'[2]

The discussions and resolutions on the growth of the left wing within Amsterdam were also predictable. The IFTU left was irresolute, ideologically formless, and wholly undependable. It was best understood as a 'barometer,' a rather inaccurate barometer, measuring only partly and inadequately the real discontent of the masses with their compromising,

[1] My basic source for the Profintern Congress is Red International of Labour Unions, *Protokoll über den Dritten Kongress der Roten Gewerkschafts-Internationale abgehalten in Moskau vom 8. bis 21. Juli 1924* (Berlin: Verlag der Roten Gewerkschafts-Internationale, [1924]). The resolutions and theses may be found in *Profintern v Rezoliutsiakh* and *Desiat¹ Let Profinterna*. Lozovsky summarized the work of the Congress in *World's Trade Union Movement*, pp. 141–4, in 'The Results of the III Congress of the RILU,' *Inprecorr*, IV, 56 (7 Aug., 1924), 596–7 and in 'Der Kampf für die Einheit der Weltgewerkschaftsbewegung,' *Die Rote Gewerkschafts-Internationale*, No. 7/8 (42/43) (July–Aug., 1924), pp. 3–6. Tomsky's important speech to the Congress was translated into English and reprinted in Tomsky, *Getting Together*, pp. 43–65.   [2] *Profintern v Rezoliutsiakh*, pp. 47–8.

strike-breaking, reformist leaders. Pressure from the dissidents below persuaded a few laggard, grudging, ideologically opportunistic leaders to give way a little, to mouth radical phrases and indulge themselves in intermittent abuse of those farther to the right than they. Although they should be supported as against their rightist colleagues, they must be tested constantly – required to prove themselves in more than words. Most of them would fail the test.

The strength demonstrated at Vienna by the slippery and undependable leftists was nevertheless immensely important. It indicated the utter disillusionment of the trade union rank and file in the west with the antiquated policies still being pursued by their organizations. The same disillusionment which produced the IFTU pseudo-left was also producing a true left in the form of minority movements within the Amsterdam affiliates. The minority movements, unlike the 'leftists,' were firmly rooted in sound ideological principles, Marxist principles, the programme and tactics of Profintern. Their political prospects were excellent and they must be energetically supported. Such judgements applied with special force, of course, to the situation in England. The British delegates were uncompromisingly harsh on the so-called leftists in the TUC General Council, and correspondingly optimistic about the prospects for the National Minority Movement. Their views were reflected in the Congress's resolutions.[1]

These conclusions were pretty much foreseeable, expressing the same attitudes which had prevailed at the Comintern Congress. The debate on international trade union unity, on the other hand, produced some surprises, and one significant policy change. Three proposals on the subject were submitted to the RILU delegates. The Soviet representatives suggested the possibility of the Russian trade unions entering Amsterdam. The Germans opposed any plan for unity with class traitors and urged abrupt rejection of all IFTU's overtures. The French delegation, opposing any Russian application for IFTU membership, also rejected surrendering the unity slogan to the reformists, and urged an intensive campaign for the other route to an all-inclusive trade union international, the route via a world congress of all affiliates of both RILU and IFTU.[2] The Executive Committee endorsed and presented the French resolution.

---

[1] *Protokoll über den Dritten Kongress*, pp. 171–200, 339–50, *Desiat¹ Let Profinterna*, pp. 119–51.

[2] The existence of the three separate proposals was acknowledged publicly six months later: *Inprecorr*, v, 12 (6 Feb., 1925), 151.

The debates began calmly enough. Dogadov's speech to the Congress, welcoming the delegates in behalf of the Russian trade unions, was hospitable, agreeable, and non-controversial. There must be no suspicion that the Russians had ever contemplated selling their revolutionary souls in return for the social democrats' mess of ideological pottage. They would never betray their comrades in the Red International, he promised, just to gain admission into Amsterdam. They were for world trade union unity, but not at any price.[1]

Offering the report from the Executive Committee, Lozovsky took acceptance of the French draft resolution for granted. He devoted very little time to the question, stressing only that in the search for unity, Profintern would not be taken in by Amsterdam's 'sly' invitation to come together on the basis of its programme and platform.[2]

It was Tomsky, fresh from his genial contacts with the TUC General Council, who dramatically re-vivified the whole dead issue in a vigorous alternate report to that offered by the Profintern Executive.[3] The reason for the report, he said, was to clarify the attitude of the Russian trade unions on the unity question. In a period of strenuous capitalist offensives all over the world, the proletariat had to concentrate all its forces to withstand the onslaught. Faltering and ineffective though it might be, IFTU represented an effort at such an amalgamation of strengths, a crude sort of effort, but nonetheless real. In the interests of the working masses, millions of whom were still members of IFTU organizations and obediently followed their reformist leaders, Communists had to make common cause with those leaders in the struggle against capitalism, the common enemy. To stand aside on the excuse that revolutionaries could never demean themselves by sitting down at the same table with class traitors was to be petty and parochial, and to jeopardize the whole proletarian cause.

The conversion of the Amsterdam left to a policy of trade union unity was, he said, the result of broad mass sentiment. He did not pretend to be an expert on the international trade union movement, he admitted. He did not even claim special competence on English trade unionism, although he had just returned from two months in Britain. He could assert, however, confidently, that the slogan of trade union unity was irresistible to the English workers, and that they would follow the leaders

[1] *Protokoll über den Dritten Kongress*, pp. 18–19. Actually, Dogadov did not employ the suspiciously Biblical 'mess of pottage' imagery. He talked about 'bean soup' instead.

[2] *Ibid.*, pp. 23–38.

[3] *Ibid.*, pp. 272–82; Tomsky, *Getting Together*, pp. 43–65.

who endorsed it. 'Whoever marches under this slogan will triumph in England.' If Profintern would make the first move toward unity, it would immediately win massive and enthusiastic support. Organizational pride should not influence the decision. It was irrelevant who first asked whom to unite. Indeed, by taking the 'revolutionary initiative,' Profintern would not lose prestige but gain it.

Tomsky was confident that the Communist cause would suffer no setback in an all-inclusive trade union international. Within it, revolutionaries could move from an opposition role to effective leadership of the organization. Amsterdam leftists might even contribute to such an effort. They might become more militant as time went by, and eventually be won over to the revolution. Some of them were sincere and trustworthy fighters. He cited Cook and Purcell, both of whom were 'sterling fellows.' They had demonstrated practical sympathy for the Russian workers (presumably by their assistance in the treaty negotiations) at a time when it was most unpopular to do so. Of course the leftists had to be tested, to see how left they really were. But if they could meet the test, Communism might win millions of adherents through their influence. To dismiss such possibilities with simplistic, ultra-left formula – all reformists are scoundrels, all reformists are traitors – was to miss the whole point of the argument. To urge a united trade union international was not opportunism, but sound revolutionary tactics.

He reassured the delegates on the projected talks with Amsterdam. The Russian unions had no intention of abandoning their Profintern comrades and entering IFTU alone. They were revolutionaries. They had always consulted with RILU and Comintern in the past, and they would continue to in the future. Not 'a single step,' he emphasized, had ever been taken, or would ever be taken, 'without the knowledge and sanction of the Profintern.' But to refuse to deal with Amsterdam, to ignore its overtures, would be idiocy. RILU should rather require the Amsterdam leaders to show their hands, to disclose their real position to the workers. The confrontation could achieve far more than some mere 'pasteboard propaganda onslaught.' It could mark 'the beginning of a definite attempt to take their fortress by storm.' A properly-waged campaign could 'storm the reformist citadel' – IFTU – and win it for Communism. The stakes were 'the real leadership of the international working-class movement.' 'We will see,' he concluded, 'to whom the victory will belong, the reformists, or the wing of the international workers' movement that is revolutionary not just in words, but in deeds.'

The German ultra-left leader, Schumacher, rose quickly to challenge Tomsky.[1] What kind of an international did he have in mind? Why no word on how such an organization would stand on socialism, on the dictatorship of the proletariat, on the liquidation of capitalism? Too much in the proposed resolution was too vague, he charged. It would look like Profintern was suddenly surrendering its principles. He foresaw in Tomsky's suggestions the slow liquidation of RILU, and that was the same as liquidating the revolution itself. To argue otherwise was in fact to assert Profintern never should have been founded. He predicted 'a fiasco of the highest order' in the coming negotiations. Tomsky was willing to pay too high a price for unity. The revolutionary movement had already suffered from too much zigzagging, too many united fronts. He proposed, instead, militancy, uncompromising devotion to principle, and stern refusal to deal with the enemy, with the elites.

Profintern hardly needed defenders like Schumacher, Lozovsky replied.[2] Unity was all to the good. RILU had always believed in it. The Russians planned no Versailles-type surrender to Amsterdam, and only Schumacher could envision such a prospect. The question was simply whether to seek unity or not to seek it. The Russian trade unions could be trusted to deal with Amsterdam responsibly, Lozovsky said. They had in the past; they would in the future. The resolutions indicated the aim of the negotiations was unity by means of an international congress at which all political viewpoints would be proportionally represented. No precipitous liquidation of RILU was contemplated, Lozovsky promised, and no liquidation at all until agreement was reached on a new united international in which both Profintern and Amsterdam would lose their separate identities. He did not consider that represented any surrender.

The resolution adopted incorporated a substantive concession to Tomsky's plea.[3] It reiterated Profintern's support for working-class unity on the broadest basis to meet the capitalist offensive. It suggested a world congress of trade unions from both existing internationals to negotiate terms for union. To persuade Amsterdam to join in calling such a congress, it authorized the RILU Executive, or its representatives (by which was meant the Russian trade unions), to deal with IFTU directly or with the British trade unionists. Insofar as the Russian

[1] *Protokoll über den Dritten Kongress*, pp. 283–6.
[2] *Ibid.*, pp. 286–8.
[3] The debates, indicating changes made in the resolution, are in *ibid.*, pp. 265–88 and especially p. 282. The resolution as adopted is in *ibid.*, pp. 351–2 and in *Profintern v Rezoliutsiakh*, pp. 54–5.

affiliate conducted the negotiations, however, it was to do so under the closest supervision of the Profintern leadership. 'Each decisive step' taken could be taken '*only* with the sanction and under the direction of the Profintern.'

All that sounds like a mere reiteration of the established line. In one key respect, however, the resolution had been amended. The original French draft had indicated that a huge propaganda campaign for unity among the masses must come first – a nod to the 'united front from below' doctrines – and then the next step 'should be' the calling of that international unity congress. In response to Tomsky's plea, the wording was changed to read 'could be.' The change was crucial. Tomsky knew there was absolutely no chance of the IFTU leaders agreeing to sit down at the same table and on an equal basis with RILU representatives. If unity could be sought only by that world congress it was not going to be achieved. But if the congress were suggested as just one possible means of attaining unity, and other means were not excluded, something might be accomplished. IFTU might agree to alter its constitution and rules enough to make them palatable to Profintern. Then the Russians, and the other RILU affiliates, could apply for IFTU membership. That might be something of a prestige loss, but it could be the only way (aside from a unity congress Amsterdam would refuse to attend) to attain unity. It could put the Russian trade unions back in the mainstream of the European labour movement, and it was therefore what Tomsky wanted. Now he had a somewhat reluctant and artfully veiled authorization to see if he could get it.

Lozovsky was clearly unhappy about the change of wording. In subsequent reviews of the Profintern meeting he kept harking back to the suggestion of a unity congress, and noting, almost zestfully, that Amsterdam's leaders were quite unlikely to agree to attend one.[1] He did not seem to care whether they did or not. The struggle for unity was aimed at winning the masses, not the leaders, he emphasized. Energetic agitation among the workers, rather than negotiations at the top, would produce results. Right after the RILU Congress, Lozovsky succeeded in pushing through the Profintern and Comintern Executives a joint statement, which, on the face of it, half-repealed the RILU's unity resolution.[2] It reaffirmed unity as a slogan, but insisted it could be achieved

---

[1] See, for example, *Inprecorr*, IV, 56 (7 Aug., 1924), 596–97, and *Die Rote Gewerkschaftsinternationale*, No. 7/8 (42/43) (July–Aug., 1924), pp. 3–6.

[2] Red International of Labour Unions, *Mezhdunarodnoe Profdvizhenie za 1924–27 gg.: Otchet Ispol'buro IV Kongressu Profinterna* (Moscow: Izdanie Profinterna, 1928), p. 44.

'only on the basis of the class struggle, only by merger of the Red International of Labour Unions and the Amsterdam International, only through an international unity congress...' 'Only'! Taken literally, that word would be fatal to Tomsky's whole effort. Tomsky seems, in fact, to have paid no attention to it. Profintern hardly worried him at all, apparently. Indeed, Profintern hardly existed at all over the next four years except in the skeleton form of its small Executive bureau. No international Congress of RILU would convene again until March of 1928. The organization's charter specified congresses were to meet, 'if possible,' not less than once a year. The Profintern Central Council would meet only once between 1924 and 1928; the charter demanded meetings not less than twice a year. Clearly, the whole organism went into a state of suspended animation for the next four years, while Tomsky, on its behalf, manoeuvred for that marriage with Amsterdam which had been so stoutly denied at the Comintern meeting.[1]

Manoeuvring was not easy. Militant leftists in the USSR were a constant source of embarrassment. A typical Comintern manifesto on July 18, 1924, proposed that all 'yellow Amsterdam trade unionists who take their orders from the bourgeois ministers and the magnates of capital' and all 'Menshevist leaders of political and trade union organizations' must be pitilessly jettisoned. 'Drive them away,' the International urged, 'expose them, boycott them, force them out of the ranks of the working class.'[2] Anti-Communist militants within Amsterdam would regularly assemble collections of such statements, translate and publish them. Zinoviev and Lozovsky were particularly reliable sources of usable quotations.[3] Few Soviet leaders were ready to contradict them openly. Of the major Party spokesmen, only Stalin supported Tomsky's campaign, and even his backing was cautious, reserved and tentative.[4]

On the other side, within the inner councils of the IFTU, the opponents of any dealings at all with the Russians seemed to be becoming more stubborn, more vocal and more militant in the last six months of 1924. Their leader was Jan Oudegeest, one of Amsterdam's three secretaries. His opinions dominated the editorial columns of the two more-or-less regular IFTU publications, the *International Trade Union Review* and the *IFTU Press Reports*. His line was straightforward and persuasive.

[1] The charter of the RILU can be found in *Desiat¹ Let Profinterna*, pp. 272–6. That source also lists meetings of the Congresses and of the Central Councils.
[2] *Inprecorr*, IV, 43 (18 July, 1924), 427–33.
[3] See, for example, *IFTU Press Reports*, No. 46 (20 Nov., 1924).
[4] An example is in his article for *Bol¹shevik* for 20 Sept. 1924: Stalin, *Sochineniia*, VI, 280–301.

RILU had been slinging mud at Amsterdam for half a decade, but had only soiled itself. Realizing the battle was as good as lost, it had come up with the high-sounding slogan of the united front. Behind the pretentious verbiage surrounding the slogan was concealed a simple and desperate plan: penetrate Amsterdam, take it over, discard much of what had been built up so painfully and carefully, enlist the rest in the cause of Bolshevism, and in the process – in fact – destroy it all. If the Russians – *just* the Russians, and not their friends among the west European trade union schismatics – wanted to apply for IFTU membership on the basis of its existing rules and in a genuine effort to strengthen it, they might be accommodated. Citing the speeches of Soviet leaders themselves, however, Oudegeest doubted whether that was what the Russians had in mind.[1]

Since Oudegeest could speak for at least five of his seven colleagues on the IFTU Executive Committee, it is hardly surprising that the negotiations with the Russians proceeded at a leisurely pace. Not until July 16 did the Executive even bother to notify the Russian trade unions, officially, of the Vienna resolution passed over a month earlier inviting them to affiliate – on Amsterdam's terms, of course, and with due regard for Amsterdam's dignity.[2] If, the Executive indicated, the Soviets agreed to negotiations 'on the basis of the principles contained in this resolution,' IFTU was ready to meet with them.

The Soviet reply came just ten days later.[3] It expressed the 'deepest satisfaction' at Amsterdam's willingness to negotiate, and its own 'full readiness to take all measures necessary to establish unity.' The Russians felt, however, that the conditions attached to the Vienna resolution represented a bar to fruitful discussions. The terms under which unity might be achieved should be the whole subject of the negotiations, and 'to put forth as a preliminary condition our acceptance of the conditions and rules of your international, as you do, is contrary to the...aim of unity.' Just as the IFTU Executive was bound by the resolutions of the Vienna Congress, so too was the All-Union Central Council of Trade Unions 'obliged to carry out the decisions of...the Congresses of the Red International.' To find some common ground for negotiation, and to achieve final integration of the divided international trade union movement, the Russians proposed 'as our starting point' a discussion

---

[1] A typical statement of Oudegeest's viewpoint was in his article, 'A Few Remarks on the Vienna Congress,' *International Trade Union Review*, IV, 3 (July/Sept., 1924), 211–16. [2] Text in *ibid.*, p. 247.

[3] Texts in *ibid.*, pp. 248–9 (English) and in Tomsky, *K Probleme Edinstva*, pp. 36–7 (Russian).

of 'the decisions of both internationals on the basis of equality and mutual understanding.' The meeting should be purely exploratory, with neither side setting any 'preliminary conditions.'

No reply other than a routine acknowledgement came back from Amsterdam for almost seven weeks. Oudegeest and his colleagues were doubtless hoping the TUC might get over its inexplicable intimacy with the Russians. The Hull Trades Union Congress, in early September, dramatically demonstrated that the liaison was as mawkish as ever.[1] The IFTU bureaucrats decided on further delaying tactics. A new letter to Tomsky went out on September 11.[2] It agreed with the Russians on the importance of trade union unity, and noted sourly that it was not Amsterdam's fault that unity had ever been lost. During the course of the split, however, certain fundamental differences had been noted between Russian policies and those of IFTU, differences which went far beyond the question of a greater or lesser degree of radicalism. Before becoming involved in detailed negotiations, therefore, it might be best to see where the two sides stood on basic principles. The IFTU wanted 'something in writing' on the subject to serve 'as a basis for discussions.' 'We therefore request you,' the note continued, 'to make written proposals from which we can judge' whether an agreement was likely.

Tomsky was irritated. He told the Soviet trade union congress later in the year that Amsterdam had a lot of 'cheek' asking the Russians to state their principles. 'The Amsterdamers were already quite familiar with our principles.'[3] He decided on a blunt reply.[4] It went out October 23. He felt it inappropriate, he wrote, to commit himself in writing to any detailed exposition of the Russian programme for unity. Nor did he feel it helpful to exchange charges about which side was responsible for the split in the movement. It was sufficient that both sides had expressed themselves in support of an all-inclusive international. The details could be negotiated in face-to-face talks.

In response, however, to the IFTU request, he was glad to spell out broadly how the Russian trade unions looked at the subject of unity. What they favoured was a trade union international including the

[1] See below, pp. 82–6.
[2] Slightly different English texts available in *International Trade Union Review*, IV, 4 (Oct./Dec., 1924), 325–6, and in *Inprecorr*, IV, 80 (20 Nov., 1924), 906–7.
[3] USSR, Central Council of Trade Unions, *Shestoi S''ezd Pronfessioal'nykh Soiuzov SSSR, 11–18 Noiabria 1924g.: Plenum i Sektsii. Stenograficheskii Otchet* (Moscow: Izdatel'stvo VTsSPS, 1925), p. 79.
[4] Similar English-language texts in *Inprecorr*, IV, 80 (20 Nov., 1924), 906–7 and in *International Trade Union Review*, IV, 4 (Oct./Dec., 1924), 326–8. Russian text in Tomsky, *K Probleme Edinstva*, pp. 39–42.

greatest possible number of organizations – IFTU affiliates, RILU affiliates, and organizations presently without any international connections at all. The sole condition for membership for national centres outside either IFTU or RILU should be their recognition of 'the principle of the class struggle.' The Russian motive in urging unity, he continued, was the most basic and obvious, to enable the workers to fight successfully against the capitalist offensive, against fascist reaction, and against the whole bourgeois social order. The most suitable means for achieving unity (he did not say the *only* means) was the convening of a world labour congress, the details of which could be worked out in the preliminary negotiations.

He expressed some perplexity about Amsterdam's stressing the differences separating them. It would be more helpful, he said, to emphasize areas of agreement rather than areas of discord. The most important possible basis of agreement, the Russians felt, was recognition of the 'irreconcilable contradiction between the interests of labour and of capital.' That contradiction demanded 'decisive class war between the wage slaves and the capitalist classes.' The workers' aim should be 'the final annihilation of the capitalist system and the emancipation of the proletariat from the oppression of capitalist exploitation and the beggary, barbarism, and slavery which it brings in its train.' The Russians would therefore propose, as a basis for the new international, 'a complete break with every form of class collaboration with the bourgeoisie.' We await your reply, Tomsky concluded. Corresponding with IFTU was splendid, but talks would be more useful and productive.

The letter was, in sum, tough, businesslike, and to the point. The Russians had not abandoned their ideological identity, but they were ready to unite on the basis of international class solidarity. The western labour press began to speculate on how the details of the Soviet proposals would look. Did, for example, abandoning all forms of class collaboration involve giving up any effort to secure reforms through the International Labour Office and the League of Nations?[1] If so, that might be one possible justification for breaking off negotiations. At least, so Oudegeest felt. On November 6 he wrote a confidential letter to Léon Jouhaux, the IFTU vice-president whose views on the subject were closest to his own.[2] He enclosed a copy of Tomsky's communication,

[1] *The Labour Press Service*, issued by the Joint Publicity Department of the Trades Union Congress and the Labour Party, 9 April 1925.

[2] The existence of the letter, and its contents, was revealed almost three years later at the Paris IFTU Congress by J. W. Brown. See the official IFTU organ, *The International Trade Union Movement*, VIII, 8 (Aug., 1927), 114–15.

noting that it appeared 'to show a sincere desire on the part of the Russians to co-operate with us.' He touched on a number of potential barriers to unity. It was possible, for example, the Russians would back away from amalgamation because of IFTU's associations with the League and the ILO. Raising the question of the 'absolute independence' of the Russian unions from outside political influences might be helpful. A contradiction might become evident between IFTU's rules guaranteeing the autonomy of individual national centres and Soviet support for Communist cell-building tactics. He suggested some private talks before the IFTU Executive met on December 1, aiming at an advance agreement on the reply to be sent to Moscow. He thought that British support for Russian affiliation might be fading. Purcell had just been defeated in his bid to return to Parliament, the MacDonald government had fallen, and a sharp reaction against Communism had set in across the channel, Oudegeest wrote. The time might be propitious to de-fuse the whole explosive unity issue.

The problem, clearly, was Britain. So long as the TUC insisted on supporting the unity campaign, Amsterdam had to take it seriously. Anglo-Russian flirtations had continued right through the summer. A rendezvous had been arranged for Hull in September and a more extended assignation was planned, in the Soviet Union itself, beginning less than a week after Oudegeest wrote that letter.

The General Council's suggestion that the Russians send a fraternal delegate to the annual Congress at Hull had come out of a meeting of the International Committee on July 17, 1924. The committee noted that even Thomas had agreed, at the 1923 Congress, that a Russian representative might be welcome at next year's TUC. The Russians, however, had not made the necessary application, presumably because they were not aware they were supposed to take the initiative. The committee recommended that the General Council invite them.[1]

By the time the General Council met, six days later, the Russians had already wired a very different proposal. The telegram went out on July 20, almost immediately following the RILU Congress's vote authorizing direct contacts with the English. It invited the TUC to send a delegation to the Soviet Union 'in order to establish permanent regular connections between the two Movements' – that Anglo-Russian Committee, presumably, Lozovsky himself had suggested at the Comintern meeting. Moscow was rushing the courtship. The General Council drew back.

[1] TUC General Council, International Committee, Minutes, 17 July, 1924, file 901, document I. C.5.

While authorizing a 'sympathetic reply' to the Soviet overture, the councillors suggested that the proposed visit might best be discussed with the Russian fraternal delegate whom they hoped would be attending the Hull Congress.[1] The Russians accepted with pleasure.

British Communist leaders were delighted. The presence of Soviet fraternal delegates at Hull might reinforce left wing tendencies in the British labour movement, *Workers' Weekly* editorialised.[2] The left wing referred to, however, was not the Purcell–Hicks–Swales left, whose efforts at Vienna were dismissed almost contemptuously. In basic principle, General Council members were indistinguishable from one another. 'The corporate solidarity of trade union officialism' was still intact, wrote R. Palme Dutt, and any reliance on the self-styled 'leftists' would produce only 'bitter disillusionment' later. The struggle to revolutionize English trade unionism would 'have to come from below.'[3] The true leftists in the National Minority Movement, about to gather for their first conference, would be, hopefully, the major beneficiaries of the Russian presence at Hull. They would eventually 'sweep away' the old trade union bureaucracy, 'which has nothing to present but class peace' and mobilize the workers for militant proletarian struggle.[4]

The NMM conference met August 24 and 25, 1924, a week before the Hull TUC.[5] Some 270 delegates took part, claiming to represent 200,000 workers. Tom Mann presided, and Harry Pollitt was named general secretary. The aim of the new movement, it announced, was neither to disrupt the old trade unions nor to create new ones. It hoped to work within existing structures to strengthen them and to prepare them for class struggle. The NMM recorded its wholehearted devotion to international trade union unity, welcoming the British initiative at Vienna but noting that it was hardly enough to call for just Russian admission to IFTU while ignoring the existence of the other RILU affiliates. It suggested the General Council demand a special meeting of the Amsterdam Executive, at which it could insist on convening a world unity congress of all Amsterdam and Profintern centres. Unity could 'only be achieved,' of course, in terms of 'a full recognition of the class struggle, and all its implications.'[6]

---

[1] General Council Minutes, 23 July, 1924.   [2] *Workers' Weekly*, 1 Aug., 1924.

[3] R. Palme Dutt, 'A Postscript,' *Labour Monthly*, vi, No. 8 (Aug., 1924) 457–71.

[4] E. Verney, 'Conference of the "Minority Movement" in Great Britain,' *Inprecorr*, iv, 61 (28 Aug., 1924), 637–8.

[5] The basic source is National Minority Movement, *Report of National Minority Conference Held August 23 and 24, 1924* (London: National Minority Movement, 1924). See also the NMM weekly, *The Worker*. For commentary see Hutt, *British Working Class*, pp. 93–4.   [6] *National Minority Conference: Report*, pp. 21–2.

The unity resolution, and lots more suggestions covering everything from the Dawes Plan to miners' wages, were sent off to the TUC General Council with a request they be placed on the agenda for the Hull Congress. The proposals were received coldly. The trade union leadership hardly deigned to notice the Minority Movement. Labour's most influential periodical, the *Daily Herald*, never even mentioned the NMM conference. The General Council was barely civil. Curtly acknowledging receipt of the resolutions, it noted that only affiliated societies of TUC were authorized to submit proposals to the Congress, a reply *The Worker* later termed 'bureaucratic sticking to formalities.'[1]

These, then, were the genuine revolutionary activists whose cause was supposed to be advanced by Tomsky's presence at the Hull TUC. He may, in fact, have felt somewhat embarrassed by their raucous devotion. That he would have preferred an uncompromisingly leftist General Council goes without saying. As a practical realist, however, he knew that the Council he would have to deal with, for a year or more, anyway, would be well to the right of the NMM. The noisy appeals of his comrades in the international movement for the abrupt dismissal of the councillors with whom he was negotiating could have made for some unpleasant tensions, and ruptured the whole delicate relationship. On the other hand, of course, the strength of the Minority Movement gave him a diplomatic weapon against the General Council. If it behaved, the NMM could be restrained. If it were obstructive, the militants could be propelled into action. Tomsky was never stupid enough either to brandish his weapon openly or to discard it. If some members of the General Council were intimidated by it, all to the good. Most, probably, were not, and Tomsky probably knew it. British trade union officialdom was disdainfully contemptuous of native Communists, uncritically respectful of Russian ones, and loth to acknowledge any connections between them. In any event, the British considered Tomsky as, basically, a trade unionist rather than a Communist. For real trade unionists, loyalty to the organization came first, ideological attachments second. If such was the case in Britain, why should it be any different in the USSR?

The General Council welcomed Tomsky then, more in spite of than because of his most vociferous English admirers. It welcomed him also in spite of the unexpected retinue he brought with him. The Council had invited only one fraternal delegate from the Soviet Union. It had ordered only one convention badge. It had missed the references in the British

---

[1] General Council Minutes, 28 Aug., 1924; *The Worker*, 13 Sept., 1924.

Communist press to delegates, in the plural.[1] Not until August 30, two days before the Congress was to open, did the Council learn that four Soviet trade unionists, plus an expert interpreter, were en route to Hull. While agreeing to accord the same hospitality to the extra four, the General Council had to notify them that only one of them could address the Congress, and the additional badges would be, unhappily, delayed.[2]

It was not only in their number that the Russians made an impact. Their appearance proved something of a shocker as well. They all wore shabby caps and slovenly work clothes and looked like they'd just dropped by on their way home from the factory. The transparent bit of ill-conceived public relations was designed to impress the delegates with the proletarian credentials of their Russian guests. It would not have worked, and Joe Cotter, of the Marine Workers' Union, had the courage and good sense to tell them so. By the time the Soviets got to the Congress hall they were washed down, brushed up, and dressed as immaculately as undertaker's assistants.[3]

Within a day of the opening formalities, the delegates got to the issue in which the Russians were most interested, international trade union unity.[4] Harry Pollitt rose to congratulate the General Council on its stand at Vienna but to criticize, at the same time, the weak-kneed resolution the IFTU had finally passed. The way to an all-inclusive international, he said, was a conference of all affiliates of both Amsterdam and Moscow, and not just Russian admission to IFTU. He hoped the General Council would bear that in mind.

The General Council leftists were a bit embarrassed. Purcell and Bramley both reaffirmed their position favouring preliminary talks between the Russians and the IFTU. If the Congress had any specific instructions on how such talks should be conducted, Purcell said, he would welcome a resolution on the subject. Tillett resented the very suggestion that the General Council might not have tried hard enough. He protested the Council's great sympathy for Russia, and noted it had been unfairly abused by reactionaries who believed it had already gone too far. The way to unity was by direct contacts with the Soviet trade unionists, he urged, who were 'men of high character and mentality and broad outlook' with whom something 'useful' could be arranged.

Not all delegates were so sure the Russians could be dealt with at all.

[1] As, for example, in *Workers' Weekly*, 1 Aug., 1924.
[2] General Council Minutes, 30 Aug., 1924, 1 Sept., 1924.
[3] W. M. Citrine, *Men and Work: An Autobiography* (London: Hutchinson, 1964), p. 89.
[4] The debate, on 2 Sept., 1924, is in *1924 TUC: Report of Proceedings*, pp. 311–18.

Will Thorne, whose trade union credentials were as well-established as Tillett's and who was a member of Parliament besides, thought the Russians were their own worst enemies in the quest for unity. Profintern's 'outrageous and abusive language' had made unity 'almost impossible.' He suggested Pollitt tell his friends in Moscow to moderate their language against colleagues 'who are doing as much as they are themselves to bring about unity.' Were it not for the efforts of those TUC leaders damned from Moscow as yellow reformists, there would never have been any prospect of creating an all-inclusive international.

C. T. Cramp of the Railwaymen was not so worried about the abusive language. 'We should be able to hold our own' in that contest, he suggested. But he was firm on the proposition that unity should be contemplated only with genuine Russian trade unionists 'and not with hangers-on of their movement in various parts of the world.' The Russians he had met he adjudged – not perhaps the angels their admirers had made them out to be – but still 'sincere and straightforward men.' That was more than he could say for 'those whom they employ in this country.' If honourable terms could be arranged with them, unity was possible, but the terms must guarantee the Communists could not dictate to the projected international. Only people 'who possess an enslaved mentality,' he said, looking at Pollitt, can accept dictatorship.

Pollitt had few defenders. Only two out of ten participants in the debate backed him. When his proposal of support for a world unity congress was offered next day, in the form of an emergency resolution, it was overwhelmingly rejected. By the time Oudegeest took the floor on September 4 for his fraternal address on behalf of the IFTU, the unity cause seemed in serious trouble. Oudegeest proceeded to try to kill it altogether.[1]

He never specifically mentioned the Russian trade unions, which would have been most uncomradely in view of Tomsky's presence, and he did express the hope that all national centres might eventually affiliate with Amsterdam. He alleged, however, that everything possible had already been done to enable them all to do so. IFTU had 'never refused the affiliation of any real Trade Union centre which sought admittance.' He then offered a definition of a 'real' centre clearly designed to nail down the coffin of any Soviet bid for affiliation. The IFTU had to assure itself, he argued, that its affiliates were genuinely autonomous. Specifically, all of them must enjoy the full freedom to criticize their own governments. That principle was 'perfectly sound,' he said, and any national

[1] *Ibid.*, pp. 393–5.

trade union federation 'which is really and truly independent' could meet it.

Tomsky's speech immediately followed Oudegeest's.[1] He was in his very best form. He was happy to be the first representative of the Russian movement to speak to a Trades Union Congress. The TUC had pioneered modern trade unionism, and Soviet workers had learned much from it. It was their conviction, however, that the struggle between workers and capitalists was not just an industrial struggle and could not adequately be dealt with in such terms as 'practical trade unionism.' It was a world-wide political struggle as well, based on a world-wide clash of class interests. For the workers to stand up for their interests, they would have to organize on an international basis.

The Russians were anxious to participate in any such international movement. In response to 'Comrade Cramp,' he happily admitted the Russians were not angels, but noted, with a theological imprecision which would have appalled John Milton, that 'angels didn't start revolutions.' Russians did not want to be treated like angels. They did demand to be treated as equals. Equality was the only precondition for building an all-inclusive international. The Soviets had no desire to impose their principles on anybody else. They did not see, however, why they should have to surrender their principles, renounce 'the ideas by which we live' in order to get unity. Surely, as workers, they could unite strictly on the basis of their broad community of interests as against the ruling and exploiting classes. Could not each side retain its own principles while coming together in the common effort against capitalism?

He denied Oudegeest's claim that the Amsterdam door was open to all. It had not been open to the Russians, he charged, in 1919 and 1920, and that was why they had felt it necessary to found their own inter-national. The RILU 'may be a good thing, or it may be a bad thing,' he admitted. 'A great many people do not like it; but the essential point is that it exists' and could not be ignored. He did not deny the IFTU–RILU split had produced harsh language, and that the Communist side might have been excessively severe on Amsterdam. But if the dispute were to be ended, the way to end it was to unite the two internationals, and in that effort, questions of 'dignity' such as the Vienna Congress had raised were irrelevant. Let us talk business, he pleaded, without any preliminary stipulations on either side. The TUC could facilitate such talks, because its word counted heavily everywhere. If the British workers insisted on unity, there could be unity. It depended on them. Let each

[1] *Ibid.*, pp. 395–400.

of us, he concluded, maintain those ideas we believe right, but let us join hands to fight the enemy attacking us both.

It was an effective speech, combining salty good humour, clear-headed logic and firm resolution. It got a splendid reception. The delegates rose in their places to cheer their visitor. Cramp himself rushed to the platform to be the first to pump Tomsky's hand. Even Oudegeest now tried, without success, to arrange a talk; he complained later that Tomsky 'fled' before he could get to him.[1] The whole Congress seemed re-energized by the speech. Within hours, Purcell announced that the unity issue, apparently dead since Pollitt's resolution was passed over, was to be briefly re-opened. All over Europe, he said, workers were 'looking to the British Trade Union Congress' to advance the cause of unity. 'If our movement is to fulfil its great destiny' they must not be disappointed. 'It seems incumbent on this Congress,' he advised, 'without any formal resolution or indulging in long discussion,' to help bring together 'the different elements of the Labour Movement in Europe' in order to 'establish that solidarity' so essential to all. He suggested the Congress 'empower the General Council, through the International Federation of Trade Unions, to take all possible steps to bring the parties together.'[2] The delegates agreed, without debate, by acclamation and enthusiastically.

Tomsky's hot fervour had not scalded everybody, however. The General Council still had before it his suggestion of July 20 that the TUC send a delegation to the USSR 'to establish permanent regular connections between the two Movements.' Many councillors were wary of any such scheme. On September 5, a day after his speech to the Congress, Tomsky appeared before the Council to discuss his proposal in more detail. He was asked to indicate 'precisely' the Soviet intention in urging such a visit. His answer was something of a surprise. Not a word was said, on this occasion, about any formal ties between the two trade union organizations. The purpose of the English visit would be purely educational. The Soviets wanted their British colleagues to acquire first-hand information on the real situation inside Russia. That was all he had in mind, Tomsky said. The councillors questioned him intensively, but his story remained the same. The resolution finally passed reflected the Council's meticulous vigilance. It recommended accepting the Russian

---

[1] Oudegeest said so at Amsterdam the following February. It is noted in Fred Bramley, *Relations With Russia: A Speech in Favour of International Trade Union Unity* (London: Trade Union Unity, 1925), p. 6.
[2] *1924 TUC: Report of Proceedings*, p. 404.

invitation but only on the clear understanding that the express purpose of the trip was to investigate conditions in the USSR and submit a report.[1] The delegates were not to be charged with any other responsibility, and surely not with negotiating those permanent regular connections suggested in July.

The British Communist press, unaware of the General Council's suspicious treatment of Tomsky's hospitable overtures, was generally well satisfied with the outcome of the Hull TUC. Holding out little hope for the Congress before it met, the CPGB was agreeably surprised with the result. The support for trade union unity was particularly progressive. Pollitt's draft resolution on the subject would of course have been preferable to the motion finally adopted, but any pledge to work for unity represented a change for the better. British Communists proudly credited the TUC's move leftwards to their own efforts.[2]

The Congress raised again the question of the CPGB's attitude toward the official trade union leftists. J. R. Campbell warned that it would be a 'complete mistake' after Hull 'to imagine that they are merely right-wingers being pushed on from behind by the masses.'[3] To rely on them would be of course 'suicidal,' but there were 'genuine progressive elements amongst them' that should be encouraged. An anonymous contributor to *Labour Monthly* was more reticent. The leftists were not 'consciously insincere,' he admitted, but they were 'mortally afraid of advancing too far in front of rank and file opinion' and the NMM would therefore have to prod them constantly.[4] Only Palme Dutt remained stolidly unimpressed by the leftists. So long as they still failed to establish a 'clear and definite division' with the right on the fundamental issue of the class struggle, they actually hindered and thwarted progress rather than furthering it, he wrote.[5]

Russian comment on Hull was closer to Dutt's position than Campbell's. Lozovsky's articles in *Pravda* were typical.[6] He saw scant reason to congratulate the General Council. It was still timid, cowardly and ideologically foggy. Its resolution on unity evaded the real issue, the world labour congress to amalgamate IFTU and RILU. Hull represented

[1] General Council Minutes, 4 Sept., 1924, 5 Sept., 1924.
[2] *The Worker*, 6 Sept., 1924, 13 Sept., 1924; *Workers' Weekly*, 12 Sept., 1924; *Inprecorr*, IV, 66 (18 Sept., 1924), 717–18 (Pollitt).
[3] J. R. Campbell, 'After Hull – What?' *Communist Review*, V (Oct., 1924), 287–93.
[4] A Delegate, 'After the Hull Congress,' *Labour Monthly*, VI, No. 10 (Oct. 1924), 627–35.   [5] R. P. D[utt], 'Notes of the Month,' *ibid.*, pp. 579–90.
[6] *Pravda*, 5 Sept., 1924, 6 Sept., 1924, reprinted in Lozovsky, *Angliiskii Proletariat na Rasputi*, pp. 91–98. See also Lozovsky, *World's Trade Union Movement*, pp. 228–30.

a real step forward in only one sense. It saw the emergence of the NMM – the real left in British trade unionism, the revolutionary left. The 'official' left in the General Council could never release the TUC from the dead hand of tradition and compromise. The NMM might.

As for the unity campaign, its success demanded even more intensive preparation from below. The Comintern launched a massive propaganda effort for it immediately after the Hull Congress. The ECCI and Profintern Executive led off with a joint statement on September 18.[1] The international capitalist class was not only attacking wage rates all over the world, it was also preparing a direct military assault on the USSR, the proletarian fatherland. Its efforts had to be resolutely resisted. The fight required an immediate end to the rupture in international trade unionism. By ignoring the call for unity, IFTU bureaucrats served only the imperialists and the bourgeoisie and sabotaged the workers' cause all over the world. They would have to be compelled to change their minds. The gain at Hull showed what the masses could achieve when they expressed their will to unity clearly and resolutely. The campaign must broaden out from there and mobilize workers everywhere for the struggle against capitalism and intervention.

A more cautious and realistic assessment of Hull came from Tomsky himself. He was very doubtful about the prospects for revolution in Britain, or in western Europe generally. Living standards there were high enough so he could see no reason for the workers to turn Communist.[2] He was impressed, on the other hand, with the General Council left, and gratified at its sympathetic interest in Soviet Russia. He paid tribute to the hospitality extended the Russian delegation even by the TUC old guard. He cited Cramp especially, who seemed to him typical of the labour aristocrats. They were reserved, but not actually hostile, on the question of integrating the Russian unions into the international trade union movement, Tomsky noted. He thought they could be won over if they could be convinced the Russians asked for no more than equality, were not plotting to dictate to other trade unions. He considered Hull a considerable success. 'The Russian trade union movement has burst through the front of the forces hostile to it,' he noted. 'There is a feeling of dismay among our adversaries.' He was confident the forthcoming visit of the TUC's delegation to Russia would strengthen the ties between the two movements.[3]

[1] *Profintern v Rezoliutsiakh*, pp. 56–8; *Inprecorr*, IV, 66 (18 Sept., 1924), 718–19. See also *The Worker*, 11 Oct., 1924.   [2] Deutscher, *Stalin*, p. 402n.

[3] A summary of Tomsky's statements to the press forwarded to London by the British Embassy in Moscow, 24 Sept., 1924, N 7715/5799/38, F.O. 371.10498.

III

Towards the end of September, 1924, the General Council selected seven of its own members, plus three expert advisors, to make the trip to Russia. The delegates were originally scheduled to leave Britain in October, but later postponed their departure until early November. They returned just before Christmas, and published their final report in February 1925. During the five months thus elapsed, the MacDonald Government fell in London, the political power-balance shifted significantly in Moscow, and official relations between the two capitals deteriorated to the lowest levels since the time of the 1923 Curzon Ultimatum. Only in relation to that rapidly changing political background does the work of the TUC delegation, and the Soviet response to it, become almost intelligible.

All Ramsay MacDonald's troubles seemed to originate in the Kremlin. The Campbell case, the treaty, the Zinoviev letter – looking back on it, it must have been difficult for MacDonald not to conclude he was the innocent victim of a shamelessly devised, diabolically planned and unscrupulously executed Muscovite plot. The Campbell case, for example, the immediate occasion of his downfall, grew out of the Comintern's annual anti-war campaign, pressed all the harder in observance of the tenth anniversary of Sarajevo. For Communism, the occasion afforded an opportunity to revolutionize the armed services. To wage war against proletarian brothers at home or against the proletarian fatherland in the USSR was both unjust and unintelligent. The proper Leninist response to any such orders was for all soldiers everywhere to turn their guns on the real enemy, the capitalists. *Workers' Weekly* made it all very clear. The headlines were big, black, inflammatory and specific. 'Prevent War Tomorrow by Fighting Capitalism Today!' 'Will You Kill Your Mates?' 'The Bosses Are Your Enemies.' 'The Next War: Murdering Kiddies: What It Will Be Like!'[1]

On 5 August, the Attorney-General, Sir Patrick Hastings, moved to prosecute J. R. Campbell, *Workers' Weekly*'s acting editor, under the Incitement to Mutiny Act. He acted on his own initiative, without consulting the cabinet. The Home Secretary, Arthur Henderson, was dismayed. So was MacDonald. Neither of them would have authorized the prosecution if they had been asked, and both took Sir Patrick to task for exceeding his authority. MacDonald nevertheless favoured going through with Campbell's trial on the grounds that dropping it would be politically

---

[1] *Workers' Weekly*, 25 July, 1924, 1 Aug., 1924.

disastrous. Sir Patrick, however, said the decision to prosecute might easily be reversed on the excuse that Campbell was, apparently, only temporary editor of the paper. The cabinet favoured that escape and, with some reluctance, MacDonald agreed.[1]

The charge against Campbell was withdrawn as maladroitly as it had been originally made. The explanations offered by the Crown prosecutor on August 12 proved very different from those Sir Patrick himself suggested to the Commons on September 30. The Tories therefore submitted a censure motion October 1, 1924. The Liberals countered with an amendment urging appointment of a Select Committee to investigate the matter. The cabinet decided to treat not only the Conservative motion but also the Liberal amendment as matters of confidence. When the Conservatives supported the Liberal amendment, therefore, the government's doom was sealed. The vote was on October 8 and the government was beaten 359 votes to 198. On the next day, Parliament was prorogued and new elections, the third in less than two years, were scheduled for October 29.[2]

The Campbell prosecution was a trivial business on which to bring down a government, however, and the only reason both MacDonald and the opposition let it swell to such critical proportions was because each knew the government's days were numbered in any event. The Russian treaty was the truly lethal issue. The Liberals, on whose votes MacDonald depended, were particularly dismayed over those financial provisions inserted August 5–6 as a result of the Labour and trade union left's last-minute intervention. Their leader, H. H. Asquith, spoke contemptuously of 'nursery diplomacy' and, on October 1 tabled a resolution rejecting the treaty. The vote was scheduled for early November, and MacDonald was certain to lose it. The Campbell fiasco just advanced the date of execution by six weeks.[3]

Communists, Russian ones and the home-grown variety, had proved MacDonald's nemesis. Not very surprisingly, the annual Labour party conference, assembling a day before the decisive vote in the Commons, voiced stern disapproval of Bolsheviks everywhere, in language almost as full-blooded as that heard in the Carlton Club lounges. They turned down the CPGB's application for bloc affiliation by 20 to 1, and by almost 4 to 1, voted to declare Communists ineligible for endorsement

[1] Cabinet Conclusions, 1924, CAB 23.48, Conclusion 40 (24) 5, 6 Aug., 1924 and 48 (24), 6 Aug., 1924.
[2] *Annual Register, 1924*, pp. 96, 104–7.
[3] *Ibid.*, pp. 97–9, 103–4.

as Labour candidates for public office. In a very close vote, Communists were ruled inadmissible even as individual party members, a virtually unenforcable regulation but nonetheless exasperating to the CPGB.[1] The Comintern's election instructions to the British Party, issued just three days later, must have elicited some wry comment among comrades at London headquarters. Communists were to continue to back Labour candidates, even while criticizing the personnel and policies of the MacDonald government. The CPGB was notified that representatives of German, French and Chinese workers would take part in the coming election campaign, and the Georgian trade union organization was to dispatch an appropriate appeal to British trade unionists. Moscow's exquisitely comprehensive insensitivity to British electoral realities was rarely displayed more lavishly.[2]

First the treaty, then the Campbell case! But what seemed Communism's most insufferable affront, just four days before the elections, was the Zinoviev letter, the direct call for Party cells in the services to prepare Red revolution.[3] The Foreign Office was apparently convinced

---

[1] *Ibid.*, pp. 107–8; Bell, *British Communist Party*, p. 96.

[2] Great Britain, Parliament, *Communist Papers*, Cmd. 2682 (1926), pp. 48–9.

[3] A lengthy digression on the fascinating subject of the Zinoviev letter is almost irresistible. A great deal of documentation is available: see, for example, Cabinet Conclusions, 1924, CAB 23.48, Conclusion 59(24)9, 12 Nov., 1924, 60(24)9, 19 Nov., 1924; Cabinet Papers, 1924, CAB 24.168 C.P. 484(24), 11 Nov., 1924; and Cabinet Commissions, 1924, CAB 27.254. A summary of the most interesting recent PRO material can be found in the *Sunday Times*, 31 Dec., 1967. A convincing investigation of the authenticity of the letter is Lewis Chester, Stephen Fay and Hugo Young, *The Zinoviev Letter* (London: Heinemann, 1967), but it was written before the discovery of a Russian-language copy of the offending document at the Harvard Law School library in 1969, which complicated the mystery deliciously. An earlier and persuasive analysis was Coates, *Anglo-Soviet Relations*, I, 181–97. The best introduction to basic published primary materials is Arthur McManus, *History of the Zinoviev Letter* (London: Communist Party of Great Britain, 1925). The diplomatic correspondence is available in English in Great Britain, Foreign Office, *Russia No. 3(1927): A Selection of Papers Dealing with the Relations Between His Majesty's Government and the Soviet Government, 1921–1927*, Cmd. 2895 (London: 1927), pp. 28–36, and in Russian in Russia, Narodnyi Komissariat po Inostrannym Delam, *Anglo-Sovetskie Otnosheniia*, pp. 77–87. Russia, Narodnyi Komissariat po Inostrannym Delam, *Antisovetskie Podlogi: Istoriia Fal'shivok, Faksimile i Kommentarii* (Moscow: Litizdat NKID, 1926) exposes a number of anti-Soviet forgeries. The Zinoviev letter is treated on pp. 43–79. The same material is available in English translation, *Anti-Soviet Forgeries: A record of some of the forged documents used at various times against the Soviet Government* ([London]): Workers' Publications, Ltd. (1927). A recent Soviet historian of the letter manages eight routine pages on it without mentioning Zinoviev's name. The forgery has become the 'Comintern letter.' See Volkov, *Anglo-Sovetskie Otnosheniia*, pp. 103–11. For current information on the status of the mystery, and whether spy-of-the-century Sidney Reilly really 'did it,' the curious are referred to W. E. Butler of

the document was genuine, as was 'C,' the head of the Secret Intelligence Service, Sir Hugh Sinclair. MacDonald therefore approved a severe protest note to the Soviets, assuming it would not be dispatched, however, until the document had been thoroughly and independently validated. The Foreign Office transmitted the protest almost immediately and made the letter itself public. The Soviets promptly denounced the letter as a clumsy forgery and demanded an apology. MacDonald sent back the Russian note, declining even to receive such abuse. Only the TUC, it seemed, retained any sympathy for the Russians. Zinoviev himself wired the General Council, a day after the letter appeared, urging it to send a special mission to Moscow to investigate the letter's authenticity.[1] It would have been a wasted trip. Polling day was at hand, and those Conservative managers who had paid £5,000 just for advance information the letter existed were ferociously getting their money's worth from election platforms all over the country. October 29 saw the Tories gain almost two and a half million votes and win close to 70 per cent of the seats in the Commons. The Liberals were smashed. Their popular vote declined by 30 per cent and they retained only 40 Parliamentary constituencies. Labour did surprisingly well, actually polling over a million more votes than it had in 1923, but the vagaries of the system of single-member districts left MacDonald with only 151 seats in the Commons to Baldwin's 413.[2] A minority in the country, the Tories were invincible in Parliament, and by mid-November they had organized their new government.

The new Conservative government, committed from the very beginning to the authenticity of the Zinoviev letter,[3] had to make an immediate decision on its attitude toward Soviet Russia. A vocal minority within the cabinet – including Winston Churchill, Chancellor of the Exchequer, Sir William Joynson-Hicks, Home Secretary, and Lord Birkenhead, Secretary of State for India – favoured a hard line, even a diplomatic rupture. Chamberlain and Baldwin led the moderates. The cabinet finally agreed to disavow MacDonald's treaty, to forbid arms exports to the Soviet Union and to reiterate to Moscow – while declining to discuss the matter further – its conviction that the Zinoviev letter was authentic. An immediate diplomatic break was rejected, however. So potent a one-

University College, London, who knows more about the topic then anybody should want to.

[1] *The Times*, 27 Oct., 1924.
[2] *Annual Register*, 1924, pp. 116–17.
[3] 179 H.C. Deb. 5s at c. 183.

time weapon, if it were used at all, should be used at a more propitious time. Instead, Chamberlain intended to 'disengage' from the Zinoviev controversy quickly, and subsequently to 'ignore the Soviet Government as much and as long as this position is tenable.'[1]

Back in Moscow, Marxist theoreticians had to make dialectical sense out of developments in London. They had only just succeeded in explaining away 'leftist' governments in both Britain and elsewhere by concocting an inevitable 'democratic-pacifist era' in capitalistic development. They interpreted MacDonald's administration accordingly as a bourgeois masquerade designed to lull the workers from their revolutionary duty and to distract them while capitalism prepared a direct attack on them. Since MacDonald had fallen, and an unashamedly bourgeois Baldwin government had moved into Whitehall, that attack must be at hand, and the Red Army was hardly strong enough yet to stand up to the threat.

Stalin was among the most vocal in calling attention to the danger and indicating how it might be met. Russia's 'most faithful and important ally' in the crisis, he said, was the European proletariat. As an instrument of revolution, it was still in a primitive stage, but its 'indirect, moral support' was of inestimable value. He was particularly impressed with 'the growth of a revolutionary mood among British workers' which had even infiltrated the TUC's General Council. He predicted an open rupture between the pro-Soviet trade unionists and the anti-Soviet Labour party chieftains. That development would be both gratifying and dangerous. It would be gratifying for Russia to have the support of the organized working class in Great Britain. It would be dangerous because the more the English proletarians gravitated toward the USSR, the more the ruling classes would turn against it. An anti-Soviet crusade might thus become at the same time more difficult to win but more likely to be launched. The preconditions for war were maturing, he said, and it might become inevitable, 'not tomorrow or the day after of course, but in a few years time.'[2]

Internally, the USSR was in a bad position to meet the threat. Condemned by the Party at its 13th Congress in May, unnaturally reticent at the Comintern's 5th Congress in June, Trotsky finally struck back at his enemies in October with his book, *The Lessons of October*. Kamenev and

---

[1] Cabinet Conclusions, 1924, CAB 23.49, Conclusion 59(24)10, 12 Nov., 1924, 60(24)9, 19 Nov., 1924, 61(24) 3(b), 20 Nov., 1924; Cabinet Papers, 1924, CAB 24.168, C.P. 484(24), 11 Nov., 1924; Viscount Cecil of Chelwood to Churchill, 20 Nov., 1924, British Museum, Additional MSS 51097.
[2] Speeches to the Communist Party Central Committee plenum, 19 Jan. 1925 and to the Moscow Party organization, 27 Jan., 1925, Stalin, *Sochineniia*, VII, 11–14, 25–33.

Zinoviev were lacerated particularly savagely, and they retaliated – rather ineffectively – in a volume entitled *For Leninism*. Party members promptly dubbed it 'the literary debate.' Trotsky clearly had to be punished. Kamenev and Zinoviev talked about expulsion from the Party, enabling the third triumvir, Stalin, to assume that attitude of sane and prudent moderation which was to prove so useful to him politically. The Central Committee, meeting in January of 1925, deprived Trotsky of only his government position, as War Commissar, and the literary debate was declared closed. Trotsky would dutifully keep his peace for the next eighteen months.[1]

Trotsky's defeat made it possible for Stalin to slough his inconvenient partners in the triumvirate. To do so required him to seek other alliances among those who would later be dubbed rightists, Bukharin, Rykov and Tomsky. The new bloc was in the making as early as January, 1925, and appeared openly in April. As far as the TUC was concerned, the shift was a godsend. Zinoviev's declamations on trade union matters were almost always unfortunate. His mischievous meddling was a major stumbling block to better relations between the English and Russian movements. Bramley had said so bluntly in Moscow in December, 1924.[2] Tomsky, on the other hand, the English considered their friend. Almost alone among the Soviet leaders, he seemed to understand them. The stronger his position in Moscow, the better the chances for fruitful cooperation with the TUC. He never seemed stronger than he did in early 1925. The Anglo-Russian trade union tie could be duly, and firmly, knotted. The only possible opposition would come from the RILU and its General Secretary, Lozovsky. Tomsky and the Russian unions could surely manage them easily.

The TUC's pilgrimage to Russia in November and December 1924 had brought the two movements closer together than ever. The members of the General Council elected at Hull ratified the recommendation of their predecessors and approved the visit on September 24. After discussing the possibility of a three or four man delegation, the Council finally compromised on ten, seven from the TUC itself and three expert interpretor-advisors. The leftists, represented by Purcell, Tillett, John Bromley of the Locomotive Engineers and Firemen, and A. A. H. Findlay of the Patternmakers, dominated the group. Smith of the Miners' Federation would probably have been classified as a moderate. John Turner of the Shop Assistants' Union was farthest to the right. Fred

---

[1] For the 'literary debate,' see Deutscher, *Trotsky*, pp. 151, 160–3, 201–9.
[2] *The Times*, 9 Feb., 1925.

Bramley, the TUC's General Secretary, dubbed himself an extreme right-winger; most of his General Council would have put him squarely in the centre.[1]

They were sane, capable people. The British *chargé d'affaires* in Moscow, who talked to most of them, was favourably impressed, and was particularly pleased that most of his fellow-countrymen were apparently not taken in by the round of extravaganzas arranged in their honour. The compliment, however, did not, 'unfortunately,' apply to Purcell, whom he never got the opportunity to meet. 'I say unfortunately,' the dispatch concluded, 'because he [Purcell] appears to be the leading spirit on the British side.'[2]

It was indeed Purcell who attracted the most attention. As immediate past president of the Trades Union Congress and incumbent president of the Amsterdam International, he was almost bound to. If his titles had not put him centre-stage, his tirades would have. Purcell sounded splendidly revolutionary in the Soviet Union. He called the USSR 'the first Bright Jewel in the World's Working Class Crown' and compared the progress being made there to the 'dirt, ignorance and prejudice' of capitalist society. He implied strongly that the English working man could save himself only as the Russians had, by armed violence against his exploiters. The thinly veiled summons to revolution at home, coupled with lavish praise for the Red Army which had 'already struck terror into the hearts of the British bourgeoisie,' added up to something close to treason as seen from Fleet Street.[3] They loved it in Red Square. The Moscow Soviet was so pleased with Purcell it made him an honorary member.[4]

Fred Bramley was not nearly as flamboyant a personality as Purcell, did not seek the limelight, and made a very negative impression to begin with. He confessed later that as a non-revolutionist, he was 'very nervous indeed' in an atmosphere so 'charged with revolutionary fervour.' In the midst of such irresistible excitement, it was not easy to keep one's sense of proportion, to maintain 'reserve and restraint.'[5] In his role as the authoritative spokesman for the General Council, however, Bramley had

[1] General Council Minutes, 24 Sept., 1924.
[2] Hodgson to Chamberlain, 21 Nov., 1924, N 8865/530/38, F.O. 371.10487.
[3] For characteristic Purcell rhetoric, see *Izvestiia*, 12 Dec. 1924. Another example, translated into English, is available in *Inprecorr*, iv, 88 (23 Dec., 1924), 1017–18. *The Times* collected and reprinted many of Purcell's indiscretions. See, for example, the issue of 22 Dec., 1924.
[4] *The Times*, 31 Mar., 1925.
[5] Bramley, *Relations With Russia*, pp. 9–10.

carefully disciplined himself back home to limit policy statements to the TUC's agreed line. The resulting reticence, caution, understatement – wholly understandable in Britain – sounded crabbed and stilted in the Soviet Union. Following Purcell to the platform, which he usually did, he was shockingly anti-climactic. It was in the conference room rather than at the podium that he was accustomed to make his impact. He was a negotiator, not an orator. The Russian workers probably never appreciated his talents, but their leaders came to. While Purcell talked, Bramley got things done. Without his 'clear head' and 'firm will,' Lozovsky said later, the cautious British would have made no contribution to the unity campaign at all.[1]

The only other member of the delegation who stood out strongly as an individual personality was John Turner. Turner praised the Russians for building hospitals and asylums and for making an effort to meet the housing shortage. Nothing else impressed him. He deplored the lack of freedom in the Soviet Union, the restrictions on speech, assembly and the press. He thought prison conditions were wretched. He complained that a fraternal autograph bestowed on an enthusiastic admirer was later attached, without his permission, to one of Ben Tillett's statements with which he did not agree. He was contemptuous of Zinoviev, a 'silly and nervous chatterbox,...fearing his own shadow,...with the heart of a hare and the appetites of a Napoleon.' He found the constant repetitions of the *Internationale* tedious. His comments were refreshingly blunt. The way he was exploited by the anti-Soviet press back in Britain was deplorable.[2]

The group was originally supposed to leave England October 16, arriving in the USSR in time to attend the 6th Soviet Trade Union Congress. When the general election required the English to postpone their departure (Purcell lost his seat at Coventry anyway), the Russians adjusted the date of the Congress for them.[3] It was a splendid gesture, no doubt producing minor administrative chaos in Moscow. The delegation finally got started November 6, and crossed the Soviet frontier three days later. The official monthly journal of the British labour movement marked the departure with cheery optimism. Trade union unity would be achieved through Russian admission to the IFTU. Such obstacles as stood in the

---

[1] Alexander Lozovsky, *British and Russian Workers* (London: National Minority Movement [1926], p. 15. For a corroborating opinion, see Bramley's moving obituary by W. Jarozki, *Die Rote Gewerkschaftsinternationale*, No. 11 (58) (Nov. 1925), 267–9.

[2] *The Times*, 31 Jan., 1925, 6 Feb., 1925; *Manchester Guardian*, 4 Apr., 1925.

[3] General Council Minutes, 16 Oct., 1924.

way were all surmountable. Practically all trade union centres on the continent now backed the British effort. If the TUC delegation could 'cement the Moscow–Amsterdam relationship' in the course of its visit, the editorial concluded, its achievement would 'mark the birth of a new era of great possibilities.'[1]

The travellers had set themselves a strenuous schedule. In the next six weeks they would cover some seven thousand miles – from London to Moscow, from Moscow to remote Transcaucasia in the south, from Transcaucasia back through Moscow again to the far north and Leningrad, from Leningrad home via Riga and Berlin.[2] Within the Soviet Union, they would spend nearly a month on a special train, with two carriages set aside for their exclusive use. Armed guards convoyed the train to protect it from bandit gangs. Untoward incidents were rare. When an unarmed bandit already on the train – presumably some railroad employee – stole Smith's watch, the Soviet trade union movement replaced it within 24 hours, and with an elaborate gold timepiece a good deal better than the one he lost.

The delegates were received ecstatically everywhere they went. The Russian reputation for heart-warming, stomach-shattering hospitality pre-dates the revolution, of course. It is a phenomenon all western visitors experience – even those of low degree – and most survive. In treating the British guests to continuous displays of mass enthusiasm, then, the Bolsheviks were employing one of Muscovy's richest and most productive natural resources. It began as soon as the delegates crossed the frontier and gathered momentum all the way to the capital. Again and again the train had to stop while delegations of trade unionists, of local government officials, and most irresistibly of all, of Young Pioneers, pronounced their effusive welcomes. At Moscow, each member of the British delegation was introduced individually to the 6th Soviet Trade Union Congress, and every one received a standing ovation. That same afternoon they all were honoured at a march-past lasting over three hours. A hundred thousand workers participated. They cheered the

---

[1] *The Labour Magazine*, III, 6 (Oct. 1924), 265.
[2] Sources for the general character of the delegates' reception in Russia are *The Times*, 9 Mar. 1925, citing Bramley's speech to an ILP meeting; Hodgson to Chamberlain, 19 Dec., 1924, N 9463/530/38, F.O. 371.10487 and 30 Dec., 1924, N 153/73/38, F.O. 371.11014; Trades Union Congress, General Council, Russia: *The Official Report of the British Trades Union Delegation to Russia and Caucasia, November and December, 1924* (London: Trades Union Congress General Council, 1925), Preface, pp. xi–xxiii; *The Worker*, 22 Nov., 1924 (Pollitt); *Inprecorr*, IV, 82 (4 Dec., 1924), 939–40; *Workers' Weekly*, 5 Dec., 1924; Ben Tillett, *Some Russian Impressions* (London: Labour Research Department, 1925).

English visitors, booed Baldwin and Curzon, bellowed revolutionary battle-songs, and unfurled flags with slogans as blunt as they were expressive. 'Follow the Example of the Russian Workers! Chase Away Your Bourgeoisie!' 'March More Boldly Forward: Seize the Bourgeoisie by the Throat!' 'English Workers, Act in the Russian Manner!' 'Long Live the Russian Workers!' some of the British shouted back. 'Long live the Soviet Republic!' Some joined in the revolutionary songs. Purcell, inevitably, made an expansive speech about unity.

The rest of the stay in Moscow was a long series of galas. The enthusiasm sometimes got out of hand. At the close of the Trades Union Congress, the participants rushed to the platform and hurled Purcell (as well as Tomsky) high into the air. He was thrown so energetically, Harry Pollitt recorded, 'I thought he was going to find in heaven the seat he lost in Coventry.' Nor did the revels cease when the delegation left the intoxicating capital. They witnessed a huge demonstration for them and for unity in Tiflis, the capital of Georgia, where the Bolsheviks were especially anxious to persuade their guests that the recent Menshevik insurrection derived solely from American gold. The last leg of their journey, from Moscow to Leningrad, was transformed into a triumphant procession. The residents of Peter's capital were as anxious as always to prove anything provincial Muscovites could do sophisticated Leningraders could do better. The railway station was decked in banners, flags and bunting. The local newspaper, *Krasnaia Gazeta*, printed half its front page in English in honour of the visitors. The march-past, led by bands of singing sailors, was the biggest, gaudiest, longest and loudest of all. The British consul reported home that his fellow-countrymen drank to excess and were noisy at the Hotel Europe that evening. They must have recovered. On the day of their departure they were shouting lustily and waving red flags from the train.

In view of the strenuous demands of the social schedule, it seems incredible that the English would have gotten anything constructive done. That they did testifies to their determination to learn all they could. The British legation in Moscow noted their eagerness to get the facts, and acknowledged they amassed 'a huge amount of information,' most of it from trade union sources.[1] The language barrier, the rigid railroad time-tables, and commonsensical Slavic reticence about mingling too closely with foreigners, all conspired to keep them from any extensive contacts with ordinary Soviet citizens. Nevertheless, they kept their eyes open, asked good questions, and did everything they could to fill out their

[1] Hodgson to Chamberlain, 19 Dec. 1924, N 9463/530/38, F.O. 317. 10487.

rather mediocre background knowledge of Russia. Most of them – Purcell is an obvious exception – managed to avoid getting carried away by the ebullient enthusiasm with which they were received. Their comments on their impressions and experiences were cautious and sound, and when pressed for speeches, they responded carefully with gratitude for the hospitality and routine expressions of goodwill.

On three specific issues, however, the delegation as a whole did take a definite position, on the Zinoviev letter, on the situation in Georgia and on trade union unity. Most delegates were convinced, even before they got to Moscow, that the Zinoviev letter was a forgery. One or two of them said so the very day they got there. After a two-hour talk with Zinoviev himself, they were all escorted to International headquarters and shown volumes purporting to be a complete register of all out-going Comintern correspondence, including confidential dispatches. The material looked authentic enough. The entries were clearly made by a number of different people and at different times. Older pages were satisfactorily smudged, more recent ones convincingly clean. Suspicious-sounding documents were pulled from the files for the delegates' inspection. No indication of anything like the Zinoviev letter was discovered. On November 26, therefore, the delegation announced, without elaboration, that it had conclusive evidence the celebrated letter was a forgery. The statement made the front pages of both *Pravda* and the *Daily Herald*. In London, the General Council agreed to hand over whatever facts its representatives had gathered to a Labour party committee already inquiring into the matter.[1]

The delegation's statement on Transcaucasia, on the basis of a two-day stay in Tiflis, was much more doubtful. A brief Menshevik-sponsored uprising in Georgia in September had been promptly, decisively and cruelly suppressed. The western press had played up the story energetically, and Bolshevism was anxious to counter the bad impression made. The Tiflis workers were mobilized for a big and demonstrative march-past with all the right slogans. The delegation thereupon issued a statement. An independent Menshevik Georgia could never have survived, it declared. It would soon have become the focus of bourgeois and monarchist reaction and have lost its autonomy. The Bolsheviks were committed to preserving the Georgian language and Georgian culture

---

[1] *Pravda*, 27 Nov., 1924; *Daily Herald*, 27 Nov., 1924; *1925 TUC, Report of Proceedings*, p. 293; General Council Minutes No. 72, 26 Nov., 1924, No. 83, 17 Dec., 1924, No. 111, 29 Dec., 1924; Hodgson to Chamberlain, 19 Dec., 1924, N 9463/530/38, F.O. 371.10487.

generally. The area was prospering under Muscovite direction. The majority of the people were devoted to their Soviet governors, in sum, and the Mensheviks were a tiny, confused minority exploited by outsiders for their own ends. Such fragile, paper evidence as was made available to the delegates could surely not sustain the weighty conclusions they built from it. The Mensheviks were livid. They left a letter at the British consulate in Leningrad, to be forwarded to Purcell, criticizing his gullibility, and chiding him for accepting Bolshevik lies. The Foreign Office – one suspects, rather gleefully – dutifully transmitted the document via TUC headquarters to Purcell. It must have arrived in Britain just about the same time as that honorary membership in the Moscow Soviet.[1]

Purcell took the lead on the issue of trade union unity. It was a subject on which he could speak authoritatively as well as forcefully. On his initiative, a reluctant IFTU had left its doors open to the Russians in June. At his suggestion, the Hull TUC in September had authorized a British effort to mediate Moscow–Amsterdam reconciliation. Both votes Purcell considered – and not without reason – personal triumphs. Now was the time to consolidate them, to enlist the Russians themselves in the cause, to persuade them merger with IFTU need not involve betraying their revolutionary inheritance. The opportunity to make his case presented itself when he, along with Bramley and Tillett, was invited to deliver a fraternal address to the Soviet trade unionists as they opened their Congress on November 11.

The wording was strictly his own. Neither the General Council nor the delegation set any rules on, nor any guidelines for, individual members' speeches. Each could say what he liked. The addresses of Bramley and Tillett proved genial but colourless.[2] The brunt of Bramley's address, a routine recitation of TUC statistics, was hardly inspirational. Tillett waxed reverently and lengthily eloquent on the virtues of Lenin, but Russians knew those virtues better than Tillett did, and he said very little of substance. Purcell, however, who spoke first, starkly posed a real issue, unity.[3] Capitalism, he said, was crumbling. The emancipation of the proletariat was at hand. To achieve it, proletarians all over the world had to unite. The union should be more than a mere formality. It should be firmly class-based and wholly committed to the struggle

---

[1] *Daily Herald*, 10 Dec., 1924; Hodgson to Chamberlain, 19 Dec., 1924, N 9463/530/ 38, F.O. 371. 10487, and 27 Dec., 1924, N 146/43/38, F.O. 371.11014.
[2] *Shestoi S''ezd Professional'nykh Soiuzov: Stenograficheskii Otchet*, pp. 51–6.
[3] *Ibid.*, pp. 49–51.

against capital. IFTU could provide the basis for such an organization, he argued, but only if the Russian centre agreed to be part of it. A trade union international without the Soviet was 'absurd,...like having Hamlet played without having Hamlet in the play.' The British were anxious to mediate between Moscow and Amsterdam. Amsterdam, of course, might prove stubborn and resist the unity campaign, but if it did, he pledged, Britain would take the initiative herself. What sort of initiative he did not say.

Tomsky's response was encouraging.[1] He likened past exchanges of invective between Moscow and Amsterdam to a lovers' spat. He reviewed the most recent correspondence in considerable detail, reserving special scorn for IFTU's request that the Soviets submit a written statement of their principles. Next they would be asking us, he said, whether we were blondes or brunettes! He absolved Purcell from any responsibility for such delaying tactics, however. German social democracy, he said, still controlled the Amsterdam bureaucracy, and Purcell, as IFTU president, had to sign many documents which obviously did not represent his personal viewpoint.

In spite of reformist obstructionism, however, progress toward unity was being made, and Purcell's pledge of the day before represented a long stride forward. Purcell had made a promise: if Amsterdam would not agree to join in a truly all-inclusive trade union international, then the English would see to constructing one on their own. That promise would be kept, Tomsky said. English workers, and their leaders, meant what they said, and acted on it.

Unity would mean, of course, that Russian workers would have to sit down at the same table with yellow social-democratic traitors who were worth as little personally as they were ideologically. The three delegates who disputed Tomsky's recommendations during the course of the debate – nobody rose to support him – all made that point forcefully.[2] Revolutionary integrity, they urged, was more important than unity. Integrity was not the issue, Tomsky replied. 'Our principles are iron.' They and we have stood the rigorous test of struggle at home. Now we must submit them to that test on a broader arena.

Capitalists had resumed the offensive, he noted, all over the world, and especially in western Europe. Wages and working hours would soon

---

[1] *Ibid.*, pp. 56–8, 78–84, 178–80. An English translation of one of Tomsky's speeches is reprinted in Tomsky, *Getting Together*, pp. 66–75. Very different translations may be found in *Inprecorr*, IV, 85 (16 Dec., 1924), 979–83.

[2] *Shestoi S''ezd Professional'nykh Soiuzov: Stenograficheskii Otchet*, pp. 118, 125, 133.

come up for renegotiation, and conflicts were inevitable. Six million
Soviet workers, controlling their own state, could count for something in
those conflicts. United with their western brothers, Soviet workers could
'take an active part' in the struggles-to-come, 'throw the whole of our
revolutionary enthusiasm...into the balance...' With all its faults,
Amsterdam still provided the obvious foundation on which to build such
unity. It was a grave error to assume, as 'some comrades' did, that IFTU
was crumbling, and that the Russians could smugly sit back and wait out
its collapse. That was Menshevik talk, and intolerable. It would cruelly
abandon millions of workers to revisionist traitors. It would sentence
Soviet workers to ignoble spectator roles during the great class-against-
class clashes in western Europe.

Tomsky's pleas for unity were not confined to the platform. He was
also active, behind the scenes, with his British guests. Not more than a
day after the delegates arrived, Bramley recalled later, they received a
letter from Tomsky and Dogadov, the Secretary of the Central Council
of Trade Unions, 'making certain proposals' and urging informal talks.[1]
The British agreed to the talks, and all members of the delegation participated. After hearing Tomsky, they asked him for a written statement
of precisely what he had in mind. He sent one November 16. Although
it was never published, it is clear what it suggested – a formal association
of English and Russian trade unionists, an Anglo-Russian committee,
pledged to promote the unity campaign.

According to Lozovsky, the proposals were 'formulated in extremely
cautious and moderate terms.' Nevertheless, he recalled, the English
greeted them suspiciously. They hesitated to commit themselves one way
or the other. It was Fred Bramley, he said, who skilfully and forcefully
manoeuvred his reluctant colleagues into the agreement finally reached.[2]
That agreement was formalized in a letter from Bramley to Tomsky dated
November 17, 1924. It was a carelessly drafted and sloppily worded
document, but its meaning was clear enough. The English delegates
pledged themselves to present the Russian unity proposals to the General
Council, and to recommend their acceptance. Specifically, they would
urge the Council to demand IFTU agreement 'to a free and unconditional immediate conference' with the Soviet trade unionists. They
would also propose that the Council seek 'full power' – from a subsequent

[1] Bramley, *Relations with Russia*, pp. 10–13.
[2] A. Lozovsky, *Das Englisch-Russische Komitee der Einheit* (Moscow: Verlag der
  Roten Gewerkschaftsinternationale, 1926), pp. 5–6; Lozovsky, *British and Russian
  Workers*, p. 15.

Trades Union Congress, presumably – to 'act jointly' with the Russians in the search for unity. They expressed confidence that such 'joint action of Russian and British trade union organizations' would stimulate progress 'towards international trade union unity.'[1]

The Russians were jubilant. Lozovsky, scheduled to speak to the Soviet trade unionists the very next day, was authorized to make the announcement, saving it for the very end of a lengthy speech devoted to the whole unity issue.[2] Generally speaking, he took as hard a line as ever. His very precise suggestions as to how a proper all-inclusive trade union international should organize itself, for example, were almost ludicrously unrealistic. Nevertheless, he professed ebullient optimism. Under the prodding of the working masses, the west European labour leadership was moving decisively leftward. The visit of the TUC delegates was dramatic proof of how much prospects for unity had improved. If Russian trade unionists, the most numerous members of Profintern, and the English trade unionists, the biggest IFTU component, if they could find some common ground, so surely could the two Internationals with which they were affiliated. And they had found common ground, he proclaimed triumphantly. He was authorized to announce that recent negotiations had resulted 'in a reciprocal and fundamental agreement upon the need to establish an Anglo-Russian Unity Committee' with the TUC. His audience responded with a standing ovation.

The agreement with the English was tentative, Lozovsky acknowledged, and was subject to ratification. It nevertheless represented a decisive step forward. The Anglo-Russian committee would be just the first of a number of committees, he promised, with a number of other partners. 'We think of setting up a whole chain of similar committees,' he confided, a whole 'network' of them. The committees would bypass all the old obstacles to unity, the narrow interests of particular nations and of particular trades. Sooner or later, the committees would be in a position to insist on the unity congress, and the all-inclusive trade union international. Within that international, finally, revolutionaries could continue and complete their great struggle, the struggle for the ideological allegiance of proletarians everywhere.

Lozovsky could hardly have done the unity cause more damage. The English had come to the USSR to urge the Russians to join IFTU. Only

[1] Text is in Trades Union Congress, General Council, *Russia and International Unity: Report to Affiliated Societies, Trades Union Congress* (London: Trades Union Congress General Council, 1925), p. 6. See also *1925 TUC: Report of Proceedings*, pp. 295–6, and Gurovich, *Vseobshchaia Stachka v Anglii*, pp. 31–32.

[2] *Shestoi S''ezd Professional'nykh Soiuzov: Stenograficheskii Otchet*, pp. 375–89.

after anguished soul-searching had they agreed to recommend to their General Council 'joint action' with the Soviets in behalf of unity. Now Lozovsky had trumpeted their consent to some formal Unity Committee, linked with scores of other Unity Committees, all of them propagandizing for a world labour congress so selected that all RILU affiliates would be represented by strong, united delegations and all IFTU centres by impotent and divided ones. It was a preposterous perversion of what the English really had agreed to.

The resolution unanimously adopted by the Congress empowered the All-Union Central Council of Trade Unions 'to organize, after suitable negotiations with the General Council of the British trade unions, an Anglo-Russian [USSR] Committee whose task it will be to coordinate the activities of the trade union movements of both countries in their struggle for international trade union unity...'[1] Tomsky hailed the resolution in his closing speech.[2] The discussions with the English delegates had convinced him 'that the cause of unity will not merely be confined to correspondence with the Amsterdam International.' The Anglo-Russian agreement would 'be followed by an Anglo-Franco-Russian, an Anglo-Franco-Russian-German agreement, until we have created a united international combining the workers of the whole world in one single family, advancing...against capitalism.' Such heroically aromatic pipe dreams quite intoxicated the Congress delegates. Purcell and Tomsky were the heroes of the hour at adjournment.

Even the dour Lozovsky, gushing out a torrent of muddy prose, could find little to criticize in the proposed Committee.[3] The agreement with leftist Anglo-Saxons was justified, in spite of the fact they clearly were not Communists. They *were* internationalists, and although they did not yet appreciate the need for a world unity congress, they could be pushed in that direction by an intensive propaganda campaign back in Britain. Any separate Russian affiliation to Amsterdam, Lozovsky repeated, was out of the question. He saw that whole suggestion as a Menshevik-inspired plot. The Bolshevik response must be to insist all the more strenuously on complete amalgamation of the two internationals, an

---

[1] *Ibid.*, pp. 440–1. English translation in Lozovsky, *British and Russian Workers*, pp. 14–15, and *Inprecorr*, IV, 85 (16 Dec., 1924), 995.

[2] *Shestoi S''ezd Professional'nykh Soiuzov: Stenograficheskii Otchet*, pp. 433–6.

[3] Some Lozovsky works dating from this time and providing the basis of the commentary which follows are: *World's Trade Union Movement*; 'Die ersten Ergebnisse des Kampfes für die Einheit,' *Die Rote Gewerkschaftsinternationale*, No. 11 (46) (Nov., 1924) 160–5; 'Ein Schritt vorwarts: Das Englisch-Russische Einheitskomitte,' *ibid.*, 12 Nov. (47) (Dec., 1924), 234–43; 'The Mensheviks, the Russian Trade Unions and Amsterdam,' *Inprecorr*, IV, 88(23 Dec., 1924), 1019–20.

amalgamation achievable only by the world unity congress. Lozovsky waxed ever more eloquent on the Congress, and ever more precise on the mechanics of calling it, convening it, and implementing its decisions. If the General Council back in London had been obliged to deal with him, rather than Tomsky, or if it had taken him seriously as an influential leader of Soviet trade unionism, Anglo-Russian trade union rapprochement would have gone no farther. Instead, the British considered him a discredited extremist, a joke or a nobody. In any event, they persisted in spite of him.

They persisted also in spite of a very bad press both in Britain and in western Europe generally. Opposition from Tory newspapers, and even Liberal ones, was of course taken for granted. The *Daily Telegraph*'s characterization of the Russian delegation's work as 'an almost incredible record of treasonable mischief' only echoed general Fleet Street opinion.[1]

The censure and displeasure of colleagues in the labour movement was a more serious matter. J. R. Clynes spoke for many of them when he scolded trade unionists whose 'energies are spent in waving revolutionary banners and in the worship of the names of Russian leaders.'[2] Continental socialists were blunter yet. Only misguided dupes would be taken in by Communism's united front manoeuvres, they insisted. The Red aim was simply to destroy democratic socialism. The slogan of trade union unity camouflaged a plan to split Amsterdam and then liquidate it. IFTU must beware of the likes of Purcell and Bramley, whose fatal susceptibility to Russian overtures was explainable only by a lamentable ignorance – evidenced in their own statements – of the real nature of Soviet tyranny.[3]

In the midst of all the turmoil and debate, the TUC General Council suffered some misgivings. Its free-wheeling representatives in the USSR sometimes seemed out of control. They had discredited the Zinoviev letter in an afternoon and settled the future of Georgia in two days. Now they seemed to have committed the TUC to some mysterious 'Anglo-Russian Committee for World Trade Union Unity.' The *Daily Herald*

[1] *Daily Telegraph*, 12 Dec., 1924. For similar comment, not always as succinctly worded, see the *Manchester Guardian*, 25 Nov., 1924; *Daily News*, 28 Nov. and 13 Dec., 1924; *Morning Post*, 12 Dec., 1924; *Daily Mail*, 12 Dec., 1924; *The Times*, 12 Dec., and 22 Dec., 1924.

[2] *Daily Herald*, 5 Feb., 1925.

[3] F. Adler, 'The True and the False United Front,' *The Labour Magazine*, III, No. 8 (Dec., 1924), 349–52; *The Times* 5 Jan., 1925; Labour and Socialist International, Second Congress (Marseilles, 22–7 Aug., 1925), *Report of the Secretariat* (London: The Labour Party, [1925]), pp. 37–8.

announced 'agreement' on such a committee on November 27, based on a mail dispatch just in from Moscow. That may have been the first news most trade union leaders in Britain had of what their junketing colleagues in Russia were up to.

Not unreasonably, the General Council, meeting just two days before the delegation arrived back home, decided to insure itself against further surprises.[1] The Council's Assistant Secretary, Walter Citrine, was instructed to meet the delegates as soon as they landed and inform them that no statement of any kind was to be made to the press until cleared by the Council. Citrine did his work well. The boat train that pulled into London on December 19 carried ten mutely obedient delegates. Neatly and evenly dispersed from the front cars to the rear ones, they presented an impossible target for interrogators from the press. The delegates eluded not only the journalists, however, but also an enthusiastic welcoming party sponsored by the ultra-left. *Workers' Weekly* condemned the 'wire pulling that must have gone on behind the scenes,' which it interpreted as an effort 'to prevent any revolutionary speeches being made.' The TUC should itself have organized an official welcome for the returning heroes, it protested. Anything less was a 'scandal.'[2]

Scandalous may have been too harsh a word, but the General Council's precautions were surely unwise. The delegation's enforced silence was atrocious public relations and would surely produce ugly rumours of Council dissensions. The press would get after the individual delegates anyway, and one or another of them was sure to say something indiscreet eventually. Bramley wisely decided a brief 'interim statement' would reduce the pressure. He produced one over the weekend and issued it December 21. A subdued and unimpassioned document, it noted the impressive economic recovery of the USSR, suggested British capital could safely, and profitably, be invested there, denied any restrictions on religious freedom, and repeated earlier statements supporting the Bolshevik regime in Georgia. The whole question of relations between British and Russian trade unions, the specific matter of the proposed Anglo-Russian Committee, and the possibility of some new all-inclusive trade union international, were all passed over in silence. *The Times* found the statement absurd. It was especially suspicious at the omission of any statement on international trade unionism. The *Daily Herald* rose to the delegates' defence. The statement, it editorialized, exposed the lies about Russia invented for and circulated by the capitalist

[1] General Council Minutes, No. 84, 17 Dec., 1924.
[2] *Workers' Weekly*, 26 Dec., 1924.

press. The delegates' conclusions confirmed those of other informed observers. They would carry extra weight with the workers, however, because the delegates were men the workers trusted.[1]

The TUC General Council did not seem as sure of the delegates' trustworthiness as was the *Daily Herald*. A number of councillors were indignant about the unauthorized release of the interim statement against their specific instructions, and dressed Bramley down at the meeting December 29. The Council then turned its attention to guaranteeing its control over the final, complete report, to be produced in January. The security precautions were elaborate. It was only by a narrow margin the Council agreed to entrust the preliminary draft to the mails – registered post, of course. The councillors were not so meticulous, however, in their consideration of the unity problem. They listened to Purcell's explanations of his speeches and Bramley's of his letters and accepted both. The next move, clearly, would have to be directed at persuading the IFTU to agree to that unconditional preliminary conference with the Soviets. The question of any further 'joint action' with the Russians could be deferred until Amsterdam made its decision. The press was informed, cryptically, that the Council had 'endorsed' the proposals its delegates made while in Russia. Nothing more was said. The delegates themselves were still under strict orders to make no public speeches and to refuse any comment to the press until their official report was approved.[2] The aloof silence imposed in Britain on men who had declaimed so passionately in the USSR was especially irritating to the delegation's noisiest supporters, the members of the CPGB. The unity campaign would quickly falter unless sustained by continuous pressure from below, from the masses. That was accepted Party mythology. Any progressive and forward-looking step the General Council ever took it took only because an aroused rank and file insisted on it. Aside from a few exceptional individuals, Purcell, perhaps, or John Bromley or George Hicks, the General Council was composed of men who substituted ringing phrases for meaningful deeds whenever they could. The unity effort, however, must not be allowed to collapse in empty rhetoric. Mass opinion, 'which forced the issue at Vienna and at Hull,' could force it again. It could get behind Purcell and his fellow delegates to the USSR, make it impossible for them to retreat from the positions they

[1] *The Times*, *Daily Herald*, 22 Dec., 1924. See also Purcell's statement protesting the press treatment of the delegation's activities, the *Daily Herald*, 23 Dec., 1924.
[2] General Council Minutes, Nos. 109, 110, 114, 115, 29 Dec., 1924; *Daily Herald*, 30 Dec., 1924.

took in Moscow and make it impolitic for the General Council or the IFTU Executive to resist them. To organize such support, the National Minority Movement, in early December, summoned a special Unity Conference for January 25, 1925.[1] The General Council, however, not only refused to have anything to do with it, but even forbade the members of the delegation to Russia to address it. It was maddening to have to generate mass support for people too intimidated to speak on their own behalf. Most mortifying of all, the General Council used its new influence with Tomsky to persuade him to snub the NMM too. The Council had information that the Russian trade unions planned to send a fraternal delegate to the Unity Conference. It dispatched a strong telegram urging reconsideration December 30. Within a day, it had been reassured. No delegate was sent.[2]

British Communists were realistic enough to have expected a few set-backs. They still insisted on the unity slogan, however, and on January 10, 1925, the Party's Executive Committee published a resolution delineating official policy on the subject.[3] Trade unionists had to unite, nationally and internationally, to meet the intensifying capitalist offensive. The General Council's efforts toward that goal were welcome. The proposals put forward by the trade union delegation to the USSR were especially promising, and the Council's endorsement of them helpful. Unity could only be achieved, however, if the working masses forced Amsterdam to join RILU in convening a World Trade Union Congress. The National Minority Movement was responsible for organizing the masses in Britain for such an effort. The CPGB urged workers to rally to the NMM, and support its forthcoming unity conference.

The Conference itself, on January 25, was not all its sponsors had hoped, but much more of a success than its detractors liked to admit.[4] 617 delegates attended, claiming to represent 750,000 workers, compared to 270 delegates and 200,000 workers at the NMM's inaugural conference five months earlier. 750,000 workers would be 17 per cent of the TUC's membership. Even the notoriously optimistic Lozovsky, just a

---

[1] *Workers' Weekly*, 5 Dec., 1924; *The Worker*, 6 Dec., 1924; Harry Pollitt, 'Der linke Flügel der englischen Gewerkschaftsbewegung,' *Die Rote Gewerkschafts-internationale*, No. 12(47) (Dec., 1924), 247–51.

[2] General Council Minutes, No. 112, 29 Dec., 1924; Bramley, *Relations With Russia*, pp. 14–15.

[3] *Inprecorr*, v, 7 (22 Jan., 1925), 73.

[4] A conference report was published separately, but I have used the transcript in *The Worker*, 31 Jan., 1925, and a copy of the conference programme in the TUC library. See also *The Times*, 23 and 26 Jan., 1925, and *Inprecorr*, v, 14 (11 Feb., 1925), 181–2.

month before, estimated NMM sympathisers at no more than 12 per cent.[1] Even allowing for almost unavoidable exaggeration on how many of his mates each delegate truly 'represented,' it was an impressive turnout. Unity was indeed a popular issue.[2]

On the other hand, the official TUC leadership boycotted the Congress almost to a man. Aside from the perennial Tom Mann, who presided, few trade unionists of national reputation attended in person. A. J. Cook sent the speech he would have given, proudly declaring himself 'a disciple of Karl Marx and a humble follower of Lenin,' but cancelled his personal appearance because of the pressure of work. Hicks sent a cautious greeting, favouring trade union unity but diplomatically vague about how to get it. Fraternal delegates attending all represented just splinter groups of RILU dissidents. No official national centre sent a spokesman. Of the 617 voting participants, only a hundred or so came from outside the capital, enabling *The Times* to scoff at the meeting as just 'a general gathering of London Communists.'

Communist sources, however, expressed delight at the work of the conference. *Pravda* headlined it as a 'big success,' and noted that the 'radicalization' already discernible in the General Council and among trade union functionaries was even more pronounced among the masses.[3] *Pravda* was being delicate. Other Communist comment was less restrained. Radical tendencies in the masses were the sole cause of radical tendencies in the General Council, it was alleged. If the Unity Conference had not occurred, the General Council would never have approved the proposals of its delegation to the USSR. It would never have published their official report, which it had already delayed for over a month. It would never have reversed its ban on the delegates making speeches. The conference blew the General Council's plans to smithereens, a CPGB leader reported to the Comintern a month later. It broke 'the conspiracy of silence' concocted by General Council reactionaries, and stiffened the resolution of the left wingers. Without the conference, the unity campaign in Britain would have died.[4]

---

[1] Lozovsky, *World's Trade Union Movement*, p. 246.

[2] The official Comintern representative in Britain, A. J. Bennet, writing two years later, said only 600,000 workers were represented at the Unity Conference: Petrowski (Bennet), *Anglo-Russische Komitee*, pp. 14–15.

[3] *Pravda*, 27 and 29 Jan., 1925.

[4] Ferguson's speech to the ECCI, 26 Feb., 1926, reprinted in Communist Party of Great Britain, *Orders from Moscow?* (London: CPGB, 1926) pp. 17–34. See also, for the same allegation, Pollitt's preface to Lozovsky, *British and Russian Workers*, pp. 9–10; Vinogradov, *Mirovoi Proletariat i SSSR*, p. 117; Petrowski (Bennet) *Anglo-Russische Komitee*, pp. 14–15.

Such interpretations were palpable self-deception and wholly un-justifiable. The Minority Movement's efforts had no detectable impact on the General Council at all, which had endorsed the recommendations of its delegates to Russia almost a month before the Unity Conference, in December.[1] It had not acted on their official report simply because that report took Bramley longer to complete than he had expected and was not ready, even in galley proofs, until the end of January. As soon as it was ready, the Council agreed to consider it, at a special meeting on February 12. When the report was approved the ban on speeches by the delegates was lifted automatically and immediately.

IV

It would provide a good plot for a naughty but sentimental Victorian novel. Three characters: the sharp-tongued, malicious, and unprincipled village gossip; the major target of her slanders, the hard-working and virtuous housewife; our heroine's husband, gullible, weak-willed, simple-minded. A seduction! The silly fool of a man beguiled into running off with the infamous purveyor of odious falsehoods. A shameless proposal! The venomous tart suggests the three of them set up housekeeping in a *ménage à trois*. As a woman of honour, the wife of course refuses indig-nantly, but as a Christian woman, offers husband forgiveness if he pledges his undivided allegiance in the future.

Nobody in the emancipated 1920s would dare concoct quite such old-fashioned plot-lines, of course, but one has the impression that the Amsterdam bureaucracy would have appreciated the allegory. It felt it had been contemptibly and shabbily dishonoured and demeaned. Its own president, Purcell, had gone off to Soviet Russia, the home of the Tempter, there to be deceived, outwitted and humbugged. Diabolical, spiteful Profintern had inveigled him into endorsing its insidious cam-paign for unity. It was outrageous. He had to choose – sever his con-nection with Amsterdam or disown his cronies in Moscow.

It was not that simple, of course. Oudegeest and his IFTU colleagues had been aware of the Anglo-Soviet entanglement for months, and were already taking steps to counter it. The very same day the TUC delegation set out for Russia, in early November, Oudegeest wrote his colleague Jouhaux that indiscreet letter already referred to.[2] Tomsky seemed to be

[1] The best evidence for that is in the Council minutes themselves. General Council Minutes, No. 110, 28 Jan., 1925.
[2] See above, pp. 79–80.

serious about the unity campaign, he reported. The two of them should therefore get together to block it. The strategy conference presumably took place sometime before the meeting of the IFTU Executive on December 1–2, 1924. The results of it became apparent at that meeting.

The opportunity was too good to miss. The Executive had before it the most recent Russian letter, a response to Amsterdam's request for a Soviet 'statement of principles.' The Executive could not, on its own authority, reject the Russian statement outright. Such agreeably drastic action was reserved for the IFTU General Council, not due to meet until February. But the Executive could write Tomsky a letter all but pre-judging the General Council's decision, and perhaps discouraging the Russians from any further overtures. Purcell, away making unforgivable speeches in Transcaucasia somewhere, could not interfere. The Russian statement provided an opening by referring briefly to the possibility of a world unity congress. The Executive wrenched the phrase out of context, seized on it, and made it central in the reply dispatched to Tomsky on December 5.[1] The Soviet statement, the letter read, did not indicate a willingness to comply with the definite and specific resolution approved by the Vienna Congress, which ruled out Russian affiliation on any other basis except that of Amsterdam's established rules and regulations. Moscow instead proposed a world labour congress. The IFTU General Council, empowered only to execute the decisions of the Congress, would compare the Russian proposals and the Congress's resolution at its meeting February 5, and the Soviets would be informed of the result.

So long as Purcell continued clamouring for camaraderie with the Russians, however, Oudegeest's cunning manipulation of the corre-spondence, however adroit, was hardly enough to reassure the timid. The Swiss Trade Union Federation was the first to sound the tocsin, on December 2, in a confidential letter to the IFTU Executive. They were uneasy at the reports coming out of Moscow concerning Purcell's visit. They wanted no part of any unity meeting. They would refuse to attend it, and they hoped other national centres would follow their example. The Russian unions were in fact nuclei of Communist agents. To let them in the International would only disrupt it, the Swiss argued.[2]

Oudegeest reassured them, publicly and officially.[3] The IFTU was

---

[1] Text in *International Trade Union Review*, v, 1 (Jan.–Mar., 1925), 11–12 and in *The Labour Magazine*, III, 9 (Jan., 1925), 429.

[2] *The Worker*, 31 Jan., 1925; *Inprecorr*, v, 12 (6 Feb., 1925), 152–3.

[3] 'Purcell in Russia,' *IFTU Press Reports*, IV, 49 (18 Dec., 1924); *ibid.*, v, 1 (8 Jan. 1925). The TUC General Council protested the first of these articles (General Council Minutes, No. 114, 29 Dec., 1924).

most concerned about the statements made by its president while in Russia, he announced. The Executive Committee would certainly pursue the matter. And before Amsterdam could ever agree to Russian membership, the Soviets would have to prove that their unions were truly independent of state control; they would have to renounce all 'cell-building' in the labour organizations of other countries; they would have to assure IFTU their struggle for progressive social legislation and for disarmament would be directed as much at their own government as at everybody else's. In fact, Oudegeest confided, the united front was purely a matter of talk. The Russian trade unions had no intention of joining Amsterdam. They admitted they received government subsidies and had no genuine autonomy. Their affiliation fees to IFTU, if it ever came to that, would come out of the state treasury, a clear violation of Amsterdam's most elementary principles. Their talk about unity could hardly be serious.

Unofficially, Oudegeest tried to find Purcell a path along which he could retreat from his Moscow entanglements.[1] The resolution of the Vienna Congress on Russian affiliation was very explicit. If the Russians could not accept IFTU's rules and regulations, they could not join. Purcell himself had signed letters to the Russians informing them of those conditions. If he had changed his mind since, he should have informed IFTU before making speeches elsewhere. But to be kind to Purcell, he perhaps just hoped to mediate between Moscow and Amsterdam, to keep them talking to one another 'until the Russian trade unions have become so far independent of the Communist Party and the Red International of Labour Unions that they can affiliate.' If that was Purcell's aim, he was guilty of no more than misguided optimism. Oudegeest could not believe the British really intended to call any international unity congress on their own initiative, as Purcell had seemed to imply in Moscow. If they did, they had better apply to Amsterdam first. 'The British General Council know very well that no Congress *not* convened by the IFTU would be attended by a single one of the affiliated national centres.'

The most influential IFTU leaders outside Britain all seemed solidly behind Oudegeest. The English delegates to Russia spoke for themselves only, not for the IFTU, said Jouhaux of France.[2] Amsterdam would never be taken in by united front manoeuvres. Purcell's speeches in the USSR were either naive or stupid, said the Dutch trade union chairman,

[1] *The Times*, 22 Dec., 1924.
[2] *Inprecorr*, v, 5 (15 Jan., 1925), 44–45.

Stenhuis.[1] The IFTU Genera Council should pass a vote of censure on him. Such was the opinion of practically every national centre in IFTU. They wanted their chairman to defend their views. If the TUC could not provide such a chairman, they would have to find one elsewhere. The feeling was virtually unanimous. The only possible excuse for Purcell – the French ventured it – was that he had been misunderstood or misquoted. If that were not the case, Paris was against him, too.[2]

Purcell was in trouble. His IFTU colleagues seemed determined to discredit him, if not indeed to dismiss him. Unable to explain his speeches in Russia until the delegation's official report was published, he could hardly defend himself convincingly. His colleagues on the TUC General Council, however sympathetic, could be of only limited help. They did elect him permanent chairman of the Council's International Committee, some show of support. And they did dispatch a curt note to the Swiss, the first to protest Purcell's speeches in the USSR. If Berne wanted accurate information on the TUC's attitude toward Russia, something better than exaggerated press reports, it was advised to listen to the British representative's address to the next IFTU General Council.[3] The TUC did not want to make the relations between the IFTU and the Russian trade unions a focus of partisan controversy. It hoped to play a mediating role between Moscow and Amsterdam, a quiet, peace-making role. 'A great deal of education has got to be done,' *The Labour Magazine* explained, to bring the continental labour organizations as far along the unity road as the British had travelled.[4] Onesided and misleading newspaper accounts had presented a distorted picture of British intentions and caused unnecessary excitement. The TUC had not deserted to Moscow. It only wanted to help bring the two sides together.

Outside of Britain, enthusiasm for the TUC position was slight. RILU affiliates on the continent, and especially in France, were encouraging. Communist activists were sometimes able to persuade local or regional labour organizations to pass appropriate resolutions. But the only national centre to support the British was the Norwegian, unattached to either RILU or IFTU. The Oslo trade union secretariat wrote Purcell in early February expressing interest in affiliating with the projected new

[1] *Ibid.*, 7 (22 Jan., 1925), pp. 72–3.
[2] *Ibid.*, 14 (11 Feb., 1925), p. 183.
[3] TUC General Council, International Committee Minutes, 20 Jan., 1925, file 901, doc. I.C. 2, 1924–25.
[4] *The Labour Magazine*, iii, 9 (Jan., 1925), 411–12.

international and asking for more information.[1] For the moment, Purcell left the letter unanswered. He, and everybody else, had to see what the IFTU was going to decide.

Prospects looked bleak. The IFTU General Council was composed of 22 members. Four of the 22 were British: Purcell, the president; J. W. Brown, one of the three secretaries; Bramley, representing the TUC; and Cook, representing the Miners' International. All four were firmly committed to the TUC's position on unity, beginning with an unconditional preliminary conference with the Russians. So was Edo Fimmen, back again in Amsterdam's high councils by virtue of his office in the Transport Workers' International. Another probable vote was that of G. J. A. Smit, representing the Commercial, Clerical and Technical Employees' International. TUC could count five votes then, and perhaps six. But twelve members, a majority, seemed sure to be lined up in opposition. The twelve included all three IFTU vice-presidents, Jouhaux, Mertens and Leipart, two secretaries, Oudegeest and Sassenbach, and the representatives of the German, French, Swiss, Dutch, Polish, Italian and Hungarian trade union movements. Even if the TUC could win over all the doubtfuls, the representatives of Spain, Czechoslovakia, Canada and Denmark, its motions would be rejected.

The effort had to be made, nevertheless. The British had committed themselves. The TUC letter was approved by the General Council on January 28, 1925, and sent to Amsterdam three days later.[2] The Council was 'deeply impressed,' it said, with the need for a unity conference between IFTU representatives and Russian trade unionists. To try to settle all differences between the two sides prior to such a conference, by correspondence, was a waste of time. The whole purpose of the conference would be to settle differences quickly, in an informal, face-to-face confrontation. If the talks were to be productive, neither side should go into them committed in advance to any specific formulae, the British advised. Following the informal talks, the parties were apparently to come together for a second round of negotiations. The British proposal on the subject was vague. Careful expository draftsmanship was not one of Bramley's strengths. What he said was that it should be understood, 'of course, that the findings of such a conference [the informal exploratory talks] should be considered as a preliminary to a mandatory

---

[1] N 5647/71/30, 6 Feb., 1925, F.O. 371.10992.
[2] General Council Minutes, No. 121, 28 Jan., 1925; Trades Union Congress, General Council, *Russia and International Unity*, pp. 6–7; *1925 TUC, Report of Proceedings*, p. 296.

conference to follow after reports of the preliminary discussions had been given to the bodies responsible for the final conclusions.' Only Bramley could untangle such verbal knots, but the reference to a second 'mandatory' conference could be interpreted as a call for that world unity congress on which Lozovsky doted so tenderly. Whether that was what Bramley meant or not, mentioning some second conference was a tactical mistake. It would be difficult enough to get the IFTU to agree to a first one.

In spite of translation problems, the Russian message to Amsterdam was both more coherent and more persuasive than the British.[1] The Moscow cable expressed surprise at the way the Amsterdam bureaucracy had distorted the Russian 'statement of principles' of the previous October. The Soviet letter was 'perfectly clear' and the IFTU Executive's comment on it reflected either 'misunderstanding or tendencious interpretation.' The Executive had made it appear as if Moscow was insisting on a unity congress of all national trade union centres. Russia did indeed believe such a congress desirable, but it was not what she had proposed. What the Soviets had urged, and urged all along, was merely a joint conference of IFTU representatives and representatives of the All-Union Central Council of Trade Unions. 'This, and this only, is our practical proposal to you at the present moment.' At the conference, both sides would try to agree on some mechanism by which an all-inclusive trade union international could be established, an international embracing the affiliates of both IFTU and RILU.

The IFTU General Council met February 5–7 to decide how to answer the Russians.[2] Everybody assumed beforehand that the British representatives would find themselves on the defensive. The Council would surely insist on reprimanding Purcell for the outrageous speeches he made while in Russia. Instead of digging in, however, the British charged. Bramley lashed out at the Amsterdam bureaucrats on the very first day. He objected emphatically to the way the official *IFTU Press Reports* had published distorted reports of the trip to Russia, pre-judged

---

[1] Text in Tomsky, *K Probleme Edinstva*, pp. 43–5; English translation in *Inprecorr*, v, 12 (6 Feb., 1925), 152 and in *International Trade Union Review*, v, 1 (Jan.–Mar., 1925), 12–13.

[2] The best brief summary of the meeting was in *The Labour Magazine*, iii, 11 (Mar., 1925), 526. See also *IFTU Press Reports* (undated and unnumbered, but late February 1925); Trades Union Congress, General Council, *Russia and International Unity*, pp. 7–10; *The Monthly Circular of the Labour Research Department*, xiv, 3 (1 Mar., 1925), Special Supplement, p. x; Bramley, 'Relations with Russia,' *International Trade Union Review*, v, 3 (July–Sept. 1925); *The Times*, 9 Feb., 1925; *Trade Union Unity*, i, 3 (June, 1925), 43–4.

policy matters not yet determined, and inserted itself into issues of purely British concern. He proposed a resolution instructing the secretariat to limit its public statements to 'general information suitable for public discussion.'

Oudegeest rose to defend himself. If Communist lies were to be answered at all, they had to be answered immediately. IFTU had to propagandize as efficiently as its opposition. He noted, for example, that one of Purcell's speeches in Russia was published in the German Communist press the same day it was delivered. Surely, Oudegeest said pointedly, the president did not want his own organization ignoring his pronouncements while the other side was so purposefully exploiting them! Jouhaux supported Oudegeest. IFTU leaders had the right to defend themselves when they were attacked, and the duty to correct Communist lies. He noted, for example, the Communists' claim that an Anglo-Russian Committee had been formed, that a similar committee would be organized in France, and that the two committees would work together to force the IFTU into a world unity congress. Any such committee in France would be composed of only RILU dissidents. Did the British really intend to collaborate with such people?

Bramley's rebuttal was brief, and only the four British members supported his motion. But the atmosphere around the council table was distinctly easier after the storm had passed, almost congenial. And the *IFTU Press Reports* would be restrained indeed for the next three months or so. Bramley's motion may have been beaten, but it had not been wasted.

The following day, Purcell spoke for himself. He claimed that the complaints about his speeches in Russia were due to a misapprehension. He had not spoken in his capacity as IFTU president, nor had he claimed to. He spoke only for himself. Nor had he sold out to the Bolsheviks. Indeed, he opposed their suggestion of a world congress as the first step toward unity. The Russians, however, had not insisted on any such congress. They had proposed it only tentatively, and as a basis of discussion.

Oudegeest did not care how they had proposed it. It was clear enough, he said, they were not prepared to accept the Vienna Congress's terms for affiliation and were still as hostile as ever toward the IFTU. Everything possible had been done to persuade Russia to accept Amsterdam membership and it was still unwilling to join. He proposed, therefore, on behalf of the Executive, that the Russians be informed 'that we regard the whole question as finished,' and that 'we should refrain from further correspondence.'

Bramley rose again to put the Anglo-Russian counter-proposal. He stressed, to begin with, the proposal had nothing to do with a world unity congress. The TUC had never even considered any such suggestion, much less endorsed it. The British urged only that IFTU agree to talk to the Russians, immediately and without preconditions, about unity. It was foolish to try to settle differences by letter when verbal exchanges were so much quicker and so much more productive. The Vienna resolution did not prohibit such exchanges. It set no conditions at all on talks with the Russians, only on their admission to IFTU.

The basic reason the British favoured talks, he continued, was simply that 'we are internationalists.' Excluding as big and important a country as Russia from international trade unionism would be 'very, very unfortunate' if not 'disastrous.' The British had come to know the Russians well during their recent visit, he said. London and Moscow had each promised to work together for international unity. That was the whole of their commitment to one another at the moment. It represented no surrender to Bolshevism, he insisted, and cited the TUC's repudiation of the Minority Movement and its Unity Conference. But if governments could negotiate with the Russians, trade unionists could too. Once the Russians were included in IFTU, the influence of the international movement generally would be enhanced, the working class would be strengthened all over the world, and Amsterdam would have made a real contribution to the establishment of international peace.

He pleaded for toleration. He was asking only for talks, unconditional talks. He urged his colleagues to consider the matter calmly and unemotionally. Most discussions involving Russia seemed to produce a 'panicky state of trembling fear and excitement and almost savage ferocity.' In such an atmosphere, reason could never prevail. He was no Communist, he assured them, and less of one now than when he went to the USSR. But for the Russians, Communism was the only possible alternative. Russian Communists were not at all like the west European variety. They were steady, constructive, logical and well-informed people, and they had done much for their country. One could deal with them. He urged the IFTU to 'set aside prejudice,' give the British proposal 'very careful consideration,' and let the 'spirit of toleration prevail.' Unity would 'make a wonderful difference' to workers everywhere.

It was a good speech, one of Bramley's best, but it failed to move a single delegate. The British got only the six votes they counted on, no more. Not a single national centre backed them. Eight centres, plus five members of the Executive, voted against them. Three members were absent.

The British had not been firm enough, or eloquent enough, to force their own motion through. They did generate enough sympathy, however, to block Oudegeest's suggestion, terminating the Moscow–Amsterdam correspondence altogether. That motion was finally withdrawn. A 'compromise resolution' was then offered by Stenhuis and Smit and accepted 14 to 5. It instructed the Executive to tell the Russians that they could be admitted to IFTU whenever they expressed a desire to be. IFTU was also willing to convene a conference with the Russians, in Amsterdam, 'with a view to an exchange of opinions,' as soon as possible after the All-Union Central Council of Trade Unions intimated its desire for admission.

In retrospect, the British were not at all unhappy with what they had achieved at Amsterdam.[1] Within a day or so, they were referring to it as a moral victory. The rightist effort to kill the negotiations altogether had been rebuffed. The resolution adopted marked a definite step forward from the position taken at the Vienna Congress a year earlier. The Congress had demanded the Russians accept Federation rules and conditions before they could join it; the Stenhuis resolution mentioned no such limitations. Tomsky might therefore be willing to say he intended to apply, and thereby get that conference he wanted. At the conference, he could press for the rules changes he sought. Bramley thought that was what Tomsky would do. He claimed to be proud of what he had achieved at the meeting. The opposition to the TUC's viewpoint, he told an interviewer, was due mainly to a misunderstanding of what it had really proposed. The atmosphere changed radically after the British explained themselves. The resolution adopted enabled the Russians to sit down with IFTU officials and explain just what their objections were to the way the Federation was presently constituted.

The opponents of unity in the IFTU were just as convinced the victory was theirs.[2] *Vorwärts*, the organ of the German Social Democrats, called the Stenhuis resolution 'a shrewd blow at the Bolshevik split-brothers.' Once the Russians committed themselves to enter Amsterdam, they committed themselves to liquidate Profintern. With Profintern disowned and destroyed, Communist splinter groups in west European trade

---

[1] Interview with Bramley in *The Labour Press Service*, 12 Feb., 1925; *Daily Herald*, 9 Feb., 1925; *The Times*, 9 Feb., 1925.

[2] *Vorwärts*, 11 Feb., 1925; *Le Mouvement Syndicale Belge*, 28 Feb., 1925 (Mertens); *The Times*, 9 Feb., 1925.

unionism would crumble away. If the Russians refused to disown Profintern, the whole affiliation issue would be dead. Either way, IFTU could only gain, Communism could only lose.

A further advantage of the Stenhuis resolution was that it should persuade the TUC to back away from the projected Anglo-Russian Committee. Moscow's continuing references to such a committee, and the TUC's tight-lipped silence, had puzzled and worried the Amsterdam bureaucracy.[1] Bramley's speech to the IFTU General Council provided the first definite information. But all that he had said was that the British had pledged 'to act jointly' with the Russians in the search for unity. That could mean anything or nothing. It need not have meant any formal Committee, however noisily the Russians urged one. *The Times'* correspondent was not being unreasonable when he suggested that the Stenhuis resolution could scotch the project altogether.[2] If Moscow agreed to talk with IFTU on the terms set, the Moscow–Amsterdam Committee would, in effect, supersede the stillborn Anglo-Russian Committee.

It all depended on the Russians. Nobody – not even the Russians themselves, at first – seemed to know for sure how they might decide to react. *Pravda*, on February 10, called the Stenhuis resolution a 'compromise' and said it represented a step forward in the cause of unity, but also called it 'hypocritical' and proclaimed the battle for true internationalism would continue. Its major concern seemed to be the impact the resolution might have on the TUC. Would Britain still go ahead on what *Pravda* now called 'the Anglo-Russian Action Committee'? A clear IFTU commitment one way or the other, for or against a conference with the Russians, would have made the Committee's future, or lack of one, clearer.

A hard line seemed to be in the making a day later. Soviet trade unions would submit to Amsterdam only if they were out-voted at a world labour congress, *Trud* declared. All revolutionary trade unions, not just the Russian, must participate in such a conference. The Stenhuis resolution was admittedly less rigid than Amsterdam's earlier line. The IFTU leftists had tried sincerely and honestly to move their recalcitrant colleagues. But the result they achieved was not good enough. The comments of the Amsterdam bureaucrats made it clear they were still, in fact, insisting on Soviet capitulation.[3]

---

[1] See, for example, Jan Oudegeest, 'The Mysterious Committee,' *IFTU Press Reports*, V, 4 (29 Jan., 1925), 1–3.
[2] *The Times*, 9 Feb., 1925.   [3] *Pravda*, 10 Feb., 1925; *Trud*, 11 Feb., 1925.

From the beginning, British Communists seemed much more convinced than Soviet ones that the die-hards, not the progressives, had won an absolute victory at the battle of Amsterdam. Harry Pollitt told an interviewer on February 9 that the Stenhuis resolution was simply a subtle effort to break up Profintern and would have to be rejected.[1] He urged immediate establishment of the Anglo-Russian Committee to 'defeat the sabotaging tactics of the reactionaries.' The Committee should then convene a world unity congress on its own responsibility, whether Amsterdam liked it or not. *The Times* took such threats seriously. The very existence of an Anglo-Russian Committee, its correspondent worried, 'would be a definite menace to the Amsterdam International, and might, within measurable time, bring about its downfall.'

Such gloriously dire predictions raised spirits in Moscow notably. The Soviet press reprinted Pollitt's interview and *The Times'* comment on February 12, and was clearly happy about both.[2] With each issue thereafter, a more uncompromisingly negative attitude toward the Stenhuis resolution emerged. The Communist press abroad reacted accordingly. The TUC General Council must now act, *Workers' Weekly* demanded.[3] Even if the Russian trade unions did accept the IFTU proposals, the prospect for talks was not very promising. The Anglo-Russian Committee must be established and must function. It was now 'the one guarantee all of us have against Right wing sabotage.'

The Russians moved to reinforce their ties to the TUC the very day after the Stenhuis resolution was passed. Shmidt, the Soviet Labour Commissar, got in touch with Bramley to urge an early Anglo-Soviet conference on trade union unity, to suggest the possibility the General Council might arrange Amsterdam–Moscow talks on its own responsibility and to urge, in any event, immediate formal establishment of the Anglo-Russian Committee.[4] Tomsky seconded these suggestions in a subsequent letter to Bramley.[5] The 'cynically frank' statements of the IFTU bureaucrats, he wrote, made it clear they intended to break up the whole unity project. The conditions set by the Stenhuis resolution he condemned as 'humiliating' and demanding, in fact, 'complete capitulation' by the Russians. The USSR could not accept them. He therefore

---

1 *The Times*, 10 Feb., 1925.
2 *Pravda, Izvestiia*, 12 Feb., 1925. By 14 Feb., *Pravda* had clearly taken the position the Stenhuis resolution was unacceptable.
3 *Worker's Weekly*, 13 Feb., 1925.
4 General Council Minutes, No. 173, 25 Feb., 1925.
5 Trades Union Congress, General Council, *Russia and International Unity*, pp. 10–11. (No date provided).

begged Bramley 'in a most urgent manner' to 'do all you can' to get the Committee established. 'If you act with determination, under your influence, the acceptance of the Anglo-Russian Committee is assured,' Tomsky continued. Bramley's ability to manipulate his trade union colleagues was still remembered in Moscow.

Once the Committee was founded, Tomsky observed, but not before, 'the Russian Unions, with its support, would be able to put the question of meeting the Amsterdam Commission.' (To *whom* he would put that question he did not reveal, but the Politburo surely reserved such decisions for itself.) 'If you consider my coming to you useful,' he concluded, 'I will try to come if the British Government gives me permission. Do not allow the right wing to break a cause of historic importance. The immediate formation of the Anglo-Russian Committee by every means is the only possible reply.'

Moscow had made up its mind. Conversations with the IFTU on the IFTU's present terms were too mortifying to contemplate. The ties to the British must first be formalized and tightened. The Committee must become a reality. Once it had, and the TUC was behind them, the Soviets would be in a strong enough position to deal with Amsterdam. The next move, however, was up to the General Council.

3

Engagement (February–September, 1925)

I

The TUC General Council meeting of February 12, 1925 was devoted exclusively to considering the draft report of its delegation to Russia. The delegates had already been back some seven weeks. The press was beginning to speculate on whether they ever would be heard from again. After issuing that brief 'interim report' in December, they had delivered no speeches, made no statements, published no sensations in the periodicals. For the CPGB, it all smacked suspiciously of a right-wing conspiracy. Trade union reactionaries were plotting to deny British workers the glorious news from their class brothers in the USSR. *The Times* and Fleet Street generally, suggested roughly the same possibility in rather different language. Perhaps sound anti-Communists in the TUC had finally resolved to resist the rank Bolshevism preached by a few noisy and misguided associates.

In fact, considering the length of the report, some two hundred pages, it was rather a triumph to have it ready as soon as it was. To whom to credit it is difficult to say. Bramley insisted the whole delegation was responsible for the whole report, and that it had been written 'either by the delegates themselves or at their direction.' *The Times* attributed authorship to the three 'expert advisors' accompanying the delegates. A. B. Swales said, much later, that the experts were used only for editing and for technical chores, and that Bramley drafted practically the entire document by himself.[1]

However it was done, it was done reasonably, quickly, and competently. It surely reads more smoothly than other documents Bramley was producing at the time. The members of the General Council treated it respectfully. They did send back the material on the Zinoviev letter for further study, but otherwise suggested only minor alterations and amendments. The report was approved for early publication. The General Council itself would sponsor the English-language edition. The Soviet trade unions were offered publication rights for foreign-language

[1] *Sunday Worker*, 29 Mar., 1925; *The Labour Magazine*, IV, 7 (Nov., 1925), 317; *The Times*, 28 Feb., 1925.

reprints. The embargo on speech-making by the delegates was lifted, and all concerned were thanked for their efforts. TUC records provide absolutely no substantiation for suggestions that pressure from Minority Movement sympathizers forced a reluctant General Council to approve a report it would have preferred to ignore or reject.[1]

The book went on public sale February 28. *The Times* that day printed a four-column summary and then condemned the report as worthless.[2] The delegates knew very little about Soviet Russia when they left, and they required more than just six weeks to make up their educational deficiencies, *The Times* decreed. 'To undertake the task in such a time and with such qualifications was itself proof of unfitness to perform it.' With an august disdain for the petty virtue of consistency, the editorialist went on to condemn the unqualified delegates for not coming to more forceful and positive conclusions. He then asserted flatly that the unqualified delegates had not written the report at all, which was in fact produced, he said, by the three interpreter–advisers to whom even he conceded the adjective, 'expert.'

The Times reflected general press opinion in Britain. The delegates were scolded for using official statistics, which were of course all falsified and therefore should have been checked. They were rebuked for not submitting their prejudiced report to unbiased anti-Bolshevik Russian émigrés for verification. They were labelled dupes, Communists or idiots, and sometimes all three. Their opinions were dismissed by the *Daily Express* as 'whitewash,' by the *Daily Mail* as 'eyewash.'[3]

Once the reviewers had their say, politicians, professors and preachers could pile into the debate. All of them – or at least all of them *The Times* found worth quoting – were hostile. The report was 'ill-informed, second-hand, and prejudiced.' It offended common decency, common sense, and the common canon of historical science. It was distorted, contradictory, false, and worst of all, revolutionary. One MP proposed to suppress it by statute. Its authors had clearly been deceived by Red agitators. The hospitality lavished on them, with money stolen from British subjects, among others, had warped their judgement.[4]

Bramley assumed responsibility for defending the delegation.[5] Its members had not urged British workers to resort to Russian methods to

---

[1] General Council Minutes, Nos. 159–62, 12 Feb., 1925; No. 197, 25 Mar., 1925; No. 240, 21 Apr., 1925.
[2] *The Times*, 28 Feb., 1925.
[3] *Daily Mail, Daily Chronicle, Daily Express*, 28 Feb., 1925.
[4] 181 H.C. Deb. 5, at cc. 351–9; *The Times*, 11, 25 Mar., 14 Apr., 1925.
[5] *The Times*, 23, 28 Mar., 1925.

emancipate themselves, he insisted. Such methods were quite unnecessary in Britain. The real issue, however, was not the evils of Bolshevism, but the evils of capitalism. Capitalism degraded the poor and demoralized the rich. Russian experience demonstrated that socialism was a valid and practical alternative to capitalism. The delegates had said so. The capitalist press lords had set out deliberately to destroy the credibility of the report, Bramley charged, so they could continue to spread lies about Soviet Russia, discredit socialism, and prop up capitalism. Their criticism should be judged in the light of their motives. The workers would not be fooled.

For both sides in the debate, what mattered, clearly, was not so much the accuracy or inaccuracy of the delegates' observations and conclusions but the impact their report might have in the clash between socialism and capitalism. The contestants seemed to prefer throwing the book to reading it. It can perhaps be evaluated more judiciously now. In retrospect, it was a commendable enough effort, not nearly so outlandish, surely, as the virulent anti-Soviet trash being circulated contemporaneously by Tory die-hards and their friends. The ten thousand or so copies sold[1] surely advanced – modestly – the cause of better Anglo-Russian relations. But whether they advanced the cause of unvarnished truth is questionable. The report will not stand comparison with that submitted by the 1920 Labour delegation. Its authors were clearly a bit naive, too reluctant to criticize what was amiss in Soviet society, too anxious to justify mistakes, too eager to locate and praise anything that seemed to have gone well.

The report speaks for itself. A few samples should demonstrate the essence of it. 'The control by the Communists of the central authority is not so absolute as is claimed.' 'The Communist organisation is becoming more distinct from the Government, more and more a religion.' 'Recent developments are towards a "democracy" in the sense of a Government based on the expressed approval of a majority of the electorate.' The Communist International was changing into something in the nature of a preaching order, like the Society of Jesus. 'The Soviet system of representation and its scheme of constitutional and civil rights...give...to the individual a more real and reasonable opportunity of participation in public affairs than does parliamentary and party government.' Apart from some housing shortages, which were only temporary, Russia was economically and financially sound and ready for more trade – with Britain, if possible. The Red Army was a trim and efficient fighting

[1] *1925 TUC: Report of Proceedings*, p. 483.

force. The moral tone of the USSR was infinitely better than that of tsarist Russia. Soviet education, Soviet art, Soviet law and the Soviet press were all praiseworthy. The prison system was much more humane than before. The workers ruled the country, and 'enjoy the rights of a ruling class.' The trade unions were therefore 'largely freed from their main function elsewhere of protecting the workers against exploitation by the wealthy' and could 'engage in educating the workers as citizens and rulers.' The right to strike was protected but it was rarely used. 'Full religious toleration' had been achieved. Some 'rights of opposition that are essential to political liberty elsewhere' had been withdrawn in the USSR. All but a 'very small minority' of Russian citizens, however, were perfectly willing to renounce such rights.[1] The Comintern was delighted with such stuff. It offered Communist Parties outside Britain the financial wherewithal to get the report published locally.[2] One can see why.

The delegation's conclusions on the Zinoviev letter, which the General Council had sent back for re-study, finally emerged in subdued form about three months later. They were approved by the General Council on May 14, after some additional amendment. They summarized the delegates' interview with Zinoviev himself, and recounted the tale of inspecting the Comintern registry book. The report was released to the press May 18 and published in pamphlet form for circulation to affiliated unions. The Prime Minister was sent a copy, along with a suggestion that Labour party representatives, plus officials of the Home Office and Foreign Office, conduct a new investigation of the whole affair. The answer from Number 10 was chilling: the TUC request was unprecedented and could not be entertained.[3]

II

Even before the General Council tidied up the paperwork on its last meeting with the Soviets, it got itself involved in arranging another one.

---

[1] Trade Union Congress, General Council, *Russia: The Official Report*. Quotations are from pp. 3, 12, 17, 136, 147, 171. The most effective criticism of the report is Friedrich Adler, *The Anglo–Russian Report: A Criticism of the Report of the British Trade Union Delegation from the Point of View of International Socialism* (London: P. S. King, 1925).

[2] *Communist Papers*, Cmd. 2682 (1926), pp. 8–13 (Plan of Work of the Agitprop Department of the ECCI for the Next Half Year, 7 May, 1925) and pp. 13–15 (Unsigned file copy of letter dated 21 May, 1925, to Secretary, Agitprop Department, ECCI, Moscow, from Agitprop Department, CPGB).

[3] General Council Minutes, No. 286, 14 May, 1925; International Committee Minutes, 26 June, 1925, file 901, document I.C. 6, 1924–5.

Bramley suggested the new get-together at the General Council's session of February 25. The Stenhuis resolution was not as clear as many Council members seemed to think, he reported. It could be variously interpreted. It might require the Russians to repudiate the Red International as a precondition for unity talks. Continental trade union leaders seemed to think it did. If so, Moscow could never accept it. Before simply rejecting Amsterdam's proposals outright, however, the Russians wanted to confer with their friends in London. Shmidt had said so, and Tomsky's letter confirmed it. Having pledged itself to act jointly with the Soviets in the campaign for unity, the TUC could hardly be so inhospitable as to turn them down now.

Bramley suggested a four-step programme to the Council. The first step was for the British to get together with the Russians, discuss the IFTU decision, and decide how Moscow should react to it. If the Anglo-Russian talks produced no mutually agreeable Soviet response, or if (more likely) the agreed response was still unacceptable to Amsterdam, step two could be tried. The TUC General Council would convene a Moscow–Amsterdam conference on its own initiative. It could mediate between the two sides, assist them to find a formula enabling the Russians to affiliate to IFTU. But if, finally, such a conference still failed to reach any agreement, the General Council would move to steps three and four. Step three would be to ask the Scarborough Congress next September to establish the Anglo-Russian Unity Committee Tomsky had been urging so energetically since last November. Step four, to see the campaign through in the meantime, would be to agree to a temporary 'informal association' with the Russians involving 'friendly consultations' on the unity problem.

Bramley's suggestions got a meticulous going-over from his colleagues, termed 'long and serious consideration' by the minutes. The Council finally made a decision characteristic of its work on other occasions: take the one almost unavoidable step but no more, and hope nothing more would be required of it. It would talk with the Russians – or more precisely, it would authorize its International Committee to talk with the Russians – about how Moscow might respond to the Stenhuis resolution. But any further action would depend on how those talks went.[1]

For Bramley, the vote was another disappointment. He had pledged himself to an Anglo-Russian Committee. Twice he had failed to sell the proposition to TUC colleagues. He had tried to convince his fellow-delegates to the USSR back in November. They had refused to commit

[1] General Council Minutes, Nos. 173–5, Nos. 177–8, 25–6 Feb., 1925.

themselves to much more than vague good intentions. Now he had failed again. The General Council itself had apparently vetoed any Committee, even as a last resort, even after all other procedures to achieve unity had been exhausted. Bramley was losing his touch. His colleagues had soundly rebuffed him. His only consolation was that there would be more talks with the Russians, and the International Committee, which would do the talking for the TUC, was much less suspicious of Moscow than was the General Council as a whole. Bramley was irrepressibly optimistic by nature. One doubts he sulked for very long.

The letter inviting the Russians to confer, 'about the difficulties that stand in the way of your becoming affiliated to the Amsterdam International,' was addressed to Shmidt and sent, presumably, on the 26th or 27th of February. Moscow received the invitation ecstatically, accepted it promptly, and blurted it out to the press almost immediately. A meeting of the All-Union Central Council of Trade Unions, originally scheduled for March 17, would be postponed until May. The conference, so 'vitally important in connection with the Anglo-Russian trade union movement for unity,' had priority. The Soviets preferred to hold the conference in London and start it on March 14, but they were willing to meet anywhere the British suggested and at any time.[1]

London found Moscow's breathless enthusiasm a bit of an embarrassment. Bramley had to assure *The Times* the fabled Anglo-Russian Committee had not yet been established. Nothing more was involved than a comradely discussion of the Stenhuis resolution and how to react to it. The International Committee had to wire the Russians that March 14 was out of the question. The British could not possibly be ready that soon. They proposed the week of March 30–April 5. London was the best location, but if the British government proved un-cooperative about visas, either Brussels or Berlin would be acceptable alternatives.[2]

Tomsky clearly had not anticipated any visa problem. Before he got the TUC's reply, while he was still hoping for a conference before mid-March, he had named his negotiating team and put in an urgent application at the British legation for the necessary travel documents. He could not have foreseen what commotion that would produce in Whitehall. The Foreign Office favoured issuing the visas. If the General Council insisted on talking with the Russians, talk it would, and to drive the dialogue underground would only make it more difficult to monitor.

[1] *The Times*, 11 Mar., 1925.
[2] *Ibid.*; International Committee Minutes, 12 Mar., 1925, file 901, doc. I.C. 3, 1924–5.

Home Office officials, on the other hand, were eager to keep the Russians out. The TUC did not really want to talk to the Soviets, they felt. It was being forced to the conference table by Minority Movement agitators. In any event, four of the Russian negotiators, including Tomsky, were *persona non grata* to Joynson-Hicks.[1]

The diplomats did their best. They sent the request along to the Home Office with a recommendation for approval attached. For twelve days, the wheels of bureaucracy ground away without result. Two more cables arrived from Moscow, pressing for a decision. Tomsky decided the British would never give him an answer. 'Your matter is under consideration,' the legation kept repeating. He resolved to arrange that alternate site in Berlin that the TUC had suggested. The German government proved almost as inhospitable as the British. At first it was unwilling to have the Russians at all. When it changed its mind on that, it insisted it could welcome them not to Berlin, where hotels were suddenly and mysteriously 'over-crowded,' but only in Frankfurt-on-the-Oder, 'a provincial agricultural town thick with Fascists,' a member of the Soviet delegation described it. The Russian negotiators left Moscow on March 27 still uncertain where they were going to do their negotiating. They just headed west and hoped for the best.

Back in London, the Home Office had finally caved in. Its first reply, on March 23, was the flat 'no' expected. Austen Chamberlain then wrote a personal letter to Joynson-Hicks urging reconsideration. The General Council made urgent representations about the same time. The Home Secretary authorized the visas March 27, and a telegram went out to the USSR that same day. It reached the Russian trade unionists on the Lithuanian border. They of course credited the happy result to the efforts of their comrades in the TUC. The realization that their chief advocate had been the monocled gentleman presiding so icily over HM Foreign Office would have been mortifying.

The Soviet delegates were already oozing confidence, even before they were absolutely sure any conference could take place at all. Tomsky told the crowd seeing them off at the station that he was sure the English and Russian trade unionists 'would be able to place the unity of the international movement on firm foundations.' The trip itself was almost

---

[1] For the Foreign Office material on the Soviet delegation, see N 1487/1/38, 11 Mar., 1925; N 1565/1/38, 18 Mar., 1925; N 1660/1/38, 23 Mar., 1925; and N 1741/1/38, 27 Mar., 1925, F.O. 371.11006. Additional material on the departure of the Soviet trade unionists derives from A. Chekin (V. Iarotsky), *Na Londonskoi Konferentsii* (Moscow: Izdatel'stvo VTsSPS, 1925), Chapter 1, pp. 5–10; *Izvestiia*, 29 Mar., 1925; *The Times*, 30, 31 Mar., 2 Apr., 1925; General Council Minutes, No. 195, 25 Mar., 1925.

uneventful. A minor hitch developed at the Dutch frontier, when the border police demanded the delegation produce one more passport. It turned out that the Dutch had assumed that N. P. Glebov-Avilov, chairman of the Leningrad trade unionists, was two people. *The Times* had made the same mistake. At Folkstone, the Communist visitors were separated from the other passengers and quizzed in a manner they found discourteous. The visas provided were valid for ten days only. The bourgeoisie was afraid of them, they concluded happily. By the early morning hours of April 2 – five days after leaving Moscow – they were safely registered at a London hotel. The General Council had put the conference back a couple of days as a result of the visa delays. It was now to begin April 6. Tomsky and colleagues were free to rest, see the sights, and fight off the journalists for four days.

Five weeks had elapsed since the General Council invited the Russians to confer. During that time, the whole political left in Britain had rallied to the cause of trade union unity. The *Sunday Worker*, first appearing March 15, best symbolized the new confraternity.[1] The Communist Party controlled it, a CPGB member edited it, and Party funds helped support it. Ostensibly, however, it was an independent newspaper, and its columns were opened to anyone with good leftist credentials. Combining a substantial main course of radical politics with appealing side dishes of daring photography and racy stories of the peccadillos – primarily sexual – of the upper classes, it lured readers by the tens of thousands. In just a few months its circulation had soared to somewhere between eighty-five and a hundred thousand, far ahead of the Party's older and duller publications. All the trade union leftists wrote for it – Cook, Tillett, Hicks, Swales, Citrine and Purcell. Unity was their favourite subject. In the very first issue, Purcell addressed himself to the topic, deploring the petty doctrinal differences which had separated Moscow and Amsterdam in the past and pleading for both sides to be less rigid in the future.

For Communists, doctrinal disputes were not petty matters, however, and some believed the dogmatic pabulum offered up by Purcell and his friends was dangerously mushy fare on which to cut good Party teeth. R. Palme Dutt and J. T. Murphy disputed the implications of it all in a series of articles in the *Communist International*.[2] The left wingers – even

[1] For some instructive comment on the early history of the *Sunday Worker*, see MacFarlane, *British Communist Party*, pp. 143–6.
[2] R. Palme Dutt, 'The British Working Class after the Election,' *Communist International*, New Series, No. 8 (Feb., 1925), pp. 13–35; J. T. Murphy, 'How a Mass

in the trade unions where they really were strong – were incapable of
leading the working class of the future, Dutt insisted. They tried to win
the masses with nothing but 'phrases and promises,' and if they ever
succeeded, they would simply dissipate their victory in some 'comic
opera fiasco.' Murphy responded almost contemptuously. He dismissed
Dutt as 'an intellectual who has lost touch with realities.' The leftists
were drawing nearer to Communism all the time. To attack them was
only to drive them away again, along with the masses who followed them.
Proper tactics were to lure them closer. Communists could bait the trap
with offers of united fronts on immediate and popular issues.

A year or so later, Dutt's argument would look, in retrospect, very
good. The general strike had indeed some elements of a comic opera
fiasco. At the time, however, Murphy seemed the winner. The united
front – from above as well as below – was producing good results. The
issue of trade union internationalism seemed especially advantageous. It
brought together leftists and Communists as had no other cause since
the end of the intervention. The *Sunday Worker* continued the unity
campaign, and intensified it, over the spring and summer of 1925.

So did the Labour Research Department. Ostensibly independent, the
LRD was also in fact Communist-controlled, and its secretary, R. Page
Arnot, was – after Dutt – the CPGB's most articulate theoretician. In
early March, 1925, the LRD put out a special supplement to its *Monthly
Circular* devoted completely to documenting the history of the unity
issue. Purcell was given the opportunity to write the preface.[1] He lashed
out at continental socialism in general and the IFTU bureaucracy in
particular for obscuring and distorting the facts of the unity campaign.
They resorted to trickery and deceit to defeat the TUC's initiatives.
Purcell cited the Stenhuis resolution, presented to the IFTU as a compromise and hailed since by its supporters as a smart piece of work to
foil the British. What was needed, he said, was a regular journal correct-
ing the lies from across the Channel. 'Already some of us have been discussing such a publication,' he remarked.

Amsterdam was stung by the criticism, especially since the author had
identified himself as IFTU president. Purcell had no right to dignify such

Communist Party Will Come in Britain,' *ibid.*, No. 9 (Mar., 1925), pp. 1–16; R.
Palme Dutt, 'The British Working Class Movement, the Left-wing and the Communist Party,' *ibid.*, No. 12 (June, 1925), pp. 97–112; J. T. Murphy, 'The Coming of
the Mass Party in Britain,' *ibid.*, No. 13 (July, 1925), pp. 99–106.

1 *The Monthly Circular of the Labour Research Department*, XIV, 3 (1 Mar., 1925),
special supplement, pp. i–ii.

a 'curious' article by citing his official position, Oudegeest insisted.[1] IFTU never authorized him to write such a thing. He defied Purcell to be specific about the alleged anti-British conspiracy. Why had he not complained of it before? What had happened since the last IFTU General Council meeting, which Purcell himself had told the press was 'cordial and comradely,' to upset him so? In the interests of clarity and truth, Purcell should explain himself.

It was a splendid scrap! The TUC General Council entered another tough new protest against using the *IFTU Press Reports* to attack in- dividual Federation members.[2] Moscow rejoiced. Amsterdam was in chaos and reformism therefore in a state of collapse.[3] It is not surprising that Purcell found the money he was looking for to establish that journal he had mentioned. It is not surprising that the journal, *Trade Union Unity*, was published at 162 Buckingham Palace Road, the office of the Labour Research Department. It is not surprising that the General Strike infected the journal with a sudden and acute financial anemia and that it died one issue afterwards. One cannot document Communist financial support for the venture. One cannot prove that support was withdrawn in May of 1926. One simply credits the Comintern with having the horse sense to seize an advantageous opportunity when it presented itself. One also assumes the International was prudent enough not to send good money after bad when the opportunities faded away. If that be slander...

The journal appeared in late March 1925, just before the Anglo- Russian trade union conference was to open. Its editors were Purcell, Fimmen and Hicks. Purcell wrote the lead editorial.[4] *Trade Union Unity* was designed, he said, to interest British workers in the doings of their brothers in other lands. It stood for unity 'because Unity means POWER. And when Unity is achieved, the next task for the working class is to use their POWER to emancipate themselves, to free the subject nations and to make an end to capitalism, and all the misery, beggary and barbarism that follow in their train.' The grammar was deficient, the style extrava- gant and the words ('misery, beggary and barbarism') borrowed from Purcell's own speeches in the USSR. But it did provide the Cause with its own platform, a platform not directly (at least provably) associated

---

[1] *IFTU Press Reports*, v, 10 (12 Mar., 1925), 1–2.
[2] General Council Minutes, No. 204, 25 Mar., 1925.
[3] Communist International, Enlarged Executive, *Rasshirennyi Plenum Ispolkoma Kommunisticheskogo Internatsionala (21 marta–6 aprelia 1925g.)*: *Stenograficheskii Otchet* (Moscow–Leningrad: Gosudarstvennoe Izdatel'stvo, 1925), pp. 251–3; Stalin, *Sochineniia*, VII, 54; *The Worker*, 23 May, 1925.
[4] *Trade Union Unity*, I, 1 (Apr., 1925), 1–2.

with any particular political party. And if the first issue showed some weakness in substantive content, the names were still impressive. Will Thorne, MP, who seemed not quite sure of the difference between the Red International and the Russian trade unions, wrote a confused little piece. Edo Fimmen wrote a much better one. At least four members of the TUC General Council sent messages of greeting.

The whole unity debate became shriller and more frenzied after the Russian trade unionists arrived in Britain for the conference. The Communist press, sensing victory, pressed its advantage hard.[1] The united front from above must be supported by a united front from below. The rank and file must demand the Anglo-Russian Committee now. The General Council had vacillated long enough. Any more delay would be intolerable. Every trade union branch, every miners' lodge, must deluge the Council with manifestos in support of the Committee. An intense joint campaign of propaganda and agitation and the job would be done.

Most propagandizing in early April, however, seemed to be coming from the other side. Fleet Street was angry at the visiting Russians, and perplexed by them. Here were a bunch of Red 'agitators' who refused to be interviewed! It was intolerable! The only way to deal with such frauds was to expose them. They were not really trade unionists at all. They could not be, since the USSR had closed down all genuine trade unions. They were cunning Old Bolshevik wolves come to devour innocent British lambs. They brought huge sums of money with them to buy up the support they needed. Russians took to intrigue like fish to water. Tomsky was not really a Russian at all, but a Jew. His colleague, Mel'nichansky, was no worker, but an intellectual, proved by the fact he spoke a few words of English. Both of them were 'firebrands creeping in under false pretenses, spreading subversive propaganda under a transparently fraudulent cloak of Trade Unionism.' Wolves, fish, Jewish intellectuals, firebrands creeping under cloaks – the imagery was dazzlingly varied, but the attitude represented was clear enough.[2] It even penetrated the venerable precincts of Westminster. How could the Home Secretary ensure us, a backbencher asked, that these Russians would not take advantage of their visit to spread Communist propaganda? The gentleman seemed to fear Tomsky might stroll through Piccadilly Circus scattering leaflets. Joynson-Hicks, however, answered the question as

[1] *The Worker*, 4 Apr., 1925; *Sunday Worker*, 5 Apr., 1925; *Workers' Weekly*, 9 Apr., 1925.

[2] The press summary is from the *Daily Dispatch, Daily Express, Daily Mail* and *Daily News* for Apr. 4 and 6, 1925. See also Chekin, *Na Londonskoi Konferentsii*, pp. 11–17, and the *Daily Herald*, 6 Apr., 1925.

earnestly as it had been posed. He assumed the Soviet delegates would confine their discussions strictly to trade union matters. 'I will not now anticipate the action which might be taken if this assumption proved to be incorrect.' The visitors had been duly warned.[1]

The Times constituted itself the special champion of the aggrieved IFTU bureaucrats, for whom its feelings, heretofore unexpressed, were apparently overwhelmingly tender.[2] The gulf between Amsterdam and Moscow was wider than the TUC seemed to realize, it announced. The divergence of principle was fundamental. Amsterdam fought the class war by legal means and for economic ends, Moscow by revolutionary means and for political ends. For years, the Russians had tried to destroy Amsterdam by frontal attack. The campaign had failed. The Reds had now turned to more devious manoeuvres, subtly sowing seeds of dissension to tear IFTU apart from within. Essential to that effort were united front techniques. By accepting the united front, the TUC was playing into Soviet hands.

By undertaking a mediating role, then, between the Russians and the IFTU – against IFTU's will – the General Council had put itself in the position of agent for Communism. Other IFTU affiliates would 'fail to understand the British attitude to a militant rival whose intrigues and attacks they are continually engaged in resisting.' The reports that Britain was considering calling unconditional unity talks on her own authority were especially distressing. Any such action would be deliberate defiance of established IFTU policy and explicit disloyalty to the organization. *The Times* quoted Amsterdam's vice-president, Jouhaux: 'Should the British trade unions,' he said, 'decide to pass over the I.F.T.U. and... call together an international congress, they would put themselves outside the International...They have a duty...to respect the rules and decisions which they have accepted.'

A subtler effort than *The Times*' to sabotage the talks with the Russians appeared in an official Labour party–TUC journal published just days before the negotiations were due to begin. Its author was C. T. Cramp.[3] As general secretary of the Railwaymen and chairman of the Labour party, he spoke with special authority. He doubted the unity effort would succeed. The Russians did not really want to affiliate with IFTU, as presently constituted, and European trade unionists did not

[1] 182 H.C. Deb. 5s at c. 1501.
[2] *The Times*, 31 Mar., 6, 7 Apr., 1925.
[3] C. T. Cramp, ' "Continental" Trade Unions: A New Plan for World Unity,' *The Labour Magazine*, III (12 Apr., 1925), 538–9.

want Soviet and non-Soviet Reds infiltrating their movement. Cramp had a counter-suggestion, continental trade union federations, five of them, one each for Europe, America, Asia, Australasia and Africa. The change would automatically solve all Moscow–Amsterdam problems. Limited to that part of Europe west of the Soviet border, Amsterdam could concentrate its efforts where they would be most effective. Moscow 'would have to sever direct affiliations with a few European Trade Unionists' but would guide the destinies of the Asiatic federation. All friction between RILU and IFTU would disappear, because there would be nothing more for them to fight about. It sounded so reasonable on the surface and was basically so utterly ruinous the Russians concluded the real source of the article could be no less than Ramsay MacDonald himself.

Facing a tough fight at home, the TUC leftists badly needed support from respectable – i.e. non-Communist – sources on the continent. Such support was hard to come by. A dozen or so encouraging resolutions from local organizations hardly neutralized the unanimous condemnation of all the national federations and their leaders. All but one, that is. The Norwegian trade unionists – resolute, if a bit remote – stayed loyal to the unity cause.[1] Purcell got another letter from Oslo, February 11, inquiring again how the negotiations were going and indicating Norway was still interested in joining the projected new International. The letter evinced particular curiosity about the Anglo-Russian Committee. It asked about the Committee's composition, its programme, and how British trade unionists felt about it. Norwegian workers would much appreciate Purcell's personal views on all these matters, the note concluded.

Purcell wrote back a week later. He tried to explain the IFTU attitude on unity, and the Stenhuis resolution in particular. He repeated, even more explicitly, the pledge he had made in Moscow: if Amsterdam would not itself call an unconditional conference with the Russians, the TUC would call such a conference on its own initiative. He promised to keep the Norwegians informed. He carefully – and judiciously – avoided answering the questions on the Anglo-Russian Committee. The topic surely embarrassed him. His General Council colleagues, moving with such maddening deliberation, showed no sign of ever agreeing to any Committee.

Opposition to the unity campaign irritated TUC leftists far more than

---

[1] The relevant correspondence is in N 4145/71/30, 16 July, 1925, F.O.371.10992) and in *Trade Union Unity*, I, 1 (Apr., 1925), 4.

it did Russians. Moscow rather enjoyed listening to the bourgeoisie scream. The enemy would not make so much noise if it did not feel genuinely threatened. Trade union internationalism must be an effective slogan. Anglo-Russian trade union rapprochment must be an astute tactic. Bolshevik leaders could officially congratulate one another on their perspicacity at the meeting of the Comintern's Enlarged Executive, the ECCI, opening March 21, 1925.[1]

They had very little else to cheer them up. Generally speaking, prospects in Europe looked poor. Capitalism had apparently extricated itself, at least temporarily, from its immediate post-war crisis. Communist dogmatics produced a descriptive phrase for that unpleasant reality, the 'partial stabilization of capitalism.' The concept was disagreeable, but the Party could hardly avoid it. Stalin, for one, accepted it emphatically. It fitted well with his new theory of the achievability of socialism in just one country.[2] Zinoviev accepted it with much more reluctance. It hardly reflected creditably on his leadership of the International.

To Comintern brethren, Zinoviev preferred to stress the positive. Capitalism might be partially and temporarily stabilized, but objective conditions remained revolutionary. He invited the International to consider the possibilities in Britain. The working classes were moving sharply to the left, tugging their reluctant leaders along with them. The political shift was apparent in the official Labour party. It was even more clearly discernible in the trade unions. It was reflected in the favourable report of the General Council's delegation to the USSR. The delegates' sympathetic interest in the Soviet experiment had nothing to do with 'the fact of their being good fellows,' Zinoviev said. It was basically a by-

---

[1] The official report of the ECCI meeting, *Rasshirennyi Plenum Ispolkoma K. I.: Stenograficheskii Otchet*, has already been cited in note 3, p. 131 above, and is the principal source for what follows. The relevant speeches are those of Zinoviev, pp. 33–80; Gallacher, pp. 154–61, 271–5; Kuusinen, pp. 204–11; Lozovsky, pp. 245–71, 295–302; and Seward, pp. 282–7. The principal resolutions to be consulted are the resolution on the report of the Executive, pp. 495–6, and the resolution on unity in the international trade union movement, p. 545. The most authoritative text for the key resolution on Bolshevization and correct united front tactics is found in *Kommunisticheskii Internatsional v Dokumentakh*, pp. 444–95. That volume does not contain the resolution on trade union unity. English language summaries of the debate are available in *Inprecorr*, v, 26, 28, 31, 32 and 34 (4–17 Apr., 1925) and 47 (4 June, 1925); and in Communist International, Enlarged Executive, *Bolshevising the Communist International: Report of the Enlarged Executive of the Communist International, March 21st to April 14th* (sic!) *1925* (London: Communist Party of Great Britain, 1925). See also Popov, *Outline History of the CPSU*, II, 282.

[2] The theory was first propounded in an essay of Dec. 1924 (*Sochineniia*, VI, 358–401). Although published in the daily press, the theory was hardly noticed at the time. His colleagues did not yet take Stalin seriously as a Marxist theorist.

product of Britain's economic decline. That decline had also produced the phenomenal growth of the National Minority Movement, the most unmistakable and dramatic evidence of the radicalization of the masses. Zinoviev credited the NMM with six hundred thousand adherents. The old right-wing labour aristocracy was clearly losing its grip. If the emerging left could be consolidated, organized, united, captured, mobilized, a mass Communist Party might yet be built in Britain. At that point, 'the centre of gravity for the further development of world revolution may gradually begin to move to England.'

Potential allies though they might be, most of these leftists were not to be trusted. Lozovsky made the point over and over again. Communists must never forget that the leftists were basically weak, half-hearted, illogical and timid, almost sure to betray the cause in moments of crisis. Communists were contemptuous of them all, and rightly so. But they could not be ignored, disregarded, or simply scorned. They wielded a lot of influence in the trade unions, a decisive influence, apparently, in the TUC. And unless the unions, the fighting organs of the working class, were first won for Communism, the revolution would never triumph in the West. The leftists must therefore be supported and encouraged whenever possible. When they acquiesced in compromise, of course, when they proved irresolute, cowardly, and unreliable, they must be condemned. That, Lozovsky declared, was the way to win the proletariat, the way to keep it moving past leftism to Communism, the way to enlist it for class war.[1]

Merely to applaud the leftists when they happened to move ahead and to carp at them when they did not might seem a passive sort of a policy for impatient activists. Both Lozovsky and Zinoviev made it clear that passivity was quite unnecessary. Objective conditions – often beyond human manipulation – created revolutionary opportunities, true, but in exploiting those opportunities rationally, Communists could in fact enlarge them. The relevant technique was the united front. Find an Issue, and an associated Cause, on which leftists and Communists could unite with enthusiasm. Publicize the Issue as strenuously as possible. Propagandize the Cause. Insist the leftists back it uncompromisingly. So long as they did, praise them. When they became reticent about it, chide them. When they compromised it, rebuke them. When they deserted it, vilify

[1] Both Lozovsky and Gallacher made these points to the ECCI. Lozovsky made them even more forcefully in *World's Trade Union Movement*, pp. 106–8, published about the same time. In a press article on the eve of the ECCI session, Stalin agreed that winning the European trade unions was a necessary precondition for making revolution in the west (*Sochineniia*, VII, 46–7).

them. In the end, some leftist leaders might be won for Communism; most would revert to type and flee to the bourgeoisie. It made no real difference. Participation in the common effort would have brought Communists and the non-Communist working masses closer together than ever. It would have given Communists the opportunity to explain themselves to the masses, and prove themselves. Workers could not help but contrast Communist resolution with reformist half-heartedness, Communist perseverance with reformist opportunism, Communist discipline with reformist disarray.[1]

The obvious issue on which to build a united front was the issue of trade union unity. It was not the sort of bread-and-butter issue on which Lenin had based his united front theories, but it had tremendous practical advantages at the moment. Economic adversity had obliged the English leftists to come out for it. The rank and file were keen on it. Capitalists and the old-line trade union bureaucrats opposed it. To pose the issue, then, to mount a massive campaign for it, would achieve two objectives. It would show the masses that their truest and most devoted friends were the militant Communists, the proletarian vanguard. It would also show them the whole range of their real enemies, not only the bosses, but also the social-democratic lackeys who did the bosses' bidding while masquerading as labour leaders.[2]

The campaign thus involved no compromise of principle, and certainly no accommodation with reformism whatsoever. Even if Amsterdam yielded to all the pressure and agreed to unity, the war on social democracy would continue on a larger scale, on the new battleground. Within the new, all-inclusive International, the fight against reformism would be waged a hundredfold more intensively than ever. It would still be Moscow *v.* Amsterdam and no quarter asked or offered. The fighting would just be done at closer range. In the end, revolutionaries would not be reformed; reformists would be revolutionized.

The campaign was only nine months old, Lozovsky pointed out, but had produced good results. It was already generating its practical organizational form, the Anglo-Russian Committee. It had already split Amsterdam apart. It had already begun to isolate IFTU's reactionary bureaucrats from the masses they led. It had already, in fact, paralysed Amsterdam, and left it in chaotic disorder. The relationship with the

[1] For these points, see especially the speeches of Lozovsky, Kuusinen and Seward to the ECCI (note 1, p.135 above).
[2] For these points, and those in the next paragraph, Lozovsky's speeches to the ECCI are the major source (note 1, p. 135 above).

British was clearly the key to such successes. Achieving any sort of accord between Soviet and British trade unionists, on any terms, was 'of extraordinary historical importance.' It was 'worth a hundred resolutions.' It would demonstrate the workability of united fronts. Revolutionaries and reformists *could* sit down together, *could* work for common ends. It would put pressure on trade union leaders in other countries to explain to their followers why they were lagging so far behind the British. Most of all, it would guarantee the achievement of trade union unity. 'Nobody in the world will be able to prevent unity,' Lozovsky declared, if the British and Russians could form any sort of a bloc for it.

The NMM could take advantage of the Anglo-Russian rapprochement to further its own interests. Sooner or later, TUC rightists – Thomas, Clynes, Cramp – would feel obliged to resist the unity effort. They would hesitate to oppose it openly, because it was so popular with the rank and file, but they would certainly try to sabotage it behind the scenes. 'This is a big opportunity,' the CPGB's Gallacher pointed out, 'for the Minority Movement to strike a wedge between the masses and the reformist leaders.' Skilful exploitation of the unity cause could thus both accelerate and give direction to the leftward tendencies in British trade unionism. The conversion of Britain, in turn, would mark the decisive shift in 'the ratio of forces in the struggle between imperialism and Communism.'

The resolution adopted reflected those attitudes. They hailed the Anglo-Russian reapprochement, and urged all workers, regardless of politics, to support the Anglo-Russian bloc 'resolutely and energetically.' Work in the trade unions was deemed 'a most important and integral part of Bolshevization' and the Comintern directed that 'a hundred times more attention than before' must be devoted to it. The unions must be liberated from reformism and made over into 'reliable instruments of the class struggle.' The way to win them was by united front tactics, and the most potent slogan on which to forge a united front was trade union unity, the slogan by which 'we shall conquer the masses.'

As usual, Communism had stated its purposes, objectives and motives bluntly, honestly and without any dissimulation. It did not trust the General Council leftists, but it was prepared to work with them for unity. It would do so not only because unity was a good idea but because the fight to get it would discredit the Amsterdam reformists and perhaps even shatter the whole Amsterdam organization. Bolsheviks sought unity not to compromise their ideological war against social democracy but to win it. The reformist leaders were still trusted by the trade union masses. The leaders were therefore to be asked to share their trade union leadership in order that they might more conveniently be sacked. Even Russia's allies in this effort, the members of the British General Council, would have to give way to their ideologically purer colleagues in the National Minority Movement. A few of them might survive, perhaps. Gallacher mentioned Purcell and Tillett. The rest of them would presumably go. The fact that they agreed to cooperate with their Soviet colleagues would make it all the easier to get rid of them. They were not, however, to interpret Russian overtures as a manoeuvre. It was all meant utterly sincerely. To be struck down by a sincere assassin, one presumes, is somewhat more comforting than being dispatched by a hypocrite.

The TUC leaders read all this. *The Times* made sure they knew about it, even if they did not subscribe to *Inprecorr*. But they did not take it seriously. Zinoviev and Lozovsky were gross, loud-mouthed Red agitators. They wanted no truck with the likes of them. They were dealing with Tomsky, one of their own kind, a good trade unionist, a man they could trust. He said he was a Communist, and professed allegiance to Comintern and Profintern, but of course, he had to. It was just a formality. Basically, he was a worker, and believed, as they did, that workers had to stick together if they were going to beat the bosses. What difference, then, did all the fine theoretical talk in Moscow make? All was well in London.

A week before the conference with the Russians began, the General Council's International Committee made up its mind on procedures to be followed. The first formal event would be a dinner on the evening of April 5 – at the TUC's expense, the committee members hoped. At the opening business meeting the next day, the first agenda item would be how to organize the conference. The British assumed the Russians would propose the TUC side designate a presiding officer. If so, A. B. Swales, as General Council chairman, was the natural choice. The Russians should then be invited to state their position on trade union unity in the light of the Stenhuis resolution. After hearing what the Soviets had to say, the British could decide what to talk about next. The records indicate no TUC plan, at this stage, to discuss any permanent Anglo-Russian Committee. If some members were privately determined to get such a committee, they were not yet ready to press the point openly.[1]

---

[1] International Committee Minutes, 31 Mar., 1925, file 901, doc. I.C. 4, 1924–5; General Council Minutes, Nos. 235, 236, 8 Apr., 1925, indicate the General Council paid for the dinner for everybody, and for the Russian delegation's expenses for the whole trip.

The British delegation was dominated by the TUC left. It included not only Bramley and his assistant, Citrine, but also Swales, Purcell, Hicks and Tillett. H. Boothman (Cotton Spinners), J. W. Bowen (Post Office Workers) and R. B. Walker (Agricultural Workers) followed the Bramley –Purcell lead. E. L. Poulton (Boot and Shoe Operatives), Britain's representative at the International Labour Organization, spoke for the rightists. The way the Russians looked at it, Poulton did the talking for their real enemies behind the scenes – Thomas, Cramp and MacDonald. He got precious little sympathy, however, from his colleagues on the International Committee. Will Thorne might back him on some points, and Julia Varley of the National Federation of General Workers (Workers' Union) on most. Otherwise, he was alone. Worse yet, he had to leave before the end of the sessions to meet a prior commitment and could not even vote against the final declarations. Robert Smillie of the Miners, who might have had some sympathy for Poulton's viewpoint, missed the meeting altogether. He was off in Scotland negotiating. Of the 12-man British team, then, no more than three could be considered rightist. The Russian delegates, one is hardly surprised to learn, enjoyed a happy unanimity on all issues. In addition to Tomsky, the Soviets had sent Olga Chernishova, N. P. Glebov-Avilov, I. I. Lepse, V. M. Mikhailov and G. N. Mel'nichansky, acting secretary of the All-Union Central Council of Trade Unions.

III

The Anglo-Russian conference began the morning of April 6, 1925.[1]

[1] The two essential sources on the Anglo-Russian Trade Union Conference, from which most of what follows derives, are both in Russian: Chekin, *Na Londonskoi Konferentsii*, and *Londonskaia Konferentsiia Edinstva 6–9 aprelia 1925 goda, s Predisloviem V. V. Shmidta* (Moscow: Izdatal'stvo VTsSPS, 1925). They contain all the essential documents plus valuable supplementary material. I am grateful to Mr Andrew Rothstein for making them available to me. Tomsky reprinted his speech to the conference in his *K Probleme Edinstva*, pp. 3–17, and an English translation may be found in his *Getting Together*, pp. 91–111. Lozovsky's history of the conference is *Anglo–Sovetskaia Konferentsiia Professional'nykh Soiuzov.* (Moscow–Leningrad: Gosundarstvennoe Izdatel'stvo, 1925), available in German as *Die Englisch–Russische Gewerkschaftskonferenz* (Berlin: 1925). Almost exactly the same material also appeared in *Die Rote Gewerkschaftsinternationale*, No. 5 (52) (May, 1925), pp. 259–72, and was reprinted in Lozovsky, *Angliiskii Proletariat na Rasputi*, pp. 99–128. Mel'nichansky gave his impressions of the conference in an article in *Izvestiia*, 16 Apr., 1925. *Trud* published all relevant documents as they were approved. English-language material is scarcer, but see *The Times* for 7–11 Apr. and 8 May, 1925; *Labour Monthly*, VII, 5 (May, 1925), 304–7; *International Trade Union Review*, V, 3 (July–Sept., 1925), 188–91; *1925 TUC: Report of Proceedings*, pp. 298–301; Hutt, *British Working Class*, pp. 104–6; *Inprecorr*, V, 45 (28 May, 1925), 593–5 (Tomsky); and *Trade Union Unity*, I, 3 (June, 1925).

Swales welcomed the visitors and assured them that Cramp's scheme for continental trade union federations, just appearing in the press, did not represent official TUC policy. Poulton then suggested the conference discuss how the Russians proposed to answer the Stenhuis resolution. Somebody pointed out the conference could not discuss anything until it had officially organized itself. The Russians dutifully suggested Swales as permanent chairman, and proposed, in addition, a formal agenda. First, they would put their viewpoint on the Stenhuis resolution. The British could then do the same, and the two statements could be compared and discussed. Third, the delegates could deal with the possibility of further joint efforts in behalf of unity. Finally, they could take up the proposed Anglo-Russian Committee. The agenda was too complicated, the British replied. They suggested the Soviets first proceed on point number one, the Stenhuis resolution and their reaction to it, so that the two sides could find out how close together they really were. Tomsky agreed, and presented his speech.

It was another splendid performance. This was Tomsky's third effort with British trade unionists, and he did better every time. He shouted no slogans; he talked facts; he avoided hackneyed Red jargon about 'the will of the broad working masses;' he threw in a little topical humour; and he held his speech to under an hour. It was not the sort of harangue native Communists bellowed out at Speakers' Corner and it probably strengthened the English impression – the wholly erroneous impression – that Tomsky could not really be a genuine revolutionary at all.

He began by defending the Soviet position on unity, defending it not in terms of revolutionary Marxist goals but in terms of simple economics. Capitalists maintained a united front, to attack wage rates more effectively. Labour must be as united as its enemy. That meant a single trade union federation in each nation, and a single trade union international. The Soviets had always favoured unity. They had tried to unite with western trade unionists way back in 1918 and 1919, but had been ignored. They finally had no alternative but to establish Profintern, their own international. A lot of harsh words had passed between east and west since. The blame was not all one-sided. The Russians, 'not being vegetarians, could give change as good as we received.' But the polemics had hardly served the cause of working-class solidarity.

The Soviets recognized they represented a very different political viewpoint from that held in western labour organizations. But certainly they all had enough in common to be able to unite. All Moscow wanted to do was to meet with Amsterdam, to talk, to see what the obstacles to unity were and try to get around them, to develop a common purpose to which both sides could subscribe. Such conversations should be conducted totally informally, and neither side should set any preliminary conditions for them. It was unreasonable of the IFTU to require the Soviets to accept its constitution and rules in advance. The conditions Amsterdam set were the sort generally dictated to vanquished enemies. Statements made by Amsterdam bureaucrats after the Stenhuis resolution was passed indicated clearly they expected the Soviets to break with Profintern, to renounce all concern for RILU friends before the negotiations even began. That was a dictated peace, Tomsky charged, a trade unionist Brest-Litovsk.

It had been argued that the Soviet trade unions were not genuine trade unions, and that they could not really contribute anything to the international federation. Tomsky scoffed at such arguments. Organized workers in Russia numbered $6\frac{1}{2}$ million men, and they ruled one-sixth of the globe! He thought they could contribute quite as much to the cause of labour internationally as did, say, the Palestinian trade unions, an IFTU affiliate of seven thousand members. In any event, it would hardly hurt Amsterdam to sit down long enough to find out. If capitalist governments, 'gnashing their teeth,' could recognize the Soviet government, IFTU ought to be able to recognize the Soviet trade unions, at least to the extent of a brief talk with them.

He scoffed at the idea the Russians might lead their European colleagues astray ideologically. Such stories were already circulating in the London press about the present conference. The reports, Tomsky noted, 'picture the British delegates as innocent little boys in swaddling clothes, and the Russians as grizzled old roughnecks with years of experience in corrupting the young! As to age, when I look around this room, I cannot see where we have the edge.' It was perhaps not the kindest remark to make. The British delegates were 10–20 years older than the Russians. But they were also a lot more experienced in trade union work, the point was well taken, and the British appreciated it.

All the Russians wanted to do, Tomsky continued, was to get together with the IFTU leaders to discuss unity. If IFTU really believed in what it stood for, it should have nothing to fear from Moscow. The terms set by the Stenhuis resolution, however, were unacceptable. They had set the unity campaign right back where it began. The Russian unions would continue the campaign, however, and they looked to the TUC, 'the only force that supported the fight for unity in the International,' for help. Together, he pointed out, British and Soviet trade unionists numbered thirteen million workers (an exaggeration of about two million). 'Surely we can overcome the conservatism and stagnation of a few leaders in other countries.' Russia wanted Britain's advice on where to go next.

The meeting adjourned after Tomsky's address had been translated. The British delegation then assembled separately and informally to pick the speech apart and decide how to reply to it. The reply took longer than expected. At ten the next morning, the agreed hour for reassembling, the TUC statement was still not ready. The Russians cooled their heels for an hour and a half in Citrine's office, inspecting his reference library, his dating stamps, his 'in' and 'out' boxes, and various other evidences of his singularly precise and tidy mind. They were impressed, but impatient too.

The British were finally ready to read their statement at 11:30 on April 7. They suggested the Russians indicate to IFTU continued interest in participating in a single trade union international. The aims of that international, and its constitution, would not differ in essentials from Amsterdam's. Since, however, present IFTU rules failed to meet a number of legitimate requirements of the Russian trade union movement, Moscow and Amsterdam should get together for preliminary conversations. The object of the talks would be to ascertain how to amend the existing IFTU structure so as to facilitate the inclusion of the Russian 'and all other' trade union organizations.

In short, Moscow should answer the Stenhuis resolution by agreeing to join something very like Amsterdam, an only slightly amended Amsterdam. The TUC would take the position such a reply complied with the conditions set by the Stenhuis resolution 'as far as can be reasonably required.' It would urge IFTU to accept it as such. Britain would counsel IFTU to so amend its rules – in the interests of unity – that they could comprehend 'variations in tradition' and allow for 'political difficulties in the various countries.'

If Moscow concurred in those procedures, the British would promise to press IFTU's Executive to convene an immediate conference with the Russians to discuss unity. If the IFTU refused, the TUC General Council would summon a meeting itself and 'promote international unity by using its mediatory influence' between Moscow and Amsterdam. The language of the British statement became somewhat imprecise at this point. The TUC promised, for example, that its peace-making efforts would 'be inspired by a full appreciation of existing difficulties,' a pledge easier to make than to define. It all reads suspiciously like Bramley's work – impassioned and inscrutable.

Generally speaking, Tomsky had no insurmountable objections to the TUC's suggestions. Such reservations as he had were about verbal niceties, whether, for example, the Russians should agree to join an international with a constitution not essentially dissimilar from Amsterdam's, or one with a constitution 'in general outlines' not essentially dissimilar. The Soviets welcomed TUC support for the unity campaign, the formal reply stated, and appreciated British concern for the special circumstances forbidding any immediate and unconditional Soviet application for IFTU membership. The Russians had the feeling that replying to IFTU might be a waste of time, and that Amsterdam would manage to avoid unity talks no matter what concessions the Russians made. If, however, the British wanted them to, the Soviets would continue to ask for a meeting. No matter what the circumstances, conversations would mark a significant step toward 'gathering together forces of all working-class organisations' into a single structure 'based on the principle of the class struggle between labour and capital.' Only by combination could labour block capitalism's economic and political offensive. Only by combination could labour prevent new fratricidal wars. In view of the critical importance of the issue, the Soviets recommended the conference issue a joint declaration of its views when it adjourned.

The whole conference then reassembled to consider both documents, the British statement and the Russian reply. Each delegation was finally able to express itself completely satisfied with the views of the other. The British fully understood, a Soviet delegate emphasized later on, that the real issue was not simply how to get the Russians admitted to Amsterdam. The USSR never had any intention of joining IFTU by herself, and the British knew it. She was interested in a truly all-inclusive international, linking all trade union organizations and not omitting Russia's RILU partners. British views 'coincided fully' with ours, the Soviets claimed.[1]

The British statement and the Soviet reply were to be submitted to the governing bodies of the two movements for ratification, and were to be kept confidential until both sides had approved them. The TUC representatives had no objection, however, to the immediate and public joint declaration the Russians favoured, and the conference appointed a special commission of five – Swales, Purcell, Bramley, Tomsky and Mel'nichansky, to work out a draft. Mel'nichansky and Bramley did the spade work, apparently – Mel'nichansky providing a basic text, Bramley tidying it up here and there. The commission of five then met early the next morning to inspect the result. The session lasted some three hours. Purcell, Tomsky

---

[1] Chekin, *Na Londonskoi Konferentsii*, p. 34.

and Swales went through the document line by line, phrase by phrase. What they had before them, what Bramley and Mel'nichansky had agreed on, was basically just an apologia for trade union unity and an appeal for a Moscow–Amsterdam conference. Not afterwards. What emerged from their review was tough, uncompromising and to the point, if somewhat old hat.

The conference affirmed, it began, that unity was essential to achieve labour's social and political aims and to maintain its economic standards. At the moment, those aims were not being fulfilled, those standards not upheld. Reaction seemed invincible. Capitalists had created an international united front in order to exploit the workers. Wage rates were under intense attack, the eight-hour day was endangered, unemployment rates were high. The post-war world had proved no improvement over the pre-war. Capitalists and politicians had 'cynically repudiated' promises made while the fighting was still going on. The exploiters were now secretly preparing new wars for workers to fight. So long as capitalism continued, wars would continue, too. They were an integral part of the system. Only one power could still save mankind from the scourge of war, defend the proletariat against oppression and tyranny, and 'bring freedom, welfare, happiness and peace to the working classes and to humanity.' That power was the power of the workers themselves, if they organized, if they were disciplined, and if they were determined to fight. To save itself, then, and save humanity, labour had to unite. British and Soviet workers would continue the work for unity they had begun the previous November at Moscow. As a first step, the British would again try to persuade IFTU 'to agree to a free, unconditional and immediate conference' with the Russians. 'The mottoes to be inscribed on our international banner,' the declaration concluded, 'must continue to be the following: "Workers of the World, Unite!" "Long Live a Worldwide Federation of Trade Unions!" '

All that was splendidly ferocious Marxist rhetoric. Delegates at a Comintern Congress listening to such a manifesto might have considered it overly obvious, even a bit banal, perhaps, but not heretical. It provided for no action, however, beyond that already agreed to in the earlier exchange of statements. It was Bramley who suggested, last-minute, that the commission go one step further. If English and Russians were to continue to work together for unity, it was only logical they should establish closer formal ties to one another. He proposed attaching an annex to the declaration, listing specific proposals for Anglo-Russian trade union cooperation.

He suggested six points. First, the delegates would declare their intention to promote bilateral collaboration 'in every way that may be considered from time to time advisable, for the purpose of promoting international unity.' Second, they would agree to exchange documents of mutual interest. Third, they would exchange memoranda 'on special subjects...with a view to joint discussion regarding important principles.' Fourth, as opportunities arose, 'a further extension of joint contacts may be devised to develop the closest possible mutual aid.' Fifth, an Anglo-Russian joint advisory council should be established, consisting of the chairman, secretary, and three additional representatives from each organization. Sixth, to facilitate communication between the two organizations, the All-Union Central Council of Trade Unions should establish a sub-committee analogous to the TUC's International Committee.

It was a remarkable bit of strategy. For five months now, although with constantly diminishing conviction, the Soviets had trumpeted the news of some Anglo-Russian Committee, occasionally called the Anglo-Russian Unity Committee or even the Anglo-Russian Action Committee. The General Council, however, had refused to make the slightest move toward actually establishing any such committee, and seemed totally disinterested in the suggestion. Commentators had begun to talk about the 'mythical' committee, and journalists had assumed, quite reasonably, the whole idea was dead. Now here it was, resurrected again, courtesy of Bramley, an apparently innocuous point number five, preceding a ludicrously innocuous point number six, in what seemed an innocuous afterthought to the main conference declaration. And that declaration incorporated such a thunderous lot of revolutionary pyrotechnics that the afterthought, the annex, was almost a relief, hardly noticeable, surely nothing to protest about. It seemed, at first glance, a grotesquely anti-climactic let-down, considering the strong stuff that preceded it. In addition, the committee it recommended was not even to be called a committee, which would have sounded like the Russians had got what they wanted, but a 'council.' The council was to be 'Anglo-Russian' and 'joint' – not a club other trade union federations could join, and it was to be 'advisory' – suggesting, counselling, recommending – no more – surely not undertaking the crusading and propagandizing role the Russians had seemed to have in mind for it. Furthermore the council was first proposed to the small commission of five, whose English members, Purcell and Swales, were strongly for Anglo-Russian cooperation and would surely agree to it. Finally, if accepted by the whole conference, the proposal would be incorporated into a declaration to be released to the press immediately.

The General Council would thus be faced by a *fait accompli*. It could repudiate the exchange of statements on the Soviet reply to the Stenhuis resolution with comparative ease, because those statements were to be kept secret until both sides ratified them. But the declaration, on the other hand, although its proposals required ratification too, was out there in the open from the beginning. To refuse to ratify it was to oppose Anglo-Russian cooperation overtly. The rightists would find their usual tactics, postponing and delaying those measures it was politically awkward to veto, somewhat more difficult this time. They had skilfully side-stepped the issue of the Committee up to now. It would be impossible to evade it much longer. Bramley's stubborn persistence, his enthusiasm for trade union unity, and his keen sense of TUC tactics, had combined to produce an impressive result.

To start, everything went beautifully. Swales, Purcell and the Russians accepted Bramley's annex without a demur and tacked it onto the declaration worked out the night before. When the expanded document then came before the whole conference for approval, the expected opposition from Poulton never materialized. Poulton got himself totally caught up in the declaration's wording on the eight-hour day. It was a minor point, Poulton achieved minor textual changes, but it took a long time to debate. Will Thorne then suggested the declaration's language on the colonial question be strengthened. This time Poulton opposed any changes, and once again, the discussion was extended. Before the delegates had ever gotten to the annex – much less to that key point number five – the session had to adjourn for lunch. Poulton had another commitment and could not attend the conference that afternoon. Julia Varley was the only delegate, therefore, to object to the annex. She could not vote for the Joint Advisory Council, she said. She did not really oppose it in principle, but neither the Hull Congress nor the General Council had empowered the delegates to recommend any such organization. Her fellow delegates finally talked Miss Varley out of a 'no' vote: she merely abstained, and only on the annex. Everybody else voted for it. The declaration as a whole then passed unanimously. All present agreed they had made significant history, and the final hours were devoted mainly to mutual admiration and congratulations. The Russian trade unionists left Victoria Station the morning of April 10 – carrying bouquets of red roses courtesy of their British colleagues – well-satisfied with what they had achieved.

IV

The British press, which had condemned the Anglo-Russian talks even before they began, denounced them all over again now that they were over. The TUC was 'coquetting with an organization whose real object is to destroy British trades unionism,' the *Daily Chronicle* warned. The acceptance of class war doctrines, decreed the *Weekly Despatch*, was 'alien to the traditions and contrary to the principles of British trade unionism.' The only real issue, the *Daily Telegraph* announced, was 'whether British Trade Unionism shall or shall not be Bolshevized.' The delegates who signed the conference declaration 'signed themselves Bolsheviks by the same act.'[1]

The Times, which had covered the conference most completely, denounced it most vigorously.[2] Eleven TUC leaders, it charged, had now determined to take the revolutionary path to socialism rather than the evolutionary. The decisions they reached were 'of a character to mark a turning point in English trade union history.' They preached militancy and class strife, espoused 'civil war, chaos, and disaster.' Such dangerous doctrines were the predictable result 'of keeping company with revolutionaries.' The conference had been called merely to discuss the difficulties preventing Russian affiliation to IFTU. It had resulted, however, in something like that Committee Communists had urged so strenuously. Red tactics had proved eminently successful. 'How ZINOVIEFF must chuckle!' The TUC seemed determined to follow 'a strange path in violent company.' It was to be hoped, however, that saner councils would prevail, and the delegation's views be repudiated.

The Times' labour correspondent was as harsh as its editorialist.[3] If the delegation's work won the endorsement of the full General Council, he wrote, it would signify that 'the Bolshevization of the British trade union movement has begun.' He was especially concerned with how continental trade unions would react to the news. The TUC was, in effect, telling Amsterdam it had no right to ask the Russians to give up their 'plans of destruction and conquest.' The moral effect of such a position on European trade unionism was 'of the gravest character.' It would only strengthen Communist minority movements everywhere.

---

[1] *Daily Chronicle*, 8 Apr., 1925; *Weekly Dispatch*, 12 Apr., 1925; *Daily Telegraph*, 13 Apr., 1925. The best summary of British press treatment of the conference is in *Londonskaia Konferentsiia Edinstva*, pp. 79–102. The Russians delighted in western denunciations of the conference. *Pravda* and *Izvestiia* translated such materials and reprinted them gleefully.

[2] *The Times*, 11 Apr., 1925.   [3] *Ibid.*

Neither the delegates nor the General Council had any authority to take such a step.

The delegation defended itself, without much conviction, via an editorial in *The Labour Magazine*, an official TUC–Labour party organ.[1] 'The paternal anxiety of the capitalist press of this country' for the future of British trade unionism was touching, the anonymous writer commented, but misplaced. It was more likely that Soviet workers would be influenced by British than vice versa. Exposed to an older and more stable trade union tradition, the Russians might well be persuaded to 'modify the principle and practise of Bolshevism.' Admission to the IFTU, and association with workers committed to political democracy, would speed that process. In any event, the commitment to unity had been made. The obstacles to it were considerable. IFTU still seemed afraid of any 'frank, free and full exchange of views' with the Russians. Such fears were unfounded. IFTU was far stronger than RILU. When the two sides finally did get to the negotiating table, Moscow – not Amsterdam – would have to make the concessions.

That sort of defence did not please everybody, at least not everybody on the TUC left. George Hicks, for one, insisted that the spirit of the Anglo-Russian conference had been unabashedly revolutionary.[2] Outwardly, the delegates had concerned themselves with 'pettifogging details,' he admitted. Ultimately, however, their 'overshadowing idea' was 'the winning of the world by the toilers of the world.' The reason the two internationals must combine was embodied in the great Marxist slogan: the workers had nothing to lose but their chains, and they had a world to win. United, they could get rid of capitalism and abolish war. That was what the campaign was all about.

British Communists were not so anxious, however, to grant revolutionary credentials to General Council leftists. These same people – to curry favour with their rightist colleagues – ignored, scorned, or even condemned the National Minority Movement, a CPGB spokesman complained.[3] They still deluded themselves on the character of the Amsterdam bureaucracy, still hoped it might be persuaded to join the unity campaign. That was absurd. The only way to get trade union unity was to ignore the reactionary IFTU functionaries and convene a world

---

[1] *The Labour Magazine*, IV, 1 (May, 1925), 27.
[2] *Lansbury's Labour Weekly*, 18 Apr., 1925.
[3] J. R. Campbell, 'The Struggle for International T.U. Unity,' *Communist Review*, VI, 1 (May, 1925), 31–4. CPGB reactions to the conference, on which I have relied for the generalizations which follow, may also be found in the *Sunday Worker*, 12 Apr., 1925 and *Workers' Weekly*, 17 Apr., 1925.

labour congress over their heads. The TUC leftists still refused to take such obvious steps. That was why they recommended only a watered-down Joint Advisory Council with the Soviets. The Anglo-Russian Committee – active, aggressive, uncompromising – would have been much preferable.

The CPGB had its reservations about some of the conference's decisions, then, but it was distinctly pleased the meeting had occurred. The two sides had taken a good long first step toward the achievement of trade union unity. The TUC had at least finally acknowledged that the new international must be truly all-inclusive, that it was not simply a matter of 'Russian trade unionists leaving their [RILU] friends in the lurch and entering the Amsterdam International.' The conferees had been right to warn the workers of the war danger, and to point out that war was an inevitable concomitant of the capitalist system. The declarations, statements and agreements, though not everything Communists hoped for, must be ratified promptly by the General Council. All that could presently be achieved by diplomacy would then have been achieved. The next phase of the struggle demanded mobilization of the rank and file through the National Minority Movement. Only the NMM could generate the force to smash through subtle right-wing obstructionism and keep the unity campaign moving.

When the General Council met to consider ratifying the conference's decisions, on April 21, the right-wing obstructionists were indeed subtle, so subtle their impact was almost indiscernible.[1] The conference documents – the joint declaration, its annex, and the British statement in reply to Tomsky's speech – were all adopted without amendment. The rightists apparently scored only two points. The proposal for a Joint Advisory Council would be submitted to the full Congress in the autumn for final approval. Copies of the Anglo-Russian statements would be sent to IFTU for information. Somebody managed to convey the impression to *The Times* that the worst was over. 'There are indications,' it disclosed two days later, 'that a steadying influence has been at work in the last few days, and that there is a wider recognition of the fact that the General Council has no authority from the Trade Union Congress to act in any way independently of the Amsterdam International.'[2] The 'extremer men' had been rebuffed. *The Times* suggested they would be repudiated unmistakably when the full Congress assembled in September. 'Plain speaking may [then] be expected from delegates who see already [how] the Russians have manoeuvred the Council.' *The Times*

[1] General Council Minutes, No. 247, 21 Apr., 1925.　　[2] *The Times*, 23 Apr., 1925.

was confident that those who had surrendered to Tomsky, without authorization from their constituency, would be censured by the rank and file.

Such optimism was rudely shaken on May 7. The General Council released the text of the British delegation's statement in reply to Tomsky's speech, the statement in which the British promised to call a unity conference themselves if Amsterdam refused to. *The Times* despaired again.[1] Those 'steadying influences' discernible only two weeks previously were now quite forgotten. The TUC had apparently given way to the Russians entirely. The 'General Council seems to be dominated now by pro-Communists.' They had agreed to join the Soviets in campaigning for a frankly revolutionary trade union international preaching class war and proletarian dictatorship. IFTU was equally firmly committed, by decisions of its international Congress and of its General Council, not to participate in such an organization. A break seemed inevitable.

Even the Tory government began to indicate public concern. Lord Birkenhead spoke out for his colleagues at a London meeting of the National Association of Trade Protection Societies on May 13.[2] The unions, he charged, were 'now undertaking responsibilities very alien to their original purposes.' 'We might contemplate them with less anxiety,' he continued, 'if we saw any signs that the older and trusted leaders of trade unionism were at the helm today.' The TUC's agreement with the Russians was inconsistent with its obligations under the IFTU charter. Apparently, however, 'unless a special meeting of the Trades Union Congress is convened, no judgement can be passed on that action, which seems to me gravely mutinous,' until the annual TUC meeting in September. In the meantime, the situation was becoming graver all the time. Zinoviev had indicated Britain was his next target, and the General Council leaders seemed determined to assist him. The trade unions had to decide, and quickly, 'whether they are going to march along the common road side by side as Englishmen, or whether they are going to accept the orders...of men who care nothing for England but whose whole philosophy of life is the insane campaign of...the world's revolution.'

The Russians were as delighted with the conference as Lord Birkenhead was chagrined. Indeed, it was the very chagrin of the Birkenheads that delighted Moscow most of all. It gave the Soviet press something to trumpet while the conference was still going on and not yet producing

[1] *Ibid.*, 8 May, 1925.   [2] *Ibid.*, 14 May, 1925; *Sunday Worker*, 17 May, 1925.

anything but routinely cryptic press releases. Russian readers got daily front-page reports on bourgeois irritation at the meeting, how Fleet Street was shocked, Amsterdam outraged, Mensheviks and Social Democrats indignant.[1] To be considered (and by such influential circles!) formidable, fearsome, dangerous – it was all heady stuff, quite gratifying. The only power to which even the most devoted revolutionary knows he must submit is the power of a yawn.

With the adjournment of the conference and the release of the declaration and annex, Soviet editors finally had some hard news to work with.[2] 'Big step on the road to trade union unity!' the headlines read. 'The will of 11 million organized workers.' Not only had the two trade union movements established closer formal ties with one another, *Izvestiia* gloated, but they had reached a 'unanimous understanding' on the tasks of organized labour internationally. That understanding was based on class war doctrines and called for proletarian unity against the bourgeoisie. Marxists could hardly fault it.

Lozovsky stressed the doctrinal purity of the joint declaration in his analysis of the conference.[3] No sacrifice of Communist canon was necessary to reach that agreement with the British, he wrote. The wording was perhaps not always quite blunt and unequivocal enough to suit Soviet tastes, but the principles were surely well within the limits of dogmatic acceptability. He was a bit disappointed, though, with the Joint Advisory Council. Its very name, he said, was a compromise. But such was the 'balance of forces' within the General Council that the leftists could not yet persuade their colleagues to accept a true Anglo-Russian Committee with power to act. Such a Committee would require the approval of a full Trades Union Congress, he explained, and that was why the conference resorted to the 'transitional' organizational form it did. Lozovsky clearly expected the Joint Advisory Council to function only until September. He assumed the Scarborough Congress would then replace it with an Anglo-Russian Committee. Perhaps Tomsky laboured under the same delusion.

The slow pace may have dismayed Lozovsky, but it could hardly have surprised him. He expected it. Many British leftists, he pointed out, had

---

[1] *Pravda, Izvestiia*, 7–10 Apr., 1925.

[2] *Pravda*, 11 Apr., 1925, *Izvestiia*, 16 Apr., 1925.

[3] See Lozovsky, *Anglo-Sovetskaia Konferentsiia* and his article in *Pravda*, 28 Apr., 1925. Lozovsky's organization, RILU, echoed his personal views. See *Mezhdunarodnoe Profdvizhenie*, pp. 48–9; *Inprecorr*, v, 40 (29 Apr., 1925), 529; *Profintern v Rezoliutsiakh*, pp. 62–3 (the date printed is incorrect; it should be 22 Apr., 1925); *The Worker*, 2 May, 1925.

not yet even come out in favour of an International Unity Congress. They were still thinking in terms of Russian affiliation to IFTU. Given time, of course, they could be educated. And in the meanwhile, the very existence of the Council/Committee would have its impact both on them and on international trade unionism generally. It would demonstrate that trade union unity was practicable and that the Communist commitment to it was sincere. The largest and most influential components of the two existing internationals had been able to sit down together, talk a common language, and reach businesslike conclusions. What more irrefutable argument could be offered for rallying to an all-inclusive international!

Somewhat ironically, the Soviets took longer to ratify the London agreements than the British had. Not until April 30 did Tomsky present them to a plenary session of the All-Union Central Council of Trade Unions.[1] A delegation of British women trade unionists, headed by Mary Quaile of the Transport and General Workers Union, was there to listen to the discussions. The west European proletarian was under attack, Tomsky announced. Capitalists threatened to reduce his wage rate and lengthen his working day. It was the duty of the Russian worker to stand by his class brothers just as they, in the days of Intervention, had stood by him. Only the British trade unions, however, had responded to the Soviet call. 'Our greatest and most lasting achievement in the treaty made with the MacDonald Government in London – and this is all that is left of that treaty – was our connection with the English trade unions.' It was only natural, therefore, that when IFTU passed the Stenhuis resolution, rejecting the Soviet call for unity, in effect, the USSR should turn to the English for consultations. The result was the London conference. Tomsky read the delegates the official conference documents. Predictably, he was proudest of the joint declaration, with its explicit recognition of the principle of class war. He was optimistic about the Joint Advisory Council. Even though it was not yet organized, it was already, 'among many millions of workers, the most popular organization in the world.' The alarm it had occasioned among right-wing leaders proved the potency of its impact.

The debate was desultory. The recommendations of the London conference were ratified unanimously. Although IFTU still indicated no interest in conversations with the Russians, the resolution stated, the establishment of fraternal relations between English and Russian

---

[1] *Inprecorr*, v, 43 (14 May, 1925), 560–1 and 45 (28 May, 1925), 593–5; *Daily Herald*, 2 May, 1925; *The Times*, 4 May, 1925; Volkov, *Anglo–Sovetskie Otnosheniia*, p. 176.

workers was an 'undoubted success' in the campaign for proletarian solidarity. The delegates instructed the All-Union Central Council of Trade Unions to continue the fight for a united trade union international, 'as it has already done up to now, in complete agreement with the general line of the Red International of Labour Unions.'

While Tomsky was presenting the conference's work to the trade unionists, Zinoviev was defending it before the Party. He addressed the 14th Conference of the CPSU April 27, offering the comrades the leadership's current thinking on revolutionary prospects generally and on the situation in Britain in particular.[1] The Comintern's statement on the partial and temporary stabilization of capitalism had been distorted, he insisted. Communists had not forsaken revolution. They just acknowledged objective facts, and the fact was that no immediate revolutionary opportunities existed.

England however, presented good prospects for Communist exploitation over the longer period. The trade union movement there had swung decidedly to the left, resulting in the rapprochement with Soviet trade unions. MacDonald and Thomas were finding themselves more and more isolated on the far right, and 'slowly but surely' a revolutionary situation was 'beginning to evolve' in Britain. The Anglo-Russian Joint Advisory Council was a way of 'advancing to meet this clearly expressed tendency in the historical development of England...towards the revolutionization of England and its labour movement.' United front tactics were paying off splendidly and must be exploited more intensively than ever. Specifically, it was no disgrace for Soviet trade unionists to yield certain points to their British colleagues, as they had at London. It was clever.

Stalin, commenting on the work of the Party Conference, was both blunter and plainer on the aims of the Anglo-Russian trade union connection.[2] In Russia, he noted, the Party had founded the trade unions, and had been able to keep them under control. In the west, it was different. Trade unionism there came first. The Party only appeared later. The worker's primary allegiance, therefore, was to his union. To create a mass Communist organization, it was necessary for the Party to penetrate the unions, take them over, and enlist their members. Trade union unity would facilitate that process. When a mass Party had been built, it could be used as an instrument of insurrection. Stalin emphasized, how-

---

[1] *Inprecorr*, v, 42 (7 May, 1925), 546 and 46 (30 May, 1925), 597–608; *The Times*, 29 Apr., 1925; Popov, *Outline History of the CPSU*, pp. 226–40.
[2] Stalin, *Sochineniia*, vii, 90–106.

ever, that world revolution might take a matter of decades to complete, and that immediate prospects were dim. He seemed more concerned, therefore, with brandishing the revolutionary stick than with actually bashing anybody with it. He saw the threat of revolution as Soviet Russia's strongest defence against a generally hostile outside world. The west still hoped to destroy the USSR by force. But if it launched any such effort, the Soviets had a response. They could call out the European proletariat. The workers were Russia's allies and would back her in the event of war. If an attack came, therefore, 'we shall take all measures to unleash the revolutionary lion in every country on earth. The leaders of the capitalist countries must realise that we have some experience in such matters.'

Both Stalin and Zinoviev, then, favoured trade union unity and both favoured it in order to build mass revolutionary parties. At that point their attitudes diverged. Zinoviev would presumably have ordered the workers to mount the barricades as soon as he felt they might be strong enough to win. He would have fired the revolutionary weapon, and if it missed the target, laboriously set about re-loading it. Stalin would have aimed it, with great care, trumpeted its existence noisily, and warned the capitalists it would be discharged if they attacked. He could hardly have fired it, however, short of actual war. To use it prematurely would have been to destroy its effectiveness as a deterrent.

Motives varied, then, for supporting the tie to the TUC. Soviet leaders were far from unanimous on what they expected the connection to produce. Was it to convert the TUC leftists, make real comrades of them, or to expose them as the cowardly, half-hearted class traitors they were? Would it culminate in a real revolution, or just enough of a revolutionary threat to have an impact on British foreign policy? Nobody seemed quite sure. But all of them, for their various reasons, supported the rapprochement – Tomsky and Trotsky, Lozovsky and Bukharin, Zinoviev and Stalin.[1]

The Anglo-Russian Trade Union Conference produced a flurry of excitement on the European continent. The Norwegians were especially intrigued. The General Confederation of Trade Unions in Oslo moved to join whatever new Anglo-Russian organization had been founded, and wrote Purcell asking about the club's admission procedures. He did not reply. Undaunted, the Norwegians voted in August to affiliate to 'the Anglo-Russian Unity Committee' and to take part in any international conference it called. They wired Purcell the good news and

[1] See the summary of opinion in James, *World Revolution*, pp. 219–20.

asked him how to get in touch with the Committee. Once again, they got no answer. Eventually, somebody thought to write Bramley. He replied that the Anglo-Russian partnership was strictly bilateral and that nobody else could crowd in on it. He could not even divulge the Joint Advisory Council's address, or the names of its individual members, he said. The Norwegian press found the whole incident ridiculously delightful. Labour leaders, and Communists, were not amused.[1]

The IFTU bureaucrats reacted variously to the Anglo-Russian Conference. Vice-President Mertens was just plain indignant.[2] The TUC was trying to force its opinions on everybody else. That was just the sort of offence of which the Russians themselves were so frequently and so maddeningly guilty. It was gross presumption. IFTU had set its conditions for talking to the Russians. The English had no right to insist on overruling that decision.

Oudegeest's response was less impulsive, and (if not quite so honest) a good deal shrewder.[3] Many Russian trade union leaders, he confided to the world, were dissatisfied with their enforced subordination to the Party leadership. 'Possessing as we do,' he revealed, 'a somewhat fuller knowledge of the negotiations between Russia and Britain than can be gleaned from general publications, we are very strongly under the impression that Tomsky and his friends are inclined to take the right path.' To help them make their break from Communist influence and control, they sought the help of organizations in other countries. Western trade unionists of course wished them well. 'We should indeed be only too glad to help our friend Tomsky and his fellow-fighters to free themselves from the tyranny of the Communist Party.' The 'instinct for self-preservation,' however, required IFTU to exercise 'discretion' in dealing with the Russians. It was not at all clear, in the first place, who was really in command of Soviet trade unionism. In theory, Tomsky was the leader, but in fact, villains like Zinoviev and Lozovsky still spoke for the movement, and claimed to speak authoritatively. 'Although they are outside the trade union movement,' they appeared to be 'the persons who control it.' Second, one could not deal with the Soviet labour movement

[1] *Arbeiderblad*, 15 July, 1925, cited in N 4145/71/30, 16 July, 1925, F.O. 391. 10992. See also N 5647/71/30, 2 Oct., 1925, F.O. 371.10992; *Trade Union Unity*, 1, 7 (Oct., 1925), 108; *Inprecorr*, v, 69 (10 Sept., 1925), 1013–14.

[2] *Le Mouvement Syndical Belge*, 9 May, 1925.

[3] Jan Oudegeest, 'Amsterdam–London–Moscow,' *IFTU Press Reports*, v, 18 (14 May, 1925), 3–5; *The Times*, 19, 20 May, 1925. Oudegeest repeated the general argument – the Russian trade unions are our friends, Lozovsky is the enemy – in another article in July: J. Oudegeest, 'Losowsky Against Unity,' *IFTU Press Reports*, v, 25 (16 July, 1925), 1–2.

in isolation from the Red International of which it was a part. Profintern took its orders from the Party, and the Party still demanded the destruction of Amsterdam. To merge with the sworn enemy would clearly be foolish.

It was a clever piece, but it was surely hypocritical. Tomsky was not Oudegeest's 'friend,' nor was it likely that Oudegeest had any special information on the Anglo-Russian talks. He had never before evidenced any particular sympathy for the Russian trade unions and had always opposed trade union unity if it meant joining hands with Communists. If he did have some private information that Tomsky and company were hoping to break the unions' Party connection and establish their organizational and ideological independence, publicizing the possibility was the surest way to guarantee it never actually happened. To give credence to such rumours could only be to weaken Tomsky, strengthen Zinoviev and Lozovsky, and make the achievement of unity just that much more difficult. Oudegeest must have been aware of what he was doing. His tactic was crude and unfair.

For the time being, however, he did not press his case very hard. He did not have to. There was no urgency. The formal Russian request for reconsideration of the Stenhuis resolution was not despatched until May 19, and the way things worked out, could be dealt with very leisurely. Moscow had delayed any response to the IFTU's decision, the Russian letter explained, to allow time for consultations with the British. Those consultations were now complete, and the All-Union Central Council of Trade Unions had decided to draft its formal reply to Amsterdam on the basis of the British recommendations.[1]

The Stenhuis resolution had created a 'most distressing impression' in the USSR, the letter continued. Press statements and interviews since February, by both Oudegeest and Jouhaux, had made it clear that Amsterdam had no intention of changing its constitution and statutes to accommodate the Russians, that Moscow would be expected to join the organization exactly as it now was, and that the Soviet trade unions would have to abandon their comrades in Profintern before they would be allowed into IFTU. Such conditions widened the breach between east and west and made the achievement of unity more difficult than ever.

The Russian trade unions reaffirmed, the letter continued, their support for an all-inclusive international standing on the principle 'of

---

[1] Russian text in Tomsky, *K Probleme Edinstva*, pp. 46–7. English translations in *International Trade Union Review*, v, 3 (July–Sept., 1925), 191–4; *Inprecorr*, v, 45 (28 May, 1925), 595; *1925 TUC: Report of Proceedings*, pp. 301–2.

the class struggle and the final emancipation of the working class from the capitalist yoke.' The precise wording of the constitution of such a body was comparatively unimportant. 'The trade unions of the Soviet Union are prepared to affiliate with a trade union international whose constitution, in essentials, would not differ vitally from the constitution of the Amsterdam International. This united federation could also include in its list of aims and objects the aims set forth in the IFTU constitution.'

The Russians had finally, then, after four paragraphs, choked out those painful words the British had suggested back in London. Much of the impact, however, was dissipated in what followed. The Soviets had not been consulted when the Amsterdam constitution got drafted, they emphasized, and they did think the statutes of the new international should make it possible for not only the Russians to affiliate, but also all other trade union organizations not presently attached to IFTU. In order to achieve all-inclusiveness, 'differences in traditions, historical connections, and political peculiarities' of the various countries had to be examined, studied and taken into account. Such must be the task of the proposed Moscow–Amsterdam conference. There was no reason to suppose such a conference should not succeed. The London talks which so strengthened 'proletarian solidarity' between British and Russian workers, demonstrated that it was not impossible for Communists and non-Communists to find a common language, 'given mutual good will.' Moscow asked the IFTU General Council, therefore, to reconsider its decision of February 5–7 and to agree to a unity conference without insisting on any preliminary conditions.

The Soviet note incorporated some words and phrases agreed on at London, but it included some interesting variations on and additions to the original understanding. The agreement at London had been that the Russians would write the Amsterdam Executive, indicating their willingness to join an organization not unlike the IFTU. The TUC would then suggest that the Soviet response had met the minimum conditions set by the Stenhuis resolution and would ask the Executive, therefore, to agree to talk to the Russians. If the Executive refused, Britain would summon such a meeting herself. But Russia had not addressed her letter to the IFTU Executive at all: it was directed to Amsterdam's General Council. No General Council meeting was scheduled until early October. And Moscow had seemed to demand not a generous interpretation of the Stenhuis resolution but its direct repeal – quite another matter. The changes in wording did make a difference. Specifically, they relieved the

British, for the moment, of the responsibility of summoning a Moscow–Amsterdam conference on their own initiative. Any such drastic action would now have to be postponed until IFTU's General Council met, a matter of some six months, at least.

The English did not see the Russian note before it was despatched, apparently. The TUC General Council first considered it on May 27.[1] Swales, Purcell and Citrine were delegated to draw up a statement on it to send on to the IFTU. The statement, urging that the Russian request be given favourable consideration and that an unconditional conference be called immediately, was not to be made public. It was approved; and sent off to Amsterdam, June 15, 1925.

The IFTU Executive was due to meet June 29–30. Moscow's letter, and Britain's note indicating support, were on the agenda. At the last minute, however, Purcell decided to contest a Parliamentary by-election at the Forest of Dean. He could not attend the Executive meeting, therefore, and neither could his deputy, George Hicks. Both Purcell personally and the TUC General Council therefore asked the IFTU to put the discussion off until the next scheduled meeting August 17. On that date, the Executive referred the whole matter to the IFTU General Council, originally due to assemble in early October, but postponed – once again, at the request of the TUC – until December 4–5. The Amsterdam Executive asked the British to meet with them on December 1, before any decision was taken on the Russian note, so that all sides could clarify their position in advance of the formal meeting. The British were agreeable.[2] The collision that seemed imminent and inevitable in April was finally postponed, then, some eight months – at least. Neither London nor Moscow seemed unduly disturbed at the delay. Both had contributed to it.

V

Official relations between Britain and the Soviet Union had remained no better than coldly correct ever since the exchange in connection with the Zinoviev letter in November and December of 1924. Moscow hoped the spring of 1925 might produce a diplomatic thaw. The Russian chargé assured Austen Chamberlain on April 1 that Soviet attitudes had changed considerably over the years and that anti-British propaganda

[1] General Council Minutes, No. 319, 27 May, 1925; *1925 TUC: Report of Proceedings*, p. 302.

[2] Tomsky, *K Probleme Edinstva*, pp. 49–50; *The Times*, 1 July, 1925; *1925 TUC: Report of Proceedings*, p. 302; International Committee Minutes, 25 Aug., 1925, file 901, doc. I.C. 7 1924–5.

was now a thing of the past.[1] Chamberlain was unconvinced, however, and continued to spurn all Muscovite overtures. The Russians got a bit discouraged. He still hoped for better relations with Britain, Rykov told the Congress of Soviets on May 17, but he could not report any improvement yet.[2] The Foreign Office seemed totally absorbed in its project for an Anglo-French treaty. In fact, Rykov suggested, 'pacts between Tomsky and Purcell' contributed more to peace than pacts between London and Paris.

Rykov's preoccupation with how to manage the war threat was characteristic of the official line over the summer of 1925. Stalin stressed the problem over and over again.[3] With capitalism stabilized and world revolution delayed, a new war of intervention was much more likely. To defend herself against attack, the USSR needed to make allies of the European working classes. The 'Tomsky–Purcell' trade union bloc could play a role in mobilizing British proletarians for the defence of Soviet Russia, their class fatherland.

Such formulations were congenial to Stalin'a general line, de-emphasizing world revolution, stressing instead the achievement of socialism in the USSR. Tomsky, along with other Politburo rightists, endorsed the ideological package. Among the oppositionists, Zinoviev was most conspicuous. He stated his case plainly in a celebrated article entitled 'The Epoch of Wars and Revolutions,' appearing in June of 1925.[4] He emphasized once again how very partially and temporarily capitalism had stabilized itself. Indeed, the stabilization was only 'relative' and might be 'overtaken' at any time 'by Bolshevization.' 'The international proletariat rests its greatest hopes,' he indicated, 'on the rapprochement between the trade unions of the USSR and of Great Britain.' The alliance suggested 'the possibility of a real union of the broadest masses of workers throughout Europe.' Such a union's first responsibility, he agreed, would be to 'wage war against new wars.' But to unite the forces of the proletariat against war, to combine for the one specific purpose, would also suggest broader possibilities, he noted, including the possibility of waging world revolution. The world was still in the midst of a revolutionary era, and Zinoviev cited China, primarily, and Britain, secondarily, as likely locations for Communism's next triumphs.

Most General Council members were happier with the role Stalin set for them – peacekeepers – than with the part envisaged by Zinoviev –

---

[1] Great Britain, Foreign Office, *Russia No. 3*, Cmd. 2895 (1927), pp. 37–9.
[2] *The Times*, 19 May, 1925.   [3] See, for example, *Sochineniia*, VII, 206–7.
[4] *Izvestiia*, 16 June, 1925.

revolutionaries. Well before the Anglo-Russian Conference, back at the Hull Congress, the TUC had committed itself to supporting the normalization of diplomatic relations with the USSR, the exchange of ambassadors, and the expansion of trade. The resolution passed at Hull became obsolescent after the MacDonald government fell, but in March of 1925, the General Council voted an amended version of it for publication and, if possible, direct presentation to the prime minister. Maintaining the peace required that Russia be accepted as part of the family of nations, the manifesto proclaimed. Trade with the USSR would help take men off Britain's unemployment rolls. Humanitarianism and self-interest coincided neatly. The General Council endorsed the resolution unanimously.[1]

The labour leaders got a chance to make their case personally when Baldwin and several government colleagues agreed to receive them on June 23. Twenty-four General Council members took part. The TUC spokesmen tended to stress the practical argument, the economic advantages of good relations with the USSR.[2] If Russia were 'admitted to the comity of nations,' something could be done to relieve Britain's 'abnormal and prolonged unemployment.' Purcell, however, ventured into more controversial areas when he condemned recent press suggestions in favour of a diplomatic rupture with the Soviet Union. If a break were attempted, he warned, it 'would be resisted, just as strenuously as war would have been resisted in August, 1920, by the entire Trade Union movement of this country.'

Baldwin was polite with the trade unionists, but sceptical about their recommendations. Russia had never been much of a market for British manufactures. If she was to come back into world trade at all, Germany would have to bring her back, once 'things became more settled in Europe.' Britain would then benefit indirectly, because by selling to Russia, Germany would be in a better position to pay her reparations debts. The prime minister denied London was trying to keep Russia out of the community of nations. The League would never be complete until both Russia and Germany were in it. It was not Britain's choice Moscow preferred not to join.

Chamberlain repeated much the same argument. Britain was taking no hostile action against Russia, he maintained. His Majesty's Government

---

[1] General Council Minutes, No. 200, 25 Mar., 1925. Volkov (*Anglo-Sovetskie Otnosheniia*, pp. 144–5) characteristically attributes the resolution to the pressure of local trade union organizations.

[2] For the meeting, see *1925 TUC: Report of Proceedings*, pp. 154, 161–70, and *The Times*, 24 June, 1925.

had no intention of breaking off diplomatic relations with Moscow, he promised, 'in spite of not a few provocations of a serious character.' It was surely pointless to do any serious negotiating with them, however, so long as the Soviets continued hostile to British institutions and influence all over the world, and so long as 'no common basis of agreement' could be found 'in respect of great principles which must crop up again and again...throughout these negotiations.'

The General Council was not totally satisfied with the government statement, but it was gratified to be reassured no diplomatic break was contemplated. The pressures on Baldwin and Chamberlain to cut the tie to Moscow altogether were considerable. Birkenhead, Joynson-Hicks, and Churchill led the die-hard group inside the cabinet itself, and Commander Oliver Locker-Lampson was the noisiest of their many sympathizers among Tory backbenchers in the Commons. As a result of their efforts, a first-class pseudo-crisis erupted in July. Workers and students had joined in great anti-foreign demonstrations in Shanghai. The die-hards attributed the plague to Communist contamination carried by Russian agents. Birkenhead, in particular, got carried away by the momentum of his own indignation, and in language as eloquent as it was immoderate, urged re-evaluation of the government's whole Russian policy. Rumours appeared in the press of a British effort to organize a 'black united front' against the USSR. Finland, Poland, Roumania, the Baltic States, and Germany were to be enlisted in a huge anti-Soviet coalition, Moscow charged. The Soviet response would be to call out the proletarian peace alliance. 'The working class of all countries, including the English working class, will put a spoke in the wheel of those who wish to start a conflagration all over the world,' *Pravda* assured its readers. 'The workers must be prepared...to stop the criminal efforts of those who are in search of new adventures.'[1]

The Soviet Foreign Commissariat, however, suggested more conventional conciliation devices. Chicherin offered to negotiate all issues dividing the two countries. Chamberlain declined the invitation on July 6. He had nothing to say to Chicherin. In relation to the events in China, the government claimed 'full liberty to take whatever action they may think required.' Chamberlain refused to respond to Labour invitations to repudiate the bellicose speeches of his cabinet colleagues.[2]

---

[1] *Pravda*, 7, 10 July, 1925. G. Zinoviev, 'The Foreign Political Situation of the Soviet Union,' *Inprecorr*, v, 77 (29 Oct., 1925) summarized the crisis from the Soviet viewpoint.

[2] 186 H.C. Deb. 5 s. at cc. 20–1.

The Foreign Secretary's statements alarmed TUC officials. They seemed to indicate a retreat from the pledges to the General Council deputation made only two weeks earlier. Citrine wrote to Baldwin on July 7 regretting the decision to reject Chicherin's bid for negotiations, deploring the 'attempt in certain quarters to break off Anglo-Russian relations,' and strongly urging the government to avoid any action which might provoke such a rupture.[1] Citrine's was not the only protest. Chamberlain decided to clarify his stand. He assured the Commons on July 8 that no proposal to sever diplomatic relations was under consideration by the government. Baldwin sent the TUC a note repeating that pledge.[2]

In a cabinet meeting that same afternoon, Anglo-Soviet relations got their first general review since the new government was organized.[3] Chamberlain won a decisive victory over his more fiery colleagues. He provided them evidence 'from several sources,' the minutes note, 'to show that what most disconcerted the Soviet Government was an attitude of indifference to them.' Bolshevism depended, for its very survival, on its extension to other countries. What most disturbed its followers, then, 'was to find themselves treated in international relations almost as though they did not exist.' 'The more they were denounced,' on the other hand, 'the greater was their satisfaction.' The wisest policy for Britain, therefore, was just to keep a 'watchful eye' on Soviet subversion, retaining freedom to act when 'sufficient evidence of their misdeeds' accumulated. In the meantime, formal relations should be kept 'as distant as possible' and there could be no yielding 'to the demand in some quarters for an early breaking off of relations.' Chamberlain appealed to his colleagues to keep those principles in mind in their public speeches. A precipitous diplomatic break would only provide 'the extremists in this country' just the sort of issue they coveted.

Chamberlain got the approval he sought for his policies, but a number of ministers felt the problem required a lot more study. On July 29 the cabinet appointed a special committee of seven to go over the whole subject of Anglo-Soviet relations all over again and make recommendations. Birkenhead and Joynson-Hicks were named to the group, but the other five were Chamberlain men, and the report, accepted on August 5, indicated there was no reason to change the current line toward the

[1] General Council Minutes, No. 383, 10 July 1925; Coates, *Anglo-Soviet Relations*, I, 207–10.
[2] 186 H.C. Deb. 5 s. at cc. 386–7; General Council Minutes, No. 383, 10 July, 1925.
[3] Cabinet Conclusions, 1925, CAB 23.50, Conclusion 36(25)3, 8 July, 1925.

USSR. The only concession to the die-hards was the agreement that the activities of 'Communist agents' in Britain should be carefully watched and that the committee would be convened again after the Parliamentary recess.[1]

With the opposition leaders effectively muzzled, the war crisis passed, and the TUC found no need to issue any further manifestos on Anglo-Soviet relations. A special Trades Union Congress on July 24 repeated the old plea for more trade with the USSR, but fresh initiatives, in the calmer international atmosphere of the late summer, seemed unnecessary, at the very least, and perhaps just plain undesirable.

In fact, Anglo-Russian trade union relations cooled a good deal during the mid-summer of 1925. The Joint Advisory Council did not meet. Swales and the Russians made tentative arrangements for a session in June, but the General Council brusquely overruled its chairman at the first opportunity. Moscow was informed that 'in view of all the circumstances' (unspecified), the TUC felt no meeting should take place. The English even seemed loth to promote informal Anglo-Russian contacts. A Soviet request for General Council help in arranging holiday excursions in the USSR for British trade unionists was rejected. The Council, unhelpfully, suggested the Russians might contact the individual unions – over two hundred of them![2]

The freeze could, in a sense, be justified. The General Council had decided to present the proposal for a Joint Advisory Council (or 'The Anglo-Russian Committee,' as almost everybody persisted in calling it) to the Scarborough Trades Union Congress for ratification. It could be argued that the Committee should not meet until its existence had been formally confirmed. But the logic was marginal, at best. Nothing in TUC rules prevented the councillors from conferring with anybody they cared to. Congress had never specifically approved the April talks with Tomsky, for example, but nobody had challenged the legality of that meeting. The Anglo-Russian Committee was only empowered to advise, not to act. If the General Council still did not care to let it meet, it was because the Council just did not care to do any more talking with the Russians – at least, not for the moment.

TUC leaders continued to protest their devotion to the cause of internationalism, but their protests must have rung somewhat hollowly as heard from Moscow. Typical of what now seemed the prevailing consensus in General Council was the attitude of Arthur Pugh, who would

[1] *Ibid.*, Conclusions 41(25)3, 29 July 1925 and 43(25)1, 5 Aug., 1925.
[2] General Council Minutes, No. 319, 27 May, 1925, No. 342, 23 June, 1925.

succeed Swales in September as General Council chairman. He was all for trade unity, Pugh wrote, not so much as an end in itself but as a step toward the greater goal of a World Commonwealth of Peoples.[1] But such a Commonwealth, he warned, could never 'be established on the basis of...class antagonisms' or by simply 'making the under-dog of today the upper-dog of tomorrow.' So much for Marxist historical theory! And for the immediate future, Pugh emphasized the economic advantages of trade union unity rather than the political. The dock worker refusing to handle blackleg goods accomplished more positive good, all by himself, than did hundreds of his fellows singing the Internationale, Pugh ventured. His contribution to unity was both 'more practical and more intelligent.' That sort of argument was surely not appreciated in Moscow. It also held no terrors for IFTU functionaries and their friends. Amsterdam markedly toned down its attacks on the British over the summer of 1925.[2]

Why were the advocates of unity suddenly so powerless in the General Council – at least, from May through July? The most likely answer is that Fred Bramley was not there to buck them up. Nobody had promoted the tie with the Russians more persistently and more imaginatively than Bramley. Purcell did the conspicuous speechmaking, but when things got done, they usually got done on Bramley's initiative. But Bramley was ill – mortally ill, as it turned out – with cancer. The conference with the Russians had completely exhausted him. The General Councillors were informed on April 21 that the Secretary required a long leave of absence to have any chance of recovery. His deputy, Walter Citrine, would manage the office while he was gone. As it turned out, Bramley would be away about five months. He would not attend another General Council meeting until September 2, just before the Scarborough Congress.[3]

Walter Citrine, who took Bramley's place from April through August, was only 37 years old at the time. The strongest points in his favour were his youth and his zeal, his courage and his integrity, and most of all, his cool, precise, sharply-honed mind. Beatrice Webb, who did not like him very much, admitted all these qualifications, but found other traits distressing. He was too ambitious and too vain. He was something of a 'hygienic puritan' in his personal life. His 'manners and clothes and way

[1] Arthur Pugh, 'What Is This Unity?' *Trade Union Unity*, I, 4 (July, 1925), 51–2.
[2] Such attacks as materialized were more likely to come from the Labour and Socialist (Second) International than from Amsterdam itself. See, for example, the statement of the LSI Secretariat in *The Times*, 8 Aug., 1925.
[3] General Council Minutes, No. 242, 21 Apr., 1925, No. 434, 2 Sept., 1925.

of speaking' reminded her 'of a superior bank clerk.' His preoccupation with exact detail verged on fussiness. He could be a bit of a bore on the subject, she felt. 'He keeps a note-book and puts down the points made in conversations; he keeps a diary in shorthand describing events as they occur; and he likes to talk about all these mental processes...'[1]

He had been brought to TUC headquarters in 1924 to set up some regular administrative system there. Bramley was impatient with what he considered picayune detail and rarely spared time for it. With some relief, he gave his deputy *carte blanche* to clean things up. Citrine waded into the chaos with relish, and created order. His meticulous care shows up dramatically in the surviving records. Archival material gets classified and numbered and filed systematically. General Council decisions are carefully noted, indexed, and cross-indexed for easy accessibility and quick reference. The sheer literary quality of TUC documents improves immeasurably. Bramley was earnest, but his draftsmanship was sloppy and his prose style heavy. Citrine was quite different. He wrote crisp, brisk prose. He may not have been as fervent and as intense as Bramley – he was not that sort of person – but he made up for it in brilliance, judgement and clear thinking.[2]

His views on relations with the Russians did not differ significantly from those of his chief. Like Bramley, he was classified among the TUC's leftists. Mrs Webb, before she got to know him better, was calling him 'communistic in sympathy.' He exhibited unqualified admiration for the Soviet experiment. Later on, after he changed his mind, he was frank to admit that in 1925 he had been 'naive' on the subject of the USSR. His enthusiasms totally overpowered the facts, he confessed. 'I accepted...practically everything that emanated from Russian official sources...I was convinced that our newspapers simply couldn't tell the truth about events in the Soviet Union. I was resolved to do all I could to bring our two trade union movements into closer relationship.'[3]

Citrine was as pro-Russian as Bramley, then, and yet, during the

---

[1] Webb, *Diaries, 1924–32*, pp. 146–9.

[2] The estimate of Citrine's character, my own, derives from his books, and especially *Men and Work: An Autobiography* (London: Hutchinson, 1964), from our correspondence and interviews, from his many speeches, especially to Trade Union Congresses, and, most of all, from the evidence of his impact in the archival material at TUC headquarters. Among other sources I have used are: Webb, *Diaries, 1924–32*, pp. 146–9; Gallacher, *Rolling of the Thunder*, p. 63 and *The Last Memoirs of William Gallacher*, p. 201; and J. H. Thomas, *My Story* (London: Hutchinson, 1937), pp. 96ff., 277–8.

[3] Citrine, *Men and Work*, p. 88. Lord Citrine confirmed these impressions in an interview with the author on 9 Nov., 1967.

summer of 1925, with Bramley away and Citrine in charge, the association with Moscow cooled noticeably. Why? At least three factors would seem to have played a part. Citrine was young, to begin with, still the rawest neophyte, from the point of view of the General Councillors. He was not yet experienced enough to manipulate his colleagues as deftly as Bramley had. Second, he did not get along personally with the councillors as well as Bramley had. His fastidiousness bothered them. He seemed aloof, austere, cold, distant. His very intelligence probably counted against him. British trade unionists were ambivalent about intellectuals: they respected them, but vaguely mistrusted them, too. Bramley was rough-hewn, blunt, simple, direct. He talked like a mate in the pub. Citrine was sensitive, somewhat haughty, wholly unable to suffer fools gladly. He was, Mrs Webb later recalled, 'contemptuous – and largely justifiably contemptuous – of the members of the General Council.'[1] Finally, however devoted Citrine was to good relations with the Russians, he did not really have the time to do much about promoting them. TUC headquarters still needed a lot of attention. With Bramley away, the routine work was more burdensome than ever. Larger issues would have to await the Secretary's return.

If the TUC's reticence and caution irritated the Russians, they did not show it. Lozovsky warned his countrymen as early as the end of May that the English only moved very slowly, that they were not really very internationally-minded, and that the main reason they had turned to the USSR was merely the hope of gaining economic advantage.[2] Nevertheless, conditions in England were favourable to the emergence of a real revolutionary movement. Trade unionists were becoming disillusioned with compromise, with mere strategic manoeuvring. The Anglo-Russian Committee would provide Communism an opportunity to take advantage of the objective possibilities and to exert a real influence on English trade unionism, Lozovsky argued. The very existence of the Committee would make the capitalists' war preparations much more difficult. An attack on the USSR would produce insurrection at home. Just as the first World War had resulted in one successful Communist revolution, the next would produce several.

If Lozovsky's view represented official policy, there was no immediate need to push matters, to make demands of the TUC. No specific action

---

[1] Webb, *Diaries, 1924–32*, pp. 146n. and 177. When Lord Citrine annotated that comment, in 1956, he recalled nothing he might have said to Mrs Webb to give her that impression. Significantly, he did not deny the impression was accurate.

[2] Lozovsky, *Angliiskii Proletariat na Rasputi*, pp. 129–38.

was required of the Committee yet. It was not even absolutely necessary the Committee meet. Its mere existence would have an impact. So insofar as the British were reminded at all of the obligations they had assumed in April, it was done very subtly and quietly, and by proxy, by surrogates, not by the Soviet trade unions directly. It was done, for example, by the Communist youth organizations, holding congress in Berlin in July.[1] They issued a special appeal to what they called the 'Anglo-Russian Committee for Trade Union Unity,' urging it to warn the international bourgeoisie that no new intervention would be tolerated. The young people were confident the Anglo-Russian Committee would 'do its international duty.'

Anti-war agitation was not the only responsibility the Russians had in mind for the Committee. The slogan of trade union unity was still on Communism's approved list, too, and the fifth anniversary of Profintern, in July of 1925, gave Moscow an obvious opportunity to repeat it.[2] The manifestos hailed the Anglo-Russian bloc, bragged about the Red International's growing strength in the colonial world, and ridiculed IFTU. Amsterdam was not actually an international at all, the RILU declared. It was almost purely European, and its membership was declining, even in Europe. A third of its members were really pro-Communists, and therefore pro-Profintern, and another third were sympathetic leftists. Its president, 'comrade Purcell,' was 'a friend of the Soviet Union.' Its continued refusal to agree to unity on RILU's terms was absurd.

Tomsky's personal statements on the unity campaign were just as blunt, and just as uncompromising.[3] The Soviet trade unionists had been asked, he said, first, why they were for unity, and second, what they could contribute to an all-inclusive trade union international. The answer to the first question, he said, was obvious. The Communist revolution was for everybody, not just Russians. That was why they wanted unity. As for what the Soviets could do to help their west European class brothers, the answer to that was also simple. Bolsheviks understood the true nature of the class struggle. It must be waged uncompromisingly, violently. There could be no other way. Once that was understood, it was clear what help the Russian proletarians could offer European comrades. The Russians had been the first to win the struggle

---

[1] *Internationale Presse Korrespondenz*, No. 128, 4 Sept., 1925, cited in Carr, *Socialism in One Country*, III, Part 2, 995–6.

[2] *Inprecorr*, v, 59 (23 July, 1925), 817–19 and 60 (30 July, 1925), 831–2; *The Times*, 25 July, 1925.

[3] Tomsky, *K Probleme Edinstva*, pp. 21–3.

against capitalism, after all, to seize their factories, and to survive for eight years without the bosses. They could show others how to do the same.

Such was the sort of argument Soviet leaders stressed all summer, with special attention to visiting delegations of west European workers. The delegations were all subjected to intensive propaganda, for unity and for the Anglo-Russian Committee. Purcell and company were presented as lonely pioneers, waging the fight for unity inside IFTU against the stubborn opposition of a pack of corrupt and reactionary Amsterdam functionaries.

It was an image that not all revolutionaries found congenial. Making heroes out of the Purcells, out of reformists, could be fatal. Trotsky made the point with characteristic vigour and wit in his book, *Where is Britain Going?*, published in the spring of 1925.[1] Pseudo-leftists, he said, were really the most reactionary people in Britain, more dangerous than the Conservative party or Oxford University or the Anglican episcopate. All those institutions clearly identified themselves as enemy strongholds. The proletarians knew how they would have to be dealt with. It was labour's ostensible friends, who could, and did, mislead the workers, or rather, not lead them at all, hold them in check, befog their consciousness, paralyse their will. Trotsky was not against British trade unions. They had a great future, after the revolution, as 'the main lever of the economic transformation of the country,' as suppliers of 'the indispensable human personnel' for the socialist state apparatus, as 'organs of administration of the nationalized industry.' But such responsibilities could only be assumed after the proletariat had seized political power. As Trotsky understood it, that seizure of power was strictly the CPGB's business, not the trade unions'. The TUC would then be assigned its specific duties by the Communist Party. All it had to do in the meantime, to make it fit for the obligations it would assume in the future, was to free itself 'of conservative officials, of superstitious blockheads, who from heaven knows where expect a "peaceful" miracle.' That was as much as could, or should, be expected of it. To assume the trade unions would actually organize revolution was to succumb to 'monstrous illusion.'

A year later, in mid-1926, British Communists would discern serious errors in Trotsky's argument. They would even claim it demonstrated uncomradely hostility towards them. Such was not, however, the

[1] Leon Trotsky, *Where is Britain Going?* Revised edition (London: Communist Party of Great Britain, 1926). For comment on the impact of the book, see Deutscher, *Trotsky*, pp. 217–23.

CPGB's first reaction. The Party press gave the volume high grades for brilliance, and apparently could not fault it ideologically. British Communists would not follow Trotsky, however, in any absolute condemnation of TUC reformists. The CPGB's 7th Congress, at the very end of May 1925, demonstrated considerable warmth toward the General Council leftists.[1] As a result of their efforts, 'we have seen a real class basis given to the propaganda and activities of what has been described as the oldest and most conservative trade union movement in the world.' Nobody denied the 'differences of opinion between our party and the General Council,' but in backing the effort for trade union unity, the TUC leftists had, whether they knew it or not, raised a question which was 'not just a question of trade unionism pure and simple' but a revolutionary question. Unity was not an end in itself. The whole point of it was to rally the workers against the bourgeoisie. The net result of an all-inclusive international would be to ensure 'the gradual development of working class power up to the point that it can overthrow capitalism.'

British and Russian trade unions must intensify the fight for unity. The joint advisory council must be transformed into a Unity Committee and must agitate and propagandize for the cause all over the world. It should agree to 'take upon itself the initiative of calling a world conference' to establish the new trade union international. That international should base itself squarely on the principle of class struggle. 'It must recognize that all concessions which it can extract from capitalism are only temporary, and that workers can only win real freedom by overthrowing the capitalist system. To this end the trade union movement must develop its organisation and must be prepared to co-operate with other working-class bodies moving to the attack on capitalism.' Unlike Trotsky, then, the CPGB clearly did have a revolutionary role in mind for trade unionism.

Not all Party members were happy about that point of view. One comrade pointed out that 'certain individuals...prominent in this fight for international unity' should be regarded 'with very great suspicion,' and suggested the campaign be delayed 'until economic forces have developed in this country a little more' and 'the ground was more fertile' for such an effort. Harry Pollitt, however, was firm. He conceded the dangers of opportunism, and admitted that 'certain individuals' in the

---

[1] Communist Party of Great Britain, *Report of the Seventh National Congress, May 30–June 1, 1925* (London: Communist Party of Great Britain, 1925). The relevant materials are Harry Pollitt's opening address, pp. 5–12, the debate on trade union unity, pp. 66–74, and the resolutions on the subject, pp. 188–94.

TUC leadership did indeed have to be treated with suspicion. It was dangerous, however, to overstress the point. It was not only British trade union leaders who were involved in the unity campaign, he recalled, but Russian ones too, 'in whom we have complete confidence.' It might be true that some General Council members only spoke out for internationalism because they were pushed into doing so by the rank and file, but if that were the case, the CPGB's responsibility was to make sure they got pushed harder, not to relax the pressure on them. That meant building up the Party organization. 'Unless there is...a strong mass Communist Party, bringing the working class under a powerful Communist lead, all the demands and attempts made to achieve trade union unity can never fructify.' A stronger CPGB, cooperating with and propelling a trade union left it did not basically trust – that was Pollitt's prescription, then, and that was what was recommended in the resolutions. For the next year, Communist attacks would be directed not at Purcell, Swales or Hicks, but just at Thomas, Cramp and Clynes. The unity campaign had had just the effect so many ultra-Reds had feared it might: Communists had gone soft on reformists. General Council leftists might be chided occasionally, scolded. They might be urged to do much more than they already were. But it was all done with un-Bolshevik gentility and delicacy. Leftists published their views in the Communist press. Leftists and Communists sponsored meetings jointly and appeared on platforms together. So long as that sort of thing continued, the ideological lines between Communism and leftism were bound to become blurred and poorly-defined. Any united front involved ideological risks. The CPGB took the risks from the spring of 1925 to the spring of 1926. The unity campaign, and the establishment of the Anglo-Russian Committee, were what prompted it to do so.

'Red Friday' – July 31, 1925 – must have persuaded many comrades the united front had fully justified itself. British labour flexed its muscles, pronounced its demands with measured determination, and prepared to fight for them if necessary. As a result, it never had to. It got everything it wanted. Unity and militancy secured for the TUC its greatest triumph since the war.

It had all begun a month earlier, on June 30. The coal mine operators gave the required one-month notice of their intention to terminate their 1921 agreement with the Miners' Federation of Great Britain.[1] The old

---

[1] Material on Red Friday is plentiful. Convenient summaries may be found in Crook, *General Strike*, pp. 285–98, Hutt, *British Working Class*, pp. 111–16, and *Annual Register, 1925*, pp. 64–7, 75–82.

agreement, the first pact on a national basis, had tied wage rates to profits. If the mines failed to show a profit at all, however, or if profits were low, MFGB members were still guaranteed a basic minimum wage rate. They had been, that is, under the old agreement. But the operators now offered new terms, under which the minimum wage would have been abandoned, pay scales would have been negotiated locally rather than nationally, and the result would have been a drop in wages of anywhere from 13 to 48 per cent, depending on the district.

The MFGB refused to accept any such outrage and appealed to the General Council to support its stand. On July 10, the General Council appointed a Special Industrial Committee of nine members, headed by Swales, to follow the negotiations carefully and to summon a special General Council meeting, if necessary, to deal with the crisis.[1] Meanwhile, the talks between miners and mine operators produced no agreement. The Baldwin government intervened at the last minute to mediate the dispute but achieved nothing. The MFGB despaired of any help from official quarters, and turned again to the General Council. If a strike were to succeed, coal users would have to be prevented from bringing in supplies from abroad. The only way to stop them was to slap a complete embargo on any movement of coal at all. The railway workers and the transport workers would have to cooperate. The General Council agreed to make the arrangements. On July 31, a thousand delegates from TUC-affiliated unions met in conference. Unanimously, virtually without discussion, they promised to mobilize the whole power of the labour movement in behalf of the miners. All key unions pledged themselves to the cause. Strike notices went out. As of midnight, July 31, no coal would move in Britain at all.

The government was not prepared for such a show of labour strength. It had a plan, an inherited plan, to maintain the flow of supplies in the event of an industrial crisis. The scheme dated from the labour unrest of the 1919–21 era. It centred on a special cabinet committee, the Supply and Transport Committee, and involved numerous sub-committees, eleven regional headquarters, and much more. The Home Secretary had revealed the existence of the plan at one of the first cabinet meetings back in 1924. It needed modernization, he noted. It assumed, for example, the existence of a large army, which Britain was no longer maintaining. Even though 'no grave emergency' was 'immediately

---

[1] 'Mining Dispute and General Strike, G. C. Decisions,' a file drawn up for use at the Special Conference of Trade Union Executives, 1927, file 1 1/2.2, decision No. 1, p. 1, TUC Archives.

anticipated,' therefore, Joynson-Hicks had proposed to spruce the plan up, and his colleagues had authorized him to do so.[1] It had not been easy, apparently. The arrangements for securing emergency services were adequate, Baldwin told the cabinet July 30, 1925, and the Supply and Transport Organization was complete, but it was, after all, 'only a skeleton and could not be put in operation until volunteers had come forward. Volunteers, however, could not be called for until an emergency was proclaimed.' The government would then require 'a few days' – a few too many, apparently – to sort out the volunteers, examine their qualifications, and enrol the most valuable in positions where they could do the most good. In short, for all of Joynson-Hicks' efforts, the government was not really ready for a showdown with the TUC. It had not expected one. It had not believed labour would really unite.[2]

With the greatest reluctance, therefore, and by a vote that was far from unanimous, the cabinet agreed, on July 30, that the payment of a subsidy to the mining industry was to be preferred to fighting a national strike. The prime minister was authorized to reverse his solemn declaration of just the day before and offer a subsidy. Miners' wages would be maintained for nine more months, until May 1, 1926, at the old rates. The government would grant the coal operators the necessary subsidies. In the meantime, a Royal Commission would make a detailed study of the whole problem. The government had bought the time it wanted.

Labour relished its success, and trumpeted the triumph immoderately. Red Friday, as July 31 was promptly dubbed, was 'the biggest victory the Labour Movement has won yet in the course of its history,' the *Daily Herald* rejoiced.[3] Solidarity had proved its might, and 'if it chooses, Labour can use this giant's strength to gain everything on which its heart is set.' The editorialist went on, of course, to note that labour's leaders were sensible and responsible people and would never abuse the power they had accumulated. It is doubtful whether the City – or the Baldwin government – were reassured by such pledges.

The British Communist Party was overjoyed by Red Friday, and indeed, even managed to claim credit for it.[4] The victory seemed to vindicate the decision of the CPGB's 7th Congress, back in May, to cooperate with TUC leftists. The left had been in complete control on Red Friday, and had won. It had rejected 'the shoddy middle-class

[1] Cabinet Papers, 1924, CAB 24.168, C.P. 496(24), 19 Nov., 1924.
[2] Cabinet Conclusions, 1925, CAB 23.50, Conclusions 42(25)1, 30 July, 1925.
[3] *Daily Herald*, 1 Aug., 1925.
[4] See Ferguson's speech to the ECCI, 26 Feb., 1926, in CPGB, *Orders from Moscow?*, pp. 17–34.

policy of the Webbs and the MacDonalds' and accepted 'the Class-War policy of the Communist Party,' Gallacher exulted.[1] The so-called moderates were no use whatsoever in the crisis. 'They weren't wanted... The leadership passed into the hands of good proletarians like Swales, Hicks, Cook and Purcell.' 'These comrades,' Gallacher continued, 'must be encouraged and strengthened...In the stern, tough voice of Swales *spoke the working-class Dictatorship.*' The faction he and his friends represented 'must be developed and stimulated so that it may be possible to pass from defensive to offensive action.'

Palme Dutt was not quite as extravagant as Gallacher, but he was clearly impressed.[2] In 1924 he had been the most vocal of Communists in deprecating the pseudo-left reformists and warning his comrades not to trust them. Now he was all for them. They were more and more taking a revolutionary line, he admitted. They had, in effect, provided the workers an alternate political leadership to that of the Labour party. He was especially encouraged by Swales' speeches. 'In the present stage,' he concluded, 'the language of the Left Trade Union leaders is the closest indication of the advance of the British working class to Revolution.'

For all its delight in the Red Friday victory, however, and its interest in the men who had achieved it, the CPGB was still uneasy. The miners had scored no positive gains, after all. They had just avoided being obliged to accept an immediate loss. What had been achieved, then, was only 'an unstable truce' and only temporary. It expired in nine months. After that, not industrial peace, but a new round of conflicts, was to be anticipated. 'The capitalist class will prepare for a crushing attack upon the workers,' the Party warned. 'If the workers are doped by the peace talks and do not make effective counter preparations then they are doomed to shattering defeat.' Labour must get ready. The General Council must be strengthened. Local Councils of Action must be formed. The need for 'relentless class struggle' must be frankly recognized. The next test could be decisive.[3]

The warnings were timely, and in retrospect, one must conclude the CPGB foresaw events more accurately than the General Council did.

---

[1] *Workers' Weekly,* 7 Aug., 1925.

[2] R. Palme Dutt, 'The Capitalist Offensive in Britain,' *Inprecorr,* v, 62 (6 Aug., 1925), 853–6. The Gallacher–Dutt opinion was not, it might be noted, unanimous. For the views of one Communist spokesman still disturbed at the TUC left, see G. Allison, 'Imperialism and the British Labour Movement,' *ibid.,* pp. 859–60.

[3] *Workers' Weekly,* 7 Aug., 1925. The warnings were repeated with more and more urgency, in subsequent editions. The CPGB continued to demand that the TUC prepare for the test in May. So did Profintern. See, for example, the manifesto in *Inprecorr,* v, 64 (13 Aug., 1925), 915–16.

The government was indeed mortified at being defeated and determined to reverse the decision at the first opportunity. Sir William Joynson-Hicks was quite explicit in an address delivered the day after Red Friday.[1] Men like Cook and Purcell, men in close touch with Moscow, men who gloried in their honorary memberships in the Moscow Soviet, were conspiring to destroy the British economy, Jix charged. The legitimate trade unions had been infiltrated by Communists. Those were the men the government had to deal with. He was convinced Zinoviev was still in touch with people in England, and was using his contacts and his revolutionary experience 'to destroy and ruin us.' Sooner or later the question would have to be faced, and one way or the other, resolved. Was England to be governed by a Parliament or by a handful of trade union leaders? If the trade unions got the upper hand, it would amount to the abolition of Parliament and the establishment of a British Soviet, he insisted.

The Home Secretary was just as forceful, and a good deal more explicit, in the privacy of cabinet meetings.[2] On August 5, he told his colleagues he was prepared to circulate to them a memorandum elaborating proposals whereby the general public could be invited to volunteer for the maintenance of vital services even before an industrial emergency arose. He also proposed to establish permanent headquarters all over Britain to direct emergency operations, to appoint permanent staff to such headquarters, and to increase the number of Special Constables. He also favoured an enquiry into the legal position of trade unions. It was not right that they could threaten the whole community with 'suffering and loss in connection with disputes with which they were not themselves directly involved.' He thought something could be done about it by new legislation. The cabinet thought so, too. A number of his proposals were adopted just two days later, and the ministers agreed to discuss the rest of them after the Parliamentary recess. The government clearly did not intend to be humiliated twice.

VI

British trade unionism never before moved as far left as it did at Scarborough in September of 1925. The delegates were all still in a kind of euphoria over their Red Friday triumph. They had stood fast, stood

[1] *The Times*, 3 Aug., 1925.
[2] Cabinet Conclusions, 1925, **CAB 23.50, Conclusions** 43(25)3(a)(b), 5 Aug., 1925, and 44(25)2, 7 Aug., 1925.

together, and faced up to the bosses without flinching; the bosses had given way. The secret of working-class power was unity, and unity became the dominant *leitmotif* at Scarborough. Unity at home implied more power for the General Council. Unity abroad required creation of an all-inclusive trade union international.

Even before the Congress began, moderates were anticipating trouble. The 'communistic T.U. leaders' had taken over the General Council, Mrs Webb informed her diary, and they were 'plunging head over ears into grandiose schemes of immediate and revolutionary changes.'[1] Swales' presidential address, opening the Congress, must have confirmed many of her worst fears.[2] He urged adoption of 'militant and progressive' policies to 'unify, consolidate and inspire our rank and file.' The General Council had to be able to marshal its resources as quickly and effectively as the bosses marshalled theirs. International unity was also essential, and that meant, in the first instance, making a place for the Russian unions in IFTU. The General Council had done what it could to mediate between Moscow and Amsterdam, and it was a pity the two sides were still kept apart by such minor differences. The TUC must persist in its efforts, Swales emphasized.

It was a good speech. It was robust, tough and assertive. It matched the mood of the Congress. The radicalism of the meeting surprised even the National Minority Movement. So long as what was involved was only a statement of left-wing principle, requiring no specific action, the delegates were ready to whoop it through with gusto. Almost unanimously, Congress approved NMM resolutions condemning the Dawes Plan, opposing imperialism, demanding withdrawal of British troops from China and expressing solidarity with 'our working class Chinese comrades.'

The most surprising vote of all was the 2-to-1 majority for a motion recommending the establishment of shop committees as 'indispensible weapons in the struggle to force the capitalists to relinquish their grip on industry.' In effect, the TUC was agreeing to organize itself for revolutionary action. The resolution carried 2,456,000 to 1,281,000.

When the resolutions got more specific than that, however, when they involved something more than pious hopes, the delegates got cautious. Or perhaps it was just that the moderate tacticians got cleverer. In any event, a number of NMM suggestions were just never considered, were

---

[1] Webb, *Diaries, 1924–32*, p. 68.
[2] *1925 TUC: Report of Proceedings*, pp. 70–5. The material on Scarborough which follows derives principally from this volume. For comment on the Congress, see *Annual Register, 1925*, pp. 91–5; MacFarlane, *British Communist Party*, pp. 155–7; Hutt, *British Working Class*, pp. 115–18.

ruled out of order, or were sidestepped. The resolution, for example, which would have conferred on the General Council the power to organize and decree a general strike 'to assist a union defending a vital trade union principle' was referred back to the Council itself. The Council was authorized to recommend such a measure to a conference of union executives, and Congress empowered the executives to make the final decision. In effect, the TUC approved the idea in principle, shelved it in practice. And when the delegates got around to choosing a new General Council, they elected out-and-out rightists. Seven new members were named to the General Council at Scarborough, none of whom were associated with the Swales–Hicks–Purcell faction. They included two councillors who had resigned their TUC responsibilities in 1924 to serve in the MacDonald government: J. H. Thomas and Margaret Bondfield. Not only did both of them speak for the far right in the TUC, both of them spoke strongly and authoritatively. Both seemed able to influence the undecided votes in the General Council – and the undecideds often constituted a majority there! Among others elected to the General Council at Scarborough, the ablest, cleverest, and most forceful of the new personalities was Ernest Bevin of the Transport Workers. Although a protégé of Ben Tillett, Bevin did not share his mentor's ecstatic devotion to the Soviet Union. He could see no point in the Anglo-Russian trade union negotiations.[1] He too would be classified – not wholly fairly – as a rightist. These were the personalities, then, who would dominate the new General Council. As their chairman, they would choose staid, safe, cautious Arthur Pugh, a totally different sort of a man from Swales. The Scarborough Congress, then, the most ebulliently radical of them all, entrusted its destinies to a prudent and circumspect General Council. Students of British national character can draw horrid lessons from such fearsome inconsistencies.

The significance of the rightist victories only became apparent later. At the time, the left seemed to be sweeping everything before it. Its most well-publicized victories came in the fields of international trade union unity and of Anglo-Russian relations. Purcell had anticipated the debate in an article appearing in a Communist periodical on the very eve of the Congress.[2] Unity was essential, he wrote, not only to maintain the workers' living standards, but also to prevent war. The masses were for

---

[1] Alan Bullock, *The Life and Times of Ernest Bevin* (London: Heinemann, 1960), I, 262–3.
[2] A. A. Purcell, 'The Burning Question of International Unity,' *Labour Monthly*, VII, 9 (Sept., 1925), 524–9.

it, and only 'a small bunch of Amsterdam leaders' opposed it. The opposition was supported by the Socialist International, itself nothing more than an 'appendix to various continental capitalist governments.' The Secretary of that same international had 'perpetrated the most unscrupulous and contemptible attack yet' on the report of the TUC delegation to Russia, he noted. Such were the enemies of unity!

Purcell proposed establishment of a new international trade union federation by a world congress of all labour organizations, the same approach the Communists favoured. He differed from the Reds, however, on the key issue of timing. While 'we cannot expect a world congress to be convened tomorrow,' he wrote, 'one important step...can be taken at once. That is the affiliation of the Russian Trade Unions to the International Federation of Trade Unions. This should and can be achieved, without more ado, by a preliminary conference of both sides.' He urged the Anglo-Russian bloc to continue to press for such a conference.

The Times found such suggestions naive and dangerous.[1] The united front was a Communist trap. Giving in to Zinoviev would be a disastrous error. The TUC did not seem to realize the gravity of the decision it was about to reach. It was urged not to be gullible, not to allow itself 'to be outwitted or outmanoeuvred for the amusement of the Bolshevist wire-pullers or their [English] accomplices.'

The delegates were not much interested in *The Times*' counsels. They were more impressed by the candid geniality of Tomsky, back for his fourth visit to Britain and his second Congress in a row. The Soviets had written the General Council in June asking it to accept another 'fraternal delegation' at Scarborough. That sounded like more than one Russian, an embarrassment of riches. The Council carefully limited its invitation to 'one representative' of the All-Union Central Council of Trade Unions. For a while, it seemed unlikely there would be any. The Home Office was as reluctant as ever to have live, unmuzzled Bolsheviks prowling the streets untended. Eventually, however, Jix relented. Tomsky – plus two uninvited friends – appeared at Scarborough. The General Council wearily authorized the purchase of a pair of extra mementos. It had already invested in an elaborate sapphire-and-pearl pendant for Madame Tomsky. (One wonders what became of it!)[2]

[1] *The Times*, 31 Aug., 1925. The same general argument was repeated in editorials on 5 and 7 Sept., 1925.
[2] General Council Minutes, No. 342, 23 June, 1925; No. 446, 3 Sept., 1925; No. 459, 4 Sept., 1925.

Tomsky gave good value for money. His speech, on September 10, made a strong impression on practically everybody but Ramsay Mac-Donald, who walked out in the middle of it and did not come back for the translation.[1] Tomsky hoped the Congress would confirm and strengthen the growing friendship between British and Soviet workers. The past year had seen notable progress, he said. The TUC delegation to the USSR had produced a powerful report, finally telling the truth about conditions in Russia. The Anglo-Soviet Trade Union Conference, in April, had then brought the two movements still closer together. Out of the Conference had come the Joint Advisory Council. While it had not met yet, the very fact of its establishment had served to win the support of 'millions of workers' for the cause of trade union unity.

He would not repeat in detail the arguments for unity, Tomsky continued. He had outlined them last year at Hull. The basic objective, 'we state frankly,' was to bring together workers all over the world 'in their struggle against the class of capitalists.' Workers everywhere could agree on the 'one common aim that unites all of us,...the emancipation of labour from the yoke of capital.' So long as nobody disputed the objective, it was not vital that they all agree on the strategy for achieving it. Everybody knew where the Russians stood. They were not ashamed of their ideas. Their whole state reflected them. But they were not demanding that everybody agree with them. Why could there not be a diversity of opinions in the new international? On essentials, after all, they aimed at the same result.

He reviewed the negotiations with IFTU since the last Congress. After conducting a wearisome correspondence with Amsterdam, the Soviets had decided that direct business-like talks would get better results. But the IFTU set conditions on negotiations. It demanded the Russians commit themselves to abandoning the Red International, to betraying their friends, to entering Amsterdam on Amsterdam's terms. Moscow could not accept such dictates. After all, two trade union internationals did exist, and the aim should be to merge them, not to destroy one of them. Surely there was no danger in unconditional conversations, just to discuss the unity problem. Why should IFTU be afraid of frank talks? Moscow made no preliminary demands. It just refused to be treated as a defeated enemy. It looked to the TUC for support. 'When the Russian unions found they were alone in the struggle for unity they turned to the British Trade Union Movement, and their experience has told them

---

[1] *1925 TUC: Report of Proceedings*, pp. 474–8.

they did right...We have started the campaign together; let us finish it together.'

Tomsky had put a powerful argument. Nobody seemed anxious to dispute it, not even the IFTU's fraternal delegate, J. W. Brown. Brown declined even to discuss Moscow–Amsterdam negotiations, confining himself to agreeing that unity was desirable and denying that IFTU opposed it.[1] The Russians seemed to have an unanswerable case, and the General Council's report all but specifically endorsed it.[2] The Anglo-Russian bloc was making real progress in the quest for unity, the Council claimed. The visit of the English delegation to the USSR almost a year earlier had produced a genuine and meaningful rapprochement. The Trade Union Conference in April had strengthened relations between the two movements. A Joint Advisory Council had been established. TUC had pledged to convene a Moscow–Amsterdam conference itself if IFTU would not agree to summon one. If the Congress would endorse what had already been done, the leadership would continue the work, carry on the campaign, in the years to come.

Fred Bramley presented the General Council's case to the Congress.[3] He was a dying man and he knew it. He had only one last fight left in him. He chose to wage it on behalf of trade union unity and Anglo-Soviet cooperation, the causes for which he had expended his energies so prodigiously over the past fifteen months. The General Council's interventions on behalf of the Russians had won it few friends, he began. Instead, the past year had produced 'an unprecedented attack' both on the British labour movement as a whole, and on the individual leaders 'who have been carrying out your instructions' in the campaign for unity. Those so slandered had made no attempt to reply to the charges. They were responsible only to Congress and to its resolutions. They now sought approval for what they had done.

Soviet workers fully merited inclusion in the international movement, he argued. They had won a great revolution, 'the first revolution in all history aiming at and securing the overthrow of economic exploitation.' Indeed, the Russians had merely given concrete expression '...under certain circumstances and from a certain point of view...to the resolutions we have passed at Trades Union Congresses for many years.' He condemned the continental powers for their continued hostility to the USSR. Other states changed their political institutions as much as they pleased, and their neighbours still left them alone. 'But if you disturb the landed interest of a country and abolish the exploitation of the wage-

[1] *Ibid.*, pp. 471–3.   [2] *Ibid.*, p. 85.   [3] Bramley's speech is in *ibid.*, pp. 482–7.

earner, deal with the factory exploiter, and get rid of the privilege, property and power possessed by a minority, then you will have to face what Russia is now facing – isolation, boycott, and international persecution.' The Soviet Union was 'a nation at bay.' The Trades Union Congress could help bring her back into the international community. He asked approval of the Council's report.

Two draft resolutions on the subject had already been presented to the Congress, one from the Tailors and one from the Miners. The Tailors offered a Minority Movement proposal, urging international unity and deliberately omitting any mention of the existing Amsterdam federation. The Miners' proposal stuck to the Purcell formula of the year before, indicating the unity effort should be directed at enlarging IFTU to include the Russians. Both were considered by a Congress committee which, without much thought, tacked some reference to IFTU onto the Tailors' draft and brought that in. The small but vigilant NMM faction noted the change, protested it, and got the offending passage altered.[1] The wording was changed from *the* International Federation of Trade Unions to *an* International Federation – all the difference in the world, from the Communist point of view. Sam Elsbury of the Tailors, a Minority Movement stalwart, then presented the final version of the resolution to the Congress. 'This Congress,' it read, 'records appreciation of the General Council's efforts to promote international unity, and urges the incoming General Council to do everything in their power towards securing world-wide unity of the Trade Union Movement through an all-inclusive International Federation of Trade Unions.'[2]

It took Congress 17 minutes to hear the resolution presented, seconded and passed. Jimmy Thomas indicated he wanted to speak to the question, but could not get the chairman to recognize him. The delegates shouted the motion through on a voice vote. *The Times'* labour correspondent was aghast.[3] He had been confidently predicting all summer that the pro-Bolsheviks on the General Council who were promoting the entry of Muscovite conspirators into IFTU would get their comeuppance at Scarborough. And all they had gotten was cheers. The resolution had been rammed through Congress relentlessly, he protested. The consideration had been 'wholly one-sided.' 'It is inconceivable that the Congress saw the implications of the policy it endorsed.' He could only conclude that 'the idea of the united front has exercised a sort of fascination over the delegates.'

[1] Petrowski, *Anglo-Russische Komitee*, pp. 19–20.
[2] Text in *1925 TUC: Report of Proceedings*, p. 569.   [3] *The Times*, 11 Sept., 1925.

The delegates were hardly concerned at *The Times'* opinion. It was rather a lark to offend the press. They even compounded the crime by voting a second pro-Russian resolution on the subject of credits. Once again, the initiative was Bramley's. Members of the Russian trade delegation had approached him with a tale of woe. They wanted to place a five million pounds order in Lancashire for textile machinery, but British banks refused to provide them any credit facilities. The General Council voted to present an emergency resolution to Congress. Swales argued the case for the resolution strongly in his presidential address. The delegates backed him, and approved a motion expressing 'concern and profound disappointment' at all the lost Russian orders and urging the government to take action.[1]

All the General Council's recommendations on relations with the Soviets had gone through Congress on voice votes. The Anglo-Russian trade union bloc never seemed solider. The rank and file were enthusiastic about it. Tomsky decided to consolidate his gains. He approached Bramley to ask him if the Anglo-Russian Committee could hold its first session right after Congress adjourned, while he and Dogadov were still there in Britain. The General Council agreed, and the meeting was set for September 17 in London.[2]

It had been a memorable Congress. Reactions to it were all very predictable. What the CPGB called 'the capitalist press' – all the daily papers but the *Herald* – was resolutely hostile. The *Daily Mail* was angriest and most virulent. *The Times*, almost as if weary of the whole controversy, merely sponsored a tediously dignified series of articles exposing Communist subversion in Britain region by region and union by union. The press reflected official government attitudes. Sir Philip Cunliffe-Lister, President of the Board of Trade, told a Conservative rally in Yorkshire that 'the men who for the time being have captured the...Trades Union Congress are determined to convert the trade union movement...into a revolutionary and Communist organization.'[3]

The Communist Party was ecstatic about Scarborough.[4] Given the current rate of progress, Harry Pollitt wrote, the Minority Movement would soon take over the TUC altogether. The resolution on international trade union unity was especially gratifying. Swales' presidential address

---

[1] General Council Minutes, Nos. 442, 463, 3 Sept., 1925, No. 58, 28 Oct., 1925; *1925 TUC: Report of Proceedings*, pp. 71, 489, 512.

[2] General Council Minutes, No. 468, 11 Sept., 1925.

[3] *The Times*, 14 Sept., 1925.

[4] For characteristic reactions, see *Workers' Weekly*, 11 Sept. (Pollitt) and 18 Sept., 1925 (Murphy), and *Inprecorr*, v, 71 (24 Sept., 1925), 1054–5 (Pollitt).

was magnificent. Bramley was never more eloquent. The comrades only found one or two features of the Congress distressing. They were not happy, for example, about the failure of Hicks, Purcell, and some other supposed leftists to speak out on key resolutions. More generally, they were regretful that the left wingers did not just crush the rightists altogether, which they certainly could have. Those claiming to be on the left had a great opportunity. They could now stand forward, with the CPGB, and take prominent places in the revolutionary movement. Indeed, they must do so. Otherwise they would inevitably revert to the right again. The future was with Communism, and the leftists had better not be left behind.

Moscow was pleased at Scarborough, too.[1] The Soviet press called the Congress one of the most significant events of recent times. It rejoiced in how the resolutions had rebuffed that ogre, J. H. Thomas, and confessed some chagrin – and perplexity – that he had nevertheless been elected to the new General Council. Still, the Congress was a victory, and its lustre could not be tarnished. The voice of Scarborough would reinvigorate the oppressed working classes of Europe, spur them back to the path of revolution. Comintern headquarters congratulated the CPGB for exerting such marked influence on the labour movement.[2] United front tactics were paying off, Zinoviev gloated.[3] Communists, socialists and non-party proletarians were finding a common cause. Treacherous western trade union bureaucrats were more and more forced to side openly with the bourgeoisie. The Amsterdam citadel was crumbling.

[1] *Pravda, Izvestiia*, 6–13 Sept., 1925; *The Times*, 18 Sept., 1925.
[2] Secretary of the ECCI and Chief of the Org. Department of the ECCI to CEC of CPGB, 26 Sept., 1925, in Great Britain, Parliament, *Communist Papers*, Cmd. 2682 (1926), pp. 18–19.
[3] *Izvestiia*, 9 Sept., 1925.

4

Marriage (September 1925–May 1926)

I

The Anglo-Russian Committee met for the first time – at Tomsky's suggestion – on September 17, immediately after the Trades Union Congress adjourned.[1] The British members were all still luxuriating in the heady Scarborough rhetoric about working-class solidarity and proletarian internationalism. They had a clear mandate for the unity movement from the rank and file. Their responsibility was to translate the sentiments of their constituency into achievement.

To start with, however, there was very little for the Committee to do except get itself organized and make sure the world knew it existed. The next substantive move in the unity game was not its to make, but Amsterdam's. The IFTU General Council had yet to respond to the Russians' May 19 bid for unconditional talks.[2] It was pointless for the English and Russians to discuss counter-strategy until that decision was made. They turned their attention instead, then, to simpler matters. There was that vexing application of the Norwegian Trades Union Federation for affiliation with the Committee, as if the Committee was to become the nucleus of some brand-new International. Bramley had brusquely, almost rudely, turned the Norwegians down quite on his own responsibility. The Russians were unhappy at the apparent discourtesy. The Committee decided to send a new, softer message, expressing appreciation for the Norwegian comrades' support, assuring them they would be kept up-to-date on the Committee's work, and informing them 'that the question of their participation in the work of the Council might be considered later on.'[3]

[1] The minutes of the meeting in the TUC Archives, File 947/220, A.R. 1, are incomplete. The English text of the final joint statement can be found in the *Daily Herald*, 24 Sept., 1925 and the Russian text in *Pravda* of the same date. See also Trades Union Congress, *Report of Proceedings at the 58th General Trades Union Congress (1926)*, Ed. by Walter M. Citrine (London: Cooperative Printing Society, [1926]), p. 245.   [2] See above, pp. 157–9.
[3] The soft reply to the Norwegian enquiry evoked additional applications for admission to the Committee – from the official Finnish trade union federation and from breakaway federations in Spain, Japan, Sweden and elsewhere. The Russians suggested accepting such applications for membership, but the English finally vetoed them all. Aleksandr Lozovsky, *British and Russian Workers* (London: National Minority Movement, 1926), pp. 17–18.

On purely structural matters, the Russians deferred completely to their English friends. The TUC's General Secretary, for example, was designated Secretary of the Committee, and his office, in the TUC building, Committee headquarters. The British, then, could shuffle the papers. In return, the Russians wanted some say in what went into the papers. In particular, they wanted this first meeting of the Committee to produce an emphatic new demand for trade union unity. Nobody objected, and the document that emerged, although some of the wording sounded a lot like Purcell, might perfectly well have been produced in Comintern headquarters. Bourgeois governments had become 'more and more reactionary and destructive to working class interests,' it alleged. The danger of imperialist war was 'nearer and more evident' in Morocco, in Syria, in China. Trade union unity was more vital than ever. An 'all-inclusive world-wide federation of trade unions' was inevitable, and proletarians everywhere were exhorted to participate in the struggle to build one now.

The manifesto got an unexpectedly critical scrutiny from the TUC's new General Council on September 22. Jimmy Thomas and Margaret Bondfield, back in the inner circles again, had already set out to rescue trades unionism from what Beatrice Webb later called 'the little knot of silly folk who led it into the Scarborough morass of pseudo-Communism.'[1] Thomas was not a regular attender at the General Council – he skipped over half its meetings during the next two years – nor did he participate with any great regularity in its International Committee, of which he was also a member.[2] But when he was there he was forceful and persistent. He had his doubts about the Russians from the beginning. He suspected they aimed at getting the Committee involved in more than just trade union matters, extending it into political questions. For Thomas, politics was the business of the Labour party, not the TUC, and he did not want the enthusiasts of the Committee committing trades unionism to stands which might embarrass his friends on the Labour front benches. So the Committee's proposed statement got a long and careful review. It was finally adopted, and approved for publication. It almost had to be. The Russians had already gone home, with Citrine and Hicks in tow, and amending the manifesto was therefore impracticable. The General Council therefore contented itself with preventing the Com-

[1] Webb, *Diaries, 1924–32*, pp. 80–1.
[2] My evidence for the lackadaisical attendance record is the General Council minutes. Thomas' autobiography (*My Story*) has nothing at all to say about the Anglo-Russian Committee. Then again, it hasn't much to say about anything else. He moves from a singularly uninformative chapter on the general strike to a singularly tedious chapter on 'Some Cherished Memories of the Royal House.'

mittee from committing such indiscretions in the future. From now on, it resolved, except in 'special emergencies,' proposed joint statements of the Committee on international questions would have to be submitted to the General Council before adoption. Even in emergency situations, the Committee's pronouncements had to accord with previously accepted General Council policies. The Council wanted its Committee under control.[1]

Nobody, however, suggested ditching the unity campaign altogether, not even Thomas. Perhaps he shared the fantasies of *The Times*' labour correspondent, who thought Tomsky might be enlisting the support of friends in the west in order to escape the domination of rivals back home.[2] The Russian trade unions might be hoping, with English support, to free themselves from the despotism of the Soviet Party and Government. Such speculations intrigued many TUC leaders. Walter Citrine and George Hicks, whom Tomsky had invited to come back with him to Russia, hoped to test them while there. Neither of them had ever been to the USSR before. Hicks was one of the few prominent TUC leftists who had not. For Citrine, the trip was inescapable. Bramley was critically ill. (He died October 14). As heir-apparent to the TUC General Secretaryship and thus, by extension, the Anglo-Russian Committee Secretaryship, Citrine had to get to know the people with whom he was going to be associated. This was his opportunity.

In retrospect, the trip probably contributed little to Anglo-Russian understanding.[3] Hicks and Citrine found the atmosphere in the USSR unsettling. Citrine recalled later that everybody seemed to be weighing their words too carefully. Nobody seemed able to say what he felt. It was as if some outside power had everybody firmly in line. Tomsky proved an especial enigma. They liked the man personally. He was genial, he was a genuine workingman, and he liked convivial talk. But he never said what they wanted him to. They pressed him on the connection between the Russian trade union movement and the Soviet Communist Party. Did the Party dominate the labour movement? Was it wise for the two to be so closely identified? Did not the unions risk losing their independence to the State?

---

[1] On Thomas' stand inside the Council, and his influence there, I am relying on the personal testimony of Lord Citrine. The resolution restricting the Committee's authority to make stands on political issues is in General Council Minutes, No. 2, 22 Sept., 1925.   [2] *The Times*, 30 Nov., 1925.

[3] My sources for the trip, and for Citrine's and Hicks' reaction to it, are Lord Citrine's personal testimony, his autobiography (*Men and Work*, pp. 95–7) and *The Times*, 30 Nov., 1925.

Tomsky professed to see no problem. It was all one movement – the proletarian movement. The trade unions were part of it; so was the Party; so was the state. 'We have hardly any real differences because we are the same people.' The line never varied. Yet, somehow, both Citrine and Hicks had the impression that Tomsky was less orthodox than he sounded, that his conception of trades unionism, in particular, was quite similar to theirs, and that he was a trade unionist first, responsible primarily to his worker constituents, and a Communist Party functionary only secondarily.

While Citrine and Hicks talked trade union unity in Russia, privately, Purcell was talking it publicly in Atlantic City, New Jersey, as the TUC's fraternal delegate to the annual convention of the American Federation of Labor.[1] He waxed eloquent about the progress made in the Soviet Union, and suggested American workers could learn much from the Russian experience. He recommended they send a delegation to the USSR, as Britain had. He urged them to join the IFTU, and work within that organization, in partnership with the TUC, for an all-inclusive labour federation including the Russian unions.

He got an icy response. William Green, the AFL president, rejected Purcell's appeal out of hand. Communism was interested only in making revolution, not in the achievement of economic gains. Americans would never be taken in by such alien doctrines, and would never collaborate with those who preached them. The delegates agreed. A resolution favouring recognition of the Soviet Union won only two votes. The Anglo-Russian Committee was denounced as an 'attempt to destroy from ambush the freedom of workers in democratic countries.' The British were advised to remain 'loyal to the free institutions' of their own country. The *Washington Post* demanded Purcell's deportation.

The German labour movement was as scandalized by the Anglo-Russian entanglement as was the American. The Socialist newspaper, *Vorwärts*, found the Committee's first communiqué 'shameful'.[2] The English trade unions had become agents of Soviet foreign policy. They must now realize how their friendship with the Russians had alienated them from their colleagues on the continent. The Amsterdam unions could no longer keep silent. 'Millions of organized European trade unionists have looked on at these negotiations for unity with a mixture of incredulity and horror.'

---

[1] See his speech in *Trade Union Unity*, I, 8 (Nov., 1925), 124–5. Green's response is in *ibid.*, 126–7. See also *IFTU Press Reports*, v, 40 (22 Oct., 1925).

[2] *Vorwärts*, 29 Sept., 1925.

The Amsterdam bureaucrats hardly needed prompting. Indeed, Secretary Oudegeest had not waited for *Vorwärts'* signal. He was writing impassioned invective against the unity campaign even while the Committee was first meeting.[1] When the joint statement appeared, Oudegeest attacked even harder, chiding his British colleagues for hypocrisy.[2] They urged unity on others, they did not even practise it themselves, witness their contemptuous disdain for the National Minority Movement. In fact, he insisted, Amsterdam was as strongly for solidarity as anyone. IFTU would be happy to welcome the Russians in, on the same terms as everybody else. They refused to ask for admission on that basis, and the British had backed them up. Indeed, the TUC had supported the Russian line 'with so much zeal that occasionally they seem in their eagerness to have come very near overstepping the boundaries of loyalty to the IFTU and its affiliated national centres.' It was a 'peculiar form of radicalism' which had infected the English comrades. It could be disastrous to international trades unionism, and it was 'highly improbable,' therefore, that continental labour organizations would be influenced by it.

The TUC leftists could pooh-pooh their bad press across the Channel. They had to pay attention, however, when their friends in the Labour party rebuked them. The party's Annual Conference met at Liverpool just three weeks after Scarborough. Many of the same people attended both meetings. This time, however, the leftists took a drubbing. Beatrice Webb attributed it to platform leadership. 'In both cases,' she observed, 'the thousand delegates trooped after the man who sat on the platform and managed the business.'[3] The man on the platform this time was the Railwaymen's C. T. Cramp. His opening address warned the delegates of the dangers of armed revolution, and called for class cooperation rather than class conflict. The Conference responded, by decisive majorities. Its resolutions denounced all Reds and Red sympathizers, decreed Communists ineligible for Labour party membership even on an individual basis, and enjoined all trade unions not to send known Com-

---

[1] *IFTU Press Reports*, V, 36 (24 Sept., 1925), 1–2.   [2] *Ibid.*, V, 37 (1 Oct., 1925), 4–5.
[3] Webb, *Diaries, 1924–32*, pp. 74–5. The report of the Conference is *Report of the 25th Annual Conference Held in the St. George's Hall, Liverpool, on September 29th and 30th and October 1st and 2nd, 1925* (London: 1925). Cramp's address is on pp. 181–9. The relevant resolutions are on p. 352. See also Annual Register, 1925, pp. 97–9. For Lozovsky's analysis of what went wrong, see 'Scarborough and Liverpool,' a report at the Printers' House, 9 Oct., 1925, in *Angliiskii Proletariat na Rasputi*, pp. 139–62. For additional comment, see Hutt, *British Working Class*, pp. 118–21 and G. D. H. Cole, *A History of the Labour Party from 1914* (London: Routledge and Kegan Paul, 1948), pp. 146, 176–8.

munists as delegates to party conferences. 'A great and welcome affirmation,' decreed *The Times*. 'A triumph for constitutionalism,' affirmed Ramsay MacDonald.

For four years, English Communists had been trying to insinuate themselves into the Labour party. This was the most unmistakable rebuff ever. Shapurji Saklatvala, the CPGB's only MP, urged 'merciless' retaliation, including a campaign to persuade trade union branches to affiliate directly with the Communist Party.[1] If Labour then threw them out, what difference did it make. The Communists were the only genuine anti-capitalists around, and they should present themselves as such to the workers. It amounted to abandoning the united front altogether.

Cooler heads, however, prevailed. Harry Pollitt did not deny the Party had suffered a defeat at Liverpool.[2] The Communist response, however, must not be to junk the united front but to extend it, to adapt the tactics which had succeeded so brilliantly at Scarborough to the Labour party. The CPGB must seek a new alliance with the Labour left. It must call for a 'common campaign' for a 'common working class policy.' If the comrades acted quickly, they might yet 'wipe away the shame and betrayal of. . . Liverpool' at the 1926 Labour Conference.

The right wing reaction so potent at Liverpool was even more conspicuous at the Conservative Conference, meeting at Brighton a week later. The Tories recommended their government ban the CPGB and gaol its leaders. In fact, the Baldwin cabinet had authorized a secret investigation of Communist subversion even before the Conference met, and on October 13, after six days' cursory explorations, decided it had enough evidence to put a dozen Red chiefs away for seditious libel and incitement to mutiny. A raid on Party headquarters netted not only the twelve culprits but also some confidential and embarrassing documents, which the government later shamelessly retailed in a white paper. It was terribly distressing, seen from Moscow. Soviet trade union leaders suggested even firmer working-class unity, nationally and internationally, as the only effective response to such infamy.[3]

The Russians were clearly in something of a dilemma as of the autumn

---

[1] Saklatvala to the Political Bureau, CPGB, 7 Oct., 1925, in *Communist Papers*, Cmd. 2682 (1926), 72–3.

[2] 'The Liverpool Labour Party Conference,' *Inprecorr*, v, 74 (15 Oct., 1925), 1099–100.

[3] For the Congress, see *The Times*, 8–12 Oct., 1925. The documents relating to the arrest of the 12 CPGB leaders are Cabinet Conclusions, 1925, CAB. 23.51, Conclusion 47(25)2, 7 Oct., 1925 and 48(25) 2A, 13 Oct., 1925. The confiscated papers were published in *Communist Papers*, Cmd. 2682 (1926). The response of the Soviet trade union leaders is in *Inprecorr*, v, 86 (10 Dec., 1925), 1301.

of 1925. In spite of the set-backs at Amsterdam, Atlantic City, and Liverpool, they finally had that organic relationship with the British trade unions which they had sought so strenuously. They were delighted with it, and expected great things from it, but they seemed to vacillate on just how to use it. The Comintern bureaucracy, still headed by Zinoviev, wanted to exploit the Committee to wage revolution in Britain. That was, after all, the whole purpose behind adopting united front tactics in the first place – to expose and discredit the trade union aristocracy and win the proletariat for Communism and militancy. What was important was not the good will of the reformist elite but 'the revolutionizing of the British proletariat' for the first time since Chartism. The purpose of the Committee, then, was not to pander to TUC hierarchs, but rather to help the British proletariat shake them off and 'turn to Russia' for guidance instead.[1]

Such tactics, however, required Communist Party members to demonstrate uncharacteristic patience and restraint over the short term. It was hardly comfortable, after all, for English comrades to watch their ideological brethren from the Soviet Union amicably hobnobbing with class traitors from the TUC magistrature during Committee meetings. Might not such associations serve to legitimize the reformists in the eyes of their followers, and thus, finally, divorce the western proletariat from Bolshevism?

Stalin, for one, saw no problem.[2] The leftward swing of the trade unions would strengthen Communist influence in the end. The old reformist leaders were already in eclipse anyway. Comrades sometimes failed to understand that. 'Instead of lending a hand to the workers moving left from social democracy, they begin to rebuke them as traitors and push them away.' That was poor Marxism and poor strategy. Western workers felt close to their unions and respected their union leaders. That must be remembered when 'exposing' reformists. To hurl abuse at them prematurely would only create the impression that Communists were out to wreck the organized labour movement. Such tactics would not win over the masses, but alienate them.

[1] For this point of view, see Agitprop Department, of ECCI, 'Theses for Propagandists on the Second Anniversary of Lenin's Death,' 14 Jan., 1926, in Degras, *Communist International: Documents*, I, 237–43. See also Zinoviev's speech to the Leningrad Soviet on 6 Nov., 1925, 'Eight Years of Revolution,' in *The Communist International*, Nos. 18 and 19 (Combined Issue) (1926), pp. 3–25. The quotations cited are from *Communist International*, pp. 8, 13 and Degras, I, 240–1.

[2] Interview with participants in a conference of the Agitation and Propaganda Department, 14 Oct., 1925, Stalin, *Sochineniia*, VII, 235–7.

Stalin was not explicitly challenging the assumption that the major purpose of united front manoevures was still the successful waging of revolution. In fact, however, he was undoubtedly considering an alternative mission for front organizations, and for the Committee specifically – as useful weapons in the armoury of the Soviet Foreign Commissariat. To enlist the English trade union movement in securing Russian national interests would be a diplomatic *coup*. The first Committee statement, ranging over foreign policy issues from Germany to China and reflecting Soviet viewpoints in every instance, must have delighted the Narkomindel. But if such was to be the Committee's major function, it would not do to alienate those reformist leaders who were so agreeably doing one's bidding. The British Foreign Office would never allow itself to be influenced by the demands of a delegation of Communist agit-prop specialists. It might, however, heed the respected and responsible opinions of distinguished labour moderates. In such circumstances, the Committee would never serve its purpose if TUC reformists were 'exposed' and ousted, nor would it help if, under Communist attack, they neglected the concerns of the proletarian fatherland, the USSR. Instead of being attacked, then, they should be propped up, sustained and coddled. Stalin of course, never mouthed such heresies openly, but he was clearly intrigued by the Committee's possibilities in the diplomatic arena, and if those possibilities were ever going to be fully exploited, it was silly jeopardizing them just to get in a few kicks at the likes of Jimmy Thomas.

Foreign policy issues seemed crucial to the Soviet leadership during the latter part of 1925, and relations with Great Britain were especially worrisome.[1] The Russians were convinced that the west was trying to seduce their only friend, Germany, into a new anti-Soviet coalition. They were anxious for a *détente*. Foreign Commissar Chicherin almost pleaded with the English to state their price for some new agreement. Chamberlain refused to bargain. His policy was to keep the USSR on ice, maintaining relations with her at the minimum correct level and no more. His cabinet colleagues, however, showed not even that much restraint, and Birkenhead, Joynson-Hicks and Churchill, in particular, indulged regularly in spirited anti-Soviet invective. The Russians responded in kind.

---

[1] The best brief summary in English is in Carr, *Socialism in One Country*. See especially III, Part I, 262–82, 414–19, 457. For the basic documents relating to Anglo-Russian relations during this period, see USSR, Narodnyi Komissariat po Inostrannym Delam, *Anglo-Sovetskie Otnosheniia* and W. N. Medlicott, Douglas Dakin and M. E. Lambert, eds., *Documents on British Foreign Policy, 1919–1939*, Series 1A, Vol. I (London: H.M.S.O., 1966). Note especially No. 65, pp. 101–3, No. 465, pp. 671–2 and No. 504, pp. 724–31.

Pravda's lead article on September 22 accused Britain of systematically preparing war against the USSR. If the Russians believed their own propaganda, if they were genuinely convinced western capitalists were indeed planning a new crusade against them, then the TUC connection could turn into a useful deterrent. The international bourgeoisie, *Izvestiia* said on September 18, was plotting 'cruel and terrible slaughter,' but western trade unionists, in collaboration with their class brothers in the Soviet Union, might yet intimidate the imperialists. The USSR needed 'a breathing space for our work of reconstruction,' Lev Kamenev wrote, and the Committee could help provide it.[1]

The association with British trade unionism, then, could be used either to promote revolution in England or to prevent Stanley Baldwin from waging war on the USSR, and although Kamenev professed to find no ambiguity in the two missions, it is easy to see, in retrospect, how they might be incompatible. There was, however, a third possible assignment for the Committee – for the British, its most obvious *raison d'être* – the construction of a single trade union international, an international not, at least to start with, likely to submit to the control of the Comintern. On his return from England, Tomsky professed to be very optimistic about the prospects for unity.[2] The obstructionist tactics of the Amsterdam bureaucrats were, after Scarborough, no longer viable, he said. Ultimately – soon – they would have to sit down and talk unity. The workers of the world were determined to unite, he concluded, and they were not going to be stopped by the likes of Oudegeest.

Such forecasts were not confined to the Soviet press. Even *The Times* predicted Amsterdam might now have to agree to talks.[3] Nobody outside Britain was enthusiastic about negotiating with the Soviets, the correspondent reported, but even those who deplored the TUC's initiatives agreed it was better for the IFTU to arrange a unity conference than to let the English summon one unilaterally. Tomsky seemed to have persuaded the TUC leadership, *The Times* continued, that the Russian trade unionists were ready to break with the Red International, abandon it, and join Amsterdam. The idea sounded preposterous, but some IFTU officials were reported at least willing to test it.

Even if the Russians did agree to apply for IFTU membership, however, the question remained as to whether Soviet labour organizations

---

[1] L. Kamenev, 'The International Situation and the Soviet Union,' *Inprecorr*, v, 86 (10 Dec., 1925), 1297–8.

[2] See the report in *Izvestiia*, 18 Sept., 1925 and the speech of 7 Nov., 1925 in Tomsky, *K Probleme Edinstva*, pp. 24–33.

[3] *The Times*, 3 Dec., 1925.

really qualified as 'trade unions' in the western sense of the term, whether, specifically, they were 'willing to put an end to their subservience to the Communist Party and assert their independence.'[1] If they were not, they might, presumably, be denied IFTU membership on those grounds.

The whole question of the role, mission and direction of trade unionism was indeed very much of an issue in the USSR in the mid-1920s.[2] The problem was that Soviet trade unions had expanded too rapidly during the early NEP years. Membership doubled just between 1922 and 1926. Numerical strength, in such cases, produced ideological weakness as a byproduct. The Party's response was to impose stricter controls and severer discipline over the union rank-and-file. The reliable Marxists at the top, in the central leadership, were to be obeyed without question. The central leadership, in turn, was subject to ever closer scrutiny by the Party organs, 'the organized vanguard of the working class,' Tomsky wrote, 'which directs the whole proletarian movement' of which the trade union movement was just one part.[3]

Publicly, Tomsky never failed to emphasize the tie of the trade unions to the Party. Russian labour organizations, he wrote, worked in closest cooperation with the Party, and under its leadership.[4] Privately, however, Tomsky may have felt differently.[5] Within Party counsels, he strenuously protested petty meddling by Communist functionaries in day-to-day trade union business. He also objected to the way basic decisions on wages and hours were being made without reference to the trade unions, by Party organs, often by managers of state enterprises with a vested interest in keeping wages low and productivity high. It could be Tomsky hoped Russian association with more conventional, reformist, western-type unions in an expanded International Federation of Trade Unions would clarify the functions of his organization back home, and augment its prestige.

He was in a good position, in late 1925, to drive hard bargains on behalf of the unions. Stalin was about to make his break with Kamenev

---

[1] *Ibid.*

[2] See the superb summary in Carr, *Socialism in One Country*, I, 409–19. See also Tomsky's assessment in his report to the 14th Party Congress: Vsesoiuznaia Kommunisticheskaia Partiia, *XIV S''ezd Vsesiuoznoi Kommunisticheskoi Partii (B), 18–31 Dekabria 1925g.: Stenograficheskii Otchet* (Moscow–Leningrad: Gosudarstvennoe Izdatel'stvo, 1926), pp. 722–49.

[3] *The Times*, 23 Feb., 1926, citing a description of Soviet trade unionism Tomsky submitted to the International Labour Office.

[4] See Tomsky's article for the special supplement to the *Daily Herald*, 28 Nov., 1925, on the Soviet trade union movement.

[5] See above, pp. 186–7.

and Zinoviev, needed all the Politburo backing he could get, and presumably was ready to pay a price for it. He might be willing to let Tomsky build his bridges to the western social democrats, and join Amsterdam. In the process, of course, the old definition of the united front as a method of exposing and ousting moderates and replacing them by revolutionaries might somehow get lost, but perhaps Stalin did not care. The prospects for world revolution never did seem to captivate him much and, as we have seen, he was intrigued by the possibility friendly reformists in the west could be useful allies of the Soviet Foreign Commissariat.

In one of the last speeches he made before the open break with Stalin, Zinoviev took pains to remind Soviet trades unionists of their responsibilities to Marxist orthodoxy and to world revolution.[1] The purpose of the united front, and specifically, of the tie to English trades unionism, was to free British workers from the bourgeoisie and its reformist lackeys, he recalled, and bring them around to the Russian point-of-view, to Communism. Soviet labour organizations would not achieve that end unless they themselves were more intensely 'Bolshevized.' As 'the vanguard of the revolutionary proletariat of the world,' they could not let themselves lapse into western-style trades unionism. 'Above all and first of all,' he continued, Soviet trades unionists 'must be, and remain, from head to foot, proletarian international revolutionaries.' The Committee, then, was there solely to help topple the bourgeoisie, in Zinoviev's opinion, and he seemed ready to challenge Tomsky – or Stalin – if they sought trade union unity either for some other purpose or as an end in itself.

As of late 1925, then, Russian leaders were divided on how they would use the Committee, whether to employ it to revolutionize the English workers, or to restrain the English Foreign Office, or to achieve a single Trades Union International of which they would be an important part. One has the feeling, without documentation, that the Politburo consensus, to start with, was to leave all options open and postpone any final decisions. The Committee was there. In that sense, the united front campaign had succeeded. The Soviets finally had an organizational link to the western proletariat. The Committee could be considered as a kind of tender sprout, the lone organic result of the strenuous efforts over almost half a decade to plant Bolshevik seed in the stony soil of the non-Communist west. The organism should be cultivated, tended and nurtured. Later, when it had grown up, one could decide how to use it most

[1] Speech to the Metal Workers' Congress of the USSR, 25 Nov., 1925, *Inprecorr*, v, 87 (17 Dec., 1925), 1309–12.

advantageously. The final judgement, of course, would be for the Communist Party to make, and any decisions on immediate tactics the responsibility of the 14th Congress of that Party, scheduled to assemble in late December.

II

Amsterdam was as uneasy about the unity movement, and how to handle it, as were the Russians. It wanted no part of any general IFTU–RILU merger. Such an amalgamation would involve the distasteful obligation to accept the legitimacy of those dissident Profintern splinter groups in Europe which had been pouring vitriol on the official trade union leadership for almost a decade. If, however, what was proposed involved only admitting the Russian trade unions into IFTU – on the same conditions as all other members – it might be advantageous to explore the possibilities further. Once the Russians joined Amsterdam they would presumably sever their connections with Profintern. Without the Russians, Profintern would shrivel up and die, and its European stooges would have to come grovelling to the legitimate trade union establishment and accept any deal they were offered. An altogether happy prospect!

A great deal depended on how hard a line the TUC took. IFTU was not as dependent on the British as RILU was on the Russians, but the English movement was – after the German – the largest single centre in the federation. To lose the TUC would be to drop almost 30 per cent of the members from IFTU, and the richest members at that. So the campaign for unity had to be taken seriously in Amsterdam and the precise nature of the commitments the English were making to Tomsky had to be explored. As early as mid-July, 1925, even before the Committee was officially in existence, Oudegeest had suggested his British colleagues sit down with him and tell him more about the projected organization.[1] He was not going to put any obstacle in their way if the English wanted to meet with the Russians, he promised, so long as Profintern splinter groups were not in on the discussions too, but he hoped to be kept informed.

The TUC was willing to talk, but felt no urgency about scheduling anything quickly. The IFTU's General Council was not planning to discuss the Russian question until mid-October anyway, and when Purcell got that invitation to address the AF of L Convention at Atlantic City, the session was set back until December 5. Oudegeest then suggested a preliminary meeting of the IFTU Executive and the TUC leadership on

[1] General Council Minutes, No. 394, 21 July, 1925.

December 1 'to exchange opinions' on Amsterdam–Moscow relationships. The English had no objections.[1]

The seven-man Amsterdam delegation arrived in London November 29. Publicly, anyway, Oudegeest sounded conciliatory.[2] He would of course like to arrange for Russian entry into IFTU, he said, so long as the terms negotiated did not make it impossible for America to join as well. The problem was not the Russians, he indicated, but their Profintern puppets, who had already split and weakened the trade union movement on the continent. He would make no concessions to them.

He was not asked to. The nineteen TUC leaders who sat down with him two days later were all courtesy and amiability.[3] They must have been misinterpreted, they insisted. TUC had not turned against Amsterdam, and it certainly had no intention of swinging over to Profintern. The only question at issue was the Russian trade union movement and how to get it into IFTU, to everybody's advantage. The British felt the first practical step to the achievement of that end was to accept the Soviet proposal for unconditional talks. If they were fruitful, RILU would presumably just wither away.

The Amsterdam representatives had their doubts. IFTU vice-president Leipert noted the Russian trade unions were not autonomous organizations at all, just Communist Party auxiliaries, and he wanted no part of them. His Belgian colleague, Mertens, attacked on another front. The Anglo-Russian Committee had been the source of much mischief on the continent. Perhaps the press exaggerated when reporting its activities, but the effect had been to encourage Communist dissidents and splitters. Oudegeest, who made the opening statement in Amsterdam's behalf, took an equally hard line. If Russia came into the IFTU, he noted, the Americans would stay out. It was hardly worth it. He was sure, in fact, the Soviets' real objective was to open the doors of international trades unionism for those Profintern schismatics who were their clients.

The English did their best to reassure everybody.[4] They even put all

---

[1] *Ibid.*, No. 429, 6 Aug., 1925; No. 23, 28 Oct., 1925.

[2] Interview in the *Daily Herald*, 30 Nov., 1925. Oudegeest was misleading when he said he did not oppose Russian entry into IFTU. See above pp. 79–80.

[3] The TUC record is in General Council Minutes, No. 115, 1 Dec., 1925. The General Council statement, which was supposed to be confidential, was printed just two days later in *Het Volk*, the organ of the Dutch Social-Democratic Party. See also *The Times*, 2 Dec., 1925, the *Daily Herald*, 3 Dec., 1925 and *1926 TUC: Report of Proceedings*, p. 247.

[4] They were so reassuring, Bennet charged later, that the Amsterdam bureaucrats went away convinced the TUC had never meant all its unity talk at all (*Anglo-Russische Komitee*, pp. 33–44).

their goodwill in writing, in a supposedly 'secret' statement which appeared almost immediately in the continental press. The document expressed the 'confident hope' that the talks had 'removed any mis-understandings of the motives and intentions of the [TUC] General Council in suggesting the convening of an unconditional conference' with the Russians. The TUC denied any allegation that anything it had done was to be construed as hostile to IFTU. In fact, its sole intention was 'to strengthen and consolidate the International Trade Union Movement.' It recognized the difficulties of initiating the Russians into the Amsterdam organization, but felt the problems could best be resolved by a meeting of both parties, 'it being distinctly understood that such Conference would be confined strictly to representatives of the IFTU and the All-Russian Council of Trade Unions,' not the RILU. TUC chairman Pugh expressed the hope that the statement would enable his 'continental friends' to engage in a fruitful dialogue with the Soviets. Although Oudegeest was making no promises, Pugh felt confident, he said, that 'something would result' from the day's work which would 'lead to a better understanding of the purpose they [the TUC] had in view.'

Assuming the talk at the conference table was as muddied as the TUC's records of it, it is hardly surprising that the two sides had in fact passed each other in the night. The TUC leadership thought it had made its point successfully, that Amsterdam would now feel safe negotiating with the Russians, and that the IFTU General Council would rubber-stamp that decision on the 5th. When the *Daily Herald* interviewed Oudegeest the day after the conference, he sounded very conciliatory. All the silly misunderstandings dividing the TUC and the IFTU, one would assume, had now been cleared up.[1]

The Amsterdam bureaucrats, however, apparently saw the talks differently. They never really wanted to negotiate with Tomsky anyway (something the British could not seem to realize). What had worried them were the reports in the Communist press that the Anglo-Russian Committee would call a unity conference on its own responsibility if the IFTU refused to. The English statement, with its fervent professions of loyalty to Amsterdam, had pretty well scotched that possibility. The British had then surrendered, in advance, the one formidable weapon they had against Oudegeest. He did not have to worry about them any more, and he could therefore afford to continue dealing with them sternly.

[1] *Daily Herald*, 3 Dec., 1925.

Just four days later, he did, on his own home grounds, back in Amsterdam. The IFTU General Council, meeting for the first time since early February, had just one item on the agenda – the Russians, and what to tell them now. The Stenhuis resolution, passed back in February, had confirmed Amsterdam's willingness to admit the Russian trade unions to IFTU whenever they submitted their application, but had refused to sanction any Moscow–Amsterdam negotiations beforehand.[1] The Russian letter of May 19, drawn up along lines suggested by the TUC, had agreed to join an international not unlike the IFTU, and asked for talks on that basis.[2] How was the IFTU to respond?

The discussion was prolonged, but surprisingly restrained and totally amicable, at least on the surface.[3] None of the repartee at London – which nobody mentioned, in any event – had persuaded anybody to budge an inch. Hicks, representing the TUC, joined with Fimmen of the Transport Workers' International to move the IFTU declare itself 'prepared to meet representatives of the All-Russian Trade Union Council in order to discuss the possibility of affiliation of the Russian Trade Union Movement.' J. W. Brown, the British representative on the IFTU Secretariat, and Frank Hodges of the Miners' International, suggested some alternative wording which would have specified the unity talks be limited to 'the terms of the resolution passed by the Vienna Congress' – stipulations requiring unconditional Russian acquiescence in the International's existing 'rules and conditions.'[4] According to *The Times*' correspondent, Oudegeest and company were prepared to fall back on the Brown–Hodges wording as a compromise if, as they feared, the propaganda efforts of the Anglo-Russian Committee had swung a significant number of votes over to the English side. As the debate proceeded, however, it became clear London had hardly any backing at all. There was no need to equivocate. An impatient Stenhuis, voicing regret at all the time wasted on the unity issue – the International was getting behind on its routine paper work, he said, and it was the TUC's fault – proposed the toughest option of all. His wording simply took note of the correspondence between Moscow and Amsterdam over the past ten months, and of the discussions at the present meeting, reaffirmed the February decision – a Russian applica-

[1] See above, p. 118.		[2] See above, pp. 157–8.

[3] For the IFTU General Council meeting, see *International Trade Union Review*, VI, 1 (Jan.–Mar., 1926), 14–15; *Trade Union Unity*, II, 1 (Jan., 1926), 7–9; *The Labour Magazine*, IV, 9 (Jan., 1926), 431; *1926 TUC: Report of Proceedings*, p. 243; and *The Times*, 7 Dec., 1925.

[4] See above, pp. 55–6.

tion for membership prior to talks – and decreed any new decision unnecessary. His motion passed, 14 to 7. IFTU was not going to budge.

The Times was exultant. The British passion for unity with the Russians had always been a 'strange delusion.' The Soviets themselves had never been interested in unity, only in promoting 'dissension and division,' and their effort to join Amsterdam was made only in order to wage civil war there. The naivete of the TUC leadership was 'astonishing.' Fortunately, it was 'attempting the impossible' because the continentals, knowing the Russians better, would never let them in.

Oudegeest was a magnanimous winner. The decision had been made, and he was sure his British friends would honour it. If they wanted to appeal the General Council's judgement, they could do so at the next IFTU International Congress, eighteen months off. If, on the other hand, they were now to convoke a unity meeting on their own, no IFTU members would come, only RILU affiliates and representatives of minority movements. But, Oudegeest continued, 'we think, in view of our friendly relations, that the British movement will not take such a step.' Purcell, interviewed the same day, seemed to confirm that impression. Given the circumstances, *The Times* suggested, about all the English could now do would be to get Tomsky and some IFTU functionaries together informally, unofficially and off-the-record. That sort of an invitation might well be accepted, the reporter indicated, but nothing more.[1]

Lozovsky was furious.[2] The English had made their presentation far too gently. IFTU had responded by demanding total surrender. Nobody mentioned the real issue, that Communists believed in class war rather than collaborating with the bourgeoisie. The Russians would never descend to the AF of L level, especially after the 'stream of abuse' Amsterdam had poured out against them and against Profintern. Even the TUC was now under attack. The campaign for unity, however, would go on, and 'he who laughs last laughs the longest.'

The next move was up to the Anglo-Russian Committee, which met at the Hotel Continental in Berlin on December 8, 1925, just three days after the IFTU General Council adjourned.[3] Hicks and Purcell had

[1] *The Times*, 7 Dec., 1925.
[2] 'The Sabotage of International Trade Union Unity Still Continues,' *Inprecorr*, v, 87 (17 Dec., 1925), 1319–20.
[3] The most complete record of the meeting is that in the TUC archives, file 947/220, document A.R. 2/2/1925–26. A. B. Swales reported sidelights on the sessions in 'London, Amsterdam, Berlin,' *Trade Union Unity*, II, 1 (Jan., 1926), 3–7. See also *The Times*, 8–11 Dec., 1925 and *1926 TUC: Report of Proceedings*, pp. 245–6.

come to Berlin directly from Amsterdam. They were joined there by Pugh, Findlay, Swales and Citrine. The eight-man Soviet delegation was headed by Tomsky, Mel'nichansky and Dogadov. The Russians were angry, and wanted to launch a tough counter-attack on IFTU, but they also had Party orders, according to *The Times'* correspondent, to maintain the association with the TUC at all costs and to make generous concessions to British views when necessary. The Anglo-Russian Committee was a major asset to the Soviet Foreign Commissariat and had therefore to be preserved, Deputy Commissar Litvinov had told them – or so *The Times* reported.

The British delegation was determined to keep the sessions orderly, calm and unimpassioned. It was all to be very businesslike. The post came first, of course. There had been a cordial letter from the Finns indicating a desire to cooperate. Secretary Citrine had already answered it, along the lines of the reply to the Norwegian salutations back in September. The correspondence was read, first in English, then in Russian. Findlay moved the Finns be sent a further communication informing them of the 'Committee's efforts to proceed with its work.' Seconded. Passed. To the embittered Russians, still smarting from the Amsterdam defeat and eager to retaliate, all the busy work must have been enormously frustrating.

The second item on the agenda could hardly have restored their spirits. The British had to report the ukase of their colleagues back home, dating from September, that the Committee's statements on international questions, from now on, 'must first be submitted to this General Council.'[1] Even in case of 'special emergencies,' the Committee could say nothing that did not reflect and accord with policies already adopted by the governing bodies of both movements. The Russians wanted all that explained, but they finally acquiesced in it. A lot more time had been lost.

Now they got down to business. Pugh reported on the discussions between the TUC leaders and the IFTU Executive on December 1, and Hicks related what had been said and done at Amsterdam four days later. The Russians were invited to comment. They had a lot to say. The IFTU decision was just one more illustration of the kind of indignity they had had to suffer for a year and a half now. Their members were

---

[1] In the confusion, the Committee passed the limiting document exactly as the TUC General Council had written it, so that it read that future statements would have to be submitted 'to this General Council.' The next session of the Committee amended the statute to read '...to the General Councils of both countries.' (A.R. 3/1925–6).

beginning to question whether the unity effort was all worth it. Oude-geest and his cronies had subjected them to continuous and shameless libels. They could reply in kind, but they had restrained themselves, as the British advised, for the sake of the unity movement. But it was straining them to endure all IFTU's abuse, not be able to respond, and not have anything to show for their self-denial. They were ready to give up the whole campaign right now, if that was what the English advised.

The English responded soothingly. All was not lost and the Committee should persist in its efforts. The next step, clearly, was to reach an agreement on immediate tactics. They suggested adjourning the general meeting and assigning the chairmen and secretaries of both sides the responsibility of drawing up an agreed statement, and some resolutions, that the Committee could then formally ratify the next day. It was late by now, after eight, and the session had gone on non-stop for almost six hours, so everybody agreed. *The Times'* correspondent, next day, ventured the guess the meeting had been acrimonious and the two sides unable to reach any consensus.

In fact, the only real problem was the stamina – or lack of it – of the participants. The four-man sub-committee had no trouble producing the required documents, which were ready for the official stamp of approval the following morning. The statement indicated that the second meeting of the Committee had been frank and cordial, that the major item on the agenda had been the IFTU's rejection of Russia's proposal for a unity conference, and that attention had also been given to the 'regrettable effort' of un-named villains to deceive the labour rank and file with regard to the Committee's objectives in pursuing the unity campaign. As a result of its deliberations, the Committee reported, it had adopted five resolutions – unanimously. Four of them were routine. They expressed regret at IFTU's latest decision. They asserted that decision reflected not the opinions of ordinary trade unionists but the bias of a few top Amsterdam officials. They denounced the 'continued and unprovoked attacks' on Soviet trade unionism, and the 'gross misrepresentations' of the policies and purposes of the Committee, and resolved to take steps – unspecified – to counteract such libels. They agreed, however, that both movements must maintain an attitude of 'moderation and dignity in the face of all irresponsible attacks directed against them.' They would carry on the fight in that spirit, and would meet again early in 1926.

All that fully justified the disdain of *The Times*, which dismissed it as a 'colourless report of pious aspirations' without practical consequences.

But the Committee had approved one resolution which the journalist should have taken more seriously. It recorded the group's judgement on what should be done next. The TUC General Council should now convene, on its own responsibility, that unity conference which Amsterdam had just turned down. Oudegeest, of course, had said back in Amsterdam that if the British summoned such a conference, nobody from IFTU would come, but no one in Berlin apparently took that threat seriously. The British had made a commitment, in public, twice, and the Committee felt that now was clearly the time to honour it.

The idea was not absurd. It was not even original. A *Daily Herald* editorialist had suggested the same course of action two days before the Committee's recommendations were made available. The Scarborough Congress had gone on record in favour of an 'all-inclusive' international trade union organization, an organization which would not necessarily be just a revamped version of IFTU. The General Council's job was to get on with generating such an association.[1] The councillors themselves, however, were not so sure. As early as December 12 *The Times*' labour correspondent was reporting unease within the TUC leadership.[2] Many officials objected to the resolutions agreed to by the Committee, he revealed, and particularly to that 'statement having the character of a manifesto.' They were wary of letting the Committee chivvy them into calling some international unity congress which probably nobody but Communists would attend anyway. Their only obligation was to try to get the Russians and the Amsterdam functionaries together around one table, and many of them were of 'a disposition...to put a limited construction on this obligation...'

It might indeed appear as if the mood of the General Council was hardening around the turn of the year 1925–6. So it was said later on. But in fact, attitudes did not change, just tactics. The Council had never taken the lead in the unity campaign anyway. It had merely acquiesced in it. Forceful, independent and influential freewheelers – Purcell, Swales, Bramley, Hicks – had gotten TUC so hopelessly tangled up with the Russians that by the time anybody realized how constricting a net it could be, it seemed impossible to disentangle. But many trades union leaders, Thomas in particular, did not at all like the propaganda the Committee was producing. They felt the Russians were getting a lot more out of the organization than they were. The Reds were using their tie to the TUC to promote, not unity, but the interests of the Comintern and of the Soviet state. It was dangerous. Britain was on the eve of an

---

[1] *Daily Herald*, 7 Dec., 1925.　　　[2] *The Times*, 12 Dec., 1925.

industrial crisis. The miners' contracts would run out in April, and all signs pointed to a major confrontation then. At such a critical juncture, to convene some great congress for international trade union solidarity – which only Communists and their sympathizers would attend – would be wretched public relations. 'We surely did not want the British people to feel we were any part of a revolutionary movement, inspired by Russia or by anybody else,' Walter Citrine recalled later.[1] The TUC leaders knew they would need all the support they could get, all over the nation, soon enough. They were not anxious to alienate people un- necessarily just to make Tomsky feel better.

All of this came out at the General Council meeting on December 16 and 17. Not only did the members not much like *what* had been done at Berlin, they did not appreciate the *way* it was done. By what right did Hicks report to the Russians on the IFTU meeting before he reported to *them*? Smillie and Bondfield proposed a motion of 'regret' at that – a motion of censure, in effect, and almost unprecented. It lost, but it did get seven votes. The councillors were dubious about the Committee's recommendation that they convoke a unity congress on their own. It was noted that the continentals seemed quite adamant against attending any such meeting, and it might be well to find out first, then, informally, just who might come if a congress were called. If only the Russians and their allies were there, if IFTU members refused to come, it would hardly be worth it.

The Council finally decided to just ask the Amsterdam Executive to reconsider that December decision, which meant, in fact, it decided to do nothing. Smillie and Thomas moved the resolution. It expressed the TUC's 'deep regret' that IFTU had not agreed to talk to the Russians and promised to 'continue to press' for such a conference.[2] Such restraint virtually guaranteed no results. The IFTU Executive met in February, 1926, declared itself not empowered to change a decision already made by its General Council, and agreed to submit the question to the next IFTU General Council if the British insisted. It was over a month later before the TUC leaders took up the problem of what to do next. Some- thing would have to be decided, Pugh noted, 'regarding the obligation of the Council in the light of the instructions of the Scarborough Con- gress.' Purcell, who was still a tiger in the public press (unity was an

---

[1] Conversation with the author, 9 Nov., 1967, from which much of the material in this paragraph is drawn.
[2] General Council Minutes, Nos. 120, 121, 122, 16 Dec., 1925; *The Times*, 17, 18 Dec., 1925.

'imperative need,' a unity congress must be held immediately, and those who opposed it must be either 'recklessly criminal or poor blind fools'),[1] was a tame house cat in the privacy of the General Council. He moved that the International Committee, which had only met twice since Scarborough, be asked 'to consider how under all the circumstances the instructions of the Congress could best be carried out.' The wording was so innocuous Mrs Bondfield seconded it. The International Committee subsequently suggested that the Anglo-Russian Committee be summoned for the week beginning May 17, the week a Migration Conference was scheduled in London. The IFTU would be represented at that Conference, so the British might be able to make an opportunity to arrange some informal and unofficial Moscow–Amsterdam *pourparlers*, thus fulfilling, in a way, their promises of the year before. It seemed a good way to get off the hook. As it turned out, however, the IFTU was not much interested, the Russians still insisted on the public, official conference they had been pledged, May 17 found the TUC in a shambles anyway, in the aftermath of the general strike, and the Migration Conference was postponed.[2]

But well before that, at least from December on, relations between the TUC and the Russians cooled markedly. Although the British did decide, in January, 1926, to invite Tomsky back to their annual Congress, they extended the same courtesy to Oudegeest, and they declined to send any fraternal delegates in return to the Soviet trade union congress.[3] When TUC vice-chairman Swales popped off to the USSR for his first trip, in April, he apparently did not bother to talk trade union politics at all. He just ran up and down mountains for six weeks and sweated off four of his twenty stone bulk.[4] Such a programme, however satisfying personally and aesthetically, hardly contributed to the Cause, but it was as if everybody were already aware that the Cause was dead. Almost nobody in England, outside the CPGB, seemed able to see any chance of it coming to anything. The Amsterdam die-hards had won.

The British Communists seemed alone in their continued exuberance

---

[1] A. A. Purcell, 'The Imperative Need for International Trade Union Unity,' *Plebs*, XVIII, 1 (Jan., 1926), 5–6.

[2] General Council Minutes, No. 207, 24 Feb., 1926 and No. 211, 23 Mar., 1926; General Council, International Committee Minutes, 13 Apr., 1926, file 901, doc. I.C. 3/1925–6; *1926 TUC: Report of Proceedings*, pp. 244–5.

[3] General Council, International Committee Minutes, 25 Jan., 1926, file 901, doc. I.C. 2/1925–6; General Council Minutes, No. 268, 28 Apr., 1926.

[4] So testified Andrew Rothstein, in a conversation on 18 Dec., 1967.

for the prospects of trade union unity.[1] They even professed to find some ray of hope in the fact that IFTU bureaucrats had not followed their real inclinations and repudiated the unity effort altogether. They no doubt wanted to, but the Scarborough decision forced them to profess an interest in international solidarity they did not really feel. They must be pushed further, and it was up to the Anglo-Russian Committee, and especially its British component, to do the pushing. Above all, TUC must insist on that unity conference, not just a conference of Russians and Amsterdam bureaucrats, except, perhaps as a preliminary, but 'an unconditional International Conference of all trade unions,' Profintern affiliates included.[2] If necessary, the British should call such a conference on their own responsibility. British Communists still professed to believe such a decision possible. They refused to recognize that TUC had given up the campaign. Moscow had so decreed, and native comrades shaped their attitudes accordingly. It may have seemed foolishness, but the true test of faith, for the devout of any denomination, is, as Tertullian observed, to believe what is absurd. CPGB members passed the test beautifully.

III

The apparent *impasse* in the unity campaign once Amsterdam issued its latest affiliate-first, talk-later pronouncement left Soviet leaders in something of a dilemma as of mid-December, 1925. Should the effort to achieve an all-inclusive trade union international be dropped altogether? Should Profintern, in virtual suspended animation for some months now, be allowed to revive? Should the old Moscow *versus* Amsterdam slogans be resurrected? If so, what would become of the Anglo-Russian Committee? What price should the Soviets pay to maintain their astonishing intimacy with the TUC reformists? What other purposes might the Committee be made to serve, assuming the dreams of an IFTU–RILU merger were beyond realization? Or should the Soviet trade unions bow to Amsterdam's iron will, ditch Profintern, join the IFTU unconditionally and – with British help, perhaps – work to subvert that organization from within? The possibilities were many, all of them were tantalizing, and it was not easy to decide among them.

[1] See, for example, *Workers' Weekly*, 11, 18 Dec., 1925, from which the next two quotations in this paragraph were drawn.
[2] The wording is from a resolution of the NMM's 'Conference of Action.' National Minority Movement, *Report of Special National Conference of Action, March 21, 1926* (London: National Minority Movement, 1926), p. 26. The resolution reflects, and summarizes, the official Party line from early January on.

At least some leaders seem to have favoured ordering the Soviet trade unions to follow the TUC's advice and join IFTU 'unconditionally and categorically.' Kaganovich was the principal advocate of that course within the Politburo.[1] Many of the Russian trade union leaders would have welcomed such instructions, or so Trotsky alleged. They resented paying Profintern's bills and submitting to its rules and were perfectly willing to liquidate the organization entirely. At their instigation and apparently without consulting the Party, some 23 Russian trade unions changed their statutes some time late in 1925 or early in 1926 in such a way as to strike out all wording about membership in RILU, substituting for it a more general reference to affiliation with some trade union international[2]

Tomsky, according to Trotsky's testimony, was more cautious. He did want to get his unions into IFTU, and was willing to eliminate RILU to do it, but only on conditions, conditions which presumably would require Amsterdam to make some accommodation for Russia's Profintern partners. His difficulty was that IFTU was so manifestly unwilling to talk about conditions of any kind. The TUC might still help break Amsterdam's resolve down, however, and Tomsky therefore favoured continuing the work of the Anglo-Russian Committee. Its unity slogans were, in his estimation, still valid, an all-inclusive trade union international would still be advantageous, and it might yet be possible to turn IFTU into such an international. The Soviets should therefore keep all options open, including Russian entry into Amsterdam, and see what developed.

Not everybody was so sanguine about the British connection. Trotsky, notably, was critical of Russia's TUC allies.[3] The so-called 'leftist' in Britain was 'without rudder and without sails,' he wrote. Even if the 'Left Wing muddlers' ever managed to get any power they would just 'hasten to hand it over to their elder brothers on their Right.' They might control the TUC General Council, and have it 'in tow' on the question of trade union unity, but it was all talk. Leftists were always most radical on international questions, and always awed by revolutions elsewhere, but they never could bring themselves to waging revolution on their own, at home. Fundamentally, all the TUC people were pro-govern-

[1] So claimed Trotsky in November of 1926: Trotsky Archives, T–3006.
[2] Trotsky Archives, T–2993 (11 July, 1926), and T–881 (July, 1926).
[3] See, for example, L. Trotsky, 'Problems of the British Labour Movement,' (Notes from a Notebook), *Communist International*, No. 22 (July (?), 1926), pp. 19–41. See also Ruth Fischer, *Stalin and German Communism* (London: Oxford University Press, 1948), pp. 560–1.

ment, and if it came, for example, to any test of strength between Britain and the USSR, they would turn against the proletarian fatherland instantly. To construct some tenuous link from the Politburo to the TUC via Tomsky and the Committee, and to think you could use such a fragile connection to manipulate the British Empire, was therefore just plain foolishness.

Stalin, Zinoviev and Kamenev, about to bring their feud into the open in the 14th Party Congress, all seemed wary of the united front issue, and the particular problem of what to do with the Committee, and loth to inject such matters into their debate. None of the triumvirate, in any event, wanted to risk offending Tomsky by questioning the British connection or challenging the accepted rhetoric about trade union unity. Zinoviev had already firmly committed himself to the Committee, anyway, as a useful tool for splitting Amsterdam and a valuable device for waging revolution in Britain. Stalin, less involved personally in the creation of the Committee, was nevertheless interested in it, more and more openly, as an adjunct to the Soviet Foreign Commissariat. If, as he was now alleging, socialism could be achieved in just the one country, the USSR, it was essential that west European workers sympathize with the Soviet experiment and support it so as 'to prevent their capitalists from launching an attack on it' and bringing it down.[1] The Committee, in his judgement, might serve that purpose admirably.

Lozovsky was in the most difficult position of all. He could not openly repudiate the Committee, because to support it was established Party policy. Yet if the result of the Committee's work were Russian entry into IFTU – on any terms – his Profintern power base would disappear and he personally would be out of a job. His tactic was to praise the Committee for all the wrong virtues, following the Zinoviev line.[2] It was a mechanism for tearing Amsterdam apart. It was useful for nudging British trade unionism further to the left. Ultimately it might serve to expose the weakness and vacillation of the TUC reformists and enhance the prospects of the genuine revolutionaries in the Minority Movement and the CPGB. Such talk might embarrass Tomsky with the British who periodically challenged him to explain it away, but it enabled Lozovsky to seem to support the Committee while simultaneously sabotaging it.

The 14th CPSU Party Congress, meeting in December, 1925 – right

---

[1] Stalin, *Sochineniia*, VIII, 95–8.
[2] See, for one good example, A. Lozovsky, 'Where is the Development of the International Trade Union Movement Heading?' *Inprecorr*, VI, 16 (4 Mar., 1926), 237–40.

after the Anglo-Russian Committee's Berlin meeting – provided Tomsky his big opportunity, and Lozovsky some of his most anxious moments.[1] In the normal course of events, when a decision had to be made on issues as significant as how to proceed with united front tactics and what to do with the Committee, the Party leadership would come to a consensus in advance and use the Congress merely to proclaim the new line publicly. This, however, was no normal Congress. It was more like a Roman spectacle. Kamenev and Zinoviev had come to do unequal battle against the Stalinist lions. For once, the debates were to be real, not just a formality, and the atmosphere was very tense. Stalin was counting on the support of the 'right' – Tomsky, Bukharin, Rykov. Kamenev and Zinoviev had the powerful Leningrad apparatus with them.

The rupture in the Party leadership was probably as much a matter of personalities as of policies. The question was not so much what was to be done as who was to do it. The debates, nevertheless, had some substance. Stalin's astonishing suggestion that the Soviet Union could achieve socialism even before the advanced countries had their revolutions was up for examination. So was the related matter of the New Economic Policy, including the substantial concessions to the peasants NEP demanded and, especially, the near-capitulation to the demands of the kulaks. But above all, the Party had to consider the problem of its own leadership. Was the CPSU surrendering the 'democratic' part of demo-cratic centralism? Was a cult of personality emerging around Josef Stalin? Was the dictatorship of the proletariat to be abandoned for the despotism of the *vozhd*?

Tomsky played a decisive role in the Congress' deliberations. Not only did he present a crucial report on the tasks of Soviet trade unionism under NEP, he also accepted the onus of defending Stalin against the

[1] The proceedings of the Congress are recorded in Vsesoiuznaia Kommunisticheskaia Partiia, *XIV S''ezd Vsesoiuznoi Kommunisticheskoi Partii (B), 18–31 Dekabria 1925g.: Stenograficheskii Otchet* (Moscow–Leningrad: Gosudarstvennoe Izdatel'stvo, 1926), from which subsequent citations will be drawn. Stalin's report is available, separately, in English, in J. V. Stalin, *Political Report of the Central Committee to the Fourteenth Congress of the CPSU (B), December 18, 1925* (Moscow: Foreign Languages Publishing House, 1925), as well as in his *Works* (Moscow: Foreign Languages Publishing House, 1952), VII, 267–403. The whole debate on trade union policy is also available in German translation: M. P. Tomsky, *Die Gewerkschafts-arbeit auf dem XIV Parteitag der Sowjet-Union: Referat, Diskussion und Schlusswort* (Berlin: Führer-Verlag, 1926). For useful English-language commentary, see especially Carr, *Socialism in One Country*, III, Part I, *passim* (and particularly pp. 586–8); N. Popov, *Outline History of the Communist Party of the Soviet Union*, ed. by A. Fineberg and H. G. Scott (London: Martin Lawrence, 1935), II, 249–54; Fischer, *Stalin and German Communism*, pp. 478–95.

Opposition's allegations of power-grabbing. Kamenev and Zinoviev were beclouding the issues, he charged.[1] Nobody was dictating to anybody in the Politburo. It made its decisions collectively, not individually. The rebuttal was blunt, strong and reassuring, and the delegates gave Tomsky a tremendous standing ovation when he was finished. The trade union leader was clearly in a superb bargaining position vis-à-vis Stalin and should have been able to dictate almost any decision he wanted with respect to the Committee and to the question of international trades unionism. One gets the impression he either did not know exactly what he wanted, or else that he was naive about taking quick advantage of the influence he had.

In presenting the majority report of the Central Committee (Zinoviev offered a 'co-report'), Stalin laid heavy stress on maintaining good relations with the western proletariat.[2] Capitalism had recovered from the crisis of the immediate post-war years, he acknowledged, and proletarian revolutions in the advanced countries were therefore, at least temporarily, unlikely. Such opportunities as now existed could be found in such areas as the 'growth of a mass movement under the banner of the struggle for trade union unity.' It was important for the Soviet Union to encourage such movements and stay close to them. The USSR needed close ties with western labour, not just to promote revolutionary action in the (lamentably!) distant future, but to win immediate diplomatic advantages. Russia needed the help of western proletarians against 'imperialism and its interventionist machinations,' for, 'without the workers, it is impossible to wage war nowadays.' If western workers refused to fight the Soviet Union, if they regarded it 'as their child in whose fate they are sincerely interested, then war against our country becomes impossible.' Stalin never mentioned the Committee, although he did refer to British trades unionism's recent 'swing to the left.' But everything he said surely indicated the campaign for international labour solidarity was to proceed, and that contacts with western workers would not be limited to those already enrolled in the ranks of the Party faithful.[3]

In his report on the work of the Comintern's Executive Committee, Zinoviev referred to the Committee explicitly, praised it lavishly, and rejected out of hand the arguments of Ruth Fischer, the German Left,

[1] His speech is in *XIV S''ezd V.K.P. (B): Stenograficheskii Otchet*, pp. 275–92.
[2] *Ibid.*, pp. 8–55.
[3] The resolutions the Congress adopted 'On the Political and Organizational Reports of the Central Committee' echoed, in rather vague language, the Stalinist approach, with somewhat more emphasis, perhaps, on the revolutionary responsibilities of western workers. *Ibid.*, pp. 956–64.

and 'other comrades' who had cited it as an example of 'opportunism.'[1] On the contrary, he argued, it was 'of immense importance all along the line.' It preserved the peace, guaranteed the USSR against the interventionists, and ensured that 'in the course of time we shall render reformism harmless in Europe.' It was one of the best examples of how to use united front tactics successfully to 'conquer the reformist masses in an era of revolutionary lull.' He admitted the creation of the Committee had been something of a surprise, but in retrospect, it was as significant a symbol of the present historical epoch in Britain as Chartism was of the mid-nineteenth century, and it would eventually make it possible for the CPGB to enlist 'powerful battalions of workers' which, up to now, had remained impervious to Marxist logic. He nurtured no illusions, he continued, about the nature of English reformists. Even Purcell, 'one of the most revolutionary-minded of the left leaders,' was no Communist, no real Marxist. Inevitably, most such people would vacillate and retreat. 'Our basic foundation in England' had therefore to remain 'the Communist Party and the trade union minority following it.' But the existence of the Committee would make their task simpler, and therefore 'I do not hesitate to repeat that the rapprochement between our trade unions and the English Left is of vast and universal historical importance, and I shall support this movement.'

It is doubtful whether Zinoviev's pledges of support were any great comfort to Tomsky. Zinoviev was now a political invalid anyway, and in no position to advance anybody's cause, even his own. And he had praised the Committee for all the wrong reasons. To argue that its major achievement would be to 'render reformism harmless' would only provide ammunition for those in the west who wanted to destroy it, especially since Zinoviev had not even mentioned the Committee's supposed 'real' goal of achieving an all-inclusive trades union international.

Tomsky, however, had his own report to make, on Soviet trades unionism, and he saved the last quarter of it for reviewing the work of the Committee – and defending it – in some detail.[2] He noted carefully, first, that everything he had done had been cleared in advance, with the Central Committee of the CPSU, with Profintern, and with the Communist International. Tactics had been carefully planned all along, then, and their success had been gratifying. It might all seem strange to some

---

[1] The speech is in *ibid.*, pp. 639–81. The passages relating to the Committee are on pp. 655–7 and 673–6.
[2] *Ibid.*, pp. 743–9.

comrades. 'The most revolutionary and at the same time the youngest trade union federation in the world, the Russian federation, creates a bloc with trade unions which up to now have been considered the oldest and most conservative...in the world.' The alliance was no historical accident, however, but the product of definite historical conditions, subject to normal Marxist analysis. English living standards were being imperilled by cheaper labour abroad. The British worker therefore reacted sharply to the 'capitalist offensive,' to the effort of the bourgeoisie to cut his wages and extend his hours, and the capitalist response was just what Marx would have predicted, to redouble the offensive and to use political as well as economic weapons against labour. The English worker had, as a result, become radicalized, and that was why, even though he got Europe's highest wages, he was still an outstanding fighter for proletarian unity and for the creation of some international organization to deal with his economic grievances effectively.

The Soviet response to those objective facts, involving the creation of the Anglo-Russian Committee, was correct, and indeed stemmed from the united front campaign already launched by Comintern and RILU. It gave that campaign practical form. It had already produced considerable stress within the Amsterdam organization, and put a great deal of pressure on the compromisers there. The Anglo-Russian bloc had concerned itself with more than just the unity of the international trade union movement, however, and Tomsky cited the statement agreed on at the first session of the Committee. That manifesto had not only demanded world-wide labour solidarity but had also protested imperialist war-mongering and the economic offensive of capital. The Committee, then, was involving itself in political issues, and its statements on those issues were, incidentally, unanimous. Unanimity was vital. 'We come to some decision unanimously or we come to no conclusion at all.' He admitted the Committee's documents were not outstanding bits of 'orthodox Communism' and that some might have preferred stronger language, like 'traitor,' 'reformist,' or 'yellow Amsterdam leader.' Such words came easily for Communists, but, in effect, the Committee had expressed the same sentiments in another way, in a form 'acceptable both to the worker and to the European trades union aristocracy.'

The current situation, he reported, was that the English had suggested they try to mediate between Moscow and Amsterdam. They would call a world unity conference if IFTU did not, but when that conference would meet, and what preparatory work would have to be undertaken first, depended on other matters. 'For the success of this conference, according to the opinion of the English – and I am in agreement with them – a whole series of preparatory steps must be undertaken.' Soundings had to be taken to see how much support the Committee had in other national federations. IFTU had to be given one more chance to reconsider its decision against unity talks. It might be that informal and unofficial meetings would have to be held between Amsterdam functionaries and the Russians. Whether, out of all those negotiations, a unity congress would emerge, could not be predicted. He was not optimistic about IFTU's attitude. It might be that it would continue to reject all overtures absolutely.

In that case, the English and the Russians would presumably call the congress on their own responsibility over Amsterdam's head. Such a meeting would get a tremendous popular response all over the world. It would be 'the greatest achievement ever of the international labour movement.' For the first time, wage earners would unite for their economic struggle, and all good Marxists knew that such a development would soon lead to union for political purposes and for class struggle. Russia's responsibility, then, was to solidify her ties with the British and continue to urge a world unity conference on the basis of proportional representation. It might not work out exactly that way, however. 'It is impossible to say what form the fight for unity might take.' Unity was worth achieving, however, no matter how it was gotten, and not just to unmask revisionists, either. 'So many have been unmasked, and again unmasked, that one does not need to go through this sort of complicated and difficult manoeuvre for their sake.' The Committee's purpose, then, was not to expose social democrats, but to wage 'the class struggle in the highest meaning of the words.' It sought labour unity against war, labour unity against the capitalist offensive, and the close cooperation of proletarians everywhere, especially those in England and Russia.

In most Party gatherings, before and since, the deliberations on an official report have been just dull routine, designed largely to see which sycophant could produce the most impressive superlatives. The 14th Congress was different, and Lozovsky rose to demand a more precise statement on just how far Tomsky intended to take all the unity talk.[1] Achieving a single labour international would not be as easy as Tomsky implied, he warned. Not only had the number of organized workers fallen over the past half decade, almost 30 per cent, but those that were still in unions were badly divided – politically, nationally, religiously, racially. Many national federations had remained aloof from both IFTU

[1] *Ibid.*, pp. 768–78.

and RILU, so even uniting the two existing internationals would still not produce world-wide trade union solidarity.

Basically, however, all labour movements found themselves somewhere between two poles. The Communists, led by the Soviet workers, were at one extreme, and the conservative, anti-socialist Americans were at the other. The rest, including both the TUC and the other IFTU affiliates, stood somewhere in between. IFTU itself, however, was split. Many of its members – perhaps one in seven – were, in fact, Profintern people, revolutionaries. Many more were 'leftists,' ideologically amorphous but clearly discontented with the old policies and tactics. Together, the 'left' and the RILU people probably constituted a majority of Amsterdam's membership already. The Anglo-Russian Committee had facilitated the leftward movement. It had split the IFTU, not just organizationally, but politically, and opened the door for even greater 'left' and ultra-left triumphs in the future.

All these gains would be jeopardized, however, if the Soviet trade unions agreed to affiliate with the IFTU. Their friends on the international scene would never trust them again after such a 'capitulation,' and Lozovsky had quotations from *The Times* to prove it. Such a betrayal would enable Amsterdam bureaucrats to crush the entire left spectrum of the workers' movement. Tomsky had said he did not know how far the negotiations with Amsterdam might go. That was not precise enough. The Party had to know how far they would go. Apart from the talks with 'our friends, the English,' in which 'all possible concessions as regards formulas are absolutely necessary,' the Soviet stand must be clear and unmistakable. 'Under no circumstances can and shall all our negotiations with the representatives of the Amsterdam International lead us to enter the Amsterdam International.' To do so could be to wreck Profintern and to split and weaken Communist Parties all over the world.

Lozovsky was unlucky in his friends. The only delegate rising to defend him in the debate that followed was N. P. Glebov-Avilov, head of the Leningrad trade unions, an associate of Zinoviev and therefore, automatically, under a cloud. He warned against the prospect of some unconditional surrender to Amsterdam.[1] He had no objection to dealing with the English, but Russia should make it clear now, with no equivocation, that her trade unions would never affiliate with the IFTU.

Mel'nichansky, among others, came to Tomsky's defence.[2] He chided Lozovsky for inconsistency. Last year he said he favoured unity. This

---

[1] *Ibid.*, pp. 784–9. See especially pp. 788–9.   [2] *Ibid.*, pp. 789–92.

year he seemed to be afraid of it. It was not good enough just to review a
lot of statistics to prove how strong Profintern was. Just what were all
those Profintern organizations doing to achieve a united trade union
movement? Lozovsky and his people talked solidarity, but never
practised it. And as for Glebov-Avilov, he need not even be taken
seriously. He was just playing at leftism for effect.

Tomsky was marvellous at spontaneous give-and-take anyway, and he
lit into Lozovsky and Glebov-Avilov with apparent relish in his concluding remarks.[1] The Profintern Secretary made no sense, he charged.
He had to defend RILU, of course. That was his job. But in this case he
was doing it badly. He was contradicting himself. He had gone down all
the statistics; he had proven there were millions of good revolutionaries
in the IFTU ranks; he had then concluded Russia should stay as far
away from IFTU as possible and leave her friends there isolated. There
was no logic to that. In fact, what Russia sought was unity. Everybody
agreed on that. In terms of precisely how unity was to be achieved, no
real issues had ever arisen in the past, and they were not likely to in the
future. The theses to be voted by the Congress, for example, had been
worked out by a three-man committee of himself, Bukharin and Zinoviev. What changes Zinoviev suggested had been made, and he had
joined in recommending the document to the Politburo. Even Glebov-
Avilov had no protest to record until just two hours ago! If so few
problems had come up in the past on how to pursue the united front
campaign, they were not likely to emerge now, and Lozovsky's insistence, therefore, on setting precise rules on how to achieve trade union
unity, was incomprehensible.

The unity movement had its false friends, he continued. Some of
them – and he pointed directly at Lozovsky and Glebov-Avilov –
promoted splitting under the cloak of the unity effort, and hoped that
nobody would notice. 'As if here there were only pure genuises, like me,
Glebov and Lozovsky, and there only simple dumb-bells like Jouhaux
and Oudegeest, who don't understand anything. And the English
leaders – they are babies who do not realize where they are being led.' It
was a 'false and ambiguous' policy, and the workers would see through
it. It was time to stop using unity slogans as mere agitation manoeuvres,
and take the campaign for trade union solidarity seriously.

The most advantageous method of achieving unity, for the USSR,
would be through an international congress, but the Soviets should not
commit themselves so wholly to that device that they closed the doors on

[1] *Ibid.*, pp. 797–804.

other possibilities. If they had been so rigid in the past, there never would have been an Anglo-Russian Committee. If someone who could really think dialectically and was not afraid of a lot of leftist phraseology could prove, conclusively, it was wise for the Russians to enter the Amsterdam International, why should the CPSU forbid it? Why should it say 'never,' 'under no conditions'? 'A Bolshevik would not so decide.' As for him, 'I would go to the devil's grandmother, the Roman pope, anywhere, if it would further the cause of the working class and of the workers' revolution.'

The resolution the Congress passed – the one Tomsky, Bukharin and Zinoviev had agreed on in advance – was innocuous and non-committal and was in fact accepted unanimously.[1] It welcomed the 'fraternal fighting alliance' of Soviet and British unions as 'the first practical step towards the establishment of international unity,' but was more enthusiastic than specific about what the next step might be. Nothing, then, had really changed. Lozovsky had not persuaded the Congress to forbid Russian affiliation with IFTU, but nobody had really supported such an idea, either. Even Tomsky had only dared suggest it as the vaguest sort of future possibility. The Party, in fact, had not yet made up its mind.

The letter the Russian trade unions wrote Amsterdam on January 6, just a few days after the Party Congress adjourned, reflected the leadership's indecision.[2] Addressed 'Dear Comrades,' signed 'With International Greetings,' and couched in the mildest of language, it noted merely that the Soviet Central Trades Union Council 'leaves in full effect its former proposal' and 'can add nothing new.' In spite of IFTU's latest decision against unity talks, the Russians would continue, 'untiringly,' the effort to create a single Trades Union International. No threats there, and no vituperation, and one can only conclude that somebody in Moscow still considered Russian entry into IFTU a real possibility.

Exactly one week later, however, the Politburo finally had made up its mind, and apparently ruled out Russian membership in IFTU on any terms.[3] The statement, from the Central Committee of the CPSU to all

---

[1] *Ibid.*, pp. 973–88; also in Institut Marksa–Engel'sa–Lenina–Stalina pri TsK, KPSS, *Kommunisticheskaia Partiia Sovetskogo Soiuza v Rezoliutsiiakh i Resheniiakh S''ezdov, Konferentsii i Plenumov Ts.K.*, Seventh Edition, 2 Parts ([Moscow]: Gosudarstvennoe Izdatel'stvo Politicheskoi Literatury, 1953), ii, 108–9.

[2] English text in *IFTU Report, 1924–26*, p. 51 and in *International Trade Union Review*, vi, 16 (Jan.–Mar., 1926), 15; Russian text in Tomsky, *K Probleme Edinstva*, p. 52.

[3] *Pravda*, 14 Jan., 1926; *Inprecorr*, vi, 6 (21 Jan., 1926), 81–2.

Comintern sections, expressly repudiated 'all the counter-revolutionary talk with regard to the alleged intended affiliation of the Soviet trade unions to the Amsterdam Trade Union Federation...' The flexible policy implied in Tomsky's addresses to the Party Congress had been, then, rejected. The victorious Stalinists perhaps no longer felt any need to bend to anybody's rightist idiosyncracies. And Stalin, personally, must have been wary all along of Soviet trade unions attaching themselves to some outside agency not under his personal control. A leader so sensitive to the encroachments of the comrades in the Communist International could hardly be less suspicious of claims the bourgeois lackeys in IFTU might make on him.

Amsterdam officialdom could hardly contain its glee over the Central Committee's statement. Obviously, it reported, that Tomsky–Lozovsky debate at the Party Congress had been staged, a sham. The Russian unions never had any intention of joining Amsterdam. All they sought was that disruptive world 'unity' congress through which they hoped in fact, to subvert the existing labour organizations everywhere. Zinoviev himself had agreed that the united front was designed merely to replace 'rotten reformism' in the trade unions by Communism. To continue to play the unity game, then, would needlessly disturb the returning tranquillity of the trades union movement. Realism dictated putting an end to the whole farce.[1]

The IFTU Executive tried to do just that at its meeting of February 11 and 12.[2] The British were informed that their request for a reconsideration of the unity issue would be referred to the next General Council meeting, which meant a postponement of almost a year. The Russians were told that their January 6 letter must be considered an unfavourable reply to the invitation to affiliate, and that it, too, then, would be passed on to the General Council for consideration early in 1927. Finally, the Amsterdam functionaries bluntly rebuked the TUC (although not by name) for indiscriminate and mischievous use of the 'unity' slogan. 'Anyone who takes on the task of mediator' between Moscow and Amsterdam 'must stand honourably and deliberately between the two, and hold out his hand to both sides.' Would-be mediators had not been totally impartial up to now. They had been far more critical of Amsterdam's policies than of Russia's. Amsterdam, obviously, had had enough of all the dangerous chatter about unity. Oudegeest and Lozovsky were now allies.

[1] *IFTU Press Reports*, VI, 10 (11 Mar., 1926), 4–5; 11 (18 Mar., 1926), 2–4.
[2] *IFTU Report, 1924–26*, p. 52; *The Times*, 22 Feb., 1926.

IV

The acrimonious bickering so characteristic of the deliberations at the 14th CPSU Congress was not repeated at the meeting of the Comintern's Executive Committee two months later.[1] The Soviets had given advance notice they would not appreciate any foreign comrades commenting publicly on the Russian Party's dirty linen,[2] and, with just one exception, the injunction was heeded. Harmony and near-unanimity prevailed, and the leadership's reports, theses, and resolutions all emerged unscathed.

The 'one exception' was the Italian left-winger, A. Bordiga, who specifically challenged the established line on united front tactics.[3] The united front had been so misinterpreted, he claimed, that Communist revolutionary cadres were in danger of degenerating into mere study groups for the examination of social relations. The campaign for RILU–IFTU merger, in particular, was a demoralizing surrender and theoretically indefensible. Amsterdam never had been and never could be a truly proletarian organization. It was a bourgeois stronghold, an adjunct of capitalism's League of Nations bastion, and it should be exposed, attacked and demolished, not joined.

Bordiga may have had friends in the audience – he probably did – but the storm of abuse exploding over the lone heretic's head seemed to strike them dumb. Neither Zinoviev nor Lozovsky, both of whom must have felt some twinge of sympathy for the ultra-left line, would concede

---

[1] The basic source for the 6th ECCI is the verbatim report, *Shestoi Plenum Ispolkoma Kominterna: Stenograficheskii Otchet*. See especially the speeches of Zinoviev (pp. 1–6, 10–56, 435–67), Bukharin (pp. 201–13), Lozovsky (pp. 271–309, 413–29), Tomsky (pp. 310–23), Hardy (pp. 323–36), Bordiga (pp. 368–73) and Geschke (pp. 390–401). Stalin never addressed the full session of the ECCI but his speeches to the French and German Commissions may be found in *Sochineniia*, VIII, 105–6, 109. English language reports on the deliberations, with some speeches translated verbatim, may be found in *Inprecorr*, VI, 18 (10 Mar., 1926), 20 (17 Mar., 1926), 22 (25 Mar., 1926). The final theses are available in Russian in *Kommunisticheskii Internatsional v Dokumentakh* and in English (not complete, but most judiciously selected) in Degras, *Communist International: Documents*. Professor Carr, as usual, provides lucid commentary: see *Socialism in One Country*, III, Part I, 490–6, 500–8, 513–14, 522–4, 588–9, 592–3.

[2] *Pravda*, 14 Jan., 1926.

[3] *Shestoi Plenum Ispolkoma Kominterna: Stenograficheskii Otchet*, pp. 368–73. Actually, one other delegate stepped inadvertently out of line on the unity issue. A German representative, whose dialectics were two months out of date, echoed the Tomsky line at the 14th CPSU Congress and urged no statement at all on the matter of Russian membership in Amsterdam on the grounds 'it would be wrong if we were to exclude any forum for trade union unity absolutely and forever.' (*Ibid.*, pp. 390–401). Nobody rebuked him, but nobody – not even Tomsky – repeated the heresy.

Bordiga anything at all. Whether deliberately or not, he misinterpreted the whole unity campaign. He seemed to suggest its purpose was to win over Amsterdam bureaucrats. In fact, the objective was the allegiance of the proletarian masses enrolled in IFTU affiliates, and to secure it, amalgamation of the two internationals would be highly advantageous. No compromise was contemplated between Communism and reformism, and in that sense, the old Moscow *versus* Amsterdam rhetoric had not been abandoned, just dialectically metamorphosed.

The leadership was not going to waste much time, however, on refuting the argument – however brilliantly pleaded – of an isolated malcontent. More positive work had to be done. The newest edition of the Party line on united front tactics had to be set forth clearly, specifically and in detail. Communists must, once again, speak with a single voice on what their aims were in the labour movement, and in particular, what their relationship was going to be with trade union organizations led by revisionist class traitors. The extended correspondence between the Russian trade union federation and IFTU, the conclusion of an alliance with TUC bureaucrats, the uncertainties and confusions evident at the recent Soviet Party Congress, the rumours of Profintern's imminent dissolution and the fact of Profintern's sluggish inactivity – all of these had aroused the apprehensions of more militant comrades, and added ammunition to the arsenal of ultra-leftist dissidents. It all had to be explained, and the explanation had to be defensible and unambiguous. Lozovsky, Zinoviev, Tomsky, Bukharin – this time they would all set forth the same argument and come to the same conclusions. Divisive debate was a luxury Communists could ill afford.

Soviet trade unions were not going to join IFTU by themselves. They had never even contemplated any such 'act of betrayal.' The aim all along had been to fuse the two existing trade union internationals at a world unity congress. Since Amsterdam refused to discuss anything at all with RILU, however, Profintern had agreed to let the Soviet trade unions approach IFTU independently, broach the possibility of their entry into the Amsterdam International, and ask for unconditional talks on the subject. But no basic change of tactics was involved. It was 'out of the question,' Tomsky assured everyone, that Profintern's Russian affiliate would ever have left 'to its fate the International which we created and the unions which we brought into it.'

Unfortunately, the tactic had been misinterpreted. It had given rise to a lot of legends. Some reformists had spread the falsehoods deliberately, some out of honest, genuine but misinformed belief. They said that the Soviet trade unions were about to abandon Profintern, cut their ties with other revolutionary trade unions, break away from the influence of the Communist Party, and pursue a more European orientation. It was all a lot of nonsense, but it had been so prevalent that even Communists had become confused. The Central Committee of the British Communist Party, for example, had twice referred to the question of the entry of the Soviet trade unions into Amsterdam in policy statements devoted to the issue of trade union unity. The mistake only got as far as draft texts, of course, and was not in the final published documents, but it was indicative of a general confusion on the topic that had even been reflected in the Party press.

Everything should now be clear. Russian trade unions had always accepted – nay, welcomed – the guidance of the Party, and still did. All negotiations with Amsterdam had been carried on under Party supervision and with full Party approval. The Soviet labour organizations 'have not conducted, are not conducting, and never will conduct any other policy than the policy of the RILU and the Comintern. Both the friends and the opponents of the Comintern should understand this.' They would never abandon Profintern – 'of which they are an organic part' – until the final disappearance of both RILU and IFTU in a larger, all-encompassing trades union international. Tomsky was not optimistic about anything happening very soon, especially since his English friends were preoccupied with the forthcoming struggle over miners' wages. IFTU seemed stubbornly unwilling to concede anything to achieve unity, and RILU had conceded all it could. The Executive Committee's final resolutions, in any event, would hardly make dealing with Amsterdam easier. 'There can be no question,' one of them read, 'of the entry of the trade unions of the USSR...into the Amsterdam International, for the latter being at present only a tool of the imperialistic League of Nations, does not carry out a class-conscious proletarian policy' and in fact just 'sabotages workers' unity.'[1]

In spite of all the obstacles, the campaign would go on. Trades union unity would be our 'principal slogan,' Zinoviev avowed, and Communists would work 'with the greatest energy in every country on earth' to achieve it. The workers would finally establish unity themselves, 'over the heads of the Amsterdam right-wing leaders,' if necessary. The revolutionary movement was making demands on Amsterdam, then, but it also offered some concessions. Most obviously, it was ready to surrender the independent existence of RILU. The Comintern

[1] *Kommunisticheskii Internatsional v Dokumentakh*, p. 549.

resolution reaffirmed its willingness to liquidate 'the Red International of Trade Unions as a separate body, and to its fusion with the Amsterdam International.'[1]

The unity campaign had its dangers, of course. Communists must not be so impatient for quick results, Lozovsky warned, that they agreed to unity at any price. There could be no premature dissolution of Profintern, for example. Indeed, until the amalgamation of RILU and IFTU was complete, Profintern must be supported and strengthened to the utmost. Tomsky himself said so. And finally, the kind of international that revolutionaries would ultimately insist on could never sanction any collaboration with the bourgeoisie. The only unity possible was unity on the basis of the class struggle and Communists would insist the new trade union confederation pursue that struggle actively and energetically until 'the full emancipation of the working masses from the power of capital' had been achieved.

It was a favourable time to press united front tactics into service. Capitalism had stabilized itself, yes, but at the workers' expense. The living standards of proletarians were being reduced, and unpopular new forms of class collaboration, most of them designed in the USA, were being imposed on them. The proletariat was reacting angrily. Its radicalization was splitting the social democratic movement. A left opposition had appeared that was beginning to shed some of its reformist illusions. In such circumstances, a Communist call for joint action against the bourgeoisie could not fail to be appealing. It was no surrender to opportunism, it was just good sense, and good sense not just for the moment but over the long haul. The united front was no mere contrivance to gain some temporary advantage, Zinoviev stressed. It was the basic Communist strategy for the entire historical epoch, and it would not be abandoned until a solid majority of the proletariat had been won for Communism.

United front tactics were particularly appropriate for use within the European trade union movement. The 'capitalist offensive' and the resulting wage squeeze had moved rank-and-file trade unionists, and some of their leaders, well to the left. The right-wing Amsterdam bureaucrats were trying to salvage their position by leaning on the reactionary bourgeois hirelings running the American Federation of Labor. The tensions within IFTU, however, had continued to mount, and the result was a three-way split – right, 'left,' and revolutionary ultra-left. The 'leftist' position was not easy to define. It varied from country to country

[1] *Ibid.*

and from individual to individual. Basically, however, the 'leftist' recognized the futility of Amsterdam's traditional methods and policies, rejected the idea of class collaboration with the bourgeoisie, sought some common understanding with the Soviet workingmen and urged trade union unity, nationally and internationally.

The 'left' and ultra-left, together, constituted a majority within the Amsterdam federation, but the rightists held the leadership positions and so far, although their position was precarious, they had nevertheless managed to win most of the battles. In such circumstances, Marxist revolutionaries had no real choice. Their response derived from 'the most fundamental principles of Bolshevik tactics.' Communists always backed 'every opposition movement within reformist...organizations which is directed against the theory and practice of those organizations.'[1] They could not stand aside from the struggles within the trade unions, then. They must intervene 'with all our energy and strength.' They must seek contacts with leftists, reach an understanding with them 'on the basis of a concrete programme of action,' work with them to emancipate the workers from reformism, and in the process, establish such close contacts among Communists, social democrats, and non-party people that, in the aftermath, a united proletariat could move rapidly to its revolutionary destiny.

The leadership seemed somewhat confused as to how close an association with trade union 'leftists' such a programme might require. Basic united front doctrine was, of course, that one linked arms with a reformist leader only to get the leverage to throw him down. On the other hand, many of these Amsterdam 'leftists' did seem to be moving toward a genuinely revolutionary stance, and no less an authority than Stalin himself said the Party could *only* triumph in the west after it won over, not only the trade unions, but the trade union leaders as well. The movement needed 'extensive connections' and 'genuine proletarian contact' with those leaders before it could capture a majority of the western working class, he noted, and short of such a majority, proletarian revolution in Europe was impossible.[2]

The best indication, in fact, of how much a Comintern functionary trusted some apparently sympathetic western trades union leader was his use – or non use – of quotation marks around the term 'leftist'. When the Russians referred to their English friends, the punctuation was almost always omitted. Communists were still in raptures about the Anglo-

---

[1] *Kommunisticheskii Internatsional v Dokumentakh*, p. 560.
[2] Stalin, *Sochineniia*, VIII, 105–6.

Russian Committee. Even the dour Signor Bordiga praised it. The only criticism, apparently – and it was never openly voiced in plenary session – came from un-named German ultra-leftists, who tactlessly suggested 'Russian necessities of State' might have had something to do with the Committee's creation. The Executive Committee resolutions rebuked them roundly for the heresy, and every speaker who had anything at all to say about the TUC connection acclaimed it.

For Zinoviev, it was a very model of how to construct a united front and make it work. It had become a bridge, bringing the 'revolutionary *avant-garde*' and the masses together. It would also facilitate the construction of more bridges, because 'our friends in England' really believed in international trade union unity and they were 'not sitting with folded hands' while Amsterdam reactionaries tried to sabotage the cause. The whole effort to construct that single trade union international, within which united front tactics could be employed on an even grander scale, depended on their efforts.[1]

Lozovsky was even more eloquent. It had not been easy to establish the Committee, he said, and Amsterdam die-hards and TUC right-wingers had both tried to obstruct it. But the rank and file had insisted on it, and its 'foundation was greeted joyfully by the masses' all over the world. It marked 'a new stage in the history of the international trade union movement' and demonstrated beyond any doubt the practicability of the proposed all-inclusive labour organization. If Russian and British workers could find a common language, so could workers all over the world. If workers so far apart ideologically could still make a common effort 'against reaction, fascism, and the capitalistic offensive,' then how could one doubt that a still wider coalition could do even more. 'The Communist International,' the Executive Committee proclaimed, 'proudly hails the rapprochement between the English and Soviet trade unions, and...will do everything in its power to aid the Anglo-Russian Committee in realizing its aims...' Communists were instructed to give the Committee 'full and unqualified support' and to struggle 'relentlessly' against those who 'sabotage its work' and 'try to disrupt the Anglo-Soviet bloc.'[2]

Lozovsky went to some lengths to assure the comrades that Russia's TUC associates were a rather special breed of reformist.[3] They did have their ideological failings, of course, but they still were less permeated

---

[1] *Shestoi Plenum Ispolkoma Kominterna: Stenograficheskii Otchet*, p. 591.
[2] *Kommunisticheskii Internatsional v Dokumentakh*, p. 562.
[3] *Shestoi Plenum Ispolkoma Kominterna: Stenograficheskii Otchet*, pp. 331–3.

with reactionary social democracy than were their opposite numbers on the continent, and more sensitive to the feelings and aspirations of the masses. The revolutionary movement had to cooperate with them, and help them widen their influence within the TUC. It would be unwise to make the kind of demands on them that one might make on fellow-revolutionaries. The sort of action programme that would be acceptable to them – and to Communists as well – would not incorporate every Bolshevik slogan. There was still a wide area of agreement; they were useful allies; and they should be cultivated.

Not everyone at the meeting seemed as devoted to the General Council bureaucrats as was Lozovsky. An English delegate, the Minority Movement's George Hardy, recalled pointedly – if inaccurately – that the TUC left got converted to unity only after the NMM whipped up a lot of rank and file enthusiasm for the idea. To get trade union functionaries moving in the right direction, he suggested, and to prevent them from deviating thereafter, one had constantly to prod them from below. While not so blunt about it, Zinoviev was obviously still a little apprehensive about the TUC connection too. A 'splendid bridge' between the working masses and the revolutionary movement it might be, but the Amsterdam die-hards were tough fighters and had great diplomatic talents and they might be able to bring it down. If so, he avowed, 'we will build three more' bridges.[1] The final resolutions incorporated both Zinoviev's short-term misgivings and his long-range confidence. 'Even if the Anglo-Russian Committee, for some reason or other, should fail to widen the scope of its work,' they read, the Communist International was still 'absolutely convinced' that the idea of international trade union unity would finally prevail.

In part because of the very existence of the Anglo-Russian Committee, the Comintern indulged itself in some ill-considered fantasies about the prospects for early revolutionary upheaval in Great Britain. Even a capitalism 'partially stabilized' elsewhere might still prove vulnerable on the island, given what Zinoviev called 'the revolutionizing of the English workers' movement.' Although minuscule numerically, the CPGB had so mastered the intricacies of united front manoeuvring, Lozovsky testified, that every card-carrying member now had the ear of literally hundreds of his fellow workers. The National Minority Movement, now with almost a million adherents, provided the most striking example of Communist success, transforming the Party almost overnight into a significant force in British politics. The comrades had learned how, 'if not to lead, at

[2] *Ibid.*, p. 591.

least decisively to influence, a mass movement,' Zinoviev proclaimed. There were still too few of them, of course – only 6,500 – and they were instructed to double that enrolment in a year, but they had taken advantage of their opportunities superbly. The Scarborough resolutions, some of them 'almost Leninist,' represented a tremendous advance. Over the next few weeks and months the prospects looked even more exciting. When the miners' wage agreement ran out, 'gigantic struggles' could be expected between British workers and their oppressors. 'The traitorous character of right-wing reformists' would become obvious, and proletarians would stop chasing the will-o'-the-wisp of seeking their emancipation in a bourgeois Parliament. In such circumstances, the comrades assured one another, assuming the CPGB campaigned as brilliantly in the future as it had in the past, prospects were excellent.

Over the period of late winter and early spring of 1926, Communists became more and more intoxicated with the exhilarating revolutionary possibilities in Britain – so much so that they tended to neglect the tedious and apparently interminable campaign for international trade union unity. It hardly got any serious attention at all at the meeting of the Profintern Central Council of March 7 to 15, right after the Comintern sessions were adjourned. Indeed, the Profintern meeting seemed listless and dispirited, as if everyone were merely going through some academic exercise, solely for show. Since Comintern had decided that RILU should be strengthened, they had to get together and talk, but nobody seemed to have his heart in it. Only 34 delegates were there, plus 18 alternates, and they met for only a week, on so relaxed a schedule that the stenographic report of every word spoken still fits easily into 111 pages of published text.[1]

Lozovsky dominated the dreary proceedings, and although he still mouthed the standard unity slogans, he was clearly pessimistic about anything dramatic happening soon. He dismissed the negotiations between the Soviet trade unions and IFTU almost peremptorily. It hardly mattered much whether they succeeded, he seemed to imply, since Amsterdam was not that important anyway. He seemed much more cautious than he had just two weeks earlier – at the Comintern meeting

---

[1] The published report is Red International of Labour Unions, Central Council, *IV Sessia Tsentral'nogo Soveta Krasnogo Internatsionala Profsoiuzov, 9–15 Marta 1926g.: Otchet* (Moscow: Izdanie Profinterna, 1926). The speeches of special interest are those of Lozovsky (pp. 3–6, 17–33, 63–71), Liss (pp. 48–9), Vitkovsky (pp. 56–9) and Carney (pp. 60–1). The resolutions adopted are included in *Profinterna v Rezoliutsiakh*, pp. 25–56. The material in *Desiat' Let Profinterna*, pp. 152–6, is woefully incomplete.

– in his attitude toward the trade union leftists. He never mentioned the Soviet Union's friends on the TUC General Council, nor did he refer even once to the Anglo-Russian Committee. Leftists were, almost by definition, sound on the question of trade union unity, he acknowledged, but they were not to be trusted on much else. Anybody not subject to Party discipline was, in essence, an enemy. The correct relationship to be reached between revolutionaries and leftists, Lozovsky concluded, varied widely, depending on the country and the circumstances of the moment, and no precise guidelines could be drawn.

Lozovsky did not go unchallenged. One of his colleagues on the Profintern secretariat chided him gently for his pessimism on the prospects for trade union unity.[1] Lozovsky spoke as if the campaign had failed utterly for 18 whole months, he observed. In fact, much had been achieved, including the construction of that valuable relationship between Russian and English trade unionists. Lozovsky was also too hard on the leftists. Surely the trade unions they controlled were at least a cut above the Fascist variety. Finally, Lozovsky had downgraded IFTU rather too much. Its strength might well be concentrated largely in Europe, but Europe was not unimportant, and world-wide proletarian solidarity would surely never be achieved without the participation of workers in Amsterdam affiliates.

Lozovsky never even bothered to answer the argument, although others spoke to it briefly, and the resolutions adopted reflected his priorities.[2] The gestures toward international trade union unity were correct but cursory. Much more emphasis was given to achieving single trade union organizations within each nation, and constructing fighting united fronts, wherever possible, against the bourgeoisie. The united front was no 'game,' Profintern affirmed, and no 'literary device,' nor was it a 'manoeuvre' against reformists, as charged in the west. It was a 'legitimate class manoeuvre of the proletariat against the bourgeoisie.' The 'Anglo-Soviet Unity Committee' – it appeared to have acquired a new name in the Profintern's books – deserved 'every possible support.' The labour troubles on the horizon in Britain offered a fertile field for IFTU–RILU collaboration. To win that imminent class struggle would require proletarian internationalism of the highest order, and Amsterdam was challenged – without much hope of acceptance – to prove itself worthy of the allegiance of its members. All of this – and this was about all there was – was buried in some fifty pages of resolutions, most of

[1] *IV Sessia Tsentral'nogo Soveta: Otchet*, pp. 48–9 (Liss).
[2] *Profintern v Rezoliutsiakh*, pp. 25–6, 38, 48, 55–6.

which were devoted to such more intriguing issues as emigration, the eight-hour day, Profintern prospects in Japan and the complexities of the Czechoslovak labour movement. The international unity slogans were not repudiated, but Lozovsky's passion for them was obviously well under control.

The National Minority Movement's so-called Conference of Action in March reflected the revised line admirably.[1] It was the most impressive gathering the NMM would ever sponsor, with 883 delegates present claiming to represent almost a million workers. International trade union unity was still on the agenda, and the Anglo-Russian Committee was urged to do more to achieve it. But international solidarity took second place, especially for the NMM, to the urgency of creating a monolithic labour front in Britain in behalf of the miners.[2] It was 'imperative' that 'all the forces of the working-class movement should be mobilized under one central leadership' to win the battle. The members of the General Council were the obvious ones to direct the mobilization, and they should immediately convene a National Congress of Action to discuss specific strategy.

The deference to the General Council may have seemed a bit strange, especially to the councillors. Communists clearly still did not trust them. Zinoviev said so again in late April – and bluntly.[3] One backed them – against the reactionaries – but one never overestimated them or relied on them. English leftists, in particular, had begun to waver ever since their vain hopes of luring the Soviet trade unions into IFTU were frustrated. Lozovsky was also nervous about the TUC leftists.[4] He sensed them 'descending toward vacillation.' The *Daily Herald* was a good example. It barely reported the NMM Conference at all, and it seemed lukewarm in its support of the miners. The right-wing compromisers appeared more and more in command. But it was still the General Council, nevertheless, which Communists insisted take the lead in the crucial class struggle to come.

[1] The transcript is in NMM's *Report of Special National Conference*. Lozovsky had ordered the NMM to hold such a meeting back on Jan. 11 (*Mezhdunarodnoe Profdvizhenie*, pp. 20–1). For Lozovsky's appraisal of the conference, see his article in *Pravda*, 2 Apr., 1926.

[2] The *Sunday Worker* only devoted one article specifically to international unity in the whole period between February and May, William Paul's piece on 14 Mar., 1926.

[3] *Inprecorr*, VI, 45 (3 June, 1926), 740–1.

[4] See, for example, *Pravda*, 10, 24 Apr., 1926, and 'Amsterdam, Profintern, and the Crisis in English Mining,' *Krasnyi Internatsional Profsoiuzov*, No. 5, cited in Lozovsky, *Angliiskii Proletariat na Rasputi*, pp. 180–92.

By the Party's analysis of the situation – and it was an exceptionally clear-headed analysis – it had very little choice. If the rest of the labour movement stood by the miners, and the operators and government did not yield, the general strike was on. A general strike meant revolution. Communists understood that, even if trade union bureaucrats did not. As far back as September, 1925, J. T. Murphy noted that a general strike could 'only mean the throwing down of the gauntlet to the capitalist state, and all the powers at its disposal.' 'Either that challenge is only a gesture,' he continued, 'in which case the capitalist class need not worry about it,' or it must develop 'into an actual fight for power, in which case we land into civil war. Any leaders who talk about a general strike without facing this obvious fact are bluffing both themselves and the workers.'[1]

Only the General Council could call such a general strike and get a response. If and when it did, then, like it or not, it would find itself in charge of an insurrection. It was badly prepared for its revolutionary role, but long-term, it could not escape it except by ignominious surrender – a surrender which, if one credited the Scarborough rhetoric, was not really likely. To wage any revolution successfully required monolithic leadership, and the General Council had to be in a position to exert such leadership. The CPGB slogan, in such circumstances, had to be 'All Power to the General Council!' and the comrades urged that doctrine as early as January, 1926. It was not easy for all the Party faithful to understand the dialectics of the situation, and see *why* they should favour thrusting power on trade union reactionaries who did not seek it, but their leaders could only offer them the hope that if the councillors got the power, and still failed to use it effectively, they might be replaced by others more militant than they.[2]

Murphy was not even sure of that. On the very eve of the strike, he reminded his fellow-revolutionaries that Communists did not hold leading positions in the trade unions, and that the Party could only offer advice, and place its forces at the disposal of a movement led by men with 'no revolutionary perspective before them. Any revolutionary perspectives they may perceive will send the majority of them hot on the track of a retreat...They are totally incapable of moving forward to face all the implications of a united working-class challenge to the state.

[1] J. T. Murphy, 'The Nine Months Truce', *Communist Review*, VI, 5 (Sept., 1925), 211–16. See also R. Palme Dutt, '"Red Friday" and After,' *Communist International*, No. 16 (1925), pp. 64–88.
[2] See Bell, *British Communist Party*, pp. 110–11 and Communist Party of Great Britain, 'Orders from Moscow?' (London: CPGB, [Aug.] 1926), pp. 50–1.

To entertain any exaggerated view as to the revolutionary possibilities of this crisis and visions of new leadership "arising spontaneously in the struggle," etc. is fantastic'.[1]

That degree of gloom, however, was peculiar to Murphy. Most British Communists were more hopeful. They were hopeful in the USSR, too, and Russian Communists joined their British opposite numbers, at the last minute, in rallying behind the General Council.[2] Profintern telegraphed the IFTU on April 17 – with a copy to the TUC in London – urging a mammoth international coalition in behalf of the miners 'in their struggle against the capitalist offensive,' and expressing confidence that 'our other differences' would not preclude 'common action.'[3] Amsterdam, predictably, was disinterested. It already was in touch with its TUC affiliate, it replied, and would cooperate with the British in any way they requested. It saw no need for any special RILU–IFTU venture in addition.

Lozovsky then fired off a wire to the members of the General Council, reminding them that Amsterdam had also resisted any cooperative effort on behalf of the miners back in 1921, and that that strike had therefore failed. The lesson was obvious. IFTU did not really support the proletarian cause at all. 'We are certain,' Lozovsky concluded, 'that the English trade unions and the General Council, having assumed the initiative in re-establishing a united world trade union movement – because in unity there is strength – will react negatively to the failure of unity of action in a cause so burning and so serious for the working class.'[4]

The TUC response must have smarted. It acknowledged with thanks Profintern's offers of support, ignored the invitation to spank IFTU, and indicated that the negotiations on behalf of the miners, which it 'hoped would be successful,' were still proceeding.[5] When the All-Union Central Council of Trade Unions and the Soviet Miners' Union offered their 'fraternal assistance,' the General Council parried their overtures with the same meaningless courtesies. The TUC leadership did not consider itself revolutionary, and was wary about moving too close to those

---

[1] *Workers' Weekly*, 30 Apr., 1926.

[2] Volkov, *Anglo-Sovetskii Otnosheniia*, pp. 209–13 and Gurovich, *Vseobshchaia Stachka v Anglii* summarize the Russian effort nicely.

[3] Russian text in *Mezhdunarodnoe Profdvizhenie*, pp. 56–7; English text in *IFTU Press Reports*, VI, 16 (29 Apr., 1926).

[4] *Mezhdunarodnoe Profdvizhenie*, p. 21.

[5] TUC Special Industrial Committee, Decisions Nos. 120, 133, 148, file 1 1/2.2, pp. 22, 24, 26.

who hoped to force it into such a role. It was outraged by charges of 'irresolution' out of Moscow, and the even more offensive warnings about the dire possibility the cause might be 'betrayed' by its own leaders.[1] The Baldwin cabinet might have been alarmed at the Third International intervening in the miners' dispute. Indeed, it was, and Chamberlain made sure the Russians knew it.[2] But the trade union leaders must have been even more distressed. With friends like Zinoviev, they hardly needed any enemies.

They had them, nevertheless, and above all, in the Tory government. Baldwin and his colleagues saw the nature of the coming trial as clearly as did the Communists, and were quite as astute in their analysis of what was really at stake.[3] To continue – indefinitely – eking out miners' wages with government subsidies was out of the question. It had cost the Exchequer 17 million pounds to finance the subsidies from August to April, 70 per cent over the first cost estimates.[4] Conservatives had no taste for such unsound extravagances from the public till. The miners would have to take their pay cuts, like it or not. And if once again, as on 'Red Friday,' the rest of the labour movement stood behind them, and if the result were a general strike, the government would be ready for it. Joynson-Hicks openly encouraged such 'unofficial' associations as the Organization for the Maintenance of Supplies (OMS) to recruit local toughs as anti-union volunteers. Indeed, the cabinet records make it clear OMS was government-sponsored. The government was even willing to accept help from the Fascists, who applied in droves for positions as Special Constables. As early as October 7 the Home Secretary was bragging to his ministerial colleagues that his skeleton organization for the industrial emergency was 80 per cent complete.[5] On February 22 he announced preparations were already so advanced that 'there is now very little remaining to be done before the actual occurrence of an emergency.'[6]

Meanwhile, the Attorney-General, Sir Douglas Hogg, was investigating the legal weapons available to the government when the general strike came. Neither the Sedition Laws nor the Incitement to Mutiny Act would be adequate to such a crisis, he suggested. Indeed, there was

[1] Degras, *Communist International: Documents*, pp. 298–9.
[2] Cabinet Conclusions, 1926, CAB 23.52, Conclusion 15(26)3, 14 Apr., 1926.
[3] See, for example, Joynson-Hicks' speech at Northampton in early August, 1925 (*The Times*, 3 Aug., 1925).
[4] Cabinet Conclusions, 1925, CAB 23.51, Decision 51(25)1, 28 Oct., 1925.
[5] *Ibid.*, Decision 47(25)2, 7 Oct., 1925.
[6] Cabinet Papers, 1926, CAB 24.178, C.P. 81(26), 22 Feb., 1926.

nothing illegal about a general strike at all, except for those actions threatening such essential public services as gas, water and electricity. Hogg was intrigued by the possibility of re-defining the crime of sedition, as the Australians had, to make it prohibit any act promoting 'feelings of ill-will and hostility between different classes of His Majesty's subjects.' Prime Minister Baldwin referred the whole problem to a special cabinet committee.[1] By the end of March, its report was ready, complete with a tough new draft law on sedition on the Australian model, providing for gaoling agitators without even a trial in the event of an emergency. The successful 'prosecution of the Communist leaders' in October had, however, 'obviated any necessity for immediate legislation,' and trade unionists would probably react so violently to the proposals that introducing them might actually precipitate the industrial crisis Baldwin hoped to avert. The cabinet therefore decided to approve the committee's draft, but delay introducing it until the situation demanded.[2]

By the end of April, the government's only worry was that it might have over-prepared. Joynson-Hicks had few last-minute suggestions to make, and nothing he proposed was really crucial. Everything had been done in advance. All that remained were details on the occupation of Hyde Park and the dispatch of troops, 'as unobtrusively as possible,' to Scotland, South Wales, and Lancashire.[3] There would be no repetition of 'Red Friday' this time!

The government was ready, then. So were the Communists, as ready as they could be with many of their key leaders still in gaol. Only the TUC bureaucrats were still improvising. They seemed more and more aware that planning a general strike amounted to preparing open rebellion against the established order, and that they had no desire to do. They were not revolutionaries, and did not want to appear to be. They may have assumed their resolution would never be tested, that the government would yield at the last minute. Or, as G. D. H. Cole suggested, perhaps they were just 'bewildered and paralysed by the course of events, and did nothing because they could not make up their minds what to do.'[4]

In any event, they seemed more and more reticent as winter gave way

---

[1] Cabinet Papers, 1925, CAB 24.175, C.P. 420(25), 9 Oct., 1925; Cabinet Conclusions, 1925, CAB 23.51, Conclusion 48(25)2, 13 Oct., 1925.
[2] Cabinet Papers, 1926, CAB 24.179, C.P. 136(26) 25 Mar., 1926; Cabinet Conclusions, 1926, CAB 23.52, Conclusion 14(26)1, 31 Mar., 1926.
[3] Cabinet Conclusions, 1926, CAB 23.52, Conclusion 19(26)6, 28 Apr., 1926.
[4] Cole, *History of Socialist Thought*, IV, Part I, 441.

to spring – more restrained, more cautious, more circumspect. Back in February they had strutted like fighting cocks. Working-men would unite to resist any cut in miners' wages. But after March 10, after the release of the Royal Commission report prescribing just such cuts, they began to look more like just cackling hens. A statement on April 9 merely reconfirmed the leadership's 'previous declarations in support of the miners' efforts to obtain an equitable settlement,' and General Secretary Citrine suggested the time was not yet ripe for 'any final declaration of the General Council's policy.' A somewhat stronger affirmation five days later, expressing the Council's 'fullest' support of the miners' decision to resist 'the degradation of their standard of life,' was softened, in fact, by J. H. Thomas' warning, that same day, that 'to talk at this stage as if in a few days all the workers of the country were to be called out was...letting loose passions that might be difficult to control.' Nobody should feel, he cautioned, that war was inevitable.[1]

In fact, it looked more and more as if it were. By the end of March, both the government and the mine operators had indicated general approval of the Royal Commission's recommendations. The miners, however, affirmed on April 9 they would never agree to a reduction of wages or a longer working day, and contemptuously rejected the draft of a national agreement the owners submitted to them on April 21. At this point, the government stepped in. Baldwin met with both sides for four days without result, and then, on April 26, invited the TUC General Council to involve itself in the negotiations. The old agreements would run out on the 30th, in just four days. The labour movement finally had to decide what it would do then. The General Council started working out its plans on the 27th, and summoned the executives of its affiliated unions to London on the 29th to give them their instructions.

In fact, the instructions were not yet ready and the negotiations were still proceeding, so the executives merely voted J. H. Thomas' resolution endorsing all efforts to find a settlement. With nothing else to do except wait out the talks, they whiled away the time singing: 'Lead, Kindly Light!' was perhaps the most appropriate of their selections. Meanwhile, in the conference room, the government and operators refused to budge, and on April 30, miners arriving at the pits were presented statements proclaiming wage cuts on a take-it-or-leave-it basis – in effect, lock-out notices. The crisis was on, and the General Council promptly provided

[1] The quotations in this paragraph are drawn from Hutt, *British Working Class*, pp. 124–6. Hutt's account of the events leading up to the strike is both exciting and persuasive.

each of its executives a memorandum amounting to Order Number One for the general strike. It listed which workers were to go out, and when. Each executive was asked to agree to it separately, and each was invited to delegate all his powers, for the duration of the emergency, to the General Council. It would all begin Monday, May 3. The support was overwhelming, and the May Day celebrations on Saturday were the biggest and most tumultuous of the decade.

Meanwhile, however, the negotiations proceeded. The government agreed to urge the operators to withdraw the lock-out notices, but only if the miners acceded to the principle of wage cuts. The miners agreed to discuss the possibility. The government nevertheless declared a state of emergency under the Emergency Powers Act, and at this point, the members of the General Council seemed ready to cave in completely. The miners would just have to take their cuts. They wired the Miners' Federation executives to come back to London to be in on the surrender. Baldwin was convinced the crisis was past. His cabinet colleagues were not so sure, and indeed, many of them urged refusing to negotiate any more at all unless the General Council withdrew its general strike threat. The labour leaders, however, assured the government they had issued no orders that could not be reversed, and they promised to press the miners to accept the pay reductions suggested.

And, of course, that should have been the end of it, except that the editors of the *Daily Mail* had taken this occasion to write a leader calling the general strike threat 'revolutionary' and urging the government to crush it, and *Daily Mail* workers had refused to print such an atrocity. The cabinet hard-liners now carried the day, and Baldwin agreed not to resume negotiations until the TUC leaders repudiated their members at the printing plant and withdrew all strike notices unconditionally. A chagrined and intimidated General Council was ready to recant, at least to the extent of dissociating itself strongly from the *Daily Mail* printers, but when its spokesmen took a note to that effect to Number 10, they were informed Mr Baldwin had already retired. It was too late. The British labour movement had been manoeuvred into a revolutionary confrontation its leaders never wanted and tried desperately to avoid.[1]

---

[1] My account of the immediate background of the strike derives from Hutt, *British Working Class*, pp. 126–36, supplemented by the government documents, especially Cabinet Conclusions, 1926, CAB 23.52, Conclusions 21(26)1, 22(26)1, and 23(26), 2 May, 1926.

5
Separation (May–November 1926)

One historian has dubbed the general strike 'labor's tragic weapon.' If, however, following Aristotle (as who would not!), one assumes 'tragedy' must evoke both pity and terror, Britain's 1926 fiasco failed half the test. Pitiable – even pitiful – it may have been. But it inspired no terror, not then, and now it prompts only a kind of aching anguish that such mammoth energies could be engaged so ineffectually, and such wondrous idealism dissipated so totally.

The story of the strike has been, as they say, 'told elsewhere.'[1] It has not been told especially well. Historians often seem embarrassed by tragedy (by *anybody's* definition) and ill at ease with lost causes. What won, what survived, must have been – in some cosmic sense – right, and vicarious participation in the triumphs of the victorious is, in any event, a much more congenial diversion than is mourning, with the losers, the intransigence of fate.

Surely no cause could have been more lost than this. A mighty and spirited army – with nobody leading it – hurled itself awkwardly and ineffectively against a smug, complacent, somewhat repulsive, but probably irresistible enemy. The result, predictably, was that the workers' movement was smashed, their organizations impoverished and enfeebled, and their leaders humiliated and discredited. The English political left was disabled for a generation, and much that was imaginative, thoughtful, humane and good in British life and thought did not again get a serious hearing until after the Second World War.

---

[1] The General Strike lacks a definitive history. The best sustained account is still Crook, *General Strike*, pp. 283–495, but much material which eluded Crook has been made available since. The Public Record Office and the TUC Library, for example, both bulge with fascinating and not yet fully exploited documentation. A more recent secondary account of the strike, using only some of the material at hand, is Symons, *General Strike*. Christopher Farman, *The General Strike: May, 1926* (London: Rupert Hart-Davis, 1972) adds little. Hutt, *British Working Class*, pp. 140–60, has a distinctive and significant viewpoint on the strike, and there is an unimpassioned and useful summary in the *Annual Register, 1926*, pp. 50–5. An interesting personal recollection is Leslie A. Paul, *Angry Young Man* (London: Faber & Faber, [1951]). For anything much more substantial than all of this, one must just take to the primary sources oneself.

Prime responsibility for the fiasco simply has to be assigned to the TUC General Council. The workers themselves were superb – disciplined, confident and enthusiastic.[1] Their leaders, on the other hand, 'unprepared and proud of it' as they went into the strike,[2] presided over the rout with about the gusto and elan of the priest directing the condemned man to the gallows. They were hesitant and apologetic from the start. The TUC officials seemed not to have made up their minds, Graham Wallas puzzled, 'as to what they expect to do or how they expect to do it.' He wondered whether they were planning their moves 'with full intellectual seriousness.'[3]

In fact, of course, the members of the General Council were in a terrible dilemma. They had not meant to call such a strike, and they had never thought it would come to that. They had been manoeuvred into a bluff, however; the bluff had been called; and lo and behold they found themselves involved in a revolutionary confrontation that was ideologically repugnant to almost all of them. Their walk-out had nothing to do with politics, they kept insisting, and they definitely had no intention of seizing power unconstitutionally. They virtually promised not to hurt anybody, and to prove it, held off calling out the so-called 'second line' workers until the very last minute, and never called out the employees in such key industries as electricity. From at least May 8 on, only five days after the strike began, they were casting about frantically for some way to adjourn the confrontation, at virtually any price.

The government did not make it easy for them. It demanded, in effect, unconditional surrender. Baldwin pronounced the walk-out unconstitutional and illegal, and even the moderates in his cabinet agreed that it would be 'a grave error' to allow the strikers 'even the appearance of success.'[4] Moderation, however, even of that doubtful variety, was not much in evidence in the highest Tory counsels. Joynson-Hicks and Churchill, notably, were uninterested in concessions of any kind at any time. They urged instead an all-out war against the TUC, including new statutes outlawing the strike explicitly and freezing union funds.[5] The ferocity evident in the cabinet records makes a mockery of those accounts

[1] Even the government acknowledged it. See the cabinet's *Daily Bulletin*, Nos. 1–11, 3–13 May, 1926, Cabinet Commissions, 1926, CAB 27.331.
[2] The phrase is Crook's (*General Strike*, p. 367).
[3] Graham Wallas to George Bernard Shaw, 8 May, 1926, British Museum, Additional MSS 50553.
[4] The 'moderate' involved was Viscount Cecil of Chelwood, Chancellor of the Duchy of Lancaster. See Cabinet Papers, 1926, CAB 24.179, C.P. 188(26), 7 May, 1926.
[5] For these matters, see Cabinet Conclusions, 1926, CAB 23.52, Conclusions 25(26), 26(26)1, 27(26)1, 7, 8 May, 1926.

of the general strike, then and later, emphasizing what a jolly lark those Oxford undergraduates had trying to run the Underground network, or recalling with bemused awe the famous and oh-so-English strikers-versus-policemen football game. In fact, this was serious business, deadly business. The government saw it that way, even if the TUC did not. The strikers were revolutionaries, no matter what their protestations, and at least some of the Tory ministers were ready to wage counter-revolution to restore the balance.

In fact, however, the government never had much of an excuse to use even a fraction of the power available to it. The assumption, in advance, that a test of strength was inevitable, and the months of planning for it, paid off handsomely. Outside the major cities, the general population was hardly inconvenienced at all. Stocks of necessities held up nicely right through the crisis, and were in an 'extremely satisfactory' state as late as the last day. What rioting there was was successfully localized and put down with precision. A 'soviet' started issuing orders from the Standard Public House in Deptford, in London's East End, but less than a week later the cabinet was assured the entire population of that area had been 'cowed by the display of force made during the past few days.' The judiciary cooperated in the intimidation campaign. One London magistrate fined a striker £10 for 'being in possession of a leaflet likely to cause disruption.'[1]

It was madness to continue an irresolute and hesitant assault on so tenacious and resourceful a foe, and the General Council knew it. It was draining its members' energies and squandering their money, and to no possible advantage. J. H. Thomas, who announced as early as May 9 that he had 'never favoured the principle of a General Strike' anyway, was quick to hand with the formula for surrender. He had been involved in secret conversations with Sir Herbert Samuel, the chairman of that Royal Commission which had recommended miners' pay cuts back in March. Acting on his own authority, not Baldwin's (the government absolutely refused to negotiate while the strike was still on), Samuel came up with a document suggesting about the same reductions in miners' wages as he had proposed in his original report. The TUC Negotiating Committee approved the document unanimously, at least as a basis for talks, summoned the representatives of the miners, informed them the strike was about to be called off, and insisted they participate in the surrender. The miners refused, but the General Council went ahead anyway, on the night of May 12. It was a humiliating finish

---

[1] *Daily Bulletin*, 5, 11, 12 May, 1926, Cabinet Commissions, 1926, CAB 27.331.

to a shameful adventure. The Prime Minister would not even receive them until they confessed they were there solely to capitulate, and the announcement of their defeat was all he would listen to. He would not even promise any help getting reinstatement of strikers who had been dismissed. They could talk about victimization, apparently, later on.[1]

The rout cost the nation dearly, some three to four hundred million pounds, according to the *Economist*. More working days were lost in just that week and a half of futility than had been forfeited in all industrial disputes of all kinds over the previous $2\frac{1}{2}$ years.[2] The strikers themselves felt outraged and betrayed. Their spokesmen had assured them that solidarity guaranteed victory. They had dutifully stayed together and obeyed orders. They thought they were winning. Only two days before the collapse of the effort, the *British Worker* had headlined 'ALL'S WELL' and relayed the General Council's instructions to 'Stand Firm' and 'Trust Your Leaders.' Those same leaders had now directed them to haul down the flag and beg for mercy. The miners, who were most directly affected, rejected any such humiliation. The rest felt they had to accept it, but they scorned and resented those who had so beguiled and deceived them. Over half a million workers quit the movement altogether over the next two years. Those who stayed in had so little money behind them – a third of their reserves had been dissipated in the strike – that their organizations would be almost totally ineffectual for the rest of the twenties. The only real gainers from the strike appeared to be the Communists. There were almost twice as many of them in September as there had been in May.[3]

It was a nice consolation prize, but at the beginning of the strike, Communists – and especially those in the Soviet Union – had hoped for much more. For a year and a half, now, they had been putting a lot of emotional energy into cultivating that comradely relationship with the TUC General Council. They now anticipated some return on their investment. Profintern had a manifesto out as early as May 4, certifying the struggle a genuine class war and calling on workers all over the world to do their proletarian duty. RILU had the slogans ready. 'Not one ton of coal to England!' 'Relentless struggle against strike breaking!' 'All, as one man, to the aid of the struggling English proletariat!' For

---

[1] Bullock, *Bevin*, I, 333–9, speaks most authoritatively on the gruesome surrender ceremony.

[2] *Statistical Abstract*, Cmd. 4801 (1935), pp. 117, 118, 121.

[3] Communist International, Executive Committee, *The Communist International Between the Fifth & the Sixth World Congresses 1924–1928* (London: Communist Party of Great Britain, 1928), p. 131.

those impatient with mere slogans, Profintern suggested donating a quarter of a day's pay to the English strikers. Once again, it invited Amsterdam to participate in the common effort. The bid got precisely the response anticipated – none whatsoever.[1]

Comintern was also active on its own. It provided its affiliates instant Marxist analysis of the strike as early as May 5.[2] The events in Britain were of 'historic importance.' The capitalists had determined to defeat and humiliate the miners (described, rather surprisingly, as 'the vanguard of the British proletariat') in a kind of 'preventive war' against the whole labour movement. It began as a purely economic struggle, over wages, but it would rapidly be transformed into a political contest of the most basic kind, a class war. The international bourgeoisie had united behind the employers and the government. The workers, all over the world, would have to respond in kind. The major threats to proletarian solidarity were the villains of 'Black Friday' and the English movement was warned to beware the treachery of the likes of Jimmy Thomas. In a separate manifesto addressed to the CPGB, English Communists were instructed to point out to the strikers that 'Thomas and Co. . . are more dangerous to the movement than all Baldwin's O.M.S.'[3] If right-wing manipulators and traitors were frustrated, all would be well. The 'gigantic struggle' in England, which the international proletariat watched with 'the greatest delight,' would inevitably lead to the Bolshevization of the proletarian vanguard and the beginning of the end for the bourgeoisie.

The Soviet government deemed it impolitic to rhapsodize over England's agony quite so openly. A diplomatic break with Britain would be inconvenient, and the Russian leaders did not want to give the hotheads in Baldwin's cabinet any excuse to insist on such a rupture. It may well have been something of an embarrassment to the top leadership when local soviets in Moscow and Leningrad addressed appeals to their constituencies urging 'every honest toiler' to contribute part of his wages to the cause as 'an expression of fraternal solidarity and sympathy with the English proletariat.'[4] If the Foreign Office wanted something to

---

[1] *Mezhdunarodnoe Profdvizhenie*, pp. 21–2, 57; *Inprecorr*, VI, 41 (13 May, 1926), 658–61.
[2] *Pravda*, 5 May, 1926; *Inprecorr*, VI, 41 (13 May, 1926), 653–54; Degras, *Communist International: Documents*, pp. 298–300.
[3] *Izvestiia*, 8 May 1926; Great Britain, Foreign Office, *Russia No. 1 (1924): Note From His Majesty's Government to the Government of the Union of Soviet Socialist Republics Respecting the Relations Between the Two Countries, and Note in Reply, February 23/26, 1927*, Cmd. 2822 (London: HMSO, 1927), pp. 9–12.
[4] *Izvestiia*, 8 May, 1926.

protest, it had better be those resolutions, the British Ambassador suggested. He had not been able to identify any other breach of international etiquette.

The state apparatus may have shown some restraint, but the press showed virtually none. Karl Radek, dismissed from his Comintern position in 1925 and now principal of the Sun Yat-sen University in Moscow, told his many British contacts that he had 'instructed the press to keep calm,' and he personally did indeed warn the public not to expect too much from the British struggle.[1] In private, he anticipated no success at all. 'Make no mistake,' he told one visiting Englishman, 'this is not a revolutionary movement. It is simply a wage dispute.'[2] One is hardly surprised, however, that the Soviet man-in-the-street, reading *Pravda*'s account of the British bourgeoisie fleeing the country in battleships, did not share Radek's detachment. The British Ambassador exaggerated only a little when he reported Russian press coverage of the strike was 'as impertinent in its comments as it was obstinate in its misinformation and obtuse in its ignorance of foreign psychology.'[3]

The dispatches of Zinoviev and Lozovsky he deemed especially outrageous. Zinoviev had indeed written enthusiastically, but the articles he submitted to the newspapers were no more inflammatory than the manifesto he issued in behalf of the Comintern. Indeed, they were virtually identical.[4] Lozovsky, in fact, was a good deal more intemperate, and as chief *Pravda* commentator on the strike, he had much more to say.[5] The general strike was the most gigantic social upheaval in English history. It had made a 'stunning impression on the whole international labour movement.' Five million men were out. (Lozovsky apparently counted each striker twice.) The TUC's General Council had been transformed into the general staff of a mighty proletarian army. Labour's right wing – MacDonald, Henderson, Thomas – feared the struggle and was trying to arrange a capitulation without the consent or agreement of the General Council and behind the backs of the workers, but such traitors would be unmasked and repudiated.[6] That was the strike as Lozovsky saw it, and it was coupled with 'news' articles printed under

---

[1] Hodgson to Chamberlain, 25 May, 1926, N 2367/1687/38, F.O. 371.11786.
[2] *Ibid.*; Robert Boothby, *I Fight to Live* (London: Victor Gollancz, 1947), pp. 81–2.
[3] Hodgson to Chamberlain, 13 May, 1926, 18 May, 1926, N 2187/1687/38, N 2260/1687/38, F.O. 371.11794.
[4] Compare, for example, his article in *Pravda*, 5 May, 1926, with the Comintern resolution of that date.
[5] His articles were collected in book form in *Angliiskii Proletariat na Rasputi*.
[6] *Ibid.*, or *Pravda*, 6–8 May, 1926.

the most extravagant of headlines. 'Class Against Class In England.' 'Strike In England Widens.' 'Strike Reaches 100 Per Cent.' 'Communications Between England And The Continent Broken.' 'Government Prepares for Repression.' 'Clash Between Strikers And Strikebreakers.' 'Workers' Blood Shed In Hull.' 'Bloody Clashes Between Workers and Police.' 'English Workers Stand Firm.' 'Councils of Action Start In Operation.' Cumulatively, it was all immensely stimulating, and terribly misleading.

The Russian people responded enthusiastically. Even before Soviet trade union leaders could transmit any specific recommendations, workers all over the country had voluntarily obligated themselves to back the English strikers financially with donations of up to two full days' wages. Hundreds of thousands of them participated in mass sympathy demonstrations, carrying placards vowing 'The Cause of the English Worker is Our Cause!' Over a hundred thousand turned out just in Kharkov. Factory meetings all over the country, in a refreshing variety of resolutions clearly *not* mass-produced in Moscow beforehand, affirmed the solidarity of Russian and English proletarians. Party agitators, of course, were in on all this, but they hardly had to do much to keep temperatures high. The feeling was already there, genuinely and spontaneously. Even the British Minister had to confess that the Russian money offered the TUC was contributed voluntarily.[1]

As early as May 7, the All-Union Central Council of Trade Unions – Tomsky's organization – had moved to direct all the enthusiasm into creative channels. Its suggestion was that trade union members contribute a minimum of a quarter of a day's wages to the cause. It anticipated, therefore, a total collection of something in the neighbourhood of two million rubles, and proposed to dispatch a portion of that, 250,000 rubles, immediately.[2]

The offer put the TUC bureaucrats in a terrible quandary. They needed the financial help badly, and had indeed asked Amsterdam for a

---

[1] Hodgson to Chamberlain, 25 May 1926, N 2367/1687/38, F.O. 371.11786. For convincing evidence of the spontaneity of the demonstrations, see *Angliiskaia Stachka i Rabochie SSSR* (Moscow: Vsesoiuznyi tsentralnyi sovet professional'nykh soiuzov, 1926). The English translation is *All Russian Council of Trade Unions, Red Money: A Statement of the Facts Relating to the Money Raised in Russia During the General Strike and Mining Lockout in Britain*, trans. Eden and Cedar Paul (London: Labour Research Department, 1926). See also *Inprecorr*, VI, 41 (13 May 1926), 658–61 and 50 (1 July, 1926), 818–20; Gurovich, *Vseobshchaia Stachka v Anglii*, pp. 169–71; Fischer, *Soviets in World Affairs*, II, 624–31.

[2] The ACCTU letter to its affiliates is in *Pravda*, 7 May, 1926, and (in English) in *Inprecorr*, VI, 50 (1 July, 1926), 819.

contribution on the very first day of the strike.[1] But Red Gold was something else, and the General Council decided immediately that it 'could not accept the money...as the offer would be wilfully misrepresented and acceptance would be misunderstood.'[2] The decision was recorded the day it was made in the *British Worker*. The Council confirmed the reports already appearing in the continental press that it had been offered Russian money to carry on the strike, and it announced it had informed the Russians 'in a courteous communication' that it could not accept the offer and that the money was being returned.[3] It did not release the text of the letter, which was in fact an ambiguous document suggesting the General Council was anxious to 'convince the public we are not pursuing any revolutionary aims,' and implying that all contributions from abroad were therefore to be declined.[4] In fact, of course, non-Communist largesse would have been welcomed, had it been forthcoming, and the government was ready to forbid the use of Russian money in any event, even if the TUC had been willing to take it. The very day the General Council sent the Russian cheque back, the cabinet agreed to prohibit banks from paying out any foreign money 'for purposes prejudicial to the public safety or life of the community.' That Red Gold was what the ministers had in mind.[5]

The Soviets were hurt, disillusioned and resentful about being rebuffed so bluntly. The Central Trade Union Council issued a carefully drawn and restrained statement devoted mostly to justifying its original benevolence. English and Soviet workers had a rather special relationship, it noted, because of the existence of the Anglo-Russian Committee, and that was why the strike had aroused such an enthusiastic popular response in the USSR. The Central Council, it continued, would make no comment on why the TUC chose to refuse its offer. It assumed (falsely, in fact) that all money from abroad was to be rejected. The Soviets would simply turn over the funds already collected to the Miners' Federation instead, and would continue to accept contributions on behalf of that organization.[6]

[1] General Council Decision No. 218, 3 May 1926, file I 1 2/2, p. 36, TUC Archives.
[2] *Ibid.*, Decision No. 247, 8 May 1926, p. 40. For final disposition of the Soviet offer, see *ibid.*, Decision No. 268, 18 May, 1926, p. 43, and Finance and General Purposes Committee, Decision No. 311, 8 June, 1926, p. 48.
[3] *British Worker*, 8 May, 1926.
[4] For the text of the General Council's reply, see *Inprecorr*, VI, 42 (20 May, 1926), p. 673.
[5] Cabinet Conclusions, 1926, CAB 23.52, Conclusion 27(26)1, 8 May, 1926.
[6] Statement in *Pravda*, 11 May, 1926; English translation in *Inprecorr*, VI, 42 (20 May, 1926), 673.

The Soviet press was not so gentle. To send back the money was a 'huge,' perhaps a 'fatal,' mistake, and a strange and disturbing mistake. It demonstrated the fundamental weakness of the TUC leadership, its stubborn refusal to acknowledge that the confrontation in which it was involved was as much political as it was economic. The General Council was still trying to maintain the absurd fiction of a non-revolutionary general strike. It was up to the councillors to recognize realities, and act on them. That meant dismissing class traitors like MacDonald, Thomas and Bevin, accepting all the international help available, and waging the fight on an overtly political basis. The TUC was engaged in a class war, like it or not. If it failed to learn the basic rules of class war, it must inevitably lose.[1]

The British Communist Party, in theory, anyway, was specially trained in those 'basic rules,' and ready to communicate them to fellow pro-letarians whenever class consciousness reached a suitably advanced state. In fact, of course, the CPGB leadership was rather surprised the confrontation had finally occurred, and was in no position, in any event, to much influence how the battle was waged. The most thoughtful Red leaders, like Murphy, conceded very early in the strike the likelihood that the General Council would capitulate prematurely.[2] Such pes-simism, however, if expressed openly, could only prove self-fulfilling, and the Party's public posture was confident and positive. At Comin-tern's direction, CPGB theorists arranged events neatly in acceptable dialectical order and CPGB agitators hurried off to the masses with the tactically appropriate slogans. The rhetoric was to get increasingly militant as the strike progressed and to become more and more overtly political, finally demanding ouster of the Baldwin government in favour of, to start with, a broadly based left-labour coalition.[3] When the news came out that the TUC had sent back that Russian money, the Party pamphleteers joined the Soviet press in lamenting the mistake. It was 'a blow at the wives and children of British workers and a wanton insult to the Russian workers.'[4] And finally, when it became clear the General Council was going to call off the action, Communists urged the workers to defy their leaders and stay out anyway. It is difficult to see, however, that all the analysis, all the sloganeering and all the pamphleteering affected the course of events in the slightest.

[1] *Pravda, Izvestiia*, 11, 12 May, 1926.
[2] MacFarlane, *British Communist Party*, pp. 163–4.
[3] George Hardy, *Those Stormy Years: Memories of the Fight for Freedom on Five Continents* (London: Lawrence and Wishart, 1956), p. 189.
[4] 'Workers' Bulletin' (typewritten CPGB newspaper), 10 May, 1926.

The poor showing might have demoralized British Communists severely had not their more rabid enemies credited their movement with sole responsibility for the Great Adventure. The *Daily Mail* announced, the day the strike ended, that the Comintern had planned it from as far back as 1918, and 'the association between the British trade unions and the Russian trade unions' had provided the opening needed. Citing some of Zinoviev's more extravagant braggadocio, gloriously out of context and in appalling mis-translation, the paper recalled Purcell's visit to the USSR in 1924 to negotiate 'a united front against the capitalists.' That, apparently, was when the evil plot had been hatched.[1] Lord Birkenhead, two days later, corroborated the *Daily Mail*'s fantasies. Both the general strike and the miners' strike were 'directed and engineered from Moscow,' he told the Junior Imperial League. It was 'beyond all dispute' that all the labour difficulties were occasioned by 'insolent orders' from the Russians, 'obeyed with imbecile servility by Mr Cook.'[2]

Right-wing Tories might have their villains nicely sorted out; identifying the enemy was more difficult in Moscow. Tomsky was not even sure there *was* an enemy. He wired the Central Trade Union Council the day the strike ended suggesting that the TUC really had no choice but to capitulate.[3] For the public record, however, more exciting explanations were in order, and the press was quick to accuse the labour right, and specifically MacDonald, Thomas, and Henderson, of acts of 'direct treachery' that occasioned the surrender. It was a bit embarrassing, of course, that Russia's 'leftist' friends had joined the Thomases to authorize an end to the strike, but decisions of the General Council, even when closely contested, were traditionally given unanimous consent, *Izvestiia* reported, and that presumably accounted for the mysterious behaviour of Messrs Purcell and Swales.[4]

Zinoviev set the general tone for the first Soviet analysis of the strike.[5] It had been doomed to defeat, he wrote, ever since the General Council denied its political implications. It was especially foolish of the TUC to allow Thomas and MacDonald to help direct such an effort. They should have been exposed and repudiated at the very outset. In spite of the scandalously inept leadership, however, the strikers still scored great victories. The English proletariat had finally demonstrated its fighting spirit. In the process, it had thrown off all its reformist illusions, and the

---

[1] *Daily Mail*, 13 May, 1926.   [2] *Daily Herald*, 16 May, 1926.
[3] The 'secret' telegram fell into the hands of the Trotskyite opposition and was published by the left Communists in Germany. See *The Times*, 15 Dec., 1927.
[4] *Izvestiia*, 14 May, 1926.   [5] *Pravda*, 13 May, 1926.

way was now cleared for militant Leninism to claim the entire English labour movement.

A more comprehensive interpretation of the events in England was produced by the indefatigable Lozovsky, who fired off an awesome barrage of prose in the first week after the strike praising the English workers ('the masses showed how to wage such a gigantic fight') but denouncing their spokesmen ('the leaders showed how not to lead it').[1] The General Council's capitulation was the result of treason and toady-ism by the likes of Bevin, Henderson, Pugh, MacDonald and Thomas, who laboured from the beginning to make the strike 'as harmless as possible for the bourgeoisie.' They had never wanted to call a strike in the first place. The miners had forced it upon them. They had not dared to oppose it openly, but had plotted from the beginning to betray it. They were terrified their followers would get out of control and turn the stoppage into a genuine revolution. Their refusal to accept Soviet money demonstrated their perfidy most brazenly. Russian and British workers had pledged themselves to friendship and mutual aid when they estab-lished the Anglo-Russian Committee. Soviet proletarians had an un-mistakeable duty to lend their class brothers a hand. To reject that offer on the grounds it might be 'misunderstood' was absurd. The workers would not 'misunderstand.' Who cared if the capitalists did!

Where was the TUC left while the cause was being betrayed? Where was the great Purcell, whose picture had been so prominently displayed in the Soviet press during the first day or so of the strike? Lozovsky sug-gested that the left had never been in fact as strong as it seemed on paper. It controlled the General Council only on international questions. On domestic matters, it had been a minority all along. It was also spineless, passive, irresolute and naive. Leftists were especially witless in their estimates of fellow trade unionists. They accepted the Jimmy Thomases as basically nice fellows, and tried to arrange ideological compromises by which they could all work together. But that united front with the labour right represented, in fact, a united front with the bourgeoisie, and inexcusable treachery against the workers. It amounted to conniving, or at least acquiescing, in class treason, and when the workers were ready to demand truly effective leadership, the 'leftists' would be repudiated as vigorously as the rightists. The entire General Council had signed its

[1] See his articles in *Pravda*, 13, 16, 18, 19 May, 1926. These and other Lozovsky commentaries are in *Angliiskii Proletariat na Rasputi*, pp. 210–51. Additional material composed at the same time can be found in Aleksandr Lozovsky, *Die Lehren des Generalstreiks in England* (Moscow: Verlag der Roten Gewerkschafts-internationale, 1926).

own collective death warrant as leader of the labour movement. The masses, who had every reason to believe they were winning their war, had been shocked at the defeat and outraged at those who had engineered it. Their faith in reformism, in constitutionalism, in Parliamentarianism, was shattered forever. So was their belief in the old-fashioned apolitical trades unions. The only real possibility now was to go over to revolution. That required new leaders. The only leftists who would be believed any longer were the revolutionaries, leftists in deed as well as in word.

The campaign for international trade union unity was probably dead for a time, Lozovsky conceded. The English labour movement had been so enfeebled by the strike effort, had lost so much money and so much prestige, it was hardly in a position to make demands on the IFTU. The Amsterdam bureaucracy would no longer even have to do Britain the kindness of listening courteously. The Soviets and Profintern would of course continue to urge international proletarian solidarity, but prospects for Amsterdam's participation in the cause were even dimmer than ever.

British Communists' first reactions to the setback were much the same as those of their Russian comrades. The decision to call off the strike was the 'greatest crime that has ever been permitted...against the working class of...the whole world,' an act of 'abject and unforgivable cowardice.' The General Council was apparently just bluffing all along, and was 'amazed and daunted' when its bluff was called. The councillors finally 'broke under the weight of responsibilities they had never seriously intended to assume.' The right wing was chargeable with 'direct responsibility' for the fiasco. But 'most of the so-called Left-wing have been no better than the right.' They used the 'false pretext of loyalty to colleagues to cover up breaches of loyalty to workers.' The rejection of the Russian money was 'one of the most humiliating aspects of the General Strike.' In the Council's concern for middle-class, English 'public' opinion, it 'forgot all about the public opinion of the Russian working class, anxious to do its bit by British Workers, and receiving an undeserved insult by way of acknowledgement.' The proper response of Communists to the dismal record of the trade union leadership was to 'Cashier the Cowards' – all of them, 'left' and right – and replace them with revolutionary militants ready to meet their leadership responsibilities.[1]

For the Party intelligentsia, anxious for something more than the latest slogans, R. Palme Dutt provided some preliminary suggestions as

[1] The quotations are from 'Workers' Bulletin' (CPGB), Strike Special No. 9, 13 May, 1926; *Sunday Worker*, 16 May, 1926; *Workers' Weekly*, 21 May, 1926.

to what it had all meant.[1] The Party had erred, he confessed, in its first, too cautious, assessments of the walk-out. In fact, the strike was 'the first stage of the revolutionary struggle of the masses for power' in England, 'the greatest revolutionary advance in Britain since the days of Chartism,' and a 'triumphant vindication of the working class.' The defeat was no disaster but a 'profound revolutionary lesson and stimulus.' By the very methods it used to suppress the strike, the British bourgeoisie had convinced the proletariat of the class character of the state. All the trappings, all the camouflage, had been exposed for what they were, and when the next confrontation came, the workers and their new leaders would strike immediately at the centre of capitalist power, the state.

The masses had not been defeated on May 12. They 'stood solid.' What was defeated was 'the old leadership, the old reformist trade unionism, parliamentarism, pacifism and democracy.' The General Council, in particular, had proved itself guilty of 'shameful humiliation and impotence; a confusion, distortion and evasion of the issues; a cringing servility and whining to the bourgeoisie; a fear and distrust of the workers.' To call a general strike without any serious intention of going through with it and without, therefore, being prepared for it 'was an act of irresponsibility,' and to call it off just on the basis of some promises by Sir Herbert Samuel 'an act of greenhorns unfit to be let out without a nurse.' Dutt was not vitriolic, nor did he consider it worthwhile indicting any specific individuals. It was the 'treachery and failure of a whole policy' that most concerned him. Rightists and leftists alike had participated in that policy. It was the entire leadership and the ideology it represented that clearly was bankrupt, and now, in the new phase of the class struggle that had just been reached, only the Communists could lead the working classes to victory.

Communists in the Soviet Union, then, and Communists in Great Britain had both certified all members of the General Council, right or left, either traitors or cowards, and legitimate targets of proletarian contempt. Lozovsky had indicated the TUC could be of little further assistance in the movement for world trade union unity. One might have concluded, therefore, that there was no point in Soviet trade union officials continuing to maintain any pretence of *camaraderie* with such scoundrels and weaklings. The Anglo-Russian Committee should be scrapped, with ruffles and flourishes, to testify dramatically and unmistakably to work-

---

[1] R. Palme Dutt, 'Britain's First General Strike,' *Communist International*, No. 21 [1926], pp. 3–26; R. Palme Dutt, 'Notes of the Month,' *Labour Monthly*, VIII, 6 (June, 1926), 323–36.

ing people all over the world that the General Council had betrayed the proletarian cause.

Nobody, however, suggested such a thing. Indeed, nobody even mentioned the Committee except to suggest, in passing, that its very existence legitimized the Soviets' sending the TUC that cheque on May 7. Nobody, that is, but Lev Davidovich Trotsky.

At the time of the general strike, Trotsky was in Berlin, incognito, consulting with doctors about those increasingly debilitating fevers which had plagued him from at least as far back as 1921. He had played no substantive role in Soviet politics for a year and a half, standing aside with frigid indifference while Stalin destroyed the other two-thirds of the triumvirate at the 14th Party Congress. Now – far too late – he was preparing to make his move. He had met secretly with Kamenev and Zinoviev in April, just before his departure for Germany. The three had not spoken since 1923, but if they were to challenge the massive power Stalin had accumulated, coalition was an obvious necessity. In addition to unity, however, they needed an issue, some unmistakable blunder they could exploit to humiliate and discredit the would-be *vozhd*. Trotsky thought he saw such an issue in the decision of the Stalinist-controlled Politburo to maintain the Anglo-Russian Committee even after the General Council's capitulation on May 12.[1]

Even while the strike was still on, Trotsky claimed later, he could foresee how it was going to end. *Pravda*'s coverage of the walkout, and particularly its naive faith in the General Council left-wingers, 'made my gorge rise.' It was 'cynical distortion of the facts,' and he challenged it, at least by implication, in a series of articles that the Party daily finally published on May 25 and 26.[2] In sum, the material constituted a devastating attack on the British trade union left. No genuine Communist movement could ever arise in England, he claimed, except 'under conditions of a continuous, systematic, unwavering, untiring and naked denunciation of the muddles, the compromises and the indecision of quasi-left leaders of all shades.' No mercy should be shown their 'loathsome, two-faced policy.' Such a left would never participate seriously in any revolutionary struggle, and if, in spite of all the efforts, the battle was finally joined, leftists would enlist in the proletarian army only to betray it. They had consistently deceived the masses as to their real motives and

---

[1] Leon Trotsky, *My Life: An Attempt at an Autobiography*, (New York: C. Scribner's Sons, 1930), pp. 526–28; Deutscher, *Trotsky*, pp. 266–9.

[2] *Pravda*, 25, 26 May, 1926; English translation in *Communist International*, No. 22 [1926], pp. 19–41.

intentions, Trotsky charged. Professing solidarity with the workers of the Soviet Union, for example, they were in fact quite as terrified as was Sir Austen Chamberlain about the prospect of Russian 'interference' in their 'internal affairs.' Such leaders did not advance the workers' movement; they were 'a brake' on it.

They would inevitably try to destroy 'the revolutionary will of the proletariat.' 'In this sense the reformists are at one with the fascist elements in the Conservative party.' If the British workers were to prevail, they must recognize the fact they could not 'cross a revolutionary stream on the horse of reformism.' Their current leaders, all of them, right and left, would have to go. Communists would have to make them see why. And specifically, Communists could no longer maintain 'any appearance of unity' with the quasi-left opportunists in the General Council.

The inferences were unmistakable, even if any specific reference to the Committee was omitted. The Party had erred in maintaining its shameful relationship with the General Council right through the agony of the strike. Surely, as of May 12, there was no longer the slightest excuse for not forcing a rupture. That, indeed, was precisely what Trotsky demanded, privately, right after the capitulation.[1] It was perfectly acceptable to have established the Committee in the first place, he conceded. 'Temporary agreements may be made with the reformists whenever they take a step forward.' But such alliances should be made only to be demonstratively broken at the first good opportunity. The aim of any united front agreement was to compromise the non-Communists who were parties to it – in this case, the members of the General Council. Stalin, Bukharin, Tomsky and the rest had seen the Committee instead as an agency for the revolutionization of the English working class, a substitute, in effect, 'for the young and too slowly developing Communist party.' In that sense, the whole conception of the Committee had been false 'from beginning to end.' It served the interests only of the TUC compromisers. Maintaining it even after their May 12 surrender was 'equivalent to criminal toleration of traitors and a veiling of betrayal.'

The CPGB had been particularly damaged by the Politburo's refusal to rupture the Committee. It was a very immature organization, barely

---

[1] 'Voprosy britanskogo rabochego dvizheniia,' 18 May, 1926, Trotsky Archives, T-2985; Trotsky, *My Life*, p. 528; Lev Trotsky, *Die Internationale Revolution und die Kommunistiche International*, trans. A. Muller (Berlin: E. Laubsche Verlagsbuchhandlung, 1929), pp. 116–24; Leon Trotsky, *The Third International after Lenin*, trans. John G. Wright (New York: Pioneer Publishers, 1936), pp. 128–31. See also Trotsky's account of the June Politburo plenum in Trotsky Archives, T-3093, 25 Sept., 1927.

more than a mere 'propaganda group of the extreme left,' and it badly needed to develop good revolutionary habits. Above all, it had to culti-vate 'a spirit of irreconcilability towards opportunist leaders of all hues and varieties.' Reformists were as much the enemy, after all, as un-repentant capitalists. Without the Purcells and Cooks, there would be no Jimmy Thomases; without the Thomases, no Baldwins. It was all one interlocking system. Purcell's 'false, diplomatic masquerade' of 'leftism,' fraternizing at the same time with churchmen and Bolsheviks, was the major constraint on the development of a revolutionary class conscious-ness in England. 'Capitalist stabilization' was in fact then just 'Purcel-lism' under another name. Destroy Purcellism and there would be no stabilization. That's why maintaining the Committee was a crime against the working masses in general, and their vanguard, the CPGB, in particular.

The great Trotsky had used unimpressive instruments before to score mighty victories. With a few hundred Red Guards, he had toppled Kerensky. With a rag-tag Red Army, he had crushed Kolchak. Now he was trying for the most spectacular triumph of all. He was proposing to pummel Stalin into oblivion with A. A. Purcell!

II

Everybody else may have gone back to work on May 13, but the miners were still out, angrier and more embittered than ever. Their brothers in the labour movement had abandoned them, leaving them to fight – alone – a desperately unequal contest against the combined power of operators and government. Indignant at the betrayal, they were reckless enough to say so in public, most pungently in A. J. Cook's pamphlet, *The Nine Days*, a 'secret history' of the general strike taunting the TUC leadership for sins ranging from weakness and vacillation to deliberate treachery. The document finally persuaded the General Council to retaliate. Its Special Industrial Committee prepared a detailed report on the late unpleasantness charging the Miners' Federation (MFGB) with major responsibility for the whole sorry fiasco. Pursuing 'a policy of mere negation,' tied inflexibly 'to mere slogans' of their own creation, the miners had conducted themselves with such wooden incompetence that the TUC had no choice but to withdraw its support for them, the report indicated. The Council proposed to circularize that defence at a Con-ference of Trade Union Executives it scheduled for June 25.

The MFGB had no choice but to seek a truce. However unfair and disingenuous the report might be, it had the weight of a good deal of embarrassing documentation behind it, and its release would have compromised the miners' cause hopelessly. Three days before the conference was to begin, the miners surrendered. If the meeting was postponed and the report kept secret, they promised to cease all attacks on the General Council from either press or platform and to stop publication and sale of *The Nine Days*. The miners were only barely able to negotiate even that shabby a deal. Many councillors objected to any concessions to them at all. It was only the tiebreaking vote of Chairman Pugh that restrained the Council from releasing its report immediately.[1]

The Soviets were incensed at the arrangement. It was nothing but 'a new manoeuvre of deceit' designed to 'screen the crimes of the leaders of the General Council.'[2] The masses must never be allowed to forget how the trade union bureaucrats betrayed them on May 12, Lozovsky warned. Cook had no business covering for colleagues who 'just yesterday helped the bourgeoisie defeat the English labour movement.' Lozovsky was particularly pained when *The Worker*, the organ of his very own National Minority Movement, endorsed the slogan 'action first, criticism afterward,' justifying, in effect, Cook's disgraceful bargain with the councillors. Revolutionaries had no interest in shoring up the failing prestige of the trade union capitulators and traitors; they should be trying to bring them down.[3]

In fact, the arrangements between the General Council and the MFGB were not anywhere near as cosy as they may have seemed from Moscow. The June 22 truce was just that – an armistice, no more. The General Council continued to support the miners verbally, but offered them very little of what they needed most, money. As early as mid-July, the councillors were debating whether it was worthwhile investing any more resources at all in what they clearly considered a lost cause. They asked the MFGB to meet them to explore the possibilities of a negotiated settlement. The miners were outraged, and the meeting was explosive.

[1] General Council Minutes, No. 289, 17, June 1926; No. 298, 22, 23 June, 1926; No. 327, 328, 14, 15 July, 1926; Hutt, *British Working Class*, pp. 169–71. The report was finally published the following year: Trades Union Congress, General Council, *Mining Dispute, National Strike: Report of the General Council to the Conference of Executives of Affiliated Unions, June 25, 1926* (London: Cooperative Printing Society, 1927). Parts of it had appeared earlier in the Locomotivemen's journal.
[2] ECCI manifesto published in *Izvestiia*, 26 June, 1926. English translation in Great Britain, Foreign Office, *Russia No. 1*, Cmd. 2822 (1927), pp. 12–15, and in *Inprecorr*, VI, 50 (1 July, 1926), 809–10.
[3] *Inprecorr*, VI, 51 (8 July, 1926), 834–5; Lozovsky, *Angliiskii Proletariat na Rasputi*, pp. 303–7.

All they asked of the General Council was cash, Cook snapped, and they were getting precious little of that. The subsequent discussions were so heated, and the MFGB people so vitriolic, that one councillor formally protested and insisted Cook withdraw his slanders or face a public rebuke. The rift was finally patched over, but the Council was so piqued at Cook and his colleagues that it was not until August that it even got around to soliciting funds on their behalf from IFTU. Only about eighty thousand pounds ever came in from that source, less than 2d. per IFTU member.[1]

Fellow countrymen were somewhat more generous. The miners raised about £450,000 in the United Kingdom, £276,000 of it from other trade unions and from the General Council. That represented something like 1 shilling 3 pence from each TUC member. It was the Russians, however, who finally paid most of the costs of the strike. Their donations totalled £1,233,788, over two-thirds of all funds collected and more than 90 per cent of the receipts from outside Britain. That averaged out to almost 3 shillings from every Soviet trade unionist, over twice as much per person as organized British workers were willing to pay. Considering Russians earned only a fraction of what their English counterparts received, it was an extraordinary total. Bernard Pares calculated that Russian miners at the time were taking home only about 22s. 6d. a week, less than their locked-out English counterparts were drawing in strike pay. It was 'disgraceful,' he observed, that the Soviets should be dunned for any contribution at all.[2]

It is hardly surprising that Herbert Smith, the MFGB president, could say of the Russian workers that 'they *understand* the meaning of solidarity.'[3] Smith assumed, of course, that all Russian donations were com-

---

[1] General Council Minutes, No. 331, 334, 14, 15 July, 1926; Lorwin, *Labor and Internationalism*, pp. 336–38. The figures on the IFTU contribution to the Miners' Relief Fund are from TUC General Council, *Mining Dispute, National Strike*, pp. 54–7.

[2] The figures on contributions are from *Miners' Relief Fund: Statement of Accounts* (London: Cooperative Printing Society Limited, 1927), with additional data from TUC General Council, *Mining Dispute, National Strike*, pp. 54–7. I have not counted, in my tallies, 'General Council' contributions which, in fact, represented funds received from IFTU. Rather different estimates of the Russian contribution (and, surprisingly, somewhat more modest ones) may be found in Volkov, *Anglo-Sovetskie Otnosheniia*, pp. 218–19, and in Gurovich, *Vseobshchaia Stachka v Anglii*, pp. 175n., 190. *The Worker* (24 Sept., 1926) contrasted how much the Russians were giving, and how little was coming in from IFTU, even while the strike was still on. The Bernard Pares estimates, and his comments, are from a confidential Foreign Office document dated 2 Nov., 1926, N 4958/245/38, F.O. 371.11785.

[3] Herbert Smith, 'The Miners' Struggle Continues,' *Labour Monthly*, VIII, 6 (June, 1926), 375–8.

pletely voluntary, and the evidence does indeed suggest that nobody had had any trouble collecting those first kopeks back in May. Whether such spontaneous enthusiasm was sustained all summer long and well into the autumn, however, is problematical. The Foreign Office thought not. Hodgson reported from Moscow as early as July 17 that Russian trade union officials were finding it increasingly difficult to persuade their members to be as generous as the Party demanded. 'I think it is safe to assert,' he ventured, 'that the great majority of the workers are entirely indifferent to the success or failure of the miners' strike, and certainly would not pay were the question put to them.'[1]

Perhaps not, but the question was never put to them, and pay they did. As early as mid-June, Profintern and Comintern were calling on them to pay more. The coal strike had to continue. It had 'enormous political significance for the working class of the whole world.' To carry on, however, the miners would need to collect twice as much money as they were now. Good proletarian internationalists would respond accordingly.[2]

The Russians themselves were prepared to respond up to some £300,000 a month, or so the chiefs of their Miners' Union suggested to Cook and W. P. Richardson, the MFGB treasurer, at a meeting in Berlin on July 7. What they had in mind was a 1 per cent levy on all wages, and they were sure Soviet trade unionists would agree to such a contribution if it was put to them. All they proposed in return was formation of an Anglo-Russian Miners' Committee to 'maintain connections between the two countries, and, ultimately, to secure the admission of the Russian Miners' Union to the Miners' International.' The British agreed such an organization might serve a useful function, and suggested, in the meantime, the Russians just send in their membership application to the International.[3]

---

[1] Hodgson to Chamberlain, 17 July 1926, N 3455/1678/38, F.O. 371.11796. He repeated that estimate in subsequent reports. See Hodgson to Chamberlain, 24 Sept. 1926, N 4068/1687/38, and 8 Oct., 1926, N 4651/1687/38, F.O. 371.11796. On the other hand, W. P. and Z. K. Coates (*Anglo-Soviet Relations*, i, 229) assert many 'independent observers' testified the contributions were voluntary. The question, by nature, can never be answered definitively.

[2] *Izvestiia*, 19, 26 June, 1926; *Inprecorr*, vi, 48 (24 June, 1926), 790; 50 (1 July, 1926), 809–10.

[3] The Berlin meeting was exceptionally well covered by the British Embassy there, which suggested that whatever Cook may have gained from the Russians, he lost by his rude and brusque treatment of German labour leaders. See Addison to Chamberlain, 9, 10, 21, 27 July, 1926, C 7660/7660/18, C 7749/7760/18, C 7835/7660/18, C 7836/7660/18, C 7837/7660/18, C 8173/7660/18, C 8369/7660/18, F.O. 371.11328. For the official communiqué of the Berlin meeting, see *The Labour Magazine*, viii, 9 (Sept., 1926), 569, and for further information, The Miners'

For at least as long as the strike was on, relations between the MFGB and the Russians stayed close. Striking miners toured the Soviet Union drumming up new enthusiasm for the struggle.[1] The 1 per cent contribution was formally proposed to Soviet trade unionists by the Presidium of their Central Council on August 31, and Tomsky wrote Smith and Cook that he was sure, given 'the ardent sympathy of the workers of the USSR toward your heroic struggle and the readiness to aid it,' the suggestion would get 'a warm response.'[2] While the warmth was being generated, an advance of three million rubles on the expectation of contributions-to-come was sent along September 4, and an additional million rubles October 30. Soviet workers, Tomsky wired, watched the miners' 'heroic fight' with 'unfailing attention and deep sympathy.' 'We firmly believe in your victory in spite of all the difficulties of fighting against the united forces of a powerful and dangerous enemy and having still more dangerous quasi-friends who are trying to weaken and to disorganize your fighting ranks. Workers of the USSR will be with you to the end.'[3]

The MFGB could hardly fail to respond. 'Every British miner will be thrilled' by the evidence of Soviet 'practical comradeship,' the strikers' newspaper exulted. 'There has never been a more striking example of international working-class solidarity.' Cook was so moved, he wired Tomsky, that 'words fail me,' and proceeded to prove the contrary at some length. If others followed the example set by the Soviets, he affirmed, the miners could not possibly lose. 'It is silver bullets that we need for victory.'[4] One wonders if the Russians were ever tempted to suggest the possibility that lead bullets were cheaper!

In any event, they never complained, and they never put any strings on the money they sent. They did, however, keep urging creation of that Anglo-Russian Miners' Committee they first suggested in Berlin in July. At the time, the British had proposed the Soviet Miners' Union apply for membership in the Miners' International. When, however, the Soviets asked the International, a month later, whether it would be willing to confer on the subject, it got a somewhat brusque reply reminding the Soviets that IFTU rules forbade the Internationals to accept Profintern members as affiliates. The British Communist press protested such an

Federation of Great Britain, *Annual Volume of Proceedings, 1926* (London: Co-operative Printing Society Limited, 1927), pp. 544–5. See also R. P. Arnot, *The Miners: Years of Struggle*, Vol. II of *A History of the Miners' Federation of Great Britain* (London: George Allen & Unwin, 1953), p. 470.

[1] *MFGB Proceedings 1926*, p. 233.   [2] *Ibid.*, p. 238.   [3] *The Miner*, 6 Nov., 1926.
[4] *Ibid.*

'insulting' response, and suggested the bilateral Anglo-Russian organization be established forthwith.[1] Crusty old Herbert Smith seemed in no hurry. He conceded the Russians had done a lot more for the MFGB than had the International, and he certainly thought the Russians should join the International, and he personally was not worried at all about their RILU connection, but he did think they had to agree to accept the International's constitution and to abide by its rules before they joined it. After they were in, they could try to change the regulations, but not before. And after they were in, the proposed Anglo-Russian Miners' Committee might be worth further study.[2]

The Soviets did not press the issue hard. Cook was on their side, they knew, and as more and more of the bitter and resentful rank and file put in their applications for Communist Party membership cards, the problem should resolve itself. When a delegation of miners visited the USSR in late October, its members unanimously recommended the Miners' Committee be established.[3] Having failed to permeate the TUC as a whole, the British chargé commented, the Soviets were now trying to undermine labour organizations in specific industries. The Miners' Committee represented the Russian hope of salvaging something from the apparent wreckage of the old connection with the General Council.[4]

The USSR's continuing support of the miners, added to the indignity of its attempt to help finance the general strike, aborted an embryonic effort to improve Anglo-Soviet diplomatic relations. Hodgson, in Moscow, had urged a *détente* back in early May, and his plea had seemed to be achieving modest results.[5] Somebody in the Foreign Office, for example, had scurried off to figure out just what was wrong with the treaties MacDonald had negotiated with the USSR back in 1924, and what amendments would make them acceptable. It was not much, but it was more of an effort than the Tories had ever made before.

It did not last long. The miners' strike killed it. Baldwin's administration – unofficially, perhaps, but nonetheless unmistakably – was backing the operators. Nobody masochistic enough to subject himself to the tedium of the Cabinet records from May to November could come to any other conclusion.[6] Equally clearly, responsible leaders in the Soviet regime were supporting the men, and although they might pretend their

---

[1] *Workers' Weekly*, 17 Sept., 1926.   [2] *MFGB Proceedings 1926*, p. 915.

[3] *The Worker*, 22 Oct., 1926.

[4] Hodgson to Chamberlain, 22 Oct., 1926, N 4884/1687/38, F.O. 371.11796.

[5] Hodgson to Chamberlain, 6 May, 1926, N 2241/387/38, F.O. 371.11786.

[6] Cabinet Conclusions, 1926, CAB 23.53, should suffice for a reference, but see in particular Conclusion 58(26)1, 18 Oct., 1926.

acts of partisanship as Communist activists had no relationship to the correct detachment they maintained as state officials, their protestations seemed unconvincing in London.

One suspects neither H.M. Foreign Office nor the Narkomindel really wanted any confrontation over the issue, but neither knew how to defuse it. The Soviets may have made some sort of an effort, albeit surreptitiously and tangentially. Their chargé in London, A. P. Rozengolts, dropped broad hints to his British friends that those donations to the miners were not only not to his liking – he had specifically advised against them, he said – but not to the liking of his superiors, either. It was foolish of his government to permit such a thing, he said, and the regime was in fact acutely embarrassed by the resultant strain on Anglo-Soviet relations, but the Comintern had stirred up so much popular feeling on the miners' behalf that the government was powerless to resist.[1]

Such ingenious apologetics were hardly good enough, however, to satisfy the hard-line triumvirate in Baldwin's cabinet, Joynson-Hicks, Churchill and Birkenhead. As they saw it, the Russians were trying to buy themselves a revolution in Britain, and they were not going to stand for it. To edify the sceptics in the cabinet, and, he hoped, convert them, Joynson-Hicks had his Home Office staff rush out a complete catalogue of Russian enormities on just three weeks notice.[2] It was a remarkable document. Capturing the TUC, Jix announced, had been the major goal of Soviet strategists for two whole years now. The Minority Movement had been organized to help achieve that end, and so had the Anglo-Russian Committee, an instrument 'for maintaining permanent and close contact between the extremists of the two countries.' Lozovsky had plotted revolutionary strategy with A. J. Cook at a secret meeting in Berlin in August, 1925, and in the following month, at Scarborough, the Russians had successfully manoeuvred the Trade Union Congress into granting the General Council the sort of 'despotic powers' required to do the British constitution effective mischief.

Ever since then the Soviets had involved themselves in intensive preparations for the decisive confrontation. Using the 'intimate and uninterrupted' connection with the General Council they had achieved via the Committee, they had conferred with their English stooges in

---

[1] Foreign Office memorandum, 11 June, 1926, N 2675/387/38, F.O. 371.11786.
[2] The document is a memorandum on 'Russian Money,' 11 June, 1926, C.P. 236(26), in Cabinet Papers, 1926, CAB 24.180. Jix had apparently started work on the document 19 May (Cabinet Decisions, 1926, CAB 23.53, Decision 33 [26] 16) and completed his report 9 June (*ibid.*, Decision 37 [26] 5 [6]). Italics in the quoted selections from 'Russian Money' were in the original.

'various' joint meetings and during 'repeated comings and goings.' When direct contacts were inconvenient, the Soviet Embassy had acted 'as a channel for the transmission of messages.' The most urgent exchanges, according to Jix's astonishing information, involved arrangements for financing the coming convulsion. Citrine had apparently pleaded the TUC's poverty so effectively, as early as January 14, that the Executive Bureau of RILU, 'a Comintern and Soviet Government agency,' agreed to an immediate transfer of funds 'to the Strike Committee of the General Council.'

Once the stoppage was on, dissimulation was deemed no longer necessary, and the Soviets had flung rubles around with reckless immoderation. Everybody knew about the attempt to lavish two and a quarter million of them on the TUC on May 8. Jix claimed credit for stopping that donation, having conveniently forgotten the TUC had rejected the money even before he forbade accepting it. Apparently, however, the Russians had already slipped some of their lucre past him via other channels. On May 4, he reported, the Bank for Russian Trade, Arcos, had paid in three cheques of £100,000 each to the Westminster Bank, to the credit of an organization the Home Secretary identified as the Wholesale Cooperative Society. The Society drew the money out again within 24 hours, £14,000 of it in silver and the rest in bills, 'and the Cooperative representative quite openly referred to it as strike pay.' Thus, Jix could announce triumphantly, a Russian governmental agency – Arcos – 'was without doubt providing money *on the first day of the General Strike* for the financing of the strike.' Such damning evidence (which of course could not be made public since it was based on 'most secret information') demanded the cabinet discuss two urgent issues. First, should Britain cut diplomatic ties with the USSR immediately and order all Russian representatives out of the country forthwith. Second, should the Home Secretary ban all donations from abroad for the miners' strike. Those Russian contributions offended Jix mightily. 'I think it is quite argueable...to say that it is not a bona fide charity on the part of Russia,...but...a definitely left-wing movement in order to...destroy the economic position of this country.'

Enjoining discretion on his colleagues, Jix was unable to practise it himself. The day before his report went to the cabinet, the Home Secretary found himself being pressed, in the Commons, on whether the Soviet government had helped finance the general strike. After a great deal of confusion and receipt of what must have been a most ambiguous message from a Foreign Office messenger, Jix popped out with the extraordinary revelation that 'some money from the Russian Government' had indeed been involved.[1] Whether or not Jix had in mind those mysterious cheques to the 'Wholesale Cooperative Society' is uncertain. More likely, he had just heard a garbled report of the protest note Chamberlain now proposed to dispatch to the Narkomindel. The Foreign Secretary had decided that since the USSR forbade transfers of its currency without special authorization of the Commissariat of Finance, and since permission had been given to forward those millions of rubles to the TUC, that the Soviet government had thereby intervened in British internal affairs in violation of international law and in a manner which 'does not conduce to the friendly settlement the Soviet Government profess to desire.'[2]

It was a mild enough statement, and one suspects it was designed as much to placate the ultras at home as it was to rebuke the Communists in Moscow. But coming as it did the day after Joynson-Hicks' allegation that the Soviet government had helped pay for the general strike, the protest aroused a storm, in Britain as well as in the Soviet Union. The Tory far right demanded a full-dress Parliamentary debate on whether to break diplomatic relations with the USSR. The Labour front bench, delighted with the prospect of watching the Conservatives stage a family fight, concurred. Citrine fired off a broadside to Baldwin denying the TUC had ever received a farthing from the Soviet government and protesting Jix's anti-union slanders 'most strongly.'[3] It was a glorious row!

They were excited in Moscow, too – everywhere, that is, except in the Foreign Commissariat, which produced a patient, reasoned and dignified defence of the Soviet government's conduct during the strike in reply to Chamberlain.[4] But the composure in the Narkomindel offices was not reflected in the streets. *Izvestiia*'s correspondent got Joynson-Hicks' Commons statement and Chamberlain's protest note hopelessly jumbled up together, and sounded the tocsin. An estimated three hundred thousand workers swarmed into Red Square to assert – noisily – their right to express their international proletarian solidarity with anybody they liked, and to protest the English government's attempt to interfere

---

1 196 H.C. Deb. 5 s at c. 1680.
2 Chamberlain to Hodgson, 12 June, 1926, N 2799/1687/38 and N 3800/1687/38, F.O. 371.11786.
3 Citrine to Baldwin, 12 June 1926, C.P. 241(26), Cabinet Papers, 1926, CAB 24.180.
4 The Russian notes are in USSR, Narodnyi Komissariat po Inostrannym Delam, *Anglo-Sovetskie Otnosheniia*, pp. 91–2, and in English in Degras, *Soviet Documents*, II, 118–19.

in Soviet trade union matters. 'Hands Off the Trade Unions of the USSR!' the signs read.[1]

Without meaning to, probably, Jix had really stirred up a hornet's nest, and it must have been terribly humiliating for him to discover, a day or so later, that the most formidable piece of evidence he had collected on that Russian gold was in fact a casual bit of ill-considered Fleet Street gossip. Those Soviet cheques (actually made out not to the 'Wholesale Cooperative Society,' which did not exist, but to the Cooperative Wholesale Society) represented in fact normal repayments on short-term loans; the funds drawn out by the trade unions at the same time and in about the same amounts were legitimate trade union reserves left on deposit with the Society; and the source of the 'most secret infromation,' apparently, was a representative of the *Daily Mail*![2]

While the Home Secretary was writhing under the obstinate spitefulness of facts, analysts at the Foreign Office were preparing a measured and persuasive response to his original memorandum.[3] They conceded Jix a great deal. True enough, the general strike was an 'illegal and unconstitutional act' and the Soviet government had no right to support it either directly or indirectly. True enough, the Communist Party controlled not only that government, but the trade unions as well, and it was fatuous, therefore, for the Soviet Foreign Commissariat to disclaim responsibility for actions taken by the unions. It was 'scarcely credible,' in any event, that the money offered the TUC really came from voluntary contributions. Finally, the Comintern had indeed devoted formidable financial resources to promoting revolution, even if 'its success has been poor compared to its efforts.' The British had shown great patience in the face of all these provocations. 'We have found it best not to take them or their offenses against international comity too seriously...One cannot but believe in the ultimate power of sanity...' In the meantime, maintaining diplomatic relations with the Soviets did facilitate trade with them, trade which was 'not negligible.' To break the tie, jeopardizing that exchange, would gain Britain nothing. Since 'Russia is almost as invulnerable economically...as she is...militarily,' she would not suffer from the trade lapse. And finally, with relations broken, the Communists would probably just intensify their propaganda barrage against the UK, since they would then have nothing whatsoever to hope for from Britain, after all, but 'the delightful spectacle of revolution and ruin.'

[1] *Izvestiia*, 15, 16 June, 1926; Volkov, *Anglo-Sovetskie Otnosheniia*, pp. 220–1.
[2] Cabinet Papers, 1926, CAB 24.180, C.P. 244(26), 15 June, 1926.
[3] *Ibid.*, C.P. 250(26), 16 June, 1926.

The Cabinet sat through two long sessions on June 16 to weigh the evidence and make a decision as between the Home Secretary and the Foreign Secretary.[1] Every man there agreed with Joynson-Hicks that the Soviet government had displayed such 'malignant hostility' to Great Britain that a diplomatic break was fully justified, but 'a large majority' decided the time was 'not opportune for a rupture.' Anglo-Soviet trade was brisk, profitable, and on the increase. And once relations were broken off, it would be difficult to reestablish them. Although the public should be 'enlightened,' therefore, on the menacing character of Soviet policy toward Britain, the advantages of a complete break with the USSR were outweighed by the practical disadvantages. Finally, since diplomatic relations were to be maintained, it was deemed not 'worthwhile' to stop the transmission of funds from Russia to the miners: such a step would be 'misrepresented.'

Jix and his friends had lost the battle, but they were not out of the war. Baldwin had thrown them a crumb – the injunction to 'enlighten' the public on the Red menace – and they proceeded to make a banquet of it. The Home Office dug out all those old papers seized from CPGB headquarters back in September and published the juiciest of them, those purporting to prove direct Soviet support of subversive activities in Britain. Churchill assured a London audience that of course the Russian government financed their 'dupes' and 'featherheaded hirelings' in Britain, and that who actually signed the cheques was unimportant. Everybody knew the Party ran everything in the USSR, and so long as one was sure of whose hand 'fired the pistol, what did it matter which finger pulled the trigger.' Birkenhead's speeches showed roughly the same degree of statesmanlike moderation, and indeed, the campaign was so shrill and so strident that even the Tory *Daily Express* felt obliged to object.[2]

Such a barrage of raucous sensationalism guaranteed an explosive Commons debate, when it finally came. Baldwin managed to put off any extended discussions until June 25, well after the Cabinet had made its decisions. In the meantime, Jix had had time to back away from his more extreme statements on Soviet gold, and Chamberlain had been able to assure the members that the Russians had already been roundly rebuked for all provable crimes.[3] It was not enough. The ultras were ready with

1 Cabinet Conclusions, 1926, CAB 23.53, Conclusions 39(26)7, 40(26)5, 16 June, 1926.
2 For Churchill's and Birkenhead's speeches, see *The Times*, 21 June, 1926, and for its editorial reaction, the *Daily Express* of the same date. The incriminating documents were published in Great Britain, Parliament, *Communist Papers*, Cmd. 2682 (1926).
3 196 H.C. Deb. 5 s at cc. 1959–64, 2471–9.

sentimental memories of the gallantry of Admiral Kolchak and as harsh calumnies against the current usurpers as the deputy speaker would allow them. The Foreign Minister presented the government's case in as strong an anti-Soviet tone as was consistent with the decision that had been taken. Lloyd George and Ramsay MacDonald, among others, spoke for the Opposition, and Mardy Jones tried vainly to get in a word on behalf of the miners. After five hours, the session was finally adjourned, without a vote, amidst 'grave disorder.' For all the jarring cacophony, the end result was that British policy toward the USSR had not really changed in the slightest.[1]

The rhetoric, however, was different. Baldwin had unleashed the diehards, and that worried the Soviets. Chicherin wrote Chamberlain that he would not dignify the 'rude and intolerable attacks' on the USSR with a direct reply, but he found it 'totally incomprehensible that such speeches by responsible members of the Government should be permitted and tolerated.'[2] That Churchill – the architect of the 1918–19 intervention – was still determined to bring the Soviet government down seemed obvious. That he might even be contemplating all-out war on the Bolsheviks could not be ruled out. Stalin was nervous, and hurried to mobilize every deterrent available to him. One such, in Britain, was the Communist Party, which was called out on an intensive anti-war campaign in July.[3] Another possibility was the Anglo-Russian Committee.

Stalin may have decided to revive his link to the General Council even before the war scare broke. The CPGB press had again acknowledged the Committee's existence as early as June 6, suggesting it might now resume the campaign for international trade union unity.[4] Churchill's blustering malice, however, made the matter more urgent. Stalin was characteristically blunt about what he was up to.[5] He granted there were a lot of other reasons for resuscitating the Committee, but they had all been discussed before. What he wanted to stress was the possibility of using it to 'protect the first Soviet Republic in the world from British intervention.' The English trade unions – reformist, even re-

[1] 197 H.C. Deb. 5 s at cc. 699–778.
[2] USSR, Narodnyi Kommissariat po Inostrannym Delam, *Anglo-Sovetskie Otnosheniia*, p. 93; English translation in Degras, *Soviet Documents*, 120–3.
[3] See *Workers' Weekly*, 30 July, 1926 and ff. The 30 July issue of the paper was to carry such detailed instructions to the proletariat on matters such as how to sabotage the armaments industry that the printers refused to run much of the copy.
[4] The *Sunday Worker*, 6 June 1926, 20 June, 1926; *Workers' Weekly*, 18 June, 1926.
[5] See his report to the Joint Plenum of the CC and CCC of the CPSU, 15 July, 1926, *Sochineniia*, VIII, 176–91. The quotations which follow are from p. 185.

actionary, though they might be – seemed willing to join the USSR's revolutionary trade unions 'in an alliance against the counter-revolutionary imperialists of their own country.' Why, he asked, 'should we not welcome such an alliance?' To refuse it would only be to play into the hands of the interventionists.

The effort to persuade the TUC to schedule another Committee meeting began in late June, within a few days of Churchill's most flamboyant anti-Soviet diatribe, and in view of Stalin's own testimony, it is difficult to avoid suggesting a cause-and-effect relationship between the two events. The cables and letters to the General Council, however, never mentioned the war scare. The purpose of the meeting, they proposed, should be to organize energetic strike action on behalf of the British miners. Since the Soviets were well aware of the strained relations between the General Council and the MFGB, and since Stalin, in that same speech in which he defended the Committee as a war deterrent, also pointed to its usefulness in widening the split between the miners and the rest of the TUC leadership,[1] the causal pattern may not be as neatly obvious as one would like it to be.

The invitation itself was sent off to the TUC June 29.[2] 'Despite its treachery,' *Pravda* explained, 'the General Council remains the leader of the British working class' and it would be difficult to mobilize the international proletariat on the miners' behalf without its cooperation. The Russians therefore requested a meeting 'as soon as possible.' Citrine wired immediately acknowledging receipt of the invitation, and followed up with a letter indicating the General Council would discuss its reply as soon as the opportunity presented itself. That was not good enough for the Soviets. Dogadov telegraphed Citrine expressing surprise at the vagueness of the answer and demanding 'a complete and clear presentation' of the TUC's proposals for aiding the miners, including a specific date for the Committee meeting. The Soviets insisted on knowing where the General Council stood.[3]

Citrine was not to be rushed. The International Committee was due to meet July 13, and the General Council the day after that, and that would be time enough. In the meantime, however, the Russians kept up

[1] *Ibid.*, pp. 188–9.
[2] That the Russians wanted a meeting, at least as early as June 25, is clear from the Soviet and CPGB press. See the statement of the secretary of the Soviet Miners' Union on that date in *Pravda*, and the *Sunday Worker*, 27 June, 1926. For the correspondence between the Soviet trade unions and the TUC relevant to the meeting, see *Inprecorr*, VI, 50 (1 July, 1926), 811; 51 (8 July, 1926), 838–9; 52 (15 July, 1926), 858–9; 53 (22 July, 1926), 883.   [3] *Pravda*, 30 June, 1926.

the pressure as best they could. If the councillors really wanted to help the miners, Lozovsky sneered, they would have responded to the Russians immediately. Indeed, they themselves would have summoned the Committee.[1] Cook and Richardson were persuaded to endorse the demand for a meeting when they met their Soviet opposite numbers in the miners' conference in Berlin on July 7.[2] *Workers' Weekly* sounded the alarm back home.[3] Why the delay, it enquired? Perhaps the General Council had been so offended by its critics in the USSR that 'out of ruffled feelings and injured dignity' it was prepared to desert the miners in retaliation. If so, 'no bigger piece of treachery to British Labour and the cause of international unity' had ever been committed.

The TUC chiefs, in fact, were already drafting their reply to the invitation.[4] The International Committee had devoted a long session to the Russians on July 13. The consensus was that meeting with them solely to discuss aid to the miners might in fact just prejudice the TUC's efforts to raise funds for the MFGB in other countries. Nevertheless, it was hard to find any excuse for refusing to meet, since the British had promised a Committee session for 'early' 1926 when their representatives last sat down with the Russians back in December. The decision was taken, then, to recommend to the General Council that it agree to another conference with the Russians, but not to talk about the miners. Rather, they would merely resume the 'regular business' of the Committee left over from the December session – how to manoeuvre the Soviets into IFTU affiliation, presumably – and also review 'recent events in their relation to International Trade Union Unity.' Although they did not say so for the record, the 'recent events' the British labour leaders wanted reviewed were, in fact, some harsh words directed at them by the Central Council of the Russian trade unions.[5] The TUC leaders had no intention of letting those slanders go unrebutted, and at least some of them were unwilling to discuss anything else at all with the Soviets until they got a public retraction of the accusations against them. Within a matter of days the CPGB press was on to the news. The councillors might refuse to discuss the miners' strike with the Russians

[1] *Ibid.*, 4 July, 1926. See also his article in *Die Rote Gewerkschaftsinternationale*, No. 7 (July, 1926), pp. 475–9, reprinted (in Russian) in Lozovsky, *Angliiskii Proletariat na Rasputi*, pp. 303–12.

[2] *The Labour Magazine*, VIII, 9 (Sept., 1926), 569. See above, p. 251.

[3] *Workers' Weekly*, 9, 16 July, 1926.

[4] General Council, International Committee Minutes, 13 July, 1926, file 901, doc. I.C. 4/1925–26; General Council Minutes, No. 331, 14–15 July, 1926; *Inprecorr*, VI, 53 (22 July, 1926), 883.

[5] See below, pp. 265–6.

at all, it reported, and insist instead on challenging the decision of Soviet trade unionists to criticize the conduct of the general strike. 'The Russian Workers have earned the right to talk straight,' the *Sunday Worker* protested, 'by their magnificent display of practical solidarity with British Labour.' It demanded the General Council heed its Soviet critics, ponder their advice, and then make a serious effort to cooperate with them in behalf of the miners.[1]

That the Committee was to be reactivated, and that Soviet revolutionaries would once again sit down at the same table with social-fascist class traitors, should have been grist to the Opposition mill back in the USSR. Trotsky, Kamenev and Zinoviev had now formally agreed to work together to bring Stalin down. A gallant undertaking it may have been – to challenge the gods always inspires a kind of gloomy awe – but prospects were bleak.[2] The three Prometheans had no real power base and no agreed common programme. Most of all, they needed an issue, some irrefutable example of Stalinist bungling that, properly explained and skilfully exploited, could shatter the Party's confidence in the wisdom and reliability of its General Secretary. In the foreign policy area, aside from the inglorious performance of the Polish Communist Party at the time of the Pilsudski *coup*, about all they could point to was the disgraceful connection to the TUC capitulators. Unfortunately, however, in this area as in so many others, they could reach only minimal agreement on how vigorously to press their advantage.[3] Trotsky might want to make the Committee a major talking point and demand its total repudiation, but he could afford to. He had been sceptical of the adventure all along, and never closely associated with it. Zinoviev, on the other hand, more involved in the creation of the Committee and on the record as supporting it, had to approach the question more cautiously. It was not until mid-July that he was ready to come out forthrightly for liquidating the TUC connection. In the meantime, although he was willing to make a case against the Committee, he did it only by indirection.[4] He concentrated his venom on the General Council 'leftists.'

[1] *Sunday Worker*, 18 July, 1926.
[2] The story of the United Opposition and its dramatic and tragic struggle, against overwhelming odds, is best told in Deutscher, *Trotsky*, pp. 271–394, and E. H. Carr, *Foundations of a Planned Economy* (London: Macmillan, 1969–   ), II, 3–53.
[3] Or so Rykov later reported to the Moscow Party organization (*Inprecorr*, VI, 57 [19 Aug. 1926], 955).
[4] For English translations of his efforts, see 'The International Significance of the General Strike in Britain,' *Inprecorr*, VI, 47 (17 June, 1926), 761–5 and 48 (24 June, 1926), 789–91, and 'The General Council's "4th of August",' *Communist International*, No. 22 [July, 1926], pp. 3–18. The originals also appeared in *Pravda*.

They had agreed to the foundation of the Anglo-Russian Committee only to foster the illusion of their 'leftism.' The general strike, however, had torn their masks away. They had all sold out – whether for money or on conviction really did not matter. Only Swales had been able to resist the 'rot,' the 'decay,' but he no longer counted. In the end it had become Thomas' General Council, a 'stinking corpse' which good revolutionaries must utterly repudiate. Good revolutionaries in the Soviet trade unions could set a splendid example by liquidating their cosy arrangements with the class traitors and abolishing the Committee.

Without mentioning his Politburo rival by name, Zinoviev scoffed at Stalin's notion that a collection of double-dealers and renegades such as those leading the TUC would ever support the USSR in the event of a new imperialist war. They had despicably betrayed the proletarian cause in May, when 'the working class had every prospect of victory, the objective situation was entirely in their favour.' They would do so again in the event of war. 'The present "Thomas" General Council would no doubt be at the beck and call of the bourgeoisie and would faithfully and truly serve the capitalists of "their" country.' To rely on proven class traitors would be madness.

The Opposition attack on the Committee touched sensitive Kremlin nerves. While the strike was in progress, the Soviet press had indeed been kind to TUC leftists. No faithful *Pravda* addict would ever have suspected, not before May 13, that they might betray the cause. Thomas was capable of such enormities, certainly, but not Purcell, not an honorary member of the Moscow Soviet. Even when he and his leftist colleagues joined the rest of the councillors voting to end the strike, *Izvestiia* had managed to find excuses for him.[1] It might be true that the press had taken a tougher stance since, but that the leftists had been protected during and immediately after those nine crucial days was undeniable, and that the existence of the Anglo-Russian Committee was partly responsible for such uncharacteristic Soviet tendernesses seemed a reasonable assumption.

It also seemed obvious that the British Communist Party had coddled 'leftists.'[2] The CPGB had never rebuked them while the strike was in progress, even when they were publicly protesting their devotion to

---

[1] See above, p. 242.

[2] One of the most comprehensive critiques of the CPGB's performance both during and immediately after the strike was P.B., 'The Communist Party and the Miners' Fight,' *Labour Monthly*, IX (Jan., 1927), 13–35. P.B. speaks most authoritatively, and although he is not otherwise identified, the article might well have been written by Petrovsky–Bennet.

gradualism and non-violence. Although the comrades did indeed respond with predictable bitterness and proper indignation the day the strike got called off, they moved subsequently toward a much more conciliatory position. An official Party statement adopted May 31 blamed only the rightists – the 'agents of capitalism in the labour movement' – for the failure of the strike. The leftists were to be forgiven, and allowed another chance to redeem themselves. Indeed, Communists were advised to cultivate the left more energetically than ever. Until the CPGB was truly a mass movement, apparently, it would suggest Purcell – not Pollitt – as the alternative to J. H. Thomas.[1]

Purcell and his friends seemed more than willing to make up. They were already issuing their apologias to 'comrades national and international,' terming the strike a great victory, dubbing its termination a 'courageous gesture for peace,' and expressing their gratitude to workers all over the world – and especially the Russians – for having come to their aid. The skirmish of May 3–12 had been only preliminary to the main battle, they insisted. Since the general strike weapon was unfamiliar, it had not been used as skilfully as it might have been. But the class struggle was not over – it was, indeed, intensifying – and their strike experience would enable the workers to fight capitalism more effectively in the future.[2]

What must have jarred them so back in Moscow was that 'leftists' were actually being allowed to print such soporific drivel in CPGB-controlled journals. Indeed, the *Sunday Worker* seemed almost ready to forgive not only the leftists, but all the rest of the councillors as well. It ran a little piece by Ben Turner arguing, in effect, that there were no 'rights' or 'lefts' in the General Council, and certainly no traitors – only 'men and women desiring to do what is right and possible.'[3] The appearance of such a suggestion in the Party's own press just seemed to prove the charges of Trotsky and the Opposition back in the USSR, that the continued existence of the Anglo-Russian Committee was serving to shield the General Council from Communist criticism, and that revolutionaries were neglecting their duty to expose compromisers and class traitors among their temporary 'allies,' the reformists.

The Party majority moved to correct the balance. The Soviet and

---

[1] The official CPGB statement was published in *Workers' Weekly*, 4 June, 1926. See also the comment in *Communist Review*, VII (June, 1926), 2, 53–6, and (a somewhat tougher statement) C.B., *The Reds and the General Strike* (London: CPGB, June, 1926). For comment see MacFarlane, *British Communist Party*, p. 167.

[2] *Lansbury's Labour Weekly*, II, 63 (22 May, 1926), 15; *Sunday Worker*, 13 June, 1926.

[3] *Sunday Worker*, 23 May, 1926.

Comintern press had already been instructed to get tougher on British 'leftists,' and to name names.[1] But that was not enough. The leaders of the Soviet Central Trade Union Council, the TUC's partners in this particular united front, had to testify personally and forcefully to the grievous failings of their Committee colleagues. It was a hard decision for the Stalinists to reach. The British might react by liquidating the Committee themselves. But confronted with Trotsky's argument and his evidence – only three choices were possible. The Party could take his advice and rupture the Committee – but that would amount to admitting the heretic had been right all along. It could resolve to save the Committee no matter what the costs, even if it meant limiting the right to abuse General Council leftists, but that would just prove the validity of Trotsky's charge that the English capitulators were being shielded. Or it could take those steps the Central Committee hurriedly decided upon the first week in June – denounce the TUC leaders roundly, while demanding the right to continue associating with them. The policy might seem ambivalent, but it was based on at least one bit of consistent logic: it conceded nothing whatsoever to Trotsky or the United Opposition.

A special plenum of the All-Union Council of Trade Unions met June 7 to vote the resolution the Party wanted.[2] Tomsky and Lozovsky assured their colleagues that the net result of the general strike would be to strengthen – not weaken – the Anglo-Soviet trade union connection. Comparing the open-handed support the Russians offered them with the grudging and miserly contributions of IFTU affiliates, British workers would realize who their real friends were. They would oust the reformist hypocrites who camouflaged bourgeois ideology behind leftist phrases, and substitute good revolutionaries who knew what class war was. That was precisely what the resolution adopted invited them to do, although it was addressed not just to the British but to the International Proletariat. It recalled how English and Russian workers had pioneered in calling for world-wide trade union unity, for joint action against the

[1] See, for example, *Pravda*, 22 May, 1926, a direct response to the Hicks–Swales–Tillett article in *Lansbury's Labour Weekly*, or *Inprecorr*, VI, 45 (3 June, 1926), 729–30 and 46 (10 June, 1926), 748–9.

[2] For the plenum, see *Trud*, 8 June 1926. For the resolution, see *Trud* or *Pravda*, 8 June 1926 (*Pravda* also published some explanatory remarks by Lozovsky), or the English translations in *Inprecorr*, VI, 47 (17 June, 1926), 772–3, or *Workers' Weekly*, 16 July 1926. Much to Lozovsky's indignation, the *Daily Herald* never printed the statement. The members of the General Council saw it, however. The Finance and General Purposes Committee had copies run off for them before the July meeting of the Council, the meeting that had to deal with the Soviet demand for another session of the Committee!

capitalist offensive. In such circumstances, it was natural for the Soviets to have taken a keen interest in the progress of the general strike. Now, after the defeat, they were duty-bound, as good internationalists, to offer their analysis of what went wrong. The defeat was not due to any defect in the strike weapon, nor to any irresolution in the English rank and file. The leaders had betrayed it, and not only the traitors on the right, like Thomas, but also the capitulators on the left, like Purcell and Hicks. Indeed, the leftists, having influence but refusing to use it, were most culpable of all. Soviet workers tried to energize and reinforce them and 'in an unprecedented expression of solidarity, collected money, copper by copper, to aid their struggling British brothers.' But George Hicks had responded with a contemptuous sneer at the 'damned Russian money' and the General Council refused to accept it. It had thus dealt the cause of international solidarity, and the Anglo-Russian Committee, a severe blow. The Soviet proletarians would not stand meekly aside, however, and let the reformist traitors cut their ties with the British working class. The Committee would not be liquidated, but reinvigorated 'as an organ of common struggle of the working class of both countries.' Such a joint effort, however, to succeed, demanded plain speaking and honest criticism on both sides. From the Russian side, it seemed clear that if British workers faced up to the lessons of the general strike, they would oust those traitors and capitulators who had so grievously misled them and find new spokesmen, class-conscious, militant and unafraid, to represent them on both the General Council and the Anglo-Russian Committee.

Tomsky's statement was echoed, a day later, in a rather lengthier document produced by the Executive Committee of the Comintern.[1] The major grievance against the councillors, obviously, remained their rejection of that Soviet money, an attempt to 'isolate the English workers from the international proletariat.' In spite of such calculated insults, however, it would be a 'wholly inexpedient' and 'infantile' gesture for the Soviet trade unionists to respond by liquidating the Anglo-Russian Committee. To urge such a course implied one had to choose either to wage revolution or to negotiate with social democratic opportunists – that one could not do both. Soviet workers had never been taken in by such false assumptions. As they saw the purpose of the Committee, it was to enable them to make contacts with the English rank and file, not the TUC bureaucrats. If those same bureaucrats now found the Committee a burden – as they well might – the Comintern

---

[1] The complete English text is in *Communist Review*, VII, 3 (July, 1926), 113–36.

virtually challenged them to withdraw from it, if they dared. To do so would only expose their treason all the more clearly, bring them into even sharper conflict with their own followers, and thus accelerate the leftward movement of the working masses.

The two chief spokesmen for the Politburo majority trumpeted the new line in parallel speeches June 8, the very day the Comintern statement appeared. Stalin made the case cautiously to railway workshop workers in Tiflis.[1] Bukharin made it more flamboyantly and at somewhat greater length to the functionaries of the Moscow Party organization.[2] Bukharin made more of an effort to confront and refute the Trotsky–Zinoviev line. The Central Committee had rejected the Opposition proposal to liquidate the Anglo-Russian Committee, he reported, because to do so would be tantamount to urging Communists to desert all reformist trade unions. The Soviets had never nurtured any illusions about those General Council bureaucrats anyway, he claimed, and had therefore not been surprised by their May 12 surrender, but as the English masses continued moving to the political left, they would change the composition of the General Council, and therefore of the Committee. To break the TUC tie, in the very midst of that process, would be the height of foolishness.[3]

It may be that at this point the Russians did not really want to keep their line to the TUC, but wanted the General Council to take the responsibility for breaking it. For all their talk about maintaining the Committee, and strengthening it, it was not for another three weeks, not until after the flurry of Churchill–Birkenhead sabre-rattling at the end of the month, that they actually wrote the TUC proposing a meeting.[4] In the meantime, they kept up their barrage of abuse against the councillors. Tomsky told the *Sunday Worker*, for example, that the only real reason the TUC turned down the Russian contribution May 7 was because the government had already moved to block transfer of the funds by law. By hiding that fact, he alleged, the General Council aided and abetted Joynson-Hicks.[5] Citrine denied it. He confessed himself 'unable to believe' Tomsky could have been guilty of such a 'serious reflection' on the good faith of the General Council. The *Worker*'s

[1] Stalin, *Sochineniia*, VIII, 155–72.
[2] *Inprecorr*, VI, 51 (8 July, 1926), 830–4 and 52 (15 July, 1926), 850–4.
[3] The Stalin–Bukharin line got dispensed in more lavish and extended form in an article by Lozovsky in *Die Rote Gewerkschaftsinternationale*, No. 6 (65) (June, 1926), pp. 383–94. Almost the whole issue was devoted to explicating the texts of the Central Council and Comintern statements of June 7–8.
[4] See above, p. 260.   [5] *Sunday Worker*, 13 June, 1926.

correspondent, admitting that a chronological check had indeed proved Citrine right, that the TUC had turned the money down before it learned the government had required it to do so, announced triumphantly that the new revelation made the TUC sin all the worse. Sending the money back had obviously just encouraged the government to issue that edict banning transfer of Russian funds.[1] The message really should have been clear at Eccleston Square. Tomsky was telling them that the only thing worse than refusing the money before Jix acted was refusing it after he acted – and vice versa. One finds it difficult to avoid the conclusion that for these two or three weeks, the Soviets were perfectly willing to goad the TUC into rupturing the Committee.

British Communists were dismayed at the Central Council's June 7 letter, and indeed, the CPGB press put off printing a translation of it for an unprecedented six weeks.[2] The Party had already reversed itself once, moving from that 'Cashier the Cowards' slogan the day after the strike to a call for reconciliation with the leftists two weeks later. Now it was being asked to go back to square one all over again, a humiliation no reference to the mysteries of the dialectic could successfully camouflage. The mortification might have been somewhat more palatable had the comrades been warned it was coming, or best of all, allowed to participate in the deliberations which produced it. Such was not the case: many of them first heard of the existence of Tomsky's manifesto when they read of it in *The Times*. Finally, local Communists had their doubts whether the statement would produce any results. The General Council was already under attack from its own rank and file anyway. The British worker was damning his leaders in expletives quite as imaginative and colourful as any current in the Comintern lexicon. When foreigners joined the chorus, however, the local reaction – however illogical it might be – was to close ranks against the outside intruder. The manifesto, then, was more of a help to Jimmy Thomas than it was to the CPGB. In short, the document was a mistake, as Andrew Rothstein was bluntly telling Rykov just a couple of weeks later. The CPGB registered its official dismay in letters to the Central Committee of the Soviet Communist Party and the Executive Committee of the Comintern, and indicated it intended to bring up the matter at the next Executive Committee meeting.[3]

---

[1] *Daily Herald*, 15 June, 1926; *Sunday Worker*, 20 June, 1926.

[2] *Workers' Weekly* finally announced the existence of an 'important manifesto by the Russian TUC' July 9 and printed it, on p. 4, July 16.

[3] This paragraph is based largely on the personal testimony of Andrew Rothstein,

The comrades might not like what had been done, but they were disciplined enough to conform to the new dispensation.[1] *Workers' Weekly* launched the now-obligatory attack on TUC leftists in its issue of June 18. It was a mild enough beginning, mostly aimed at Purcell and chiding him for returning to his old 'class struggle' patter only now, after the real class struggle was over. He had to act, not just talk, the editorialist insisted, and unless he did, the workers would reject him.[2] The *Communist Review* took a similar line, stressing in particular 'the shameful, inexcusable, unforgettable act of refusing the Russian workers' help' and noting the rumour of 'a renegade and disgraceful speech from George Hicks against taking the money.'[3] Palme Dutt mounted the harshest attack of all.[4] He pronounced them guilty of having 'completely failed to provide any alternate leadership during the crisis,' and cited Hicks, Bromley, Purcell, and Tillett as the worst offenders. The lesson to be learned was that there was no substantial difference between the left and the right. The left was impotent in practice because it had no positive programmes, nothing to offer, in fact, but opportunism.

However distasteful the CPGB may have found Moscow's instructions on the TUC and on the Committee, then, it had adapted to them, which was more than the United Opposition seemed willing to do back in the Soviet Union. Trotsky, Zinoviev and Kamenev had rejected the decisions taken in early June, and in mid-July a joint plenum of the CPSU's Central Committee and Central Control Commission, was convened to hear, and reject, the Opposition's case.[5] The three dissidents had a lot more to talk about than just the Committee, of course. But their principal complaint against Stalin was his doctrine of socialism in one

supplemented by the material in Murphy, *New Horizons*, pp. 226–35, and in MacFarlane, *British Communist Party*, pp. 167–8.

[1] The CPGB was. The NMM, a much more chaotic organization, had to be reminded to toe the line. See *Mezhdunarodnoe Profdvizhenie*, p. 50.
[2] *Workers' Weekly*, 18 June, 1926.
[3] *Communist Review*, VII, 3 (July, 1926), 101–5.
[4] R. Palme Dutt, 'Notes of the Month,' *Labour Monthly*, VIII, 7 (July, 1926), 387–8.
[5] The major source for the plenum is *Izvestiia*, 25 July, 1926. Stalin's speech to the meeting, in an abridged version, is in Stalin, *Sochineniia*, VIII, 176–91. The Declaration of the Opposition is in the Trotsky Archives, T-880, and their Draft Resolution on the General Strike in *ibid.*, T-881. There is further information in Trotsky's account of the Committee written 25 Sept., 1927, Trotsky Archives, T-3093; in B. A. Abramov, 'Razgrom Trotskistko-Zinov'evskogo Antipartiinogo Bloka,' *Voprosy Istorii K.P.S.S.*, No. 6 (1959), pp. 25–47; in Lev D. Trotskii, *The Strategy of the World Revolution* (New York: Communist League of America [Opposition], 1930), pp. 54–5; in *Inprecorr*, VII, 4 (12 Jan., 1927), 75, 80; and in Deutscher, *Trotsky*, pp. 275–80.

country, and their major objection to that slogan was that it seemed to involve a perversion of united front doctrines in order to allow shameful accommodations with counter-revolutionary reformists and opportunists. The Anglo-Russian Committee was the most obvious example of what the Oppositionists objected to, and they proceeded to club the *vozhd* with it for nine successive days of tough Party infighting.[1]

They did not have any new charges to bring. Trotsky and Zinoviev had said it all before, and they would repeat it all later. The Committee represented a retreat from revolutionary militancy. It had become a united front from above only, a link between elites, and no such organization could ever provide Communists any meaningful connection with the social democratic masses. The Committee was useless, then, in terms of revolutionizing the English workers, or furthering the class struggle in Britain. Instead, it just confused potential sympathizers. They were told their trade union leaders were traitors, cowards and opportunists, but at the same time, leftists with proven credentials – Russian revolutionaries – were still willing to work in tandem with them. In such circumstances, how could the rank and file ever know just who their enemies were?

Nor would the Opposition accept the argument that the Committee might serve to deter the British government from taking hostile action against the USSR. To assume such a thing, one had to assume the English members of the Committee were trustworthy and reliable proletarian militants, and they had proved themselves quite the contrary May 12. Indeed, with the likes of Thomas, MacDonald and Purcell at the head of the labour movement, the bourgeoisie had nothing to worry about at all. The reformist cowards were sure to keep the masses unprepared and confused. To encourage workers in either Britain or the USSR to rely on them was to maintain fatal illusions. Only by relentlessly unmasking such traitors and ousting them from the trade union leadership could the imperialists be restrained from waging war on the USSR.

The connection with the General Council should be liquidated forthwith, then, and the councillors no longer allowed to posture as friends of the USSR. The break had been delayed too long already. It should have been made May 12. The most active and class-conscious English proletarians had been ready to oust the reformist TUC timeservers then and

---

[1] 14–23 July, 1926. The deliberations were so heated that after ranting through one especially lengthy bit of invective, Dzerzhinsky suffered a heart attack and died right there in the meeting hall.

there, and it was disgraceful that the Soviets had lacked the courage to back them up. The Politburo majority had helped pull Purcell and company through the crisis. Now, presumably, they had no special use for the Committee any more, and might, indeed, consider it an inconvenience. They would probably try to sabotage it on some trivial organizational technicality. To let them thus seize the initiative and liquidate the Committee on their own terms would be an unforgivable mistake, a crime against the working class. The Russians must strike first. That was the sort of united front Lenin recommended, and Trotsky had the quotations from the canon to prove it.

It was a strong argument, but votes, not sophistry, was what counted in this power struggle, and Stalin had the votes. His supporters slashed away at the Opposition for various heresies: for repudiating united front tactics, trying to isolate the Communist Party from the working class, and demonstrating uncomradely hostility toward the CPGB. Such deviations were all unscientific and un-Marxist and maybe even a bit suspiciously bourgeois. In attacking the trade unions, for example, the Opposition seemed to be echoing Stanley Baldwin's attitudes. He, too, was sceptical of too powerful a TUC. Objectively, then, the Opposition and the bourgeois imperialists stood together. In fact, of course, however backward or reactionary the present leaders of British trade unionism might be, they still represented a definite stage in the development of proletarian political consciousness in Britain, and they could not be overthrown – from Moscow – without the help of the British masses. The Committee provided a contact with those masses. It made it easier to win them over from reformism to Communism. Its very existence extended the breach between Amsterdam and the TUC, 'a rift which exists and which we shall widen in every way possible.' Most of all, it inhibited the imperialistic warmongers in Baldwin's government. 'The Anglo-Russian Committee can and will play a tremendous role in the struggle against every intervention directed against the USSR,' read the theses presented by the Moscow Party organization. 'It will become the organizational centre of the proletariat in the struggle against every effort of the international bourgeoisie to concoct a new war.' Its liquidation, therefore, would only serve the interests of the Birkenheads and the Churchills, and Stalin too could cite the conventional number of quotations from Lenin to prove his case.

Given the immediate circumstances, Stalin's position had some merit. Relations with Britain were indeed grim, and the USSR needed all the friends on the island it could find. The Soviet trade unions had not neglected their ideological duty: they had rebuked their Committee colleagues roundly, and gotten away with it, too. Indeed, word had just been received that the General Council had finally consented to another Committee meeting – because it had to, Stalin explained, because Cook and Richardson, friends of the Russians, had obliged it to. The TUC leaders did not dare risk an open fight with the miners. They could not liquidate the Committee, therefore, however uncomfortable it made them and however much the Russians used it to expose them, to their own rank and file, as class traitors. For the Soviets to surrender such a useful organization would just be to break contact with the British masses, throw them into the arms of the Sassenbachs and Oudegeests, and delight the hearts of the Churchills and Thomases – with nothing to show in return for all those losses. It would be a cheap theatrical gesture, Stalin scoffed, 'ridiculous and adventurist,' reminiscent of Trotsky's anti-Leninist behaviour at the time of Brest-Litovsk.

The plenum saw things Stalin's way. Why dissolve an organization that produced so much pain among reformists, at so little risk to revolutionaries. The General Council's telegram agreeing to another Committee meeting – arriving at such a crucial moment – had shattered the Opposition's case totally. It was hardly surprising Lozovsky presented the wire to the plenum so triumphantly, with such melodramatic flourishes. It was flaunted as a victory over the Opposition, not over the TUC, Trotsky recalled later. The Stalinists jeered at their rivals, taunted them for their imbecility, and turned down their programme overwhelmingly, on the Committee issue as on every other. Zinoviev was dropped from the Politburo for presuming to challenge the will of the majority. Stalin had taken personal responsibility – for the first time, really – for the future of the Committee, and offered his colleagues lavish assurances as to its usefulness.

III

Prospects for the next meeting of the Anglo-Russian Committee, scheduled for Paris beginning July 30, were not particularly bright. The Soviet side wanted to discuss aiding the locked-out British coalminers, and make as much political capital as they could out of the fact they were doing more for the strikers than were the member organizations of TUC. The English wanted to protest the Russian trade unions' June 7 statement dubbing all General Council members traitors and cowards and proposing their ouster in favour of Communist militants. Neither delegation seemed especially concerned with the problem of international trade union unity, which had presumably been the major reason for establishing the Committee.

Only the TUC leftists, targets of the Soviets' harshest abuse since June, seemed able to recall what the Committee was all about. In the last issue of a by now obviously obsolete journal, *Trade Union Unity*, Hicks and Purcell urged that nothing be allowed to 'impair the effective continuence of the work of the Anglo-Russian Committee until its task is completed.'[1] They confessed their 'Russian comrades' seemed to have been taken in by 'many distorted statements' as to 'what actually transpired here' during the general strike. The Central Council's June 7 statement was therefore 'incorrect in many details and far from complete.' But to haggle over such 'little things' would be tragic 'when there are so many big things that can and must be done,' and they urged the Committee to concentrate on the major issue – trade union unity and how to achieve it.

It was a futile gesture. The Soviets were no longer interested in any sort of unity except unity on their own terms. The hope of manoeuvring them – somehow – into IFTU was at least seven months out of date. Indeed, the British Communist press was now proposing a much simpler solution to the problem of trade union internationalism: the TUC should just ditch the IFTU and join Profintern.[2] The unity campaign, then, was in a state of suspended animation. The English 'leftists' who had once pretended to back it could hardly be expected to continue the fight, Lozovsky admitted, now that their Russian colleagues were savaging them so successfully.[3] The cause would therefore lose some of its pretended partisans, but it never needed the backing of cowards anyway. Ultimately, they would be replaced by 'thousands and tens of thousands of *working* campaigners' ready to demonstrate 'proletarian decisiveness' and march 'hand in hand with the revolutionary wing of the labour movement.'

Assuming Lozovsky's attitude represented official policy, the Paris meeting just had to be a fiasco. If the two sides could not discuss trade union internationalism, there was hardly anything to discuss at all. Their talks had been successful in the past largely because they could share their exasperation with some mutual enemies, those incorrigible and

---

[1] *Trade Union Unity*, 11, 6 (Aug., 1926), 81–2. The journal must have appeared during the last two weeks of July. There had been no numbers dated June or July.

[2] *The Worker*, 17 June, 1926.

[3] *Die Rote Gewerkschaftsinternationale*, No. 6 (65), (June, 1926), pp. 471–2.

unprincipled mules at the head of the Amsterdam bureaucracy. If that topic were now exhausted, they would be reduced to talking about one another, meddling scandalmongers on the one side, cowardly traitors on the other. It was hardly a promising agenda.

Nor was the membership of the Russian delegation a particularly good omen. The one Russian the British liked and trusted, the one they considered a 'real trade unionist,' the one who had joined with them most energetically for proletarian unity – Tomsky – had sent his regrets.[1] He had worked himself too hard, he reported, and his doctor had ordered two months convalescence. He was very sorry he had to miss the meeting because the sessions would be very important. He hoped the Committee might 'extend its work' in order to support the miners, and he trusted differences of opinion on other matters would not inhibit cooperation on behalf of the MFGB. Andrei Andreev, only just named alternate member of the Politburo, would lead the Russian delegation in his stead.

In fact, Tomsky's convalescence may have been ordered by his colleagues, not his doctors. He was not the sort of man to mouth the tough new Soviet line convincingly. He was too close to the British leaders personally, and too genial and gregarious a soul in any event to make a convincing show of malevolence. Andreev, a hard, calculating *apparatchik* of the new breed, could do that sort of thing superbly. So it was he, plus Dogadov, Mel'nichansky, Lepse and Schwarz who sat down opposite Pugh, Findlay, Purcell, Hicks and Citrine at 11:15 am, Friday, July 30, at the Cayres Hotel in Paris for the Committee's third – and stormiest – session.[2]

---

[1] The letter was reprinted in *Trud*, 13 Aug., 1926.

[2] Andrew Rothstein is my source for the suggestion Tomsky's illness may have been more diplomatic than medical. For the Committee meeting, the two essential documents are Andreev's detailed report to an Extraordinary Plenary Session of the Soviet Central Trade Union Council, as published in *Trud*, 13 Aug., 1926 and (in English) in *Inprecorr*, VI, 58 (26 Aug., 1926), 987–91 and 60 (2 Sept., 1926), 1024–8, and the minutes in the TUC Archives, file 947/220, doc. A.R. 3. 1925–6. Andreev's report has to be read carefully, since he so blends his account of *what* happened at the meeting with his comments on *why* it happened it is difficult to distinguish one from the other. See also Petrowski (Bennet), *Anglo-Russische Komitee*, pp. 24–31. The British press, even the Communist press, had almost nothing to say about the meeting, but see the *Daily Herald*, 2 Aug, 1926, *Workers' Weekly*, 6 Aug., 1926 and *Sunday Worker*, 15 Aug., 1926 (a summary of Andreev's report). The General Council said almost nothing about the meeting at the 1926 Congress (*1926 TUC: Report of Proceedings*, p. 246) and only very little more was revealed to the 1927 Congress (Trades Union Congress, *Report of Proceedings at the 59th Annual Trades Union Congress* [*1927*], Ed. by Walter Citrine [London: Cooperative Printing Society, 1927], p. 200). Purcell sat in at the Committee meeting for Swales, who apparently had another engagement.

The delegates enjoyed about five minutes of relaxation – the time it took to read the letter from Tomsky and vote him the Committee's condolences. Then Pugh rose to the attack on behalf of the TUC. The English were in some doubt, he reported, whether they should continue to participate in the Committee at all, given the cruel and unwarranted slanders their Russian colleagues had directed against them in connection with the general strike. Ordering that stoppage, managing it, and concluding it were the exclusive responsibility of the General Council, and the Council could not accept the right of any outsiders to try to dictate to it how it should have conducted its affairs. It was therefore 'imperative,' before the Committee moved to the next item on its agenda, that the Central Council's June 7 statement 'be unreservedly repudiated and publicly withdrawn.'

It smacked of a Jimmy Thomas harangue, Andreev reported to fellow trade unionists back home two weeks later, but even the TUC 'leftists' present refused to disown it. The Russians, however, would not give an inch. The British were overly sensitive, Andreev retorted. The circumstances under which the June 7 statement was issued were, of course, 'exceptional,' but to call the Central Council's criticism 'interference' was absurd. The Committee's own constitution specified that the struggle against capitalism was world-wide, so how could the General Council relegate so titanic an event as a general strike to the obscurity of a purely English affair? The Soviets believed in proletarian internationalism, and that meant they were always ready both to offer criticism, and take it, across national boundaries. When the General Council surrendered to the bourgeoisie and deserted the miners, the Soviets could find no other term for the sum total of what had been done than 'treachery.' It was, admittedly, a tough word, but 'proletarian class frankness' demanded it be used. In any event, it was silly to argue about history. The miners were still fighting, and they could still win, but they needed assistance from all over the world to do it. Andreev suggested the Committee proceed to discuss how to organize such an effort.

It had been over two hours, and the delegates needed a lunch break. When they returned to the meeting room, an hour and a quarter later, they were refreshed but not reconciled. Round two would go over five hours, to 8 pm, and both sides were as unyielding as ever. Citrine said he did not see how, in an atmosphere of such hostility, any cooperation was possible. Purcell raised the subject of the Russian money, admitting it was a mistake to have sent it back, but arguing that accepting it would have been wrongly interpreted by the government as an agreement to be bribed into continuing the strike. The Soviets said it all stank of coward-ice to them. Hicks rose to deny 'categorically' he had ever talked about any 'damned Russian money' or that he and Purcell had ever voted to recommend a 10 per cent reduction in miners' wages, as the Soviets had charged. It was a 'lie' and he wanted it retracted. The Russians were not ready to back down. If the TUC representatives wanted to raise the issue, however, they were willing to discuss 'the activity and the attitudes of the General Council in all its details during the general strike.' Citrine replied the British delegation was not empowered to discuss General Council decisions within the Committee. The Russians retorted they were not empowered to discuss their Central Council's statements, either.

Purcell insisted the British were for unity, but they also believed in autonomy, and as they saw it the Soviet statement struck at that fundamental principle of international trades unionism. The Russians clearly had a lot to learn about their British associates, he proceeded. The distinction between 'rights' and 'lefts' in the British trade union movement, for example, was just absurd. The Russian declaration had made it terribly difficult to work with them effectively, and they would just have to do something 'to liquidate the position' into which they had put the TUC. Findlay was harsher yet. As far as he was concerned, the Soviets had destroyed the very basis of the Anglo-Russian partnership, and unless they could give the TUC the assurances it demanded, the General Council should simply refuse to participate in the Committee's work any longer.

Andreev replied with a lecture. The two sides had had differences of opinion before, he recalled, but they had still been able to find a common language in the interests of international trade union unity. He had hoped they would find a common language now, to discuss how to help the miners, the principal current targets of the capitalist offensive. He provided the British delegation a brief Marxist analysis of the current international economic situation, and a few moments of *dicta* on the nature of a general strike. It was a splendid weapon, he noted, when wielded *politically*, but it could not be used just to resolve wage problems. The 'connection between economics and politics is understood by every simple worker in the Soviet Union,' he noted, 'but the leaders of the General Council have not grasped it.'

Invincible ignorance, however, was the least of the councillors' failings. Andreev pointed out that they had also dragged their feet on the unity campaign. They had promised to convene a meeting between the Russian trade unions and the IFTU, and they had not done so. The

Soviets wanted an explanation of the delay. They also wanted some response to the dangers of imperialist war-mongering all over the world. They wanted a declaration by both parties on the continued existence of the Committee. Most of all, however, they wanted to go into a whole catalogue of possibilities on how to aid the MFGB. Pugh replied the British were not authorized to discuss the miners' strike with the Russians, and they suspected raising the issue would do more harm than good. In any event, the matter was outside the Committee's competence; the Russian proposals, if they had them down in writing, should just be referred directly to the General Council. For now, all the British wanted was a disavowal of that June 7 statement. They seemed in a great hurry to get home, Andreev commented later.

Perhaps they were just in a hurry to get to dinner. A long afternoon of debate – and no tea break! – had left everybody's teeth on edge. The evening session was a disaster. They tried to discuss what kind of a statement they might issue to the press, and could not even agree on that. They met again the next morning and each side presented a memorandum incorporating its impressions of what had happened the day before. The British, predictably, emphasized the intolerable Central Council statement of June 7. The Soviets stressed the matter of aid to the miners, and included a draft resolution, which the British rejected, covering that subject, the war threat, trade union unity and the future of the Committee. The two memoranda were so far apart that both sides agreed it would be best to make no statement to the press at all. The English proposed that the meeting should be regarded as just suspended, with another session to follow in two to three weeks. The Russians replied future meetings would have to be negotiated. The good-byes were perfunctory and chilly.

It was only a matter of a week before the British Communist press had a pretty fair idea of what had happened at Paris, and an agreeable set of explanations as to whose fault it was.[1] The Committee had achieved no results at all, *Workers' Weekly* reported, and the dirtiest roles in the 'sordid story' had been played by the so-called 'leftists,' Hicks and Purcell. They had become mere *'screens and handrags for J. H. Thomas.'* They intentionally obstructed the Committee's deliberations in order to prevent the Russians from extending the miners any additional practical help. Obviously, 'leftists' had broken completely away from the principles they once claimed to stand for, and they should all be ousted from the General Council in favour of trustworthy revolutionaries.

[1] *Workers' Weekly*, 6 Aug., 1926.

From August 13 on, the Russians supplied official documentation for that position. The Soviet press published Andreev's account of the Paris debacle, and the subsequent resolution of his Central Council colleagues accusing the TUC leadership of persisting in a policy of sabotage and capitulation.[1] Assuming the Committee were a mere bloc between élites – dissoluble by either side at its convenience – the English had decided to rupture the organization, the statement charged. The Soviets would resist all such efforts. They saw the Committee as an expression of solidarity among the working masses in the two countries, and not to be liquidated, therefore, unless the rank and file so decided. Meantime, they demanded the right to continue to tell the truth about their opposite numbers on the General Council. Their fellow proletarians in Britain needed ideological as well as material help, and the Russians were determined to provide it.

Profintern and Comintern rushed out manifestos echoing the Central Council statement and enlarging upon it.[2] The miners' cause was in serious trouble. The official TUC leadership, the Miners' International and the IFTU had joined the British bourgeoisie in a campaign against the strikers. That was why the General Council sabotaged the Paris meeting. The British proletariat had to compel its leaders to fight the miners' fight through to the end. That involved mobilizing Amsterdam's affiliates in the MFGB's behalf, rejecting any settlement requiring the miners to make concessions, maintaining the Committee, and using it to organize a massive new effort to win all the strikers' demands.

Whether or not the members of the General Council took the Soviet propaganda barrage very seriously is hard to say. They knew, however, the Russians could reveal what had been said at Paris, and some of that might indeed be embarrassing. Their instructions from the Scarborough Congress, after all, had been to cooperate with the Soviets in the unity campaign, and it would seem childish and petulant of them to neglect that responsibility out of what could be interpreted as mere personal pique. And the Russian offer to provide the miners still more aid could not be dismissed casually either – not without some good justification. The MFGB needed help, certainly, and Amsterdam had offered very little.[3] Finally, the next annual Congress was less than a month away,

[1] The Central Council resolution was published in *Trud*, 13 Aug., 1926 (the same day as Andreev's report) and was reprinted in *Profsoiuzy SSSR: Dokumenty i Materialy*, II, 555–57. *Workers' Weekly* echoed its major points in an editorial entitled 'Keep the Committee' in its issue of 20 Aug.

[2] *Inprecorr*, VI, 58 (26 Aug., 1926), 965–7; *Mezhdunarodnoe Profdvizhenie*, pp. 49–50.

[3] IFTU loaned the TUC £380,000 in July, 1926, but did not really begin an energetic

and the councillors surely did not want to provide their enemies a lot of new ammunition to use against them. They had little enough good will anyway after the way they had conducted the general strike! In any event, and for whatever the reason, they decided to back down. After a lengthy discussion August 13, the General Council voted to seek another meeting with the Russians, by August 20 if possible, 'to continue the purposes for which the Committee was appointed.'[1] The TUC leadership had decided to drop its demand that the Soviets retract that June 7 statement. It was also now at least willing to listen to what they had to say about the miners' strike.

While the members of the General Council were changing their minds in London, the leaders of the British Communist Party were having theirs changed for them in Moscow. The scene was a meeting of the presidium of the Comintern's Executive Committee. Murphy was there, for the CPGB, to reiterate the Party's objections to the Soviet trade unions' June 7 statement criticizing the TUC leaders and urging their ouster. It was unnecessarily harsh; the CPGB should have been consulted before it was published; the General Council might dissolve the Committee in retaliation; it would encourage the anti-Soviet cabal in the government; and it would not work: British workers would resent outsiders interfering in a domestic quarrel and rally to the councillors. Profintern might issue such pronunciamentos, Murphy conceded, but for the Soviet trade unionists to do so was to indulge in futile and ineffective gestures.[2]

The argument was a bit unreal. Trotsky and Zinoviev – not Hicks and Purcell – had been the real targets of that June 7 statement anyway. It was designed to cut the ground out from under the Opposition. Stalin knew perfectly well, in fact, that one could not hurl a brickbat from Moscow and demolish the General Council in London. He had already

effort on behalf of the miners until the latter part of August. It never compared with the Russian effort. See *IFTU Press Reports*, VI (1926), *passim*. See also *Lansbury's Labour Weekly*, 28 Aug., 1926.

[1] General Council Minutes, No. 369, 13 Aug., 1926. See also *Sunday Worker*, 15 Aug., 1926.

[2] Murphy, *New Horizons*, pp. 226–35. Murphy's memoir has to be used cautiously. He confuses the Central Council's June 7 statement with the telegram Tomsky later sent the Bournemouth TUC, and he quotes Stalin as conceding that the statement might break up the Committee, which would be most regrettable, but to care too much about mere forms that had no proletarian, revolutionary value any more would just prevent Communists from bringing the truth to the workers. A pretty speech, except we know very well he said nothing even vaguely like that until almost a year later, on 1 Aug., 1927: Stalin, *Sochineniia*, x, 3–59.

said so, in response to the Opposition demand for the Committee's liquidation. Having parried the attack from the left, then, he was now confronted with some of his own arguments when assaulted from the right. But Stalin was an old hand at walking a dialectical tightrope, and he practised that art again now.[1]

He would concede just one point to Murphy: the CPGB should indeed have been consulted before the June 7 document was published. There had not been time. The statement had been cleared through Profintern and Comintern, however, as well as the Central Committee of the CPSU, so the international movement had a chance to look it over in advance. Stalin rejected Murphy's further suggestion Profintern should have issued the manifesto itself. RILU was neither particularly well-known in Britain nor especially popular. Nothing it said, the *vozhd* admitted cheerfully, would carry much weight. The Central Council of the Russian Trade Union Federation, on the other hand, was well-known and well-liked. To make an effective impact on the British, therefore, Tomsky had to do the talking, and judging by how loudly the general councillors were protesting what he had said, one could only assume he had hit the mark.

Stalin pooh-poohed Murphy's concern that the General Council might retaliate by dissolving the Committee. In view of how much aid the Russians were providing the miners, such a move was 'almost out of the question.' Nobody, in fact, was more afraid of a break-up than Hicks and Purcell, who had built their reputations at home, after all, by cultivating the Russians. The English might threaten a rupture, then, to try to intimidate the Central Council, but they would never dare go through with it. And even if they did, the loss would not be crucial. The Soviets could surrender the Committee if they had to. They certainly would not stay in it if to do so they had to give up their freedom of criticism. The whole purpose of the alliance with the English, Stalin recalled, was to work together in the interests of the workers. If the General Council itself betrayed the workers' interests, thus making joint action impossible, the Russians had the duty to say so. And if saying so discredited some TUC reactionaries, no great harm had been done. The sooner they were exposed and removed, the better.

It would all take time, however, and Stalin warned his fellow-Communists not to become impatient. That was the mistake Trotsky made when he demanded the Soviets liquidate the Committee immediately. To follow his advice would just be to indulge in a lot of pointless

---

[1] His speech is in Stalin, *Sochineniia*, VIII, 194–203.

theatrics. It would be equally unsound, however, to go to the other extreme and resolve to save the Committee at the price of ignoring the General Council's treacheries, from the May 12 capitulation up to the Paris Committee meeting. Such duplicities had to be publicized. Silence would be interpreted as approval, an act of 'political and moral suicide' for the International. Stalin contemptuously dismissed Murphy's contention that non-Englishmen should not interfere in the 'internal affairs' of the British. It was a deplorable argument, reminiscent of what Purcell, Citrine and Pugh had said at Paris. To criticize the General Council was to serve the British workers, not to insult them, and Soviet trade unionists would continue to rebuke the TUC leadership when it deserved rebuking.

Stalin had not yielded much, but he had answered the CPGB argument in almost every particular, and Murphy himself, a month later, was ready to admit he had made a mistake. The Party made its submission even earlier, just two days after Stalin's address.[1] The 'so-called "Left-Wingers" on the General Council' deserved their scolding, the resolution affirmed. 'At every critical moment during and since the General Strike' they had capitulated to the trade union reactionaries, and not only that, by their very silence they had helped protect the rightists from the wrath of the rank and file. Nevertheless, for the Soviet trade unions to respond by withdrawing from the Committee would just be to deal the world unity movement 'a particularly heavy blow' at an especially unfortunate time. The suggestions for a break-up, 'dictated either by despair, or by an over-estimate of the degree of revolutionization of the British Worker, come well enough from the emotional and confused armoury of Comrade Trotsky,...but they are not to be expected from the Chairman of the ECCI,' the British noted, and indicated they would therefore support Stalin's proposal to oust Zinoviev from the Comintern leadership.

As of mid-August, then, both sides had decided not to scrap the Committee altogether. Neither partner, however, was willing to concede much to the other just to make the organization a success, and that became perfectly clear when the two again sat down together, in Berlin, on August 23.[2] The TUC had given way some, just enough to make con-

---

[1] 'Resolution of the Political Bureau of the C.P. of Great Britain on the Discussion in the C.P.S.U.,' 9 Aug., 1926, mimeographed (TUC Library); *Inprecorr*, VI, 57 (19 Aug., 1926), 963–4.

[2] Two admirably complete records of the meeting are available, the TUC's minutes, Doc. A.R. 4 1925–6, file 947/220, TUC Archives, and Andreev's report to the Presidium of the Central Trades Union Council, 31 Aug., 1926, in *Trud*, 1 Sept.,

versations possible. It had dropped its demand that the Russians repudiate their Central Council statement of June 7. The issue that had seemed so crucial at Paris never got raised at all in Berlin. Stalin had gambled on the assumption the General Council could not afford to scrap the Committee – not so long as the miners were still locked out and Soviet support for them so lavish – and though his logic might have been tenuous, his conclusions seemed borne out.[1]

Having given in on the one issue, however, the English were ready to be obstinate on others, and Pugh began the proceedings by reprimanding the Russians for publishing Andreev's account of the Paris meeting. As he understood it, both parties to that fiasco had agreed not to make any statements to the press. Not so, Andreev replied. We only agreed to postpone the publicity until both sides reported to their respective parent bodies. The Committee was no secret society, and Russian workers were intensely interested in what it was up to. Pugh was not convinced, but did not press the point. He suggested they proceed to the question of trade union unity, first, and then consider Russian views on aid to the miners. Not so, Andreev replied again. The matter of the miners was more urgent, and should come first. He had several concrete proposals to advance. That could all wait, Pugh interjected. The primary function of the Committee, after all, was to achieve trade union unity, and that had to take priority. Parliamentary procedures dictated that old business got considered before new business. Those were the General Council's instructions.

The Soviets were probably unfamiliar with *Roberts' Rules of Order*, but they were more than ready to deny the proposition the Committee's only purpose was to achieve organizational unity. It was also charged with 'resolute joint struggle against the capitalist offensive,' they insisted, and right now that involved taking practical measures on behalf of the

1926, and available in English in *Inprecorr*, VI, 62 (16 Sept., 1926), 1056–9, 63 (23 Sept., 1926), 1071–6, and in *Workers' Weekly*, 10 Sept., 1926. See also Petrowski (Bennet), *Anglo-Russische Komitee*, pp. 24–31. Hodgson, in Moscow, sent a copy of Andreev's report back home to London, where 'C.W.O.', a Foreign Office functionary, marked it 'distinctly amusing.' 'I imagine,' he commented, 'that the British members of the Committee wish it had never been formed.' Hodgson to Chamberlain, 8 Sept., 1926, N 4209/4031/38, F.O. 371.11802.

1 Bennet said later the TUC had been intimidated by the publication of Andreev's account of the Paris meeting. The Council may have considered the possibility of such a report 13 Aug., when it made its decision, but it could not have known the Soviet press was indeed publishing the document that very day. The English did not hear of the report until Aug. 15, when a much abbreviated version of it appeared in the *Sunday Worker*

miners. Their struggle had reached 'a particularly difficult stage.' Their families were suffering privation and hunger. Practically nobody but the Russians had done much for them. Workers all over the world were waiting to see what action the Committee would take. To respond, with despatch, was its 'direct and bounden duty.' Those were the Central Council's instructions.

After the debate had droned on for $2\frac{1}{2}$ inconclusive hours, the two sides agreed to adjourn for private consultations. By mid-afternoon, the Russians had a written statement ready – conceding nothing. Their orders were inflexible and they could not yield. After another hour's recess, the British gave way – under protest. They would have preferred to maintain orderly procedures, they noted, but they were willing to listen to what the Russians had to say.

The Russians, it turned out, had a lot to say. Indeed, they had two statements ready, one recapitulating all the arguments for insisting on their agenda rather than the TUC's, and the second listing the 14 'concrete' measures they proposed to take on behalf of the miners. The Soviet proposals contained nothing really new, and many of them were hardly very 'concrete' after all. One, for example, merely put the Committee on record as supporting the miners' 'heroic' struggle. Another praised the Russians for their generosity to the MFGB. A third condemned the IFTU for not doing enough. The major thrust of the document, however, was to propose an international embargo on shipments of 'scab coal' to and within Britain. In addition to the embargo, the miners needed strike funds. Once again, the non-Communist Internationals should be asked to contribute more (the Communists were doing enough already), but the TUC would have to raise most of the money at home. The Russians suggested the 1 per cent charge on wages they were considering levying on their trade unionists might also be appropriate in Britain.

Pugh said the proposals disappointed him. He appreciated the Russian willingness to help, but not one of their suggestions could be accepted. They were trying to use the Committee to dictate to the TUC, and the General Council would not tolerate such a thing. In any event, everything they recommended that was worth trying had already been tried. The TUC had proposed an international embargo on coal shipments, for example, but many foreign unions refused to cooperate. To appeal that decision to the masses over the heads of the leaders would be to antagonize everybody unnecessarily and do more harm than good.

During the debate that followed, all the proprieties got forgotten.

Everything the Russians suggested, one of them complained later, was rejected: either the proposal was deemed unnecessary, or it was impractical, or it was an unwarranted intervention in the TUC's internal affairs.[1] Andreev finally accused the English of a deliberate attempt to evade the issue and to sabotage the cause of the miners, just as they had done at Paris. If they did not like the Soviet proposals, they should suggest their own alternatives. Their professions of support for the miners were all rank hypocrisy, and Andreev found them disgusting. The General Council had struck a terrible blow at the Committee, he charged, when it refused to discuss the Russian suggestions seriously.

The British were stunned at the ferocity of the attack. Perhaps Andreev was expressing only his personal views. Maybe his colleagues were less adamant than he. Citrine and Swales were impertinent enough to say so openly – a patent attempt to divide us, Andreev commented later. And if what he had said did represent the official Soviet position, the British warned, the General Council might consider dissolving the Committee when it heard the news. Go ahead, Andreev retorted. 'We will see what the British working classes have to say about that!'

The two delegations adjourned for the night at this point, the Russians to get some rest, the British to draft a statement formally rejecting the Soviet proposals for aid to the miners. They had hoped, they began, to get some suggestions involving 'lines of activity and sources of support for the miners which had not already been explored or carried out.' They had always been willing to examine such proposals, but the Russians did not offer any. The proposed condemnation of IFTU for alleged inactivity was not all justified, and was outside the Committee's jurisdiction in any event. The embargo question had already been 'fully considered' back home anyway, and for the Committee to prescribe such a measure, when it could not itself implement it, would be 'rightly resented' as 'unwarranted interference' in other people's affairs. The General Council had already investigated all possible sources of financial aid for the MFGB, both at home and abroad, and the Russian propositions were unlikely to produce additional money. Indeed, implementing them would arouse such resentment that both the miners and the cause of international trade union unity might suffer. Achieving unity, the British suggested, was what the Committee was really all about, and they urged the Russians to move to that part of the agenda.

As far as the Soviets were concerned, it was really a waste of time. To debate 'petty resolutions about unity' while ignoring the plight of a

[1] Vinogradov, *Mirovoi Proletariat i SSSR*, pp. 165–6.

million miners locked in a crucial struggle for survival was unconscionable.[1] They were sceptical, as well, of the General Council's sudden fervent interest in those Scarborough unity resolutions it had ignored or sabotaged for some eleven months now. They were willing to yield, nevertheless, at least for the moment, and let the TUC's General Secretary review the current state of the campaign. The Central Council had rejected any unofficial pourparlers with IFTU officials on the occasion of the Migration Conference, Citrine recalled,[2] and insisted instead on those unconditional unity talks – presumably public – which the TUC was pledged to arrange. The English had referred the matter once again to the IFTU General Council, he reported, and were awaiting its decision before proceeding further.

The Russians professed to find the statement appalling. The English had not even honoured the promises they had already made. They had said that if IFTU would not convene a meeting, they would, and they had not. The Central Council had done everything it promised. It had conducted an interminable correspondence with Amsterdam, with no results. Actually, the whole thing had been so discouraging the Russians had pretty much given up the idea of talking to Amsterdam on their own, Mel'nichansky confessed. What they suggested now was a joint IFTU–RILU unity conference, with all unaffiliated workers' organizations invited as well. The British were appalled. They had been confronted with what, to them, was an absolutely new proposal, never discussed before, and they had no authority whatsoever to agree to it. In that case, Mel'nichansky came back genially, he would yield, but only on condition the Committee pass a resolution specifically confirming its decisions of last year – that the TUC, in effect, re-pledge itself to summon that unconditional conference of the IFTU and the Russian unions if Amsterdam refused to call such a meeting on its own. The British agreed to charge a subcommittee with drafting such a motion.

If the TUC representatives thought, however, that the question of the MFGB was now to be shelved, they got a rude jolt that evening. The Russians had spent the afternoon scribbling, and they had a long statement ready deploring the 'patent unwillingness' of the English side to cooperate in behalf of the strikers. The rejection of their programme was just one more example of the 'intolerable' and 'criminal' passivity of the General Council which had led to 'the effective isolation of the miners.'

[1] The quotation is from Petrowski (Bennet) *Anglo-Russische Komitee*, p. 29, where the point is made very strongly.
[2] See above, p. 204.

The Tory government and the capitalists were thus provided 'full freedom to go on crushing the miners.' The reluctance of the General Council's spokesmen to respond to the Soviet proposals, or indeed to make any suggestions of their own, was 'quite inadmissable' conduct, 'at direct variance with the mood of the widest masses,' and the argument that the Russian programme was outside the Committee's competence was just 'a new attempt to break up the Committee' and a blow 'at the friendship and unity of British and Russian trade union movements.' The Soviets believed in the Committee, and would fight to maintain it, but they insisted it be active, and so did the masses of British workers. The Russians protested 'categorically' Pugh's suggestion they were trying to dominate English trades unionism. The leadership of the TUC was up to the British working class to determine, and when the leaders proved inadequate, when they made mistakes in relation to the miners' struggle, for example, the rank and file would rectify the situation in their own way.

The British were furious at being confronted with such a manifesto, and Hicks and Findlay, in particular fought back with vigour. After a short intermission for consultation, the TUC delegates finally submitted a reply expressing their 'emphatic protest at the attack upon their motives and sincerity' and recording their 'amazement' that their 'reasoned arguments' had evoked such a harsh response.

To go back to a discussion of 'unity' after that altercation may have seemed absurd, but the subcommittee had completed its draft resolution before the flare-up began and it was now ready to submit its recommendations. The motion expressed regret at the unwillingness of IFTU to agree to unconditional talks with the Russian trade unionists and pledged both the TUC and the Soviets to continue the unity campaign anyway. 'As a first and essential step in this direction,' the Committee confirmed the resolution passed in Berlin the previous December, 'that the General Council...should immediately implement the undertaking agreed upon at the Anglo-Russian Trade Union Conference' and summon 'under its own auspices' a 'preliminary conference without conditions' between Moscow and Amsterdam. The Committee proposed to the General Council that the talks be scheduled for 'not later than the end of October.'

After twenty hours of brawling, it must have been a relief to have come upon a collection of words which could be accepted unanimously, and within minutes after the resolution was approved, the Committee members were packing to go home. The session had hardly been a success, but it had not failed as abysmally as had the Paris deliberations, and at least it now appeared neither side was going to dispense with their association altogether. Stalin, presumably, wanted to keep the Committee to restrain British foreign policy makers, and indeed, Andreev's report back to the Central Committee emphasized once again the Committee's role in preventing 'the imperialist war now being prepared.'[1] Considering that the war threat never got mentioned at all in Berlin, however, one can only conclude Stalin was not quite as alarmed at the verbal onslaughts of Churchill and Birkenhead as he had been a month or so earlier.

It is possible, of course, that he was just hoping to defer unleashing the Committee on the warmongers until he had a more sympathetic TUC leadership to deal with, after the Bournemouth Congress in September, presumably. The Russian delegation at Berlin had expressly reserved its right to continue to 'criticize' the General Council, and would be exercising that privilege – with unseemly gusto – within a matter of days after the Committee adjourned. If the British rank and file responded with appropriate proletarian verve, and propelled the worst of the villains into political oblivion, the chastened survivors might be suitably intimidated and conveniently docile – perhaps that was the hope. If it was, the comrades should have known better. When their failings were exposed, TUC leaders got hot collars, not cold feet.

The General Council meeting September 3 was a case in point.[2] The councillors found the minutes of the Berlin meeting infuriating. Whether it was worth maintaining the Committee at all, if it required them to endure such slanders, was doubtful, and they instructed the British representatives at Berlin to consider their 'recent experiences' and report back to the new General Council just what they thought the Committee's functions should be. They also decided, on Bevin's motion, to circulate all documents relative to the Paris and Berlin meetings to affiliated unions for comment. Such deliberations would of course take time, which made it difficult to fulfil the Committee's unanimous recommendation that the TUC convene a conference between the Russians and the IFTU by not later than the end of October. The General Council moved to defer consideration of that suggestion for three months – until early November, then. In effect, the councillors had stamped their veto on the only positive result of those twenty hours of bilingual bickering at Berlin.

The Russians would not hear of the indignity for a week or so, but they had already decided to turn the unity issue into a major propaganda

[1] *Trud*, 1 Sept., 1926. [2] General Council Minutes, No. 398, 3 Sept., 1926.

weapon against the TUC leadership at the Bournemouth Congress. They did not have much else to use. Chairman Pugh had banned any debate on the conduct of the general strike. That issue had to be dealt with first by a Conference of Executives, he ruled, and under the terms of the agreement with the miners, such a Conference would not be convened until the MFGB gave the signal. So if the councillors were to be got at, it had to be on their lack of commitment to the cause of trade union internationalism. By mid-August, an NMM leader was already predicting that unity – and the General Council's failure to promote it – would be the most important item on the Bournemouth agenda.[1] The rank and file demanded the TUC convene that conference between the Russians and the IFTU it promised over a year and a half ago, he stressed. The NMM's annual meeting, towards the end of the month, echoed those sentiments.[2] Having damned the councillors for 'failure of leadership' and 'criminal neglect,' labelled them all 'knaves and cowards' and 'utterly incapable,' and suggested they 'could not run a fried-fish shop, let alone a general strike,' it then insisted they call a unity conference. They had done nothing for unity so far but talk about it, *Workers' Weekly* charged.[3]

The General Council's failure to get Oudegeest to the negotiating table with Tomsky was worth making a fuss about, from the Communist point-of-view, but it was not nearly as self-evident a proof of the councillors' criminal incompetence as was their record during the general strike. The Bournemouth delegates could not raise that issue, once Pugh ruled it out of order, but the 'fraternal representative' of the Soviet trade unions could say whatever he liked. If Joynson-Hicks had been clever enough to let Tomsky into the country, therefore, he could have put the TUC in an uproar. Poor Jix! With his unerring gift for making the worst decision at the most impropitious moment, he had finally decided not to let any more Russians seduce any more trade unionists from King and Country. Tomsky was denied his visa. The General Council, some of whose members must have been ecstatic at the result, condemned the Home Secretary sternly.[4] It was a matter of 'profound disappointment' to them to realize Joynson-Hicks would 'use his office to prevent responsible Trade Unionists, against whom no personal charge can be imputed, from engaging in legitimate Trade Union activities.' The TUC

---

[1] G. Hardy, 'The Fight for a Militant T.U. Movement,' *The Communist Review*, VII, 5 (Sept., 1926), 225–33.

[2] *The Times*, 30 Aug., 1926.

[3] *Workers' Weekly*, 3 Sept., 1926.

[4] General Council Minutes, No. 387, 2 Sept., 1926; No. 415, 3 Sept., 1926.

could only conclude the decision was 'animated by political prejudice and party bias'; the Council registered its 'strong protest.'

The words were not strong enough, as far as Tomsky himself was concerned. His exclusion from the country was 'not unexpected,' he confessed.[1] After all, the British bourgeoisie was involved in waging class war on the workers. Everybody knew that except the dullards on the General Council. His presence in the country would therefore be inexpedient. It was significant, he noted, Joynson-Hicks had not excluded the fraternal delegates from the AF of L or the IFTU. They would neither inconvenience the bourgeoisie nor embarrass the TUC incompetents. He demanded those incompetents announce 'openly and frankly' precisely what action they had taken to get him his visa.

He had no intention, in any event, of being denied the opportunity to say his say to the Bournemouth delegates. On September 5, he addressed a long telegram to them, outlining the address he would have given could he have been there.[2] It was an extraordinary document, uncompromisingly candid, brutally frank, and pitilessly mistranslated. Whether the mistranslation was done at the Moscow end of the line or in London is hard to tell. It would seem some of the incomprehensibility derived from an effort to pack the most possible abuse into the fewest possible words and thus save a few rubles on telegraph charges. In any event, the infelicities of the English did not add to the pungency of the message, and when the General Council decided to circulate the telegram to the Congress, it mischievously left all the warts in.

The Russians sent their greetings to all present, especially the miners, 'who continue defend their rights, their living standards, and their past historic gains despite. . . betrayal via certain leaders general strike and capitulating mentality others.' Aiding the locked-out MFGB should be the Congress' first priority business, he suggested. He regretted that the dictatorship of 'manufacturers, bankers, mineowners and landlords' that called itself a Tory government had excluded him, and he attributed the

---

[1] *Inprecorr*, VI, 61 (9 Sept., 1926), 1032–3.

[2] The telegram is in *1926 TUC: Report of Proceedings*, pp. 509–11. Somewhat later in the month, Tomsky spoke to the Moscow Trades Union Council on the general strike, and gave them a rather different version of what he would have said to the Bournemouth Congress. In this address, he emphasized that the general strike had been political and international, whether the General Council liked it or not, and that fraternal proletarians therefore had a *right* to support it financially and to criticize the way it was led (or mis-led) and betrayed. He criticized Pugh's TUC speech ('pitiful doddering') and urged strengthening the Committee into a fighting proletarian alliance that could wage class war with vigour. *Inprecorr*, VI, 64 (30 Sept., 1926) 1087–91; 65 (7 Oct., 1926), 1102–6; *The Times*, 13 Oct., 1926.

atrocity to the fact that the Russians were 'giving of their last penny re help class brothers in great fight.' Visas were available, he noted to fraternal delegates from America and from Amsterdam 'who either blackleg on miners or shamefully talk of loans on interest, that is, speculate like usurers on unheard of distress miners, on tears and misery workers' wives and bairns.' Soviet trade unionists were indignant at the injustice, Tomsky reported, and were convinced 'blame must be laid herefor on bend-the-knee attitude toward Government of TU leaders like Thomas,...main instigator defeat General Strike.'

If he had been able to address them, Tomsky continued, he would have liked to have provided them a Soviet evaluation of the events of May 3–12, an evaluation based on the experience of 'numberless General Strikes fought via our working class' before Red October. The message might seem harsh, 'but when it comes to choosing between empty compliments meaning nothing to leaders and serving working masses will always choose latter course.' The plain proletarian truth was that the general strike should have been won. If it had not been called off it 'would have led to glorious victory and you would already have long been freed of your Government aristocrats and mineowners.' The TUC leaders betrayed a winning battle. They were 'prepared shirk fight...and even go straight over to enemy.'

The most immediate problem facing the TUC leadership was the lock-out of the miners. If the bourgeoisie scored another triumph there, the whole of the English working class would be the losers. The Central Council of the Soviet trade unions therefore 'particularly regrets confirm fact that at Paris meeting Anglo-Russian Committee British Delegation categorically refused discuss question assisting miners.' Nor was that all! 'Soviet CCTU likewise regrets confirm at Berlin meeting Anglo-Russian Committee delegation completely turned down all our proposals re assisting miners including embargo and 1 per cent levy for benefit strikers suffering but fighting determined not be slaves to mineowners.' Not only would the English not adopt the Russian suggestions, they would not even 'discuss them business-like fashion,' which Tomsky found 'unexplainable.' The Soviets would nevertheless not be deterred from continuing to show 'proletarian solidarity' with the MFGB. They would adopt that 1 per cent charge all by themselves, providing the cause some three million rubles. They were sure that British proletarians would return the favour if Soviet trade unionists ever had to ask for their help. 'More than once [the British workers have] withheld mailed fist British Bourgeoisie hanging over our Workers' State,' Tomsky recalled, and he assumed they might be asked to do so again. For these various, and mutually advantageous, purposes, the Anglo-Russian Committee, 'symbol International Trade Union Unity, symbol Brotherly bonds existing between British and Soviet Workers,' should be maintained, consolidated and strengthened, the telegram concluded.

IV

The members of the General Council first read this pungent prose September 6. They decided to circulate the telegram to the Bournemouth delegates, along with a stiff response Citrine composed.[1] The reply registered the councillors' 'strongest possible protest' at the 'most regrettable abuse of the ordinary courtesies of Fraternal Delegates.' The Soviet trade union organization had 'asserted to itself the right to indulge in unwarrantable censure of the General Council of Congress, to abuse personally certain of its members, and to make an unprovoked attack upon other fraternal delegates.' The British leadership considered the message an 'intolerable interference in British Trade Union affairs,' and expressed its confidence the Bournemouth delegates would confirm that judgement.

The councillors indeed seemed to have their constituency with them this time. The CPGB was unhappy, of course, accusing the TUC leadership of 'an intolerable blow at working-class solidarity' designed – quite deliberately – to encourage the Tories in a 'new attack on Russia.'[2] But the only prominent non-Communist taking that position was Cook, who growled he would have savaged the councillors even more emphatically than had Tomsky had he not made the mistake of pledging himself to silence.[3] The rest of the movement seemed behind its leaders. The *Daily Herald* protested Tomsky's message 'emphatically' and pronounced his judgements both on individuals and on tactics 'neither helpful nor sound.'[4] The Bournemouth delegates would probably have concurred, but they were never really given the chance. No discussion of the Tomsky telegram was permitted, on the grounds fraternal messages were never debated, and when somebody moved to 'adopt' the General Council's

---

[1] General Council Minutes, No. 420, 6 Sept., 1926; No. 432, 8 Sept., 1926; No. 437, 9 Sept., 1926. Citrine's first draft of a response did not please 5 Council members, and it was amended before being finally adopted. The final TUC answer is reprinted in *1926 TUC: Report of Proceedings*, p. 511.

[2] *Workers' Weekly*, 17 Sept., 1926.

[3] *Sunday Worker*, 12 Sept., 1926.

[4] *Daily Herald*, 10 Sept., 1926.

reply – which had already been dispatched in any event – no debate was allowed on that, either, nor a vote tally recorded. The chairman simply ruled the motion carried.[1] It may have been true enough, as a Communist observer later reported, that the delegates received the Russian telegram 'in a very thoughtful manner.'[2] Making sense of the garbled English did indeed demand concentration. But that any substantial number really felt that it was the only document received at the Congress dealing 'boldly with the real problems of the British working class' is doubtful.

Boldness was not really in fashion at Bournemouth anyway. The 'feeling of elation and bursting self-confidence' so characteristic of Scarborough a year earlier was nowhere in evidence, Beatrice Webb reported.[3] The issue of trades union internationalism, which came up a full three days after the Congress began, provided some of the few animated moments in an otherwise dispirited routine.

The CPGB had been anticipating the unity debate with relish. Campbell had instructed Minority Movement sympathizers to wade into the discussions and demand the General Council disclose precisely what it proposed to do next to achieve international unity. They were also to inquire about the meetings of the Anglo-Russian Committee at Paris and Berlin, asking particularly whether the question of aid for the miners had been raised. 'We know,' Campbell confided, 'that the result was unfavourable to the miners, favourable to international unity, but we want this brought out at the Congress.'[4] Unfortunately for the Communists, the General Council had somehow found a copy of those instructions, and when the crunch came, the leadership had its counterattack prepared.

Pugh had tried defusing the issue the very first day of Congress, in his bland and insipid presidential address. True unity grew out of a common will and purpose, common aims and methods, he lectured, and one could not create it by mechanically manipulating the multiplicity of existing organizations into one super-organization of the future. He was of course in favour of unity, but it had to be 'a living unity of mind and heart' and spring from 'a genuine spirit of friendship and understand-

---

[1] *1926 TUC: Report of Proceedings*, p. 447.
[2] Earl Browder, 'Der Kongress der Trade Unions in Bournemouth,' *Die Rote Gewerkschaftsinternationale*, No. 9/10 (68/69) (Sept.–Oct., 1926), pp. 632–36.
[3] Webb, *Diaries, 1924–32*, p. 115.
[4] Walter M. Citrine, *Democracy or Disruption? An Examination of Communist Influences in the Trade Unions* (London: Trades Union Congress, 1928), p. 17; *The Times*, 11 Sept., 1926.

ing.'¹ Given the contents of the Tomsky telegram, one could interpret the speech only one way: the president might again exert himself for unity when the Russians stopped saying all those nasty things about him.

The IFTU's fraternal delegate took much the same line, three days later. Amsterdam had sent one of the TUC's own – J. W. Brown – to speak for it. He spoke with great care.² He had no criticism to make at all, he began, at the relationship between the TUC and the Russians. He believed international trade union unity was indeed a worthwhile objective, and he even cited Tomsky to nail the point down. But unity did not mean uniformity. Complete autonomy for the member organizations was the *sine qua non* of any all-inclusive trade union international. No one affiliate should try to dictate to the others, or interfere in the affairs of the others, and until that principle was accepted by everybody, progress would be minimal.

Not everybody at Bournemouth, apparently, found autonomy that fascinating a topic, and not more than a few hours after Brown's speech, the NMM spokesmen at Congress were insisting on talking about unity. By what right, one of them inquired, had the General Council gone on record in opposition to an all-inclusive world trade union conference, with RILU's unions as well as Amsterdam's in attendance? Admittedly, to start with, IFTU was only being asked to meet with the Russians, but that was just as a preliminary in order to achieve a wider unity later on. He protested 'emphatically.'³

Nor was that the Council's only enormity, another critic interjected.⁴ A promise made had not been honoured. Back in April, 1925 the leadership had pledged the Russians a meeting with the IFTU, and had vowed to call such a meeting itself if IFTU would not. That undertaking had been ratified at Scarborough in September, but nothing had been done about it. The General Council was 'sabotaging world unity' and he demanded to know why.

Pugh had had enough. When a third NMM member rose to speak, he gavelled him down and moved on to a brief statement on the Anglo-Russian Committee. He had little to say. The Committee had met, in Paris and in Berlin, the British members had submitted their report and it would be circulated to the affiliated unions. The leadership had decided to defer any further consideration of the Committee's recommendations for three months. Was it true, Pugh was asked, as Tomsky had charged, that British representatives on the Committee had refused to discuss the

---

¹ *The Times*, 7 Sept., 1926.   ² *1926 TUC: Report of Proceedings*, pp. 405–9.
³ *Ibid.*, pp. 435–6.   ⁴ *Ibid.*, p. 437.

question of aid to the miners? Not true, Pugh replied. Are you sure, the inquisitor persisted? 'I gave you the answer to that,' Pugh snapped back. 'It was in the negative.'[1]

Purcell, who had not even gone to Berlin, rose to clear everything up – particularly the matter of why the General Council had not convened those Moscow–Amsterdam talks. It was an appallingly muddled effort.[2] A World Trade Union Unity Congress would not work just yet, he argued. Everybody would bicker and nothing would be achieved. One could not force people into unity. Britain had to convert her old friends in IFTU first. They were, admittedly, anti-Russian, but it was not so much because they disliked the Russians themselves as it was they disliked Russia's association with RILU dissidents. Russia had disrupted their labour movements. The TUC had 'to get the Russians to ease the position and themselves help us to bring about this unity.' If you start charging us with sabotage – he was now addressing the NMM people – and the IFTU with sabotage, you will just make things more difficult and you will encourage all those dissidents on the continent who are the main obstacles to unity. 'There is still a chance of bringing the Russians to our side and getting the IFTU to take up the attitude we think they ought to take up.' But if the TUC called some 'huge International Congress,' things would only get worse.

Purcell had not responded to the question at all, and an NMM delegate was quick to tell him so. A 'huge International Congress' was not the issue – just a meeting between the IFTU and the Russians to discuss how to achieve unity. That was what had been promised, that was what the Scarborough Congress had demanded, and nothing had been done. The NMM had a resolution ready, putting the Congress once again on record as favouring 'one United Trades Union International,' expressing regret that such an organization had not yet been established, and instructing the General Council to 'continue their efforts to bring this about.'[3]

That was a resolution almost everybody could vote for, even the councillors themselves. They could not accept the spirit behind the speech moving the resolution, they said, but they agreed with the proposed wording.[4] They would not acquiesce, however, in a tough amendment to the original motion, also proposed by the NMM. It would have instructed the General Council to 'insist' the IFTU sit down to a unity conference with RILU – 'in order to endeavour to lay the basis for International Trade Union Unity.'[5]

¹ *Ibid.*, pp. 437, 439.   ² *Ibid.*, pp. 437–9.   ³ *Ibid.*, pp. 439–41, 502.
⁴ *Ibid.*, p. 443.   ⁵ *Ibid.*, pp. 442–3.

John Bromley spoke for the General Council on that one. He had some sympathy for the Russians, but none for RILU, which had 'been trying to ride rough-shod in some of the nations of Europe.' Its affiliates had presumed to dictate to everybody else, and just disrupted trade unionism in the process. Concessions to such dissidents only encouraged them. Ultimately, even the TUC might find itself under the control of outsiders, and he cited a circular which had been distributed to some of the delegates sitting in front of him by which non-members of TUC were presuming to send 'instructions to delegates here that their representatives...' They would not let him finish the sentence. The hall was in an uproar. The Minority Movement people were livid. They were the victims of 'low-down, dirty innuendo,' but they were too angry to be coherent about it. One tired realist got up to announce he was voting against the whole package, resolution *and* amendment, because they were both absurd. The amendment was fatuous and the resolution meaningless, a 'pious aspiration' and no more. Pious aspirations, however, were in good odour at Bournemouth. Congress voted the resolution by more than 3-to-1, and turned down the amendment almost 2-to-1. Not really a bad showing for the NMM – a million and a quarter 'votes' were registered for that crucial amendment – but no major triumph, either.[1]

In fact, aside from one resolution on imperialism, Communists found nothing at all to cheer about at Bournemouth.[2] All the 'leftists' had disappointed them. The NMM seemed to have no reliable allies at all. It would have to take over the TUC on its own. The pressures of the class struggle had driven 'all the posers and mouth artists' straight into the ranks of the enemy. Hicks, Purcell, Bromley – they had all betrayed the cause. They had talked left only so long as Thomas and Co. had been around to prevent anything really happening. When things happened anyway, much to their chagrin, they dropped the poses and proved themselves just 'lickspittles of capitalism' like all the rest. Even Cook had compromised, when he agreed not to debate the general strike issue at Congress. There could be no compromise with lickspittles.[3]

What most disturbed Lozovsky about the Bournemouth proceedings was the way the British had made that 'non-intervention' nonsense stick.[4] It was disgraceful that Tomsky had been excluded from the sessions, and

[1] *Ibid.*, pp. 443–6.
[2] Communist Party of Great Britain, *The Eighth Congress of the Communist Party of Gt. Britain, Held at Battersea Town Hall on October 16 and 17, 1926. Reports, Theses and Resolutions* (London: Communist Party of Great Britain, 1927), p. 30.
[3] *The Worker*, 17 Sept., 1926; MacFarlane, *British Communist Party*, p. 172.
[4] Lozovsky, *Englisch-Russische Komitee*, pp. 14–16.

even worse that the delegates could not respond to his telegram in open debate. Nobody had any business telling English and Russian workers that they could not communicate with one another. The General Council members were afraid of the contact. They might be criticized. They might not be able to get away with their '*schweinerei*' so easily! But proletarians everywhere simply had to be alert to – and respond to – the situation of proletarians anywhere. 'Non-intervention' theories had no place in the workers' movement, and one could never achieve international trade union unity until such ideological rubbish was cleared away.

The TUC's General Council – with only minor exceptions, the same tired veterans who had ornamented the Council chamber during the general strike disaster – was unimpressed with that sort of argument. The new chairman was Hicks, now skipping nimbly to the political right. The reactionaries named him to the top job, the Communist press charged, to reward him for deserting the cause of trade union internationalism.[1] Although such grumbling sounds just petulant, Hicks did indeed keep the Russians at a safe distance for the rest of the autumn. At one point, for example, Purcell suggested the Council hold a special meeting on relations with the Soviets and international unity generally. Hicks turned him down brusquely.[2] The Council even refused to send a fraternal delegation to the Russians' biennial Trade Union Congress. Since the whole matter of relations with the Soviets was under general review, Moscow was informed, such good will gestures would be inappropriate. When Tomsky wrote back regretting the decision, Purcell and Findlay reopened the question in the General Council, but got beaten back, 11 votes to 9.[3] It was part of a general tactic of surrender to the capitalists, the CPGB charged, and a conscious move to rupture the Anglo-Russian Committee.[4]

British Communists were just beginning to get their own signals straight on the Committee, and indeed, on policy toward the TUC generally. That unpleasant altercation between Murphy and Stalin back in August[5] had required the Party leadership to do a bit of fencemending. Where the CPGB had been decreed in error, some judicious self-criticism was in order; where its judgements had been sustained, some

1 *Workers' Weekly*, 1 Oct., 1926.
2 General Council Minutes, No. 11, 22 Sept., 1926.
3 *Ibid.*, No. 16, 22 Sept., 1926; No. 74, 76, 24 Nov., 1926.
4 Communist Party of Great Britain, *The Ninth Congress of the Communist Party of Gt. Britain* (*Held at Caxton Hall, Salford, October, 1927.*) *Reports, Theses & Resolutions.* (London: Communist Party of Great Britain, 1928), p. 51.
5 See above, pp. 279–81.

discreet self-advertisement might be advantageous. The theses prepared for the 8th Party Congress, scheduled for mid-October, did a bit of each.[1]

The Party had performed brilliantly during the general strike, its leaders reported. The General Council would never have exerted itself even to the limited extent it did had not the comrades prodded it so persistently. Trotsky's charge that the CPGB had in fact served as a brake on revolution was wholly false. The comrades had criticized defeatism both on the right and the left, and even warned of the possibility the General Council might surrender to the bourgeoisie. Immediately after the capitulation, it had sternly rebuked the entire TUC leadership for betrayal. The Comintern itself had confirmed that the CPGB line was correct all along.

The strike had utterly discredited the TUC leftists, mere 'phrase-mongers who had won easy fame as "revolutionaries" on the issue of international trade union unity.' The Party had condemned them right after the strike, but 'missed one or two opportunities' to drive the point home thereafter.[2] 'One or two technical mistakes were made, owing to inexperience.'[3] On the whole, however, it had maintained a 'systematic exposure' of reformist traitors since May 12. Even Cook had been subjected to an occasional CPGB scolding, the Party pointed out, notably when he agreed in late June to tone down his criticism of the General Council.

The campaign for trade union internationalism should be maintained. Proletarians everywhere understood the need for unity – particularly since the failure of the general strike – and insisted their leaders work for it. When the leaders refused, their own men would repudiate them. The CPGB pointed to the General Council's embarrassment over its failure to keep that promise to convene a world unity congress. As an integral part of the unity campaign, the Anglo-Russian Committee had to be kept alive. Trotsky's contention that the Russian unions should rupture the relationship with the TUC was 'absolutely incorrect.' The Committee had justified itself in action – when the Russians sent all that help to the locked-out miners – and it should be strengthened, not discarded.[4]

The leadership defended the Party's performance at Bournemouth. The Communist faction at the TUC was 'small in number,' even counting

---

[1] The available record is CPGB, *Eighth Congress: Reports, Theses and Resolutions.* The material relevant to the Party's attitude toward the TUC, the Committee, and trades union unity may be found on pp. 6–12, 17, 18, 26–31, 36, 60, 68–70.

[2] *Ibid.,* p. 12.   [3] *Ibid.,* p. 17.   [4] *Ibid.,* p. 68.

non-Party sympathizers, but nevertheless provided a 'very effective' opposition to the General Council, almost 'the only opposition, with a definite policy, that raised its voice at the Congress.'[1] Given the growth of the Party, with some five thousand new members, mostly miners, it could expect even more impressive results in 1927.

If the leadership hoped its acknowledgement of 'one or two' little mistakes was going to suffice, it learned otherwise very quickly, and from two of its own members, at that. J. T. Murphy and Robin Page Arnot, writing in a Comintern journal, accused their CPGB colleagues of serious rightist vacillations right after the general strike.[2] In a misguided effort 'to preserve the Anglo-Russian Committee at any cost,' the Party 're-fused to criticize sharply the treacherous conduct of the General Council leaders.' The capitulators of the Purcell variety had been treated particu-larly gently, and Cook – who had now surely lost his leftist credentials entirely – had hardly been criticized at all. The failure of such tactics had been obvious both at the NMM's annual conference and at the Bourne-mouth TUC. The General Council had been damned so faintly, on both occasions, that even its responsibility for the general strike disaster had been muted.

Coming from Murphy, who had publicly attacked the Soviet trade unions for being too harsh on the General Council, the rebuke sounded absurd, but Murphy cheerfully acknowledged, in a special telegram to the journal, that he was as much to blame as anybody, 'especially in relation to the policy regarding the Anglo-Russian Committee for which I was probably more responsible than others.' It was the leadership as a whole that had erred, however, and the leadership as a whole should own up to its mistakes. The editors of the journal, in a postscript, con-curred, and noted that the Comintern's Executive Committee felt the same way.

The CPGB, the spoiled little darling of the International, had never had its knuckles rapped so smartly before, and it howled back in agony and anger. If the Party had been naughty, Arnot and Murphy were as responsible as anybody else, the comrades replied.[3] They were members of the Central Committee, too. If the Comintern Executive did not like what the CPGB had done, why had it not said so itself? It was a full three weeks since Bournemouth, after all, and the Executive had had

[1] *Ibid.*, p. 18.

[2] J. T. Murphy and R. Page Arnot, 'The British Trades Union Congress at Bourne-mouth,' *Communist International*, III, 1 (Oct., 1926), i–iv.

[3] Executive Committee, CPGB, 'Our Party and the T.U.C.,' *ibid.*, 2 (30 Oct., 1926), pp. 12–15.

plenty of time to write if it had something to say. Indeed, the reply went on – a bit petulantly – 'the Party wishes to state clearly that it has not received a single detailed criticism of any action or policy from the ECCI since the beginning of the General Strike, just as it did not receive a single lead from the Presidium which it had not already decided upon and in most cases applied itself.' So there, too!

The Murphy–Arnot article, the CPGB chiefs alleged, was erroneous and deceptive. They acknowledged some sins of omission right after the general strike, but to charge them with general right deviationism was false. The Party press had criticized the General Council, ever since the end of the strike. It had not exempted 'lefts' of the Purcell–Hicks type, and it had even reprimanded Cook, 'repeatedly.' At Bournemouth, it had carried on the struggle intensively and productively. The general councillors had been publicly labelled traitors, cowards and fools. Arnot–Murphy had apparently forgotten, the article charged, those strong speeches when the issue of international unity came up.

It all had a gorgeous irony to it. The aim of creating the Committee, supposedly, was to split up the reformists, and expose them as imbeciles and betrayers. What it was doing, instead, was splitting the ranks of the Communists, and arousing distinct suspicions as to the good sense and/or real loyalty of some of the comrades. Not only was the CPGB in turmoil over the issue, so was the CPSU.

In the Soviet Union, of course, lots more was at stake than just the Committee. But the Committee was one of Trotsky's favourite issues – he would keep banging away at it for almost a year and a half – and it was one of the most embarrassing for the Party regulars. They could not defend the TUC connection too vigorously, or estimate it too highly, or it would appear they were staking too much on an organization those General Council cowards and traitors could, after all, smash anytime they wanted to. On the other hand, if the Party estimated the Committee too modestly, comrades might begin to wonder why anybody had bothered to establish it in the first place, and with such fanfare, at that, and who had been responsible for celebrating it so lavishly – and so deceptively – prior to May.

Lozovsky was good at dealing with such questions. To construct an elaborate and intricate theoretical framework imprisoning great masses of inconveniently squirming realities seemed his favourite sport. He used arguments as if they were rubber truncheons, hammering his opposition over the head with them with such dull perseverence the poor reader or listener was finally clubbed into leaden acquiescence. Putting together a consistent and tenable argument for the Committee was an assignment that suited him perfectly, and he now proceeded to do it.[1]

After a lengthy review of the origins of the Committee, Lozovsky asked himself whether the Committee should now be broken up, as the Opposition was demanding. Summarizing Trotsky's argument – and very fairly, at that – he finally rejected it on the grounds it neglected the reactions of the British rank and file. They considered it their Committee, not the General Council's, and given that attitude, they would not understand why some Soviet ultra-leftist would want to take it away from them. In any event, revolutionaries could still use the connection, Lozovsky argued, to get to the masses and show them the superiority of revolutionary tactics to reformism.

If the Committee was so convenient for Communists, why did not the ultra-right TUC reactionaries break it up themselves? They must want to, Lozovsky reasoned, and they must know they could no longer hope to use the Committee for any purposes of their own. The Russians would not let them. But they also knew the masses would not stand for a rupture, so they did not dare take the initiative in a break. They must be hoping the Soviets would follow Trotsky's advice and smash the Committee for them.

The Committee had strengthened the fraternal ties between the English and Russian proletariats, Lozovsky continued. The British worker now saw who his real friends were. The Russians acted, offered real comradely help. The IFTU just talked, and offered proclamations and $4\frac{1}{2}$ per cent loans. The ordinary worker would recognize the difference. The leaders of the two movements might draw further apart, but the masses would continue to come together. At such a time, it would obviously be stupid to break the Committee up, to destroy the most obvious symbol of the common interests of workers in both countries.

The General Council would continue to try to sabotage the Committee, Lozovsky concluded, to limit it, minimize its functions, restrain it from any practical work. The councillors would not really exert themselves enough to get that Moscow–Amsterdam conference. The only sort of unity they really favoured was a unity as meaningless as that represented by IFTU itself, a unity of affiliates so completely autonomous in everything that mattered that they could not offer one another any help at all. The Soviets wanted no part of any such travesty anyway, so the

[1] The book is A. Lozovsky, *Englisch-Russische Komitee*, which is almost (but not quite) identical with the volume he published about the same time entitled *British and Russian Workers*.

Committee, for the time, was paralysed. The TUC would weaken it; the Russians would try to strengthen it, or at least maintain it. Out of the tension within the Committee, however, might come some good. It posed to the 'broad masses' the question of with whom and against whom they should stand – with the Central Council, the RILU and revolution, or with the General Council, Amsterdam and reformism. Lozovsky was sure the rank and file would make the right choice.

It was as good an argument, probably, as anybody could have put together, and for a time, in any event, it looked like scoring debating points against Trotsky might no longer be necessary. The Oppositionists seemed ready to surrender in early October. Their campaign had not gone well. Their speakers had been heckled and their meetings broken up and all seemed hopeless. Kamenev and Zinoviev, so confident back in the spring, were doleful now, sorry they had ever gotten into the mess. They were ready for a truce, and had persuaded Trotsky to go along. Stalin seemed amenable, at first, but he had hardly made the agreement, on October 4, than he violated it himself, attacking the three as social-democratic deviationists in a Politburo meeting October 25. Trotsky snapped back with allusions to Thermidor and that famous characterization of Stalin as the 'gravedigger of the revolution.' The Georgian stomped out of the council chamber in a rage. Within 24 hours, Trotsky had lost his Politburo seat and Zinoviev his position on the Comintern Executive. It was a fearsome row, and it guaranteed the comrades attending the 15th Party Conference a lively session. The Conference opened October 26.[1]

The Oppositionists were now cornered. They were virtually obliged to fight it out with Stalin, and on the issues he selected, most obviously, 'socialism in one country' versus 'permanent revolution.' That insured a ventilation of the whole matter of Soviet relations with western Communist Parties, western workers and western trade unions. The matter of the TUC connection would hardly be avoided. Trotsky had prepared

---

[1] For a good, brief summary of the Opposition's May-to-October campaign, see Deutscher, *Trotsky*, pp. 281–97. The record of the 15th Party Conference is *XV Konferentsia Vsesoiuznoi Kommunisticheskoi Partii (B). 26 Oktabria–3 Noiabria 1926. Stenograficheskii Otchet* (Moscow: Gosudarstvennoe Izdatel'stvo, 1927). The resolution on trade union problems is in *KPSS v Rezoliutsiiakh*, ii, 108–9, and the resolution on the Opposition bloc in *ibid.*, pp. 214–18. For English-language summaries of the debates, see *Inprecorr*, vi, 72 (4 Nov., 1926), 1245–60; 73 (11 Nov., 1926), 1261–72; 75 (18 Nov., 1926), 1281–1300; 76 (18 Nov., 1926), 1301–2; 77 (20 Nov., 1926), 1317–34; 78 (25 Nov., 1926), 1335–61; 79 (25 Nov., 1926), 1363–88; 80 (25 Nov., 1926), 1397–8 and 82 (30 Nov., 1926), 1421–8. See also Popov, *Outline History of the CPSU*, ii, 296–307.

his statement on it well in advance, as a matter of fact, even before concluding that abortive truce with Stalin.[1] The very existence of the Committee conveyed to the masses an unfortunate impression, he argued, the impression that the Soviet revolutionaries were willing to acquiesce in what Trotsky called 'Purcellism.' Since by Trotsky's logic, Baldwin's bourgeois imperialists were depending on the Purcells to keep trade unionism tame, it was madness to maintain the Committee. When Stalin cited that 'partial stabilization of capitalism' which made revolutionary efforts in the west temporarily impracticable, he referred to a stabilization he himself was helping create. Knock away Baldwin's prop, Purcell, and capitalism might prove a good deal less stable than Stalin claimed.

The theses proposed by the Politburo majority rejected that position entirely. The partial stabilization of capitalism was a fact. The revolution was not being abandoned, but it would be delayed. To despair at that, and to go over to ultra-left adventurism and putschism, showed a lack of faith in the ultimate good judgement of the masses. United-front tactics, which the Oppositionists did not seem to understand, were still valid, and that was why the Party would reject their demand to break up the Committee. To abandon it would be to mislead the English workers. They would interpret the rupture as a signal from the Soviets to quit their trade unions altogether, and many of the most revolutionary of them might do so. The leaders of the General Council would of course be delighted to see them go, and so would the Amsterdam diehards, but Communism would be the worse for their isolation.

The international situation was the first order of business at the Conference. Bukharin presented the Central Committee's report.[2] He made it immediately and abundantly clear that he had no intention of letting the Oppositionists take the high ground as super-revolutionaries. He was as much of a fire-eater as any Trotskyite. Capitalism had indeed partially stabilized itself – that was central to the whole Stalinist position – but that did not mean the revolution had been put off indefinitely. On the contrary, prospects were excellent indeed, especially in Britain and in China. The miners' strike had produced an 'enormous transformation' in the English proletariat, and as a result, he announced, Soviet policy toward Britain could move to more advanced tactical levels.

That was where the Committee came in. Bukharin had to justify creating it, and maintaining it – even past May 12 – but given the fact the TUC might break it up any day, he could not appear to be staking too much

---

[1] T-894, T-3006, Trotsky Archives.   [2] *XV Konferentsiia VKP*, pp. 3–45.

on its continuance. So he defended it, and only very briefly, for what it had been, not what it would be. 'A little while ago' it had been central to Russian policy, he recalled. One of the Party's major political 'manoeuvres' had been to link the Russian trade unions with the TUC in the cause of international trade union unity. That involved putting some limitations on Profintern, Bukharin admitted, and postponing direct revolutionary agitation among the lowest levels of the English proletariat. No longer! What was suitable and successful policy at one stage of dialectical development was not necessarily appropriate to the next stage. Since May, the English masses had really begun to move toward revolution. Communists must now help lead the English proletariat to the furthest reaches of revolutionary struggle. Specifically, that would involve a much more active role for Profintern, and less of a role for the Russian trade union movement. The Russian unions should now re-emphasize their connection with RILU, and devote themselves more energetically to playing an exemplary role within RILU.

The CPGB could play a major part in all this. It had been guilty of a number of rightist mistakes earlier in the year, but had managed to correct itself and could now proceed with 'the revolutionizing of the English working class.' It was bound to succeed. Any form of class cooperation between the English workers and their bourgeoisie was out of the question. The British proletariat would move 'more and more toward revolution and the idea of proletarian dictatorship.' Capitalism was in a state of final and complete collapse in the UK, and 'in the measured step of the English miners,' the working class was marching toward its inevitable triumph.

Now that was very heady rhetoric indeed, but it was also a bit confusing. How could one proclaim capitalism partially stabilized and at the same time announce its imminent collapse? How could one both defend the Committee and affirm its obsolescence? The delegates were confused, and Bukharin had a lot of explaining to do, a day later, when he got up to present his 'concluding remarks.'[1]

Because he had emphasized the crucial nature of Profintern's mission, he ventured, and urged the Russian trade unions to work more closely with Profintern, some comrades seemed to assume he was announcing some change in the Party line on the Anglo-Russian Committee. They misinterpreted him. 'In no circumstances' was it necessary to rupture the Committee. Of course, the other side might break it up, but even if, therefore, the organization did not last much longer – 'one must consider

[1] *Ibid.*, pp. 88–101.

such possibilities,' he admitted – it had still achieved a great deal. And the Anglo-Russian Miners' Committee would be there in any event, he pointed out.[1] Given the opportunities now opening up in Britain, however, further steps had to be taken. The English workers were achieving a higher stage of revolutionary development, and in such circumstances, Profintern could be expected to play rather more of a role than it had before, more of a role than could the Soviet trade unions alone, apart from Profintern.

He saw no contradiction between his confident predictions of an English revolution and his stand on the stabilization of capitalism. The only way capitalism managed to stabilize itself was by stamping on the proletariat, thus sharpening class tensions. That was what had happened in England, and the CPGB had shown how to take advantage of the resultant opportunities. A year ago it had been the 'smallest embryo,' almost laughably weak. Nobody took it seriously. Now it was growing at a fantastic rate, and was 'one of the few' parties in Britain with any real influence in the trade union movement. People in the TUC now listened to Communists respectfully. 'Because of the Minority Movement,' Lozovsky growled from his chair. 'Yes, because of the Minority Movement,' Bukharin agreed from the platform.

The miners' strike had accelerated the leftward movement. Even if the MFGB lost, it had already taken the English proletariat a long way down the revolutionary road, and there was no going back. Bukharin could not promise the miners would *not* lose. He had heard dire rumours of a betrayal, to which even Cook might be a party. Communists had to be prepared for the possibility of bad news, then, but in the meantime, the CPSU must continue to support the miners' strike with everything it had. 'And that is why,' he concluded, his final words to the Conference had to be 'Long Live the English Miners!'

Bukharin having managed the issue of the Committee – albeit somewhat ineptly – later speakers did not have to waste a lot of time on it. Tomsky only devoted a couple of minutes, at the very end of his speech, to the international scene.[2] He did take time, however, to chide the Oppositionists for seeking to rupture the Committee just to make some 'revolutionary gesture.' What Trotsky was saying, Tomsky argued, was that Communists should not associate with class traitors. If Communists

---

[1] He was premature. The MFGB had not officially ratified the creation of a Miners' Committee yet, and in fact, never would. See below, pp. 329–30.

[2] *XV Konferentsiia VKP*, pp. 266–95. The references to the international scene are on pp. 294–5.

took such notions seriously, of course, they would all get out of reformist trade unions altogether. But to do so would be absolutely fatal. The trade unions were where the masses were, and until the Communists had won the trust of the masses, they would never be able to achieve political power.

The Conference had been in session for four days, now, and it appeared more and more as if the only item on the agenda of any significance was the vilification of the United Opposition. The issue of the Committee was not raised for its own sake, but just to slap down Trotsky, Zinoviev and Kamenev. Even though the three had not yet said a word in their own defense, they had been abused, ridiculed, debunked, humiliated and pilloried by one speaker after another. The agony would go on for another three days before, on November 1, Stalin decided his associates had drawn enough blood. He now moved in personally for the kill.

It took him several hours.[1] He went through the whole history of the mutiny, step by step. He supplied a detailed catalogue of the Opposition's errors. Rejecting the socialism in one country doctrine was the most obvious of their recent mistakes, but their record of anti-Party, anti-Leninist deviationism went far back. Stalin described their ideological trespasses in loving detail. He quoted copiously from Lenin. It was a fearsome performance.

The Opposition had utterly misinterpreted Lenin's policy toward workers in capitalist countries, Stalin charged. Lenin knew that the USSR would have to live with the possibility of capitalist intervention for a long time. That meant cultivating the friendship of proletarians in other nations. If workers in capitalist states were devoted to the cause of socialism and sympathized with the USSR, they could make it impossible for their bourgeoisies to wage any anti-Communist crusade effectively. Eventually, of course, the workers would match the socialist revolution in Russia with revolutions of their own at home, but they had not yet reached that stage. They were already, however, in a position to block the imperialists from making war on the USSR, if their sympathies were aroused. The USSR depended on their goodwill.

It was the traditional Stalinist argument for maintaining the Committee, although he had not yet mentioned that organization by name. He proceeded to accuse the Opposition of hiding Menshevism and social democratic reformism behind ultra-left phraseology, both domestically, in their call for super-industrialization, and abroad, in their predilection

[1] *Ibid.*, pp. 421–62.

for empty ultra-left phrases and gestures. Rupturing the Committee would be such a gesture. They did not seem to have any sense of timing in these matters. To persuade the masses of the correctness of the Party programme would require a lot of patient preparation. In Britain, millions of workers were involved. The CPGB was pursuing, basically, the right line, but impressing it on the British proletariat would take awhile. Not really trusting the working masses, however, fearful they would never see the light unless dazzled by some dramatic stroke, the Opposition proposed breaking up the Committee. It was just playing at revolution! It was absurd adventurism, and it would only benefit the bourgeoisie.

The speech demanded an answer, and the Oppositionists finally rose to defend themselves. Kamenev was restrained, measured, perhaps too timid.[1] Zinoviev was ready to grovel.[2] Only Trotsky really stood up to the ordeal with dignity and wit.[3] Point by point, item by item, he refuted those charges that his position had been in some sense 'social-democratic.' The official account of capitalism's stabilization he found absurd. Britain, for example, could hardly be termed economically stable! How, then, did the British bourgeoisie survive? Not by Baldwin's efforts, not even by Thomas's, but by Purcell's. 'Purcellism is the pseudonym for what is otherwise now called "stabilization" in England,' he repeated. That was why he had argued that to show any direct or indirect solidarity with Purcell at the time of the general strike was fundamentally wrong. That was why he had proposed the break-up of the Anglo-Russian Committee. How was that suggestion 'social-democratic,' he demanded.

It was a brilliant defence, but power – not logic – was what is being tested on this occasion. The spokesmen for the majority ripped the Oppositionists apart for another day and a half for their newest lapse – presuming to defend themselves.

It was not much of an argument, but it was good enough to persuade the delegates to sanction the expulsion of all three Opposition leaders from all responsible Party positions. Stalin had had his way. Perhaps, however, the Opposition charge that he was something less than a totally committed revolutionary had stung. The extremist rhetoric directed at England became a good deal sharper around the time of the Conference. A new Comintern manifesto on the miners' strike, for example, warning bluntly of the possibility of new 'treasonous machinations' by the General Council, called for an international sympathy strike on behalf

---

[1] *Ibid.*, pp. 463–92.   [2] *Ibid.*, pp. 555–77.   [3] *Ibid.*, pp. 505–35.

of the MFGB, the forcible ouster of the Tory regime, and the immediate establishment of a real Workers' Government in Britain.[1] One is tempted to chalk up such runaway maximalism, in part, to sheer desperation. The seven-months-old miners' strike, the biggest and costliest labour dispute in British history, was finally fading. The Russians had invested a lot in the struggle, emotionally and financially. If it went on for a few more months, the CPGB might be able to take over the Miners' Federation entirely, and from that base, win the whole of the trade union movement for Bolshevism. Everybody in Moscow, from right to left, from Trotsky to Bukharin, had seemed dazzled by such glittering fantasies. Now they would have to confront a sobering reality. The miners had been broken. Rabble-rousing, tub-thumping, sloganeering, ideologizing – who could respond to any of that any more when one's wife was hungry, one's children cold, and a long winter was coming on. The MFGB leadership was negotiating for a settlement by the end of October and had one by November 13. The owners got almost everything they ever asked. It was a cruel and brutal end to a long and bitter battle. If the Soviets still hoped to win over the British working man, they would have to devise new strategies to do so.

[1] *Inprecorr*, vi, 67 (14 Oct., 1926), 1151–2.

6

Divorce (November 1926–September 1927)

I

When the editors of *Who's Who* asked Commander Oliver Stillingfleet Locker-Lampson M.P., C.M.G., D.S.O., R.N.A.S., and Chairman of the 'Clear Out the Reds Campaign,' to list his principal recreation, he replied 'refusing honours.' Such becoming personal modesty is hard to square, however, with a pamphlet his anti-Red organization produced in early 1927. In just one year, the brochure crowed, the Campaign had already toppled two established Soviet leaders. 'Zinovieff, the arch-propagandist of Russia, has been flung from power, and Trotsky, England's enemy, has been driven from the councils of the Soviet.' To maintain that glorious momentum, the Campaign insisted on the immediate expulsion of all Russian representatives in England. They were intervening in Britain's domestic affairs, the organization explained, and trying to topple established leaders.[1]

It was all such mad nonsense one wonders that anybody could ever have taken it seriously, except that the Commander and his diehard friends did seem to get themselves heard. They might not have the Prime Minister with them, or even the Foreign Secretary, but Joynson-Hicks, Birkenhead and Churchill were all quite openly on their side, and so was the Tory rank and file. The Conservative party Conference carried one of their resolutions by acclamation in early October, 1926. Protesting the subversive activities of 'Soviet agents' within the British Empire, it pledged to support the government 'in any steps they may take to end this menace to our freedom and stability.' He was a peace-loving man, Locker-Lampson announced, seconding the motion, but he would never consent to see Britain bound and gagged while the enemy spat in her face and stabbed her in the back. All Russians must be 'drummed out of England' forthwith. It brought down the house.[2]

[1] The peculiarities of the pamphlet were pointed out in Commons by Ramsay MacDonald on 3 Mar. 1927: 203 H.C. Deb. 53 at cc. 621–2.
[2] *The Times*, 8 Oct., 1926. Locker-Lampson repeated the speech a week later at a 'Clear Out the Reds' mass rally at the Albert Hall. See Coates, *Anglo-Soviet Relations*, 245–6.

It was not until mid-December, however, that the topic came up in a cabinet meeting.[1] The ultras were obviously frustrated. They were positive the members of the Russian diplomatic and trading missions were fomenting subversion in Britain, but they could not prove it. They could make a better case by relying on the open record, especially those gloriously incendiary declarations, theses and manifestos with which Comintern regularly tried to roast the international bourgeoisie. Chamberlain promised to give the whole matter another review, early in 1927, but would concede no more.

That probably would have been the end of it, had not a crisis in China forced the Foreign Secretary's hand. On January 4, 1927, a Nationalist mob stormed the foreign concession area in Hankow. British residents fled the city in panic, and Baldwin sent a battalion of marines to the area to restore stability. Chinese of every political persuasion joined to condemn the intrusion. The Soviets were of course ecstatic. There was no reason to suppose the USSR had itself engineered the mischief. Chamberlain himself had given the Russians a clean bill of health in December, specifically rejecting the charge that the Kuomintang was Bolshevik-controlled.[2] But the fact remained that Communists were egging the Nationalists on with all the boisterous exuberance once reserved for striking British coalminers. Comintern was demanding its friends in Britain launch a 'Hands Off China' campaign. For the diehards, the record was absolutely conclusive. The Russians were surely as generous with their roubles as they were with their words, and if Soviet guns and grenades were *not* pouring into China, it was only because Communists were so notoriously inefficient in matters of business. In any event, the British needed a scapegoat, and the Russians were always convenient. By January 17, the Foreign Office was hard at work compiling an up-to-date catalogue of anti-British slanders originating in Moscow, with emphasis on statements relating to China. Chamberlain was ready to protest the various discourtesies, he informed his colleagues, and invited them to consider the evidence with him.[3]

Within the week, he had sent around two documents for them to look at. One was a draft protest note, citing offensive Russian statements from as far back as May, 1926, noting that the slanders were being reprinted in official government publications, rebuking the Soviets for countenancing the libels, and concluding that HM Government would

[1] Cabinet Conclusions, 1926, CAB 23.53, Conclusion 65(26)3, 15 Dec., 1926.
[2] *Ibid.*, Conclusion 65(26)4, 15 Dec., 1926.
[3] Cabinet Conclusions, 1927, CAB 23.54, Conclusion 2(27)1, 17 Jan., 1927.

'welcome a cessation' of such unfriendly speeches and writings.[1] The other was a Foreign Office memorandum summarizing the arguments for and against breaking diplomatic relations with the USSR.

The arguments in favour of a break were unimpressive, but there were a few. The Soviet government was to all intents and purposes at war with Britain anyway, the memorandum noted, and a rupture, if 'staged-managed' properly, might indeed have some propaganda value, especially in the Orient where governments were 'traditionally reported to understand only a display of strength.' The 1923 Curzon Ultimatum had produced a gratifying 'panic in the Bolshevik camp,' and perhaps a new crisis in relations with England might again weaken the Reds domestically. The arguments on the other side centred largely on how the continental states would react to the move. Germany, trying to cultivate west and east simultaneously, would deplore it. Pilsudski's Poland might be encouraged into dangerous adventurism at Russia's expense. Finland and the Baltic states would be alarmed and the unrest, overall, might jeopardize the settlement achieved at Locarno. Finally, it might be difficult to resume relations once they had been broken. An extended rupture was not even worth contemplating, and short term, the Soviets would surely be no better behaved than they had been before. Indeed, they would probably be more truculent than ever. It would therefore be as difficult to find an excuse to *mend* the break as it would be to find a justification for *making* it.

The arguments, the memorandum concluded, seemed fairly well balanced, 'and though a negative policy suggests a certain paralysis, a positive policy in this case is unlikely to make things...any better than they are at present. Being a leap in the dark, it might easily make things worse.' It might satisfy Britain's emotional needs, the writer suggested, at the expense of her diplomatic needs. It would cut off useful sources of information in Moscow, and make it impossible for London to use whatever influence it had with the Bolsheviks to dissuade them from even greater enormities in the future.

Transmitting that evaluation, Chamberlain made it clear that he still felt the arguments against a rupture were decisive. It would not really hurt the Soviet Union, nor persuade her to mend her ways. Communist propaganda would only become more vitriolic, all over the world. Anglo-Russian trade would suffer, and the consequent rise in unemployment would hurt the Conservatives at home. It would provide the Labour party and the trade unions just the kind of issue around which

[1] Cabinet Papers, 1927, CAB 24.181 C.P. 17(27), 21 Jan., 1927.

they could unite again. The Tories had everything to lose, then, and nothing whatever to gain, from following Locker-Lampson's advice.

The only three ministers to submit written comments on Chamberlain's views, Steel-Maitland, Churchill and Birkenhead, all concentrated their attention on the proposed protest note, and all took the hard line. Churchill proposed the note make it clear that England would break relations if British blood were shed in China.[1] Birkenhead suggested the Bolsheviks be ordered to call off their anti-British campaign 'forthwith.'[2] London would reserve the right to break diplomatic relations without any further notice if Moscow did not comply.

The hard-liners seemed to be carrying the ministerial fencestraddlers along with them. The cabinet discussions of February 16 and 18 produced general agreement the note had to be beefed up.[3] Given the gravity of the charges being preferred, imposing only a suspended sentence on the Reds was absurd. A breach of relations was 'almost inevitable,' the ministers agreed, 'given the state of public opinion in this country.' They also concurred, however, in the Foreign Office estimate that 'the present moment was not opportune for a rupture.' 'No preparation for such an eventuality had been undertaken' and 'no especially significant event had occurred, comparable to the publication of the Zinovieff letter or the intervention in the General Strike.' China would do it, as Churchill had suggested, if there were bloodshed there 'as a result of a policy instigated by the agents of Soviet Russia.' But without that blood, without even a forgery or two, the ministers were frustrated. All they could do was instruct Chamberlain to produce a stronger protest which, if it 'failed to produce a better attitude on the part of Soviet Russia,' could still 'be a useful first step in preparing the way, both at home and abroad, for a rupture of relations if this should later become inevitable.'

The Foreign Secretary did as he was told. His amended draft, ready a day later, concluded with a much more formidable *dénouement*. It warned the Russians 'in the gravest terms' that there were limits 'beyond which it is dangerous to drive the temper of a self-respecting people,' and declared that 'a continuance of such acts as are here complained of must sooner or later render inevitable the abrogation of the Trades Agreement. . .and even the severance of ordinary diplomatic relations.'[4] With

---

[1] Cabinet Papers, 1927, CAB.185, C.P. 61(27), 16 Feb., 1927.
[2] Cabinet Papers, 1926, CAB 24.181, C.P. 27(27), 26 Jan., 1927.
[3] Cabinet Conclusions, 1927, CAB 23.54, Conclusions 10(27)3, 16 Feb., 1927 and 12(27)1, 18 Feb., 1927.
[4] Cabinet Papers, 1927, CAB 24.185, C.P. 64(27), 19 Feb., 1927.

a few minor adjustments in wording, that was how it went to the Soviet *chargé d'affaires* February 23.[1] The very day Chamberlain was telling the Russians a diplomatic break might be inevitable, however, he was still urging his colleagues to make a rupture unnecessary. If a rupture could be averted, the more moderate factions in the USSR 'which inclined to a less unfriendly attitude toward this country' might yet prevail.[2]

It was surely no moderate, however – at least, not by any definition the diehards would accept – who dictated Moscow's reply to the British protest just three days later.[3] The Soviets admitted relations were indeed unsatisfactory, but denied all responsibility for the unpleasantness. The Trade Agreement had not obliged the Russian government to forbid its citizens to criticize the British, any more than it enjoined British subjects from finding fault with the USSR. Comintern's statements were irrelevant. The Soviet government did not own the International, its member parties did, and they retained as much right to express theii viewpoints as did the members of the Conservative party in England. As for individual members of the Soviet government, if the Trade Agreement did indeed oblige them to refrain from expressing any anti-British statements, it was strange that Churchill, Birkenhead and Joynson-Hicks felt no necessity to reciprocate. Finally, the press attacks on the USSR from Fleet Street more than matched the anti-British sentiments appearing in Russian newspapers. The Narkomindel refused to be intimidated by threats of an economic and diplomatic rupture. The Soviet Union would continue to pursue its peace-loving and non-aggressive policy, and would sincerely welcome any evidence the British government might do the same.

The reply was both dignified and restrained, even though it conceded Chamberlain nothing. Behind the scenes, the Narkomindel indicated it was still interested in a general settlement,[4] and publicly, Stalin discounted the likelihood that Britain would persist in the threatened break.[5] She had more to lose from a rupture than did the USSR, he argued. As for the possibility of general war, although the danger was

---

[1] For the final text, see Great Britain, Foreign Office, *Russia No. 1 (1927)*, Cmd. 2822, pp. 2–20 or *Russia No. 3 (1927)*, Cmd. 2895, pp. 45–63.

[2] Cabinet Papers, 1927, CAB 27.185, C.P. 66(27), 19 Feb., 1927; Cabinet Conclusions, 1927, CAB 23.54, Conclusion 13(27)1, 23 Feb., 1927.

[3] Great Britain, Foreign Office, *Russia No. 1 (1927)*, Cmd. 2822, pp. 20–5 or *Russia No. 3 (1927)* Cmd. 2895, pp. 64–9. The Russian-language version of the correspondence leading up to the diplomatic break is in Russia, Narodnyi Komissariat po Inostrannym Delam, *Anglo-Sovetskie Otnosheniia*, pp. 100–34.

[4] Cabinet Conclusions, 1927 CAB 23.54, Conclusion 17(29)4, 18 Mar., 1927.

[5] Stalin, *Sochineniia*, IX, 170.

still there, he did not think hostilities were imminent. Western workers would never agree to fight the proletarian fatherland.

Stalin's renewed confidence in the goodwill of the British wage earner was not entirely just wishful thinking. The Labour party and the TUC had been challenging the Tories on foreign policy issues since mid-January, with more and more gusto, concentrating on the intervention in China and the anti-Soviet harangues of the diehard ministers. The news of the February 23 protest note prompted them to demand a full-scale Commons debate a week later, and Chamberlain found himself hard-pressed indeed. Locker-Lampson was of course delighted at the Foreign Office's catalogue of Soviet improprieties, but complained 'the early brave words' of the complaint lodged with Moscow 'degenerated into the feeblest of official bleats' at the end. The Labour and Liberal opposition wanted to know why, if the offenses complained of were really so grave, the Foreign Office had waited for them to accumulate in such impressive quantities before protesting them.[1] The Foreign Secretary was taking it from both sides, and he defended himself against the Labourites with such vigour the diehards could not understand why he was still insisting on maintaining relations at all. His colleagues in the cabinet, dismayed at his performance, instructed him that evening to go back to the House at his earliest convenience and explain his opposition to a rupture, as forcefully as he could, without giving the USSR the impression Britain was 'powerless and tied.'[2]

It was surely no coincidence that later that same evening somebody delivered some new 'highly secret' information to Chamberlain concerning 'the activities of Soviet Russia in this country.' The charges were of so delicate a nature that the cabinet records only hint at them, but the Foreign Secretary's statement to his colleagues next day, plus the report of the Attorney-General, Sir Douglas Hogg, two weeks later, make it clear what was involved was some communication from Comintern headquarters to the CPGB, possibly transmitted via the Soviet diplomatic or trade missions. Sir Douglas had no doubt the informant was trustworthy and his allegations reliable, but the matter was of such sensitivity that, were the evidence to be published, the government required a week's delay in order to protect its source.[3] It all smacked splendidly of cloaks and daggers, just the kind of thing Birkenhead, Churchill and Joynson-Hicks had been looking for.

[1] 203 H.C. Deb. 5s at cc. 599–675. The Locker-Lampson quotation is at c. 643.
[2] Cabinet Conclusion, 1927, CAB 23.54, Conclusion 14(27)1, 3 Mar., 1927.
[3] *Ibid.*, Conclusions 14(27)1A, 4 Mar., 1927 and 17(27)4, 18 Mar., 1927.

Once again the Foreign Secretary had his way, but the cabinet minutes no longer record general consensus on the issue. This time it was only by 'a majority' that the government agreed to keep its derogatory information to itself and to maintain relations with the USSR 'on their present footing.' Perhaps it was on this occasion that an exasperated Birkenhead said of his friend Chamberlain that he was 'generally right on everything except Foreign Affairs.'[1]

The Foreign Secretary was fighting a virtually unwinnable war. To maintain relations with the USSR he had to carry his cabinet colleagues with him every time. The diehards, on the other hand, had to command a majority just once to banish all the Red rascals indefinitely. Additional evidences of Soviet perfidy, for use in the next ministerial showdown, were available enough in any event, and China, in particular, provided the hard liners a bonanza. New anti-foreign demonstrations erupted in both Shanghai and Nanking shortly after the beginning of spring. The Nanking rioters killed two resident Englishmen and wounded dozens more. British warships retaliated by lobbing high explosives into the city's more disaffected areas, mostly working-class districts, dispatching perhaps as many as a hundred Chinese. Chamberlain took a stern tone in Commons, insisting such outrages – he meant the killing of the two Englishmen, of course, not the scores of Chinese – could not go un-punished. The possibility of a major British military effort in China seemed real enough, for awhile, and the Soviet and Communist press raised the hue and cry with ferocious energy. Comintern termed the Nanking 'massacre' a 'great and inhuman crime' which had 'destroyed and annihilated' one of the great cities of the east. The corpses, the International reported gleefully, were 'heaped mountain high.'[2]

It all smacked of a Red conspiracy back in London, particularly after an April 6 raid on the USSR's Peking Embassy by Chinese police produced a set of papers purporting to prove the Kuomintang was little more than a Communist front organization. Jix must have envied the Orientals such deliciously incriminating documents, and it was not long afterwards he began to explore the possibility of acquiring some similar goodies in London. Influential English businessmen were soon warning

---

[1] Robert Rhodes James, ed., *Memoirs of a Conservative* (J. C. C. Davidson) (London: Weidenfeld and Nicolson, 1969), p. 203.

[2] Degras, *Communist International: Documents*, II, 357–8. The victims of the British bombardment, or many of them, had been trade unionists, and *chargé d'affaires* Rozengolts, in London, suggested the Chinese trade unions might send a message to the TUC stressing that fact and asking for fraternal help (Cabinet Conclusions, 1927, CAB 23.55, Conclusion 32(27)2, 19 May, 1927).

their Russian contacts that a police strike on the Soviet Embassy might be expected any day.[1]

Moscow had to defend itself. To counter Joynson-Hicks, it would appeal to the British proletariat. The Narkomindel was gathering detailed reports on English workers' anti-war activities from early February on. There had been a demonstration at Bolton. The Labour party constituency organization at Wakefield had passed an agreeable resolution. Thirty thousand organized workers in Barnsley had been 'represented' at a protest meeting there.[2] It was all very gratifying, but it was also very localized. On a national level, some big names in the Labour party and the TUC had signed petitions and appeared at rallies,[3] but the rhetoric was all much too restrained, as Moscow saw it. The General Council should snarl, not whine. It should make it perfectly clear that labour's immediate response to an attack on the USSR would be to call a new general strike. The councillors did not seem to take the war threat seriously enough. Domestic concerns preoccupied them almost totally, and domestically, they seemed more anxious to bash Communists – especially Minority Movement people – than Conservatives.[4] J. H. Thomas was urging loyal cooperation with industry and talking about 1926 as a 'disaster' and nobody was throwing rocks at him. Meanwhile, the government was introducing measures in Parliament designed to neutralize the general strike threat indefinitely.

The bill was the infamous Trades Disputes and Trade Union Act of 1927, legislation so patently unfair and vindictive that the Labour Minister himself – within the privacy of the cabinet room – had opposed it.[5] Its major impact domestically would be to put severe limitations on the Labour party's traditional source of campaign money, the trade unions. The bill also outlawed general strikes. Any industrial action

---

[1] Fischer, *Soviets in World Affairs*, II, 685.

[2] These actions were not usually significant enough to warrant mention in the national press, but the Soviet mission in London collected news of them assiduously, and the reports ended up in the Foreign Policy Archives in Moscow. Soviet historians since have used them regularly. The reports cited derive from Volkov, *Anglo-Sovetskie Otnosheniia*, pp. 266–8.

[3] The biggest rally was perhaps the one on Feb. 5 at the Albert Hall. An 'appeal to the country on the Chinese situation,' urging also maintenance of diplomatic relations with the USSR, appeared that same day. Nine of the 34 members of the TUC General Council signed it. (*Sunday Worker*, 6 Feb., 1927).

[4] The General Council demanded on 25 Mar., 1927, for example, that trades councils disaffiliate with the NMM or drop their connection with the TUC.

[5] Cabinet Papers, 1926, CAB. 24.182, C.P. 394(26), 22 Nov., 1926, for Steel-Maitland's protest. For a good analysis of the bill itself, see Crook, *General Strike*, pp. 477–89.

designed to coerce the government or to intimidate the community was specifically forbidden. From Moscow, that seemed the key provision of the bill. Clearly, the Tories had decided on all-out assault on the USSR, and they were trying to make sure English trade unionists could not respond. It was urgent and vital that the bill be withdrawn. If the government refused, the right to call a general strike in the future must be preserved by calling one immediately. That was the response Moscow demanded, and the CPGB was told to subordinate everything else to its campaign against the bill and against the war threat.[1]

The TUC General Council was no happier about the bill than were the Bolsheviks back in Moscow. The legislation was a 'violent attack on the workers' rights,' it charged, 'striking at the living spirit of trades unionism.' But a special Conference of Executives of TUC affiliates, meeting the end of April, overwhelmingly rejected CPGB proposals to kill the bill with a new general strike. Subsequent Communist efforts to goad the General Council into stronger action against the bill were as strident as they were inadequate. The official leadership continued its sedate, dignified, and totally ineffectual rearguard action against the legislation right up to the time of its passage in late July.[2]

II

The General Council was taking no orders from the Russians, then, but it had reconsidered its earlier decision not to talk with them at all. What had made those last two meetings of the Anglo-Russian Committee so intolerable, after all, and prompted the councillors to veto any further sessions, was the impasse over the miners' lock-out. That was finally over. Within a matter of just days after the MFGB settled, the General Council's International Committee was voting to recommend repeal of that decision taken back in September (and inexplicably, never implemented) to distribute the documents on the Paris and Berlin Committee

[1] An example of Comintern invective against the bill is the statement of 15 April, 1927 cited in Degras, *Communist International: Documents*, II, 362–3. The 8th ECCI drew up the instructions for the CPGB's campaign against the bill. See the relevant sections of the Resolutions on the Situation in Great Britain, the English text of which may be found in CPGB, *Ninth Congress: Reports, Theses & Resolutions*, pp. 120–4.

[2] See the *Annual Register, 1927*, pp. 31–65. The quotation cited is from p. 31. For samples of later Communist efforts against the bill, see *The Worker*, 10 June, 1927, or L. Zoobok, 'Der Kampf gegen das Gewerkschaftsegesetz,' *Die Rote Gewerkschaftsinternationale*, No. 6 (77) (June, 1927), pp. 360–7.

meetings to affiliated unions, and to await their reaction before risking further altercations with the Russians.[1] The TUC's representatives on the Anglo-Russian Committee had met November 16, three days after the miners' strike ended, and suggested trying to find an accommodation with Tomsky instead. What they had in mind was a new clause to be added to the Committee's by-laws. The proposal would require both parties to recognize 'the complete authority and autonomy' of the other, and their exclusive right 'to organize and conduct the work of the Trade Union Movements in their respective countries.' No provision in the Committee constitution, the draft continued, 'shall be interpreted as authorizing any act of interference or intervention by either party in the internal affairs of the Trade Union Movement of the other party, nor shall any matter concerning the British Trade Union movement be brought before the...Committee except at the direct request of the TUC General Council, and a similar procedure to apply to the Russian Trade Union movement.' The International Committee liked that wording, and the General Council approved it, too.[2] The freeze on contacts with the Russians was repealed, by a 12-to-6 vote, and Citrine and Hicks authorized to draft a letter to Tomsky forwarding the new proposals and suggesting a conference on them.

The English were demanding a high price for reviving the Committee. The guarantee of the General Council's exclusive right to direct British trade unionism might be interpreted as requiring the dissolution of the Minority Movement. The non-intervention pledge, had it been in effect the previous June, would have proscribed that statement of the Soviet trade unions criticizing the TUC's conduct of the general strike. The final provision would presumably have made it impossible for Tomsky to raise the question of the miners' strike at a Committee meeting. In effect, the British were requiring the Russians to make a choice: either accept the TUC's interpretation of the Committee role – a very limited role indeed – and refrain from criticizing the TUC leadership, or stand aside helplessly while the General Council let the Committee die of neglect. The British seem to have felt they were now negotiating from strength, that the Soviets needed the alliance more than they did.

The Stalinists must have found the TUC initiative a considerable embarrassment. They first learned of it, presumably, sometime in early

---

[1] See above, p. 287. The record of the Nov. 23 meeting of the International Committee is in the TUC archives, file 901, doc. I.C. 1. 1926–7.

[2] The General Council's decision was No. 74, 24 Nov. 1926 (mis-dated 23 Nov. in the General Council Minutes).

December. Lozovsky referred to a British plan to change the Committee's constitution in a speech December 6, but did not elaborate.[1] For over a month thereafter, almost nothing would be heard of the matter at all. The proposal posed a real dilemma for the Russian leadership. To turn the British down, and stand by while they broke up the Committee in retaliation, would make the Politburo majority look silly and ineffective. They had claimed, after all, the Committee constituted a serious impediment to Baldwin's bourgeois warmongers; why, then, forfeit so valuable an asset on a mere technicality? If, on the other hand, the Committee was to be maintained, on the TUC's terms, the Trotskyites could claim the Soviet trade unions had abdicated their responsibility to expose the General Council for opportunism and cowardice. It was not an easy decision to make.

The discussions in the 7th plenum of the Comintern's Enlarged Executive, beginning in late November, did little to un-complicate the problem for them.[2] As against the claims of the Opposition, the majority repeated its conviction that the prospects for immediate revolution in the west were dim, that capitalism had achieved a 'partial, temporary stabilization.' Bukharin, obviously ill-at-ease with the whole premise, insisted the stabilization was itself 'unstable' and stressed the happy prospects for the not-too-distant future in Britain and China. Stalin, more cautious, could foresee an extended period of 'respite,' long

---

[1] Communist International, Enlarged Executive, *Puti Mirovoi Revoliutsii: Sed'moi Rasshirennyi Plenum Ispolnitel'nogo Komiteta Kommunisticheskogo Internatsionala, 22 Noiabria–16 Dekabria 1926g. Stenograficheskii Otchet*, 2 vols. (Moscow–Leningrad: Gosudarstvennoe Izdatel'stvo, 1927), I, 541.

[2] The transcript of the proceedings is Communist International, Enlarged Executive, *Puti Mirovoi Revoliutsii*. The most important speeches and reports relating to the united front and to the Anglo-Russian Committee are those of Bukharin (I, 1, 19–30 and 30–112), Gallacher (I, 5–7), Kuusinen (I, 113–36), Smith (I, 202–6), Murphy (I, 466–87 and 568–70), Lozovsky (I, 528–57 and II, 269–77), Remmele (I, 558–62), Vuiovič (II, 180–83), Shatskin (II, 183–92), Kamenev (II, 193–205), Buck (II, 223–6), Thaelmann (II, 240–55), and Katayama (II, 286–8). Stalin touched these matters tangentially in his speeches to the ECCI's Chinese Commission. See *Sochineniia*, IX, 18–19, 25–8, 139–43. The final resolutions were reprinted in *Kommunisticheskii Internatsional v Dokumentakh*. See especially 'The International Situation and the Tasks of the Communist International,' pp. 626–43; 'Resolution on the Tasks in the Trade Unions,' pp. 648–54; and 'Resolution on the Situation in England,' pp. 655–68. See also the relevant part of the 'Resolution on the Opposition Bloc in the CPSU (B),' pp. 685–6. Degras, *Communist International: Documents* II, 312–54, reprints selections from the major resolutions in English translation, and the debates may be followed in English editions of *Inprecorr*, VI, 83 (1 Dec., 1926), 1429–36, 85 (3 Dec., 1926), 1449–80, 88 (20 Dec., 1926), 1505–46, 89 (23 Dec., 1926), 1547–80, 91 (30 Dec., 1926), 1589–1616, 92 (30 Dec., 1926), 1612–38 and VII, 8 (26 Jan., 1927), 153–72, 9 (27 Jan., 1927), 173–87 and 11 (3 Feb., 1927), 217–42.

enough to enable him to build socialism in the USSR. Both agreed, however, that the Trotskyites, by refusing to accept unpalatable historical realities, demonstrated a lack of faith in the basic inner strength of the Marxist cause. To despair at the postponement of world revolution and to propose, therefore, a dangerous adventurism and putschism, hardly advanced the interests of the proletariat anywhere.

The delegates agreed that the only way the western imperialists had been able to achieve their reprieve was by enlisting the social-democratic trade union leaders as allies. Reformism had therefore become – 'objectively' – far more dangerous than Fascism, Otto Kuusinen charged. It was only with the help of reformist class traitors that the capitalists could maintain themselves at all. The renegades must be exposed and smashed. That demanded more attention than ever to united front tactics, which the comrades ruled 'necessary and obligatory' for Communist Parties everywhere.[1] The resolutions suggested stronger emphasis on the united front from below – with the rank and file union member rather than his reformist spokesmen – and only on the basis of concrete action programmes to achieve specific, definable objectives. Subject to those stipulations, the Executive recommended creation of a whole series of 'proletarian unity committees,' from the plant and factory level on up, culminating in the struggle for a single, world-wide trade union federation. The new international envisaged, Lozovsky emphasized, would be wholly unlike the IFTU in that it would be dedicated unmistakably to waging and winning class war. The way to get it was by that World Unity Congress Communists had been proposing for three years, and the way to persuade the faltering Amsterdam social fascists to acquiesce in such a meeting was to strengthen Profintern, forge even closer contacts with the social-democratic masses, and show them how to slough off those opportunistic traitors who now claimed to speak for them.[2]

Bukharin found united front prospects particularly tantalizing in Great Britain, where the extended miners' strike had made an already desperate economic crisis just that much more acute. Their economic difficulties made it impossible for the capitalists to continue to obscure their implacable animus against the working masses. The whole panoply of bourgeois institutions – government, monarchy, Parliament, Church, army, police, press – now stood revealed as mere instruments of the capitalist dictatorship. Even the trade union bureaucrats had been

---

[1] *Kommunisticheskii Internatsional v Dokumentakh*, p. 686.
[2] *Ibid.*, pp. 639, 650–4; *Puti Mirovoi Revoliutsii*, I, 540–3.

obliged to fall in, more or less openly, with their bourgeois paymasters. On the other hand, the proletarian masses were achieving a more and more intense class consciousness, as demonstrated by the growing influence of the Minority Movement and the Communist Party. As the workers became more radicalized and lost their reformist illusions, the right-wing TUC bureaucrats would find their influence waning.[1] The united front would accelerate their obsolescence, since it presupposed 'ruthless criticism and exposure of all reformist treachery, defeatism, wavering and desertion to the enemy.'[2]

Not everybody, however, had such confidence in the English proletarians. Stalin seemed perplexed by them. He found it hard to understand why the British had never simply tossed Jimmy Thomas down a well and drowned him – 'liquidation' in its most elementary form, presumably! Russian workers would have done just that: they did not tolerate opportunists. But at Bournemouth, the delegates actually re-elected all the Thomases to the General Council, and by acclamation, at that. British opportunism did not even have to camouflage itself, Stalin noted sadly. It presented itself shamelessly for what it was, and the British workers embraced it willingly. So long as unrepentant compromisers still had the confidence of the masses, one could presume that Baldwin was safe. The English had only just begun to develop a revolutionary tradition, Stalin concluded. They might feel enough sympathy for socialism to resist any bourgeois orders to march against the proletarian fatherland, the USSR, but their complete emancipation from capitalism might have to be deferred until after the old regime had been fatally weakened by the economic successes of a socialist Russia.[3]

The reformists might still be dominant in the British labour aristocracy, but the revolutionaries were coming up fast, the Comintern pointed out, enlisting new recruits at a rate of almost a thousand a month. The CPGB might not yet have reached the exalted status of a 'mass party' but it was clearly headed in that direction. Admittedly, it had been 'inadequately decisive' in exposing and denouncing the trade union 'leftists,' and it had misunderstood the indictment against the General Council presented by the Soviet trade unions. Murphy, confessing such sins back in October, had attributed them to the Party's anxiety not to rupture the Anglo-Russian Committee. One assumes the Stalinists had not found that explanation congenial. It would only seem to confirm Trotsky's allegation – that the Committee had paralysed the

---

[1] *Puti Mirovoi Revoliutsii*, I, 92–6.   [2] *Ibid.*, p. 98.
[3] Stalin, *Sochineniia*, IX, 18–19, 26–8.

CPGB and left it unable to meet its revolutionary responsibilities properly. At the plenum, therefore, the resolutions never mentioned the Committee in connection with the CPGB's little misdemeanours, and aside from one revealing indiscretion by the apparently irrepressible Murphy (the mistakes had only been made 'in order to save the Anglo-Russian Committee'),[1] those who spoke to the issue did so cautiously. The errors were made innocently, it was finally decreed, and most of them, with the help of 'fraternal criticisms and suggestions' from the Comintern's Executive, had already been corrected. The CPGB leaders now agreed unanimously that they had indeed been naughty, and promised to do better in the future.[2]

The chastened British comrades were assigned heavy responsibilities by their Comintern colleagues. They must work much harder at penetrating the trade union movement. They must do something to beef up the NMM organization (it was now more an 'influence' than an 'activity'). They must make more concerted efforts to oust the reformist TUC bureaucrats. Most of all, they must continue the campaign for a single trade union international, 'as a guarantee against international economic and political reaction and the menace of a new world war.' Since the Anglo-Russian Committee had been founded to promote the unity campaign, the Communists were to urge its revival, and condemn the efforts of the TUC reformists to sabotage it. Doing all that effectively would involve extensive participation in united fronts. If the British comrades wanted to learn how best to exploit such opportunities, they were advised to examine the techniques of the expert, Tomsky. 'The continued participation of the Soviet Russian unions, under CPSU leadership, in the Anglo-Russian unity committee, notwithstanding the criticism and exposure of the treachery and sabotage of the General Council,...provided a practical demonstration to Communists in Britain and throughout the world of the importance of united front tactics as a means to unite the workers in the struggle against capitalism

---

[1] *Puti Mirovoi Revoliutsii*, I, 485.
[2] They had already well begun to correct their 'errors,' most obviously, perhaps, in an article by J. R. Campbell, 'The General Strike and Its Lessons,' *The Communist Review*, VII, 8 (Dec., 1926), 357–63. For the earlier CPGB statement criticizing the Comintern for not offering enough helpful 'fraternal advice,' see above, p. 299. The ECCI noted, in response, that during the period May–Dec. 1926 it had issued 39 reports directly concerning Britain, to which could be added an additional 13 bulletins from the agitprop department. See Degras, *Communist International: Documents*, II, 314. For the 7th ECCI's resolutions on the CPGB, see *Kommunisticheskii Internatsional v Dokumentakh*, pp. 639–40, 655–68. See also *Puti Mirovoi Revoliutsii*, I, 105–6 (Bukharin), 118–20 (Kuusinen) and 485–7 (Murphy).

and to compel the reformist leaders to reveal themselves for what they really are.'[1]

The Committee – Bukharin was already calling it the 'so-called' Committee – might not survive much longer. But any attempt by the TUC bureaucrats to liquidate it would make their two-facedness all the plainer, and discredit them with their own followers all the more. For the Soviets to have accepted Trotsky's advice, however, and ruptured the Committee themselves would have been a 'crude error.' It would have ruled out any possibility of a combined Anglo-Russian effort on behalf of the miners, and would have made the Soviets, rather than the reformist General Council traitors, seem responsible for sabotaging the MFGB cause.[2]

To break up the Committee, then, would have been a mistake, but it would have been an even more serious mistake to maintain it at the cost of surrendering the right to criticize its British members. That was the social-democratic line, the Comintern decreed. The Communist counter-argument held that class solidarity did not stop at national frontiers, and that revolutionaries 'have intervened, do intervene, and furthermore will intervene' in any labour dispute, anywhere, 'in order to extend their assistance in the struggle against the exploiters.' The Committee was never intended as a bloc of trade union leaders, nor was its aim to establish friendly relations between the Russian and British labour elites. So when the General Council bureaucrats neglected their obligation to struggle against the capitalists, it was up to the Soviet trade unionists to rebuke them for their failings publicly and to alert the TUC rank and file – Russia's Committee allies – to the possibility their leaders might be contemplating further delinquencies. That was precisely what Tomsky had done in June, and although it produced the crisis in the Committee, British and Soviet proletarians were actually more closely aligned now than ever before. The Soviets, then, would continue to insist on the maintenance of the Committee, and they also would continue to criticize those TUC members of the Committee who had sabotaged the general strike and miners' strike.[3]

Such, then, was the decision on the Committee recorded in the plenum's formal resolutions, a re-statement and amplification, in effect, of the judgements of the 15th CPSU Conference. The men who mattered most at the meeting did not seem particularly disposed either to explicate the texts or to challenge them. Bukharin paid the Committee routine

---

[1] *Kommunisticheskii Internatsional v Dokumentakh*, pp. 655–68.
[2] *Ibid.*, pp. 638–9.   [3] *Ibid.*, pp. 648–9.

tribute in his opening statement, spoiling the effort somewhat with an over-elaborate explanation of why it was just the Russian trade unions, and not RILU as a whole, which had concluded the alliance with the British.[1] Profintern was unpopular in England, he confessed. It was too closely identified with Comintern. On the other hand, the Russian trade unions were associated with the Soviet state apparatus, which the islanders apparently admired. It had been advantageous, therefore, to cater to their quaint misconceptions. At least, it had in the past. From now on, however, RILU would assume much more significant responsibilities on its own. The Russian trade unions would ginger up the effort by participating more energetically in Profintern's work than they had previously.

Lozovsky, too, dealt with the Committee somewhat cursorily.[2] In the past, it had enabled Communists to bring together various undifferentiated 'leftist' movements on the basis of a common struggle for trade union unity. That was in the old days, however, before the general strike, when leftist sentiments had been formless and undefined. Now leftism was taking on a more distinct character. The crisis in the Committee, the clash between its Soviet and British components over the question of the general strike, had crystallized out a new, more genuine left, whose British adherents were enlisted under the banner of the National Minority Movement. The Committee had been instrumental in the growth of the NMM, Lozovsky seemed to be saying, so creating it was defensible, and there was no special reason to cast it aside now, but it was the NMM, not the Committee, that would be the focus for future united front activities in Britain.

All this was vague and equivocal, but it seemed, at first, as if nobody at the plenum wanted to dispute it. The Russian Oppositionists were strangely silent. Kamenev, later on, would declare the fate of the Committee 'one of the most significant questions of our tactics,' but aside from mocking the idea the organization could play any role in preventing imperialist wars, he seemed loth to pursue the topic further.[3] Trotsky and Zinoviev never mentioned it at all, in $2\frac{1}{2}$ hours of impassioned rhetoric. They had made their case, presumably, to the CPSU, and may have considered it a waste of time to debate the issue all over again in the Comintern. It was the comrades from outside the USSR who finally insisted that the Committee question get ventilated, and it was they who had to take most of the responsibility for conducting the review.

[1] *Puti Mirovoi Revoliutsii*, I, 102–3.   [2] *Ibid.*, pp. 540–3.
[3] *Ibid.*, II, 196–7.

The German Communist leader, H. Remmele, initiated the debate.[1] The plenum must not adjourn, he argued, 'without making a decision on the question of the continued existence of the Anglo-Russian Committee.' He was for keeping it. He deemed the Opposition's case 'absolute nonsense.' To dissolve the organization would only be to confess the bankruptcy of the whole united front policy. The Committee provided the Soviets an opportunity to continue influencing, and revolutionizing, the English proletariat, and he urged it be retained.

A Comintern *apparatchik*, the Yugoslavian Trotskyite V. Vuiovič, presented a rebuttal for the Opposition.[2] He was not even sure there was a Committee any more. If it really existed, it should be doing something. Since evidence of any activity at all was nonexistent, however, it could be presumed dead. He saw no reason to resurrect it. Its British members were just class traitors, and they should be cashiered, not conferred with. The connection should have been broken back in May. That way, the British rank and file would have been prompted to ponder the enormity of their betrayal, and to draw the necessary conclusions. The opportunity was thrown away, and as a result, the Committee had become so innocuous that now probably even Thomas would be willing to let it survive. The most pressing responsibility of the revolutionary movement, however, was to help the British workers oust their Thomases. To do so, united front tactics should be limited to the united front from below. Join with the masses, spurn all blocs with the betrayers who misled them, break the Committee!

Of the five delegates rising indignantly to refute the Trotskyite heresies, only one – Lozovsky – was Russian, and he hardly said anything new at all.[3] Much of the rhetoric was defensive and confused. The Committee might be a weak instrument against imperialism, confessed one speaker, but one had to use everything available. The Committee might generate 'a certain energy' in the economic struggle-to-come in Britain. Then again, another comrade admitted, the organization might break down – nobody had even claimed it was supposed to last forever – but even if that happened, the reformists would have trouble explaining the disappointment to their constituency. Only one speaker seemed really forthright about it all. We know the English trade union leaders are opportunists and traitors, Japan's Katayama declared, but united front tactics dictate we mix with them in order to win over those who follow

---

[1] *Ibid.*, I, 558–62.   [2] *Ibid.*, II, 180–3.

[3] The relevant speeches in *Puti Mirovoi Revoliutsii* are those of Shatskin (II, 183–92), Buck (II, 223–6), Thaelmann (II, 240–55), Lozovsky (II, 269–77), and Katayama (II, 286–8).

them. 'We must shake hands with the traitorous,...opportunist labour leaders for, behind the backs of those opportunist leaders, we want to make contact with the English workers.' That was the rationale for establishing the Committee, he pointed out, and unless the Party lacked confidence in the ultimate wisdom of the proletarian masses, no harm could come of maintaining it.

Hardly an enthusiastic endorsement, that, but it reflected a general disinterest in the Committee. Even the Trotskyite attack on it now seemed pretty perfunctory, to the great relief, no doubt, of the Politburo majority. The Stalinists, on their part, were content to praise the Committee for its past achievements, insist, noisily, that the English participate in it, and in fact let the TUC bureaucrats bear the responsibility for rupturing it at their convenience. The General Council's proposal for reviving the tie – subject to mortifying conditions – must have been too distasteful to contemplate just yet. Having pledged themselves – openly – to continue to smear the English duffers, deceivers, and deserters and to make every effort to get them tossed out of the trade union leadership, the Soviet bosses would find it difficult to turn around and sign a pledge not to interfere in the TUC's 'internal affairs.' So questionable a *volte-face* might not ever be necessary, however. If Communist Party membership continued to snowball in Great Britain, and if the National Minority Movement grew proportionally, and if revolutionary activists finally took over the Miners' Federation, the Soviets might not need the General Council any more. Stalin would have amassed an even more reliable collection of allies with which to menace Austen Chamberlain than those he had enlisted via the Committee.

He was to be disappointed, disappointed three times over, in fact. CPGB membership began to shrink just as soon as the miners' strike ended. As early as the end of January, two thousand ex-enthusiasts had let their cards lapse, and by October, the comrades numbered only 7,377. Optimists might cite that figure as a gain of almost 25 per cent since April, 1926. Realists pointed out it represented a 33 per cent loss since November of the same year.[1] Enthusiasm for the NMM also began to wane. The revolutionary trade unionists never did quite manage to sign up the elusive millionth member. At their 1926 conference, they had boasted of 956,000 adherents, but a year later, by August of 1927, they were only claiming 800,000, a drop of some 16 per cent.[2]

[1] Communist International, Executive Committee, *The Communist International Between the Fifth & the Sixth World Congresses*, p. 131.
[2] *Mezhdunarodnoe Profdvizhenie*, pp. 160–8.

The miners were the biggest disappointment of all. The Soviets had invested a lot of rubles in the MFGB, and were hoping for some ideological dividends. When Bukharin welcomed his fellow delegates to the plenum of the Comintern's Enlarged Executive, he addressed his very first remarks to the 'fighting British miners.' Many of their own leaders had deserted them, he admitted, but his information was that the rank and file were still carrying on, and he urged even greater exertions than ever on their behalf.[1] CPGB representatives confirmed those reports. The miners had paralysed British imperialism, Gallacher proclaimed, and made it impossible for the capitalists to go to war against the lackeys of the General Council. The Party's influence among them was enormous. In fact, 'we are leading them.'[2]

Even by the time the plenum adjourned, however, such buoyancy seemed passé. With the last of the strikers now back in the pits, the plenum's resolutions expressed disappointment at the collapse of the effort. MFGB leaders, even Cook, had proved too willing to compromise. Nevertheless, the Party still had immense strength in the coalfields, Cook had arrived in the Soviet Union and proclaimed himself for the overthrow of capitalism, and the long-trumpeted, oft-deferred Anglo-Russian Miners' Committee – an organization 'destined to play an historic role in the development of our international revolutionary movements' – seemed about to become a reality at last.[3] The Comintern refused to despair.

Cook had come to the USSR to sit in on the 7th Soviet Trade Union Congress, as fraternal delegate of the Miners' Federation. The General Council, much to the 'shame and indignation' of the CPGB,[4] had refused to send anybody representing the TUC as a whole, so Cook would be the only Englishman there. He was hoping, he announced before his departure, to convey to the Russians the gratitude of the British miners for all that Soviet assistance during the recent strike. And to cement the friendship, he said, he also had a 'practical object' in mind. 'I intend to form an Anglo-Russian Miners' Committee, which will meet for mutual

---

[1] *Puti Mirovoi Revoliutsii*, I, 1, 96.
[2] *Ibid.*, pp. 5–7.
[3] The quotation is from *ibid.*, II, 226. The general question of Comintern's relationship with the MFGB was dealt with in the plenum's 'Resolution on the Situation in Great Britain.' *Kommunisticheskii Internatsional v Dokumentakh*, pp. 655–68.
[4] The phrase quoted obviously represented the official Party line. The *Sunday Worker* used it 5 Dec. and the *Workers' Weekly* 14 Dec. *Workers' Weekly* said the TUC's failure to send a delegation to the USSR was an attempt to rupture the Committee, and suggested that if either the Committee or the General Council had to be dismissed, British workers would do better finding themselves a new General Council.

aid in difficulties and struggles.'[1] That was precisely, of course, the organization the Russians wanted too, so even though they were denouncing Cook in the Comintern for vacillation and compromise, they proceeded to provide him one of the most enthusiastic receptions any foreigner had received for a year or more. A delegation of Soviet miners met him at the border on December 4 and escorted him in triumph the rest of the way to Moscow. He arrived in the capital to a rapturous reception, and got lionized continuously for the next two weeks. The Russians, as always, carried their hospitality to the limits of gastric endurance.[2]

Cook responded effusively. He said 'precisely what was required of him,' Hodgson reported back to Chamberlain, 'that His Majesty's Government are preparing an attack upon the Soviet Union, but that the British proletariat will not allow this villainy to be consummated.' He reviled all his colleagues in the TUC leadership as 'traitors,' and announced that 'the toiling masses of England are slowly but surely becoming leavened with the revolutionary idea.'[3]

His major public appearance was at the Soviet Trades Union Congress, where he was received with 'stormy applause.'[4] Tomsky had warmed the delegates up for him.[5] The Committee was in trouble, he had admitted. The TUC bureaucrats were trying to break it up. That was why they now refused to keep that promise – four times repeated – to convene a Moscow–Amsterdam unity conference. That was why they sent no fraternal delegate to address Soviet trade unionists, 'an unfriendly act' by anybody's definition. That was why they demanded so 'obstinately and insistently' those amendments to the Committee constitution. It was all very subtle, Tomsky noted. The councillors might have been more direct. They could have just said to the Russians, you are too rude, when you shake hands you crush our bones, so go away! But to be that blunt would be to alienate the English working masses, so

---

[1] *The Miner*, 4 Dec., 1926.

[2] For details of Cook's visit, I have consulted the Soviet daily press, and also a report drawn up for the British Foreign Office, Hodgson to Chamberlain, 17 Dec., 1926, N 5719/5558/38, F.O. 371.11803.

[3] Hodgson to Chamberlain, 17 Dec., 1926, N 5719/5558/38, F. O. 371.11803. The report was not unjust: see, for example, *Izvestiia*, 6 Dec. and 12 Dec., 1926.

[4] There is a published stenographic report of the Congress, but I have been unable to locate a copy. *Trud*, however, printed transcripts of the major speeches, and the Congress was very well covered in *Izvestiia*. I have relied on those sources, therefore, plus English-language texts of the resolutions adopted in *Inprecorr*, VII, 5 (13 Jan., 1927), 105–7. For Cook's speech, see also *The Worker*, 17 Dec., 1926.

[5] The speech was published in *Izvestiia*, 8 Dec., 1926.

the councillors tried to achieve the same result by indirection. All of which left the future of the Committee very much in doubt. Relations between the rank and file on both sides were closer than ever, however. The generous contributions of the Soviet trade unionists to the MFGB – in fact, to the 'cause of class warfare' – had shown the ordinary English working man what proletarian solidarity was all about, and the miners, in particular, were now devoted friends of the USSR.

Cook agreed.[1] The General Council was full of cowards and traitors, and he reviled them – or at least, the rightists among them – by name. Their conduct of the general strike was reprehensible. He echoed Tomsky's sentiments about the warm feelings of MFGB members towards their brothers in the Soviet Union, and claimed they all favoured an Anglo-Russian Miners' Committee. Just what the objectives of that organization should be had occasioned some debate, he confessed. Some of his colleagues wanted to use it to help get the Russian miners into the International Miners' Secretariat. Others, himself included, deemed the existing Secretariat 'far too rotten to be reorganized' and would sooner liquidate it altogether. The English and Russians could then join to build a new organization in its place. Either way, the two movements had much to talk about, and much to do, and he was for getting on with it.

The Congress' resolutions, however, rather strangely, said nothing about the proposed Miners' Committee. They routinely approved united front tactics in general, however, on the basis of full 'freedom of mutual criticism.' Western reformists were rebuked for dragging their feet on unity, and for propping up capitalism and the bourgeoisie. The General Council was denounced for trying to sabotage the Anglo-Russian Committee. The November 30 proposals for reorganizing the Committee were noted in passing, but no details were revealed as to the specific provisions and the texts provided no clue as to how Tomsky might respond. One would assume, however, from the vigour with which he had defended his right to abuse the councillors, that he was unlikely to make the sort of commitment the TUC had in mind.

In any event, he might still strike a bargain with Cook, and he seems to have tried to. The talks must have gone well. Just a few days after the MFGB leader left for home, the Soviet press announced that 'preliminary negotiations' for that Miners' Committee had been completed, that Cook was determined to create such an organization, and that he would get the formal assent of his colleagues as soon as he got back to

[1] *The Worker*, 17 Dec., 1926.

Britain. The first regular meeting of the Committee would be held either January or February, *Izvestiia* reported, the exact date to be set as soon as the MFGB Executive gave the word.[1]

Cook must have found out very quickly he was going to have to break his promises. The MFGB Executive could not possibly have managed a January meeting with the Russians anyway. Most of the month was spent getting ready for that Conference of Trade Union Executives – already deferred over six months at the miners' request – that was to sort out what went wrong in May of 1926 and whose fault it was. When the 1,200 labour leaders met, on January 21, talk was blunt, but tempers were restrained. The General Council had the support of the overwhelming majority of those present, and its report on the general strike was accepted by almost 3 to 1 over that of the MFGB, 2,840,000 'votes' to 1,095,000. No other major union backed the miners. Eight hundred thousand of the votes they received were their own.[2]

The reaction of the MFGB was not to hurl itself ardently into the arms of the Russians, however, as Moscow must have hoped, but to stand back and ponder how it could mend its fences at home. The Soviets were told that the Executive would talk some more about the possibility of forming that Committee, some time in mid-March, but it was not yet ready to make any promises. The talks, when they finally were held, were inconclusive, and by June the Comintern had decided the miners' leaders were going to refuse to act, and was condemning them for it. The whole issue finally went to the MFGB's Annual Conference in July, where a resolution directing the Executive to create that Anglo-Russian Miners' Committee was presented by the NMM-controlled Scottish district. The Forest of Dean offered an alternative motion, a meaningless collection of words urging the Executive to 'take the necessary steps for securing a world-wide Miners' International...' Herbert Smith opposed both proposals. If the Russians wanted to come in the Miners' Secretariat, they were perfectly free to do so, he argued (under the existing 'rules and conditions,' of course), and once they joined, he would be more than willing to talk to them. Not before. Cook, predictably, supported the Forest of Dean resolution, but never said a word on behalf of his Committee, which was subsequently rejected, 557 votes to 215. The other

[1] *Izvestiia*, 1 Jan., 1927.
[2] See the *Annual Register, 1927*, p. 7. About the time the Conference met, RILU rushed into print with texts of the major documents involved, including the two 'secret' General Council reports and the MFGB's response. Lozovsky wrote a preface to the volume and Harry Pollitt a postscript. See *Chetyre Dokumenta* (Moscow: Izdanie Profinterna, 1927).

resolution, simply favouring the all-inclusive International, was passed 511 to 261, thanks largely to the backing of respectable non-Communists like Julia Varley, MP. *Pravda* was outraged at the result. A new collection of so-called 'leftists' had exposed themselves as traitors and lick-spittles. Cook's unwonted reticence on the subject of the Committee was 'completely inexplicable,' and Smith's whole argument was 'infamous'. The rank-and-file miners would not forget, the paper warned, who had stood by them so generously 'in the great months of their heroic struggle.' The Anglo-Russian solidarity then achieved would prove 'stronger than resolutions Mr Herbert Smith might force upon the miners on the orders of Lord Birkenhead.'[1] It was a suitably pitiful obituary for a policy – 14 months in the making – that had failed utterly. The blunt fact was that the MFGB could not be bought. It was a hard lesson for the Soviets to learn.

III

The proposals the General Council made in late November, 1926 for changes in the Committee constitution elicited no direct response at all from Moscow for over six weeks.[2] Indeed, they barely were mentioned. While demanding that the Committee be strengthened and denouncing the General Council for plotting to destroy it, the Russians never suggested the two sides actually meet, and insisted noisily on their duty to keep vilifying their British partners no matter what. If the TUC bureaucrats cared to retaliate for such offenses by breaking up the Committee, the Soviets virtually challenged them to do so, and suffer the wrath of their own rank and file as a consequence.[3]

The TUC responded to all the provocations with infuriating *sang*

---

[1] *Pravda*, 29, 30 July, 1927. For the MFGB Conference debates, see Miners' Federation of Great Britain, *Annual Conference, 1927. Report* (London: Cooperative Printing Society, 1927), pp. 142–57, 158–60. For the negotiations with the Russians preceding the Conference, see *The Miner*, 12 Feb. and 26 Mar., 1927. For the Comintern's June statement, see *Inprecorr*, VII, 36 (23 June, 1927), 768 (the ECCI's 'Resolution on the Situation in Great Britain').

[2] The only communication from the Central Council to the General Council during this period was a Jan. 5 Russian telegram requesting the TUC to join it in protesting the arrest and execution of Communists and left-wingers in Lithuania. (*Inprecorr*, VII, 5 [13 Jan., 1927], 97). The TUC did its protesting independently, instead, via an interview with the Lithuanian Minister and an appeal for ILO action in behalf of labour's right to organize (International Committee Minutes, 18 Jan., 1927, file 901, doc. I.C. 4 1926–7).

[3] See, for example, the *Sunday Worker*, 12, 19, 26 Dec., 1926 and 2 Jan., 1927. See also the CPGB resolution of 31 Dec., 1926 in *Ninth Congress: Reports, Theses & Resolutions*, p. 52.

froid. The whole Anglo-Russian relationship got another close going-over when the General Council met December 22.[1] The councillors even debated whether now might be the time to convene that Moscow–Amsterdam unity conference they had promised so often. The final decision, however, was to defer action until they got some Russian reaction to their proposals on the Committee constitution. In the meantime, while Tomsky was presumably making up his mind, Oudegeest might yet be persuaded to change his. The British resolved to suggest the possibility of Moscow–Amsterdam talks all over again when IFTU's General Council met in January. It was a cheap delaying tactic, the CPGB charged. To keep going back to the IFTU bureaucrats and begging was just one more 'public indication' of a General Council decision to force a break with its Soviet partners.[2]

If the comrades really believed that was what the councillors were trying to do, they were surely more convinced of it than ever after reading the *Daily Herald* for January 7. The newspaper featured a long interview with TUC General Secretary Walter Citrine, and the subject was the publication of Lozovsky's pamphlet, *British and Russian Workers*.[3] Citrine was appalled at the document. It was as if it had been written for the explicit purpose of prompting a break between the two movements. 'It could scarcely have been more violently abusive.' Lozovsky mistook 'vituperation for argument, verbosity for eloquence, and scurrility for pertinency,' and 'I think personally that the limit of our tolerance has been reached.' Lozovsky had called Pugh a liar, Purcell, Hicks and Tillett 'slippery eels,' and all the councillors 'traitors.' He charged they had transformed the Committee into a weak and ineffective instrument. 'One would imagine,' Citrine commented, 'that a committee of this description was scarcely worth keeping, . . . but Lozovsky laboriously emphasises that the proper tactics are to keep the committee in existence and appeal to the British worker over the head of the General Council.' Such tactics would not work, the General Secretary affirmed. The TUC leadership would want to know 'pretty clearly' whether Lozovsky's views were those of the Russian trade unions. If not, it would insist it 'be publicly told so.' The General Council had a perfect right to demand the Russians stop interfering in the TUC's internal affairs.

---

[1] General Council Minutes, No. 101, 22 Dec., 1926; *The Times*, 23 Dec., 1926.

[2] *Workers' Weekly*, 31 Dec., 1926; *Ninth Congress: Reports, Theses & Resolutions*, p. 51.

[3] Aleksandr Lozovsky, *British and Russian Workers* (London: National Minority Movement, [Dec., 1926]). See above, p. 300. For Citrine's own account of the circumstances surrounding the interview, see Citrine, *Men and Work*, p. 92.

According to *The Times*, the General Secretary's interview reflected not only his own judgements but those of the majority of the General Council as well.[1] Perhaps so, but three of his colleagues went to some pains to dissociate themselves from Citrine's views publicly.[2] The Council had not met since the appearance of Lozovsky's volume, R. B. Walker pointed out, so Citrine could speak only for himself. What he had said was ill-advised. It only played into the hands of labour's enemies. With the Baldwin government preparing war against the USSR, the Committee was 'more essential than ever.' Ben Tillett concurred. Only the TUC could prevent hysterical Tories from launching an armed attack on the Soviet state. Citrine should not let himself be goaded into such an unfortunate outburst. Lozovsky's 'six-month-old, stale and flatulent' bit of political invective was just 'blatant charlatanism' and of no importance at all. Hicks joined in the chorus. Citrine's reaction was understandable, he wrote, but injudicious. Russian trade union leaders did indeed indulge themselves in indiscriminate namecalling, but that was only because they were badly informed as to what was really going on in Britain.

Nerve-racking though some of his colleagues at home might find Citrine's shock-treatments, however, they seemed to produce gratifying results in Moscow. Within a matter of days, the Russians were giving those proposals for changing the Committee constitution another close look. It was about this time, and for the first time, apparently, that the Comintern apprised western comrades of the terms set by the TUC for reviving the Committee. Nobody seemed particularly happy about the proposals, *The Times* reported.[3] The Committee rules the British suggested might commit the Russian trade unions to policies quite incompatible with the procedures Profintern dictated. The General Council might even insist, for example, that Tomsky repudiate the Minority Movement. The Russians could never accept such a humiliation, *The Times* stated.

Indeed they could not, but they also had no way of knowing the TUC

1 *The Times*, 13 Jan., 1927.
2 See *Daily Herald*, 8 Jan., (Walker, Tillett, Cook) 11 Jan. (Hicks), 12 Jan. (Nathan), 13 Jan. (Davis) and 17 Jan. 1927 (Richards), Walker, Tillett, Hicks and Richards were General Council members, and of these, only Richards supported Citrine. For CPGB comment on the interview, see *Sunday Worker*, 9 Jan., 1927.
3 *The Times*, 13 Jan., 1927. *Workers' Weekly* charged, a week later (21 Jan., 1927), that Citrine had deliberately leaked the possibility of a demand for the NMM's abolition in order to sabotage talks with the Russians. It is just as possible, however, that the Soviets were nervous the British might demand such a concession, and were trying to explore the possibility by publicizing it.

really contemplated making such demands. It might be at least worth it to find out. It seems likely, in any event, that by this time the Russians had come to the realization that the Miners' Federation was not in their pocket, that the CPGB and the NMM were both fading fast, and that the connection with the General Council might therefore be worth maintaining after all. With the Chinese cauldron bubbling up towards a full head of steam again, the Stalinists could hardly afford to alienate any potential supporters in Britain – even cowards and traitors. And Vuiovič's taunt at the Comintern meeting, that since the Committee never did anything it was not really in existence anyway, must have stung. It was time to shift gingerly into reverse. It was done casually, almost off-handedly. Mel'nichansky (not the top man, Tomsky, just his deputy) wrote a letter (no telegram, therefore, presumably, no urgency) to the General Council expressing regret that the TUC had not consulted the Russians before making that unilateral decision of theirs to alter the Committee constitution. If, however, the British had set their minds on some changes, the Soviets were willing to discuss the matter. Would the General Council like to get together sometime and talk?[1]

Talk was what the councillors did best, of course, and they seemed to have an insatiable appetite for it, but Moscow would have to wait her turn. Amsterdam was next stop on the declamation schedule, with the meeting of IFTU's General Council January 13. George Hicks was there, with an eloquent plea for trade union unity and a new motion committing the Federation to an exchange of views with the Russians.[2] It was only their isolation from the rest of the trade union movement that prompted the Soviets to act like such boors, he argued. Bring them into the club and they would learn to be civilized. He assured his colleagues the Russians could not possibly dominate any all-inclusive trade union international, and begged them to relent at least enough to talk to the Reds.

It was all old hat, and they were bored with it. Stenhuis rose to move to shut off the debate, and *cloture* passed, 9 to 8. Hicks' proposal was

---

1 International Committee Minutes, 18 Jan., 1927, file 901, doc. I.C. 4 1926–7. The minutes do not reveal the date of the letter, but it was received after Jan. 8, the date of Citrine's *Daily Herald* interview (Citrine, *Men and Work*, p. 92). The TUC instructed Citrine to reply that the British proposals for constitutional changes in the Committee were not meant to preclude Russian counter-proposals, and that the British would meet providing it was clearly understood amendments to the Committee constitution were the subject for discussion.

2 See *1927 TUC: Report of Proceedings*, pp. 216–17; *The Times*, 14, 15 Jan., 1927. *Pravda* (15 Jan.) reported the story without embellishment on an inconspicuous corner of page 2. There was no suggestion the TUC had not made that motion sincerely. The editors just seemed uninterested in the story.

then quickly rejected, 12 to 6, and that was that. The British had never looked more impotent. *The Times* pronounced the whole topic of Moscow–Amsterdam talks dead. The TUC could, of course, raise the issue all over again at the IFTU's triennial Congress, in August, but it would do no better then. And if the English presumed to call a unity conference of their own, they would be rebuffed more unmistakably than ever. IFTU affiliates would simply refuse to attend.

The Times' analysis was probably accurate, but the British found it hard to take. Hicks was furious at the curt treatment he had received, and the TUC General Council voted to enter a protest with Amsterdam. 'Contrary to all accepted amenities of debate,' the British proposal had been denied a real hearing. The councillors also expressed 'regret' that the motion had not been passed, and enquired how the IFTU Executive would react if the TUC convened a Moscow–Amsterdam conference on its own responsibility? Would they be correct in assuming the IFTU Executive would refuse to participate? If so, why?[1]

The Times first pronounced the General Council's persistence 'in a losing cause' downright puzzling. Surely Amsterdam's answer was hardly in doubt. A week later, however, the correspondent reported the situation had become clearer. TUC was just looking for some way out of its pledges on east–west talks, some loophole through which it could extricate itself from those constricting commitments.[2] The writer was untypically perceptive. The Council had indeed decided that if IFTU responded negatively, it would consider the advisability of urging the Russians 'to reconsider the question of making an application to the IFTU.'[3] Since the Soviets no longer had any intention of applying for IFTU membership under any circumstances, the procedures contemplated would in fact put paid to the whole unity campaign.

Nobody told Oudegeest, however, what TUC's real intentions were. He just could not understand, therefore, why the British kept flogging a dead horse, and he wrote back February 15 inquiring.[4] Citrine's response has disappeared from the files, but whatever he said, it did not seem to convert anybody. On February 25 the Amsterdam Executive officially informed the British that it was bound by the decisions of the 1924 IFTU Congress, and by the IFTU General Council resolutions of February and December, 1925, and it could not, therefore, consent to

---

[1] International Committee Minutes, 18 Jan., 1927, file 901, doc. I.C. 4 1926–7; General Council Minutes, No. 124, 19 Jan., 1927.
[2] *The Times*, 20, 27 Jan., 1927.
[3] General Council Minutes, No. 124, 19 Jan., 1927.
[4] International Committee Minutes, 28 Feb., 1927, file 901, doc. I.C. 6 1926–7.

confer with the Russians until they announced their intention to apply for membership. The British might ask their Moscow friends, Oudegeest suggested icily, whether any such application was forthcoming.[1]

Within a matter of just hours after hearing from Amsterdam, the General Council also got word from Moscow. For over a month, the Russians had maintained their pose of nonchalance in regard to the Committee. The stiff protest note Sir Austen Chamberlain dispatched February 23 may have been what prodded them out of their inertia. By the 28th, the Soviets were telegraphing an explicit invitation to another Committee session and they wanted it quickly, too – by March 15.[2] In addition to discussing the TUC's programme for changes in the Committee constitution, and that proposed Moscow–Amsterdam unity conference, they wanted to consult on the international situation and the threat of war. The date was too early for the TUC, but the agenda was agreeable, just so long as it was understood amendments of the Committee constitution came first. The British must have been a bit bothered, however, by the Soviet suggestion they again go over the possibility of talks with the IFTU. To counter that proposition with a blunt proposal that the Russians not bother with Amsterdam any more – what the TUC had planned to do – might seem undiplomatic. Instead of following through on that idea, then, the General Council decided to refer the whole Russian problem back to the IFTU Congress, scheduled to meet in Paris in August. Maybe they could get a more constructive response there. In the meantime, they would go to Berlin and talk with Tomsky.[3]

Talking with Tomsky, however, had proved a risky business in the past. Every time British trade unionists sat down in the same room with him, they ended up surprising, embarrassing or dismaying the General Council – sometimes all three. A number of councillors – Ernest Bevin, most vociferously – therefore decided the time had come to rein in the TUC's representatives on the Committee, to make sure they said and did only what the Council majority wanted them to, no more. On Bevin's motion, the councillors had agreed, back in February, that they would give the whole subject of relations with the Russians a meticulous inspection before undertaking any further meetings with them, and that was what they proceeded to do March 22. They scrutinized the proposed agenda for the Berlin deliberations item by item, and debated and

[1] *Ibid.*; *The International Trade Union Movement* (official IFTU organ), VII, 3 (Mar., 1927), 33; *The Times*, 26 Feb., 1927.

[2] *1927 TUC: Report of Proceedings*, p. 217.

[3] International Committee Minutes, 28 Feb., 1927, file 901, doc. I.C. 6 1926–7.

decided the line the British representatives were to take on every possible point. So cautious were the councillors, and so insistent their instructions be followed to the letter, that it was doubtful, *The Times* reported, whether the Berlin meeting could achieve any positive results at all. It would surely go nowhere unless the Soviets would pledge themselves not to interfere in the TUC's domestic affairs. As far as the General Council was concerned, that was the *sine qua non* of the Committee's survival, and if the Russians stood pat on their particular version of 'proletarian internationalism,' the British were ready to rupture the relationship with them then and there.[1]

The TUC's insistence on 'trying to form a watertight constitution' for the Committee was just a waste of everybody's time, the British Communist press charged. The councillors should get on with the unity campaign and stop trying to abolish the Committee by indirection.[2] As the official trades union spokesmen saw it, however, making sure the Russians would not become 'functionally involved' in Britain's 'purely domestic affairs' was no waste of time, but hard practical politics. Once that problem was cleared up, the Committee could proceed to the matter of Moscow–Amsterdam talks, 'an undoubtedly ticklish problem,' and the tense international situation. The English expected the deliberations to produce positive results, they announced. 'All indications favour the belief the discussions will result in a real advance towards the establishment of a world-wide front against which international capitalism would hurl itself in vain.'[3]

The records of the meeting – the Committee's last formal session, as it turned out, but also the most extended – are pitifully scanty.[4] They reveal who was there, Hicks, Purcell, Swales, Findlay and Citrine for the

---

[1] So Lord Citrine told the author in Nov., 1967. For the General Council debates on relations with the Russians see General Council Minutes, No. 142, 23 Feb. and No. 169, 22 Mar., 1927 and *The Times*, 21, 23 Mar., 1927. For Bevin's sudden interest in the Committee, see Bullock, *Bevin*, I, 384–6. On the final arrangements for the meeting, see International Committee Minutes, 17 Mar., 1927, file 901, doc. I.C. 7 1926–7.

[2] *The Worker*, 1 Apr., 1927.

[3] Editorial, *The Labour Magazine*, v, 12 (Apr., 1927), 555.

[4] The only available record in English is in the TUC Archives, file 947/220, doc. A.R. 5. 1926–7. Tomsky had some very few additional comments to make on the meeting when he reported to an extraordinary plenary session of the Soviet trade unions' Central Council on 28 June 1927. See the article in *Izvestiia* for 1 July, 1927, or in *Inprecorr*, VII, 39 (7 July, 1927), 865–71. *The Worker* also reprinted Tomsky's speech: see the issues of 15, 22 July, 1927. The text of the resolutions adopted appeared in *Workers' Life*, 27 May, 1927, in *1927 TUC: Report of Proceedings*, pp. 201–2 and (last of all!) in *Inprecorr*, VII, 53 (15 Sept., 1927), 1183–9.

TUC, Tomsky, Andreev, Dogadov, Lepse and Mel'nichansky for the Russians, and they note the dates of the conference, Tuesday, 29 March–Friday, 1 April inclusive. They record the three resolutions passed, with some additional marginal gloss on one of them. They indicate the two sides contemplated another regular meeting in August, around the time of the Paris IFTU Congress. But that is as far as they go. Both parties were aware, apparently, that to keep any verbatim account of the proceedings might tempt them to speak to posterity rather than to one another. They agreed, therefore, on the very first day, to confine the written record to summary minutes.

How the debate developed, therefore, may never be known, but that Tomsky ended up giving the British virtually everything they wanted is patently obvious. Even he would admit, later on, to having made 'very considerable concessions' at Berlin. The English, he reported, were really only there just to try to persuade the Soviets not to scold them as roundly as they had after the general strike. 'You must moderate your abuse a little,' Tomsky recalled them saying. 'It makes a very bad impression on "public opinion" in Great Britain when you abuse us and mention names.' Somebody doubtless brought up Lozovsky's pamphlet, *British and Russian Workers* – the subject of Citrine's caustic *Daily Herald* interview. Lord Citrine recollected, much later, calling Tomsky's attention to the 'intolerably abusive' prose in that document, and getting the response, 'Oh, that's just Lozovsky. Well what can you expect from Lozovsky!' Such a rejoinder must have been a real debate-stopper![1] The British, however, persisted, and although they did not get Russian assent to the precise wordings proposed back in November, the resolution passed must have been very gratifying.

It came in eight parts. It began by reaffirming the commitment of both sides to trade union internationalism, and proposed the 'firm fraternal union' of the English and Soviet labour organizations as an 'essential condition for success' in the struggle to unite 'Labour against Capitalism' all over the world. The 'existing friendly relations between the two movements' should therefore be strengthened, and they should move toward 'more active mutual aid and support.' It was especially 'valuable and necessary,' however, that the two sides try to coordinate their activities 'in the sphere of international policy.' All that verbiage was a sop to the Russians who, Tomsky testified later, were still hoping to make the

---

[1] The Tomsky quotation was recalled to the author by Lord Citrine in 1967. Tomsky's own recollections of the meeting are from his report to the Central Council in June, *Izvestiia*, 1 July, 1927.

Committee over into a truly active and decisive organization. It took a lot of persuasion to get the English to endorse those words, he recalled. Perhaps so, but it is also true that the bread the TUC thus cast upon the waters came back looking like fillet steak. The Russians promised 'unconditional recognition of the principle' that the 'Trades Union Congress and its General Council' was 'the sole representative and medium of expression of the Trade Union Movement of Great Britain.' They agreed their 'fraternal alliance...cannot and must not in any degree whatsoever impair the internal authority of the...General Council...or infringe or limit their rights and autonomy...or allow any intervention in their internal affairs.' The Committee would henceforth limit its deliberations to an agreed agenda, drawn up in advance – and in precise detail – by the chairmen and secretaries of the two organizations. If an agenda item was not agreeable to both sides, the Russians promised to accept that decision 'in a proper spirit' and not 'to exploit the situation by public reference to the matter.' Those words were not part of the official text of the resolution adopted, but they were recorded in the minutes, on the insistence of the British, as part of the agreement. The Soviets were not to cite anything said in the preliminary conference on the agenda in order to score propaganda points against the General Council. Those sessions would, then, be considered 'closed,' and after considerable wrangling, Tomsky agreed to accept 'the consequences that would arise therefrom.' The two sides decided to put together the various resolutions they had passed concerning the Committee and its functions into a single document, and directed the secretaries of the two organizations to prepare a possible draft. The resolution then concluded on a positive note, expressing the conviction of the Committee that the two trade union movements would draw closer together in the future and that they would persist 'unwaveringly' in the struggle for international labour unity.

The revision of the Committee constitution was what the British had come to Berlin for, but they picked up a nice bonus, as well, in a second resolution adopted, on international unity. The statement expressed the Committee's deep regrets that the 'controlling bodies' of IFTU had stifled the campaign for labour solidarity by their 'complete unwillingness' to engage in talks with the Russians, and acknowledged that barring some change in Amsterdam policy, 'further efforts' by the British to convene such a conference 'would evidently not be successful.' The delegates agreed 'to return to the discussion of this question before or immediately following the forthcoming Paris Congress' of the Amsterdam Federation. Without unduly emphasizing the fact, then, the resolution finally released the General Council from that two-year-old, unfulfilled, and increasingly mortifying promise to summon a Moscow–Amsterdam conference on its own initiative if IFTU refused to agree to one voluntarily. The British, of course, no longer had any intention of keeping that pledge anyway. In effect, the Russians had now agreed not to chivvy them about their delinquency.

In return for all they got, the British had to give a little, and what they gave was recorded in the third resolution, ostensibly a review of the work of the Committee since its foundation. The declaration repeated all the familiar old slogans about the dangers of the capitalist offensive. It noted the continued growth of fascism, militarism and imperialism since the two sides first met, and cited the dangers of capitalist war-mongering in Nicaragua, Albania, Corfu and – most of all – China. Labour had to unite, to defend itself against capitalist, fascist chauvinists. Close ties between the English and Russian trade union movements were especially important, 'as recent events have most clearly shown, in averting the danger of aggression against the Soviet Union, the home of the first Workers' Republic.' An attack on the USSR 'would give rise to another Great War, condemning the workers of both countries to suffering and privations.' It was a major responsibility of the Committee to help prevent such an attack.

That, of course, was just the sort of commitment Stalin wanted. He had undoubtedly hoped for a good deal stronger statement on China, however, and Tomsky did make an effort to get one. He urged a joint protest on the British bombardment of Nanking, an atrocity he tried to document on the basis of evidence cabled in from the Soviet Foreign Office. The British, however, wired back to London, and discovered the stories of the bombardment circulating there were not quite the same as those current in Moscow. No resolution, therefore, could be agreed upon. 'It was the greatest concession we ever made,' Tomsky recalled later, 'that we did not take them by the throat, so to speak, then and there, and demand: "Deal with China, make a clear statement about the situation in China!" Instead, we contented ourselves with that reference to China in the general resolution.'[1] The English felt ill-at-ease with genuine political issues, Tomsky concluded, and it was considerably of an achievement, therefore, to get them to put their names to anything positive at all.

---

[1] *Izvestiia, loc. cit.* For evidence on the Narkomindel effort to sell the TUC its version of the events in China, see Chamberlain to Rozengolts 26 May, 1927, *Russia No. 3 (1927)*, Cmd. 2895, pp. 69–70.

Three months later, Tomsky undertook a concise summary of what he thought the Committee had achieved at Berlin. The Russians pledged themselves, he conceded, 'to treat the General Council carefully,' but the English, in turn, promised to help make the Committee over into a more active organization, 'in particular with regard to the struggle against the danger of war.' The TUC would help further Soviet foreign policy objectives, then, in return for a better press in the USSR. But, Tomsky continued, the Russians never gave up their right to find fault with the General Council, and their right to express their opinions freely. 'None of us ever dreamed of such a thing. . . It never occurred to us to abandon our right to criticize.'[1]

One doubts he made the point that strongly at Berlin, however, or the British would not have been so pleased with what they had achieved. 'We never chortled' about the agreement, Lord Citrine said later on. The Russians had not 'capitulated,' and the problem of enforcing the understanding reached was self-evident all along. Nevertheless, the two sides had achieved what seemed to be a meeting of the minds, and the statement they issued to the press April 1 reflected their mutual satisfaction. They announced 'complete unanimity' had been achieved on all topics. The Committee proceedings had been 'cordial throughout' and 'marked by an appreciation of the need for maintaining and still further strengthening the fraternal ties' between the two movements.[2]

The Committee's succinct and cryptic statement was hardly calculated to set off a run on the newspaper stands, and for the next few days, almost nothing appeared in the press about the Berlin meeting. Tomsky's arrival back in Moscow was made the occasion for a brief statement in the Soviet dailies, but aside from a few conventionally harsh words about Amsterdam, capitalists, and imperialism, he had little to say.[3] His major concern seemed to be to establish that the Committee 'does exist and will continue to exist,' contrary to Vuiovič's slanderous allegations at the recent Comintern meeting. Vuiovič was not mentioned by name, however, only 'enemies of the working class,' whose hopes for the Committee's dissolution had now been 'completely shattered,' according to Tomsky. The Anglo-Russian alliance had been useful in the past, he argued, and would continue to play a functional role in the future.

The story in *The Times*, the same day, was a good deal more eye-catching.[4] Perhaps Citrine was not 'chortling' about those Russian concessions – not in public, anyway – but at least one of his colleagues must

---

[1] *Izvestiia, loc. cit.*   [2] *Pravda, Daily Herald*, 2 Apr., 1927.
[3] *Pravda*, 5 Apr., 1927.   [4] *The Times*, 5 Apr., 1927.

have found outwitting the Russians irresistibly delightful, and blurted out his glee to a reporter. The piece was headlined 'Russian Unions' Surrender' and if Trotsky saw it, it must have made his day. The Soviets had caved in completely at Berlin, the correspondent reported. They had taken back all those tough words of the year before. They had agreed never to interfere in the British labour movement again, and they had raised no objection at all when the TUC reneged on its pledge to convene a Moscow–Amsterdam conference. The only explanation for such a complete capitulation was that the Russians were desperate for support in the Chinese crisis.

The Times' account must have rankled them back in Moscow. The Berlin resolutions might not be everything one might have hoped for, but they were hardly a 'surrender' and the best way to prove it was to make them public as quickly as possible. Tomsky fired off a telegram to the TUC urging quick ratification of the statements and asking permission to publish them immediately in the USSR.[1] The General Council responded at its meeting April 13. Not all the councillors, obviously, were prepared to accept the texts offered them as evidence of any Russian 'capitulation.' The rumour that percolated back to Moscow was that it was only after 'the very greatest difficulties' that the Council endorsed the statements on China, on the war danger, and on the expansion of the functions of the Committee.[2] The minutes indicate just that the Committee report was finally adopted, with two negative votes recorded. Past Soviet sins were now to be forgiven, and the absolution was formalized by putting the Russian trade union federation back on the list of organizations invited to send fraternal delegations to the September Congress.[3] The texts of the Berlin resolutions were released to the press two days later. *The Times* printed the story with very little comment, and no more talk of 'surrender.' The CPGB press praised the agreements, and termed them a real 'eye-opener to many leaders of the Amsterdam International' who had assumed, and hoped, the Committee was dead.[4]

The Politburo majority, and those who followed its lead, might find the resolutions acceptable: the Opposition found them inexcusable and intolerable. Trotsky and his allies had been uncharacteristically self-controlled over the winter of 1926–7. They had scarcely been heard from at all for some three months, not since the December meeting of the Comintern's Enlarged Executive. A CPSU Central Committee plenum

[1] International Committee Minutes, 11 Apr., 1927, file 901, doc. I.C. 8 1926–7.
[2] *Izvestiia*, 1 July, 1927. [3] General Council Minutes, No. 191, 192, 13 Apr., 1927.
[4] *The Times*, 16 Apr., 1927; *Workers' Life*, 27 Apr., 1927.

in February had been so uneventful as to be almost dull. It was as if the Opposition had gone into hibernation. Now, however, it was spring, the political sap was rising, and Trotsky had two first-rate new examples of Stalinist incompetence to trumpet. One was the Russian failure in China. The other was the ignominious Committee meeting in Berlin.

Trotskyites were gagging at the drivel the Committee released to the press even before they were made privy to the greater enormities embodied in the resolutions. It was just disgusting to talk about 'full unanimity' and 'cordial understanding' with the likes of 'the notorious Citrine,' a German Opposition group charged.[1] For all the unprincipled 'secret diplomacy' at Berlin, it was patently obvious that nothing of any importance had come of all the talk. The Russians should insist on another meeting immediately, at which they would demand TUC participation in a militant action programme. When the General Council vetoed that programme – as of course, being reformist traitors, they would – the Committee could be dissolved immediately, and with fanfare. Revolutionaries would be better off without it.

Trotsky got his chance to make that case in person April 13–16, when a CPSU Central Committee plenum met to consider international questions generally – with special reference to China – and to hear reports from Tomsky, Andreev and Mel'nichansky on their sessions with the English at Berlin.[2] Trotsky was ready, armed with a draft resolution

[1] The quotations are from an Opposition resolution presented to the Berlin Party Workers' Conference of the German Communist Party in April, 1927. The date is not provided, but the text indicates a date between Apr. 1 (when the press release appeared) and Apr. 15 (when the resolutions themselves were made public). The full text of the document is in *Der Kampf um die Kommunistische Internationale: Dokumente der russischen Opposition nicht veröffentlicht vom Stalin'schen ZK* (Berlin: Fahne des Kommunismus, [1928]), p. 173. The word in the press release that most enraged the Trotskyites was clearly the adjective 'cordial.' Forty years after the event, with a rueful smile, Andrew Rothstein admitted full responsibility for selecting the unfortunate expression. He served at Berlin as official translator for the Russian delegation.

[2] Information on the plenum is scanty. Even so careful a scholar as Isaac Deutscher was apparently unaware of its existence. He claimed (*Trotsky*, pp. 333–8) that the Opposition was unable to force a debate on the issues of England or China from October, 1926 until the 8th ECCI in May, 1927. Stalin refused to call a Central Committee meeting to debate those matters, he says. In fact, those were precisely the two issues to which the April plenum was devoted, but we have no precise record of exactly what was said. *Pravda* published a brief bulletin on the plenum 19 Apr., 1927, which is cited in *KPSS v Rezoliutsiiakh*, II, 238. *Inprecorr* revealed nothing at all. I have had to rely, therefore, on the materials in the Trotsky Archives: the draft resolution he presented the plenum, T–3045, 15 April, 1927, T–3046, 16 April, 1927 and his references to the meeting in T–3058, 16 May, 1927 and T–3093, 25 Sept., 1927.

rejecting the Berlin agreements and scolding the men who had made them. The pledge of non-interference in the TUC's 'domestic affairs' he found particularly offensive. It amounted to a capitulation, a betrayal of the first principles of proletarian internationalism. In view of the General Council's refusal to accept Russian money during the general strike, and its subsequent rejection of all Soviet proposals for joint action in behalf of the miners, securing its commitment to 'mutual aid and support' was a mockery, he charged. The Council was simply a collection of well-placed strikebreakers. For Tomsky to recognize it as the 'sole medium of expression' of British trades unionism meant that Soviet trade unionists would have to go along with the councillors, from now on, whenever they decided to break a strike. It was absurd for revolutionaries to put themselves in such a position. To assume further, as the Berlin agreements did, that the General Council strikebreakers could help create some fighting new trade union international was just ludicrous. The anti-war resolutions agreed to were a swindle, a typical bit of pacifist deception designed to lull the proletariat to sleep and leave it unprepared to act when the critical moment came. All one could ever expect from the likes of Hicks, Swales and Citrine was betrayal. All they did was trail along after MacDonald and make secret deals with the Tories at the expense of their own followers. They would be no more reliable in the event of a war emergency.

The effort to preserve the Committee, while preserving as well the right to revolutionary criticism of the General Council leaders, had failed. All the talk of 'unanimity' and 'mutual understanding' and 'cordial ties' had only served to rehabilitate and legitimize the Council renegades. Such phrases struck a particularly severe blow at the Minority Movement. So long as accredited Russian revolutionaries could assure the world they were on such good terms with the councillors, what excuse could the NMM present for recommending they all be ousted? What revolutionary trade unionists in Britain wanted – and there were more and more of them – was an opportunity to wage direct war on the TUC's 'left' wing. The continued existence of the Committee just frustrated their efforts. To become involved in some bureaucratic hocus-pocus about codifying all the Committee's resolutions, or to get concerned all over again with those stereotyped pledges on trade union unity, was just to waste time. The Committee should be liquidated forthwith.

It was a formidable brief, and Trotsky apparently had little to add to it orally. He was convinced the Committee would not last anyway. If it was to go, it was wiser for the Soviets to rupture it now, at a time convenient for them and over issues of their own choosing, rather than leave it to the English to break up later, at some more critical moment. He scoffed at the efforts to defend the Berlin resolutions on the basis of those few phrases of protest against 'the policy of the imperialists in China.' It was all just words. The General Council had consistently refused to risk any action against British imperialism, he pointed out, and it was unlikely to be any more venturesome in the future. Perhaps it meant something, he suggested, that the British had signed that Berlin agreement on April Fools' Day. 'It means we fooled them!' growled Kaganovich from his chair.[1]

The defence of the Berlin accords at the Central Committee meeting was entrusted exclusively to trade unionists. The Opposition, they charged, was 'hopelessly mired in the swamp of its own mistakes.' The Russians had not lost at Berlin; they had won. They sought, for example, a direct and clear statement from the English on the future of the Committee, and they had got one: the TUC had committed itself not only to continue the organization but to make it truly active. The Russians had also hoped to persuade the TUC to recognize the dangers of war and imperialism, and the English had done so – not in 100 per cent Bolshevik phraseology, naturally, but the best possible result under the given circumstances. Trotsky just did not understand trade union ways in these matters, the Berlin negotiators charged. One had to work with the existing leadership, however distasteful, and one had to achieve unanimity as best one could. One could not, therefore, expect to achieve everything one might hope for. One worked for the best compromise arrangement available. The Berlin accords were a very good compromise. To reject them, to break with the English trade unionists and thus cut them off at the very moment when imperialists were mobilizing against the USSR, would be thoughtless and dangerous.

The Central Committee majority felt the same way, of course, and the Berlin resolutions were not repudiated. Whether Tomsky and his trade union colleagues found that result particularly gratifying, however, is problematical. Significantly, nobody from outside their ranks had risked coming forward to endorse the Berlin accords personally. The statement appearing in *Pravda*, announcing that the Central Committee had 'approved' the Politburo's policies in international questions generally, went on to say only that the Committee had 'heard' the report of the trade unionists on the meeting with the English. It could hardly be taken

---

[1] Trotsky Archives, T–3093, 25 Sept., 1927, citing p. 31 of the unpublished stenographic report of the plenum.

as a resounding vote of confidence, and Tomsky may have suspected that if anything went wrong, Stalin was ready to disown the Berlin agreements and blame them all on him. Trotsky was concerned about that possibility:[1] it would have been surprising if it had not occurred to Tomsky. Some defensive manoeuvring was in order. He had left himself particularly vulnerable, obviously, when he pledged not to interfere in the TUC's 'internal affairs.' He had to prove, somehow, that that under-taking would not inhibit him in the slightest from meeting his obligation, as a good Bolshevik, to throw mud at social-democratic, reformist class traitors. He proved it by his famous *Workers' Life* interview of May 13.[2]

It was datelined Moscow, May 8 and entitled ' "A Bill to Crush the Workers." – Tomsky.' The subject was the Tory government's trades union bill,[3] and Tomsky complained that the TUC had not done all it could to stop the legislation. 'Certain leaders' would apparently 'be very little grieved' if it went through – the same people who, a year earlier, 'were not sorry to defeat the General Strike and later the miners' strike.' Tomsky named some names – MacDonald (a familiar villain), Havelock Wilson of the 'unpolitical' Seamen's Union, and J. H. Thomas, 'the King's Privy Councillor' who found the class struggle so 'vexing.' Thomas was the only General Council member specified, although Tomsky said 'many others' on that body must secretly favour the legislation. Why else would they not resist it more energetically? To struggle against the bill 'only or mainly by Parliamentary methods' was 'tantamount to the renunciation of the struggle' and 'a preliminary to defeat.' Instead of launching a vigorous and militant campaign against the union-bashers, however, instead of mobilizing 'against the onslaught of the capitalists,' the General Council had turned its attention to waging war on the left, to baiting 'Communists and the revolutionary minority.' It was a 'disgraceful' performance, 'the greatest and most unpardonable mistake' the General Council ever made. Once the British proletarians

---

[1] *Ibid.*, T–948, Trotsky to T. Tsardim (?) (manuscript indecipherable), 26 Apr., 1927.
[2] *Workers' Life*, 13 May, 1927. The interview was not printed in an especially con-spicuous location; it was under a two-column headline on p. 2. It had appeared a day earlier – in a slightly different translation – in *Inprecorr*, vii, 29 (12 May, 1927), 587–8, and was datelined Moscow, May 8. It must have been designed specifically for British consumption, or it would not have gotten into the hands of the CPGB editors so quickly. One doubts, in retrospect, that it ever would have been printed if Tomsky could have foreseen the Arcos raid May 12. By that time, of course, it was too late to call the item back. The most readily available source for the whole *Workers' Life* incident – the interview itself plus the subsequent correspondence on it, is *1927 TUC: Report of Proceedings*, pp. 207–10.
[3] See above, pp. 315–6.

found the right leaders, they would oust 'the traitors within their own camp' and get on with the neglected job of fighting their class enemies.

The correspondent of *The Times* was obviously thrilled with the interview. There it was, a 'clear transgression' of that non-intervention pledge Tomsky made at Berlin, and within just a month of the ratification of the agreement.[1] How would the TUC respond? The response, in fact, was deliberate, measured and cautious. Citrine wrote it up and sent it off within the week, on his own initiative.[2] He reminded the Russians of their promise not to intrude themselves into the TUC's internal affairs. In view of that commitment, he continued, he could not believe that the responsible leader of Soviet trades unionism could possibly have expressed the views attributed to him in *Workers' Life*. The article must be a 'travesty' of Tomsky's 'real' speech. It would be helpful to the councillors to know the extent to which the remarks attributed to him in *Workers' Life* really represented Tomsky's views.

Citrine was offering Tomsky an opportunity to make a graceful retreat. The whole untoward incident could be blamed on some anonymous translator. The Russian did not rise to the bait. His reply, some 18 days later, was blunt, unyielding and belligerent.[3] The article rendered the text of his remarks substantially accurately, Tomsky began. He was surprised that the General Council wanted to waste its time discussing it, however. Surely the councillors had 'more important and more vital work to do,' like planning how to sabotage the Baldwin government's war preparations. He certainly did not deny, however, the councillors' right to consider anything they wanted – even his pamphlets, if that suited them. Nevertheless, he continued, 'I must decidedly object to the claim on anybody's part to limit my personal freedom of speech or to establish any control over it.' He would account to the Russian trade unions, to the Communist Party, and to the 'labouring masses' for the content of his speeches, but to agree to renounce his convictions to suit the fancy of the General Council would be 'monstrous.' The Berlin resolutions never implied any control over his 'personal utterances.'

Tomsky had won his battle – and lost the war. True enough, Oppositionists back home would never again be able to accuse him of sparing his friends on the General Council the therapeutic shock-treatment of Bolshevik invective. But to establish his orthodoxy in Russia, Tomsky had had to surrender his credibility in Britain. The TUC leadership would never trust him again, and the possibility of resurrecting the Com-

---

[1] *The Times*, 17 May, 1927.   [2] *1927 TUC: Report of Proceedings*, p. 209.
[3] *Ibid.*, pp. 209–10.

mittee as a viable instrument of Anglo-Russian cooperation was practically nil.

Tomsky could hardly have known, on May 8, when he granted his 'interview,' that he had picked the worst possible time to compromise his arrangements with the General Council. On May 12, at 4 o'clock in the morning, British plainclothesmen burst into the Moorgate offices of Arcos Ltd., the Russian state trading agency.[1] Those ubiquitous snoopers in the secret service had reported that an Arcos employee was in possession of a missing official document. The cabinet diehards, ecstatic at the newest evidence of Communist chicanery, had demanded action. Chamberlain had caved in and given his consent. The search warrant authorized the police not only to inspect the Arcos premises but also to search the headquarters of the official Soviet trade delegation, housed in the same building. The raiders' unexpected appearance created gratifying disarray among the few suspicious-looking characters still around at that unspeakable hour. Some of them were caught trying to make a bonfire of the evidences of their wickedness.

The investigators happily ransacked the place for three full days. The mysterious missing document never showed up, but the intelligence people carted off everything they could find that looked incriminating and sifted through it all from the 15th to the 18th. It was a disappointing jackpot. It did establish that one Arcos employee had recruited some seamen for the National Minority Movement. It indicated the trade delegation had been used as a channel for transmitting Profintern manifestos

---

[1] The Arcos affair, and the subsequent expulsion of the Soviet diplomatic mission, are best followed via the Commons debates, 206 H.C. Deb. 5 s. at cc. 799–804, 914–20, 1170–2, 1344–8, 1816–17, 1850–62, 2015–18, 2203–34. The *Annual Register, 1927* summarizes events on pp. 45–51, and *The Times*, 13–27 May, 1927, is helpful. The final diplomatic exchanges are most readily accessible in *Russia No. 3*, Cmd. 2895, pp. 69–72. The relevant cabinet documents available are Cabinet Conclusions, 1927, Conclusions 32(27)2, 19 May, 1927 (with annex), 33(27)1, 23 May, 1927 and 34(27)1, 25 May, 1927. Conclusion 32(27)1 indicates no decision to make a diplomatic break had been made as late as 19 May, which is confirmed by the cover comment on N 2289/2187/38, 18 May, 1927, F.O. 371.12602 (Scotland Yard Special Branch's report on the Arcos raid). That the decision to break was a foregone conclusion May 22, the day before the cabinet finally made it, is indicated by Preston to Chamberlain, 8 June, 1927, N 3004/209/38, F.O. 371.12593, which refers to a 22 May message from the Moscow embassy to the Leningrad consulate to prepare for immediate evacuation. The Arcos documents, or such of them as the government saw fit to print, are in Great Britain, Foreign Office, *Russia No. 2 (1927). Documents Illustrating the Hostile Activities of the Soviet Government and Third International against Great Britain*, Cmd. 2874 (London: H.M.S.O., 1927). It amounts to a collection of trivia. For a sane overview of the whole incident, see Fischer, *Soviets in World Affairs*, ii, 680–98.

on the Hands Off China campaign and the agitation against the
trades union bill. The investigators could find nothing, however, linking
the Soviet diplomatic mission to any irregular proceedings, and as late
as May 19, the cabinet was still debating just the status of the trade
delegation. The diehards had to concoct a better case for themselves than
the documents warranted, but they were an indefatigable lot and managed it. By May 22, after some miraculously efficacious last-minute
exertions, somebody was able to locate 'overwhelming secret evidence
of unquestionable authenticity' to prove the Soviet *chargé d'affaires* and
his staff 'had also been engaged in interference in the affairs of this
country,' and the cabinet meeting the following day resolved to break
with the USSR altogether. The government announced its intentions
May 23 and the crucial Commons debate was set for the 26th. Clynes
presented the opposition's case, with wooden reserve, stressing the unfortunate economic impact of losing Russian orders. Lloyd George was
brilliant, and the ILP's Maxton magnificent, but the result was a foregone conclusion. Commander Locker-Lampson assured his colleagues,
in his roundest Albert Hall periods, that once they did their duty and
cut the cable to Moscow, that 'monstrous idol' – Bolshevism – would be
doomed forthwith. The government won, 377 to 111, and the Soviets
were ordered out a day later.

It was for use in just such circumstances, of course, that Stalin had
insisted on preserving the Anglo-Russian Committee. Within a matter
of hours after hearing of the Arcos raid, Tomsky was wiring Citrine
suggesting the Committee meet to discuss the crisis.[1] The British leaders
were preparing an armed attack on the USSR, he charged. Proletarians
everywhere should work out some concerted response to the menace. If,
of course, the General Council did not consider a Committee meeting
possible for some reason or another, the Soviets would not insist on one.
They assumed the General Council would, in any event, 'fulfill its
fraternal obligation and raise its voice emphatically against the policy
of... aggression against the USSR.'

Citrine, in fact, had already protested the Arcos incident, in a letter
to the Prime Minister dated May 13.[2] It was hardly a strong protest, and
one can even understand Tomsky's later characterization of it as 'a
toothless, drivelling, double-faced document.'[3] But Citrine was in a diffi-

---

[1] *Pravda*, 18 June, 1927, provides the Russian text. For English translations, see
Inprecorr, VII, 36 (23 June, 1927), 753–4 or *The Times*, 28 June, 1927.
[2] *1927 TUC: Report of Proceedings*, p. 213.
[3] Quoted in *The Times*, 5 July, 1927; for confirmation see *Izvestiia*, 1 July, 1927.

cult position. J. H. Thomas, for example, deemed it presumptuous of the General Secretary to make any statement at all on the raid without first consulting the General Council, and dressed him down for his fore-handedness.[1] Thomas was in no mood to do the Russians any favours. He had been, after all, a major target of that *Workers' Life* interview, and that still rankled. On his recommendation, the General Council's International Committee voted May 23 not to have anything more to do with the Russians until Tomsky provided some satisfactory explanation of his indiscretion. Even Purcell went along with the freeze, tabling a motion agreeing 'no object would be served' in convening another Committee meeting over the Arcos crisis.[2]

Within a matter of hours of that decision, Baldwin announced his intention to break diplomatic relations with the USSR. Tomsky promptly telegraphed a second, more urgent plea for an immediate meeting of the Committee,[3] but it only arrived after the General Council had made other, rather different plans for protesting the break. The councillors instructed all members of the International Committee to put in an appearance in the Commons' gallery May 26 – when the Prime Minister was to make his statement on the rupture – as an expression of the TUC's concern. They were then to consult with the Parliamentary Labour party, and were authorized to make any statement both sides deemed appropriate.[4]

The plan produced a lot of officious bustling about, but very little action. The Labour members of Commons were too preoccupied to be able to arrange a conference with the trade unionists on the 26th, and when they did meet, the next morning, the MPs would only agree some joint statement should be drafted sometime later on. They all then proceeded to a luncheon, at which Hicks presided, honouring Soviet *chargé d'affaires* Rozengolts and bidding him farewell. The prandial gesture might have carried more symbolic weight had the participants not tried – unsuccessfully – to keep the news of their banquet quiet.[5] Tomsky scoffed at the whole ceremony, which he erroneously reported as a breakfast. 'Admittedly' he said, 'for certain people with a certain mentality

[1] International Committee Minutes, 23 May, 1927, file 901, doc. I.C. 10 1926–7.
[2] *Ibid.* The Russians almost immediately (and accurately, this time) attributed the General Council's lack of support to Thomas. Baldwin had counted on Thomas's backing when he decided on the break, the Soviets charged. *Pravda*, 31 May, 1927.
[3] *Pravda*, 18 June, 1927; *The Times*, 27 June, 1927.
[4] General Council Minutes, No. 225, 25 May, 1927. For the story of the International Committee's subsequent fumblings, see its Minutes for 2 June, 1927, file 901, doc. I.C. 11 1926–7.
[5] *The Times*, 28 May, 1927, reported the event a day later, with a complete guest list.

and under certain conditions, even a breakfast is to a certain extent a revolutionary act. It is possible that for some people a breakfast with Comrade Rozengolts is a very definitely revolutionary act, but. . .it is hardly an act demanding any great sacrifices from the participants.'[1]

The trade unionists, of course, had not intended it to seem as though their concern over the diplomatic break ended with the last sip of after-dinner coffee. They kept pressing the Parliamentary party to work out that joint statement with them, but the politicians resisted. The MPs vetoed any meeting of the National Joint Council,[2] refused to convene the Labour party Executive, and finally just suggested the TUC issue its own statement on the break. Hicks, Pugh and Citrine eventually came up with a draft so innocuous even a suspicious J. H. Thomas found he could back it. It was released to the press June 9, over two weeks after the diplomatic rupture was first announced. It argued that the evidence the government presented hardly justified the 'grave step' it had decreed in response. It called the break a 'menace to the world's peace' and entered its 'vigorous protest.' Most of all, the TUC deplored the economic losses the break would entail, a catalogue of which took up fully two-thirds of the text. It concluded by expressing the TUC's hope 'that Russia will rise superior to retaliatory desires, . . .inspire the confidence of the people of the world, and play her full part in the establishment of peace. . .among the nations.'[3] Such sentimental bilge would hardly wash down well in Moscow, but as far as the trade unionists were concerned, they had now done everything possible in behalf of their Russian associates, and they could turn their attention to other matters.

Tomsky was not one to be shunted aside so casually. The TUC had informed him as early as May 28 that his second bid for a Committee meeting, the one he wired May 25, was going to be rebuffed as stonily as had his first, gentler overture. It was time to speak with emphasis. A long letter dispatched June 3 pronounced the international situation 'very serious.' It was perfectly clear, Tomsky charged, that the Tories were trying to force the Soviet Union into a war. 'All that remains ob-

---

[1] *Izvestiia*, 1 July, 1927.
[2] The NJC was the official coordinating body of the Labour party and the trade union movement.
[3] International Committee Minutes, 9 June, 1927, file 901, doc. I.C. 12 1926–7; *1927 TUC: Report of Proceedings*, pp. 214–15. For a characteristic Soviet analysis of the document, see Volkov, *Anglo-Sovetskie Otnosheniia*, pp. 313–14. Deutscher (*Trotsky*, p. 348) erred when he said that TUC 'had not uttered even a word of protest' over the diplomatic break. The words were not very impressive, but there were some. *The Labour Magazine*, vi, 2 (June, 1927), 72–4 – a joint TUC–Labour party organ – also carried an editorial opposing the rupture.

scure is where the attack will take place, and when.' The Committee
had a clear responsibility to map out an active programme against the
war menace. The Russians expected an immediate answer from the
TUC, agreeing to a meeting and setting an early date for it.[1]

While Tomsky put the pressure on from Moscow, the CPGB applied
it at home. The General Council's lethargy in the face of the critical war
danger and its persistent sabotage of the Committee were intolerable,
the Party fumed.[2] Apathetic and inert today, 'MacDonald, Henderson,
Clynes, Thomas, Hicks and Company' would probably turn out to be
'Baldwin's recruiting sergeants tomorrow.' The CPGB urged the establishment of new Councils of Action to thwart the warmongers, and
announced plans to call another general strike if Baldwin persisted in his
anti-Soviet jingoism. Looking back on the campaign, several months
later, the Party noted with satisfaction that its efforts had produced
'scores of resolutions' against the war threat, demonstrating 'that there
was a widespread understanding among the workers of the need to
fight the break.'[3]

The Soviets were depending on that support. They admitted it from
the beginning. Their millions of proletarian friends abroad would once
again have to rescue them from the machinations of the bourgeois
militarists, just as they had in 1920. Tomsky himself said so – without
specifically mentioning the Committee, incidentally – the very day after
the diplomatic break.[4] So long as proletarians maintained their class
solidarity, *Pravda*'s editorialist promised, the imperialists were helpless.
But Baldwin had his allies among the workers, the social-democratic
reformists who would try to break the united proletarian front just as
they had in August, 1914. Russia's true friends had to rebuff all compromisers and all pacifist dreamers. They had to organize, class against
class, and prepare now, while there was still time, to 'turn the imperialist
war...into a social revolution.'

It is hard to assess how much the Russian leaders themselves believed
all the war talk.[5] The newspapers were certainly full of it, and Comintern

---

[1] The texts of the correspondence referred to in this paragraph may be found in
Pravda, 18 June, 1927 or *The Times*, 27 June, 1927.

[2] *Workers' Life*, 3 June, 1927.

[3] *Ninth Congress: Reports, Theses & Resolutions*, p. 54.

[4] *Izvestiia*, 29 May, 1927. For what follows in this paragraph, see *Pravda*'s editorial,
'After the Break,' 29 May, 1927, and *Pravda*, 18, 19 June, 1927 or *Inprecorr*, VII,
37 (30 June, 1927), 774ff. (Bukharin's report to the Moscow CPSU Committee on
the 8th ECCI).

[5] There is a good analysis of the problem in Fischer, *Stalin and German Communism*,
pp. 579–602.

sounded the tocsin with ear-splitting stridency over and over again. The set-backs in China, the break with London, the assassination a few days later of the Soviet ambassador in Warsaw by a monarchist émigré – if one was of a mind to put two and two together and come up with 22, it all smacked of a plot. The Soviet people were apparently convinced. Louis Fischer, thinking back on it much later, recalled how his acquaintances in Moscow were all terrified, and kept asking him when and where he expected the ferocious capitalist onslaught to begin. Peasants began to hoard salt, he reported, their traditional response to a war crisis, and anxious villagers held back grain deliveries to the city, just in case. In fact, Fischer concluded, Stalin manufactured the panic deliberately, to get at Trotsky. No less an authority than Foreign Commissar Chicherin told him so, he testified. Chicherin had been in western Europe when the break came with England, and when he got back to Moscow, everybody was talking war. 'I tried to dissuade them,' Chicherin confided to Fischer. ' "Nobody is trying to attack us," I insisted. But then a colleague en-enlightened me. He said, "Sh! We know. But we need this against Trotzky." '[1]

Whether the Stalinists were indeed all that diabolical is problematical. More probably, they just saw an opportunity and they took it. What with the Russian humiliations in China and Tomsky's ill-advised 'cordialities' at Berlin, Trotsky was beginning to draw blood. A first-class war crisis might emasculate the ogre for good. A nation in mortal danger from its enemies abroad could hardly afford the luxury of Oppositionists at home. Indeed, any Oppositionist who insisted on continuing to oppose might seem to be in league with those foreign enemies. It surely was no accident that Stalin's first move, on hearing of Britain's decision to make the diplomatic break, was to go before the Comintern's Executive Committee and announce the formation of 'something like a united front from Chamberlain to Trotsky.'[2] To threaten the USSR with political faction-

---

[1] Louis Fischer, *Men and Politics* (New York: Duell, Sloan & Pearce, 1941), pp. 88–9. One problem with Fischer's theory is that not all Soviet leaders were trumpeting the imminence of war in June of 1927. Voroshilov, for example, on June 9, said the USSR was 'approaching' a time when her class enemies would inevitably force her into hostilities, but said Britain was not strong enough to launch the attack yet and that it would not come for another 'one or two years.' War in 1927 was 'unlikely'. *Inprecorr*, VII, 36 (23 June, 1927), 753–5. It is true enough, however, that other Soviet leaders were much more alarmist than Voroshilov.

[2] Stalin, *Sochineniia*, IX, 311. Even 30 years later, after Stalin's death, a Soviet historian (Volkov, *Anglo-Sovetskie Otnosheniia*, p. 282) could still give the impression a Chamberlain-to-Trotsky anti-Soviet conspiracy was in existence in 1927.

alism at a time of such grave national peril was undoubtedly dangerous and perhaps, Stalin was hinting, even treasonable.

Stalin needed all the arguments he could concoct. His concessions to the TUC reformists had proved an acute embarrassment, and the *apologia* Tomsky presented for them at the Central Committee's April plenum appallingly feeble. The *Workers' Life* interview had served to repair some of the damage, but it would hardly be enough to mollify the intractable Trotsky. The Oppositionists were sure to raise the issue again when the Comintern's Executive Committee met on May 18. Their guns had to be spiked in advance, and Bukharin undertook to do the job at a preliminary meeting of the Executive Committee's presidium on May 11.[1] The Soviet Union's precarious diplomatic situation had required her to accept those unusual Berlin arrangements, he explained. She had to enlist all available recruits – even General Council opportunists – in the struggle to frustrate Baldwin's imperialist warmongers. The compromises Tomsky made may have been unpalatable, but they were justified by the critical circumstances of the moment.

The argument was not new. Stalin had commented often on how useful the Committee could be in the event of a war emergency. Bukharin was just making that case more brazenly and explicitly than usual. If, however, he expected his eloquence to silence the Oppositionists, he was quickly disabused. As far as Trotsky was concerned, the Committee ranked with Stalin's hamhandedness in China as one of the two biggest mistakes the Party ever made, involving matters of world-wide historical significance, and he was not going to let anybody sweep it all under the rug.[2] To get his thoughts in order, and get them down for the record, he now sat down to chronicle the whole sordid story of the bloc with the TUC – and the Stalinists' cynical efforts to make excuses for it – from the time of the general strike to the present.[3]

Nobody could out-manoeuvre Trotsky in a war of words and he

[1] The speech was never published, but Trotsky referred to it extensively in his statement on 'The Struggle for Peace and the Anglo-Russian Committee,' 16 May, 1927, and Bukharin never denied Trotsky had represented him accurately. See Trotsky's account, then, in the Trotsky Archives, T–3057 or T–3058, or in *Der Kampf um die K. I.*, pp. 110–13.

[2] Trotsky to Presidium, CCC, 16 May, 1927, T–3059, Trotsky Archives.

[3] 'The Struggle for Peace and the Anglo-Russian Committee,' 16 May, 1927, T–3057, T–3058, Trotsky Archives, available in German in *Der Kampf um die K. I.*, pp. 110–25. It was addressed to the Secretariat of the Central Committee and the Presidium of the Central Control Commission of the CPSU (Trotsky Archives, T–954, 18 May, 1927) but it probably circulated among the delegates to the 8th ECCI as well. Bukharin complained later that the Opposition had dumped some 500 pp. of 'essays, speeches and declarations' on the ECCI (*Pravda*, 18 June, 1927).

marshalled the language as brilliantly as ever on this occasion. The Stalinists had now presented two excuses for that shameful Berlin capitulation, he proposed. The two were mutually exclusive, and neither was logically defensible. The one excuse – Tomsky's – at least had some tradition behind it. It assumed the purpose of the Committee was to enable revolutionaries to penetrate – and eventually take over – reformist trade union organizations. It was an example of united-front tactics, standard Communist strategy during those historical epochs when the working masses were still unprepared to admit the cowardice and opportunism of their social-democratic spokesmen. If united-front tactics were to succeed, one must, of course, maintain contact, for a time, with those same muddled-headed class traitors one was trying to oust. One could not maintain one's bridges to the masses unless one came to some sort of an understanding with their leaders. That was the way things were done in the labour movement. That was the way things had to be done at Berlin.

The difficulty with that argument, Trotsky continued, was that it was a gross perversion of the whole united front concept. The basic rules of the game demanded one never surrender one's right to expose and discredit those bourgeois lackeys one was trying to cashier. One criticized, abused, and reviled them, and at the right moment, one ostentatiously broke with them. The 'right moment' with the General Council had come and gone at least twice – when the councillors betrayed the general strike in the spring and when they let the miners down in the autumn. Both times the Opposition called for a break. Both times it warned that to maintain the Committee was only to prop up traitors. The majority had plainly chosen to keep the Committee at any price, and that was never clearer than at the Berlin meeting. Since then, the 'fundamental fact' of the international working class movement was that Tomsky had capitulated to Purcell, that they had proclaimed their 'cordial ties' with one another, that they had boasted of achieving 'absolute understanding and unanimity.'

Given the circumstances, Trotsky speculated the Stalinists must have realized they could no longer defend the Committee as a revolutionary instrument. Tomsky's concluding speech at the April plenum, by evading all the Opposition's arguments, had in fact validated them. So Bukharin had rummaged around and come up with a new, and very different, explanation of the Berlin misadventure. The agreement was necessitated by the difficult international situation, he had suggested. The Committee was being retained, at considerable cost, not to persuade the proletarian masses to be violent, but to persuade Tory hard-liners not to be. It was, Bukharin had said, a 'special' political bloc, to defend the USSR against the war danger. That was the new explanation of the Committee, then.

The two explanations for the Berlin capitulation – Tomsky's and Bukharin's – were diametrically opposed to one another, Trotsky argued. One could not play the game both ways: praise the traitors in unanimous joint manifestos for diplomatic advantage, and then damn them in whispers in the hope of winning the class war. The only thing Tomsky and Bukharin had in common was that each offered 100 per cent 'lies and hypocrisy,' tenuous nonsense dragged in by the hairs to cover up the sordid sacrifice of principle at Berlin. In fact, to depend on the social democrats to restrain the imperialists was sheer madness. The social democrats were imperialists themselves. They were of course delighted to join the Soviets in signing peace statements. That way they could tranquillize the masses, allay their unrest, make them sleepy. They called it 'pacifism,' but pacifism, as everybody knew, was a counter-revolutionary illusion. It assumed war was an exceptional event, an aberration, to be prevented by sentimental appeals to good sense and good principles. Marxists knew better. They knew that war was intrinsic to monopolistic capitalism, essential to it. The only way to win the struggle against war was to make revolution and bring down the bourgeoisie.

That was why the bourgeoisie found its 'pacifist lackeys' enormously useful. It was no exaggeration to call the Purcells Chamberlain's agents in the labour movement. They threw sand in the eyes of the proletariat. When the crisis came, they would just totter away as they always had. That was why the Committee had been so passive every time it was most needed, when the general strike was on, when the miners were locked out, when British troops were first packed off to China. To maintain 'cordial' relations with the General Council was to hang a millstone around the neck of the proletariat. By making pacifist illusions seem credible, the Committee weakened Russia's real friends among the workers, those who were prepared to fight the class war now.

It was all immaculate Marxist logic, and Trotsky repeated the key points in a lengthy address to the Comintern May 24.[1] The Berlin agreement betrayed the CPGB, betrayed the Minority Movement, knuckled under to Communism's most dangerous enemies in the TUC. The pseudo-left – Purcell and his cronies – had made common cause with the Thomases and the MacDonalds, and together they were serving to prop

[1] T–3061, Trotsky Archives.

up a failing British imperialism. Tomsky's claim that he had arranged at Berlin to 'widen' the Committee's area of activity was absurd: in the first place, he had arranged no such thing, and in the second place, it would be no achievement at all if he had, since to do so would only be to give the opportunists a better chance than ever to betray the workers' interests. Break with the Committee, support the CPGB and the Minority Movement in an intensified struggle against all pseudo-leftism in the labour movement, and Chamberlain would soon find himself in real trouble. That was the Opposition's recommendation.[1]

The Comintern's Executive Committee gave it an extended hearing.[2] The comrades had reserved themselves almost two weeks in which to talk, and scheduled just three items to talk about – China, Britain, and the danger of war. Baldwin and Chamberlain really had the delegates agitated. A British attack on the USSR, and on 'the working classes and Communism all over the world' as well, seemed imminent. Russian Bolsheviks needed the help of their proletarian friends abroad more than ever before. Without endorsing any 'vulgar pacifism' (the Movement would not dispute Trotsky on that point), the Comintern had to summon workers everywhere – and in England most especially – to defend the Russian Revolution. At the crucial moment, when Moscow gave the signal, proletarians must counter the warmongers with a general strike and armed insurrection.

The Oppositionists had no counter-proposals to make on the war danger at all, Bukharin charged later, not a single one. They made up for the poverty of their philosophy, however, by the opulence of their

---

[1] The text of the proposals submitted to be ECCI may be found in *Der Kampf um die K. I.*, pp. 138–42.

[2] The 8th ECCI plenum (18–30 May, 1927) was one of the least well documented. The stenographic transcript has never been published. *Pravda* announced the opening of the meeting May 19, but said little more than that it was an 'extremely important' session coming at a 'dangerous historical moment.' A ban was imposed on the publication of all speeches delivered at the plenum, although the Opposition material later became available anyway (see notes 2, 3, p. 353, and 1, p. 355 above). Bukharin made a lengthy report on the session to the Moscow Party organization which was reprinted in *Pravda* 18–19 June, 1927 and (in English) in *Inprecorr*, VII, 37 (30 June, 1927), 773–9 and 39 (7 July, 1927), 879–84. The 'Resolution on the Statements of Comrades Trotsky and Vuyovitch' (Vuiovič) is in *ibid.*, 35 (16 June, 1927), pp. 735–77, and Trotsky's response in *Der Kampf um die K. I.*, pp. 134–7. The 'Resolution on the Situation in Great Britain' is in *Kommunisticheskii Internatsional v Dokumentakh*, pp. 729–40; *Inprecorr*, VII, 36 (23 June, 1927), 764–8; or CPGB, *Ninth Congress: Reports, Theses & Resolutions*, pp. 116–26. For the 'Theses on War and the Danger of War,' see *Inprecorr*, VII, 40 (14 July, 1927), 889–96. For a summary of the whole session, written right after it ended, see 'The May Plenum of the E.C.C.I.,' *Communist International*, IV, 10 (30 June, 1927), 186–91.

invective. They had never been so rude, Bukharin complained, so brusque, or so clearly determined so split the Movement from within. At a time of critical war danger, when the very survival of the Soviet revolution hung in the balance, Trotsky 'uttered not a word on all these matters.' He avoided the fundamental questions altogether and instead, brought up 'one issue only: the issue of the Anglo-Russian Committee.' To Trotsky, that seemed 'the only issue worth attending to.' Bukharin had no patience with such imbecility. The Committee was not worth all the fuss. It was just one of many 'defensive weapons' in the 'enormous [anti-war] arsenal...at the disposal of the international labour movement.' There was also the Comintern and its affiliates, RILU, the Chinese revolutionaries, all of which would have to be 'mobilized against the danger of war.' The Oppositionists, however, concentrated only on the Committee, and told Russia's 'foreign comrades' that by maintaining its TUC link the CPSU had betrayed the proletariat.

The Executive Committee passed a tough resolution against the Opposition, directed specifically against Trotsky and Vuiovič, his closest Comintern associate. Their 'gross and intemperate' attacks on the International, delivered 'with unprecedented violence,' had just 'interfered with and discredited' the struggle against the imperialist warmongers. They had suggested no anti-war measures themselves except to keep reiterating their demand, 'repeatedly rejected by the Communist International, to break up the Anglo-Russian Committee.' To insist on a rupture so noisily amounted to disguising Menshevik views behind pseudo-left phrases, and the two heretics were enjoined to cease their factional disruption forthwith or face expulsion from the Comintern Executive.

We do not delude ourselves, Bukharin confided later, 'that the British representatives on the Anglo-Russian Committee would help much during or before a war,' but given the circumstances, it was a dangerous time to make an open break with them. Of course all General Council members – left and right – were 'opportunists, reformists, scabs, slaves of British imperialism, and everything else the Opposition has called them.' The question, however, was whether in the midst of an 'extremely difficult' international crisis, it was expedient to liquidate the Committee. To keep the TUC bureaucrats formally tied down to the organization at least made it difficult for them to go over openly to Chamberlain. It seemed advisable, then, to 'make a number of concessions' to the English at Berlin. None of them, however, denied the Russians the right to criticize their Committee partners. Tomsky's *Workers' Life* interview made that clear, Bukharin insisted. The General Council might retaliate for that rebuke by dissolving the Committee itself. 'This is not impossible.' If the councillors did so, of course, they would just 'unmask their own treachery' to their constituency.

For Communists to rely on them, of course, would be foolish. The CPGB itself would therefore have to take most of the responsibility for signing up workers for the anti-war campaign. The Committee would hardly be much help in any such effort, and the Party 'must explain to the workers' that 'the sabotage of the whole General Council from Hicks and Purcell to Thomas' was what had made it impossible for the Committee to meet its responsibilities adequately. It was not Tomsky's fault his link to the TUC had proved so inauspicious. He had demonstrated his sincere desire for unity over and over again. It was his total commitment to proletarian internationalism that had prompted him to concede the British what they wanted at Berlin. The CPGB proposed a face-saving formula to explain away that embarrassment, and the Comintern approved it enthusiastically. The Russians may have signed the Berlin agreements, it conceded, but the General Council was 'entirely responsible' for them. The pact each signed therefore demonstrated both Tomsky's good faith and Purcell's treachery. *Workers' Life* would explain the dialectics of it all – somehow – to the British proletariat.

On this occasion then, as on so many others, the Stalinists had rebuked Trotsky for his impertinence, scorned his logic, and then all but adopted his recommendations. The Committee was no longer to be accounted one of Comintern's major instruments in the struggle against imperialism. It was a second-rate weapon with a distressing recoil problem and its sights needed adjusting. Communists had better defences available. In a crisis, of course, one held on to everything in one's arsenal – even peashooters – so Trotsky was wrong to urge precipitous liquidation of the Committee. It would be retained, therefore, but at the same time its British members would be cursed and vilified for betraying their proletarian responsibilities. When they could stand the abuse no longer and ruptured the organization themselves, they would be cursed and vilified for that, too.

Such a stand was not good enough for Trotsky, who rejected the Comintern's decision the day it was made[1] and appealed the whole issue back to the CPSU. In spite of his setback in the International, Trotsky

---

[1] Statement of Comrades Trotsky and Vuiovič, undated (presumably 25 May, 1927), *Der Kampf um die K. I.*, pp. 134–7. The document would later be endorsed by several hundred additional sympathizers.

could speak with new confidence at home. Eighty-three prominent CPSU members had openly pledged him their support, and their joint statement, dispatched to the Party's Central Committee May 26, specifically criticized the Stalinist leadership for having surrendered to the General Council traitors, as well as for various other crimes and misdemeanours.[1]

It was the Opposition's first open breach of its pledge back in October not to engage in factional activity, and its leaders were summoned before the presidium of the Party's Central Control Commission on June 24 to explain themselves.[2] Trotsky was adamant, on the Committee issue as on every other. Maintaining that the link to the TUC bureaucrats was making it impossible to develop a real revolutionary movement in the English working class, it conferred all 'the authority of Leninism' on the General Council traitors. The Stalinists did indeed 'criticize' a Purcell – 'ever more mildly, ever more rarely' – but they remained tied to him, and he could continue to boast of how he worked 'hand in hand' with Tomsky himself. How could one allege Purcell an 'agent of imperialism' when members of the Politburo itself claimed him as an ally? 'In a devious way' the Stalinists had 'put the entire machinery of Bolshevism at Purcell's disposal.' They had made Purcell credible to the English workers, and he had used the prestige they conferred on him to back up Thomas, who in turn backed up Chamberlain. By insisting on supporting Purcell, the majority weakened the USSR and strengthened imperialism, Trotsky charged. The Control Commission leaders, not unreasonably, decided he had not recanted. He and his friends had indeed broken their promise not to promote factionalism, and 'the question of the removal of Comrades Zinoviev and Trotsky from their membership in the Central Committee' was therefore referred to a forthcoming joint meeting of the Central Committee and the Central Control Commission scheduled for the end of July.

IV

Once the Russians had decided – however obliquely – to make no further effort to keep the Committee, and indeed, to chivvy the English into liquidating it, it was clearly in their interests to get the organization disbanded as quickly as possible. How else could they hope to silence the ferocious Trotsky! The tone of the correspondence between the Soviets

[1] T–941, T–955, 26 May, 1927, Trotsky Archives: *Der Kampf um die K. I.*, pp. 149–64.
[2] For the meeting, see *Pravda*, 26 June, 1927. For Trotsky's statement, see T–3160, 24 June, 1927, Trotsky Archives, or the abridged version in *Der Kampf um die K. I.*, pp. 126–48.

an d the TUC changed markedly, therefore, after June 3. Tomsky and
Dogadov's joint letter of that date, urging a Committee meeting to
discuss the war crisis, was emphatic but not discourteous. Three days
later, however, when Tomsky dashed off his defence of the *Workers' Life*
interview, all civilities had already been abandoned: he was rude,
abusive and uncompromising.[1] Sometime between the 3rd and the 6th,
the Politburo may have given him his final instructions: goad the
General Council into a break just as fast as you can.

The onslaught caught them by surprise back in London. The members
of the International Committee, meeting June 9, were obviously unprepared for any showdown. They thought they were going out of their
way to be conciliatory. They had before them that Russian letter of the
3rd, which had only arrived the day before. They could not agree to
Tomsky's proposal for a Committee meeting, they felt, without General
Council approval, and the Council was not due to meet for another two
weeks. In view of the critical international situation, however, and the
urgency of the Russian plea, it seemed unreasonable to stick too closely
to formalities. Perhaps, they suggested, the chairman and secretary of
each trade union organization could meet informally in Berlin and
discuss the problem. They wired their decision to the Russians that very
evening, proposing Tomsky and Dogadov meet Hicks and Citrine June
17–18 'for the purpose of a preliminary examination of those questions
which you wish to bring before the Anglo-Russian Committee.'[2]

If the English hoped a soft answer might turn away Soviet wrath,
they were to be disappointed. Indeed, Moscow had already wired its
wrath: it just did not arrive quite in time for the International Committee to be intimidated by it. 'Despite the extremely tense situation,'
Tomsky scolded, the TUC had yet to respond to the Russian demand for
a Committee meeting. Soviet workers were most concerned about the
apparent inactivity of the Committee. 'This obliges us, unless we receive
a definite answer by the 14th of this month, to publish the correspondence between us on the subject.'[3] Considering it was only a week since
the Soviets had asked for the meeting, and that they had transmitted that
suggestion by post, the ultimatum could only have been meant as a
deliberate provocation.

[1] For the two messages, see above, pp. 346, 350–1.
[2] International Committee Minutes, 7 June, 1927, file 901, doc. I.C. 12 1926–7. The
     telegram to the Russians was reprinted in *Pravda*, 18 June, 1927 and *The Times*,
     27 June, 1927.
[3] Central Council to General Council, 10 June, 1927, *Pravda*, 18 June, 1927; *The
     Times*, 27 June, 1927.

By the time the Russian challenge got delivered in London, however, it was already obsolete. The Soviets had Citrine's counterproposal – preliminary four-man talks June 17. It was not good enough. The Central Council had no objection to preparatory discussions on agenda matters, Mel'nichansky wired back June 11, but it had to 'insist...categorically' that all the English members of the Committee be there in Berlin, and that they meet with the Russians in plenary session. Further delays were unacceptable.[1] Unless the British indicated otherwise – immediately – Mel'nichansky would assume they agreed. He got his reply a day later.[2] No plenary session could be scheduled without the General Council's specific approval, and the Council would not meet until the 22nd. If the Soviets had anything to talk over with Hicks and Citrine, they had better let them know right away. Moscow had been outbluffed. Mel'nichansky's final cable in the hectic series, on the 14th, promised he and Tomsky would show up in Berlin at the agreed time.[3]

The English had got their way on the meeting, but the Russians could still retaliate, and did. *Pravda*, on June 18, divulged all the supposedly confidential correspondence between the General Council and Central Council from the time of the Arcos raid on.[4] Various labour organizations, the paper explained, had expressed some concern about the Committee's inactivity at a time the international situation seemed so grave. The correspondence spoke for itself. The TUC's insistence on 'formalities' was the problem. The Soviets would continue to try to get the English to reactivate the Committee, the Central Council promised, and would resist all the TUC's efforts to condemn the organization to 'passivity and impotence.'

It was another calculated insult, a direct violation of that Soviet pledge, given only two months earlier, not to try to score propaganda points against the General Council by publicizing differences of opinion over the Committee agenda. It was also a carefully-timed insult. If the four-way conversations at Berlin had taken place on schedule, *Pravda* would have been publishing the correspondence just about the time the British were packing to go home. The *Sunday Worker* would feature an

---

[1] Central Council to General Council, 11 June, 1927, *ibid.*
[2] Citrine to Mel'nichansky, 12 June, 1927, *ibid.*
[3] Mel'nichansky to Citrine, 14 June, 1927, *ibid.*
[4] It may not be a coincidence that the same issue of *Pravda* which criticized the British for sabotaging the Committee, and printed the correspondence between the General Council and Central Council, also carried Bukharin's report to the Moscow Party organization on the 8th ECCI, rebuking Trotsky for suggesting the Committee be abolished.

English translation of the offending documents a day later, which should give Citrine and Hicks a well-deserved jolt as they arrived back in London.[1] In fact, the meeting at Berlin got put off a day because the Russians had visa problems, so the chronology did not work out as neatly as they may have hoped in Moscow. And the British were not really particularly dismayed by the revelations after all. It was one more proof, of course, that one could not trust Tomsky to keep his promises, but that was no news. Otherwise, the written record did not really make the TUC leaders look that bad. *The Times* probably reflected general informed opinion when it noted the Russian workers had apparently been led to expect much more from the Committee than they ever had any right to.[2] Some of their leaders seemed to have staked their domestic political reputations on the connection they had established with the TUC. They were now being called to account, pressed to show some results for all their involved manoeuvring. To get out of the trap they had dug for themselves, they had to abuse the councillors.

Given the circumstances, it was hardly likely that Hicks, Citrine, Tomsky and Mel'nichansky would achieve much at Berlin.[3] The British were angry, angry at those peremptory Russian summonses to a Committee meeting, angry at the *Workers' Life* interview, angrier yet at Tomsky's arrogant defense of the interview. *Pravda*'s publication of their confidential correspondence added one more item to their list of grievances, but the list was so long anyway one additional wickedness hardly made much difference. Citrine recalled later how he and Hicks surprised the Soviets with the bluntness with which they spoke their minds. The discussions were not bitter, he noted, but they were frank and straightforward, and a lot of harsh words got spoken.

The Russians began the talks, the morning of the 18th, with their estimate of the international situation. It was 'extremely serious,' they said, and war might break out at any time. The Committee had been established to deal with just such dangers, and it must convene in

---

[1] The *Sunday Worker* did indeed print the correspondence 19 June. The editor must have received it well before that date. *Workers' Life*, 24 June, 1927, hailed its Sunday counterpart's 'decision' to publish, and urged mass pressure on the General Council to break its 'silent sabotage' of the Committee.

[2] *The Times*, 20 June, 1927.

[3] For the Berlin meeting, I am relying on Lord Citrine's own recollections (supported by his personal papers), the account in the TUC archives, file 947/220, doc. A.R. 6. 1926–7, and Tomsky's colourful report to the extraordinary plenary session of the Central Council, 28 June, 1927, *Izvestiia*, 1 July, 1927. For English translations of that report, see *Inprecorr*, VII, 39 (7 July, 1927), 865–71 or *The Worker*, 15, 22 July, 1927.

plenary session immediately. To delay would be to pass a death sentence on the Committee. They had to move quickly, and the Soviets had no patience with the way the TUC kept dragging its feet.

It was all very well to talk about the war danger, the British replied, but nobody had declared war yet. There was no point crying 'Wolf! Wolf!' when there was no wolf. In any event, the TUC's International Committee was not convinced the Committee could really do much to prevent a war.[1] If the Russians had some practical proposals to make, of course, Citrine and Hicks would be glad to take them under advisement. They were more interested, however, in settling the matter of that *Workers' Life* interview. Tomsky's defence of the article in that letter to the TUC would hardly 'allay the friction already caused,' they suggested. They were also quite sure the General Council would regard the Russian telegram of June 11, demanding a Committee meeting, as 'dictatorial and provocative.' Finally, the decision to publish the correspondence was deemed 'unfortunate,' producing 'unnecessary friction and misunderstanding.' If the Russians could 'clear up' these various matters, especially that *Workers' Life* piece, perhaps they could get on to discussing other common concerns.

Tomsky was furious. Reporting on the event ten days later, he still found the British response unbelievably petty. 'Really, at a time when the whole world is threatened by the danger of war,...it is astounding to see an organization whose main plank is the struggle against war postponing its meetings while the representatives on both sides...waste their time discussing a Tomsky interview.' It might be flattering, he conceded, to have some remarks of his to the press put on the same level as a major international crisis, but the people who put them there must either be very stupid or else be 'very much interested in avoiding other unpleasant questions.' The interview was not worth discussing. He would never renounce his right to free speech just to suit the English: he never had. 'It would be silly and ridiculous, after twenty years in political life, to permit one's hands to be tied for the sake of the beautiful eyes of the Anglo-Russian Committee.' He wanted to deal with the war threat. The English had said that was crying wolf when there was no wolf. Perhaps, he replied, but by the time the wolf's fangs were at one's throat, it would be too late to make any cry at all. To postpone a

---

[1] Tomsky later reported Hicks and Citrine had said a General Council majority was against a Committee meeting. The British record indicates they said the International Committee had its doubts. The English version is the more likely. Not having met since May 26, the General Council had not committed itself to a meeting one way or the other.

Committee meeting any longer or to continue to try to evade one would be even more damaging than a point-blank refusal to meet. It would prove the TUC's 'unmistakable intention to abandon the Russian workers in the hour of their need.'

The English asked for some particulars. The Committee had only limited powers, after all. Even the Russians did not deny that. Just exactly what anti-war measures did Tomsky have in mind? It seemed an embarrassing question. Tomsky had no specific proposals to make beyond a vague suggestion that perhaps, 'if events developed,' the Committee might appeal to workers not 'to manufacture or transport munitions.' Some such declaration could 'have a big influence on the situation,' he ventured. The Committee was hardly the 'body entitled to make such international pronouncements,' the British replied. The countries most likely to be involved in any new war of intervention – apart from Britain herself – were the countries along Russia's western frontier, all of whose trade unions were affiliates of IFTU. Amsterdam, then, would be the 'most appropriate body' to issue whatever statements the Russians deemed necessary. The Russians indicated they doubted IFTU's willingness to sponsor any decisive anti-war measures. Besides, they could not wait for Amsterdam to act. The TUC would better understand the urgency once its representatives came to a Committee meeting. Tomsky had some special information to submit to them which he could not make public. If, afterwards, the General Council still felt IFTU should be brought into the discussions, it might suggest Amsterdam call an international conference on the war danger.

In the meantime, to clear up the misunderstanding about that June 11 telegram, Tomsky suggested the British put their objections to the document in writing. Citrine did so, in a letter dated June 19, repeating his opinion that the telegram had produced 'misunderstandings' and that the General Council would find it 'challenging and dictatorial.' Mel'nichansky wrote out a response the same day, expressing surprise at any such interpretation and denying the Russian message was meant to contain anything 'insulting.' The Central Council was only communicating its 'justifiable fears' that the Committee might not meet at such a critical time, and its 'determination to... mobilize public opinion and all the forces of the working class for the struggle against the obviously approaching war.'

Citrine's protest and Mel'nichansky's reply added two more items to what was now a small mountain of documentation the TUC General Council had to consider June 22, when it was supposed to decide what next to do about the Committee. J. H. Thomas had all but resolved on dissolution. The Russians were meddlers, and they could not be persuaded to stop. They subsidized splitters and dissenters inside his own union. They slandered, abused and libelled him. It was all a waste of their money, of course. They could not engineer a revolution in Britain no matter how hard they tried. But they could be, and were, disruptive. Even when Tomsky had been told to stop 'such foolishness' – and agreed – he was at it all over again within a few days. Thomas complained bitterly to his fellow railwaymen.[1] He spoke 'with great emotion,' a reporter noted. 'We must have plain dealing and straight talking,' he said. The Russian masses must be told what 'humbugs' those people were who pretend to speak in their name.

It was time for the TUC to stop coddling Tomsky, then, according to Thomas, and he proposed to his Council colleagues that no further Committee meetings take place until September.[2] The whole documentary record could then be referred to Congress, and it could make the final decision. That would certainly slap the Russians down, but to some of the councillors, it seemed a bit too severe. One of them, E. L. Poulton, moved a substitute motion, directing the International Committee to review the whole record and report back to the Council, with recommendations, in July. All meetings with the Russians would be prohibited until such time as the Council made its decision.

The discussion was strenuous and not always relevant. The crucial issue – of Anglo-Soviet state relations – was being neglected, some of the councillors protested, while the lesser question – of Tomsky's rudenesses to the TUC – dominated the debate. They finally managed to manipulate parliamentary procedures adroitly enough to permit Hicks to present a third motion, agreeing to another Committee meeting, and asking the Russians to submit that secret information of theirs – on the war danger – in advance. The General Council could then examine all the evidence and, if necessary, urge IFTU to call an international conference to deal with the crisis. As for Tomsky's indiscretions, Hicks' motion would have 'followed up' that question 'in accordance with the new constitution of the Anglo-Russian Committee.'

The votes on the three alternatives showed how closely the councillors were divided on relations with the Soviets. Hicks' motion was declared 'not carried' on a 13-to-13 tie vote. Poulton then got his motion substituted for Thomas's by 14 to 12, and his resolution, throwing the whole issue back to the International Committee for a recommendation,

[1] *Daily Herald*, 9 July, 1927.   [2] General Council Minutes, No. 233, 22 June, 1927.

finally passed, 16 to 9. It would be at least a month, then, before the
TUC could meet with the Russians.

To the CPGB, it was all 'treachery' and 'sickening hypocrisy,' just
more proof of the General Council's 'venomous hostility' against the
Russian working class.[1] To put off a Committee meeting for at least a
month was 'sabotage of the worst possible description' and 'nothing
short of criminal.' It amounted to 'an open incitement to the Conservative Government to intensify its war preparations against the Soviet
Republic.' The Party urged its members and sympathizers to bombard
the General Council with protest resolutions, insisting it 'reverse its
treacherous decisions' and agree to an immediate Committee meeting.
Subsequently, of course, British proletarians would have to purge their
movement of all 'these allies of Baldwin' who betrayed them from
within the General Council.

The comrades in Moscow were quite as angry as their ideological
cousins in London. Tomsky called a special meeting of the Soviet trade
unions' Central Council to air his grievances publicly.[2] He had known
all along, he began, that he was dealing with reformists, not Communists, when he went to Committee meetings, that he would have to
make unpalatable compromises to achieve any agreements with them at
all, and that they would tend to vacillate – or even go directly over to the
capitalists – at critical moments. All that was clear from the beginning.
He had received the TUC leaders with enthusiastic acclaim when they
made their pilgrimages to the USSR, of course, but his applause was
never meant for the Purcells personally – only for the Purcells as representatives of trade unionism 'in a country with the greatest working
class in the world.' So much for that mortifying honorary membership
in the Moscow Soviet!

Tomsky reviewed the involved negotiations between the Central
Council and General Council since March, culminating in the TUC's
decision to postpone any Committee meeting at least until July. The
British had decided to disrupt the Committee and to break off the
alliance with the Soviet workers. All the fine words professing support
for their Russian class brothers had turned out to be 'nothing but
empty phrases.' The councillors were now sounding the retreat. They
were afraid of the capitalists and afraid of the Conservative government

---

[1] The CPGB prose in this paragraph is taken from *The Worker*, 1 July, 1927 and from
the Party manifesto, as reported in *The Times*, 28 June, 1927 and reprinted in
Ninth Congress: Reports, Theses & Resolutions, pp. 53–5. See also *Workers' Life*,
special supplement on world trade union unity, 8 July, 1927.
[2] *Izvestiia*, 1 July, 1927.

and were trying to protect themselves by forming a 'moral bloc with the bourgeoisie.' It was 'disgusting,...the worst form of treachery against the workers of the Soviet Union.'

The Russians had done everything they could to maintain the Committee, Tomsky affirmed. They tried all along to 'increase its activity,' to transform it 'into an effective organ of class struggle,' to make it 'over into a centre for the mobilization of all organizations dissatisfied with the policy of the Amsterdam International.' They had hoped to make it possible for the Committee to play a major role in the campaign against war, the struggle against the capitalist offensive, and the fight for international trade union unity. They tried to maintain the organization on that basis even when the TUC opportunists wavered and faltered. They had criticized their British partners on such occasions, admittedly, but that was their right, one which they had never surrendered. Even while rebuking the general councillors, however, they had still tried to make common cause with them, and to maintain and consolidate the work of the Committee.

The effort had failed, and it was time the workers of the world knew why it had failed and whose fault it was. The bureaucrats on the General Council were 'very bad leaders,' Tomsky charged, who had not stood the test. They had promised, as recently as March, to cooperate with the Russians against the war danger, and they now acted as if that undertaking never existed. When pressed, they hid behind 'formalities.' It was 'criminal.' Tomsky demanded the councillors tell him, and tell their own rank and file, just how they proposed to mobilize the proletariat against the imperialist warmongers. He doubted they would dare reply. The working masses in both countries could then judge for themselves where the councillors really stood.

What he was asking for was an obituary for the whole unhappy venture, and his colleagues dutifully voted him one.[1] The English were still refusing to agree to a Committee meeting, even in the midst of a critical war crisis, the Central Council proclaimed. All Russia's efforts to convene such a session were met by 'tactics of evasion, procrastination, and sabotage.' The masses must have the truth, and the truth was the British had embarked on a deliberate policy of liquidating the Anglo-Russian trade union connection. They had resisted every

---

[1] *Ibid.* The declaration was, of course, translated promptly into English and appeared in the *Sunday Worker*, 3 July, 1927, *Inprecorr*, VII, 39 (7 July, 1927), 871–3, and *Workers' Life*, 8 July, 1927. The General Council also had it reprinted in the *1927 TUC: Report of Proceedings*, pp. 210–13.

'proletarian initiative' the Soviets attempted, from the time of the general strike on. It was all part of a consistent pattern. The General Council was on the bourgeoisie's side. That was why it failed to make any effective protest against the counter-revolution in China, the Arcos affair, or the diplomatic break. That was why it refused to permit a Committee meeting.

Russia wanted to preserve the Committee, and make it effective. Liquidating it would only play into the hands of splitters and warmongers. The organization was particularly important at such a critical juncture in international relations, when the Tory government was pursuing such a 'criminal, arrogantly provocative, bandit policy.' The workers must rebuke the imperialists, 'resolutely, sternly, ruthlessly.' 'Only a traitor to the proletarian cause' would remain passive to the danger. The masses had to be as resolute as the bourgeoisie. At such a time, it was 'absolutely intolerable' that the Committee 'should not meet, should be silent, doomed to inactivity.' It should be proposing 'practical measures' for the struggle against militarism. That it had not was the General Council's responsibility.

The Soviets could hardly have expected the Committee to survive a statement like that. *The Times* advised the General Council to kill the organization off quickly.[1] It was only a vehicle for Communist propaganda anyway. The councillors had 'invited the ills of which they now complain' by agreeing to the Committee in the first place, and the remedy was 'obvious' to the editorialist. It was apparently less obvious, however, to the General Council's International Committee. It met July 12 – the day of *The Times'* editorial – to do what the Council had instructed it to do – consider the whole problem of Anglo-Russian trade union relations all over again and come up with a recommendation.[2] Citrine had something ready for the members, a detailed recapitulation of Soviet efforts to interfere in TUC affairs going back over a year. It was an impressive indictment, and it seemed only reasonable to let the accused have a look at it. The resolution adopted suggested that the statement be sent along to Moscow, and the Russian request for a Committee meeting 'be considered upon receipt of and in the light of the reply received.' The General Council adopted that proposal July 27, and the bill of particulars was promptly shipped off to Tomsky.[3] It cata-

[1] *The Times*, 12 July, 1927.
[2] International Committee Minutes, 12 July, 1927, file 901, doc. I.C. 13 1926–7.
[3] General Council Minutes, No. 249, 27 July, 1927. For the statement itself, see *1927 TUC: Report of Proceedings*, pp. 202–7, or *Inprecorr*, VII, 53 (15 Sept., 1927), 1182–4.

logued all Moscow's sins from June, 1926 on, in 24 paragraphs. The British had shown the 'utmost patience and restraint' under all these provocations, the statement claimed, but they found it hard to see how they could continue to cooperate with people who publicly stigmatized them as 'traitors, renegades and capitalist lackeys.' They had tried to save the Committee in the past because they thought it would do the Russian workers no good to be isolated from the rest of the international trade union movement. That was why they had suggested those changes in the Committee constitution – to make it possible for them to preserve the organization. But 'no constitution,...however worded, can be efficacious unless honourably and loyally accepted, and honoured both in letter and spirit, by all concerned.' The General Council was not convinced the Russians had kept their end of the bargain, and before it met with them again, it wanted to hear their comment on the list of grievances.

Moscow delayed any formal reply to the TUC for over a month, but Russian leaders had signalled their attitude well in advance. The Soviets were determined to keep pillorying all labour leaders who refused to take the war threat seriously, Stalin warned.[1] The pacifist lies they spread were only designed to lull the workers to sleep, and make life easier for the imperialist aggressors. Such capitalist lackeys would be unmasked.

Unmasking them was Profintern's primary responsibility, Stalin told a joint plenum of the Party's Central Committee and Central Control Commission on August 1.[2] But the Committee could help, too – a little. The link to the General Council was one useful point of contact between the USSR's revolutionary trade unions and Britain's 'reformist and reactionary' ones, and it could be exploited to help 'isolate the labour aristocracy' in the TUC from the rank and file it so woefully misled. The Committee served as a kind of auxiliary of RILU's then, not a major channel to the masses – not like Comintern or Profintern – but a 'temporary, subsidiary, episodic channel and, therefore, not permanent, not always reliable, and sometimes quite unreliable.' The Party had realized that all along. To make a major issue of the TUC link, as the Opposition had, was just 'babbling.'

---

[1] Stalin, *Sochineniia*, IX, 322–8.

[2] *Ibid.*, x, 3–59, and especially pp. 36–41. No stenographic report of the plenum is available, but see Rykov's account in *Pravda*, 10 Aug., 1927. Trotsky's speech is in the Trotsky Archives, T–987, 988, 3085, and repeated in L. Trotsky, *The Stalin School of Falsification*, trans. John G. Wright (New York: Pioneer Publishers, 1937), pp. 162–77. Stalin's second address to the plenum is in *Sochineniia*, x, 60–84. The plenum's resolution on the Committee is available in *KPSS v Rezoliutsiiakh*, p. 246.

The Committee had come in handy. It had made it more difficult, for example, for the yellow reformist traitors to go over openly to the class enemy, and it had facilitated Communist penetration of the trade unions they controlled. The members of the General Council had been criticized 'ruthlessly,' however, and they might well now retaliate by rupturing the Committee. 'Let them do so.' That was their privilege. It would only discredit them with their own followers. Coming when it did, with war likely to break out at any time, it would just demonstrate how reactionary trade union leaders in fact supported imperialist militarism. 'It can hardly be doubted that in such circumstances, a rupture brought about by the English would make it easier for Communists to overturn the General Council, because the war issue is now the fundamental issue of the day.' If, on the other hand, the TUC did not make the break, it would mean the USSR had 'established' its right to keep on abusing the opportunists and exposing 'their treachery and social-democratism' indefinitely. The Russians could not lose; the General Council could not win.

The way Stalin was now putting it, of course, Trotsky could not win either. The Committee was marginally useful, it did not matter one way or the other if the English broke it off, so what was the Opposition complaining about? Given the war crisis, to make a major issue over a matter of so little consequence was intolerable, and some of Trotsky's own supporters obviously found it uncomfortable being trapped in that hole Lev Davidovich had dug for them. Krupskaya, for example, Lenin's widow, now publicly dissociated herself from the Opposition ranks. The imperialists were conspiring to crush the revolution altogether, she affirmed. At such a time, all good Party stalwarts must rally to the established authorities.[1]

Trotsky never defended himself more brilliantly. He understood the war danger as well as the Stalinists, he insisted. He also knew – better than they seemed to – what to do about it. One could not stay harnessed to the counter-revolutionary reformists running the TUC and still direct the revolutionary struggle against war. One could not maintain an alliance with traitors like Purcell and Hicks and still persuade the working-class masses to risk general strikes and armed insurrections against the imperialists. He was all for defending the revolutionary fatherland, but was the defence to be Bolshevik – and succeed – or trade unionist – and fail? That was 'the crux of the question.'

The Party had certified the Committee as the 'organizational centre for the international proletarian army in the struggle against...a new

[1] *Pravda*, 3 Aug., 1927.

war.' Moscow *apparatchiks* had been told 'that in the event of a war danger our working class would be able to seize hold of the rope of the Anglo-Russian Committee.' It was all false, Trotsky argued. The rope was rotten. *Pravda* itself testified to the existence of a 'united front of traitors' in the General Council. Even A. J. Cook, 'Tomsky's beloved Benjamin,' had not come out forthrightly against Baldwin's warmongering. '"An utterly incomprehensible silence!" cries *Pravda*. That is your eternal refrain: "This is utterly incomprehensible!"' It had been 'incomprehensible' in China, where the Party pinned its hopes first on Chiang Kai-shek, then on Wang Ching-wei, and got betrayed by both. In Britain, too, Communists first pinned their hopes on Purcell and Hicks, and then on Cook, only to be betrayed again and again. The CPGB had been by-passed, ignored and fatally weakened, while Moscow looked vainly around for more influential friends. 'You rejected the small but sturdier rope for the bigger but utterly rotten one,' Trotsky charged, and learned nothing from the resulting disaster. The majority persisted in pursuing that 'policy of rotten ropes on an international scale...In the event of war,...the rotten ropes will fall apart in your hands.' The CPGB itself was therefore in trouble, 'poisoned by centrism and conciliationism' as a result of the Movement's flirtations with the likes of Purcell and Cook. To continue the liaison was inexcusable.

It was a brave show – and splendid dialectics – but the Stalinists had still managed to de-fuse the issue in advance. By pooh-poohing the Committee's importance, and then demanding monolithic Party unity to counter the imperialists, the majority had left the Oppositionists helpless. The dissidents finally issued a statement pledging their loyalty to the USSR and promising to defend it, and disavowing any intention of sponsoring separatist parties in Russia or elsewhere. It was a half-hearted half-apology, and the majority found it quite inadequate. It was just good enough, however, so that the leadership put aside a motion to expel Trotsky and Zinoviev from the Central Committee, contenting itself instead with presenting them a 'severe reprimand and warning.'

On the very day the Russians were trying to out-do one another damning Purcell in Moscow, he was lavishing praise on them in Paris. The occasion was the IFTU's fourth Congress.[1] Given the circumstances, the wonder is there ever was a fifth. The British delegation was angry –

[1] The record is International Federation of Trade Unions, *Report of Proceedings at the Fourth Ordinary Congress of the International Federation of Trade Unions, Held at the 'Grand Palais,' Paris, from August 1st to 6th, 1927* (Amsterdam: International Federation of Trade Unions, 1927). See also *The Times*, 2, 3, 4, 6, 8 Aug., 1927.

angry at the way Oudegeest and his friends had rebuffed the TUC on the unity issue, angry, too, at the way they had squandered the Federation's money. Some members of the General Council had become so disgusted with the organization, way back in April, they even toyed with the idea of quitting it then and there.[1] One reason they decided to stay in was they still had hopes of persuading Congress to open the Federation's doors to the Russians. The draft resolution proposed was carefully drawn. It did not mention the USSR at all. It merely expressed regret that Amsterdam had not yet become a truly all-inclusive international, and called for the appointment of a four-man committee 'to make such recommendations as may eventually lead to an increase in the number of affiliated bodies, in order that the Federation may become an organization of universal scope and influence.'[2]

The report the IFTU Executive submitted to Congress showed no change of heart on the unity issue.[3] The Russians could come into Amsterdam any time they liked, on the same conditions as everybody else. They would have to learn, however, to extend their fellow-members of the Federation the same respect they demanded for themselves. They could no longer 'seek to force Communist methods' on other trade union federations, and demand their submission to Marxist dogmas. IFTU wanted them in. Their membership would be 'of incalculable importance to the international working class' and 'their wishes,' the Executive promised, 'if in harmony with the principles and policy of the IFTU, would always be taken into consideration.' But Amsterdam's present affiliates refused to have Russian policies jammed down their throats, and they would not tolerate the kind of intervention in their affairs Russia seemed to be claiming as a matter of right in its running debate with the TUC.

The Executive's statement played down the misunderstandings between Amsterdam and London. The creation of the Anglo-Russian Committee had produced a lot of wild rumours, Oudegeest acknowledged, and it was true the Committee had seemed to occasion 'some unfounded criticism of us which made our work more difficult.' Such disagreements as still existed between Amsterdam and the British, however, were rooted 'not in principles, but in purely tactical considerations,' and the Executive was sure the remaining differences could all be patched up.

---

1 General Council Minutes, No. 199, 27 Apr., 1927, No. 211, 25 May, 1927.
2 International Committee Minutes, 9 May, 1927, file 901, doc. I.C. 9 1926–7.
3 *Fourth Congress: Report of Proceedings*, pp. 53–8.

The English themselves were not so sure. They still had their doubts about Amsterdam's fiscal competence and they still wanted to see some progress on that unity issue. Added to which they were furious about the Mexican incident![1] The Mexican trade unionists had invited the IFTU to send a fraternal delegate to their Congress. Amsterdam had first accepted, and then reversed itself when it discovered Profintern had been invited too. J. W. Brown (the British secretary on the IFTU Executive) decided to go anyway, on his own. Brown's colleagues on the secretariat pronounced him guilty of a breach of organization discipline. He had a reply ready, and was to produce it, with melodramatic flourishes, once the Congress was underway.

Even had Brown been in a less irascible mood, however, Purcell's presidential address was almost bound to produce an explosion.[2] Purcell had not seemed quite himself for over a year, ever since the end of the general strike. Friends noticed he was acquiring something of a drinking problem, and his speeches – confused, ambiguous, hesitant – often seemed to reflect it. At Paris, however, he was his old self – assertive, strong, outspoken, blunt and tactless. His enemies might have forgiven him his opinions had he continued to articulate them so badly. When he was in form, however, people listened to him, and that was inexcusable.

He waxed eloquent about the Soviet Union. Russian workers, 'with boundless courage,' had seized control of their own country and abolished exploitation forever. 'In spite of the military and economic opposition of world capitalism, and in spite of the most tragic mis-understandings with the workers of Western Europe,' they had 'held aloft the Red Flag for ten years.' The IFTU needed them. It needed 'their freshness of outlook, their boldness, vigour and courage.' It was 'the most extraordinary and childishly silly thing that for three years past the Russians and ourselves have been engaged in calling each other names.' The 'stupid intrigues' had profited nobody. Russia was now being threatened by 'grave dangers.' 'Capitalist imperialism' was pre-paring to attack her. To isolate the Soviet workers from the international trade union movement at such a time was inexcusable. For himself, 'I would be prepared to agree to the complete re-moulding of the IFTU tomorrow if such would ensure the complete massing together of our forces. I am prepared to adopt any means – an all-in world Congress or any other methods, if such means would add to our strength.'

It was shocking heresy! One might have thought Lozovsky himself

[1] The incident is nicely summarized in *Labour Monthly*, ix, 10 (Oct., 1927), 634.
[2] The address is in *Fourth Congress: Report of Proceedings*, pp. 24–34.

had addressed the Congress. *Peuple*, the French trade union organ, only mentioned the speech to deplore it, and to assure its readers they did not really have to take Purcell seriously. Léon Jouhaux announced to the delegates, to 'prolonged cheers,' that neither he, Oudegeest, Mertens, Leipart or Sassenbach could ever 'accept the ideas which Purcell has expressed.'[1] The entire IFTU Executive, then, with the sole exception of Brown, had ranged itself immediately in opposition to its president.

It was the English against 'them foreigners'[2] and the men of the TUC were not about to desert their own. Hicks defended his colleague the next day.[3] The British delegation agreed with most of what Purcell had said, he affirmed, and it resented the unfair attacks on him both at the Congress and in the French labour press. It was absurd to exclude the Russians from IFTU just because they had 'unpleasant ways of expressing their criticism.' They were quite as impolite with one another as they were with outsiders, Hicks pointed out. It was just their way.

Hicks had been somewhat conciliatory. Brown was not.[4] The Amsterdam bureaucrats' attitude toward the Russian trade union was neither honest nor dignified, he charged. Their vendetta against the English was just disgusting, a 'net of intrigue which dooms all activities to sterility.' There was an actual conspiracy, and he could present evidence of it – a letter from Oudegeest to Jouhaux dated November 6, 1924.[5] The document proved conclusively the existence of an anti-Russian and anti-British cabal within the IFTU Executive that was prepared to go to any lengths to sabotage the effort to achieve trade union unity. Brown read out some damning extracts – Oudegeest's expression of horror that the Russians might sincerely desire to cooperate with IFTU, his proposals on how to cool their ardour, his reference to Purcell's 'communist sympathies' and his suggestion the anti-Russian clique in the Amsterdam Executive meet separately, in advance, to plot strategy against the Soviet splitters and their English cronies.

It was a sensation. The TUC delegates were 'shocked' and 'gravely alarmed,' the *Daily Herald* reported, and IFTU faced the gravest crisis in its history.[6] Citrine told the Congress that he could scarcely believe his ears when he heard Brown's revelation.[7] He was 'astounded' and he questioned whether anyone who could compose such an epistle had any

---

[1] *Ibid.*, p. 35.
[2] That was even the way *The Labour Magazine* put it, IX, 10 (Oct., 1927), 654.
[3] *Fourth Congress: Report of Proceedings*, pp. 46–7.   [4] *Ibid.*, pp. 49–51.
[5] For the text of the offending letter, see *ibid.*, pp. 85–6, and for more on its contents, see above, pp. 79–80.
[6] *Daily Herald*, 4 Aug., 1927.   [7] *Fourth Congress: Report of Proceedings*, pp. 51–3.

right to stay on as IFTU secretary. Oudegeest himself was confused and chastened. If he did write the letter, he was ready to resign, but it was a long time ago and he could not remember.[1]

The Congress adjourned in an uproar. Jouhaux denied ever receiving the offending document, but Oudegeest acted more and more like the little boy caught with his hand in the cookie-jar. Perhaps, he suggested, the English translation made the letter sound somewhat more reprehensible than it really was. The whole scandal was referred to the Congress's Staff and Finance committee for judgement, and two days later, Oudegeest resigned. He acknowledged writing the letter, while still insisting the translation made it look worse. The committee's report indicated its members could not reach the customary unanimous verdict on the matter because 'the British representative, Mr Citrine, was unable to accept the findings of the other members.'[2] Aside from the lonely recalcitrant, the committee agreed that the letter was authentic, and that it was 'unhappily worded' and should never have been sent. The report also rebuked Brown, however, for having hoarded away his incriminating document for $2\frac{1}{2}$ years, letting several occasions slip by for dealing with the matter inoffensively. It should not have been sprung on the Congress as a surprise, the committee majority complained.

All in all, Brown had taken as much of a beating as Oudegeest, and Citrine was as irate as ever. The report was 'a deliberate and definite attempt to whitewash Oudegeest' and to suppress the irrefutable fact that most members of IFTU's Executive had been sabotaging the unity campaign all along, deliberately.[3] Oudegeest was just as upset.[4] Dark forces were at work trying to weaken the international, he charged. 'The agents of Russia, Purcell and Brown,' would continue to attack the organization, no matter who succeeded him in the secretariat. He clearly had the Congress on his side. The majority report on the Oudegeest letter was accepted, 66 to 14, in spite of British objections, and when elections were held for a new IFTU Executive committee, Purcell, the TUC's agreed nominee, was rejected in favour of Hicks, who brusquely declined the honour in advance but was named anyway. The British delegates walked out *en masse* in protest, and the Congress broke up in confusion shortly thereafter.

It looked like Amsterdam was done for, and at least some of its

[1] *Ibid.*, pp. 53–4.
[2] For the text of the report, see *The International Trade Union Movement*, VII, 8 (Aug., 1927), 114–15 or *1927 TUC: Report of Proceedings*, pp. 504–5.
[3] *Fourth Congress: Report of Proceedings*, p. 82.
[4] *Ibid.*, pp. 83–4.

supporters apparently began to have second, hard thoughts the morning after. Stenhuis wrote a piece for the organ of the Dutch trade union federation suggesting the International change tack and talk with the Russians after all. 'The British are suspicious of the I.F.T.U.,' he acknowledged, 'and as a result it has been bereft of all power. Negotiations with the Russians would restore this lost confidence.' Even Jouhaux seemed ready to relent a bit. He told a reporter for the Soviet press that he would welcome the Russians in IFTU, and that so long as the USSR did not slander western labour leaders, he believed it would have their 'active sympathy.'[1]

The conciliatory gestures seemed to have little effect in London. Brown told the *Daily Herald* the Paris Congress had demonstrated Amsterdam's 'financial, intellectual and moral weakness' and made it 'impossible even for the most ardent defender of the status quo openly to support continuance on the same lines.'[2] Trade union unity was necessary, but it would have to be built on an entirely new base, and he suggested that world congress the Russians had been urging for so long. 'The greatest blow that Internationalism could suffer,' he concluded, 'would be the patching up of the I.F.T.U. in the old form so that it could continue on its unstable, haphazard and ineffective way.'

Brown was not alone. A number of TUC leaders suggested throwing the whole problem over to the delegates at the forthcoming Edinburgh Congress, who would almost certainly have quit Amsterdam on the spot with any encouragement whatsoever from the higher-ups. The councillors voted instead, however, to ask Congress to authorize the new General Council and its International Committee to give the whole IFTU connection a thorough going-over and then take whatever measures seemed appropriate. The councillors would avoid all contacts with the IFTU Executive until that review was completed.[3]

One would have expected the Communists – Russian and British alike – to rejoice in IFTU's disintegration, and perhaps even claim credit for it. It was the issue of international trade union unity, after all, that was bringing Amsterdam down, just as the Soviet leaders had said it would. The Anglo-Russian Committee might indeed be on the point of blowing up, but that was what a high quality explosive was supposed to do. It had served its purpose. It had undermined the foundations of the

---

[1] For both Stenhuis' and Jouhaux' articles, see *IFTU Press Reports*, VI, 31 (1 Sept., 1927), 4–7 or the *Daily Herald*, 3 Sept., 1927.

[2] *Daily Herald*, 2 Sept., 1927.

[3] General Council Minutes, No. 270, 1 Sept., 1927.

Amsterdam citadel, and that capitalist bastion was about to fall to pieces.

Such a reaction might have been logical, but it was not evident in the Party press.[1] The comrades seemed perplexed by the Paris Congress from the very beginning. How could one account, for example, for Purcell's strong pro-Russian speech? It was just a lot of 'left phrases,' the press decided. Purcell had always been good at that. The 'practical effect' of such a speech was nil, and Purcell knew it. If he really believed in trade union unity he would long since have abandoned the 'decrepit, corrupt bureaucracy' of IFTU. The Oudegeest letter was no surprise: Communists had always known he was intriguing against them. The General Council's dramatic walkout was a sham, designed only to try to deceive the delegates to the Edinburgh Trades Union Congress in September. The Council knew it was in for trouble at Edinburgh. It would be challenged on its sabotage of the Anglo-Russian Committee. By creating a lot of fuss over the IFTU meeting, Hicks and his cronies hoped to distract the delegates' attention away from the real issues of trade union internationalism.

Neither the English nor the Soviets even made a pretense of courtesy any more. The Reds virtually dared the General Council to try to liquidate the Committee. Why was not such a motion on the calendar for the Edinburgh Congress? Probably, *Pravda* taunted, because the councillors did not even have the spunk to act on their own real convictions.[2] If the Russians expected a reply to such gibes, they were to be disappointed. The TUC leaders remained icily non-communicative toward their opposite numbers in the USSR from late July on. The General Council was still awaiting a reply to that comprehensive list of grievances it had submitted. The Russians seemed in no hurry, however, to enter their plea to the indictment.

It was not until early September, just a few days before that Congress was to convene, that the General Council heard from the Russians officially again.[3] Tomsky was finally responding to the Council's charges

[1] The analysis that follows draws from *Pravda*, 2, 4, 9, 10 Aug., 1927; Giovanni Germanetto, 'Die Amsterdamer Internationale und der Parisier Kongress,' *Die Rote Gewerkschaftsinternationale*, No. 8/9 (79/80) (Aug.–Sept., 1927), pp. 482–4; Clemens Dutt, 'War Preparation and the T.U.C.,' *Labour Monthly*, IX (Sept., 1927), 515–23; Harry Pollitt, 'The Paris Conference of the I.F.T.U.,' *ibid.*, pp. 524–7; 'The Paris Conference of the I.F.T.U.,' *The Communist*, II, 8 (Sept., 1927), 78–80.

[2] 'Amsterdam and the General Council,' *Pravda*, 10 Aug., 1927.

[3] Central Council to General Council, 30 Aug., 1927, in *1927 TUC: Report of Proceedings*, pp. 495–501 or *Inprecorr*, VII, 53 (15 Sept., 1927), 1185–7. The Russian-language version was published in *Pravda*, 3 Sept., 1927.

of five weeks earlier, and he was rejecting them totally. The Soviets affirmed once again every criticism they had ever made of the TUC leadership. The British were only picking a fight with Tomsky to evade the really important issue of their own treachery. They wanted to break up the Committee 'in order to assist the Conservative Government to continue its military preparations unhampered.' They were thus involved in 'crimes against the working class' and the Soviets would never consent to cover up for them.

The General Council's July letter seemed to assume the Committee's only purpose was to set up a Moscow–Amsterdam conference, Tomsky continued. He 'categorically' rejected any such attempt 'to minimize the significance of the...Committee.' It had been established for bigger purposes – to combat the capitalist offensive, to resist the war menace, to fight 'for a united class-conscious Trade Union International.' In order to justify liquidating the organization, however, the British stressed only its secondary functions, and Tomsky protested. Even when the Baldwin government was making its final preparations for a new attack on the USSR, all the British could propose was submitting the question to IFTU, a suggestion 'meant to give the matter a first class funeral.' The men who betrayed the miners last year were betraying the peace cause in 1927.

Just in case that message was not clear enough, the Russians put it more bluntly yet just three days later in a telegram addressed to the delegates of the Edinburgh Congress.[1] The Home Office had once again denied Tomsky a visa, so he could not deliver the abuse personally.[2] It seemed none the less pungent for coming by wire. The Soviets sent their 'greetings' to the British workers – and their sympathies. It had been a bad year! The 'capitalist and imperialist lackeys' of the General Council had betrayed the general strike, sabotaged the cause of the miners, acquiesced in the shocking Trade Disputes Act, connived in the intervention in China and refused to protest the war preparations against the USSR. They were now urging the pernicious doctrines of class peace and fostering dangerous 'illusions as to Parliamentary Government's ability solve all working class problems.'

The British workers had some hard tasks before them, the message

---

[1] *Pravda*, 3 Sept., 1927. English translations in *1927 TUC: Report of Proceedings*, pp. 493–5 and *Sunday Worker*, 4 Sept., 1927.

[2] TUC records indicate the General Council made a modest effort on Tomsky's behalf, but Joynson-Hicks was stubborn. See International Committee Minutes, 23 Aug., 1927, file 901, doc. I.C. 14 1926–7 and General Council Minutes, No. 292, 5 Sept., 1927.

continued. They had to check the capitalist predators at home, resist Baldwin's imperialist adventurism in China and struggle relentlessly against the projected attack on the USSR. To persist in such efforts, and prevail, demanded 'first of all substitution of old bankrupt leadership by fresh bold honest working class leaders.' Under its new management, the TUC could once again take up the campaign for international proletarian unity. IFTU, of course, was hopeless. What was needed was a new fighting international to mobilize the masses against capitalism and imperialism. The Anglo-Russian Committee could help found such an organization. But the General Council leaders, who 'have chosen way of Baldwin's Government instead of workers' way,' were sabotaging the Committee. The Soviets wished the British the best of luck finding worthier men to speak for them, and signed themselves 'Yours very truly and fraternally!' It was a harsh message, *Pravda* admitted, but the councillors deserved every word of it.[1] If they wanted to dissolve the Committee in retaliation, they would have to suffer the consequences. Sooner or later, the British masses would exact their own penalties for such betrayal.

For the TUC to maintain the Committee in spite of so intense a propaganda barrage would just make its spokesmen look spineless and absurd. Of the British labour leaders who mattered, only A. J. Cook still held out for the Russian connection. The Soviets were being abused because they helped the miners, he alleged.[2] The General Council and the Labour party Executive had formed a bloc with the Tories in retaliation. He, however, felt a 'great deal of gratitude' to 'our Russian comrades' and he was not going to betray them just to get 'bouquets from Cabinet ministers.' Cook's, however, was a lonely voice. An editorialist in *The Labour Magazine* advanced the more typical argument.[3] The 'extraordinarily ill-natured and incapable methods of the Russian Trade Union leaders' had only served to hinder and obstruct the campaign for international unity,' the writer charged. They had turned the Committee into 'an instrument of disruption,' not a force for reconciliation. The TUC had shown 'forbearance and restraint,' but there was a limit to its patience.

The writer may have had some inside information. In fact, on September 5, the day Congress opened, the General Council examined all the correspondence with the Russians all over again, decided to distribute the documents to the delegates, and appointed a sub-committee

---

[1] *Pravda*, 3 Sept., 1927.   [2] *The Miner*, 3 Sept., 1927.
[3] *The Labour Magazine*, VI, 5 (Sept., 1927), 217.

of four – Hicks, Pugh, Swales and Citrine – to 'draft a recommendation to Congress' in order to get a 'definite decision on the policy to be adopted toward the All-Russian Council of Trade Unions.'[1] Everybody must have known what that would mean, and by the 7th, the sub-committee had its report ready, a statement Citrine would read to Congress proposing abolition of the Committee. The councillors accepted it unanimously.[2]

By that time, the Edinburgh Congress was already two days old. Although the CPGB claimed 12 of the delegates as Party members, and praised, in retrospect, their 'clear revolutionary criticism of the reform-ists,'[3] Beatrice Webb was closer to the mark when she contrasted Edinburgh and Scarborough and concluded the TUC had now come full circle.[4] Revolutionary sentiments ebbed and flowed like ocean tides, she mused, sweeping 'the British proletarian mind backwards and for-wards decade after decade – without effecting any substantial achieve-ment to compensate for the disturbance of the nation's life.' Just as Scarborough registered the high water mark of the revolutionary current, so Edinburgh delineated the low. It completed 'the breach with the grandiose policy of class war trumpeted...only two years ago.'

The brief presidential address had set the tone of the meeting.[5] Hicks had shown his 'real scab face,' *Pravda* commented, in his call for industrial peace and class collaboration.[6] He had very little to say about international problems, however, except to note, towards the end of his speech, that 'a great deal of resentment is felt among us against what might be termed the crude arrogance of the Russians in telling us how to conduct our affairs.' ('Hear, hear!' shouted the delegates). Hicks asked the Congress to remember the Russians had been 'reared in a hard and terrible school' and that their leaders saw the world 'with that experience as a background.' The British had to be as sympathetic and generous as possible, and 'whatever happens,' must not allow 'the conquests of the Russian workers' to be menaced by outsiders.

It was about as much as Hicks could say, of course, since the General Council had not yet formally voted its final decision for a rupture, but his failure to make any specific statement on the Committee, as well as his silence on the Amsterdam Federation, surely indicated the leadership was doing some major last-minute rethinking of all the TUC's inter-

---

1 General Council Minutes, No. 292, 5 Sept., 1927.
2 *Ibid.*, No. 298, 301, 7 Sept., 1927.
3 CPGB, *Ninth Congress: Reports, Theses & Resolutions*, pp. 20, 61.
4 *Beatrice Webb's Diaries, 1924–32*, pp. 152–3.
5 *1927 TUC: Report of Proceedings*, pp. 69–70.   6 *Pravda*, 7 Sept., 1927.

national connections. While the responsible people were coming up with their recommendations, Congress could devote itself to domestic concerns, and most especially, to battering the National Minority Movement.[1] The relevant resolution stressed the sinister outside influences dominating NMM, its outside sources of money, and the organization's use of 'wrecking tactics' against established leaders. The revolutionaries lost the decisive vote by 25 to 1, 3,746,000 to 148,000. It was the worst drubbing the Minority Movement had ever taken.

It was not until September 8 that Citrine strode to the podium to present the General Council's report on the Anglo-Russian Committee.[2] Ramsay MacDonald had just spoken, warming the audience up with some hot anti-Communist invective, but Citrine hardly really needed such help. His was a carefully phrased, unemotional and restrained discourse, free of invective, grandiloquence or tub-thumping. Practically the same people, he began, who took the initiative in starting the Committee two years ago, were now coming before Congress to report that in their considered opinion no good purpose would be served by continuing the organization. So long as 'the present attitude of the Russian Trade Union Movement' was maintained, it was 'impossible to go on.' It was not just a matter of the General Council's 'injured dignity,' he emphasized, but of two very different conceptions – the Russian and the British – of what purpose the Committee was supposed to serve.

The councillors could now discern at least three fundamental differences keeping the two organizations apart. The first difference derived from the very special historical experience of the Russian labour movement. Its leaders believed that 'in some way Moscow is a stage upon which the revolutionary battle of the workers is being fought, and that the rest of the world's Trade Unionists are interested spectators in the auditorium.' Unless others adopted their methods and principles, their revolutionary movement would be menaced, they felt. They did not understand why others refused to follow their example, and because of that, unfortunately, they discerned enemies 'in people whose only real desire is to be their sincere and warm friends.' That, then, was one point of friction with the Soviets.

A second derived from the Soviet effort to make the Committee over into some new international, and to get it involved in pronouncements extraneous to the two trade union movements. The British felt the purpose of the organization was only to bring English and Russian workers

---

[1] See especially *1927 TUC: Report of Proceedings*, pp. 324–31.
[2] *Ibid.*, pp. 358–60.

together, and to make it possible for the Soviets to affiliate to Amsterdam: nothing more. The TUC had yielded at times, Citrine acknowledged, and accepted Soviet suggestions for statements on China, for example, but it did feel it had to draw the line somewhere. The Russians apparently disagreed.

Finally, there was the matter of the Soviet's persistent abuse of their Committee partners. We were told in the USSR, Citrine explained, that 'such terms as "traitor" and "lickspittle" had become so common in the inner Councils of the Russian Movement that nobody took any notice of them, and they wondered we should be disturbed by it.' The General Council was disturbed, however, particularly after the Russians sent that scandalously abusive telegram a year ago to the Bournemouth Congress. It had made one last effort to iron things out, however, and finally got Tomsky to sign that non-interference pact at Berlin. 'Hardly was the ink dry on that agreement,' however, when the Russians were claiming the right to violate it. They insisted the TUC leadership take their orders on how to counter the war threat, and exploded when they did not get their way. In fact, if the danger really were so acute, 'is it too much to ask the Russians to refrain from attacking those who are willing to help them?' The TUC could work for peace, in fact, whether the Committee survived or not – and it surely would. But the Council saw no reason to maintain any formal tie to the Soviet trade unionists as things stood. If the Russian attitude changed, the Committee might be revived in the future, but for now, the 'unanimous and considered' judgement of the General Council was to liquidate the organization forthwith.

The debate on the resolution was prolonged and strenuous.[1] The Committee's defenders stressed the war danger, suggesting that a break with Tomsky would only encourage the ultras around Baldwin. The General Council's suggestion that the Russians discuss their military predicament with Amsterdam was absurd, an insult.

The argument had some merit, and drew support from some unexpected quarters. C. T. Cramp, for example, of the Railwaymen – Jimmy Thomas's union! – spoke out against dissolution. He did not like what the Russians put in their correspondence, he confessed, but he did not like the General Council's letters any better. 'Excessive adulation' on the one side confronted 'excessive denunciation' on the other. The TUC's leaders had gone 'very far on the path of humiliation and abasement' to keep their line to the USSR, and he understood their reluctance to go any further. But the overriding consideration was the war danger. A

[1] The verbatim report is in *ibid.*, pp. 351–70.

break would be interpreted as a gesture of support for the Tory hard-liners, and to give them any encouragement at such a critical time would be most unwise.

A well-known and established right-winger like Cramp might have swung a few marginal votes over to the Committee, but they surely swung right back again after the Woodworkers' J. Strain, an NMM militant, presented his emotional and extravagant defence of the organ-ization. The councillors were too sensitive, he suggested. If they thought what Tomsky was saying about them in Moscow was so awful, they should hear what their own rank and file were saying down there on the factory floor! Their recommendation to break with the Russians was 'hellish,' he blustered, and if the delegates accepted and supported it, 'it meant a declaration of war tomorrow against Russia.' The speech 'aroused a good deal of feeling,' the minutes recorded, 'and at times there was considerable commotion.'

For the most part, the members of the General Council had to conduct their own defence against such assaults. The only delegate to speak up for them from outside their ranks was John Clynes, the deputy leader of the Parliamentary Labour party. He was surprised they had not decided on a rupture much earlier. The Soviets had been offensive and dictatorial and the Committee was a sham. To continue to pretend a solidarity that was not really there at all would be pointless. 'Unity in appearance only is a unity without value.'

The councillors agreed. To keep the Committee would be to destroy the dignity of the British labour movement. It would just confirm the Russians in their arrogant conviction that they could terrorize the TUC leadership at will, and finally bend it to their liking. It was false to keep harping on the war issue: British trade unionists would of course never allow the Tories to wage war on the USSR – but that was not what was being decided. The question was whether the English were free to run their own labour organizations in their own way without Soviet inter-ference. To keep the Committee was to deny them that right.

The most astonishing contribution to the discussion was that of A. J. Cook. He was confused. He did not know how to vote. Admittedly, the Russians had said some nasty things, but so had the British. Perhaps if he had more time he could decide what should be done next. He could poll the MFGB's local organizations, for example. To enable him to do so, he suggested the whole matter be referred back to the new General Council. Otherwise, he was afraid that what he would encounter in the newspapers next day would be 'big black headlines...stating that the

Trades Union Congress which condemned the break with Russia has now endorsed it by breaking with Russia themselves.'

We cannot base our decisions on what might appear in tomorrow's capitalist press, Bevin replied sternly, and his eloquent and moving speech wound up the debate. The General Council's recommendation was accepted 2,551,000 'votes' to 620,000, a majority of better than 4 to 1. Most of the ballots for retaining the Committee came from Jimmy Thomas's Railwaymen. The Miners' Federation, beneficiary of a million pounds of Soviet *largesse* just a year earlier, abstained. Just in case the Tories might assume the TUC was now as anti-Russian as they, Congress quickly shouted through a resolution deploring Chamberlain's decision to sever diplomatic relations with Moscow and authorizing the General Council to publicize the unfortunate economic consequences of that break.[1]

With those issues out of the way, all the TUC had left to do was to snarl at Amsterdam a little for those indignities a month before at the Paris Congress. IFTU's fraternal delegate had tried to be conciliatory when he addressed the Congress, but the leadership refused to be mollified. It presented a resolution empowering the next General Council 'to review the whole question of the international relationship of Congress' in the light of the events at Paris and to take appropriate action. The delegates voted their leaders the big stick requested without dissent, but rejected, by over 2 to 1, an additional NMM resolution which would have committed the General Council to press for a joint Amsterdam–Profintern world labour congress.[2] Purcell wound up the Edinburgh meeting with a personal explanation of the crisis within IFTU.[3] The organization was dominated, he suggested, by 'astute and clever and capable men' who were nationalists first, Europeans only second, and internationalists not at all. They exhibited 'a very strong and very fierce anti-Russian bias' which was understandable, in view of the invective Moscow hurled at them constantly, but nonetheless unfortunate.

He, Purcell, was an internationalist. He was also frankly pro-Soviet, 'proud of what my class has achieved in Russia' and full of 'profound admiration for the real greatness of our Russian comrades.' Most of all, however, he was just for 'this great confraternity of Labour,' and that was what got him into trouble in IFTU. He regretted his personality had

[1] *Ibid.*, pp. 371–3, 501–2.
[2] The IFTU fraternal delegate's speech is in *ibid.*, pp. 345–8; the deliberations on TUC's future relationship with IFTU are in *ibid.*, pp. 373–5.
[3] *Ibid.*, pp. 376–81.

become an issue between London and Amsterdam, but he had no regrets for standing on the principles he did, and he believed that anybody else espousing them would have experienced the same hostility he did. What mattered however, was achieving 'real international solidarity' among trade unionists, and he hoped the next General Council could 'put a stop to the recriminations and criticisms' and get on with that task.

It was one of the more dramatic moments in a generally drab Congress. Edinburgh would be remembered, however, not so much for the break with the Russians, nor for the threat to break with IFTU, but for Hicks' almost frantic and somewhat pathetic pleas for industrial peace at home. A Minority Movement resolution condemning such bloodless sentimentalities was turned down overwhelmingly. The strike weapon had failed. Class war rhetoric had failed too. English trade unionists were ready to talk terms with the bourgeoisie. The Scarborough era was definitely at an end.

Not surprisingly, the Baldwin government was well-satisfied with Edinburgh, and particularly pleased with the vote to abolish the Committee. The Labour Minister even felt he had to warn his colleagues against making too much of that 'rather spectacular decision.'[1] 'To outward appearance,' he confessed, the rupture might seem 'to show a definite break from the aims and policies of revolutionary Moscow.' In reality, however, the Congress was only reflecting the views of the vast majority of rank and file trade unionists, 'who are in no way revolutionists.' The TUC had just come back, then, to 'where it was before the glamour of Moscow caught a few prominent leaders.'

Not all the Tory incumbents, however, contained their glee as successfully as did Steel-Maitland. Lord Birkenhead noisily congratulated the labour chiefs for their good sense in reaching 'a decision which is practically identical with the decision of the government.'[2] Joynson-Hicks, even more heavy-handedly, suggested the TUC propose him a vote of thanks for warning them, years ago, of the insidious Communist menace. 'Really, I am the best friend of the Trades Union Congress. I am trying to help them in their warfare against Russian Communism.'[3] The Chancellor of the Exchequer chimed in on the self-congratulations.[4] Churchill was delighted the TUC now saw things his way. He had always

[1] Cabinet Papers, 1927, CAB 24.188, C.P. 246(27), 18 Oct., 1927.
[2] *The Times*, 30 Sept., 1927.
[3] *Ibid.*, 21 Sept., 1927.
[4] *Ibid.*, 13 Sept., 1927. The CPGB later said Churchill's statement praising the liquidation was 'an outstanding justification of the Party's policy' of trying to keep it going: *Ninth Congress: Reports, Theses & Resolutions*, p. 61.

realized no one could achieve anything constructive trafficking with 'a band of political sectaries' like those Muscovite rascals. To try to come to an accommodation with them was like trying 'to make a pet of a poisonous snake.'

Such fulsome expressions of Tory support were a terrible embarrassment to the TUC leaders. A number of them rushed into print to assure everybody they had not joined any anti-Russian bloc and had not even ruled out further meetings with Tomsky some time in the future.[1] Before that could happen, however, the Soviets would have to ponder what was said at Edinburgh, tone down their 'distressingly hackneyed invective' against the General Council, and promise once again never to interfere in the TUC's domestic affairs.

Aside from loyal CPGB members, British labour leaders hardly seemed to care much about the split one way or the other. Cook expressed 'regret' about it in his own union's journal (and 'indignation' in the Communist-controlled *Sunday Worker*), but only because the rank and file had not been 'consulted' on the decision and because it could be misinterpreted as an indication of TUC support for Baldwin and Chamberlain. The Soviets could hardly take comfort, however, from the editorial on the break appearing in the MFGB's house organ, regretting Congress had 'felt it necessary' to abolish the Committee, but concluding: 'We can only hope that the drastic decision may cause the Russians to modify their attitudes.'[2]

British Communists found the MFGB's sermons particularly galling. Its leaders had 'betrayed the confidence of a million working miners' by refusing to vote 'no' on dissolving the Committee. They had, in effect, allied themselves with the General Council in bringing the long campaign to betray the Russians to a successful conclusion. It was all 'part and parcel of the capitalist preparations for a war on the Workers' Republic,' the CPGB charged. Those 'leftists' who had once expressed enthusiasm for the Committee in fact only backed it 'so long as it did nothing,' the Party explained. They were thus enabled 'to make splendid perorations and empty gestures about international solidarity.' As soon as the Russians insisted on using the organization to unmask cowards in the TUC leadership, however, they joined with the reactionaries to liquidate the embarrassment. The Committee must be revived, the CPGB decreed, and

[1] The summary derives from a *Daily Herald* editorial of 9 Sept., 1927, interviews with Hicks and Citrine in *ibid.*, 12 Sept., 1927, and Walter M. Citrine, 'Where are the Trade Unions Going?' *The Labour Magazine*, VI, 6 (Oct., 1927), 246–9.

[2] *The Miner*, 10 Sept., 1927. For Cook's statements, see *ibid.*, 17 Sept., 1927 and *Sunday Worker*, 11 Sept., 1927.

new committees established in individual industries. An Anglo-Russian Miners' Committee, presumably, would be among the first.[1]

The English comrades were too enthusiastic. The Russians themselves were not contemplating any more Committees. They insisted only they would 'devise ways and means' to keep in 'fraternal contact' with the British working class, no matter how offensive the connection might be to Baldwin's agents on the General Council.[2] The councillors had no backing any more anyway – except from the exploiters. A *Pravda* cartoon showed a fat tycoon chortling happily about how 'our people on the General Council are behaving themselves like real gentlemen.' The councillors had been sabotaging the interests of the proletariat for years, of course, but once having been obliged to break up the Committee, they could no longer hope to camouflage their treachery. The Soviets sent 'fraternal greetings' to the TUC rank and file who would, 'in the near future,' drive all the scoundrels 'into the cesspool' and install 'true revolutionaries' in their places.

If the TUC's leaders were really so wicked, why had the Soviets ever agreed to consort with them at Committee meetings? Had it really been wise to create the Committee, to hang on to it for so long, to let the British take the initiative in breaking it up? Andreev assured the faithful that the Party's record was flawless. The Committee linked the working masses of the two countries, not their leaders. The councillors had only agreed to the Committee when their rank and file required them to. Many of them tried to sabotage it from the beginning; all of them tried to after the general strike. The Soviets knew then the Committee was moribund, but they astutely avoided rupturing it so that they could unmask the councillors down to the last snivelling crypto-leftist. The English working masses, still solidly pro-Russian, would surely not tolerate their

[1] Material on CPGB reaction to the break derives from *Ninth Congress: Reports, Theses & Resolutions*, p. 56; *Workers' Life*, 16, 23 Sept., 1927, and *Sunday Worker*, 11 Sept., 1927.

[2] For sources on the official Soviet reaction to the break, see *Pravda* and *Izvestiia*, 9, 10, 11, 12 Sept., 1927 (especially Dogadov's interview of 9 Sept.); the Central Council's 'Statement to the Workers of England and the Soviet Union' in the newspapers for 12 Sept., 1927 and reprinted in USSR, Central Council of Trade Unions, *Professional'nye Soiuzy SSSR, 1926–1928. Otchet V. Ts.S.P.S. k VIII S''ezdy Professional'nykh Soiuzov* (Moscow: Knigoizdatel'stvo V. Ts.S.P.S., 1927), pp. 1–7; and (most fulsomely), Andreev's report in late Sept. to the Railway Workers' Union in Moscow, reprinted as Andrei A. Andreev, *Sryv Anglo-Russkogo Komiteta i Nashi Zadachi* (Moscow–Leningrad: Gosudarstvennoe Izdatel'stvo, 1927). For a good brief summary of Soviet reactions, consult V. I. Popov, *Anglo-Sovetskie Otnosheniia, 1927–1929* (Moscow: Izdatel'stvo Instituta Mezhdunarodnykh Otnoshenii, 1958), pp. 142–6.

leaders' newest and most blatant betrayal. The Minority Movement, therefore, would be strengthened, and the General Council weakened. The Soviets could form new united fronts, over the heads of the discredited leaders, with the labouring masses.[1] All would turn out for the best in this, the best of all dialectically possible worlds.

The dissolution of the Committee was a cruel blow to Trotsky and the Oppositionists. The Edinburgh decision deprived them of one of their last best issues in the battle against Stalinism. Trotsky obviously had not anticipated the TUC might go through with the break. The Committee was still a major issue in the Oppositionist 'platform' for the forthcoming 15th CPSU Congress, sent off to the Central Committee September 6.[2] To continue to flirt with social democrats – especially General Council traitors – would only confuse the international proletariat, the manifesto warned. To seek 'hearty accords' with TUC counter-revolutionaries was an especially dangerous tactic in a war emergency; it gave them the opportunity to betray the cause at the most crucial moment. The Stalinists were wrong on the Committee as they were wrong on China and wrong on their agricultural policy back home, and it was time the Party and the working class were told the truth before, not after, 'the heavy consequences of a policy that was false to the bottom had crashed over their heads.'

A joint meeting of the Politburo and the Central Control Commission considered the Oppositionist statement September 8, the same day the TUC voted to terminate the Committee. Stalin spoke at some length; his rivals were not allowed to speak at all. Their platform was an impertinence, they were told, and they were neither to publish nor circulate it.[3] Trotsky refused to be gagged. He and his friends decided to distribute their manifesto covertly. The authorities were made aware of the insubordination almost immediately, and as early as September 11, *Pravda* was again denouncing the Opposition publicly. Two days later, the secret police discovered one of the illegal printing presses producing the Trotskyite invective, shut it down, and reported all the culprits to the Central Control Commission. The stage was set for the last decisive confrontations.

The first of them came September 27, at a joint meeting of the Presidium

[1] Profintern was to play a major role in all this. See RILU's instructions to its sections' agit-prop specialists in *Profintern v Rezoliutsiakh*, p. 63.
[2] The platform was reprinted in Lev Trotsky, *The Real Situation in Russia*, trans. Max Eastman (London: G. Allen & Unwin, 1928), pp. 23–195. For the argument relating to the Committee, see pp. 32–3, 162, 169–70, 178–9.
[3] T–1015, 1027, Trotsky Archives.

of the Comintern's Executive Committee and the International Control Commission.[1] It was 9 in the evening when the session began, a chilly, snowy night, and all the delegates had worn heavy overcoats to keep out the cold. The coat rack was jammed. When J. T. Murphy's secretary saw Trotsky standing there looking around impatiently, he asked if he could help. Trotsky replied: 'I'm afraid not. I'm looking for two things – a good Communist and somewhere to hang my coat. They are not to be found here.'

If it had been an Oxford Union debate, Trotsky probably would have won it. He was well prepared. On the Committee issue, he had typed out 4,500 words summarizing the debacle, a closely argued final balance sheet on the liaison with the TUC.[2] Much of the same material went into his speech, which lasted over two hours. It was a magnificent statement for the prosecution, listing Stalin's sins, errors and stupidities all over the world. He found the latest attempts to defend the Committee policy appalling. The plain fact was that a cabal of flagrant counter-revolutionaries in Britain had been practically invited to betray the proletarian cause at a moment of their own choosing – when it would most benefit the imperialists, presumably.

Stalin responded just as belligerently. The Opposition had wobbled on the Committee issue as on every other. Zinoviev had once claimed the organization would 'render reformism harmless,' having forgotten, apparently, that the British members of the Committee were themselves reformists. When he finally did realize it, at the time of the general strike, he joined Trotsky in demanding an immediate break with them, deluding himself that he could overturn them all from a thousand miles away in Moscow. It was typical of the Opposition that it just swung from 'one stupidity to another.' The Committee had been managed well. The rupture, coming when it did, dramatized the war danger and the need to combat it. It confronted the workers unmistakably with the treachery of the General Council, and that was what the Party had intended all along.

The debate was all academic, of course, and all just history – the dreariest possible combination, as any schoolboy knows. Stalin was going to be remorseless, no matter who scored the debating points. Only Vuiovič supported Trotsky, and both were expelled from the Comintern Executive for their heresies. Two weeks later, the *vozhd* got Trotsky

[1] For what little we know of the meeting, see *Pravda*, 1 Oct., 1927, and Murphy, *New Horizons*, pp. 274–7. Stalin's speech is in *Sochineniia*, x, 153–67. For his comments on the Committee, see especially pp. 157–8. For Trotsky's reply, see T–3094, 3095, 27 Sept., 1927, Trotsky Archives.

[2] T–3093, 25 Sept., 1927, Trotsky Archives.

ousted from the CPSU Central Committee as well, and on November 14, after a pitiful Opposition effort to publicize itself during the celebrations marking the Revolution's tenth anniversary, the triumphant majority threw Trotsky out of the Party altogether. In one of the glorious ironies that make the historical discipline so appealingly enigmatic, British trade unionists, in 1927, played a modest role in achieving that objective which had eluded British infantrymen a decade earlier: the great Trotsky had finally been humbled.

7

Epilogue

I

Five months after the TUC liquidated the Anglo-Russian Committee, international Communism renounced united-front tactics altogether in favour of a tough, 'class against class,' ultra-left sectarianism.[1] To associate with yellow social-fascists was to expose oneself to ideological contamination, and the Party elect would no longer risk it. When, of course, a reformist dupe was ready to repent his idiocy and make his confession, the Communist priesthood might still absolve him. Revolutionaries dubbed that quaint sacrament 'the united front from below only,' so some familiar phraseology from the old liturgy, then, had found its way into the new catechism. But the substance was gone. Any further negotiations with the likes of a Purcell or a Cook, and any deals with the organizations they controlled, were now out of the question.

---

[1] To follow the shift in tactics in the primary sources, one should consult the records of the 15th CPSU Congress, the 9th ECCI plenum, the 4th RILU Congress and the 6th Comintern Congress. Available documentation includes *XV S''ezd Vsesoiuznoi Kommunisticheskoi Partii (B). 2 Dekabria–19 Dekabria 1927g. Stenograficheskii Otchet*, 2 vols. (Moscow: Partizdat TsK, KP [B], 1935). See especially Bukharin's Report from the ECCI, I, 543–604, and the resolution derived from that report, II, 1244–6. The CPGB put out an English-language transcript of most of the Congress. See *Report of the Fifteenth Congress of the Communist Party of the Soviet Union* (London: Communist Party of Great Britain, 1928). For the 9th ECCI, see *Kompartiia i Krizis Kapitalizma: 9-i Plenum I.K.K.I. Stenograficheskii Otchet* (Moscow: Partizdat, 1932). The key resolution on the 'Tasks of the British Communist Party' can be found in *Kommunisticheskii Internatsional v Dokumentakh*, pp. 729–40, and that material was translated into English and published in P. Braun, *At the Parting of the Ways: The Results of the Ninth Plenum of the Comintern* (London: Communist Party of Great Britain, 1928). For the 4th RILU Congress, see *Desiat' Let Profinterna*, pp. 157–233, *Mezhdunarodnoe Profdvizhenie* (the report of the RILU Executive to the Congress), and *Report of the Fourth Congress of the R.I.L.U.* (London: Published in England for the Red International of Labour Unions by the Minority Movement, 1928). For the 6th Comintern Congress, see *Protokoll: sechster Weltkongress der Kommunistischen Internationale, Moskau, 17 Juli–1 September 1928*, 4 vols. (Hamburg: C. Hoym, 1928–9). The resolutions are reprinted in *Kommunisticheskii Internatsional v Dokumentakh*, pp. 768–875 and deliberations may be followed in English in *Inprecorr*, VIII, 39 (25 July, 1928), 92 (31 Dec., 1928), 669–1771. Among the more interesting secondary sources on these matters are Degras (see her comment in *Communist International: Documents*, II, 424); Deutscher, *Trotsky*, pp. 397–401; Max Schachtman (see his introduction to

If it had been tactically sound to make coalitions with the reformists in 1921 – or even 1926 – why was it such a terrible mistake to do so in 1928? Because, the Party decreed, the era of partial capitalist stabilization was over. The west was entering a new epoch of economic and political crisis, the so-called 'Third Period,' which would see the final collapse of bourgeois regimes all over the world. In a frantic effort to postpone their Armageddon, the imperialists had moved sharply to the political right and demanded their stooges in the socialist movement and the trade unions come along with them. The old labour 'left,' then, had disappeared. The social democrats had capitulated totally to the bourgeoisie and were now nothing more than fascist hirelings. Trying to reach any agreement with them would be just ludicrous.

Had the International not jettisoned the united front in 1928, it is questionable whether Adolf Hitler would ever have come to power in Germany five years later. To stop Hitler would have demanded a close alliance of the whole of the political left. By the new dogmas, however, for the Reds to participate in any such venture was simply out of the question. Communists considered reformists as irredeemable as fascists. Indeed, the two were almost indistinguishable. Stalin himself had said so way back in 1924.[1] The socialist actually did the Party more damage because he lured away Communism's most likely convert, the ordinary workingman. The Red faithful must therefore direct most of their energies to exposing reformists, the Comintern decreed – and decreed it only a matter of six months before the Nazis took over the Chancellery in Berlin. Numbed by muddle-headed fantasies like that, the German proletariat let Hitler come to power without firing a shot. Hundreds of thousands of Party members, and millions who had followed their lead, capitulated to the Nazis with hardly a murmur. The most powerful Red apparatus in all Europe – except for the one in the USSR – had signed its own death warrant. 'Without Stalin, no Hitler!' So claimed the non-Communist German left in 1933. That, of course, is a slogan, not history, and the might-have-beens of the past are dazzling dead-ends professional chroniclers do well to avoid. One cannot but wonder, however, what kind of a Germany might have emerged – and what kind of a Europe – had those who led the Comintern only given Adolf Hitler as resolute a battle as – say – the quaking reformist relics on the TUC's

Trotsky, *Third International*, pp. xxvi–xxxv); and Thomas Weingartner, *Stalin und der Aufstieg Hitlers* (Berlin: Walter de Gruyter & Co., 1970), pp. 10–18.

[1] J. Stalin, 'Main Factors in the International Situation,' *Communist International*, No. 6 (New Series) (1924), pp. 3–16.

General Council put up against Stanley Baldwin in 1926. To speculate on such possibilities, of course, is not only historically unsound, but ideologically mischievous.

What made the International veer so sharply to the left in 1928? What was the 'real story' behind the repudiation of united front tactics? What came over Stalin to persuade him to authorize that suicidal sectarianism characteristic of the 'Third Period'? The most common explanation of these events is also the least likely. It goes – somewhat crudely, perhaps – like this: having finally defeated the CPSU ultras – Trotsky, Zinoviev, Kamenev – Stalin was now ready to turn on the moderates – Bukharin, Rykov, Tomsky. Since they were on the 'right,' he could humiliate and isolate them by ordering the Comintern to move 'left.' It sounds reasonable enough, but it derives from an unsophisticated fixation on those 'left' and 'right' labels. Bukharin might be on the 'right' in his tender regard for the New Economic Policy, but he was no moderate when it came to his enthusiasm for making revolution abroad. Quite the contrary! His Comintern speeches reveal him as much more of a swashbuckling adventurer than Stalin ever was, and much more impatient with the idea capitalism was even partially 'stabilized.' That was Stalin's theory, not Bukharin's. It was Stalin who warned it could be 15 to 20 years before Bolsheviks could topple another government. So insofar as 'Third Period' theories repudiated such notions, proposing instead the premise that capitalism was in a state of immediate collapse and that short-term revolutionary prospects were excellent, it was Stalin, not Bukharin, who was made to look like the ideological greenhorn.

An alternative explanation of Comintern's move 'left' – also assuming the 'real' reason for the shift lay in the USSR's domestic concerns – cites Stalin's disillusionment with the New Economic Policy. He had made the decision to expropriate the NEP-men and kulaks, the argument goes. He was ready to launch his so-called 'second revolution,' creating an industrialized economy and a collectivized agriculture in barely a decade. That meant Soviet Communists would have to break with their own bourgeoisie and wage class war at home again, and foreign comrades should logically do the same. To do so effectively, of course, they would have to rule out any deals with social-democratic class traitors. That's the theory, and it's an improvement over its predecessor, but it is still unconvincing. Had the Comintern decision to move left come in 1930 rather than in 1928, it would have to be taken more seriously. By then, Stalin had indeed decided he could not collectivize his recalcitrant peasants except by waging class war on them. But he had not come to that conclusion in 1927 or 1928. He still thought he could make his second revolution by persuasion. He did not believe force would be necessary. What could he possibly gain, then, from ordering proletarians to the barricades abroad. Indeed, if they followed those instructions, they might conceivably jeopardize the *vozhd*'s whole programme. The Five-Year Plan assumed massive Soviet imports of capital equipment from the west. If, however, the west took offence at Russia's militant allies in the Comintern, its reaction might be to deny Stalin those machines. What a terrible price to pay for the doubtful satisfaction of spouting a lot of extra-inflammatory rhetoric – particularly when Stalin surely realized the odds on any significant revolutionary triumphs were almost nil.

That Stalin ordered the renunciation of united front tactics, then, in order to achieve some devious political advantage domestically, seems unlikely. Indeed, Stalin may not have initiated the new strategy at all. Bukharin hinted, later on, that Russia's sister-organizations in the International, not the CPSU, first proposed the tougher line.[1] It makes sense. The comrades had spent six years dutifully trying to make contact with a pack of frustratingly unresponsive reformist do-nothings, and for the most part, they had failed. Where they had temporarily succeeded, as in Britain and in China, they were no better off for their success, and quite probably worse off. Britain, however, not China, was decisive. One could hardly generalize from the complicated Chinese model anyway, except to note that as an economically primitive society with a numerically minuscule proletariat, it had never been the most promising of Comintern targets in any event. England was different. It was a fully developed imperialist bastion. It should have been riddled with economic contradictions, among the likeliest candidates for early disintegration. Any revolutionary techniques Communists could devise which were appropriate to the island should hold for the rest of the advanced capitalist world as well. The Anglo-Russian Committee was a key part of the strategy finally elaborated for Britain. The Tomsky–Purcell alliance had been advertised as much more than just a pact between the Soviet trade unions and the TUC. It had been proposed as the Comintern's strongest link to the European labour movement, to the overwhelming majority of proletarian class brothers in the most advanced countries on earth. If the errant dupes of western social democracy were ever to be won over by negotiation and conciliation, this was the organization through which to win them. But the Committee had

[1] Degras, *Communist International: Documents*, II, 424.

achieved nothing. The reformists seemed no more moved by calls to reconciliation in 1927 than they had by summonses to insurrection in 1917. They had rejected the Bolsheviks as revolutionaries a decade ago; they rejected them as conciliators and collaborators now.[1] The effort to find a common language with renegades and traitors had just demoralized the Movement, and its members wanted no more part of any such shameful equivocations.

Moscow had no reasons of its own to persist in the old tactics. They had not advanced Soviet state interests, as Stalin had once hoped; they divided the Party, and they provided the *vozhd*'s critics with a lot of deadly ammunition to use against him. How much wiser to let the foreign comrades go chase their revolutionary rainbows, if that was what they wanted. They were unlikely to embarrass Stalin by succeeding. All he wanted to do, anyway, was build a socialist bastion in Russia undisturbed. The Comintern – and all the nit-picking scholastics who ran it – had just unsettled and inconvenienced him. If they now wanted to go their lonely sectarian way, why shouldn't they be encouraged to do so! Zinoviev had once affirmed that the Committee would 'render reformism harmless' in Europe. Perhaps Stalin was hoping the collapse of the Committee, and the renunciation of the whole strategy it embodied, would render his fellow-revolutionaries harmless, and leave him free to make the USSR over into the economic and military superpower of which he dreamed.

'Third Period' doctrines dictated some drastic changes in the campaign for a single trade union international. To keep trying to talk the Amsterdam bureaucracy into such a venture would be an exercise in futility. Only the IFTU 'leftists' had ever shown any real interest in unity, and they had all disappeared. The rupture of the Committee had shattered the Amsterdam left. Some of its adherents, especially among the rank and file, had subsequently come over to Communism, but the rest, including practically all the leaders, had retreated, with the bourgeoisie, far to the right. They were now preaching class peace, Parliamentarianism, and nationalistic chauvinism, and negotiating with them would be a waste of time.[2]

Given the circumstances, the Comintern considered the possibility of abandoning the unity slogans altogether, withdrawing all Party members

---

[1] Deutscher, *Stalin*, pp. 398–9, makes the point well, and I borrow his ideas gratefully.

[2] For samples of this argument, see Braun, *Ninth Plenum*, p. 25; *Mezhdunarodnoe Profdvizhenie*, pp. 51–3; *Program of the Communist International Adopted at the Sixth World Congress in 1928* (Calcutta: Radical Book Club, [1945]), pp. 51–2.

from reformist trade unions, and setting up separate, ideologically pure, Communist labour organizations.[1] It would be good showmanship, the Reds decided, but poor politics. True enough, the unity campaign involved some risks. Even Profintern had occasionally seemed to be urging 'unity at any price,' and the comrades chastised themselves for that error at their 4th Congress.[2] It was also true, however, that sooner or later – by 'Third Period' reckoning, sooner! – the proletariat would have to come together to wage class war. Marx said so. The united front therefore still made sense, but under the new dispensation, it would have to be a united front from below only, unity on Moscow's terms, unity for revolutionary action. As capitalism's crisis deepened, the working masses would see the need to consolidate their strength quickly. They would lose patience with the Amsterdam dawdlers and go ahead without them. Only Communists could direct such an effort. The way to a unity that would matter, then, was to persuade the trade union rank and file to oust the treacherous lickspittles from their easy chairs in the executive headquarters and appoint fighting Party regulars to head the labour movement. That was clearly what was demanded by the tactics of 'united front from below.'

Outside the USSR, Profintern was now to take principal responsibility for implementing that policy. RILU had seemed a bit anaemic since 1924. Its fourth congress had been postponed almost three years. The problem was the apathy, or even hostility, of Profintern's most influential affiliate, the Soviet trade union federation. So long as Tomsky had been exchanging cordialities with Purcell and Citrine, Lozovsky and his cronies had been only an embarrassment to him. Now, however, the 15th Party Congress instructed Tomsky to 'put relations between the Central Trade Union Council and the Profintern in order.' RILU had to be revived, turned into something more than just a 'publishing company,' made over into a truly active organizational centre.[3] Lozovsky and his associates promised to do their best, and the Soviet trade unions pledged their cooperation.

Profintern's best, in Great Britain, did not seem much good, nor did Tomsky's 'cooperation' appear to make much difference. The Minority Movement duly adopted the new 'class against class' rhetoric in 1928, and the Russian trade union federation bestowed its official blessing by

---

[1] Degras, *Communist International: Documents*, II, 432–3.
[2] *Fourth RILU Congress: Report*, pp. 5–7, 20; *Desiat' Let Profinterna*, pp. 181–3.
[3] See *XV S''ezd VKP (B)*, I, 572 (Bukharin), 605–16 (Lozovsky), 686–91 (Mel'nichansky).

sending a fraternal delegate to the NMM's 1929 annual conference.[1] It didn't help. Leftists voted against the NMM with their feet, deserting it first by the thousands, later by the hundreds of thousands. Walter Citrine was in on the kill, with a sledgehammer attack on the Movement beginning right after the Edinburgh Congress.[2] The General Secretary amassed his evidence majestically, mobilized the language superbly, and produced an inspired brief for the prosecution proving – beyond much question – that NMM took Moscow's directions and served only Moscow's purposes.

It is doubtful, however, whether the Minority Movement would have survived even had Citrine restrained himself. The stern demands of 'Third Period' orthodoxy were just too much for pragmatic English workingmen. By 1930, the Movement was a shambles. Even Profintern admitted it. The NMM was 'practically isolated from the masses,' it confessed.[3] Its membership was way down, its publications did not sell – and all of this in objective circumstances, a major international business crisis, that should have enabled it to achieve dramatic results. The NMM bosses themselves were to blame for not carrying out RILU's policy of 'the independent leadership of economic struggle.' What that meant was that NMM enthusiasts participating in an industrial dispute were to do so in such a way as to batter the reformist trade union bureaucrats as badly as they did the capitalist bosses. Not surprisingly, it was a tactic the rank-and-file worker neither understood nor appreciated. The Minority Movement continued to fade in the first years of the thirties. By 1932, it was claiming only 700 members, and a year later, Profintern allowed its client organization to disappear.[4]

Adjusting to the new 'class against class' orthodoxy put as big a strain on the British Communist Party as it did on the NMM. The CPGB was not in a particularly healthy condition at the time anyway. In October, 1927, when the comrades gathered for their Ninth Congress, membership

---

[1] For his speech, see *Now For Action. The Policy of the National Minority Movement. A Report of the Sixth Annual Conference. Aug. 24–25, 1929* (London: National Minority Movement, 1929), pp. 24–32. The delegate, a certain A. M. Zikhon, had his signals crossed. He called for recreating the Anglo-Russian Committee, which was not the Party line at the time at all.

[2] Walter M. Citrine, 'Democracy or Disruption,' *The Labour Magazine*, VI, 8 (Dec., 1927), 342–5, 9 (Jan., 1928), 387–91, 10 (Feb., 1928), 438–41 and 11 (Mar., 1928), 487–91. The articles were later published in book form (London: Trades Union Congress, 1928). For a Communist reaction, see Braun, *Ninth Plenum*, p. 23.

[3] *Report of the Fifth Congress of the R.I.L.U.* (London: Published in England for the Red International of Labour Unions by the Minority Movement, 1930), pp. 107–14.

[4] For the NMM's death agonies, see the concluding sections of Martin, *Communism and the British Trade Unions*.

The United Front

rolls had shrunk by a third in just twelve months. The leadership, however, assigned most of the blame for the drop to forces outside its control – 'victimization, evictions, police intimidation, unemployment and abject poverty'[1] – and hardly anybody at the Congress seemed unduly concerned about Party prospects. The delegates went through all their traditional rhetorical rituals as if nothing had happened. The rupture of the Committee was deplored and its re-establishment demanded. The leaders of the TUC, and of the Labour party, were castigated as opportunists, cowards, lackeys and traitors: Communists were then instructed to drop by the renegades' offices, sign up, and try to take over their organizations from within.

It was the immobility, ineptitude and arrogance of the Communist establishment in Britain that so exasperated Comintern associates. One of them, a few years later, would label the CPGB the International's 'most useless toy.'[2] Its failings were not entirely the Central Committee's fault, he admitted. The 'mental attitude of the British worker' made it hard to recruit him. But the leadership made things much worse. It seemed absolutely set in its ways, 'more and more averse,' a sympathetic chronicler confessed later, 'to any suggestions involving departure from existing traditions and methods.'[3] Ideologically, it left everything to Moscow, taking Russian orders with an air of perfunctory nonchalance that irritated more philosophically-inclined comrades. One of them, the Ukrainian Communist, Manuilsky, finally exploded on the subject, with some eloquence.[4] 'How does it happen,' he demanded, that the British never seems to be stirred by 'all the fundamental problems' the International has to deal with. The CPGB passed all the prescribed resolutions, of course, but still seemed quite detached from the argument, without 'any profound organic connection' to it. The Party was becoming just 'a society of great friends.' To the ideologically fervent, the islanders' self-possession in matters of dogma was both threatening and infuriating.

For just a little while, however, from the end of 1927 until late 1929, the British comrades actually did discuss doctrine. By continental standards, it must not have seemed like much of a scrap, but for the CPGB, it was indeed 'the keenest battle of ideas the Party has so far known.'[5] Palme Dutt and Harry Pollitt initiated the debate, urging the

---

[1] *Ninth Congress: Reports, Theses & Resolutions*, pp. 15–16.
[2] Jan Valtin (R. J. H. Krebs), *Out of the Night* (London: William Heinemann. [1941]). pp. 286–7.   [3] Hutt, *British Working Class*, pp. 192–3.
[4] The outburst came at the 10th ECCI in 1929, and is cited in Pelling, *British Communist Party*, pp. 45–6.   [5] Hutt, *British Working Class*, p. 193.

time had come for the Party to cut its ties to Labour altogether and strike off on its own. Conditions had changed since 1921. Ramsay Mac-Donald's organization was just a 'third bourgeois party' now. It no longer represented the interests of the rank-and-file worker to any degree. Given the deterioration of the economic situation in Britain, the time was ripe for the growth of a mass revolutionary movement. If Communists were to lead it, they had to detach themselves from the Labourites.[1]

The practical effect of the proposed change would not seem, to an outsider, all that startling. Instead of urging a Labour government, Communists would propose a 'revolutionary workers' government.' Instead of supporting MacDonald's men for the House of Commons, Communists would offer candidates of their own. Instead of J. R. Campbell, William Gallacher and Albert Inkpin running the CPGB, Palme Dutt, Harry Pollitt and Page Arnot would speak for it. Who cared? The comrades were not that numerous anyway, and no matter what strategies they adopted, they were not likely to make much of an impact on the British political scene in any event.

That, however, reflects the attitudes of cynical, bourgeois pedants: enthusiastic devotees saw things differently. The break with tradition would be decisive, one way or the other. Dutt and Pollitt were proposing the CPGB declare its independence from the discredited old Labour aristocracy and strike off on its own. It was an exhilarating, but also somewhat frightening, challenge. If the premises all proved true, if the 'broad working masses' really were moving left with all that resolute determination the Party propagandists attributed to them, then it should work. If, on the other hand, current CPGB slogans represented only daydreams and wishful thinking, it would fail, and the Party would degenerate into a disgruntled clique of sectarian ultras.

To the majority in the Central Committee, the new line seemed much too risky – as well as doctrinally unsound – and they rejected it. Dutt and Pollitt appealed to the International for a re-hearing. Given the sharp

---

[1] The best source for the new doctrine is Dutt's column, 'Notes of the Month,' in *Labour Monthly*. See especially Vol. IX, 12 (Dec., 1927), 707–27 and Vol. X, 1 (Jan., 1928), 5–22 and 4 (Apr., 1928), 195–214. See also Arnot's speech to the 9th ECCI (Feb., 1928) in *Communist Policy in Great Britain: The Report of the British Commission of the Ninth Plenum of the Comintern* (London: Communist Party of Great Britain, [1928]), pp. 17–27. For secondary accounts of the tactical shift, see Pelling, *British Communist Party*, pp. 45–50; E. H. Carr, *Studies in Revolution* (New York: The Universal Library, 1964), pp. 176–8; Hutt, *British Working Class*, pp. 192–3; Joseph Redman (Brian Pearce), *The Communist Party and the Labour Left, 1925–1929*, 'Reasoner Pamphlets. Number One' (Hull, England: [1957)], pp. 10–16.

move to the left there, it is hardly surprising they quickly lined up the support they needed. Bukharin told the 15th Soviet Party Congress in December, 1927, that Lenin's instructions to the CPGB were now officially out of date. The British comrades should have realized that for themselves. Some of their leaders were clearly prone to 'serious errors of a Rightist character.'[1] It was obvious which way the decision was going to go, and the Comintern's Executive Committee pronounced the final judgement for Dutt and Pollitt in February of 1928.[2] The Labour party moguls – 'left' and right – were deemed as ideologically incorrigible as the traitors and cowards on the TUC's General Council. Capitalism and reformism had coalesced, and Communists could only come to power over the dead bodies of both. To keep trying to nudge MacDonald and his cronies to the left was fatuous and foolish. It was as silly as trying to revive those old connections to Hicks and Purcell. They were all blatant stooges of the bourgeoisie, Comintern decreed, and there was no hope for any of them. The CPGB Central Committee, having strayed into error, duly repented, and the old leaders ceded their positions, with a minimum of unpleasantness, to the new. By July, Bukharin could proclaim a complete break 'with all the old traditions of the English labour movement.'[3] There would be no more coalitions between reformists and revolutionaries.

II

The Russians might not be interested in trade union internationalism any more – except on their own terms, of course – but the General Council had not given up on it entirely. The link to Moscow was presumably shattered beyond any hope of quick repair, but the association with Amsterdam might yet be resumed. IFTU was certainly willing. The TUC was the Federation's richest and strongest member, and without its support, Amsterdam would probably just fall apart. To get back its English affiliate, however, IFTU would have to make some concessions. The problem of Britain's right to select her own representative on Amsterdam's Executive had to be cleared up. And the General Council still wanted some assurance that 'all other Trade Union centres' – the Soviets included – would be welcomed into the International.

---

[1] *XV S''ezd VKP (B)*, I, 573, 596.

[2] For the 9th ECCI's decisions on the CPGB, see Degras, *Communist International: Documents*, II, 427–32; *Communist Policy in Great Britain;* and Braun, *Ninth Plenum*. The 6th Comintern Congress ratified the ECCI decisions in September. See *Kommunisticheskii Internatsional v Dokumentakh*, pp. 729–40.

[3] Degras, *Communist International: Documents*, II, 446.

The two sides tried to iron out both problems at a meeting November 8, 1927.[1] The British went to some pains to deny they had ever taken orders from the Russians, or from anybody else 'fomenting dissension and forming dissident unions.' They had always been loyal to IFTU. They just wanted to make it over into a stronger and more representative organization. As to the matter of Britain's presence on the Executive, the TUC hoped the continentals might put aside unfortunate personal animosities and just concede the English the right to choose for themselves the man who would speak for them.

The Amsterdam people were conciliatory. They would accept the British proposal to invite all unaffiliated centres into the club. They conceded that nobody but the English had any business nominating the TUC's representative on the Executive. They did say, however, that whoever the British put up should get an affirmative vote from IFTU's Congress (in normal circumstances) or from its General Council (in the current state of emergency).

The English were agreeable. They again proposed Purcell. The continentals turned him down. The TUC thereupon refused to nominate anybody else. The deadlock lasted until May of 1928, when Purcell finally withdrew his name voluntarily. The English selected Hicks to replace him, but Hicks declined the honour, and Walter Citrine got nominated as Britain's third choice.[2] He was acceptable to everybody. The IFTU General Council confirmed his election in September, 1928, and promptly elected him Amsterdam president. Ben Turner was able to tell the 1928 Congress that the 'difficulties' with IFTU 'have now been overcome,' that Britain was again represented on the Amsterdam Executive, and, 'so far as can be judged, will continue to have the Presidency.'[3]

The effort to get the Russians into IFTU was more of a disappointment, however. Amsterdam did specifically invite Tomsky to put in an application, but the Soviets rebuffed the overture decisively.[4] Amsterdam was a fraud, Moscow announced. It had not even agreed to common

---

1 General Council Minutes, Nos. 52, 53, 7 Nov., 1927 record the TUC's preparations for the session, and Nos. 56–64, 8 Nov., 1927, chronicle the meeting itself. See also *Report of Proceedings at the 60th Annual Trades Union Congress (1928)*, ed. by Walter Citrine (London: Cooperative Printing Society, Limited, [1928]), pp. 69, 248–9. IFTU had already agreed to the kind of administrative reorganization the TUC demanded. See *1927 TUC: Report of Proceedings*, p. 504.

2 General Council Minutes, No. 242, 23 May, 1928.

3 *1928 TUC: Report of Proceedings*, p. 69.

4 The Russian statement was issued after a conference with Norwegian and Finnish trade unionists in November of 1927. For the text, see *Professional'nye Soiuzy SSSR, 1926–1928*, pp. 18–21.

action in such basic and uncontroversial matters as how to assist the British miners. The Russian unions would of course talk to the IFTU, any time, on how to create an international based on 'the unconditional revolutionary class war of labour versus capital.' Tomsky doubted, however, that Amsterdam would be much interested in talking over that subject.

He was right. In July of 1928 the IFTU Executive once again rejected a proposal – this time from the Finns and Norwegians – that it confer with the Soviet trade unions.[1] The Russians clearly had no intention of applying for membership in IFTU, Amsterdam said, so what was there to talk about. With the Soviets now committed so strongly to 'Third Period' doctrine, the estimate was not unrealistic. Ben Turner told Congress that autumn that IFTU had made a real effort to become 'a world-wide organization' but that 'our Russian comrades' still were not interested.[2] Instead, they persisted in backing Profintern, an 'opposition body' which divided the movement and weakened the 'common struggle against...capitalism and militarism.'

Clearly, so long as the Comintern held to its class-against-class sectarianism, Moscow–Amsterdam negotiations were out. Neither side wanted them. By the end of 1933, however, the Russians were beginning to change tactics.[3] 'Third period' dogmas were gradually discarded, or just by-passed, in favour of a new effort to achieve broadly-based coalitions with the reformists. The Reds had finally realized, tragically late, how serious an enemy Hitler was. They invited other working-class organizations to join them in 'popular fronts' to resist the Nazi barbarians.

They got a chilly reception. Too many of those they wooed were still bitter at the abuse they had had to endure a decade earlier. The popular front might not represent precisely the same technique as the united front had, but many socialists were still convinced that they – not the fascists – remained Comintern's prime targets. They were wary about getting burned a second time. In Britain, the official Labour organization brusquely dismissed all CPGB overtures as just devious Muscovite

---

[1] *The Times*, 25 July, 1928.

[2] *1928 TUC: Report of Proceedings*, p. 69. See also pp. 250–1.

[3] The shift to the popular front was confirmed at the 7th (and last) Comintern Congress in 1935. See 84th Congress, 2nd Session, House, Committee on Un-American Activities, *The Communist Conspiracy. Strategy and Tactics of World Communism*. Part I. *Communism Outside the United States*. Section C. *The World Congresses of the Communist International*, House Report 2242 (Washington: Government Printing Office, 1956), pp. 292–372.

manoeuvring. A 1933 Transport House pamphlet, *The Communist Solar System*, cited Comintern officials themselves to prove the point. They had once named George Lansbury – along with Adolf Hitler – as among the most dangerous enemies of the international proletariat, the pamphleteer pointed out. Nobody as ideologically myopic as that could ever be a trustworthy co-campaigner.[1]

The CPGB did the best it could. Harry Pollitt gave his solemn oath the popular front was not proposed 'as a manoeuvre or for any concealed aims,'[2] but only a small minority of the Labour establishment ever believed him. Rejecting all the most recent Red overtures became an annual ritual at party conference. Sir Stafford Cripps might favour an accommodation, as might Aneurin Bevan, Ellen Wilkinson, William Mellor – the whole of the so-called Tribune group. The partisans of coalition could probably boast the party's best brains, then, but their opponents consistently mustered most of the votes. It was tragically wrong-headed for the party chieftains to be so stubborn, G. D. H. Cole commented, but he had to admit it was to some degree comprehensible. 'The Communist Party has spent so long saying and thinking the worst about nearly everybody who holds a leading place in the official Labour or Trade Union movement that the victims now suffer from an obsession about it,' he wrote. The old united front of the twenties did indeed involve 'a considerable element of pretense' and was 'dangerously disruptive.' Communists probably now found it difficult 'to unlearn their earlier tactics,' just as the leaders of the Labour party and the trade unions found it difficult 'to forget what those tactics had been.' Getting the old antagonists together was bound to be difficult.[3]

The TUC proved as unapproachable as the Labour party. The 1933 Congress affirmed resolute disinterest in the CPGB's first tentative overtures for coalition. Would Britain choose democracy or dictatorship – that, Congress proclaimed, was the crucial issue, and Communists had opted for the wrong alternative. Citrine was particularly adamant against any popular front alliances with the Reds. Neither the Russians

---

[1] For a general account of the popular front episode in Britain, see John F. Naylor, *Labour's International Policy: The Labour Party in the 1930's* (London: Weidenfeld and Nicolson, 1969). For interesting primary material, see such Labour publications as *The Communist Solar System*, 1933; 'British Labour and Communism,' in The Labour Party, *Report of the 36th Annual Conference Held in the Usher Hall, Edinburgh, October 5th–October 9th 1936* (London: Transport House, 1936), pp. 296–300; *The Labour Party and the Popular Front*, 1938; and *Unity – True or Sham?* 1939.

[2] Cited in Naylor, *Labour's International Policy*, p. 165.

[3] G. D. H. Cole, *The People's Front* (London: Victor Gollancz, 1937), pp. 36–43.

nor their stooges in England were acceptable partners for good trade unionists, he insisted. They had duped the Movement once: they must never be allowed to do so again.[1]

The TUC was still willing, however, to try to manoeuvre the Russians into IFTU. Amsterdam was in a bad way in the 1930s. The withdrawal of the German trade unions after Hitler's assumption of power deprived the organization of one of its two strongest affiliates. By March of 1935, IFTU had dwindled away to fewer than 9 million members, less than half the 1920 count. At that point, when RILU again proposed a formal unity conference, both sides to be represented 'proportionally,' IFTU had no choice but to reject the offer. Since Profintern could boast 42 million members as of 1935 (almost half of them Russians), Amsterdam would have been swamped at any such meeting.

The Federation was still interested, however, in getting the affiliation of just the Russians, especially if other, more conservative labour federations could be lured into the international at the same time to act as a balance.[2] The IFTU's London Congress, in 1936, launched a determined campaign to persuade Americans, Australians, New Zealanders, Latin Americans, Chinese – and Russians – to sign up. A number of them responded, including the AF of L, the Norwegian federation, and the Mexican. Some of the existing IFTU affiliates, especially the French, were themselves expanding rapidly at about the same time, so Amsterdam's membership surged back up to 20 million again by 1939.

The Russians, at first, did not reply to the IFTU's overtures at all. They claimed the formal invitation somehow never got delivered in the USSR. They finally came back, however, with their old 1925 suggestion of an unconditional preliminary conference. This time IFTU accepted. Secretary-General Walter Schevenals and Vice-President Jouhaux, plus an interpreter, trotted off to Moscow for four days in November, 1937, to see what could be arranged. It was a grim pilgrimmage. Schevenels was obliged to submit to a search at the frontier, and almost turned back on the spot. The great confrontation finally occurred, however, and the Russians announced they wanted to discuss common action against fascism. The IFTU people demurred, preferring to talk about whatever it was that was keeping the Soviets out of their international. The

[1] Not only did Citrine take that position in the 1930s, he was still prepared to defend it, in private conversation, in the 1960s.

[2] For the story of the negotiations between IFTU and the Russians in the 1930s, I have drawn from Lefranc, *Les Expériences syndicales internationales*, pp. 33–5, 65–70 and Schevenels, *Quarante-cinq années*, pp. 158–61.

Russians finally drew up a list of the things they did not like about Amsterdam, the rules they would have to have changed before they could affiliate. The IFTU people suggested they negotiate the changes *after* they came in. Moscow was adamant, and so was Amsterdam, so after only four days of discussions, the conference broke up. At the 13th IFTU Congress in Zurich in July, 1939, the delegates adopted a declaration deploring Russia's unwillingness to compromise and calling off all further negotiations. The minority strongly objected, stressing the urgency of an east–west workers' alliance against Hitlerism. About six weeks later Stalin signed his treaty with Hitler. For the next two years, trades union internationalism was a dead issue.

In the euphoria of Second World War camaraderie, Russian and British trade unionists came together once again. The TUC authorized establishment of an 'Anglo-Soviet Trade Union Council' in September of 1941, and the organization continued to function for the rest of the war years. The abolition of RILU in 1943 'in the interests of trade union unity' was gratifying enough to the English to persuade the Southport TUC in September of that year to call on all labour organizations, regardless of their ideological predispositions, to agree to that long-anticipated world unity congress. The CIO backed the idea strongly from the United States, and the first sessions were scheduled for June 5, 1944 in London. D-day forced a postponement, but the meeting was finally held in February, 1945, and plans drawn up for a brand-new World Federation of Trade Unions to replace both Amsterdam and Profintern. The founding Congress assembled in Paris that September, and delegates of 65 federations from 56 countries formally declared a new all-inclusive international in being. Seventy million workers were represented. Only the Catholic trade unions and the AF of L stayed aloof. The IFTU officially declared itself liquidated December 14, 1945 at a Congress in London.[1]

The WFTU was an early victim of cold war rivalries. The federation constitution made it possible for the affiliates with the most members to dominate WFTU's executive organs, and the Russians, therefore, with

[1] The Catholics founded their own organization, the International Federation of Christian Trade Unions, since (1969) re-named the World Confederation of Labour. For these matters I have consulted Coates, *Anglo-Soviet Relations*, I, 684–85; *Bol'shaia Sovetskaia Entsiklopediia*, Gen. Ed. S. I. Vavilov, 2nd Edition (Moscow: Gosudarstvennii Nauchnii Institut 'Sovetskaia Entsiklopediia,' 1947), pp. 1759–60; *Ibid.*, (1950), II, 405–6, 408–9; V. Rubtsov, 'World Federation of Trade Unions,' *International Affairs* (Moscow) (Nov., 1970), pp. 120–1; Schevenels, *Quarante-cinq années*, pp. 177–211; Foy D. Kohler, *Understanding the Russians* (New York: Harper & Row, 1970), pp. 259–60.

twice as many trade unionists as anybody else, found themselves in a position to dictate the organization's policy pronouncements. The international's statements on such issues as the Communist insurrection in Greece reflected Moscow's judgements in every particular, and when, in 1948, the Executive voted an absolute rejection of the Marshall Plan, the non-Communists decided to walk out. The TUC and the CIO joined with the Dutch, the AF of L, and 47 other organizations to found the International Confederation of Free Trade Unions in January, 1949. It claimed to speak for some 48 million workers, and reached a peak of 123 organizations in 95 countries, representing 63 million workers, twenty years later. By that time, however, the TUC was again suggesting the possibility of a rapprochement with the Communists, and the AFL–CIO therefore withdrew from ICFTU in mid-1969. The confederation still survives, but it has remained weak and ineffective.

The WFTU has not done much better. By the early 1960s it had enlisted some 60 million members, but half of them were in Soviet trade unions, and even though representatives of 96 other nations appeared at the organization's Seventh Congress in 1969, they were no longer taking directions as dutifully as they once did. Some west European affiliates were openly deploring the Russian intervention in Czechoslovakia, for example, and the Chinese even indicated some doubt whether the Soviets' Marxist credentials were still in order. The WFTU might continue to boast of how it could 'intervene...actively in the social conflicts in the capitalist world, establish firm contact with the masses influenced by reformist ideology, and strive for the workers' broader unity of action in their anti-imperialist struggle.' Such brave words almost sound like a nostalgic attempt to revive the rhetorical idiosyncracies of the 1920s! In fact, however, the federation has never been particularly influential or prestigious outside the Communist bloc, and it is doubtful whether the Russians have gotten value for money out of the millions of rubles they have poured into it.[1]

That history repeats itself is a hoax, perpetuated by mischievous metaphysicians and no longer credited by anybody but university freshmen. That labour history, however – and especially the history of trades union internationalism – has often demonstrated a deplorable lack of inventiveness is obvious to anybody dabbling in it. Almost half a century after the great RILU–IFTU debates of the 1920s, leaders of the WFTU and

---

[1] The quotation is from Rubtsov, 'World Federation,' *International Affairs* (Nov., 1970), p. 121. I have also drawn from Kohler, *Understanding the Russians*, pp. 260–1, from standard encyclopedias and from the daily press.

ICFTU were still reciting the same tired clichés at one another that their predecessors mouthed. In spite of five decades' talk of proletarian solidarity, the workers of the world had yet to achieve any meaningful organizational unity. The British continued to assay the role of east–west mediator on occasion, and continued to get their knuckles rapped every time they did. As late as 1973 an American trade union leader was growling darkly about the evil machinations of a 'Moscow–London Labour axis.'[1] The more things have changed, then, the more they have remained the same, and one might be tempted to conclude that pursuing the history of international trades unionism is like chronicling the peregrinations of a soap-bubble: however attractive its shiny, shimmery surface, there is nothing there of substance at all, and it will never get anywhere in any event.

III

Inconsequential though these topics might seem in retrospect, they were real enough at the time, and Trotsky, for one, had been concerned enough over the alleged mis-application of united front tactics to risk political annihilation over the issues involved. The triumphant Stalinist majority at the 15th CPSU Congress in December of 1927 pronounced him and his ex-colleagues in the no-longer-United Opposition in error on every particular. The dissenters were to be given no quarter. 'There are splitters in the Party,' a certain comrade Morozkina announced menacingly the very first day. 'We say to them,' she proceeded, 'don't put your hopes on the First Moscow Chintz Factory, because there are no splitters among us!'[2] The 'stormy applause' for the lady's remarks indicated the Second Chintz Factory – or anybody allowed to speak for it – probably shared her uncharitable sentiments. The Oppositionists had just never appreciated the subtleties of a genuinely Leninist employment of united-front tactics, Stalin charged. They had become 'foolishly and unjudiciously' infatuated with Purcell and Hicks to begin with, and just petulantly disillusioned with them later on. They were wrong to have ever set so much store by the Committee anyway, and then wrong again when they turned around and recommended discarding it so precipitously.[3]

It seemed silly to keep arguing about the Committee, Kamenev protested gently, and unnecessarily harsh to require repentant Oppositionists to renounce all their views on the subject. After all, the

---

[1] *The Guardian*, 21 Feb., 1973, quoting George Meany.
[2] *XV S''ezd VKP (B)*, I, 27. [3] *Ibid.*, p. 76; Stalin, *Sochineniia*, x, 344–5.

organization had 'died an infamous death' anyway, so why quarrel over
a corpse? The majority was adamant. A voice from the floor called back
'Yes, and you died an infamous death, too!'[1] The unidentified heckler
was more of a prophet than he could have realized. Rykov, who followed
Kamenev to the podium, demanded grovelling submission from the
Opposition, on the Committee issue as on every other,[2] and most of the
heretics complied.

Trotsky, of course, was the notable exception. He was prepared to
defend everything he had ever said about the Committee from beginning
to end. It was reasonable enough to create the organization, he admitted,
if its purpose was simply to compromise and subvert the opportunist
cowards on the TUC General Council. The Stalinists, on the other hand,
had come to nurture more elaborate ambitions for their creation. They
hoped to turn it into a semi-permanent institution 'for the systematic
revolutionizing of the English working masses.'[3] They became so
intoxicated with its possibilities, finally, that it became almost sacred to
them. The institution became more important than the purpose – class
struggle – it was originally designed to serve. That was why they
maintained it even after the May, 1926 betrayal, an 'obstinacy' that
amounted to an act of 'criminal carelessness.' The stubbornness of 1926
became 'direct servility' in 1927 at the 'disgraceful Berlin session.' The
whole episode represented one of the three most disastrous mistakes the
Comintern ever made, the other two being the abortive effort to make
Germany Bolshevik in 1923 and the even more ruinous attempt to
revolutionize China in 1926–7.[4]

Neither then nor since, however, has the CPSU or its devotees in the
historical discipline ever admitted the Committee was anything less than
a brilliant success. It served to expose the crypto-left reformists in the
TUC as capitalist stooges and splitters. It enabled the CPGB to make
enormous gains in the trade union movement and thus proved 'a powerful agent for the radicalization of the British masses.' It made it possible
for the Comintern to propagandize its slogan of world trade union
unity in every country on earth. It popularized 'the achievements of
socialist construction in the USSR among the masses of the British
workers' and furthered the Red campaign 'against war and imperialism'
and for the 'defence of the Soviet Union.'[5]

---

[1] *XV S''ezd VKP (B)*, I, 245.   [2] *Ibid.*, pp. 248–57.

[3] Trotsky, *World Revolution*, p. 50. The analysis that follows derives from Trotsky's
1928 commentary on the Comintern's new draft programme in *ibid.*, pp. 45–56.

[4] Trotsky, *Third International*, p. 127.

[5] The quotations are from Bertram D. Wolfe, *The Trotskyite Opposition: Its Signific-*

It was only with the greatest reluctance the General Council ever agreed to establish the Committee in the first place, Party historians emphasize. Intense pressure from rank and file workers forced the councillors into an association they never really wanted. They launched a concerted effort to persuade the Soviets to liquidate the organization after the general strike, but Moscow refused to cooperate. Instead, it exploited the Committee more intensively than ever to criticize and expose the councillors, and finally, 'by forcing them to break off their relations under the fire of such criticism,' obliged them to reveal themselves unmistakably as enemies of the working class. Had the Soviets followed the Opposition's advice, and broken off the Committee themselves, they would have surrendered all these advantages just for the sake of a cheap, ultra-left gesture. That J. H. Thomas and L. D. Trotsky were working to achieve the same goal was no surprise, of course: enemies of the people always sound much alike! But the Party leadership had persisted in its carefully calculated strategy, and the net result was that Soviet and British workers were even closer friends after the Committee broke up than they had been before.[1]

To a bourgeois westerner, neither the Trotskyite interpretation of the Committee, nor the Stalinist riposte, ring true. One envies the partisan chroniclers their quaint proletarian certainties – it must be a joyous experience to live again in the uncomplicated world one knew as a child – but for us, craggy mountains of hard documentary evidence have made the joys of never-never land gallingly inaccessible.[2] All Communist commentaries on the Committee seem just plain simplistic. They err fundamentally in assuming the organization ever really counted for very much in Britain. In the USSR, the tie to the TUC obviously mattered. The policies of the Committee, its goals, composition and prospects, were the subjects of continuous and intensive scrutiny and review by the very highest organs of political power, including the Politburo. The organization got extensive coverage in the daily press: *Pravda*'s readers

ance for American Workers, Workers' Library Number 5 (New York: Workers' Library Publishers, 1928), p. 48 and Popov, *Outline History of the CPSU*, II, 283. For more of the same sort of argument, see Vinogradov, *Mirovoi Proletariat i SSSR*, p. 113, and Degras, *Communist International: Documents*, II, 432.

[1] The quotation is from Volkov, *Anglo-Sovetskie Otnosheniia*, p. 383. For the kind of analysis summarized in this paragraph, see *ibid.*, pp. 383–8 and 411–13; Wolfe, *Trotskyite Opposition*, pp. 48–9 and *Bol'shaia Sovetskaia Entsiklopediia* (1950), II, 405–6.

[2] For the Soviets, documentary evidence sometimes seems scarcely any problem at all. The article on the Committee in the 1950 *Bol'shaia Sovetskaia Entsiklopediia* cited just two sources on the subject, both of them speeches by Stalin!

probably got more news of the activities of A. A. Purcell than did the clientele of *The Times*! Since the intimacy with the General Council was valued so highly in Moscow, it must have been difficult for the Soviets to accept the distasteful possibility that London felt much less involved. Such, however, was the case. Associating with Tomsky may have resolved ego problems for sentimental English leftists, and allowed them to direct their highly theoretical Marxist exuberance into purely verbal and therefore socially acceptable channels, but nobody who mattered much ever really took the Committee very seriously for very long. It came up in cabinet meetings only once or twice, in connection with the general strike, and hardly ever got referred to in Parliament at all. The press mostly just ignored it. An organization that hardly ever met any-way, and only issued another set of dreary manifestos when it did, would hardly sell papers. Even loyal *Daily Herald* readers would yawn at such stuff.

For any genuine understanding of what the Committee really did signify to Britain, the Purcells – the 'leftists' – are the key. Their 'leftism' – more sentimental than ideological, more impulsive than systematic – was a characteristic British phenomenon of the 1920s.[1] It was artless and ineffectual, but it was neither hypocritical nor shallow. They really were concerned over injustice and exploitation and they did indeed agonize over the humiliated, the brutalized and the oppressed of the world. The formidable complexities of social reconstruction quite overwhelmed them, however, and most often, their only response to an evil was to attend a demonstration against it. What did it matter if it were some Communist who organized the rally? The Cause surely transcended mere matters of dogma, and for the resolute few who were on the side of the angels to go around tut-tutting at the tarnish on one another's halos would be both undignified and self-defeating.

The Comintern could hardly have asked for likelier subjects on which to test out united front theories. The Purcells were more than ready to be recruited. Present them some emotionally charged issue (preferably one rather remote from their own country and their own immediate experi-ence), give them the illusion they could really do something about it, and they would stand in line to sign up. In this case, the issue presented was

[1] On this subject, David Thomson, *England in the Twentieth Century* (London: Jonathan Cape, 1964), pp. 99–100 has some interesting things to say – though where he got the figure of 200,000 for the Sacco–Vanzetti protest meeting Aug. 22, 1927 I do not know. The biggest rally was on Aug. 10, anyway, not the 22nd, and *The Times* estimate of 10,000 participants is unlikely to have been off by more than perhaps 100 per cent. That makes 20,000, not 200,000!

the Russian workers, and whether they would ever get the opportunity to arrange their own future in their own way. British trade unionists were still lost in wonder and admiration over what was being achieved in the USSR. For the first time in history, working people were running their own country. They had dedicated themselves to the abolition of exploitation and the achievement of social justice. For that heresy, they had incurred the implacable wrath of aggressive imperialist bosses all over the world. Somebody had to plead their cause, and what more logical candidates for that honour than fellow proletarians in Britain. With the TUC's help, the Russians could once again become full-fledged members of the international proletarian brotherhood, and join their might with that of comrades elsewhere for the achievement of socialism, justice and peace all over the world. If the dream lacked definition (dreams generally do), the first steps to achieving it were nevertheless obvious enough – get the Soviet trade unions into IFTU, unite the workers of the world, show the capitalist governments that they could never hope to conquer the toiling masses of the USSR by isolating them. To the Purcells, that all made perfect sense.

It must have been terribly frustrating to them when neither the Russians nor IFTU seemed able to cooperate in so uncomplicated a programme. The Russians kept suggesting supplementary tasks for the Committee to undertake. It should condemn the Locarno pact, support the left Kuomintang, undertake an investigation of rightist outrages in Lithuania. Such questions involved 'political' issues, not 'trade union' issues, and the TUC traditionally preferred to defer to the Labour party when it came to politics. The Soviets, however, were insistent, particularly when the Committee was first being negotiated. For them, as good Bolsheviks, 'political' matters and 'trade union' matters were all of a piece. The General Council yielded, yielded much more, in retrospect, than it could ever have meant to. It pledged itself not only to seek trade union unity but also to work cooperatively with the Soviets to resist the threat of war and to counter the capitalist offensive. To subscribe to such words was easy enough to begin with. No British trade unionist would come out for war, and very few for capitalism. But what nobody in the TUC seemed to anticipate was that the Soviets might require them to take such pledges seriously, and worse yet, to act on them. Many of the strains that finally tore the Committee apart derived from that basic misunderstanding. Tomsky wanted the English to take positive stands on specific issues. He wanted them to back their judgements by threatening to take action. If that meant blacking military shipments to, say,

Poland, so be it. That was the direction the Russians seemed to want to take, and it would move them a long way away from the comparatively simple matter of arranging their entry into IFTU. To the Purcells, it was a disillusioning distraction.

Amsterdam was uncooperative too. Tomsky was a Communist and Communists were slanderers and splitters and the IFTU bureaucrats would do them no favours. Reds disorganized the labour movement, maligned its leaders, and even set up separatist organizations of their own. The only country in which they had evidenced even a modicum of good behaviour was Britain, and they only restrained themselves there because they were still so weak on the island. Once they were stronger, they would be more truculent. In the meantime, they manipulated heavy-handed, loud-mouthed, arrogant dupes like Purcell to subvert and destroy IFTU. The united front was a trap, and the real motive in offering it was to enable the Communists to first smash, and then take over, traditional trade union organizations. The Reds threw you a rope in order to get your neck in a noose. Only a fool would pay any attention to them.

The British found IFTU's attitude alternately perplexing, irritating, and just plain sad.[1] It was unkind of the continentals to be so intolerant of fellow proletarians. The Soviets could not possibly be the monsters an Oudegeest said they were. Not Tomsky, good old Tomsky, the 'real' trade unionist! Time healed all wounds, however, and it would even mellow the disputants in Moscow and Amsterdam eventually. Britain could wait them out. In the meantime, the TUC could keep its own relationship with Tomsky at a formal level, resist his more extravagant proposals for precipitate action, and hope for the best.

After the general strike, of course, the mood in London changed dramatically. The Russians bared their teeth, maligned all their old colleagues as traitors and cowards, and called for their replacement. The 'leftists' – the only ones who had ever really interested themselves in the Committee anyway – were savaged as brutally as the rightists, who had never really paid much attention to the organization previously. They paid attention now, however, and insisted, in effect, that the price of maintaining the Committee was that Soviet non-intervention pledge. If Moscow would stop abusing them, and stay out of their affairs, they would keep trying to get the Russians into IFTU. They might even sign an occasional anti-war statement. That, however, was all they would do, and if it did not suit the Soviets, so much the worse for them. The

---

[1] On this, see Citrine, *Democracy or Disruption*, p. 5.

'leftists' – still in a state of shock after the general strike anyway – could hardly protest. The terms were proposed, the Russians found it impossible to abide by them, and that was that.

From the very beginning, then, the General Councillors' problem was how to limit the Committee, how to make sure that it did very little. The Soviets, on the other hand, wanted it to do too much. They assigned it far too many disparate responsibilities, and never seemed able to make up their minds which ones should have first priority. Technically, to begin with, the Committee was simply a straightforward example of a united front organization. The Comintern was always quite blunt about what such alliances were for. Reds linked themselves to reformist partners – temporarily – in order to promote certain specific and definable ends. So long as one's allies continued to exert themselves for those ends, one stayed with them. When they faltered, or deserted the cause – as, being reformists, they inevitably would – one reviled, exposed and destroyed them. In this case, the specific and definable end sought was a single trades union international. If such an organization did indeed come into being – with all dissident Profintern affiliates included, of course – Communists would continue the employment of united front tactics, on a larger scale, within the new organization. The Purcells would have gotten themselves a temporary reprieve, in effect, while Reds tackled the even more despicable Oudegeests. If, on the other hand, Amsterdam refused Moscow's terms for the new international, the Committee would still be useful, short-term, to drive a wedge between the TUC and her sister organizations in IFTU, and possibly bring down the Amsterdam citadel altogether. At the same time, since the Committee was also pledged to two other goals – checking imperialist warmongers and countering the capitalist offensive – one could press the Purcells to do something forceful and positive about those issues, and once they refused, once they proved themselves to be the yellow lickspittles they were, one could rupture the organization, exposing the cowardice of one's ex-partners and trumpeting their betrayal to their followers. When the dust cleared, they would all be discredited, and Communists would be in a position to take over the trade union movement. It might all seem fanciful, but that was nevertheless what the united front was all about.

Nobody in the Soviet leadership would ever have repudiated the sort of description of the Committee's function suggested above. Zinoviev articulated it most consistently. The Committee would help revolutionize the British trade union movement. It would 'render reformism harmless.'

In some mysterious way, every time Tomsky sat down to talk with Purcell, the National Minority Movement would be a bit better off for the contact. The CPGB would be too, of course, except that Zinoviev got so entranced at the NMM and Red gains in the trade unions that he sometimes seemed to discount the CPGB altogether. A Red-dominated TUC would serve as surrogate for the Party in bringing British capitalism to its knees. Zinoviev's vision of the Committee's role was surely quite consistent with Lenin's original instructions, and none of the Red chieftains ever explicitly dissociated himself from such views.

Tomsky came the closest, when he noted the reformists had already been exposed again and again and it was hardly worth going through a lot of elaborate additional manoeuvring just to expose them one more time. For him, and for his senior colleagues in the Soviet trades union movement, what seemed most intriguing about the TUC connection was the chance it might indeed facilitate the achievement of a single trade union international, thus ridding them of Profintern.[1] So long as that was a real possibility, Tomsky was perfectly willing to postpone 'exposing' Purcell almost indefinitely. From his point-of-view, RILU had been a disaster from the beginning. It established a super-bureaucracy on top of the regular trade union apparatus, headed by a rival – Lozovsky – for whom Tomsky had very little respect. With RILU eliminated, Tomsky's power base at home would be much more secure. The association with independently-minded western labour organizations might even enable him to achieve a greater degree of independence for his unions in the USSR – independence not from the Party (Tomsky was a good Communist), but independence from the petty meddling of middle-ranking Party *apparatchiks* in matters that were none of their business. Finally, Tomsky may really have hoped he might even be able to move some of his timid Amsterdam colleagues into more militant and decisive class confrontations back in their own countries. In any event, there was much to be gained, as Tomsky saw it, by negotiating Russian entry into Amsterdam, and precious little lost even if the price demanded were the surrender of RILU. If the Committee could expedite the negotiations, he was all for it.

As early as January of 1926, Tomsky's dream for the Committee had already been shattered. After some months of uncharacteristic indecision, the Politburo had finally decided to deny the Soviet trade

---

[1] Trotsky ascribed this heresy to the upper strata of the trade unions, representing the best-paid workers and the office employees. See *Where is Britain Going?* (London: Communist Party of Great Britain, 1926), pp. 11–13.

unions the right to enter Amsterdam all by themselves on any conditions. Simultaneously, IFTU had decisively reaffirmed its determination not to make any concessions to the Profintern organization as a whole. At that point, trade union unity was nothing more than a useful slogan for the propagandists. It was clearly not about to become a reality. By then, however, at least part of the Muscovite leadership was exploring the possibility of new uses for the Committee – not to achieve international proletarian solidarity, not as a conventional instrument of united front tactics, but as a brickbat with which to intimidate H.M. Foreign Office.

It was Stalin who was most blatant in proposing the new line, and his suggestions in fact reflected a wider Soviet dilemma – the tension between the expectations of world revolution and the desire to promote it, on the one hand, and, on the other, the need to develop reasonably normal state relations with other nations if the USSR were to survive as an independent entity in a dangerously hostile external political environment. Theoretically, the Committee could be used to further either purpose. By conventional united front theories, it might prove a convenient mechanism for the promotion of industrial strife in Britain, the furtherance of the aims of the National Minority Movement in the Trades Union Congress, and the ultimate penetration of the British labour movement, and perhaps even of the European labour movement, by a more militant and revolutionary ideology. Conversely, it could be a useful tool of the Soviet Foreign Commissariat, generating TUC pressure on successive British governments whenever their policies and those of the Soviet state seemed to be on a dangerous collision course. But the Committee could not serve both purposes. A TUC leadership committed to revolutionary extremism – if the Russians ever achieved such a thing – would hardly be able to carry much weight with a Tory Foreign Minister. A professional bureaucracy of comfortably ensconced trade union autocrats, on the other hand, who might command some respect in Downing Street, were hardly likely to interest themselves in secret revolutionary conspiracies, and if one 'exposed' and 'reviled' them – as united front tactics specified one must – their sympathy for Soviet diplomatic interests might quickly evaporate.

Before May 12, 1926, the Russians could explore both possibilities for the Committee simultaneously, but not afterwards. Trotsky was right: if the organization were to be used for united front manoeuvring in a Leninist sense, it should have been liquidated immediately after the General Council caved in to Stanley Baldwin and called off the general strike. The Politburo, however, failed to make the break then. Perhaps some of the Soviet leaders were concerned about how the rank and file in Britain would react if the Russians seemed to be abandoning them at such a crucial moment. Perhaps others hoped they might use the Committee to salvage the cause of the miners. Stalin certainly hoped the Committee could still advance Soviet state interests somehow. And, of course, once Trotsky had come out with his demand for the Committee's dissolution, it simply had to be retained. It would never do to seem to yield to the directives of the arch-heretic.

From May on, in fact, the future of the Committee was really in Trotsky's hands. Whenever he attacked, and remined the Politburo of Lenin's strictures on running united front organizations, Tomsky had to up-stage him by writing another baleful Manifesto denouncing the opportunistic TUC traitors. That happened in June of 1926 and again in May of 1927. Whenever Trotsky was silent for awhile, Tomsky surreptitiously repaired the line to London again as best he could, as in March and April of 1927. The supreme test for the Committee came after the Arcos raid and the diplomatic break in May, 1927. If Stalin's hopes were to be realized, the General Council should then have moved resolutely to the defence of the proletarian fatherland. He was disappointed, of course. Resolution was not chic in the TUC after the collapse of the general strike. The *vozhd* had been wrong, then, and Tomsky got his orders to rid him of the embarrassment quickly. He dutifully savaged the General Council unmercifully from June until September, 1927, when the English finally cut the line. And that was that.

United front tactics had failed, then. That was the conclusion drawn in Moscow, which is a major reason why they were so decisively abandoned, with such unfortunate consequences, from 1928 to 1934. In a sense, however, they had never really been tried. The rules Lenin laid down in 1921 had never been followed. It can be argued they had been unrealistic all along. They required a greater talent for the difficult vice of hypocrisy than the species has yet achieved. To lionize a Purcell, call him 'comrade,' make him an honorary member of the Moscow Soviet – all simply in order to manipulate him into a position from which you can castigate him as a traitor and a coward – that takes special aptitudes that not even the most dedicated Marxist militant would find easy to master. It was probably inevitable (everything is inevitable after it happens!) that once the Reds actually sat down with the social-democratic, reformist lickspittles – and exchanged a few jokes and a few drinks – both sides would risk ideological contamination. And once one decided the opportunists were nice chaps (even if they weren't revolutionaries) and sincerely meant to be one's friends, one was well on the road to ultra-right deviationism. If Purcell was really a significantly more acceptable fellow than Chamberlain, and if, indeed, one might even suggest recruiting the Purcells as allies against the Chamberlains, the whole distinction between the elect and the heretics, the proletarian vanguard and the bourgeois lackeys, Communism and reformism, began to break down. The united front may have been designed to menace the social democrats, then, but it menaced the Reds, too. It called into question their whole claim to a special vision of the Truth. All great religions have made the same discovery: the world, the flesh and the devil are irresistibly corrupting, and the only safe place for the truly pure in heart is in monastic seclusion.

And yet, in retrospect, all men have to live in the real world, the same world, and live in it together, and anything that separates men from one another makes us all just that much less human. It was not only the Communists who were hurt by the failure of Lenin's united front strategies, and it was not only non-Communists who would have been better off if, somehow, they could have been made to succeed. The dreamers and visionaries of this world – and the cynics and critics – each need the other. The creative tension between those who know the Truth and those who doubt there is One provides the dynamic energy which makes intellectual history move. No matter what the original motives may have been on either side, the united front brought opposites together – the very stuff of dialectical progress. Its collapse drove them apart again. Both paid a heavy price for the separation.

Classified bibliography

YEARBOOKS, DICTIONARIES, ENCYCLOPEDIAS

The Annual Register, 1924–1927. Ed. by M. Epstein. New Series. London: Longmans, Green, 1925–8.

Bol'shaia Sovetskaia Entsiklopediia. 1st Edition, Gen. Ed. O. Iu. Shmidt. Vol. II (1926), 720–1, 'Anglo–Sovetskii Komitet Edinstva;' Vol. XLVII (1940), 403–26, I. Yuzepovich, 'Professional'nye Soiuzy.' Moscow: Aktsionernoe Obshchestvo 'Sovetskaia Entsiklopediia,' 1926, 1940. 1947 Edition, Ed., S. I. Vavilov et als. *Soiuz Sovetskikh Sotsialisticheskikh Respublik.* N. Rytikov, 'Sovetskie Profsoiuzy,' pp. 1743–60. Moscow: Institut 'Sovetskaia Entsiklopediia,' 1947. 2nd Edition. Gen. Ed. S. I. Vavilov. Vol. II (1950), 405–6, 'Anglo–Ruskii Komitet Edinstva;' Vol. L (1957) 278–80, V. M. Tsyganov, 'Professional'nye Soiuzy.' Moscow: Gosudarstvennoe Nauchnoe Izdatel'stvo 'Bol'shaia... [etc.],' 1950, 1957.

Communist International. *Jahrbuch für Wirtschaft, Politik, und Arbeiterbewegung, 1925–1926.* Hamburg: Hoym, 1926.

Khoziaistvo, Politika i Rabochee Dvizhenie v Kapitalisticheskikh Stranakh za 1924–1927 gody. Ed. by T. L. Akselrod and others. Moscow–Leningrad: Gosizdat, 1928.

Dictionary of National Biography, 1931–40. Ed. by L. G. Wickham Legg. London: Oxford University Press, 1949.

Dictionary of National Biography, 1941–50. Ed. by L. G. Wickham Legg and E. T. Williams. London: Oxford University Press, 1959.

Institute for the Study of the U.S.S.R., Munich, Germany. *Biographic Dictionary of the USSR.* New York: Scarecrow Press, 1958.

International Federation of Trade Unions. *Third (Fourth, Fifth) Year Book of the International Federation of Trade Unions.* Amsterdam: 1925–7.

Internationales Handwörterbuch des Gewerkschaftswesens. Ed. by Ludwig Heyde. Berlin: Werk und Wirtschafts Verlagsaktiengesellschaft, 1931–2.

The 1925, (1926, 1927, 1928) Labour Year Book. London: 1925–8.

McGraw Hill Encyclopedia of Russia and the Soviet Union. Ed. by Michael

T. Florinsky, New York, Toronto, London: McGraw Hill Book Company, Inc., [1961].

Statistical Abstract for the United Kingdom. For each of the fifteen years 1913 and 1920 to 1933. Seventy-eighth Number. Cmd. 4801. London: H.M.S.O., 1935.

Who Was Who, 1941–50. London: Adam & Charles Black, 1951.

Who Was Who, 1951–60. London: Adam & Charles Black, 1961.

UNPUBLISHED MANUSCRIPTS, DISSERTATIONS, ETC.

Anglo-Russian Joint Advisory Council. Minutes, 1925–7. File 947/220. Trades Union Congress Archives.

Viscount Cecil of Chelwood Papers. Special Correspondence. Correspondence with Winston Churchill. Correspondence with the Marquis of Salisbury. British Museum Additional MSS 51986, 51085.

Communist Party of Great Britain. 'Resolution of the Political Bureau of the C.P. of Great Britain on the Discussion in the C.P.S.U.' Adopted August 9, 1926. Mimeographed. Trades Union Congress Library.

Great Britain, Cabinet. Cabinet Commissions, 1924–6. CAB 27.254, 27.331–4. Public Record Office.

Cabinet Conclusions, 1923–7. CAB 23.46–55. Public Record Office.

Cabinet Papers, 1924–7. CAB 24.166, 168, 175, 178–82, 184, 185, 188, 190.

Great Britain, Foreign Office. Foreign Office Papers. Northern Department. Political. 1924–7. F.O. 371. 10487, 10498, 10992, 11006, 11014, 11015, 11020, 11328, 11757, 11785, 11786, 11788, 11794, 11795, 11796, 11802, 12567, 12585, 12586, 12593, 12602.

Bernard Shaw Papers. Special Correspondence. Correspondence with Graham Wallas. British Museum Additional MSS 50553.

Shaw, Theodore K. 'British Reaction to the Soviet Union, 1924–1929: A Study of Policy and Public Opinion.' Ph.D. dissertation, University of Indiana, 1953.

Trades Union Congress, General Council. Minutes, 1923–8. Trades Union Congress Archives.

Trades Union Congress, General Council, International Committee. Minutes, 1923–8. File 901. Trades Union Congress Archives.

Trades Union Congress. 'Mining Dispute and General Strike, G. C. Decisions.' (A record of the decisions of the General Council and its various Committees relevant to the General Strike and Miners

Strike, 1925–7. Compiled for use at the Special Conference of Trade Union Executives.) File 1 1/2. 2. Trades Union Congress Archives.
Trotsky Archives. Harvard College Library.

LETTERS AND INTERVIEWS

Arnot, Robin Page. Interview, 24 Jan., 1968, 48, Byne Road, London SE 28.
Citrine, Walter M. (Lord Citrine of Wembley). Interview, 9 Nov., 1967, Electricity Council Building. Letter, 14 Feb., 1968.
Rothstein, Andrew. Interviews, 18 Dec., 1967, 16 April, 1968, Marx Memorial Library, London.

PERIODICALS

Bulletin of the International Federation of Trade Unions, 1924–8.
Bulletin of the Labour and Socialist International, 1925–7.
Communist International, 1925–7. (Comintern).
Communist Review (from 1927, *The Communist*), 1924–8 (CPGB)
Daily Chronicle, 1925.
Daily Herald, 1924–8.
Daily Mail, 1925–6.
Daily Telegraph, 1924–5.
International Federation of Trade Unions Press Reports 1924–8.
International Press Correspondence, 1924–8. (Comintern).
International Trade Union Review (From 1927, *International Trade Union Movement*), 1924–8. (IFTU).
Izvestiia, 1924–7. (USSR Central Executive Committee).
The Labour Magazine, 1924–8. (Labour Party and TUC).
Labour Monthly, 1924–8.
The Labour Press Service, 1924–7. Issued by the Joint Publicity Department of the Trades Union Congress and the Labour Party.
Lansbury's Labour Weekly, 1925–8.
Le Mouvement Syndical Belge, 1924–7.
The Miner, 1926–8. (MFGB).
Monthly Circular, 1925–7. (Labour Research Department)
Nation, 1925.
Plebs, 1924–8. (National Council of Labour Colleges).
Pravda, 1924–8. (CPSU)
Die Rote Gewerkschaftsinternationale, 1924–8. (RILU)

Sunday Worker, 1925–8.
The Times, 1924–8.
Trade Union Unity, 1925–6.
Trud, 1925–7. (All-Union Central Council of Trade Unions)
Vorwärts, 1924–6. (German Social-Democratic Party)
Weekly Dispatch, 1925.
The Worker, 1925–8. (National Minority Movement)
Workers' Weekly (From 1927, *Workers' Life*), 1924–8. (CPGB)

BIOGRAPHIES AND AUTOBIOGRAPHIES

Amery, L. S. *My Political Life*. Vol. II, London: Hutchinson, 1953.

Balabanova, Angelica. *My Life as a Rebel*. London: Hamish Hamilton. 1938.

Baldwin, A. W. *My Father: the True Story*. London: George Allen and Unwin, 1955.

Bell, Thomas. *Pioneering Days*. London: Lawrence and Wishart, 1941.

Blakland, William G. *J. H. Thomas: A Life for Unity*. London: Frederick Muller, 1964.

Bondfield, Margaret. *A Life's Work*. London: Hutchinson, 1949.

Boothby, Robert. *I Fight to Live*. London: Victor Gollancz, 1947.

Brockway, Fenner. *Inside the Left: Thirty Years of Platform, Press, Prison and Parliament*. London: George Allen and Unwin, 1942.

Bullock, Alan. *The Life and Times of Ernest Bevin*. Vol. I, London: Heinemann, 1960.

Citrine, W. M. (Baron Citrine). *Men and Work: An Autobiography*. London: Hutchinson, 1964.

Clynes, J. R. *Memoirs*. 2 Vols. London: Hutchinson, 1937.

Deutscher, Isaac. *The Prophet Unarmed: Trotsky: 1921–1929*. London and New York: Oxford University Press, 1959.

Stalin: A Political Autobiography. Rev. Ed. Harmondsworth: Penguin Books, 1966.

Eastwood, G. G. *George Isaacs*. London: Odhams Press, 1952.

Fischer, Louis. *Men and Politics*. New York: Duell, Sloan and Pearce, 1941.

Gallacher, William G. *Revolt on the Clyde*. London: Lawrence and Wishart, 1949.

Rolling of the Thunder. London: Lawrence and Wishart, 1947.

The Last Memoirs of William Gallacher. London: Lawrence and Wishart, 1966.

Hamilton, M. A. *J. Ramsey MacDonald:* London: Jonathan Cape, 1929.

Hannington, Wal. *Never on our Knees.* London: Lawrence and Wishart, 1967.

Hardy, George. *Those Stormy Years: Memories of the Fight for Freedom on Five Continents.* London: Lawrence and Wishart, 1956.

Horner, Arthur. *Incorrigible Rebel.* London: MacGibbon and Kee, 1960.

James, Robert Rhodes, ed. *Memoirs of a Conservative: J. C. C. Davidson's Memoirs and Papers, 1910–37.* London: Weidenfeld and Nicolson, 1969.

Jones, Jack. *Unfinished Journey.* London: Hamish Hamilton, 1939.

Lawson, Jack. *The Man in the Cap: The Life of Herbert Smith.* London: Methuen, 1941.

Murphy, J. T. *New Horizons.* London: John Lane, 1941.

Paul, Leslie A. *Angry Young Man.* London: Faber and Faber, 1951.

Pollitt, Harry. *Serving My Time: An Apprenticeship to Politics.* London: Lawrence and Wishart, 1940.

Pritt, D. S. *Autobiography.* Two Parts. London: Lawrence and Wishart, 1965–6.

Russell, Bertrand. *The Autobiography of Bertrand Russell,* Vol. II, London: George Allen and Unwin, 1968.

Samuel, Viscount. *Memoirs.* London: The Cresset Press, 1945.

Serge, Victor. *Memoirs of a Revolutionary, 1901–1941.* Trans. and ed. by Peter Sedgwick. London: Oxford University Press, 1963.

Snowden, Philip. (Viscount Snowden of Ickornshaw). *An Autobiography.* Vol. II, 1919–1934. London: Ivor Nicholson and Watson, 1934.

Thomas, J. H. *My Story.* London: Hutchinson, 1937.

Tillett, Ben. *Memories and Reflections.* London: John Long, 1931.

Some Russian Impressions. London: Labour Research Department, 1925.

Trotsky, Lev. *My Life: an Attempt at an Autobiography.* New York: Charles Scribner's Sons, 1930.

Turner, Ben. *About Myself.* London: Cayme Press, 1930.

Valtin, Jan (R. J. H. Krebs). *Out of the Night.* London: William Heinemann, 1941.

Webb, Beatrice. *Beatrice Webb's Diaries, 1924–32.* Ed. Margaret Cole. London: Longmans Green, 1956.

DOCUMENTS (PUBLISHED)

GREAT BRITAIN

General

Hansard. *Parliamentary Debates. House of Commons.* 5th Series. Vols. 167–212. (1923–7).

Hansard. *Parliamentary Debates.* House of Lords. 5th Series. Vols. 60–69. (1924–7).

Great Britain, Foreign Office. *Russia No. 1 (1927): Note From His Majesty's Government to the Government of the Union of Soviet Socialist Republics Respecting the Relations between the Two Countries and Note in Reply, February 23/26, 1927.* Cmd. 2822 (1927). London: H.M.S.O., 1927.

Russia No. 2 (1927): Documents Illustrating the Hostile Activities of the Soviet Government and Third International Against Great Britain. Cmd. 2874 (1927). London: H.M.S.O., 1927.

Russia No. 3 (1927): A Selection of Papers Dealing with the Relations Between His Majesty's Government and the Soviet Government, 1921–1927. Cmd. 2895 (1927). London: H.M.S.O., 1927.

Great Britain, Parliament. *Communist Papers: Documents Selected From Those Obtained on the Arrest of the Communist Leaders on the 14th and 21st October, 1925.* Cmd. 2682 (1926). London: H.M.S.O., 1926.

Medlicott, W. N., Dakin, Douglas, and Lambert, M. E., eds. *Documents on British Foreign Policy, 1919–1939.* Series 1A. Vol. i. London: H.M.S.O., 1966.

Labour Party

Labour Party. *British Labour Delegation to Russia, 1920: Report.* London: Trades Union Congress and Labour Party, 1921.

Report of the 25th Annual Conference Held in the St. George's Hall, Liverpool, on September 29th and 30th and October 1st and 2nd. 1925. London: 1925.

Report of the 26th Annual Conference Held in the Pavilion & Winter Gardens, Margate, October 11th to 15th, 1926. London: 1926.

Report of the 27th Annual Conference Held in the Hippodrome, Blackpool, October 3rd to 7th, 1927. London: 1927.

Communist Party

C. B. *The Reds and the General Strike.* London: Communist Party of Great Britain, 1926.

Communist Party of Great Britain. *Speeches and Documents of the Sixth (Manchester) Conference of the Communist Party of Great Britain. May 17, 18 and 19, 1924.* London: Communist Party of Great Britain, 1924.

Report of the Seventh National Congress, May 30–June 1, 1925. London: Communist Party of Great Britain, [1925].

The Eighth Congress of the Communist Party of Gt. Britain, Held at Battersea Town Hall on October 16 and 17, 1926: Reports, Theses and Resolutions. London: Communist Party of Great Britain, 1927.

The Ninth Congress of the Communist Party of Gt. Britain (Held at Caxton Hall, Salford, October, 1927): Reports, Theses & Resolutions. London: Communist Party of Great Britain, [1928].

Orders from Moscow? London: Communist Party of Great Britain, 1926.

The International Situation: Report to the Eighth Congress of the Communist Party of Great Britain, October 16 and 17, 1926. London: Communist Party of Great Britain [1926].

Trades Union Congress

Trades Union Congress. *Report of Proceedings at the 56th Annual Trades Union Congress (1924).* Ed. by Fred Bramley. London: Cooperative Printing Society Limited [1924].

Report of Proceedings at the 57th Annual Trades Union Congress (1925). Ed. by Walter Citrine. London: Cooperative Printing Society Limited [1925].

Report of Proceedings at the 58th Annual Trades Union Congress (1926). Ed. by Walter Citrine. London: Cooperative Printing Society Limited [1926].

Report of Proceedings at the 59th Annual Trades Union Congress (1927). Ed. by Walter Citrine. London: Cooperative Printing Society Limited [1927].

Report of Proceedings at the 60th Annual Trades Union Congress (1928). Ed. by Walter Citrine. London: Cooperative Printing Society Limited [1928].

General Council. Miners' Dispute, National Strike: Report of the General Council to the Conference of Executives of Affiliated Unions, June 25, 1926. London: Cooperative Printing Society Limited, 1927.

National Strike Special Conference: Report of Proceedings. London: Cooperative Printing Society Limited, 1927.

Russia: The Official Report of the British Trades Union Delegation to Russia and Caucasia, November and December, 1924. London: Trades Union Congress General Council, 1925.

Russia and International Unity: Report to Affiliated Societies, Trades Union Congress. London: Trades Union Congress General Council, 1925.

Chetyre Dokumenta. Moscow: Izdanie Profinterna, 1927.

Miners' Federation of Great Britain

Miners' Federation of Great Britain. *Annual Volume of Proceedings, 1925.* London: Cooperative Printing Society, 1926.

Annual Volume of Proceedings, 1926. London: Cooperative Printing Society, 1927.

Annual Volume of Proceedings, 1927–28. London: Cooperative Printing Society, 1929.

Miners' Relief Fund: Statement of Accounts. London: Cooperative Printing Society, 1927.

National Minority Movement

National Minority Movement. *Report of National Minority Conference Held August 23 and 24, 1924.* London: National Minority Movement, 1924.

Report of Fifth Annual Conference, 1928. London: National Minority Movement, 1928.

Report of Sixth Annual Conference, 1927. London: National Minority Movement, 1927.

USSR

General

Angliia I SSSR: Sbornik Statei, Materialov i Dokumentov, Moscow–Leningrad: Moskovskii Rabochii, 1927.

Degras, Jane, ed. *Soviet Documents on Foreign Policy.* Vol. II, 1925–1932. Issued under the Auspices of the Royal Institute of International Affairs. London–New York–Toronto: Oxford University Press, 1952.

Eudin, X. J. and Fischer, H. H. *Soviet Russia and the West, 1920–1927.* Stanford, Cal.: Stanford University Press, 1957.

U.S.S.R. Narodnyi Komissariat po Inostrannym Delam. *Anglo-Sovetskie Otnosheniia so Dnia Podpisaniia Torgovogo Soglasheniia do Razryva (1921–1927 gg.)*: *Noty i Dokumenty*: Moscow: Izdanie Litizdata Narodnogo Komissariata po Inostrannym Delam, 1927.

Anti-Sovetskii Podlogi: Istoriia Fal'shivok, Faksimile i Kommentarii. Moscow: Litizdat NKID, 1926. English version. *Anti-Soviet Forgeries: A Record of Some of the Forged Documents Used at Various Times Against the Soviet Government.* [London]: Workers' Publications, 1927.

Communist Party of the Soviet Union

Institut Marksa–Engel'sa–Lenina pri TsK, VKP(B). *Vsesoiuznaia Kommunisticheskaia Partiia (Bol'shevikov) v Rezoliutsiiakh i Resheniiakh S''ezdov Konferentsii i Plenumov Ts.K.* Sixth Edition. Ed. by M. B. Mitin, A. M. Poskrebyshev, P. N. Pospelov. 2 Parts. [Leningrad]: Politizdat pri Tsk, VKP(B), 1941.

Institut Marksa–Engel'sa–Lenina–Stalina pri TsK, KPSS. *Kommunisticheskaia Partiia Sovetskogo Soiuza v Rezoliutsiiakh i Resheniiakh S''ezdov, Konferentsii i Plenumov Ts.K.* Seventh Edition. 2 Parts. [Moscow]: Gosudarstvennoe Izdatel'stvo politicheskoi literatury, 1953.

Vsesoiuznaia Kommunisticheskaia Partiia. *XIV S''ezd Vsesiouznoi Kommunisticheskoi Partii (B), 18–31 Dekabria 1925 g.: Stenograficheskii Otchet.* Moscow–Leningrad: Gosudarstvennoe Izdatel'stvo, 1926.

Stalin, J. V. *Political Report of the Central Committee to the Fourteenth Congress of the C.P.S.U. (B) December 18, 1925.* Moscow: Foreign Languages Publishing House, 1950.

Tomsky, M. P. *Die Gewerkschaftsarbeit auf dem XIV Parteitag der Kommunistischen Partei der Sowjet-Union: Referat, Diskussion und Schlusswort.* Berlin: Führer–Verlag, 1926.

Vsesoiuznaia Kommunisticheskaia Partiia. *XV Konferentsia Vsesoiuznoi Kommunisticheskoi Partii (B), 26 Oktabria–3 Noiabria, 1926: Stenograficheskii Otchet.* Moscow: Gosudarstvennoe Izdatel'stvo, 1927.

XV S''ezd Vsesoiuznoi Kommunisticheskoi Partii (B): 2 Dekabria–19 Dekabria 1927g.: Stenograficheskii Otchet. 2 Vols. Moscow: Partizdat TsK, KP(B), 1935.

Report of the Fifteenth Congress of the Communist Party of the Soviet Union. London: Communist Party of Great Britain, 1928.

Stalin, J. V. *Political Report of the Central Committee to the Fifteenth Congress of the C.P.S.U. (B), December 3, 1927.* Moscow: Foreign Languages Publishing House, 1950.

Der Kampf um die Kommunistische Internationale: Dokumente der russischen Opposition nicht veröffentlicht von Stalin'schen ZK. Berlin: Fahne des Kommunismus, [1928].

All-Union Central Council of Trade Unions

Angliiskaia Stachka i Rabochie SSSR. Moscow: Vsesoiuznyi tsentralnyi sovet professional'nykh soiuzov, 1926. English version: All-Russian Central Council of Trade Unions. *Red Money: A Statement of the Facts Relating to the Money Raised During the General Strike and Mining lockout in Britain.* Trans. by Eden and Cedar Paul. London: Labour Research Department, 1926.

All-Russian Central Council of Trade Unions. *Trade Unions in the U.S.S.R., 1922–1924: Short Report.* Moscow: A.C.C.T.U., 1924.

Delegatsiia Britanskogo Generalnogo Soveta Professional'nykh Soiuzov v SSSR. Moscow: Vsesoiuznyi tsentralnyi sovet professional'nykh soiuzov, 1925.

Londonskaia Konferentsiia Edinstva, 6–9 Aprelia 1925 goda, s Predisloviem V. V. Shmidta. Moscow: Izdatel'stvo VTsSPS, 1925.

Shestoi S''ezd Professional'nykh Soiuzov SSSR, 11–18 Noiabria 1924g.: Plenumy i Sektsii: Stenograficheskii Otchet. Moscow: Izdatel'stvo VTsSPS, 1925.

Profsoiuzy SSSR: Dokumenty i Materialy. 4 Vols. Vol. II. *Profsoiuzy v Period Postroeniia Sotsializma v SSSR, Oktabria 1917g.–1937g.* Moscow–Leningrad: Izdatel'stvo VTsSPS–Profizdat, 1963.

U.S.S.R. Central Council of Trade Unions. *Professional'nye Soiuzy SSSR, 1926–1928: Otchet VTsSPS k VIII S''ezdy Professional'nykh Soiuzov.* Moscow: Knigoizdatel'stvo V. Ts.S.P.S., 1928.

Third (Communist) International (Comintern)

Degras, Jane, ed. *The Communist International, 1919–1943: Documents.* 3 Vols. London and New York: Oxford University Press, 1950–65.

Dix années de lutte pour la révolution mondiale. Paris: Bureau d'Edition, 1929.

Kun, Bela, ed. *Kommunisticheskii Internatsional v Dokumentakh, Resheniia i Vozzvaniia Kongressov Kominterna i Plenumov IKKI, 1919–1932.* Moscow: Partizdat, 1933.

Radek, Karl. *Piat*[1] *Let Kominterna.* 2 Parts. Moscow: Izdatel'stvo 'Krasnaia Nov',' 1924.

Tivel', Aleksandr Iu. and Kheimo, M., eds. *Desiat Le't Kominterna v Resheniiakh i Tsifrakh (Spravochnik po Istorii Kominterna).* Moscow –Leningrad: Gosudarstvennoe Izdatel'stvo, 1929.

Communist International, 5th Congress. *Piatyi Vsemirnyi Kongress Kommunisticheskogo Internatsionala,17 iiunia–8 iiulia1924g.: Stenografficheskii Otchet.* 2 Parts. Moscow–Leningrad: Gosudurstvennoe Izdatel'stvo, 1925.

Fifth Congress of the Communist International: Abridged Report of Meetings held at Moscow June 17th to July 8th 1924. [London]: Published for the Communist International by the Communist Party of Great Britain [1924].

Zinoviev, G. *Towards Trade Union Unity! (Speech at the 5th Congress of the Comintern).* London: Published for the Communist International by the Communist Party of Great Britain, 1925.

Communist International, 6th Congress. *Protokoll sechster Weltkongress der Kommunistischen Internationale, Moskau, 17 Juli–1 September 1928.* 4 Vols. Hamburg: C. Hoym, 1928–9.

Sixth World Congress of the Communist International, July–August 1928 [Vienna: F. Koritschoner, 1928].

Program of the Communist International Adopted at the Sixth World Congress in 1928. Calcutta: Radical Book Club [1945].

Communist International, Executive Committee. *Rasshirennyi Plenum Ispolkoma Kommunisticheskogo Internatsionala (21 marta–6 aprelia 1925g.): Stenograficheskii Otchet.* Moscow–Leningrad: Gosudarstvennoe Izdatel'stvo, 1925.

Bolshevizing the Communist International: Report of the Enlarged Executive of the Communist International, March 21st to April 14 [sic!], *1925.* London: Communist Party of Great Britain, 1925.

Shestoi Rasshirennyi Plenum Ispolkoma Kominterna (17 Febralia– 15 Marta 1926g.): Stenograficheskii Otchet. Moscow: Gosudarstvennoe Izdatel'stvo, 1927.

'Report on the Activities of the Executive Committee of the Communist International for the period March/April 1925–January 1926.' Moscow: 1926. (Mimeographed).

Tatigkeitsbericht der Exekutive der Kommunistischen Internatsionale 1925–26: Ein Jahr Arbeit und Kampf. Hamburg: C. Hoym, 1926.

The Communist International Between the Fifth & the Sixth World Congresses, 1924–28. London: Communist Party of Great Britain, 1928.

Erweiterte Exekutive (Februar–März 1926): Thesen und Resolutionen. Hamburg: C. Hoym [1926].

Puti Mirovoi Revoliutsii: Sed'moi Rasshirennyi Plenum Ispolnitel'nogo Komiteta Kommunisticheskogo Internatsionala, 22 Noiabria–16 Dekabria 1926g.: Stenograficheskii Otchet. 2 Vols. Moscow–Leningrad: Gosudarstvennoe Izdatel'stvo, 1927.

VIII. Plenum Ispolnitel'nogo Komiteta Kommunisticheskogo Internatsionala 18–30 Maia 1927g.: Tezisy, Rezoliutsii i Vozzvaniia. Moscow: Gosizdat, 1927.

Kompartiia i Krizis Kapitalizma: 9–i Plenum IKKI: Stenograficheskii Otchet. Moscow: Partizdat, 1932.

Novaia Taktika Angliiskoi Kompartii: Sbornik (Materialy IX Plenum Kominterna). Moscow–Leningrad: Gosizdat, 1928.

Resolutionen und Beschlüsse über der IX Plenartagung des Erweiterten Exekutiv-Komitees der Komintern in Moskau, Februar, 1928. Hamburg: C. Hoym, 1928.

Communist Party in Great Britain. *The Report of the British Commission of the Ninth Plenum of the Comintern.* London: Communist Party of Great Britain, 1928.

Braun, P. *At the Parting of the Ways: The Results of the Ninth Plenum of the Comintern.* London: Communist Party of Great Britain, 1928.

Red International of Labour Unions

Desiat' Let Profinterna v Rezoliutsiiakh, Dokumentakh i Tsifrakh. Compiled by S. Sorbonsky and ed. by A. Lozovsky. Moscow: Izdatel'stvo VTsSPS, 1930.

Profintern v Rezoliutsiakh. Compiled by S. V. Girinis and ed. by A. Lozovsky. Moscow: Izd. Profinterna, 1928.

Red International of Labour Unions, 3rd Congress. *Protokoll über den Dritten Kongress der Roten Gewerkschafts-Internationale abgehalten in Moskau vom 8.. bis 21. Juli 1924.* Berlin: Verlag der Roten Gewerkschafts-Internationale, 1924.

The Tasks of the International Trade Union Movement: being the Resolutions and Decisions of the Red International of Labour Unions, Moscow, July, 1924. London: The Minority Movement [1924].

Red International of Labour Unions, 4th Congress. *Die Internationale Gewerkschafts-bewegung in den Jahren 1924–1927. Proletariar aller Länder – Vereinigt Euch! Bericht des Vollzugsburos der Roten Gewerkschafts-Internationale an dem 4 Kongress in Moskau am*

15 März, 1928. Berlin: Führer, 1928. Russian version: *Mezhdunarodnoe Profdvizhenie za 1924–27gg.: Otchet Ispol'buro IV Kongressu Profinterna.* Moscow: Izdanie Profinterna, 1928.

Report of the Fourth Congress of the R.I.L.U. London: Published in England for the Red International of Labour Unions by the Minority Movement, 1928.

Red International of Labour Unions, Fifth Congress. *Report of the Fifth Congress of the R.I.L.U.* London: Published in England for the Red International of Labour Unions by the Minority Movement, 1930.

Red International of Labour Unions, Central Council. *IV Sessia Tsentral'nogo Soveta Krasnogo Internatsionala Profsoiuzov, 9–15 Marta 1926g.: Otchet.* Moscow: Izdanie Profinterna, 1926.

INTERNATIONAL FEDERATION OF TRADE UNIONS

The International Federation of Trade Unions. *Report on Activities during the Years 1924, 1925 and 1926: Submitted to the Fourth Ordinary Congress, Paris, August, 1927.* Amsterdam: 1927.

Report of Proceedings at the Fourth Ordinary Congress of the International Federation of Trade Unions Held at the 'Grand Palais,' from August 1st to 6th, 1927. Amsterdam: International Federation of Trade Unions, 1927.

INTERNATIONAL LABOUR OFFICE

International Labour Office, Studies and Reports, Series A (Industrial Relations), No. 26. *The Trade Union Movement in Soviet Russia.* Geneva. International Labour Office, 1927.

LABOUR AND SOCIALIST INTERNATIONAL

Labour and Socialist International, Second Congress, Marseilles, 22nd to 27th August, 1925. *Report of the Secretariat. Congress Report.* London: The Labour Party, 1925.

UNITED STATES

U.S. Congress. 84th Congress, 2nd Session. House Committee on Un-American Activities. *The Communist Conspiracy: Strategy and Tactics of World Communism.* Part I. *Communism Outside the United States.* Section C. *The World Congresses of the Communist International.* Section D. *Communist Activities Around the World.* House

Reports 2242, 2243. Washington, D.C.: Government Printing Office, 1956.

80th Congress, 2nd Session. House. Committee on Foreign Affairs. *Report on the Strategy and Tactics of World Communism.* Supplement 3. *Country Studies.* 5 Vols. House Report. Washington, D.C.: Government Printing Office, 1948.

PAPERS, SPEECHES ETC.

Bramley, Fred. *Relations with Russia: A Speech in Favour of International Trade Union Unity.* London: Trade Union Unity, 1925.

Lenin, V. I. *Sobranie Sochinenii.* Vol. XVII. Moscow: 1926.

Lozovsky, A. (Solomon A. Dridzo). *Angliiskii Proletariat na Rasputi: Sbornik Statei.* Moscow: Izdanie Profinterna, 1926.

Rykov, A. I. *Sotsialisticheskoe Stroitel'stvo i Mezhdunarodnaia Politika SSSR:* Moscow–Leningrad: Gosudarstvennoe Izdatel'stvo, 1927.

Stalin, J. V. *Sochineniia.* Vols. VI–X. Moscow: Institut Marksa–Engel'sa–Lenina pri TsK, VKP (B): Gosudarstvennoe Izdatel'stvo politicheskoi Literatury, 1946–54.

Works. Vols. VI–X. Moscow: Foreign Language Publishing House, 1952.

Tomsky, M. *Getting Together: Speeches Delivered in Russia and England 1924–25.* London: Labour Research Department [1925].

K Probleme Edinstva Mezhdunarodnogo Professional'nogo Dvizheniia. Moscow: Izdatel'stvo VTsSPS, 1926.

The Trade Unions, the Party, and the State: Extracts from Speeches by Comrade Tomsky at a meeting of the III session of the Profintern on June 27, 1923, and at the joint meetings of the Presidium of the All-Russian Central Council of Trade Unions with foreign workers' delegations, on August 11 and November 7, 1926. Moscow: Commission for Foreign Relations of the Central Council of Trade Unions of the U.S.S.R., 1927.

BOOKS, JOURNAL ARTICLES

Abramov, B. A. 'Razgrom Trotskistko–Zinov'evskogo Antipartiinogo Bloka,' *Voprosy Istorii K.P.S.S.*, No. 6 (1959), pp. 25–47.

Adler, Friedrich. *The Anglo-Russian Report. A Criticism of the Report of the British Trade Union Delegation from the Point of View of International Socialism.* London: P. S. King & Son, 1925.

Andreev, Andrei A. *Sryv Anglo-Russkogo Komiteta i Nashi Zadachi*, Moscow–Leningrad: Gosudarstvennoe Izdatel'stvo, 1927.

Angell, Norman. *Must Britain Travel the Moscow Road?* London: Noel Douglas, 1926.

Arnot, Robin Page. *The Impact of the Russian Revolution in Britain*. London: Lawrence and Wishart, 1967.

The General Strike, May, 1926: Its Origin and History. London: Labour Research Department, 1926.

The Miners: Years of Struggle. Vol. II of *A History of the Miners' Federation of Great Britain*. London: George Allen and Unwin, 1953.

Twenty Years: The Policy of the Communist Party of Great Britain from its Foundation, July 31st, 1920. [London], Lawrence and Wishart, [1940].

Bell, Thomas. *The British Communist Party: A Short History*. London: Lawrence and Wishart, 1937.

Bennet, A. J. (David Aleksandrovich Petrovsky). *The General Council and the General Strike*. London: Communist Party of Great Britain, 1926.

Borkenau, Franz. *The Communist International*. London: Faber and Faber, 1938.

Carr, Edward H. *A History of Soviet Russia. Socialism in One Country, 1924–1926*. 3 vols. New York and London: Macmillan, 1950–64.

A History of Soviet Russia. Foundations of a Planned Economy, 1926–1928. 3 vols. New York and London: Macmillan, 1969– .

Chekin, A. (V. Iarotsky). *Na Londonskoi Konferentsii*. Moscow: Izdatel'-stvo VTsSPS, 1925.

Chester, Lewis; Fay, Stephen and Young, Hugo. *The Zinoviev Letter*. London: Heinemann, 1967.

Citrine, Walter M. *Democracy or Disruption? An Examination of Communist Influences in the Trade Unions*. London: Trades Union Congress, 1928.

I Search for Truth in Russia. London: Routledge, 1936.

Coates, William P. and Zelda K. *A History of Anglo-Soviet Relations*. 2 vols. London: Lawrence and Wishart, 1943–58.

Cole, G. D. H., and Postgate, Raymond William. *The Common People*. 4th Ed. London: Methuen, 1956.

Cole, G. D. H. *A History of the Labour Party from 1914*. London: Routledge and Kegan Paul, 1948.

A History of Socialist Thought, Vol. IV. *Communism and Social Democracy, 1914–1931*. 2 parts. London: Macmillan, 1958.

A Short History of the British Working Class Movement. Revised ed. London: George Allen and Unwin, 1948.

The People's Front. London: Victor Gollancz, 1937.

Crook, Wilfrid H. *The General Strike: A Study of Labor's Tragic Weapon in Theory and Practice.* Chapel Hill, N.C.: University of North Carolina Press, 1931.

Davis, Jerome. *Contemporary Social Movements.* New York and London: The Century Co., 1930.

Deutscher, Isaac. *Soviet Trade Unions: Their Place in Soviet Labour Policy.* London: Royal Institute of International Affairs, 1950.

Dunn, Robert W. *Soviet Trade Unions.* New York: Vanguard Press, 1928.

Farman, Christopher. *The General Strike: May, 1926.* London: Rupert Hart-Davis, 1972.

Fischer, Louis. *The Soviets in World Affairs: A History of the Relations Between the Soviet Union and the Rest of the World, 1917-1929.* New York: J. Cope and H. Smith, 1930.

Fischer, Ruth. *Stalin and German Communism.* London: Oxford University Press, 1948.

Florinsky, Michael T. *World Revolution and the U.S.S.R.* London: Macmillan, 1933.

Footman, David, ed. *International Communism.* St. Antony's Papers, No. 9. London: Chatto and Windus, 1960.

Godden, Gertrude M. *The Communist Attack on Great Britain.* London: Burns, Oates, 1935.

Goldstein, Joseph. *The Government of British Trade Unions: A Study of Apathy and the Democratic Process in the Transport and General Workers Union.* London: Allen and Unwin, 1952.

Gordon, Michael. *Conflict and Consensus in Labour's Foreign Policy, 1914-1965.* Stanford, Cal.: Stanford University Press, 1969.

Graubard, Stephen R. *British Labour and the Russian Revolution, 1917-1924.* Cambridge, Mass.: Harvard University Press, [1956].

Grigor'ev, L. and Olenev, S. *Bor'ba SSSR za Mir i Bezopastnest' v Evrope, 1925-1933.* Moscow: Gosudarstvennoe Izdatel'stvo politicheskoi literatury, 1956.

Gurovich, P. V. *Vseobshchaia Stachka v Anglii 1926g.* Moscow: Izd. Akad. Nauk SSSR, 1959.

Hammond, Thomas K. *Soviet Foreign Relations and World Communism.* Princeton, N.J.: Princeton University Press, 1965.

Havighurst, Alfred. *Twentieth Century Britain.* 2nd Ed. New York: Harper and Row, 1966.

Hutt, George Allen. *The Condition of the Working Class in England*. London: Martin Lawrence, 1933.

The Post-War History of the British Working Class. London: Victor Gollancz, 1937.

James, Cyril L. R. *World Revolution, 1917–1936: the Rise and Fall of the Communist International*. London: Secker and Warburg [1937].

Kohler, Foy D. *Understanding the Russians*. New York: Harper and Row, 1970.

LeFranc, Georges. *Les Expériences syndicales internationales; des origines à nos jours*. Paris: Aubier, 1952.

Lerner, S. *Breakaway Unions and the Small Trade Union*. London: Allen and Unwin, 1961.

Lorwin, Lewis L. (Louis Levine). *Labor and Internationalism*. London: Allen and Unwin, 1929.

Lozovsky, Aleksandr (Solomon Dridzo). *Anglo-Sovetskaia Konferentsiia Professional'nykh Soiuzov*. Moscow, Leningrad: Gosizdat, 1925. German edition: *Die Englishch-Russische Gewerkschaftskonferenz*. Berlin: 1925.

British and Russian Workers. London: National Minority Movement, 1926.

Das Englisch-Russische Komitee der Einheit. Moscow: Verlag der Roten Gewerkschafts-Internationale, 1926.

Die Lehren des Generalstreiks in England. Moscow: Verlag der Roten Gewerkschafts-Internationale, 1926.

The World's Trade Union Movement. London: National Minority Movement, 1925.

Lyman, Richard. *The First Labour Government, 1924*. London: Chapman and Hall, 1957.

MacFarlane, L. J. *The British Communist Party: Its Origin and Development until 1929*. London: MacGibbon and Kee, 1966.

MacManus, Arthur. *History of the Zinoviev Letter*. London: Communist Party of Great Britain, 1925.

Maddox, William P. *Foreign Relations in British Labour Politics*. Cambridge, Mass.: Harvard University Press, 1934.

Martin, Roderick. *Communism and the British Trade Unions, 1924–1933*. Oxford: Clarendon Press, 1969.

Molchanov, Iu. L. *Komintern: U Istokov Politiki Edinogo Proletarskogo Fronta*. Moscow: Izdatel'stvo 'Mysl',' 1969.

Mowat, Charles L. *Britain Between the Wars, 1918–40*. London: Methuen, 1956.

Naylor, John F. *Labour's International Policy: the Labour Party in the 1930's.* London: Weidenfeld and Nicolson, 1969.

Nollan, Gunther. *International Communism and World Revolution: History and Methods.* London: Hollis and Carter, 1961.

Page, Stanley W. *Lenin and World Revolution.* New York: New York University Press, 1959.

Pelling, Henry. *The British Communist Party: A Historical Profile.* London: Adam and Charles Black, 1958.

A History of British Trade Unionism. London: Macmillan, 1963.

Petrowski, D[avid Aleksandrovich]. (A. J. Bennet). *Das Anglo-Russische Komitee und die Opposition in der KPSU.* Hamburg–Berlin: Verlag Carl Hoym Nachfolger [1927].

Ponomarev, B. N. (and others). *History of the Communist Party of the Soviet Union.* Moscow: Foreign Languages Publishing House, 1960.

Popov, N. *Outline History of the Communist Party of the Soviet Union.* Ed. by A. Fineberg, H. G. Scott. Vol. ii. London: Martin Lawrence [1935].

Popov, V. I. *Anglo-Sovetskie Otnosheniia, 1927–1929.* Moscow: Izdatel'-stvo instituta mezhdunarodnykh otnoshenii, 1958.

Possony, Stefan T. *A Century of Conflict: Communist Techniques of World Revolution.* Chicago: Regnery, 1953.

Redman, Joseph (Brian Pearce). *The Communist Party and the Labour Left, 1925–1929.* Reasoner Pamphlets. Number One. Hull, England: [1957].

Schevenels, Walther, *Quarante-cinq années: Féderation syndicale internationale, 1901–1945.* [Brussels]: Editions de l'Institut E. Vandervelde, 1964.

Seton-Watson, Hugh. *The Pattern of Communist Revolution.* London: Methuen, 1953.

Sworakowski, Withold S. *The Communist International and its Front Organizations,* Stanford, Cal.: The Hoover Institution, 1964.

Symons, Julian. *The General Strike.* London: The Cresset Press, 1957.

Thomson, David. *England in the Twentieth Century.* London: Jonathan Cape, 1964.

Trotsky, Lev D. *La défense de l'U.R.S.S. et l'Opposition.* Paris: Bibliothèque de l'Opposition Communiste, 1929.

The First Five Years of the Communist International. 2 Vols. New York: Pioneer Publishers, 1945–53.

Die Internationale Revolution und die Kommunistische Internationale. Trans. by A. Muller. Berlin: E. Laubsche Verlagsbuchhandlung G.m.b.H., 1929.

The Lessons of October. Trans. by John G. Wright. New York: Pioneer Publishers, 1937.

The Real Situation in Russia, Trans. by Max Eastman. London: George Allen and Unwin, 1928.

The Revolution Betrayed. London: Faber and Faber, 1937.

The Stalin School of Falsification. Introduction by Max Shachtman. Trans. by John G. Wright. New York: Pioneer Publishers, 1937.

The Strategy of the World Revolution. New York: Communist League of America (Opposition), 1930.

The Third International after Lenin. Introduction by Max Shachtman. Trans. by John G. Wright. New York: Pioneer Publishers, 1936.

Where is Britain Going? (Rev. ed.) London: Communist Party of Great Britain, 1926.

Vinogradov, B. *Mirovoi Proletariat i SSSR.* Book 5 of *Desiat¹ let Kapitalisticheskogo Okruzheniia SSSR.* Gen. ed. E. Pashukanio and M. Spektator. Moscow: Izdatel'stvo Kommunisticheskoi Akademii, 1928.

Volkov, F. D. *Anglo-sovetskie Otnosheniia, 1924–1928gg.* Moscow: Gosudarstvennoe Izdatel'stvo Politicheskoi Literatury, 1958.

Weingartner, Thomas. *Stalin und der Aufsteig Hitlers.* Berlin: Walter de Gruyter & Co., 1970.

White, Stephen. 'Labour's Council of Action 1920,' *Journal of Contemporary History,* vol. 9, no. 4 (Oct., 1974), pp. 99–122.

Wolfe, Bertram D. *The Trotskyite Opposition: Its Significance for American Workers.* Workers' Library Number 5. New York: Workers' Library Publishers, 1928.

Zinoviev, Grigorii. *Die 21 Bedingungen der Leninschen Komintern.* Berlin: Verlag der 'Fahne des Kommunismus,' [1927].

Index

Adler, F., 105n, 178
Afghanistan, 26
All Power!, 30
All-Russian Central Council of Trade Unions, *see* Central Council (Soviet trade unions)
All-Union Communist Party (Bolsheviks) (later CPSU), 21, 22, 358; and the Comintern, 5, 63, 393; and the Russian trade unions, 21–2, 215–16; thirteenth congress (1924), 48, 93; fourteenth conference (1925), 154–5; fourteenth congress (1925), 195, 207–15, 217; and Anglo-Russian Committee, 215, 269–72, 301–6, 359, 370–1, 408–9; fifteenth conference (1926), 301–7, 322; fifteenth congress (1927), 388, 396, 407–8. *See also* Central Committee (CPSU)
All-Union Trade Union Congress [formerly All-Russian Trade Union Congress]: membership, 15, 142, 193; relationship to RILU, 15, 20, 23, 68–9, 72–6, 77, 154, 206, 218–20, 303–4, 323, 332, 369, 396, 402, 414; relationship to Soviet state, 20–4; and IFTU, 24–5, 53–7, 67–70, 72–80, 110–21, 156–7, 184, 195–7, 198–201, 206, 273, 285–6, 333–5, 339, 364, 367, 372, 395, 400–2, 404–5, 411–12, 414–15; sixth congress, 97, 100–3; relationship to CPSU, 21–4, 186–7, 193; support for British miners (1926), 250–4; and TUC, 271–2, 276, 303–4, 318, 323, 332, 335, 380, 396–7, 405–7; seventh congress, 326–8; and WFTU, 405–6. *See also* Central Council (Soviet trade unions), Anglo-Russian Committee, Tomsky, M.
Amalgamated Engineering Union, 38
Amalgamated Union of Building Trade Workers, 38
American Federation of Labor (AF of L), 15n, 187, 190, 195, 199, 220, 404–6
Amsterdam International, *see* International Federation of Trade Unions (IFTU)
Andreev, A., 274–8, 282, 284, 337, 342
Anglo-Russian Committee, 155–6, 254, 394–5; first proposals for, 67, 80, 102–6, 126–7, 137, 139, 141; IFTU reaction to, 116, 119, 372–3, 376–7; Communist pressure for establishment, 120–1, 132, 152, 168–71; recommended by t.u. conference (1925), 146–7, 150; does not meet, summer, 1925, 164–7; established, 179–82; first meeting (London) and reactions to it, 182, 184–5, 187, 188, 190, 192, 194–5; second meeting (Berlin) and reactions to it, 199–205; Communist comment on and defense of, 207–15, 221–3, 243, 245,